A
CHECKLIST OF
AMERICAN IMPRINTS
for
1844

Items 44-1–44-6827

compiled by

CAROL RINDERKNECHT
and
SCOTT BRUNTJEN

The Scarecrow Press, Inc.
Metuchen, N.J., & London
1993

Library of Congress Catalog No. 64-11784
ISBN 0-8108-2654-2

PREFACE TO 1844

These volumes continue to incorporate the ideas presented by reviewers of earlier editions of *The Checklist*.

Beginning with the volume for 1840, the entry numbers have taken a new form. Prior to the 1840s, each entry was numbered sequentially. The numbers had no meaning. One review of the indexes for the 1830s noted that it would be helpful to know which volume to examine after finding the entry in the index. In these volumes the entry number has as a prefix two digits representing the year. Thus 42-1 is the first item for the 1842 volume and 43-2 is the second item in the 1843 *Checklist*. When the indexes are compiled for the decade of the 1840s, the user will not have to examine the entry numbers on the spines of the individual *Checklists* to find the correct volume.

One reviewer questioned how the location symbols were constructed and where one could find a table listing the library represented by the symbol. The *Checklist* uses the National Union Catalog (NUC) symbol for the library. This system was developed by Frank Petersen in the 1920's. Petersen's system was expanded by Douglas C. McMurtrie, the primary leader of the American Imprints Inventory; the governmental agency which listed most of the raw material that the compilers use in identifying the items for each volume of the *Checklist*. A further discussion of McMurtrie, The American Imprints Inventory, and the NUC symbols can be found in *Douglas C. McMurtrie, Bibliographer and Historian of Printing* by Scott Bruntjen and Melissa L. Young published by Scarecrow Press in 1979. A fairly complete list of NUC symbols is appended to volume 200 of *The National Union Catalog, pre-1956 Imprints* published by Mansell in 1972.

Previous editions of the *Checklist* used "dash-on entries" for representing the same author in the second and subsequent items in the same volume. This technique is well documented for use in bibliographies but the compilers found it confusing when one author, such as the City of New York, might have fifty entries in a volume. The reader was forced to look back to the first entry to determine the author of the item. Beginning with 1840, the author is provided in full for each entry. As this is a reference work to be used one item at a time, this change should make it easier for the reader.

Carol R. Rinderknecht and Scott Bruntjen

Eldora, Colorado

September, 1993.

A

A Beckett, Gilbert Abbott, 1811-1856. The comic Blackstone of "Punch." With illustrations by Cruikshank. Philadelphia: Carey and Hart, 1844. 94 p. CU; DLC; MB; NN; WaU. 44-1

A Beckett, Gilbert Abbott, 1811-1856. The comic Blackstone of "Punch." With illustrations by Cruikshank. Philadelphia: Carey and Hart, 1844-1845. 2 v. in 1. CtY; MdBP; PPULC. 44-2

A Beckett, Gilbert Abbott, 1811-1856. The comic Blackstone of "Punch." With illustrations by Cruikshank. Philadelphia: Carey and Hart, 1844-1846. 3 v. in 1. CtY; LU; MWA; PP; WU-L. 44-3

Abbot Female Academy. Andover, Massachusetts. Catalogue of the officers and members of Abbot Female Academy, Andover, Massachusetts, June, 1844. Andover: Allen, Morrill and Wardwell, printers, 1844. 12 p. MAnA. 44-4

Abbot, Anne Wales, b. 1808. Doctor Busby and his neighbors; a story illustrated by the games of Doctor Busby and Master Redbury. Salem: 1844. CtY; MH; MHi. 44-5

Abbot, Anne Wales. b. 1808. Willie Rogers, or, temper improved. [By Anne W. Abbot] Boston: Samuel G. Simpkins, 1844. 104 p. MBC; MBSi; MSwam; OO. 44-6

Abbott, Abiel, 1770-1828. The spirit of the temperance pledge. A poem, written for the celebration of the anniversary of the Declaration of Independence, and delivered before the Washington Temperance Benevolent Societies and citizens of Jersey City, in Washington Hall, July 4, 1843. New York: J.M. Elliott, 1844. 24 p. RPB; TxU. 44-7

Abbott, Jacob, 1803-1879. Cousin Lucy on the sea-shore. Boston: Massey, 1844. DLC; MB: MH; NNC. 44-8

Abbott, Jacob, 1803-1879. Cousin Lucy's conversations. By the author of the Rollo books. Boston: B.B. Mussey, 1844. MH. 44-9

Abbott, Jacob, 1803-1879. Jonas a junde; or, law among the boys, by the author of the Rollo books, Jonas's stories, etc. Boston: William D. Ticknor, 1844. 179 p. RPB. 44-10

Abbott, Jacob, 1803-1879. Marco Paul's adventures in pursuit of knowledge. City of Boston. By the author of Rollo, Jonas, and Lucy books. Boston: T. Harrington Carter and company; New York: A.V. Blake, 1844. [9]-144 p. TJoV; ScCliTO; ViU. 44-11

Abbott, Jacob, 1803-1879. Marco Paul's travels and adventures in the pursuit of knowledge. City of New York. Boston: Carter, 1844. 144 p. OO. 44-12

Abbott, Jacob, 1803-1879. Marco Paul's travels and adventures in the pursuit of knowledge. On the Erie Canal. Boston: T.H. Carter and company, 1844. 144 p. CSmH; CtY; MH. 44-13

Abbott, Jacob, 1803-1879. Marco Paul's travels and adventures in the pursuit of knowledge. On the Erie Canal. Third edition. Boston: T.H. Carter and company, 1844. 144 p. MH; NNC; OO; PSt; Vt. 44-14

Abbott, Jacob, 1803-1879. Marco Polo's [Paul's] adventures in pursuit of knowledge, state of Vermont. Boston: T.H. Carter and company, 1844. 144 p. CtY; Vt. 44-15

Abbott, Jacob, 1803-1879. The teacher; or, moral influences employed in the instruction and government of the young. New stereotype edition, with an additional chapter on "the first day in school." Cooperstown: H. and E. Phinney, 1844. 314 p. ICU; MB; MBC; MH; NPStA. 44-16

Abbott, John Stevens Cabot, 1805-1877. A visit to the mountains: or a narrative of an excursion into the country. A book for young people. Boston: Crocker and Brewster, 1844. 10-179 p. MeB; PCDHi. 44-17

Abbott, Simon B. The southern botanic physician.... a treatise on.... diseases of men, women and children of all climates.... Charleston: Burges and James, printers, 1844. 395 p. NNN; ScC; WU-M. 44-18

Abell, Lucia Elizabeth Balcome, d. 1871. Recollections of the Emperor,

Napolen. New York: Mowatt, 1844. NN. 44-19

Abercrombie, John, 1780-1844. Inquiries concerning the intellectual powers, and the investigation of truth.... Boston: Otis, Broaders and company, 1844. 284 p. CoCsC; CSt; InEvW; TNT; WMMU. 44-20

Abercrombie, John, 1780-1844. Inquiries concerning the intellectual powers, and the investigation of truth. From the last Edinburgh edition. New York: Harper and brothers, 1844. 376 p. IEN-M; MoS; OCo; NdU; WHi. 44-21

Abercrombie, John, 1780-1844. The philosophy of the moral feelings. ....From the last Edinburgh edition. New York: Harper and brothers, 1844. 236 p. InUpT; MeAu; OTifH; PLT. 44-22

Abernethy, John, 1764-1831. Family physicians; or ready prescriber in cases of illness and accident, where medical attendance is not desired or cannot be procured. Revised and enlarged by Homer Bostwick. First American from the thirtieth London edition. New York: Burgess, 1844. 120 p. PPCP. 44-23

Accidents upon railroads; their causes, and the mode of prevention, discussed in communications addressed to the Baltimore American. Baltimore: John Murphy, 1844. 23 p. ICJ; MdHi; MdLR; NNE. 44-24

An account of Julia Moore, a penitent female, who died in the eastern penitentiary of Pennsylvania, 1843. Second edition. Philadelphia: 1844. 20 p. PHi; PPULC. 44-25

An account of the celebration of the mass. New York: 1844. DLC. 44-26

An account of the religious experience and some of the trials of Susanne Lightfoot. Manchester: 1844. PSC-Hi. 44-27

Adam, Alexander, 1741-1809. Adam's Latin grammar, with some improvements, and.... additions: rules for the right pronunciation of the Latin language; ....tables, showing the value of the various coins, weights, and measures, used among the Romans. By Benjamin A. Gould.... Northampton: J.H. Butler; Buffalo: J.H. Butler and company, 1844. 299 p. GMM; NjP; NNP; PHi; ScU. 44-28

Adam, Alexander, 1741-1809. Rudiments of Latin Grammar, with numerous expansions and additions, designed to make the work more elementary and complete.... By D. Johnson. Improvements of the third New York from the last English edition of Adams. New York: W.E. Dean, 1844. 252 p. ArAT; ViL. 44-29

Adam, William. Winter classes for ladies. [Boston: 1844] MHi. 44-30

Adams, Charles Francis, 1807-1886. Texas and Massachusetts resolutions. Boston: Eastburns' Press, 1844. 54 p. CSmH; MdBJ; MeB; Nh; TxU. 44-31

Adams, Daniel, 1773-1864. Adam's new arithmetic. Arithmetic, in which the principles of operating by numbers are analytically explained, and synthetically applied. Keene, N.H.: J. and J.W. Prentiss, 1844. 180 p. NCanHi; OClWHi; WBHi. 44-32

Adams, Daniel, 1773-1864. Adam's new arithmetic. Arithmetic, in which the principles of operating by numbers are analytically explained, and synthetically applied. Keene, N.H.: J. and J.W. Prentiss, 1844. 254 p. NRU-W. 44-33

Adams, George J. A lecture on the authenticity and scriptural character of the Book of Mormon. By G.J. Adams, minister of the gospel. Delivered at... Charlestown, Massachusetts... Boston: printed by J.E. Farwell, 1844. [3] 4-24 p. MH; MMal; UPB; WHi. 44-34

Adams, George J. A lecture on the doctrine of baptism for the dead; and preachings to spirits in prison. New York: printed by C.A. Calhoun, 1844. 12 p. MH. 44-35

Adams, George J. A letter to his excellency John Tyler, president of the U.S. touching the signs of the times and the political destiny of the world. New York: Printed by C.A. Calhoun, 1844. 16 p. MoInRC; USIC; WHi. 44-36

Adams, Henry. The safety of those who die in infancy; a sermon delivered....by Henry Adams....Boston: press of Crocker and Brewster, 1844. 28 p. MAnp; MBC; Mid-B; NNG. 44-37

Adams, John Quincy, 1767-1848. The character of Hamlet, by ex-president Adams and James H. Hackett. Edited by a lady. New York: Mowatt, 1844. 7 p. MH; MHi; NBuG; PP. 44-38

Adams, John Quincy, 1767-1848. Speech delivered at North Bridgewater, on Wednesday, November 6th [Boston: 1844] [1] p. MH. 44-39

Adams, John Stowell, d. 1893. Sam Squab, the Boston boy.... founded on fact. Boston: Justin Jones, printer, 1844. 48 p. DLC; MB; MiD-B; NIC; RPB. 44-40

Adams, Jonathan. Extension of the Fitchburg Railroad. Route of the Winchendon, Keene, and Bellows Falls Railway, as surveyed by Jonathan Adams. Keene, New Hampshire: 1844. 12 p. ICJ; MBAt. 44-41

Adams, Thomas F. Typographia: or, the printer's instructor; a brief sketch of the origin, rise, and progress of the typographic art, with practical directions for conducting every department in an office, hints to authors, publishers, &c. Second edition, with numerous emendations and additions. Philadelphia: 1844. 282 p. MdBS; MiD-B; NIC; PHi; WHi. 44-42

Adams, William, 1807-1880. Conversations on the distant hills.... New York: 1844. RPAt. 44-43

Adams, William, 1807-1880. Conversations on the shadow of the cross. By the Rev. W. Adams.... [a sequel to the shadow of the cross] From the London edition. New York: General Protestant Epsicopal Sunday School Union, 1844. 42 p. OO; RPAt. 44-44

Adams, William, 1814-1848. The distant hills: an allegory. By the Rev. W. Adams, M.A. From the London edition, with engravings from original designs, by Chapman. New York: General Protestant Episcopal Sunday School Union, 1844. 104 p. MH; RPAt; ViU. 44-45

Adams, William, 1807-1880. Sacred allegories, by the Rev. W. Adams, M.A. 1. The shadow of the hills. 2. The distant hills. New York: General Protestant Episcopal Sunday School Union, 1844. 104 p. MBMu; NCanHi; NNG; RPr; WNaE. 44-46

Adams, William, 1814-1848. The shadow of the cross.... By the Rev. W. Adams.... From the London edition.... New York: General Protestant Episcopal Sunday School Union, 1844. 96 p. DLC; MB; NBuDD; WWauHi. 44-47

Adamson, Thomas. A reply to "consideration and arguments, proving the inexpediency of an international copyright law, by John Campbell". By Thomas Adamson. New York: Bartlett and Welford, 1844. 20 p. MBAt; MdBP; MHi. 44-48

Addicks, Barbara O'Sullivan. Pocket manual, treating of the science of the French language.... under the heads of 1st, orthography, 2d, etymology, 3d, syntax. ....First number. Of orthography.... Philadelphia: 1844. 103 p. DLC; MH; PPL-R. 44-49

An address composed and delivered by Frances Jane Crosby, a pupil of the New York Institution for the Blind, at the hall of the House of Representatives, in the presence of the Senate and Representatives of the United States, on the occasion of an exhibition given by seventeen pupils from the institution, at Washington, January 24, 1844. press of M. Day and company, 1844. NcHiC. 44-50

Address of the Democratic Association of Norwich. To the people of Connecticut. n.p.: 1844. CtHWatk. 44-51

Address of the carrier of the Newport Mercury, wishing its patrons a happy new year. Newport, January 1, 1844. Broadside. RNHi. 44-52

Address of the Democratic Association. Washington: 1844. NcD. 44-53

Address to the people of the United States as relates to the constitution adopted by Rhode Island in 1842. [Providence: 1844. 15 p. MB; MBAt; MH; NN; RPB. 44-54

Address to the people of the United States.... with documents.... concerning T.W. Dorr. Providence: 1844. 15 p. MB. 44-55

An address to the stockholders of the Schuylkill Navigation Company in reply to a pamphlet circulated by the Reading Railroad Company. Philadelphia: printed for the author, 1844. 20 p. DBRE; DLC; PPULC. 44-56

The advent Herald. [Weekly] Boston: 1844-1847. 6 v. in 2. MB. 44-57

The advent messages to the daughters of zion. Boston: J.V. Himes, 1844-1848? MH-AH. 44-58

The advent shield and review. Edited by J.V. Himes, S. Bliss, and A. Hale. Boston: Joshua V. Himes, 1844-. 144 p. DLC; MBAt; MeBat; OClW; PPULC. 44-59

Advice to young tradesman on the formation of business habits, etc. calculated to form the character on a solid basis and to insure respectability and success in life. Compiled from the writings of Franklin Abbott and others. Improved

edition. Steubenville, Ohio: J. Turnbull, 1844. 224 p. MnSM. 44-60

Aeschylus. Aeschylus. By author, prebendary of Norwich [New York:] Harper and brothers, 1844. 76-342 p. LNT; MH; NN; OClW; TNAg. 44-61

Aeschylus. Works. Translated by R. Potter. New York: Harper, 1844. 342 p. IaCorn. 44-62

Aesopus. The fables of Aesop and others. Philadelphia: Thomas, Cowperthwait and company, 1844. 25-358 p. CtHT. 44-63

Aesopus. The little Aesop. Philadelphia: Smith and Peck, etc., etc., 1844. MH; NN. 44-64

Agricultural almanac. n.p.: John Bear, 1844. MWA. 44-65

Aikman, James. Annals of the persecution in Scotland from the restoration to the revolution.... First American edition.... Philadelphia: Presbyterian Board of Education, 1844. 2 v. GDecCT; LNH; MnHi; NNUT; TBri. 44-66

Aikman, James H. The Washingtonian harp; a collection of original songs, adapted to famliar airs, and arranged to be sung either as solos or choruses. Designed for the use of Washington Temperance Societies. New York: Saxton and Miles, 1844. 71 p. MH; NReHi; TxHuT. 44-67

Ainsworth, S.H. Exposition of the deleterious effects of alcohol upon the human body and mind, physiologically and phrenologically considered.

Rochester: Strong, 1844. 35 p. D; IEG; OO. 44-68

Ainsworth, William Harrison, 1805-1882. Dick Turpin, the highwayman, or rookwood: A romance. Philadephia: Lea and Blanchard, 1844. 161 p. KSalW. 44-69

Ainsworth, William Harrison, 1805-1882. Old St. Paul's, a romance. Boston: 1844. 75 p. MB; MH. 44-70

The Akron buzzard. Akron, Ohio: Lane and Chamberlin, 1844. 1 v. CSmH. 44-71

Alabama. Acts passed at the annual session of the General Assembly of the State of Alabama: begun and held in the city of Tuscaloosa, on the first Monday in December, 1843. Tuscaloosa: John McCormick, State printer, 1844. 247 p. A-SC; In-SC; L; W. 44-72

Alabama. Annual report on the contingent fund. Tuscaloosa: Jno M'Cormick, State printer, State Journal and Flag office, 1844. NN. 44-73

Alabama. Journal of the House of Representatives of the state of Alabama at a session begun and held at Tuscaloosa, December 4, 1843. Tuscaloosa, 1844. 292 p. A-SC. 44-74

Alabama. Report of the committee of ways and means in relation to the state debt. James W. McClung, Chairman. Tuscaloosa: Jno. M'Cormick, State printer, State Journal and Flag office, 1844. 7 p. TxU. 44-75

Alabama. Statement of the cost of each species of manufacture, carried on in the penitentiary. Tuscaloosa: Jno.

M'Cormick, State printer, 1844. 7 p. TxU. 44-76

Alabama. Tabular statement of the census of Alabama taken in year 1844: also the census or enumeration of 1838 and 1840 and an estimate showing the increase and decrease in each county since 1838; compiled by W. Garrett. Tuscaloosa: McCormick, 1844. 11 p. A-Ar; NN; TxU. 44-77

Albany, New York. Department of Education. By-laws of the school commissioners and regulations of the public schools, in the city of Albany. Albany: C. Van Benthuysen and company, printers, 1844. 18 p. MB; NjR. 44-78

Albany, New York. Select Family School for Young Ladies. Catalogue and circular. Albany: 1844. 15 p. MB; PHi. 44-79

Albany, New York. Valatie Fire Engine Company, Number 4. Act of incorporation and constitution. Albany: 1844. 8 p. MHi. 44-80

Albany Academy for girls. Exercises... Third anniversary, July, 1844. Albany: 1844. 35 p. NN. 44-81

Albany Atlas. Albany: 1844-. V. 1-. CtY; DLC; NN; PPL. 44-82

Albany city guide, being a general description of the public buildings, literary, charitable, and benevolent institutions, etc., with numerous useful tables and statistics, relating to the city. Albany: 1844. 144 p. NjR; NIC; NN; WHi. 44-83

Albany Medical College. Albany, New

York. Catalogue and circular of the Albany Medical College. Albany: Printed by J. Munsell, 1844. 20 p. MBC; OC. 44-84

Albany religious spectator; a family paper devoted to religious and general intelligence. Albany, New York: E.H. Pease, 1844-1845. V. 1. 208 p. CtY; DLC. 44-85

The albion. Choice selections from the New York albion... Second edition. New York: 1844. NN. 44-86

The albion. Doctrines and discipline of the African Methodsit Episcopal Church. Brooklyn [New York] 1844. 256 p. NB. 44-87

Albro, John Adams, 1799-1866. The interpretation of the Bible.... Written for the Massachusetts Sabbath School Society, and revised by the committee of publication. Boston: Massachusetts Sabbath School Society, 1844. 124 p. CtMW; DLC; MH. 44-88

Albro, John Adams, 1799-1866. On the parables of the New Testament. Part II. For the higher classes. Revised edition. Boston: 1844. 90 p. RPB. 44-89

Albro, John Adams, 1799-1866. Scripture questions.... on the parables of the New Testament. For the higher classes. Revised edition. Boston, Massachusetts: Sabbath School Society, [1844] 90 p. DLC; IEG; MB; MDeeP; VtMidSM. 44-90

The album of love. [New York: Morris and Willis, 1844] 32 p. CLU; MWH; NN; RPB. 44-91

Alcala Yanez y Rivera, Geronimo, 1563-1632. Life and adventures of Alonso, the chattering lay brother and servant of many masters; Translated with notes. New York: 1844. DLC; MBAt, NjR. 44-92

Alcantara, Peter de. A golden treatise of mental prayer with diverse spiritual rules and directions. Translated into English, by Giles Willoughby. Philadelphia: M. Fithian, 1844. 216 p. MBBCHS; MdCatS; MoFloSS; WMMU. 44-93

Alcott, William Andrus, 1789-1859. A boy's guide to usefulness. Designed to prepare the way for the "Young man's guide." Boston: Waite, Peirce, and company, 1844. 180 p. FU; MH; MWA; NjP; PCC. 44-94

Alcott, William Andrus, 1798-1859. The house I live in; or, the human body. For the use of families and schools. Tenth edition. Boston: 1844. 264 p. MBM. 44-95

Alcott, William Andrus, 1798-1859. The house I live in; or, the human body. Eleventh stereotype edition. Boston: 1844. MNan. 44-96

Alcott, William Andrus, 1798-1859. No king in Israel: or, the importance of discipline. New York: 1844. MBC. 44-97

Alcott, William Andrus, 1789-1859. The story of Ananias and Sapphira. Revised by the editor, D.P. Kidder. New York: G. Lane and C.B. Tippett, for the Sunday School Union of the Methodist Episcopal Church, 1844. 72 p. DLC; MBC. 44-98

Alcott, William Andrus, 1789-1859.

The story of Anna the prophetess. By a Sabbath school teacher. New York: Carlton and Porter, 1844. 48 p. MBC. 44-99

Alcott, William Andrus, 1798-1859. Tobacco: Its effects on the human system... New York: 1844. 149 p. DLC; MB. 44-100

Alcott, William Andrus, 1798-1859. The use of tobacco; its physical, intellectual, and moral effects on the human system. Boston: G.W. Light, 1844. 86 p. DLC; NcD; PP; PPM. 44-101

Alcott, William Andrus, 1798-1859. The young man's guide. Sixteenth edition. Boston: 1844. 392 p. DLC; MDeeP; MFalm; NcD. 44-102

Alcott, William Andrus, 1798-1859. The young wife; or, duties of woman in the marriage relation.... Ninth stereotype edition. Boston: Waitt, Peirce, 1844. 376 p. PU; RPB. 44-103

Alexander, Archibald, 1772-1851. The immediate choice. Philadelphia: Presbyterian Board of Publication, 1844. 12 p. ViLxW. 44-104

Alexander, Archibald, 1772-1851. Outlines of moral science. New York: Charles Scribner, 1844. OkDurO. 44-105

Alexander, Archibald, 1772-1851. Thoughts on religious experience. To which is added an appendix, containing "Letters to the aged," Third edition. Philadelphia: Presbyterian Board of Publication, 1844. 397 p. ABBS; ICBB; NhPet; TxU; WBeloC. 44-106

Alexander, John Henry, 1812-1867.

Second report on the manufacture of iron; addressed to the governor of Maryland. Annapolis: W. McNeir, printer to the Senate, 1844. 189 p. CtY; MH-BA; MdHi; PPFrankI. 44-107

Alexandria, Virginia. The laws of the corporation of the town of Alexandria, D.C. Revised and published by authority of the common council of Alexandria. Alexandria, D.C.: Alexandria Gazette office, 1844. 124 p. DLC; NUtHi; PPB; WHi. 44-108

Alger, F. Phillips elementary treatise on minerology. Boston: 1844. NjNBR. 44-109

Alison, Archibald, 1757-1839. Essays on the nature and principles of taste. By Archibald Alison.... With corrections and improvements by Abraham Mills.... New York: Harper and brothers, 1844. 461 p. CoOrd; DeWi; NjP; PPA; ViRU. 44-110

Alison, Archibald, 1792-1867. History of Europe, from the commencement of the French revolution in 1789, to the restoration of the Bourbons in 1815. New York: Harper and brothers, 1844. 4 v. ArHa; DLC; NcDaD; PSal. 44-111

Alison, William Pulteney, 1790-1859. Outlines of pathology and the practice of medicine. Philadelphia: Lea and Blanchard, 1844. 424 p. ICJ; MB; NhD; TxU-M; WMMU-M. 44-112

Alleine, Joseph. An alarm to unconverted sinners. New York: American Tract Society, 1844. 190 p. IaPeC. 44-113

Allen, A.B. The American agriculturist

almanac for 1845. New York, 1844. 36 p. MB; MH. 44-114

Allen, George. An appeal to the people of Massachusetts, on the Texas question. Boston: C.C. Little and J. Brown, 1844. CtHWatk; IaGG; ICN; MH; WBeloC. 44-115

Allen, J. Adams. Index rerun. Boston: Crocker, 1844. ICU-R. 44-116

Allen, Richard L., 1808-1873. Historical, chemical and therapeutical analysis of the principal mineral fountains at Saratoga Springs; ....by R.L. Allen, M.D. ....Saratoga Springs: B. Huling; New York: W.H. Graham, 1844. 71 p. CtHT; KU; MH-M; NNS; PHi. 44-117

Allen, Thomas, 1813-1882. A pamphlet, on private property west of the Mississippi, protected by the treaty of 1803. Washington: 1844. 8 p. CSmH; MoSM; NcD; OC. 44-118

Allen, W. Poem delivered at the Berkshire Jubilee, August 22, 1844. [Albany: 1844] MWelC. 44-119

Allen, William, 1784-1868. Report on popery accepted by the General Association of Massachusetts, June, 1844. By William Allen, D.D. Boston: Charles Tappan, 1844. 28 p. CtMW; KWiU; MAnP; MWA; NcMHi. 44-120

Allens, Emma F. The jewel; a holiday gift for boys and girls. New York: 1844. 160 p. DLC; MWA. 44-121

The almanac and Baptist register, with astronomical calculations for the year of our Lord and Saviour Jesus Christ 1845.... Philadelphia: American Baptist Publication Society, [1844] 36 p. IAlS; MHi; MPeaHi; PCA; WHi. 44-122

Almanac of the American Temperance Union for the year 1845.... New York: American Temperance Union, [1844] 35 p. Ct; NjR. 44-123

Alphonsus, Liguori S. Instructions on the commandments and sacraments. Boston: Patrick Donahoe; New York: P. O'Shea, 1844. MdW. 44-124

Alverson, James L. An address delivered before the Philomathesian Society of the Oneida conference seminary on mental discipline, July 15, 1844. Auburn: Published by the society, 1844. 21 p. NCH. 44-125

The amateur's first book, or the flute without a master. Containing an analysis on an entirely new system of progressive lessons. By an amateur. Buffalo: Rince, 1844. 42 p. MB. 44-126

Amazons... nation of female warriors in the vicinity of the Amazon. New York: 1844. PPL. 44-127

Ambler, John V. A sermon on the day of the annual state of thanksgiving; delivered at Lanesboro, Massachusetts, November 30, 1843. Pittsfield: Printed by Charles Montague, 1844. 22 p. CSmH; NjR; NHC-S. 44-128

American agricultural almanac, 1845. New York, New York: Samuel S. and William Wood, [1844] MWA. 44-129

American agricultural almanac, 1845. New York, New York: Saxton and Miles, [1844] MWA. 44-130

American agriculturist almanac. By
A.B. Allen. New York: J. Winchester,
1844. MWA. 44-131

American agriculturist almanac, for
1845.... By A.B. Allen, editor of the
American agriculturist. New York:
Saxon and Miles; Boston: Saxton, Peirce
and company; Philadelphia: Thomas,
Cowperthwait and company, [1844] 36 p.
Ct. 44-132

The American almanac 1845.... Boston:
James Munroe and company, 1844. 329
p. IaHi; MSbri; MWHi; RP; RPaw. 44-
133

American and Foreign Sabbath Union.
First annual report of the American and
Foreign Sabbath Union.... Boston: press
of T.R. Marvin, 1844. 60 p. MBC; MH-
AH; NjR; OO; WHi. 44-134

American anti-slavery almanac for
1844. Boston: Webster and Southard,
1844. MoSHi. 44-135

The American anti-slavery almanac for
1844, compiled by D.L. Child. New York:
American Anti-slavery Society, 1844. 36
p. RNHi. 44-136

American Board of Commissioners for
Foreign Missions. Maps and illustrations
of the missions. New York: 1844. PPL.
44-137

American Board of Commissioners for
Foreign Missions. Missionary paper. The
divine method of raising charitable contributions. Boston: Press of T.R. Marvin,
1844. 19 p. MH-AH; NjR. 44-138

The American Chesterfield, or way to
wealth, honour or distinction; being

selections from the letters of Lord
Chesterfield to his son. Philadelphia:
Grigg and Elliott, 1844. 6-286 p. KyDC;
NIC. 44-139

American comic almanack. Boston:
Redding and company, 1844. MWA. 44-
140

American farmer's almanac, 1845. Cal-
culated by David Young. New York, New
York: Greeley and M'Elrath, [1844]
MWA; WHi. 44-141

American farmer's almanac, 1845.
Philadelphia, Pennsylvania: Turner and
Fisher, [1844] MWA. 44-142

American Industrial Union. Articles of
confederation, entered into by the
several associations hereinafter named:
Jefferson County Association...
Rochester: Printed by C.S. McConnell
and company, 1844. 8 p. NRHi. 44-143

American Industrial Union. Articles of
confederation, entered into by the
several associations hereinafter named:
Jefferson County Industrial Association,
Bloomfield Union Association, Sodus
Bay Phalanx, and Rush Industrial Association. Rochester: printed by C.S. Mc-
Donnell and company, 1844. 8 p. NRHi.
44-144

American Institute of Homeopathy.
Transactions. Phialadelphia: 1844-. 1st-.
DLC; KU-M; NjP; OrU. 44-145

American Institute of the City of New
York. Documents in relation to the
manufacture of silk and of cotton and
woolen goods in the city of New York.
New York: 1844. 16 p. NNMuCN; PHi;
RPB. 44-146

American Institute of the City of New York. Report of the commercial intercourse of the United States and Great Britain. New York: Jared W. Bell, printer, 1844. 12 p. DLC; MdBP; NjP; MH-BA. 44-147

American Institute of the City of New York. Report of the commercial intercourse of the United States and Great Britain. New York: Jared W. Bell, printer, 1844. 56 p. NBu. 44-148

American Institute of the City of New York. Report of the commercial intercourse of the United States and Great Britain. New York: Jared W. Bell, printer, 1844. 8 p. DLC; MH-BA. 44-149

American Institute of the City of New York. Report of the commercial intercourse of the United States and Great Britain. Fourth edition. [New York: 1844?] 8 p. IU; NN. 44-150

The American journal of psychiatry. Baltimore: The Johns Hopkins Press, 1844-. V. 1-. AU-M; CoU; IU-M; MH; OClW. 44-151

American Land Company. Catalogue of 96,046 acres of land belonging to the American Land Company situated and lying in the state of Arkansas... November, 1844. New York: 1844. 28 p. MHi; NIC. 44-152

The American mechanics' and manufactures' almanac, for 1845. Published under the patronage of the Mechanics' Institute. New York: E. Kearney, [1845] 35 p. MB; MWA; NNMuCN; PPL. 44-153

American messenger. Philadelphia:

American Tract Society: 1844-1875. NjR. 44-154

The American minstrel: being a choice collection of original and popular songs, glees, duetts, choruses, etc. New and revised edition. With select music. Philadelphia: H.F. Anners, 1844. CtY; MH. 44-155

American Mutual Insurance Company. Charter, by-laws, etc. Philadelphia: 1844. 12 p. PHi; PPULC. 44-156

American Party. Address to the native and naturalized citizens of the United States. Philadelphia: 1844. MBAt. 44-157

American Party. New York. Address to the people of the state of New York, by the General Executive Committee of the American Republican Party of the city of New York. New York: 1844. 8 p. NoLoc. 44-158

American Peace Society. Progress of peace. [Boston: 1884] 12 p. CtY; MB; MH; MH-AH; PU. 44-159

The American pioneer. A monthly periodical, devoted to the objects of the Logan Historical Society; or to collecting and publishing sketches relative to the early settlement and successive improvements of the country. Cincinnati: J.S. Williams, 1844. 2 v. C; MoSHi; MWA; OMC; OS; PPiU. 44-160

American practical navigator. Fourteenth edition. New York: 1844. MB. 44-161

American Protestant Association. First annual report of the American Protestant Association, together with the addresses at the first anniversary, November 18, 1843. Philadelphia: printed for the association, 1844. [3]-27 p. DLC; NjPT; PPPrHI; PPULC. 44-162

American Protestant Association. The quarterly review... Philadelphia: H. Hooker, 1844-. MiU; NjR; PHi; TKC; WaPS. 44-163

American Republican Association. Charleston, South Carolina. Constitution and by-laws and an address to all the American citizens of the parishes of St. Philips and St. Michaels. Charleston, South Carolina: 1844. 11 p. IU. 44-164

American Republican Association. Flushing, New York. An address to the people of Queens County, to which is appended the constitution, by-laws, etc., of the American Republican Association of Flushing. Flushing: Printed by Charles R. Lincoln, 1844. 24 p. NNQ; NSmb. 44-165

American Republican Party, New York City. Address to the people of the state of New York, by the General Executive Committee of the American Republican Party, of the city of New York. New York: General Executive Committee, 1844. 8 p. ICN; NjR. 44-166

American Seamen's Friend Society. Seamen's hymns and devotional assistant; prepared under the direction of the American Seamen's Friend Society. New York: the society, 1844. 443 p. MdBD; NNUT. 44-167

American Shipwreck Society. Constitution. New York: 1844. NoLoc. 44-168

The American songster, containing a

choice selection of eighty three songs; including Tyrone Power's favorite songs... Philadelphia: W.A. Leary, 1844. 189 p. RPB. 44-169

American Statistical Association. Constitution and by-laws of the American Statistical Association. With a list of officers, fellows, and members, and an address. Boston: press of T.R. Marvin, 1844. 24 p. DLC; MB; MeHi; MWA; PPL. 44-170

American Statistical Association. Memorial of the American Statistical Association, praying the adoption of measures for the correction of errors in the returns of the sixth census. [Washington, D.C.: 1844] 18 p. CSt; MBL; MiU; OO; TxU. 44-171

American Sunday School Union. Good better best: or the three ways of making a happy world. Written for the American Sunday School Union, 1844. KyHop; ICBB; MB; NIC; PPPrHi. 44-172

American temperance union almanac for 1845. New York, New York: American Temperance Union [1844] MWA. 44-173

The American text book of popery: being an authentic compend of the bulls, canons, and decretals of the Roman hierarchy. New York: S.W. Benedict and company, 1844. 540 p. GDecCT; MiD. 44-174

American themis: a journal of jurisprudence and judicature, January, February 1844 New York: Trevett, 1844. 32, 54 p. Mi-L. 44-175

The American themis; a journal of

jurisprudence and judicature. New York: Benjamin G. Trevett and company, 1844- . 1 v. MH-L; Mi-L; NNLI; WaU. 44-176

American whig. V. 1. August 19-November 9, 1844. Baltimore: 1844. MTaHi; PHi; PPULC. 44-177

The American woman. Philadelphia: 1844-1845. PHi. 44-178

American women! Will you save your country? New York: 1844. 110 p. MHi. 44-179

Americanischer stadt und land calender for 1845. Philadelphia: Conrad Zentler [1844] MWA; PReaHi. 44-180

The American's guide: comprising the Declaration of Independence; the articles of confederation; the constitution, and the constitutions of several states composing the union... Philadelphia: Hogan and Thopmson, 1844. 419 p. MBAt; MBr; MHi; MnHi. 44-181

Amery, Robert. Chester's triumph in honor of her Prince.... Reprinted from edition of 1610, with notes. [by T. Corser] [Manchester] 1844. 36 p. CtY. 44-182

Amesbury, Massachusetts. Annual report of the receipt and expenditures of the town of Amesbury from March 1, 1843 to April 1, 1844. Amesbury: 1844. Broadside. MAm. 44-183

Amesbury, Massachusetts. Second Congregational Church. Manual. Newburyport: 1844. 12 p. MBC. 44-184

Amherst College. Catalogue, 1844-1845. Amherst: J.S. and C. Adams, printers, 1844. 20 p. MBC; MeB; MiD-B; MWHi. 44-185

Amistad. Arguments of J.Q. Adams... in the case of the United States vs. Cinque and others. Africans, captured in the schooner Amistad... with a review of the case of the antelope... New York: 1844. PPL. 44-186

Anacreon. Odes of Anacreon, translated into English verse by Thomas Moore. New York: 1844. 32 p. CtY; DLC; MB; MCR. 44-187

Anacreon. Works.Translated by Thomas Bourne. New York: Harper, 1844. 66 p. CLSU; CtHWatk; MAm; PP. 44-188

The ancient and modern ballads of Chevy Chase. [n.p.] 1844. MH. 44-189

Ancient history of the Egyptians, Carthagenians.... from Rollin and other sources. New York: 1844. 4 v. MBC. 44-190

Anderson, Alexander, 1794-1869. The letter of Alexander Anderson, of Tennessee, in reply to the Committee of invitation to attend a dinner given by the Democracy of Maury, Tennessee, on July 13, to the delegation from that state to the national convention [n.p.: 1844] 27 p. DLC. 44-191

Anderson, Alexander, 1794-1869. People of China; or summary of Chinese history. Philadelphia, 1844. 234 p. VtU. 44-192

Anderson, Christopher, 1782-1852. Book for parents. The genius and design of the domestic constitution, with its intransferable obligations and peculiar advantages. From the Edinburgh edition. New York: 1844. CtY; NjMD. 44-193

Anderson, James, fl. 1840. Strictures on American Methodism. Lancaster: 1844. OKentU. 44-194

Anderson, Rufus, 1796-1880. American Board of Commissioners for Foreign Missions. Reported to the Prudential Committee of a visit to the missions in the Levant... Also, a letter to the committee from the Rev. Dr. Hawes... Boston: printed for the Board, by T.R. Marvin, 1844. 54 p. MoSpD; MeLewB; MH-AH; NCH; NjR. 44-195

Anderson, Rufus, 1796-1880. Report to the prudential committee of a visit to the missions in the Levant. By Rufus Anderson. Also, a letter to the committee from the Rev. Dr. Hawes. Boston: T. R. Marvin, printer, 1844. 54 p. CBB; MH; MWA; NNNr; RPB. 44-196

Andover, Massachusetts. Friendly Fire Society. By-laws of the Friendly Fire Society, formed in Andover S. parish, January, 1829. Andover: Allen, Morrill and Wardwell, printers, 1844. MBNEH. 44-197

Andover Theological Seminary. Society of Inquiry and the Porter Rhetorical Society. Order of exercises at the united anniversaries 1844-1846, 1848, 1850, 1852, 1853. MBC; MH. 44-198

Andral, Gabriel, 1797-1876. Pathological haematology. An essay on the blood in disease. By G. Andral.... Translated from the French by J.F. Meigs, M.D., and Alfred Stille, M.D. .... Philadelphia: Lea and Blanchard, 1844. 129 p. CU-M; ICJ; LNT-M; MeB; PPM. 44-199

Andrews, Charles Wesley, 1807-1875. Memoir of Mrs. Anne R. Page. By Rev. C.W. Andrews. Philadelphia: H. Hooker, 1844. 101 p. InThE; NbOP; PHi; ViRuT; WBeloC. 44-200

Andrews, Ethan Allen, 1787-1858. First lessons in Latin, or, an introduction to Andrews and Stoddard's Latin grammar. Sixth edition. Boston: Crocker and Brewster, 1844. MH; MLaw; RPB. 44-201

Andrews, Ethan Allen, 1787-1858. the first part of Jacobs and Doring's latin reader: adapted to Andrews and Stoddard's Latin grammar. Ninth edition. Boston: Crocker and Brewster, 1844. 266 p. CtMW; IaMp; IaU; PIm; TKinJ. 44-202

Andrews, Ethan Allen, 1787-1858. Grammar of the Latin language.... Tenth edition. By Ethan A. Andrews and S. Stoddard. Boston: Crocker and Brewster, 1844. IGK; LNL; MdBD; MH; PPM. 44-203

Andrews, Ethan Allen, 1787-1858. Latin exercises; adapted to Andrews and Stoddard's Latin grammar. By Professor E.A. Andrews. Sixth edition. Boston: Crocker and Brewster, 1844. 336 p. CU; GMM; MeHi; MFiHi; MH. 44-204

Andrews, Ethan Allen, 1787-1858. Leisure hours; a choice collection of readings in prose. New illustrated edition. Boston: T.H. Carter and company and B.B. Mussey, 1844. [5]-340 p. DLC; IaDuU; MB; MBevHi; MB-FA. 44-205

Andrews, James. Progressive drawing book of flowers, for beginners. New York: Collins and brothers and company, 1844. 24 p. NoLoc. 44-206

Andrews, Stephen Pearl. The phonographic class book. Boston: 1844. 23 p. NN. 44-207

Andrews, Stephen Pearl. The phonographic class book. Second edition. Boston: 1844. 23 p. MH-BA. 44-208

Anecdotes of the American Indians, illustrating their eccentricities of character. By the author of "evenings in Boston," "Ramon the rover of Cuba," etc. New York: A.W. Blake, 1844. 252 p. CtY; NjR; OkU; PP; WBeloC. 44-209

Anecdotes of the American Revolution; selected from Garden's anecdotes, Garden's letters, New Hampshire historical collections, Massachusetts historical collections, New York historical collections, American anecdotes, historical anecdotes and other works on history and biography. New York: Alexander V. Blake, 1844. 252 p. NGlf; WWaupu. 44-210

Angell, Joseph Kinnicut, 1794-1857. A treatise on the law of carriers of goods and passengers by land and water. Boston: C.C. Little and J. Brown, 1844. 791 p. CSt; NNIns. 44-211

Angell, Oliver. Angell's union series of common school classics. Number Three. Stereotype edition. Philadelphia: E.H. Butler, 1844. 206 p. ICBB. 44-212

Angell, Oliver. The select reader, or, union no. 6. Designed for the higher classes in academies and schools. Being the sixth of a series of common school classics. Revised stereotyped edition. By Oliver Angell, A.M., principal of the Franklin High School, Providence. Philadelphia: Butler and Williams, 1844. 504 p. MH; MHolliHi. 44-213

Angell, Oliver. The union, number five. Revised stereotype edition. Philadelphia: Butler and Williams, 1844. MH. 44-214

The Anglican reformation; or the church of England but half reformed. Originally published in the Edinburgh Presbyterian Review, January, 1843. Philadelphia: Presbyterian Board of Publication, Paul T. Jones, publishing agent, 1844. 66 p. CSansS; MAnP; MeBat; NjR; PPLT. 44-215

Ann Eliza; or the conflict and victory of faith. Boston: Sunday School Union, 1844. ICP; MBC. 44-216

Anna Bailey; and image worship. Philadelphia: American Baptist Publication Society, 1844. 79 p. DLC; OOC. 44-217

The annexation of Texas and separation of the United States. ["signed by Sundy" 1844?] 24 p. MHi. 44-218

The annualette. A Christmas and new year's gift. Edited by a lady. Boston: printed by Freeman and Bolles. Published by T.H. Carter and company, 1844. [13]-142 p. MHi; MWA; PP; RPB; WU. 44-219

Anthon, Charles, 1797-1867. Anthon's Latin grammar. New York: Harper and brothers, 1844. 2 parts. KyU; ODaB; OUrC. 44-220

Anthon, Charles, 1797-1867. The classical dictionary, containing an account of the principal proper names mentioned in ancient authors and intended to elucidate all the important points connected with the geography, ...and fine arts of Greeks and Romans. Together with an account of coins.... with tabular values of the same.... New York: Harper, 1844. 1451 p. CL; PAtM; ViU. 44-221

Anthon, Charles, 1797-1867. First Greek lessons, containing all the inflexions of the Greek language. Together with appropriate exercises in the translating and writing of Greek, for the use of beginners. New York: Harper, 1844. 238 p. ICU; ViU. 44-222

Anthon, Charles, 1797-1867. First Latin lessons, containing the most important parts of the grammar of the Latin language, together with appropriate exercises in the translating and writing of Latin, for the use of beginners. New York: Harper and brothers, 1844. 362 p. AMob; CtMW; InGrD; LNB; MWiW. 44-223

Anthon, Charles, 1797-1867. Latin grammar. New York: [Harper and brothers] 1844-1845. 2 v. WU. 44-224

Anthon, Charles, 1797-1867. The system of Latin prosody and metre, ...New York: Harper and brothers, 1844. 216 p. CSansS; CtHT; FTU; InGrD; LNL. 44-225

Anthony, Susanna, 1726-1791. Memoir of Miss Susanna Anthony, consisting chiefly in extracts from her writings and observations respecting them. Boston: Sabboth School Society, 1844. 180 p. MBC; MWHi; OO; VtFaH. 44-226

Anthony, Susanna, 1726-1791. Memoir of Miss Susanna Anthony. Extracts from her writings. Second edition. Boston: Sunday School Society, 1844. 180 p. OO. 44-227

The anti-annihilationist. Philadelphia: J. Litch, 1844. V. 1. No. 1. MBAt; MWorHi. 44-228

Anti-Draco, a monthly periodical, issued under the auspices of the American Society from the Collection and diffusion of information in relation to the punishment of death. New York: March, 1844. 8 p. P. 44-229

Anti-slavery examiner. The constitution pro-slavery compact or selections from Madison papers, etc. New York: 1844. 123 p. PHi. 44-230

Anti-Texas legion; protest of some freemen, states, and presses against the Texas rebellion against the laws of nature and of nations. Albany: 1844. 72 p. MB; MH; NN; TxU; WHi. 44-231

An apology for not joining the Protestant Episcopal Church. By a Presbyter. Philadelphia: Presbyterian Board of Publication [1844] 24 p. CtHC; IaDuU; MAnP; MH; NjPT. 44-232

Appleby, William I. A dissertation on Nebuchadnezzar's dream; also the rise and faith of the most notable orthodox societies of the present day, together with a synopsis of the origin and faith of the church of "Latter-day Saints," comparing their faith with the faith of other societies. Philadelphia: Brown, Bicking and Guilbert, printers, 1844. 24 p. MH; MH-AH. 44-233

Appleton, James, 1786-1862. Missouri compromise; or the extension of the slave power. Boston? 1844. CtHWatk. 44-234

Appleton, Nathan, 1779-1861. Labor, its relations in Europe and the United States compared. Boston: Eastburn's Press, 1844. 16 p. CU; DLC; MWA; PCA; WHi. 44-235

Arblay, Frances Burney de, 1752-1840. Memoirs of Madame d'Arblay. New York: J. Mowatt and company, 1844. 2 v. in 1. CtY; MBBC; MH; NcU; NjR. 44-236

Arch, John. Memoir of John Arch, a Cherokee young man, compiled from communications of missionaries in the Cherokee nation. Revised by the committee of publication. Fifth edition. Boston: Massachusetts Sabbath School Society, 1844. 36 p. DLC; MBC; MH. 44-237

Archer, William Segar, 1789-1855. Speech of Mr. Archer, of Virginia, delivered in the Senate of the United States, in secret session, May, 1844. on the treaty for the annexation of Texas. Washington: Printed by Gales and Seaton, 1844. 22 p. MHi; MiD-B; Tx. 44-238

Arguments proving the inconsistency and impolicy of granting to foreigners the right of voting; abstracted from a pamphlet published in the year 1810, by a disciple of the Washington School, and one who is personally a warm friend of the Irish. Revised by the author. Philadelphia: for sale by T.G. Auner, 1844. 8 p. CtY; DLC; MBAt; MiD-B; PHi. 44-239

The arithmetical table book; or first lessons in arithmetic. Newark, New Jersey: Benjamin Olds, 1844. MH. 44-240

Arithmetical tables for the use of schools. New York: Samuel S. and W. Wood, [1844?] MH. 44-241

Arithmetical tables, suited to the capacity of boys and girls of an early age. Designed for schools. Philadelphia: Henry M'Grath, 1844. 48 p. PU-Penn. 44-242

The ark and odd fellows western monthly magazine; a monthly periodical devoted to the cause of Odd Fellowship; Alex. E. Glenn, ed. Columbus: O.A.E. Glenn, 1844-. OClWHi; WHi. 44-243

Arlington, Massachusetts. Catalogue of books in the West Cambridge Juvenile Library. Also the by-laws of the institution. Somerville: Edmund Tufts, 1844. 32 p. OClWHi. 44-244

Arms, James Carleton. A continuous family genealogy and record of events. In three parts. Hartford: 1844. 239 p. PHi. 44-245

Armstrong, John, 1758-1843. A key to the western calculator, containing the solution of all the examples and questions for exercise, with reference to the pages where they stand. To which is added, some useful rules, designed chiefly to facilitate the labor of teachers; and assist such as have not the opportunity of a tutor's aid. Fifth edition, revised and corrected. Pittsburgh: Johnston and Stockton, 1844. 139 p. CSmH; CtY; NNC; OClWHi; PWCHi. 44-246

Armstrong, John, 1758-1843. Lives of

Anthony Wayne and Sir Henry Vane. New York: Harper and brothers, 1844. 403 p. CSmH; KyBgW; RPE. 44-247

Arnold, Isaac N. Argument before the United States Supreme Court in the case of John L.H. McCrackan, a citizen of the state of New York, Complainant, and Charles Hayward, a citizen of the state of Illinois, Defendant, involving the constitutionality of the Acts of the Legislature of the state of Illinois passed 17th February, 1841, and of 6th January, 1843, commonly known as the "Appraisal or Two-Thirds Valuation Laws." n.p., 1844. 15 p. MWA. 44-248

Arnold, Thomas, 1795-1842. Miscellaneous works. Second American edition. New York: 1844. 545 p. PHC. 44-249

Arnold, Thomas Kerchever, 1800-1853. A practical introduction to Latin prose composition. By Thomas Kerchever Arnold, M.A. ....Carefully revised and corrected by Rev. J.A. Spencer, A.M. Twelfth American edition. New York: D. Appleton and company, 1844. 356 p. KyU. 44-250

The arrest, trial, conviction and condemnation of King Alcohol. New York: 1844. 24 p. ICartC; MH-AH. 44-251

The art of acquiring memory... illustrated by diagrams and engravings. Pittsburgh: J. M'Millins, printer, 1844. 71 p. NNC. 44-252

Arthur's ladies' magazine of elegant literature and the fine arts. Edited by T.S. Arthur. Philadelphia: Ferrett, 1844-. V. 1-. ICN; ILM; PP. 44-253

Arthur's magazine of elegant literature and fine arts. Ladies magazine. Philadelphia: 1844. 2 v. in 1. MB. 44-254

Arthur, Timothy Shay, 1809-1885. Cecilia Howard; or the young lady who had finished her education... New York: John Allen, 1844. 92 p. MB; MH; TxDaM. 44-255

Arthur, Timothy Shay, 1809-1885. The hand without the heart. New York: Charles Scribner and company, 1844. 237 p. IaPeC. 44-256

Arthur, Timothy Shay, 1809-1885. Insubordination, or the shoemaker's daughters; an American story of real life. Philadelphia: R.G. Berford, 1844. 77 p. MH; MWA. 44-257

Arthur, Timothy Shay, 1809-1885. The lady at home; or leaves from the every day book of an American woman, by Mrs. Mary Elmwood [pseud.] New York: J. Allen, 1844. 96 p. ICU; RPB. 44-258

Arthur, Timothy Shay, 1809-1885. Pride or principal [sic], which makes the lady. Philadelphia: R.G. Berford, 1844. MHad. 44-259

Arthur, Timothy Shay, 1809-1885. Prose fictions, written for the illustrations of true principles, in their bearing upon every day life. Philadelphia: G.B. Zeiber, 1844. 2 v. in 1. RPB. 44-260

Arthur, Timothy Shay, 1809-1885. Temperance tales; by T.S. Arthur.... Philadelphia: E. Ferrett and company, 1844. 2 v. in 1. DLC; ICT; RPB. 44-261

Arthur, Timothy Shay, 1809-1885. The two sisters; or, life's changes.... Philadelphia: G.B. Zieber, 1844. 94 p. RPB. 44-262

Ashland songster. Comprising the most poular national songs, for western New York. Rochester: Smith and Raymond, printers, 1844. 32 p. NRHi. 44-263

Aspin, Jehoshaphat. A view of the world, as exhibited in the manners, costumes, and characteristics of all nations. With seventy-two engravings. Originally written by J. Aspin, esq., and now improved and adapted to the use of American schools, by Rev. J.L. Blake... Fifth edition, revised. Cooperstown, New York: H. and E. Phinney, 1844. 365 p. OClW; TBriK. 44-264

Aspin, Jehoshaphat. A view of the world, as exhibited in the manners, costumes, and characteristics of all nations....now improved and adapted to the use of American schools by J.L. Blake. Sixth edition. Cooperstown: Phinney, 1844. 365 p. OClW; TBriK. 44-265

Associate Reformed Synod of the West. Pennsylvania. Extracts from the minutes of the proceedings of the First Associate Reformed Synod of the West, held in the city of Allegheny, September 30, 1844; and continued by adjournment. Pittsburgh: Franklin office, 1844. 28 p. NcMHi. 44-266

Association for Domestic, Missionary and Other Purposes. Circular letter to churches asking for funds for missionary and other objects. Boston: 1844. 3 p. MHi. 44-267

Association for the Religious Instruction of the Negroes. Annual report. Savannah: 1844. MH. 44-268

An astronomical diary, for 1845.... By Thomas Spofford.... New York: Nafis and Cornish, [1844] NjR. 44-269

Atchison, David Rice, 1807-1886. Speech of Mr. Atchison, of Missouri, on the resolution of Mr. Semple in relation to the Oregon Territory: in the Senate of the United States, February 22, 1844. Washington: Printed by Blair and Rives, 1844. 14 p. CSmH; MoHi. 44-270

Atherton, Charles Gordon, 1804-1853. Speech of Mr. Atherton, of New Hampshire, on the tariff; delivered in the Senate, May 25, 1844. Washington: Printed at the Globe office, 1844. 12 p. Nh. 44-271

Atkinson, Matthew. The family director... containing plain directions, for washing wool, colouring wool, woolen yarn and flannel and mixing colours.... Carrollton [Ohio] Printed by J. Hudson, 1844. 48 p. DLC; OClWHi; PPULC. 44-272

Atkinson, Thomas, 1807-1881. Authoritive ministerial teaching; a sermon preached at the opening of the convention of the Diocese of Maryland, May, 1844. Baltimore: Brunner, 1844. 19 p. CtHT; MdBD; MH; NcU; PHi. 44-273

Atkinson, Thomas, 1807-1881. A sermon, in reference to the catastrophe which occured on board the United States ship Princeton, on February 28, 1844, viewed as a national calamity, delivered on Sunday, 10th day of March, by Rev. Thomas Atkinson, rector of St. Peter's Church. Baltimore: D. Brunner, 1844. 16 p. MdBD; MWA; PPL; NcU; NGH. 44-274

Atkinson, William Mayo, d. 1849. A sermon delivered at the installation of the Rev. John M.P. Atkinson, as pastor of the church at Warrenton, Fauquier County, September 15, 1844. By the Rev. William M. Atkinson. Winchester: printed at the Republican office, 1844. 24 p. CSansS; MWA; NjPT; PHi. 44-275

Atlantic Dock Company. Report of the committee to examine Gilberts' Balance Dry Dock. n.t.p. [1844] DNA; MBAt. 44-276

Atlee, Washington Lemuel, 1808-1878. Case of extirpation of bilocular ovarian cyst of large peritoneal section... April 17, 1844. Philadelphia: T.K. and P.G. Collins, 1844. 29 p. RPB. 44-277

Atlee, Washington Lemuel, 1808-1878. Lecture introductory to the course of medical chemistry in the medical department of Pennsylvania College. Philadelphia. For the session 1844-1845. Philadelphia: Published by the members of the class, William S. Young, printer, 1844. 16 p. MB; NBMS; OC; PHi. 44-278

Attleborough, Massachusetts. Second Congregational Church. Catalogue of the members of the Second Congregational Church of Attleborough, Massachusetts. Pawtucket: 1844. 16 p. CtY; MWA. 44-279

Atwater, Caleb, 1778-1867. Mysteries of Washington City, during several months of the session of the 28th congress. By a citizen of Ohio. Washington, D.C.: printed by A. Sage, 1844. 218 p. CU; ICN; MdBE; OCHP; PPL. 44-280

Atwater, Lyman Hotchkiss, 1813-1883. The importance of good rulers, considered especially with reference to the preservation of national peace: a sermon preached on the day of the annual fast, April 5, 1844. New Haven: Printed By B.L. Hamlen, 1844. 15 p. CtY; MBC; MiD-B; NNUT; PPPrHi. 44-281

Atwood, A. An exposure of Rev. Mr. Major's misktakes and a reply to his apology for wicked ministers in "The Episcopal Succession." Harrisburg: Isaac G. M'Kinley, 1844. 35 p. NjPT. 44-282

Auburn Theological Seminary. Catalogue of the officers and students of Theological Seminary at Auburn, New York. Auburn: Merrell and Hollett, 1844. 12 p. CSmH; NAuHi; NCH. 44-283

Augsburg Confession. Die augsburgische confession, oder das glaubens bekentniss der protestanten, des Kaiser Karl V vorgetragen und ubergeben, 1530. New York: Ludwig, 1844. 48 p. PPLT. 44-284

Augustinus, Aurelius. The confessions of St. Augustine. New York: Wiley and Putnam, 1844. 285 p. GEU-T; MHi; NjPT; ScDuE; TSewU. 44-285

Austin, J.M. A voice to youth, addressed to young men and young ladies, by Rev. J.M. Austin. Seventh edition. New York: C.L. Stickney, 1844. 390 p. NCaS. 44-286

Austin, John Mather, 1805-1880. Arguments drawn from the attributes of God in support of the doctrine of universal salvation. Boston: A. Tompkin, 1844. 218 p. MB; MiD; MMeT-Hi; NBuU; NCaS. 44-287

Austin, John Mather, 1805-1880. A

source and perpetuity of republicanism. A discourse delivered.... October 27, 1844. Auburn, New York: Merrell and Hollett, printers, 1844. 22 p. CSmH; MMeT; NCH; NRHi; OClWHi. 44-288

Austin, William. Peter Rugg, the missing man. From Jonathan Dunwell [pseud.] to Herman Krauff. Boston: 1844. 16 p. MB; MH. 44-289

Aydelott, Benjamin Parham, 1795-1880. The secret of a sound judgment: an address delivered at the commencement of Woodward College on the 28th of June, 1844. By Rev. B.P. Aydelott.... Cincinnati: G.L. Weed, 1844. 43 p. CSmH; DLC; MeHi; NNUT; OClWHi. 44-290

B

Babcock, Daniel Hutchinson. Scenes of the past. Collections of poems on various subjects. By Rev. D.H. Babcock. Boston: printed for the author, 1844. 72 p. MB; MCoh; MeB; OClW; RPB. 44-291

Babcock, James Staunton, 1815-1847. Memoir of Captain Nathan Hale.... New Haven: S. Babcock, printer, 1844. 16 p. Ct; DLC; ICN; MB; Nh-Hi. 44-292

Babylonish captivity. Boston: Massachusetts Sabbath School Society, 1844. 72 p. DLC; NNUT. 44-293

Bache, Anna. Little Clara; by Mrs. Anna Bache. Second edition. Philadelphia: James K. Simon, 1844. 10-168 p. NoLoc. 44-294

Bache, Franklin. Introductory lecture to the course of chemistry, delivered in Jefferson Medical College, November 6, 1844, by Franklin Bache, M.D. Published by the class. Philadelphia: B.E. Smith, printer, 1844. 24 p. DLC; MH; MoSMed; NNNAM; PU-S. 44-295

Backey, T. The history and mystery of puffing, or a few fragrant whiffs of the weed, evolving sundry hints touching the poetry of smoking, enlivened with anecdotes. By T. Backey [pseud.] New York: Burgess, Stringer and company, 1844. 61 p. MH; NN. 44-296

Backus, Isaac, 1724-1806. Church history of New England, from 1620 to 1804 containing a view of the principles and practice, declensions and revivals, oppression and liberty of the churches, and a chronological table... Philadelphia: American Baptist Publication and Sunday School Society, 1844. 250 p. CtY; GDecCT; KHi; NcD; PCA. 44-297

Backus, Jay S. The Lord our righteousness. A serman delivered before the Baptist Church in Auburn. Auburn: Printed by Henry Oliphant, 1844. 12 p. N. 44-298

Backus, M.M. Roman relics. New York: S.W. Benedict and company, 1844. 48 p. ICMe. 44-299

Bacon, David Francis, 1813-1865. Progressive democracy; discourse on American politics. New York: 1844. CtY; DLC; MBAt; PU. 44-300

Bacon, Delia Salter, 1811-1859. The bride of Fort Edward; founded on an incident of the revolution. Philadelphia: G.B. Zieber and company; New York: Burgess, Stringer and company, 1844. 174 p. NNC. 44-301

Bacon, Ezekiel, 1776-1870. A lecture delivered before the Young Men's Association of the city of Utica, December 15, 1843. Utica, New York: R.W. Roberts, 1844. 48 p. CtY; DLC; MB; MWA; NjPT. 44-302

Bacon, Ezekiel, 1776-1870. Odes and hymns, written and designed for the

Berkshire Jubilee. Utica, New York: 1844. 12 p. CSmH; DLC; NN; RPB. 44-303

Bacon, Francis, 1561-1626. Essays, moral, economical, and political, by Francis Bacon.... The conduct of the understanding by John Locke.... With an introductory essay by A. Potter.... New York: Harper and brothers, 1844. 299 p. IGK; MF; NbOM; OMC; RPAt. 44-304

Bacon, Francis, 1561-1626. Moral, economical and political essays. A new edition. Boston: T.H. Carter and company, 1844. MeWC; MH. 44-305

Bacon, Francis, 1561-1626. The works of Francis Bacon, lord chancellor of England. A new edition with a life of the author, by B. Montagu.... Philadelphia: Carey and Hart, 1844. 3 v. CSto; InThE; KyLx; OCY; PWW. 44-306

Bacon, Henry, 1813-1856. The endurance of faith. A sermon by Henry Bacon.... Providence, Rhode Island: 1844. 18 p. MMeT-Hi; RPB. 44-307

Bailey, Charles. The jilted doctor; or, "circumstances make the man." Springfield: B.F. Brown, 1844. 40 p. MnU. 44-308

Bailey, Charles. The reclaimed student: a tale of college life.... Springfield: Benjamin F. Brown, 1844. 60 p. MH; NN. 44-309

Bailey, Ebenezer, 1795-1839. First lessons in algebra; being an easy introduction to that science; designed for the use of academies and common schools. Twenty-third improved stereotype edi-

tion. Boston: Jenks and Palmer, 1844. 252 p. MB; MH; MiU; Nh; OMC. 44-310

Bailey, Ebenezer, 1795-1839. A key to the first lessons in algebra, ...by Ebenezer Bailey.... Boston: Jenks and Palmer, 1844. 84 p. DAU; MDovC; MH. 44-311

Bailey, Ebenezer, 1795-1839. The young ladies' class book; a seletion of lessons for reading, in prose and verse. ....Twenty-sixth stereotype edition. Boston: Gould, Kendall and Lincoln, 1844. 408 p. MB; MHi; PPULC; RJa. 44-312

Bailey, Jacob Whitman, 1811-1857. Account of some new infusorial forms discovered in the fossil infusoria from Petersburg, Virginia, and Piscatoway, Maryland. By professor J.W. Bailey. From the American Journal of Science, vol. XLVI. New Haven: B.L. Hamlen, printer, 1844. 7 p. DLC; MB; MBHO; MH; RPB. 44-313

Bailey, Samuel, 1791-1870. Essays on the formation and publication of opinions.... Boston: Ticknor and Fields, 1844. 422 p. NRivHi. 44-314

Baily, William. Anatomy of geography, or, the world in a pamphlet. Heaton, St. Clarisville, Ohio: 1844. OCo. 44-315

Baines, Peter Augustine, 1786-1843. The eucharistic mystery, taken from a lecture on the same subject. By the late Bishop Baines. Published for the Catholic Tract Society. Baltimore: 1844. 12 p. DLC; MdBD; MdBS; MWA; NNG. 44-316

Baird, Robert, 1798-1863. Religion in America; or an account of the origin, progress, relation to the state, and present conditions of the evangelical churches in the United States. New York: Harper and brothers, 1844. 343 p. CU; MH; PPPrHi; RPB; WaU. 44-317

Baird, Washington. A discourse on ordination and church polity; in which it is shown that the arrogant assumptions of high-churchism are inconsistent with scripture, with reason, and with facts. By the Rev. Washington Baird.... New York: J.F. Trow and company, printer, 1844. 31 p. GDecCT; MBC; NcWHi; NjPT; PPPrHi. 44-318

Baker, Abijah Richardson. Christ's desire for the presence of his people in heaven; a sermon occasioned by the death of the Rev. Isaac Orr. Boston: William S. Damrell, printer, 1844. 23 p. CBPSR; MB; MWA; RPB. 44-319

Baker, Benjamin Franklin, 1811-1889. Baker's American school music book; containing a thorough elementary system with songs, chants common schools.... Boston: Otis, Broaders, 1844. 143 p. NNUT; RPB. 44-320

Baker, Benjamin Franklin, 1811-1889. The Boston Musical Education Society's collection of church music, including compositions adapted to the service of the Protestant Episcopal Church. Edited by Benjamin F. Baker and I.B. Woodbury. Seventh edition. Boston: Saxton and Peirce and company, 1844. CtY; MB; MH. 44-321

Baker, James Loring. The Washington reform, an address, delivered before the Hingham Total Abstinence Society, June 16, 1844. By James L. Baker. Published by request of the government of the society. Hingham: Jedidiah Farmer, printer, 1844. 20 p. ICN; MH; MWA; NNG; PPL. 44-322

Bakewell, W.J. The distinctive principles of orthodoxy: a discourse, delivered in Trinity Church, the fifth Sunday after Easter, by W.J. Bakewell, assistant minister. Published by request. Pittsburgh: George Parkin, printer, 1844. 30 p. MiD-MCh; NjR; NNG; PHi. 44-323

Baldwin, Charles N. A universal biographical dictionary containing the lives of the most celebrated characters of early age and nation; to which is added a dictionary of the principal divinities, and heroes of the Grecian and Roman mythology. Hartford: S. Andrus and son, 1844. 444 p. Nh-Hi; OClWHi; TJoT. 44-324

Baldwin, William H. Speech of Mr. Baldwin of Clinton, Ohio. in the Senate, January 30, 1844... to fix and apportion the representation in the General Assembly. Columbus: 1844. OClWHi. 44-325

Balfe, Michael William, 1808-1870. The Bohemian girl. The new grand opera in three acts of "The Bohemian girl," first performed in America at the Park Theatre, November, 1844... New York: J.C. House, 1844. 24 p. MB; MiD; MH. 44-326

Balfe, Michael William, 1808-1870. The new grand opera in three acts of the Bohemian girl. First performed in America at the Park Theatre, November, 1844. New York: J.C. House, 1844. 24 p. CSt; MH; NNC. 44-327

Balfe, Michael William, 1808-1870.

Quadrilles from Balfe's Bohemian Girl, arranged for pianoforte. New York: 1844. CtY. 44-328

Ballou, Hosea, 1771-1852. Select sermons, delivered on various occasions, from important passages of scripture. [Second edition] Boston: A. Tompkins, 1844. 350 p. IEG; MBUGC; MH. 44-329

Ballou, Hosea, 1771-1852. A series of lecture sermons, delivered at the Second Universalist Meeting, in Boston. By Hosea Ballou, pastor. Third edition, stereotyped. Revised by the author. Boston: A. Tompkins, 1844. 375 p. MH-AH; MWeA; NCas; NcD; RPE. 44-330

Ballou, Hosea, 1771-1852. A treatise on atonement, in which the finite nature of sin is argued, its cause and consequences as such; the necessity and nature of atonement, and its glorious consequences in the final reconciliation of all men to holiness and happiness. Sixth edition. Boston: A. Tompkins, 1844. 228 p. LNB; MB; MMilf; RPE. 44-331

Ballou, Hosea, 1796-1852. A collection of psalms and hymns for the use of Universalist Societies and families. Fifteenth edition. Boston: 1844. 540 p. MBUPH; MiGr; NNUT. 44-332

Ballou, Hosea, 1796-1852. Opinions and phraseology of the Jews concerning the future state: from the time of Moses to that of their final dispersion by the Romans. By Hosea Ballou, 2d. Philadelphia: Gihon, Fairchild and company, 1844. 20 p. ICBB; MH; MMeT-Hi; MWA; PPL-R. 44-333

Baltimore, Maryland. St. Paul's Church. Address of the vestry of St. Paul's Parish,

Baltimore, to the members of the congregation. Baltimore: 1844. CtHT; MdBP; MdHi; PPL. 44-334

Baltimore and Ohio Railroad Company. Memorial to the legislature of Virginia, at the session, December, 1844 [Baltimore? 1844] 22 p. DBRE; MdBP; PHi; PPULC. 44-335

Baltimore and Ohio Railroad Company. Two replies of the Baltimore and Ohio Railroad Company, to interrogatories propounded to the said company, by the House of Delegates of Maryland, on the 25th of January, and 10th of February, 1844. Baltimore: James Lucas and E.K. Deaver, 1844. 23 p. MdBP; MdHi; NNE; PHi; PPLRC. 44-336

Baltimore Society for Promoting the Observance of the Lord's Day. Minutes of the convention of the friends of the Lord's day from Maryland, Delaware and the District of Columbia..... Baltimore: publication rooms of the Evangelical Lutheran Church, 1844-,. 1st-. CSmH; MBC; MdBE; MdBP; PHC. 44-337

Balzac, Honore de, 1799-1850. Cousin Pons. Boston: E.B. Hall and Locke company, 1844. 315 p. NJost. 44-338

Balzac, Honore de, 1799-1850. Cousin Pons. New York: John W. Lovell and company, 1844. 297 p. NdDiT. 44-339

Balzac, Honore de, 1799-1850. Gonderville mystery and the muse of the department. With photogravures. Boston: E.B. Hall and Locke company, 1844. 844 p. NJost. 44-340

Balzac, Honore de, 1799-1850.

Jealousies of a country town; Lost illusions; the atheist's mass. New York: Harper and brothers, [1844?] 654 p. MDanv. 44-341

Balzac, Honore de, 1799-1850. The philosopher's stone. A novel by H. de Balzac. Translated from the French by a lady. New York: J. Winchester, 1844. 77 p. MH. 44-342

Balzac, Honore de, 1799-1850. Rise and fall of Ceasar Birotteau; the middle classes. New York: Harper and brothers, [1844?] 364 p. MDanv. 44-343

Bancroft, Aaron, 1755-1839. The life of George Washington, commander-in-chief of the American army, through the Revolutionary War, and the first president of the United States. Boston, Massachusetts: Lewis and Sampson, 1844. 2 v. CSmH; IaDmD; MBAt; PHi; PPULC. 44-344

Bancroft, George, 1800-1891. History of the colonization of the United States. Tenth edition. Boston: Charles C. Little and James Brown, 1844. 3 v. CoCsC; MdBJ; NIC; OC. 44-345

Bancroft, George, 1800-1891. History of the United States, 1492-1782. Boston: 1844-1874. 10 v. KyLx; MdBJ; NGos; PRea. 44-346

Bancroft, George, 1800-1891. History of the United States from the discovery of the American continent. Boston: Charles C. Little and James Brown, 1844. 8 v. LNB. 44-347

Bancroft, George, 1800-1891. History of the United States, from the discovery of the American continent. Boston:

Charles C. Little and James Brown, 1844[-1866] 9 v. IU; MoFloSS. 44-348

Bancroft, George, 1800-1891. History of the United States from the discovery of the American continent. Tenth edition. Boston: C.C. Little and J. Brown, 1844. 3 v. DLC; IU; MH; MiD-B; WM. 44-349

Bancroft, George, 1800-1891. The necessity, by reality, and the promise of the progress of the human race. Oration delivered before the New York Historical Society. n.p.: n.p., 1844. 96 p. NjR. 44-350

The band of niggers! from "ole Virginny state" song with accompaniment for the pianoforte. Boston: Prentiss, 1844. 5 p. MB. 44-351

Bang, Theodore. The mysteries of Papermill village. Fitchburg: Charles Shepley, 1844. 28 p. MFiHi. 44-352

Bangor, Maine. Mayor. Address of the mayor of Bangor, to the city council, March 22, 1844, together with the annual reports of the superintending school committee, city treasurer, street commissioner, overseers of the poor, and chief engineer of the fire department. Bangor: Smith and Sayward, printers, 1844. 32 p. MeB. 44-353

Bangs, Nathan, 1778-1862. A history of the Methodist Episcopal Church. New York: G. Lane, and P.P. Sanford, 1844. 4 v. AB; CSf; DLC; MsJMC; OBerB. 44-354

Bank of Pennsylvania. Proceedings of the stockholders at their annual meeting,

February 5, 1844. Philadelphia: 1844. 8 p. PHi. 44-355

Bank of South Carolina. The bank case; a report of the proceedings in the cases of the Bank of South Carolina and the Bank of Charleston upon scire facias to vacate their charters for suspending specie payments... in the Court for the Correction of Errors of South Carolina, in the year 1842, and 1843. Charleston: Riley, 1844. 550 p. AB; IaU; IU; MdBB; NcD. 44-356

Bank of Virginia. Proceedings of the stockholders of the Bank of Virginia, at a general meeting in 1844. Richmond: Printed by Sheperd and Colin, 1844. 29 p. NcU. 44-357

Banning, Edmond Prior, b. 1810. One weakness of the body. Boston: 1844. MBAt. 44-358

Banning, Edmund Prior, b. 1810. Common sense on chronic diseases; or a rational treatise on the mechanical cause and cure of most chronic affections of the truncal organs of both male and female systems. Boston: Waite, Pierce and company, 1844. CtY; KyBC; NNN; PPCP; WBeloC. 44-359

Banning, Edmund Prior, b. 1810. Popular lectures on the mechanical nature and physical cure of chronic diseases of the human trunk. By Dr. E.P. Banning. Boston: Samuel N. Dickinson, 1844. 58 p. MBC; MiD-W; MWA. 44-360

Banvard, Joseph. A topical question book, on subjects connected with the plan of salvation, arranged in consecutive order; with hints for the assistance of teachers, designed for Sabbath schools and Bible classes, by Rev. Joseph Banvard. Fifteenth edition. Cincinnati: Jewett and Mason, 1844. 122 p. ICP. 44-361

Baptist almanac for 1845. Philadelphia, Pennsylvania: American Baptist Publication and Sunday School Society, [1844] MWA. 44-362

Baptists. Alabama. Tuskaloosa Association. Minutes of the twelfth annual session of the Tuskaloosa Baptist Assocation held at Spring Hill meeting house, Tuskaloosa County from the 14th to 17th of September, 1844. Tuskaloosa: Printed by M.D.J. Slade, 1844. 16 p. ICU. 44-363

Baptists. Colored Baptist Association. Minutes [6th].... Wood River, Madison County, August 8-10, 1844. Alton: Telegraph office, 1844. 8 p. IAlB. 44-364

Baptists. Connecticut. Ashford Association. Minutes of the Ashford Baptist Association, held with the Baptist Church in Stafford, Connecticut, May 29 and 30, 1844... Hartford: Burr and Smith, printers, 1844. 21, 3 p. Ct; NHC-S. 44-365

Baptists. Connecticut. Fairfield County Association. Minutes of the seventh session of the Fairfield County Association, held in the meeting house of the First Baptist Church, Danbury Connecticut, October 9, and 10, 1844. New York: Wm. C. Martin, printer, 1844. 15 p. PCA. 44-366

Baptists. Connecticut. Hartford Association. Minutes of the fifty-fifth anniversary of the Hartford Baptist Association, held with the Baptist Church in Bristol, September 11 and 12,

1844. Hartford: Burr and Smith, printers, 1844. 16 p. Ct. 44-367

Baptists. Connecticut. New London Association. Minutes of the New London Baptist Association. Held with the Colchester Borough Baptist Church, September 25 and 26, 1844. Norwich: J.G. Cooley, printer, 1844. 14 p. Ct; NHC-S. 44-368

Baptists. Connecticut. State Convention.Twenty-first annual meeting of the Connecticut Baptist Convention, held at New Haven, June 11, 12 and 13, 1844. Hartford: Burr and Smith, 1844. 45 p. PCA. 44-369

Baptists. Delaware. Delaware Association. Minutes of the Delaware Baptist Association, held with the church at Rock Spring, Lancaster County, Pennsylvania, May 25, 26, 27, 1844. New Vernon, New York: printed at the office of the signs of the times, 1844. 8 p. PCA. 44-370

Baptists. General Convention for Foreign Missions. Minutes of the eleventh triennial meeting of the Baptist General Convention for Foreign Missions. Together with the thirteenth annual report of the Board of Managers, Philadelphia, April 24-30, 1844. Boston: Press of John Putnam, 1844. 92 p. ICU; PCA. 44-371

Baptists. Georgia. Ebenezer Association. Minutes of the thirtieth anniversary of the Ebenezer Association, convened at Rocky Creek Church, Laurens County, on the 21st, 22d, and 23d of September, 1844. Macon, Georgia: Printed by S. Rose and Company, 1844. 12 p. PCA. 44-372

Baptists. Georgia. Georgia Association. Minutes of the Georgia Baptist Association, held at Antiock, Oglethorpe County, Georgia, on the 11th, 12th and 14th of October, 1844. Penfield, Georgia: Benjamin Brantly, printer, 1844. 11 p. NHC-S. 44-373

Baptists. Georgia. Ocmulgee Association. Minutes of the Ocmulgee Baptist Association, convened at Providence meeting house, Henry County, Georgia, on the 7th, 8th, 9th, and 10th of September, 1844. Forsyth, Georgia: Printed at the Little Georgian office, 1844. 7 p. NoLoc. 44-374

Baptists. Georgia. State annual. Minutes of the twenty-third anniversary of the Georgia Baptist Convention, held at Cave Spring, Floyd County, Georgia, May 17th, 18th, 20th and 21st, 1844. Penfield, Georgia: Benjamin Brantly, printer, 1844. 24 p. PCA. 44-375

Baptists. Georgia. Western Association. Minutes of the sixteenth session of the Western Baptist Association, held at Antioch, Troup County, Georgia, on the 14th, 15th 16th and 17th days of September, 1844. LaGrange, Georgia: Printed at the Herald office by P.S. Bronson, 1844. 16 p. NoLoc. 44-376

Baptists. Illinois. Clear Creek Association. Minutes of the thirteenth annual meeting held with the Cedar Creek Church, Jackson County, Illinois, August 10, 11, 12, 1844. Sparta, Illinois: Printed by O.F. McMillan, for the Association, 1844. 6 p. IAlB; NHC-C. 44-377

Baptists. Illinois. Clear Creek Association. Minutes of the thirteenth annual meeting of the Clear Creek Baptist Association held with the Cedar Creek Church, Jackson County, Illinois. August 10, 11, 12, 1844. Sparta, Illinois: Printed by O.F. M'Millan, for the Association, 1844. 5 p. NHC-S. 44-378

Baptists. Illinois. Franklin United Baptist Association. Minutes of the fourth session begun and held with the Gum Spring Church, Johnson County, Illinois, Friday preceding the third Lord's day, and the three days following, in September, 1844. [Shawneetown: J.S. Roberts, printer, 1844] 8 p. IAlB. 44-379

Baptists. Illinois. Illinois River Association. The eighth anniversary of the Illinois River Baptist Association held at Washington, June 13th, 1844. 6 p. NHC-S. 44-380

Baptists. Illinois. North Association. Minutes of the seventeenth annual meeting of the North Baptist Association. September sixth, Anno Domini, 1844. Carrollton: Printed at the Advocate office, 1844. 4 p. NHC-S. 44-381

Baptists. Illinois. Saline Association. Minutes, eleventh annual meeting.... Nine Mile Church, Perry County.... September 6, 1844. Belleville: office of the Belleville Advocate, 1844. 8 p. IAlB. 44-382

Baptists. Illinois. State Convention. Proceedings of the Illinois Baptist convention, held at Belleville, St. Claire County, Illinois, on the 3d, 4th and 5th days of October, 1844. Springfield: S. Francis and company, printer, 1844. 15 p. PCA. 44-383

Baptists. Indiana. Flat Rock Association. Minutes of the twenty second an-

niversary of the Flat Rock Baptist Association, held with the Sand Creek Church, Decatur County, Iowa, commencing on the fourth Saturday in August, 1844. Greensburg, Iowa: Printed by Mills and Thomson, 1844. 8 p. NHC; PCA. 44-384

Baptists. Iowa. Des Moines Association. Minutes of the sixth anniversary of the Des Moines Baptist Association, held with the Long Creek Church, at Danville, Des Moines County, Iowa on the 30th and 31st of August, 1844. Keosauqua: J.M. Shepherd, printer, 1844. 7 p. NHC-S. 44-385

Baptists. Iowa. State Convention. Minutes of the third anniversary of the Baptist Convention of Iowa: held with the Church at Mt. Pleasant, Henry County, the 31st of May, and the 1st of June, 1844. [n.p.: 1844] 8 p. IaHA. 44-386

Baptists. Kentucky, Bracken Association. Minutes of the forty-fifth session of the Bracken Association of United Baptists, held at Two Lick Meeting House, Mason County, Kentucky, on Saturday, 6th day of September, 1844 and continued until the Monday following inclusive. Maysville, Kentucky: printed at the Eagle office, 1844. 16 p. PCA 44-387

Baptists. Kentucky. Long Run Association. Minutes of the forty-first annual meeting of the Long Run Baptist Association, held at Burk's Branch meeting house, Shelby County, Kentucky, on the 6th, 7th and 8th of September, 1844. Louisville, Kentucky: W.C. Buck, 1844. 12 p. TxDaHi. 44-388

Baptists. Kentucky. Nolynn Association. Minutes of the twenty-sixth annual meeting of the Nolynn Association of Separate Baptists, held at Mt. Zion Church, Hart County, Kentucky, on the 28th, 29th and 30th days of September, 1844. Elizabethtown, Kentucky: Eliot and Gunter, printers, 1844. 8 p. PCA. 44-389

Baptists. Kentucky. State annual. Minutes of the Kentucky Baptist General Association, the Kentucky and Foreign Bible Society and the China Mission Society, held in Georgetown, October, 1843. With tables of the Baptist associations, churches and ministers in Kentucky. Louisville: printed at the office of the Baptist Banner, 1844. 48 p. PCA. 44-390

Baptists. Louisiana. Mississippi River Association. Minutes of the second annual meeting of the Mississippi River Baptist Association, held with the Hephzibah Baptist Church, East Feliciana Parish, Parish, La., October 24th, 25th, and 26th, 1844. Clinton, Louisiana: Printed by Carman and Green, 1844. 8 p. TxFS. 44-391

Baptists. Maine. Bowdoinham Association. Minutes of the fifty-eighth anniversary of the Bowdoinham Baptist Association, held with the church in Bowdoinham Village, September 25 and 26, 1844. Hallowell: Glazier, Masters and Smith, 1844. 15 p. MH-AH; NRAB; PCA. 44-392

Baptists. Maine. Cumberland Association. Minutes of the thirty-third anniversary of the Cumberland Baptist Association, held with the church in Bath, August 27, 28, and 29, 1844. Portland: Charles Day and company, 1844. 15 p. MeHi; NRAB; PCA. 44-393

Baptists. Maine. Damariscotta Association. Minutes of the second anniversary of the Damariscotta Baptist Association, held with the Baptist church in New Castle and Alna, October 3 and 4, 1844. Gardiner: Printed by Hiram W. Jewell, 1844. 12 p. NRAB; PCA. 44-394

Baptists. Maine. Hancock Association. Minutes of the tenth anniversary of the Hancock Baptist Association, held in the Baptist meeting house in East Trenton, September 3, 4, and 5, 1844. Portland: Printed by Charles Day and company, 1844. 16 p. PCA. 44-395

Baptists. Maine. Kennebec Association. Minutes of the fifteenth anniversary of the Kennebec Association, held with the Baptist church in Farmington, September 17, 18 and 19, 1844. With a view of the state of the churches. Farmington: Swift and Sprague, printers, 1844. 16 p. PCA. 44-396

Baptists. Maine. Lincoln Association. Minutes of the fortieth anniversary of the Lincoln Baptist Association, held with the Baptist church in Hope, September 18 and 19, 1844. Portland: Printed by Charles Day and company, 1844. 20 p. PCA. 44-397

Baptists. Maine. Oxford Association. Sixteenth anniversary. Minutes of the Oxford Baptist Association, held with the Baptist church in Denmark, September 17, 18 and 19, 1844. Portland: Printed by Charles Day and company, 1844. 12 p. MH-AH; NRAB; PCA. 44-398

Baptists. Maine. Penobscott Association. Minutes of the nineteenth anniversary of the Penobscot Baptist Association, held with the First Baptist

Church in Bangor, September 18 and 19, 1844. Portland: Printed by Charles Day and company, 1844. 16 p. MeBa; NRAB; PCA. 44-399

Baptists. Maine. Piscataquis Association. Minutes of the sixth anniversary of the Piscataquis Baptist Association, held at Foxcroft and Dover Village, September 24, 25 and 26, 1844. Portland: Printed by Charles Day and company, 1844. 15 p. MeBa; NRAB; PCA. 44-400

Baptists. Maine. Saco River Association. Minutes of the third anniversary of the Saco River Baptist Association, held in the Baptist meeting house at Kennebunkport, September 4 and 5, 1844. Together with a view of the state of the churches. Portland: Printed by Charles Day and company, 1844. 15 p. NRAB; PCA. 44-401

Baptists. Maine. Saco River Association. Minutes of the Worcester Association, held with the Baptist Church in Grafton, on August 22 and 23, 1844, Worcester: Printed by Henry J. Howland, 1844. 22 p. PCA. 44-402

Baptists. Maine. State. Convention. Minutes of the Maine Baptist convention, held at China, June 19, 1844. Portland: Charles Day and company, 1844. 36 p. MeBa; NRAB; PCA. 44-403

Baptists. Maine. Waldo Association. Minutes of the sixteenth anniversary of the Waldo Baptist Association, held with the First Baptist Church in Belfast, September 10, 11 and 12, 1844. Belfast, Maine: Lewis Richardson, printers, 1844. 11 p. NRAB; PCA. 44-404

Baptists. Maine. Washington Association. Minutes of the tenth anniversary of the Washington Baptist Association, held in the Baptist meeting house in Harrington, September 25th and 26th, 1844. Eastport, Maine: C.C. Tyler, printer, 1844. 14 p. PCA. 44-405

Baptists. Massachusetts. Berkshire County Association held with the Baptist Church in Becket, Massachusetts, October 9th and 10th, 1844. Pittsfield: Charles Montague, printer, 1844. 16 p. MPiB; PCA. 44-406

Baptists. Massachusetts. Boston Association. The thirty-third anniversary of the Boston Baptist Association held in the Tremont Temple, Boston, September 18 and 19, 1844. Minutes of corresponding associations, and other documents relating to the Boston Baptist Association, may be directed to W.H. Shailer, Pastor of the Baptist Church, Brookline, Mass. Boston: John Putnam, printer, 1844. 19 p. CBB; M; PCA. 44-407

Baptists. Massachusetts. Convention. The forty-second annual report of the Massachusetts Baptist Convention, presented by the Board of Directors, at the anniversary in Boston, May 30, 1844. Boston: William Ticknor and company, 1844. 27 p. PCA. 44-408

Baptists. Massachusetts. Millers River, formerly Wendell Association. Minutes of the twentieth anniversary of the Wendell Baptist Association, held with the Baptist Church in Amherst, Massachusetts, September 25 and 26, 1844. Amherst: J.S. and C. Adams, printers, 1844. 14 p. PCA. 44-409

Baptists. Massachusetts. Old Colony Association. Twenty-second anniversary.

Minutes of the Old Colony Baptist Association, held with the Baptist Church in Raynham, Wednesday and Thursday, October 2 and 3, 1844... Boston: Printed by John Putnam, 1844. 16 p. PCA. 44-410

Baptists. Massachusetts. Salem Association. Minutes of the seventeenth anniversary of the Salem Baptist Association, held in the meeting house of the First Baptist Church in Lowell, September 25-26, 1844. Boston: John Putnam, printer, 1844. 24 p. PCA. 44-411

Baptists. Massachusetts. Sturbridge Association. Minutes of the forty third anniversary of the Sturbridge Baptist Church in Hardwick and Ware, Mass. Wednesday and Thursday, August 28 and 29, 1844, including the circular letter and the proceedings of the Sabbath School Convention. Worcester: printed by Henry J. Howland, 1844. 19 p. PCA. 44-412

Baptists. Massachusetts. Taunton Baptist Association. Minutes of the 9th, 26th 28th anniversary of the Taunton Baptist Association, 1844-1863. Providence, Fall River, etc., 1844-1863. 3 v. OClWHi. 44-413

Baptists. Massachusetts. Wachusett Association. Second anniversary. Minutes of the Wachusett Baptist Associaiton, held with the Baptist Church in Sterling, on Wednesday and Thursday, September 11 and 12, 1844. Worcester: Printed by Henry J. Howland, 1844. 12 p. PCA. 44-414

Baptists. Massachusetts. Westfield Association. Minutes of the thirty-fourth anniversary of the Westfield Baptist Association, held with the Baptist Church in Westfield Farms, Massachusetts, September 4 and 5, 1844. Springfield: Wood and Rupp, printers, 1844. 20 p. PCA. 44-415

Baptists. Massachusetts. Worcester Association. Minutes... held with the Baptist Church in Grafton, on August 22 and 23, 1844. Worcester: Printed by Henry J. Howland, 1844. 22 p. MiD-B; PCA. 44-416

Baptists. Massachusetts. Worcester Association. Ninth anniversary minutes of the Sabbath school teachers' convention held at Worcester, Massachusetts, June 11, 1844. Worcester: Printed by Henry J. Howland, 1844. 15 p. MiD-B. 44-417

Baptists. Mississippi. Chickasaw Association. Minutes of the seventh anniversary of the Chickasaw Baptist Association held with the Aberdeen Church, Monroe County, Mississippi on the 6th, 7th, 8th, and 9th days of September, 1844. Ripley, Mississippi: printed by J.F. Ford, 1844. 8 p. MsCliBHi. 44-418

Baptists. Mississippi. Choctaw Association. Minutes of the sixth anniversary of the Choctaw Baptist Association, held with the Church at Black Water, Kemper County, Mississippi on the 2d to 4th of November, 1844. Macon, Mississippi: Printed by A. and A. H. Marschalk, 1844. 13 p. MsCliBHi. 44-419

Baptists. Mississippi. Mississippi Association. Minutes of the thirty seventh anniversary of the Mississippi Baptist Association. Held with the Galilee Church, Amite County, Mississippi, October 5th, 6th, and 7th, 1844. Clinton, Mississippi: Carman and Green, 1844. 8 p. LNB. 44-420

Baptists. Mississippi. Noxubee Primitive Association. Minutes of the third anniversary of the Noxubee Primitive Baptist Association convened at Salem Church, Kemper County, Mississippi; on Saturday, before the fourth Sabbath in October, 1844. Macon, Mississippi: Jeffersonian office, 1844. 10 p. NoLoc. 44-421

Baptists. Mississippi. Union Association. Minutes of the twenty fourth anniversary of the Union Baptist Association, held with the Bethel Church, Hinds County, the 19th - 21st of October, 1844. Jackson: Printed at the Southern Reformer office, 1844. 18 p. MsCLiBHi. 44-422

Baptists. Missouri. Blue River Association. Minutes of the eleventh annual session of the Blue River Association of United Baptists held with Clear Creek Church, Benton County, Missouri commencing on Saturday September 14th, 1844. Lexington, Missouri: Printed at the Express office, 1844. 7 p. MoLiWJ. 44-423

Baptists. New England. The doctrine of baptismal regeneration. From the New Englander for July, 1844. New Haven: printed by B.L. Hamlen, 1844. 20 p. LNB; MBC; MdBJ; MoWgT; NRSB. 44-424

Baptists. New Hampshire. Dublin Association. Thirty-fifth anniversary. Minutes of the Dublin Baptist Association, and of the Sabbath school convention, held with the Baptist Church in Swanzey, New Hampshire, Tuesday, Wednesday and Thursday, September 3, 4 and 5, 1844.... Concord: printed at the Baptist Register office, 1844. 12 p. PCA. 44-425

Baptists. New Hampshire. Meredith Association. Minutes of the fifty-fifth anniversary of the Meredith Baptist Association, held with the Second Baptist Church in Meredith, New Hampshire, September 11 and 12, 1844.... Concord: printed at the Baptist Register office, 1844. 16 p. PCA. 44-426

Baptists. New Hampshire. Portsmouth Association. Minutes of the sixteenth anniversary of the Portsmouth Baptist Association, held at Hampton Falls, on Wednesday and Thursday, October 2 and 3, 1844.... Portsmouth: Charles W. Brewster, printer, 1844. 12 p. PCA; TxFwSB. 44-427

Baptists. New Hampshire. State Convention. Proceedings of the New Hampshire Baptist State Convention, together with the New Hampshire branch of the National Baptist Education Society, New Hampshire Foreign Bible Society, and the Baptist Anti-slavery Society, at their annual meetings, held at Cornish Flat, June 25 and 26, 1844. Concord: printed at the Baptist Register office, 1844. 40 p. PCA. 44-428

Baptists. New Jersey. Central Association. Minutes of the Central New Jersey Baptist Association held at Sandy Ridge, October 15th, 16th and 17, 1844. Philadelphia: Kind and Baird, printers, 1844. 16 p. PCA. 44-429

Baptists. New Jersey. East New Jersey Association. Minutes of the third anniversary of the East New Jersey Baptist Association, held in the meeting house of the Second Middletown Baptist Church, June 4 and 5, 1844. New York: printed by W.B. and T. Smith, 1844. 16 p. ICU; PCA. 44-430

Baptists. New Jersey. State Convention. Minutes of the fifteenth anniversary of the New Jersey Baptist State Convention; and of the seventh annual meeting of the New Jersey Baptist Education Society, held in the meeting house of the Baptist Church at Mount Holly, November 12, 13, 14, 1844. New York: printed by John Gray, 1844. 24 p. PCA. 44-431

Baptists. New Jersey. West New Jersey Association. Minutes of the thirty-third anniversary of the New Jersey Baptist Association, held with the Church at Moorestown, September 10, 11, and 12, 1844. Burlington: printed by J.L. Rowell, 1844. 20 p. MID-B; PCA. 44-432

Baptists. New York. American Home Missionary Society. The twelfth report of the American Baptist Home Mission Society, with an appendix.... New York: John Gray, printer, 1844. 79 p. ViRu. 44-433

Baptists. New York. Black River Association. Minutes of the thirty fifth anniversary of the Black River Baptist Association, convened at Adams, Jeff. Co., June 12th and 13th, 1844. With the circular and corresponding letters. Adams: Printed at the Democrat office, 1844. 9 p. PCA. 44-434

Baptists. New York. Buffalo Association. Minutes of the twenty-ninth anniversary of the Buffalo, formerly Holland Purchase Baptist Association, held with the Baptist Church in Evans, on the 10th, 11th and 12th of September, 1844. Springville, New York: Printed by Edwin Hough, 1844. 16 p. PCA. 44-435

Baptists. New York. Cattaraugus Association. Minutes of the ninth anniversary of the Cattaraugus Baptist Association, held with the Church in Rushford, July 9 and 10, 1844. Warsaw, New York: Printed by E.L. Fuller, 1844. 11 p. PCA. 44-436

Baptists. New York. Cayuga Association. Minutes of the forty-fourth annual meeting of the Cayuga Baptist Association, held with the Baptist Church in Owasco, Cayuga County, New York, September 19, and 20, 1844. [Auburn: H. Oliphant, 1844] 16 p. NHC-S; NRCR. 44-437

Baptists. New York. Cortland Association. Minutes of the seventeenth annual meeting.... held at Groton Village, September 12, and 13, 1844. Homer: Press of Reed and Walker, 1844. 16 p. CSmH. 44-438

Baptists. New York. Dutchess Association. Minutes of the tenth anniversary of the Dutchess Baptist Association, held in the meeting house of the First Baptist Church, Fishkill Plains, New York, October 2nd and 3rd, 1844. New York: John Gray, printer, 1844. 16 p. PCA. 44-439

Baptists. New York. Education Society. Twenty-seventh annual meeting of the Baptist Education Society, of the state of New York, held at Hamilton, August 20, 1844, with the reports of the board, treasurer, agents, etc. Utica: Bennett, Backus and Hawley, [1844] 32 p. DLC; IAlS; MWA; NN; PCA. 44-440

Baptists. New York. Genesee Association. Minutes of the twenty-sixth anniversary of the Genesee Baptist Association, held with the First Church in Middlebury, [Wyoming County, New York] June 18th and 19th, 1844. Perry,

New York: D.D. Curtiss, 1844. 16 p. PCA. 44-441

Baptists. New York. Hudson River Association. The twenty-ninth anniversary of the Hudson River Baptist Association held in the Baptist meeting house in the city of Hudson, June 18, 19 and 20, 1844. New York: George B. Maigne, printer, 1844. 52 p. ICU; PCA. 44-442

Baptists. New York. Ketocton Association. Minutes of the Ketocton Baptist Association. Held with the Happy Creek Church, Front Royal, Warren County, Virginia, on the 16, 17, and 18 of August, 1844. New Vernon, New York: printed at the office of the Sign of the Times, 1844. 4-8 p. ViRu. 44-443

Baptists. New York. Livingston Association. Minutes of the thirteenth annual meeting of the Livingston Baptist Association. Held with the Church in Lakeville, New York, June 26th and 27th, 1844. Rochester: Canfield and Warren, printers, 1844. 12 p. NHC-S. 44-444

Baptists. New York. Madison Association. Minutes of the thirty-sixth annual meeting of the Madison Baptist Association, held at Cazenovia Village, Madison County, New York, on September 10 and 11, 1844. Cazenovia: W.H. Phillips, printer, 1844. 16 p. PCA. 44-445

Baptists. New York. Missionary Convention. Proceedings of the twenty-third anniversary of the Baptist Missionary Convention of the state of New York; held with the Second Baptist Church in Rochester, October 16 and 17, 1844. With the reports of the board, agents, and treasurer, list of auxiliary associations, life directors, life members, constitution,

etc. Utica: Press of Bennett, Backus, and Hawley, 1844. 51 p. NN; PCA. 44-446

Baptists. New York. Monroe Association. Minutes of the seventeenth anniversary of the Monroe Baptist Church held in the meeting house of the First Baptist Church in Parma, October 1, 2 and 3, 1844. Rochester: Printed by Canfield and Warren, 1844. 21 p. NRCR; PCA. 44-447

Baptists. New York. New York Association. Minutes of the fifty-fourth anniversary of the New York Baptist Association, held in the meeting-house of the First Baptist Church, New York, on Tuesday and Wednesday, May 28 and 29, 1844. New York: John Gray, printer, 1844. 24 p. PCA. 44-448

Baptists. New York. Oneida Association. Minutes of the twenty-fourth anniversary of the Oneida Baptist Association, held at Durhamville, Oneida County, New York, September 3 and 4, 1844. Utica, 1844. 16 p. NRCR. 44-449

Baptists. New York. Ontario Association. Minutes of the Ontario Baptist Association held with the Baptist Church in Waterloo, September 26 and 27, 1844. Rochester: Printed by Canfield and Warren, 1844. 16 p. NHC-S; NRCR; PCA. 44-450

Baptists. New York. Orleans Association. First anniversary. Minutes of the first anniversary of the Orleans Baptist Association, held in the meeting house of the Baptist Church, in Knowlesville, Orleans County, New York, June 5th and 6th, 1844. Albion: J. and J.H. Denis, printers, 1844. 16 p. PCA. 44-451

Baptists. New York. Rensselaerville Association. The forty-sixth anniversary of the Rensselaerville Baptist Association, held in the Baptist meeting house of Preston Hollow, September 18th and 19th, 1844. Albany: Printed by J. Munsell, 1844. 12 p. MHi; PCA. 44-452

Baptists. New York. Steuben Association. Minutes of the twenty-seventh anniversary of the Steuben Baptist Association, held in the meeting house of the First Baptist Church in Milo, New York, September 3rd and 4th, 1844. Dundee, New York: Booth and Butman, printers, 1844. 16 p. PCA. 44-453

Baptists. New York. Union Association. Minutes of the thirty-fourth anniversary of the Union Baptist Association, held in the meeting house of the Baptist Church at Cross River, Westchester County, New York, Wednesday and Thursday, September 4th and 5th, 1844. Peekskill: G.K. Lyman, 1844. 15 p. PCA. 44-454

Baptists. New York. Union Association. Minutes of the thirty-fourth anniversary at Cross River, Westchester County, New York, September, 4 and 5, 1844. Peekskill: printed by G.K. Lyman, 1844. 15 p. PCA. 44-455

Baptists. New York. Warwick Association. Minutes of the Warwick Baptist Association, held with the church at Warwick, Orange County, New York, June 5th and 6th, 1844.... New Vernon, New York: printed at the office of the signs of the times, 1844. 8 p. PCA. 44-456

Baptists. New York. Wayne Association. Minutes of the tenth annual meeting of the Wayne Baptist Association, held at Rose, Wayne County, New York, September 26th and 27th, 1844. Rochester: Canfield and Warren, 1844. 16 p. PCA. 44-457

Baptists. North Carolina. Liberty Association. Minutes of the twelfth anniversary of the Liberty Association, held at Abbotts Creek meeting house [near Browntown] Davidson County, North Carolina, August 17, and 19, 1844. Salem: Blum and son, printers, 1844. 7 p. PCA. 44-458

Baptists. North Carolina. Pee Dee Association. Minutes of the twenty-ninth annual meeting of the Pee Dee Baptist Association, held with the church at New Union, Montgomery County, North Carolina, October 18-21, 1844. Fayetteville: Edward J. Hale, printer, 1844. 24 p. PCA. 44-459

Baptists. Ohio. Cleveland or Rocky River Association. Minutes of the thirteenth anniversary of the Rocky River Association. Convened at Granger, Medina County, Ohio. Akron, Ohio: Printed by Lane and Coggshall, 1844. 15 p. CSmH. 44-460

Baptists. Ohio. Columbus Association. Minutes of the twenty-sixth anniversary of the Columbus Baptist Association, begun and held with the St. Albans Church, Licking County, Ohio, August 14 and 15, 1844. Columbus: Cross and Journal office, 1844. 16 p. CSmH. 44-461

Baptists. Ohio. Mad River Association. Minutes of the Mad River Baptist Association, at its thirty-second anniversary, held with the Kings Creek Church. Springfield: Gallagher and Halsey, 1844. 18 p. PCA. 44-462

Baptists. Ohio. Marietta Association. Minutes of the nineteenth anniversary of the Meig's Creek Baptist Association, held at Duncan's Falls, August 14, 15, and 16. Zanesville, Ohio: printed by Edwin C. Church, 1844. 120 p. PCA. 44-463

Baptists. Ohio. Miami Association. Minutes of the Miami Association of regular Baptists, held with the First Baptist Church of Middletown, Ohio, September 6th and 7th, 1844. Dayton, Ohio: printed at the journal office, 1844. 16 p. PCA. 44-464

Baptists. Ohio. Scioto Association. Minutes of the 39th, 42nd, 47th, 50th, 52nd, 56th-59th, 61st, 62nd, 76th anniversary of the Scioto Association. Zanesville, Ohio: Printed by Edwin C. Church, 1844-1881. 13 v. CSmH. 44-465

Baptists. Ohio. Scioto Association. Minutes of the thirty-ninth annual meeting of the Scioto Baptist Association, held at Frankfort, Ross County, Ohio, August 29 and 30, 1844. Zanesville, Ohio: printed by Edwin C. Church, 1844. 8 p. CSmH; PCA. 44-466

Baptists. Ohio. Wooster Association. Minutes of the fifth anniversary of the Wooster Regular Baptist Association. Wooster: 1844. OClWHi. 44-467

Baptists. Pennsylvania. Beaver Association. Minutes of the thirty-fifth anniversary of the Beaver Baptist Association, held with the Providence Church, Beaver County, Pennsylvania, August 22nd, 23rd, and 24th, 1841. Pittsburg: J.B. Shurtleff, printer, 1844. 8 p. PCA. 44-468

Baptists. Pennsylvania. Bradford As-sociation. Minutes of the tenth annual session of the Bradford Baptist Association held in the chapel in Springfield, Wednesday and Thursday, June 5, 6, 1844. Towanda, Pennsylvania: Printed by E.S. Goodrich and Son, 1844. 18 p. PCA. 44-469

Baptists. Pennsylvania. Bridgewater Association. Minutes of the nineteenth anniversary of the Bridgewater Baptist Association, held by appointment in the Baptist meeting house of the Jackson and Gibson Baptist Church, Jackson, Susquehanna County, Pennsylvania, September 18 and 19, 1844. Montrose, Pennsylvania: Fuller and Turrell, printers, 1844. 16 p. PCA. 44-470

Baptists. Pennsylvania. Central Union Association. Minutes of the twelfth annual session of the Central Union Association of Independent Baptist Churches, held in the meeting house of the Holmesburg Baptist Church, May 28 and 29, 1844. Philadelphia: King and Baird, printers, 1844. 24 p. PCA. 44-471

Baptists. Pennsylvania. Centre Association. Minutes of the Centre Baptist Association, at their fourteenth annual meeting, held with the Lewistown Baptist Church, Mifflin County, Pa., August 28 and 29, 1844. Hollidaysburg, Pennsylvania: John Dougherty, printer, 1844. 13 p. NRAB; PCA. 44-472

Baptists. Pennsylvania. Northumberland Association. Minutes of the twenty-third annual session of the Northumberland Baptist Association....1844. Muncy, [Pennsylvania]: W.P.I. and G.L.I. Painter, printer, 1844-. 1 v. CSmH. 44-473

Baptists. Pennsylvania. Pennsylvania Baptist Association. Minutes of the 136th, 137th and 138th anniveraries.... Philadelphia: King and Baird, printers, 1844. MiD-B. 44-474

Baptists. Pennsylvania. Pennsylvania Baptist Convention. Minutes of the eighth anniversary of the Pennsylvania Baptist Convention for Missionary Purposes, held at Milton, Northumberland County, Pennsylvania, October 25th, 26th, and 28th, 1844. Philadelphia: King and Baird, printers, 1844. 56 p. MiD-B; PCA. 44-475

Baptists. Pennsylvania. Pennsylvania Baptist Convention. Minutes of the seventh anniversary of the Pennsylvania Baptist convention for missionary purposes, held in Hollidaysburgh, Huntingdon County, Pennsylvania, October 26th and 28th, 1843. Philadelphia: King and Baird, printers, 1844. 44 p. MiD-B; PCA; PScrHi. 44-476

Baptists. Pennsylvania. Philadelphia Association. Minutes of the 137th anniversary of the Philadelphia Baptist Association, held by appointment in the meeting house of the Second Church, Southwark, Philadelphia, October 1st, 2nd, 3rd, and 4th, 1844. Philadelphia: King and Baird, printers, 1844. 35 p. PCA. 44-477

Baptists. Rhode Island. Baptist Sunday School Convention. Minutes for 1844. Providence: H.H. Brown, printer, 1844. 12 p. PHi; RHi; RPA; RPB. 44-478

Baptists. Rhode Island. Fourth Baptist Society. Charter of the Fourth Baptist Society in Providence, granted in 1820 with the amendments to the charter,

made in 1844. Providence: Printed by H.H. Brown, 1844. PHi. 44-479

Baptists. Rhode Island. Providence Association. Minutes of the first anniversary of the Providence Baptist Association, held with the Baptist Church in Woonsocket, September 18 and 19, 1844. Providence: Printed by H.H. Brown, 1844. 19 p. PCA. 44-480

Baptists. Rhode Island. Providence Stonington Union Association. Minutes of the twenty-seventh anniversary of the Stonington Union Association, held with the Plainfield Union Baptist Church, Wednesday and Thursday, June 19 and 20, 1844. Providence: H.H. Brown, printer, 1844. 8 p. PCA. 44-481

Baptists. Rhode Island. State Convention. Proceedings of the Rhode Island Baptist State Convention, held in the third Baptist meeting house, in Providence, on Tuesday and Wednesday, April 9 and 10, 1844. Also, proceedings of the Baptist Education Society, of the Warren Association, auxiliary to the Northern Baptist Education Society at the annual meeting held in the third Baptist meeting house Providence, April 9 and 10, 1844. Providence: Printed by H.H. Brown, 1844. 35 p. RPB. 44-482

Baptists. Rhode Island. Stonington Union Association. Minutes of the twenty-seventh anniversary of the Stonington Union Association held with the Plainfield Union Baptist Church, Wednesday and Thursday, June 19th and 20th, 1844. Providence: H.H. Brown, printer, 1844. 15 p. NRAB; RWe. 44-483

Baptists. Rhode Island. Warren Association.Minutes of the seventy-seventh anniversary of the Warren Baptist Association held with the First Baptist Church in Providence, on Wednesday and Thursday, September 11 and 12, 1844. Providence: Printed by H.H. Brown, 1844. 20 p. PCA; RHi. 44-484

Baptists. Tennessee. Cumberland Association. Minutes of the Cumberland Baptist Association, convened at Wilson's Creek, Williamson County, Tennessee, Saturday before the fourth Lord's day in September, 1844. Franklin: Cameron and Neal, printers, 1844. 16 p. MoSM. 44-485

Baptists. Tennessee. Mt. Zion Association. Minutes of the Mt. Zion Association of Baptists, begun and held at Pleasant Hill Meeting House, White County, Tennessee on Saturday before the third Sabbath in September, 1844. and on days following. Sparta: William Clayton, printer, 1844. 7 p. PCA. 44-486

Baptists. Tennessee. Tennessee Association of United Baptists. Minutes of the Tennessee Association of United Baptists, convened at Dumplin Creek, Jefferson County, on Friday before the first Saturday in October, 1844. Knoxville, Tennessee: Printed at the Register office, 1844. 8 p. PCA. 44-487

Baptists. Texas. Union Association. Minutes of the fifth anniversary meeting of the Union Baptist Association, convened at Plum Grove Church, Fayette County, Texas, August 29, 1844 and days following. Washington, Texas: Printed at the Vindicator office, 1844. 14 p. TxFwSB. 44-488

Baptists. Texas. Union Association. Minutes of the fourth anniversary meeting of the Union Baptist Association convened at Providence Church, Washington County, October 6, 1843, and days following. Washington, Texas: Printed by Thomas Johnson, 1844. 8 p. TxFwSB. 44-489

Baptists. Vermont. Addison County Association. Minutes of the Addison County Baptist Association, held with the church in Addison, September 24 and 25, 1844. Middlebury, Vermont: Maxham's, printer, 1844. MH-AH; MNtCA. 44-490

Baptists. Vermont. Vermont Association. Minutes of the Vermont Baptist Association, held with the church in Brandon, October 2nd, and 3rd, 1844. Middlebury, Vermont: Maxham's, printer, 1844. 12 p. NRAB; PCA. 44-491

Baptists. Vermont. Vermont Convention. XIXth anniversary. Minutes of the Vermont Baptist Convention, held with the church in Grafton, October 9 and 10, 1844.... Middlebury, Vermont: Maxham's, printer, 1844. 24 p. VtMidSM. 44-492

Baptists. Virginia. Albemarle Association. The fifty-third anniversary of the Albemarle Baptist Association held in the meeting house of the Ebenezer Church, Amhurst, August 17, 18 and 19, 1844. Charlottesville: James Alexander, printer, 1844. 19 p. ViRu. 44-493

Baptists. Virginia. Appomattox Association. Minutes of the Appomattox Baptist Association, held at Rock Church, in Prince Edward County, Virginia, August 10-12, 1844. Richmond: printed at the office of the Religious Herald, 1844. 4-26 p. ViRu. 44-494

Baptists. Virginia. Columbia Baptist Association. Minutes of the twenty-fifth annual meeting of the Columbia Baptist Association held by appointment at the Broad Run Meeting House, Fauquier County, Virginia. August 22, 23 and 24, 1844. 18 p. ViRu. 44-495

Baptists. Virginia. Concord Association. Minutes of the thirteenth annual session of the Concord Baptist Association, held with the Church of Bethlehem, Mecklenburg County, on August 17, 18 and 19, 1844. Richmond: H.K. Ellyson, printer, 1844. PCA; ViRu. 44-496

Baptists. Virginia. Dover Association. Minutes of the sixty-first annual session of the Dover Baptist Association, held with Hampton Church, Elizabeth City County, Virginia, October 11-14, 1844. Richmond: printed by H.K. Ellyson, 1844. 3-21 p. ViRu. 44-497

Baptists. Virginia. General Association. Minutes of the Virginia Baptist anniversaries, held in the First and Second Baptist Church, Richmond, June, 1844. Richmond: printed by H.K. Ellyson, 1844. 39 p. PCA. 44-498

Baptists. Virginia. General Association. Proceedings of the twenty-first annual meeting of the Baptist General Association of Virginia, assembled at Richmond, Virginia, June 1-4, 1844. [n.p.: 1844. 40 p. ViRu; Wv. 44-499

Baptists. Virginia. Goshen Association. Minutes of the Goshen Baptist Association, held at Zoar Church, in Orange County, Virginia, September 4-6, 1844. Richmond: printed at the office of the Religious Herald, 1844. [3]-16 p. ViRu. 44-500

Baptists. Virginia. Middle District Association. Minutes of the Middle District Baptist Association, held at Tomahawk M.H., Chesterfield County, August 1-4, 1844. Richmond: printed at the office of the Religious Herald, 1844. 8 p. ViRu. 44-501

Baptists. Virginia. Portsmouth Association. Minutes of the fifty-fourth session of the Virginia Portsmouth Baptist Association, held at the Cumberland Street Meeting House, in Norfolk Borough, May 24, 25, and 27, 1844. Portsmouth, Virginia: Public Index Press, 1844. 15 p. PCA; ViRu. 44-502

Baptists. Virginia. Rappahannock Association. Minutes of the second annual session of the Rappahannock Baptist Association, held with Mattaponi Church, King and Queen County, August 3, 4, and 5, 1844. Richmond: H.K. Ellyson, printer, 1844. 25 p. ViRu. 44-503

Baptists. Virginia. Salem Union Association. Minutes of the 12th annual meeting of the Salem Union Baptist Association, held by appointment with the North Fork Church, Loudon County, Virginia. Fredericksburg, printed at the Recorder office, 1844. 13 p. ViRu. 44-504

Baptists. Virginia. Valley Association. Minutes of the two semi-annual meetings, of the Valley Association in the year 1844. The first session held with the Mill Creek Church, Botetourt County, Virginia, on the 17, 18, 19 of May. The second session held with the Buchanan Church, Botetourt County, Virginia on the 23, 24, and 25 of September. Lexington, Virginia: Samuel Gillock, printer, 1844. 8 p. ViRu. 44-505

Baptists. Virginia. Western Virginia Association. The minutes of the first annual meeting of the Western Virginia Baptist Association held in Lewisburg, Virginia on the 28, 29, and 30 of August, 1844. Lexington, Virginia: Samuel Gillock, printer, 1844. 3-8 p. ViRu. 44-506

Baptists. Wisconsin. Wisconsin Association. Minutes of the sixth anniversary of the Baptist Association, of Wisconsin. Held with the church at Spring Prairie, on June 26 and 27, 1844. Racine: Advocate office, printer, 1844. 11 p. ICU; NHC-S; PCC; WHi. 44-507

Bar, M. Ro., pseud. Mary the Maniac; or the mother her own victim. In eight letters, to a young lady of the south. New York: Nafis and Cornish, 1844. 120 p. MBAt; MWA. 44-508

Barbarous, Charles Oge. L'histoire des Etats-Unis d'Amerique par C.O. Barbaroux.... Ed. rev. ear. pour l'usage des ecoles. Philadelphia: Hogan and Thompson, 1844. 304 p. LNB; LNDil; MiNazC. 44-509

Barber, James. The weaver of Lyons; or, the three conscripts, a farce in one act. New York: Samuel French, [1844?] 19 p. OCl. 44-510

Barber, John Warner, 1798-1885. Elements of general history; being a collection of facts relating to the history of man, empires, states, and kingdoms, from the earliest period to the present time, for the use of schools. Second edition. New Haven: Durrie and Peck, 1844. 288 p. Ct; CtY; CtHWatk; MH; ScGaL. 44-511

Barber, John Warner, 1798-1885. Historical collections of the state of New Jer-

sey; ....with geographical descriptions of every township in the state. ....By John W. Barber.... and Henry Howe.... New York: S. Tuttle, 1844. 512 p. CSmH; FSa; OHi; PEaL; WaS. 44-512

Barber, John Warner, 1798-1885. Historical collections of the state of New York; containing a general collection of the most interesting facts, traditions, biographical sketches.... By John W. Barber.... and Henry Howe.... New York: S. Tuttle, 1844. 616 p. Ct; DLC; LNT; MBC; WHi. 44-513

Barber, John Warner, 1798-1885. Historical collections, being a general collection of interesting facts, traditions, biographical sketches, anecdotes, &c., relating to the history and antiquities of every town in Massachusetts, with geographical descriptions. Illustrated by 200 engravings. ....Worcester: W. Lazell, 1844. 624 p. CSt; DLC; ICU; MBAt; VtU. 44-514

Barber, John Warner, 1798-1885. The history and antiquities of New England, New York, New Jersey and Pennsylvania.... by John Warner Barber, member of the Connecticut Historical Society. Hartford: Case, Tiffany and company, printers, 1844. 624 p. CtSoP; IaHi; MeLewB; Wv. 44-515

Barbour, I. The silk culture in the United States; embracing complete accounts of the latest and most approved modes of hatching, rearing, and feeding the silk-worm, managing a cocoonery, reeling, spinning, and manufacturing the silk, etc. ....Compiled from the most approved and reliable works.... New York: Greeley and McElrath, 1844. 80 p. CoFcS; DLC; ICJ; MH; MWA. 44-516

Barclay, Kate. The odd fellow's gift....
1845. New York: [1844?] ICN. 44-517

Bard, William, 1777-1853. Statements
in relation to the New York Life Insurance and Trust Company. New York:
H. Ludwig, printer, 1844. 36 p. CtY;
DLC; NN; WHi. 44-518

Barham, Richard Harris, 1788-1845.
The Ingoldsby legends, or Mirth and
marvels. By Thomas Ingoldsby, esq.
[pseud] Philadelphia: Carey and Hart,
1844. CtHT-W; MBAt; MH; MiD; ViW.
44-519

Barker, Jacob, 1779-1871. Hear both
sides. New Orleans: J.A. Noble, printer,
1844. 48 p. LNHT; LU; MdBJ; NcD;
PPL. 44-520

Barker, Theodore T. The heart that's
devoted to me. Boston: Reed, 1844. 5 p.
MB. 44-521

Barnard, Daniel Dewey, 1797-1861.
The finances of the United States, or, the
present situation of the national debt,
and the question as to the authors of such
debt, clearly settled. [Washington?
1844?] 13 p. OClWHi. 44-522

Barnard, Daniel Dewey, 1797-1861.
Letter of Hon. D.D. Barnard, of New
York: in review of the report of the Committee of Ways and Means on the finances and the public debt. [Washington:
printed at Gideon's office, 1844] 8 p.
ICN; MBAt; PPL; Vi; WHi. 44-523

Barnard, Daniel Dewey, 1797-1861.
Speech of Mr. Barnard, of New York, in
the House of Representatives of the
United States, December 29, 1843, and
January 2, 1844. On the bill to refund the
fine imposed upon General Jackson.
Washington: Gales and Seaton, printers,
1844. 20 p. CtHT; NNS. 44-524

Barnard, Daniel Dewey, 1797-1861.
Speech of Mr. Barnard, of New York, on
the report and resolutions of the committee on elections, relative to the elections
by general ticket in the four recusant [sic]
states of New Hampshire, Georgia, Mississippi, and Missouri. Delivered in the
House of Representatives of the United
States February 13, 1844. J. and C.S.
Gideon, printers, 1844. 16 p. MB;
MeWaC; MH; MsJs; PHi. 44-525

Barnard, Daniel Dewey, 1797-1861.
Speech of Mr. Barnard, of New York, on
the tariff bill reported from the Committee of Ways and Means. Delivered in the
House of Representatives of the United
States on Friday, May 14, 1844.
Washington: J. and G.S. Gideon, 1844.
32 p. ICU; MB; MiD; MiD-B; NNC. 44-
526

Barnard, Henry, 1811-1900. Condition
of education in the United States, ...with
a sketch.... of common schools....
[Hartford: 1844] 16 p. CtHWatk. 44-527

Barnard, Henry, 1811-1900. School
houses. Document setting forth the evils,
etc., of badly constructed school houses
and such plans [etc.] for the erection and
arrangement of school houses as have
been sanctioned by extensive experience. Providence: 1844] 72 p. CtY;
DLC; MH; NNU-W; RPB. 44-528

Barnard, R. Every youth's book; or, interesting conversations on arts and sciences, for the use of schools and families.
New York: Collins brothers; Philadel-

phia: Hogan and Thompson, 1844. 160 p. DLC. 44-529

Barnes, Albert, 1798-1870. The missionary enterprise dependent on the religion of principle for a success; a sermon...Worcester, Massachusetts. Boston: Press of Crocker and Brewster, 1844. 53 p. CBB; ICMe; MBC; NjR; OCl; PPPrHi. 44-530

Barnes, Albert, 1798-1870. The position of the Evangelical party in the Episcopal Church. Philadelphia: Perkins and Purves, 1844. 54 p. IU; MAnP; MCET; PPLT; RPB. 44-531

Barnes, Albert, 1798-1870. Reply to a review of the tract on the position of the Evangelical party in the Episcopal Church, contained in the Episcopal Recorder of March 16, 23, and 30, 1844. By Albert Barnes. Philadelphia: Perkins and Purves, 1844. 143 p. CtY; LNB; MH-AH; MNtCA; PHi. 44-532

Barnes, Albert, 1798-1870. A sermon preached in Worcester, Massachusetts, September, 1844, before the American Board of Commissioners for Foreign Missions, at their thirty-fifth annual meeting. By Rev. Albert Barnes.... Boston: Crocker and Brewster, printers, 1844. 43 p. MeBat; MNtCA; NjR. 44-533

Barnwell, William H. The impiety and absurdity of duelling. Sermon in Charleston, June 9, 1844. Charleston: Walker and Burke, 1844. 16 p. DLC; KBB; NN; PHi. 44-534

Barrett, Benjamin Fiske, 1808-1892. Few comments upon a pamphlet by Mr. John Douglas, purporting to be a statement of the difficulties between the first

New Jerusalem Society of New York and himself. New York: 1844. 14 p. PBa; PPULC. 44-535

Barrington, Edward. Standard works on anatomy, medicine, surgery.... Philadelphia: Edward Barrington and Geo. D. Haswell, 1844. PPL; PPULC. 44-536

Barrow, Alexander, 1801-1846. Address of Mr. Alexander Barrow, of Louisiana, to his constituents, upon the annexation of Texas [Washington: 1844] 8 p. CtY; TxU. 44-537

Barrow, Isaac. Treatise of the pope's supremacy. By the Rev. Isaac Barrow, D.D. Second American edition. New York: Stanford and Sword, 1844. 430 p. CtY; DLC; IES; MCET; MiD. 44-538

Barrow, John, 1764-1848. Description of Pitcairn's island and its inhabitants, with an authentic account of the mutiny of the ship Bounty, and of subsequent fortunes of the mutineers. New York: Harper and brothers, 1844. 303 p. MeAu; MFi; MnHi; OCo; PPFr. 44-539

Barrow, John, 1764-1848. The memoir of the life of Peter the Great. New York: Harper and brothers, 1844. 320, 4 p. MeAu; MWA; NCaS; OCo; TxU. 44-540

Barrow, John, 1764-1848. Pitcairn's Island and its inhabitants, with an authentic account of the mutiny at the ship Bounty and of the subsequent fortunes of the mutineers. New York: Harper, 1844. 303 p. LN; PPFr; PPULC. 44-541

Barrows, L.D. Anti-slavery address, at annual fast of 1844. Before Methodist Episcopal Church of Nashua and Nashville. Nashua: Murray and Kimball, 1844. 16 p. MBNMHi. 44-542

Barrows, L.D. The substance of an anti-slavery address, delivered on the annual fast of 1844, before the congregation of the Methodist Episcopal Church of Nashua and Nashville.... Published by request of the anti-slavery society.... Nashua: Murray and Kimball, 1844. 16 p. MB; MiD-B; WHi. 44-543

Barry, William. The rights and duties of neighboring churches. Two sermons preached to the First Parish in Framingham, Sunday, February 11, 1844. By William Barry, minister of the parish. Boston: Benjamin H. Greene, 1844. 43 p. ICMe; MiD-B; MWA; NNUT; RPB. 44-544

Barry, William. Thoughts on Christian doctrine. A candid answer to candid inquiries. By Rev. William Barry.... Boston: James Munroe and company, 1844. 26 p. CBPac; DLC; MeBat; MH; PPL. 44-545

Barry, William. Two sermons preached to the first parish in Framingham, February 11, 1844, by William Barry. Boston: Greene, 1844. MeB; MFm; P. 44-546

Barth, C.G. The Huguenot galley slaves; translated from the German. By Rev. C.G. Barth. Philadelphia: Presbyterian Board of Publication, 1844. 82 p. NjPT. 44-547

Bartlett and Welford, New York. Bartlett and Walford's catalogue. Part III. Literature. Catalogue of ancient and modern books comprising standard, rare, and valuable works. Comprising upward of twenty five thousand volumes in the various departments of literature and science. New York, 1844. 3 v. in 1. IU; MdHi; MHi; RPB; ViU. 44-548

Bartlett, Elisha, 1804-1855. An essay on the philosophy of medical science. ....By Elisha Bartlett, M.D. ....Philadelphia: Lea and Blanchard, 1844. 312 p. ICJ; MB; MdBJ; NhD; TxU. 44-549

Bartlett, Elisha, 1805-1855. The head and the heart, or, the relative importance of intellectual and moral education: a lecture delivered before the American Institute of Instruction, in Lowell, August, 1838. By Elisha Bartlett, M.D. Philadelphia: Anti-slavery office, 1844. 30 p. MiD-B; MWA; PHi; PPL. 44-550

Bartlett, John C. La polka quick step, composed for the pianoforte. Boston: Ditson, [1844] 2 p. MB. 44-551

Bartlett, John Russell. The progress of ethnology. New York, 1844. 25 p. DLC; NIC. 44-552

Bartol, C.A. A sermon delivered at the West Church, in Boston, January 28, 1844, By C.A. Bartol, its junior pastor. Boston: Benjamin H. Greene, 1844. 16 p. MNe. 44-553

Bartol, Cyrus Augustus, 1813-1900. Confession of faith; a sermon delivered at the West Church, in Boston, January 28, 1844.... Published by request. Boston: Benjamin H. Greene, 1844. 16 p. CtY; MBAt; MWA; PPL; WHi. 44-554

Barton, Bernard. Poems, by Bernard Barton.... Philadelphia: Henry F. Anners, 1844. 256 p. InRchE; MH; MWA; OSW; TxElpL. 44-555

Barton, Seth, 1795-1850. Address of "Randolph of Roanoke," to the Baltimore convention. Richmond: 1844. PPL; PPULC. 44-556

Barwell, Louise Mary Bacon. Infant treatment with directions to mothers for self management before, during and after pregnancy. First American edition, revised, enlarged, and adapted to habits and climate in the United States by a physician of New York, Valentine Mott. New York: James Mowatt and company, 1844. 148 p. CtY; DLC; MB; NBMS; TMeT. 44-557

Bates, Isaac Chapman, 1780-1845. Speech of Mr. Bates, of Massachusetts, in the Senate, in defence of the protective system. Delivered February 21, 1844. Washington: Printed by Gales and Seaton, 1844. 18 p. CSmH; OClWHi; OO. 44-558

Bates, Merritt. Reasons for seceding from the Methodist Episcopal Church. Troy, New York: Kneeland, 1844. PPPr-Hi. 44-559

Baxter, Richard, 1615-1691. A call to the unconverted with an introductory essay by Thomas Chalmers. Boston: O.L. Perkins, 1844. 240 p. MB-W. 44-560

Baxter, Richard, 1615-1691. A call to the unconverted; now or never; and fifty reasons. With an introductory essay by Thomas Chalmers. New York: Robert Carter, 1844. 216 p. InSb. 44-561

Baxter, Richard, 1615-1691. The saints' everlasting rest. By the Rev. Richard Baxter. Abridged by Benjamin Faucett, A.M. Boston: Gould, Kendall and Lincoln, 1844. 35 p. MB; NcD. 44-562

Baxter, Richard, 1615-1691. Select practical writings of Richard Baxter, with a life of the author. By Leonard Bacon.... Fourth edition with additions. New Haven: Durrie and Peck, 1844. 2 v. MiU; OAU; PEaL; ScCoT; WU. 44-563

Bayley, Frederic William Naylor. Jack the giant killer. With illustrations by Leech. New York: Wilson and company, 1844. 96 p. MH. 44-564

Bayly, Thomas Haynes, 1797-1839. Songs and ballads, grave and gay. By Thomas Haynes Bayly. With a memoir of the author. Philadelphia: Carey and Hart, 1844. 167 p. GDecCT; IU; MB; OMC; TxU. 44-565

Beach, Wooster, 1794-1868. The family physician; or the reformed system of medicine; on vegetable or botanical principles... Fourth edition. New York: published by the author, 1844. 782 p. CSt-L; MBM; MH-M; MWA; PPCP. 44-566

Beach, Wooster, 1794-1868. The family physician; or the reformed system of medicine; on vegetable or botanical principles... Fifth edition. New York: 1844. 782 p. MB; MdBM; NNNAM. 44-567

Beaconsfield, Benjamin Disraeli, 1804-1881. Coningsby, or The new generation. New York: George Routledge and sons [1844] 477 p. ViPet. 44-568

Beaconsfield, Benjamin Disraeli, 1804-1881. Coningsby; or The new generation, New York: Knopf, 1844. 503 p. GU. 44-569

Beaconsfield, Benjamin Disraeli, 1804-1881. Coningsby, or the new generation.

New York: Lovell, Coryell and company [1844] 317 p. ILM; MoSCBC. 44-570

Beaconsfield, Benjamin Disraeli, 1804-1881. Coningsby, or The new generation. New York: W.H. Colyer, 1844. 136 p. DLC; MWA; NjR; NN; TxDaM. 44-571

Beaconsfield, Benjamin Disraeli, 1804-1881. Coningsby, or The new generation. Philadelphia: Carey and Hart, 1844. 627 p. MBAt; MdBP; PWerv. 44-572

Beaconsfield, Benjamin Disraeli, 1804-1881. Coningsby; or The new generation. Philadelphia: Carey and Hart, 1844. 159 p. CoGuW; DSG; GU; MH; OU. 44-573

Bear Mountain Railroad Company. Act of incorporation of the Bear Mountain Railroad Company, with facts and explanatory remarks. New York: James Van Norden and company, printers, 1844. 16 p. PPM. 44-574

Beardsley, Eben Edwards, 1808-1891. An address delivered in St. Peter's Church, Cheshire, October 1, 1844, on occasion of the fifth anniversary of the Episcopal Academy of Connecticut. New Haven: Stanley and Chapin, printers, 1844. 46 p. CtY; NjR; NjPT; OClWHi; RPB. 44-575

Beardsley, Samuel, 1790-1860. Remarks of Mr. Beardsley, of New York, on the right of petition: delivered in the House of Representatives, January 4, 1844. Washington: Globe office, 1844. 8 p. KHi; MH; NcD; NCH; NUt. 44-576

Beattie, James. Poetical works. Boston: Little, Brown and company, 1844. 239 p. IaB; MnM; VtU. 44-577

Beattie, James. Poetical works, with a memoir of the author. New York: Turner and Hayden, 1844. 308 p. IaAS; ICLI; OMC. 44-578

Beatty, Adam, 1776-1858. Essays on practical agriculture including his prize essays carefully revised, by Adams Beatty.... Maysville, Kentucky: Collins and Brown, 1844. 293 p. CtY; ICU; KyDC; MWA; NcD. 44-579

Beck, John B. The effects of opium on the infant subject. By John B. Beck, M.D. [New York: 1844] 7 p. DSG; NN; NNN. 44-580

Beck, Lewis Caleb, 1798-1853. A manual of chemistry; intended as a text book for medical schools, colleges and academies. Fourth edition, revised and illustrated with numerous wood cuts. New York: W.E. Dean, 1844. [13]-480 p. LNT-M; NjR; PPM; ViRMC. 44-581

Beck, Theodoric Romeyn, 1791-1855. Analysis of the testimony on the trial of Alvin Cornell for murder and the subsequent proof which led to the commutation of his punishment. [Albany: 1844] 22 p. MB. 44-582

Becklard, Eugene. Physiological mysteries and revelations in love, courtship and marriage; ....By Eugene Becklard, M.D. Translated from the third Paris edition, with revisions and additions of the sixth Paris edition, by Philip M. Howard. ....Illustrated with sixteen engravings. New York: Holland and Glover, 1844. 256 p. DNLM; NNC. 44-583

Beckwith, George C. A universal peace society, with the basis of co-operation in the cause of peace. [A letter to John Lee, LL.D., president of the London Peace Society] Boston: 1844?. MB. 44-584

Becon, Thomas. Prayers and other pieces of Thomas Becon.... edited for the Parker Society by John Ayre. ....Cambridge: printed at the University Press, 1844. 644 p. GDecCT; MBAt; NjR; OWoC; WBeloc. 44-585

The bee, by William Augustus Munsell. Albany: Munsell's Press, 1844-1845. 9 nos. in 1 v. DLC; ICU; MB; NAL; NN. 44-586

Beecher, George. The biographical remains of Rev. George Beecher. ....New York: Leavitt, Trow and company; Boston: Crocker and Brewster; Philadelphia: Perkins and Purves; Cincinnati: William H. Moore, 1844. 345 p. ICP; MB; NNUT; OO; PHi. 44-587

Beecher, Henry Ward, 1813-1887. The means of securing good rulers; a serman, delivered on the occasion of the death of Noah Noble, late governor of Indiana. Indianapolis: Chamberlain, 1844. 27 p. CtY; Ia; In; MWA; OCHP. 44-588

Beecher, Henry Ward, 1813-1887. Seven lectures to young men, on various important subjects; delivered before the young men of Indianapolis, Indiana, during the winter of 1843-4. By Henry Ward Beecher. Indianapolis: T.B. Cutler; Cincinnati: W.H. Moore and company, 1844. 195 p. CSmH; DLC; ICP; MWA; PU. 44-589

Beecher, William H. A letter on animal magnetism, by Rev. Dr. Beecher, of the Presbyterian Church. Philadelphia:

Brown, Bicking and Guilbert... 1844. 7 p. MMal; PPCP; PPM. 44-590

Beer's Carolina and Georgia almanac for 1845. Charleston, South Carolina: Samuel Weir, by Charles Prindle [1844] MWA. 44-591

Beer's Connecticut almanac. New Haven: Durrie and Peck, 1844. MWA. 44-592

Beer's Connecticut almanac. New Haven: S. Babcock, 1844. MWA. 44-593

Beer's Connecticut almanac. Norwich: T. Robinson, 1844. MWA. 44-594

Beet, H.P. Review of Mr Mann's report. [New York: 1844] MB; MH. 44-595

Belcher, Joseph, 1794-1859. Facts for girls. New York: 1844. DLC. 44-596

Belcher, Joseph. Scripture narratives, illustrated and improved. By the Rev. Joseph Belcher, D.D. From the second London edition. New York: Robert Carter; Pittsburg: Thomas Carter, 1844. 284 p. MNS; OSW. 44-597

Belcher, Joseph. Scripture narratives; illustrated and improved, by Joseph Belcher. New York: n.p., 1844. MiD; NjMD; PReaAt. 44-598

Belknap, Jeremy, 1744-1798. American biography with additions and notes by F.M. Hubbard. New York: Harper and brothers, 1844. 3 v. DLC; LN; MWA; PAnL; TNP. 44-599

Bell, Henry Glassford. Life of Mary Queen of Scotts... New York: Harper and brothers, 1844. 2 v. CLU; ICMe; MeAu; MNan; OCX. 44-600

Bell, John, 1797-1869. An Address, delivered before the Alumni society of the University of Nashville, October 3, 1843... Nashville [Tennessee] W.F. Bang and company, printers, 1844. 42 p. CSmH; MdBP; MH; PPM; THi. 44-601

Bell and Goodman's almanac for 1845. Rochester: Bell and Goodman, [1845] MBC; NN. 44-602

The belle, the blue and the bigot; or three fields for women's influence, by the author of Wreaths and branches for the church.... Samuel C. Blodget. Providence: B.F. Moore, 1844. 322 p. MAshiHi; RBr; RHi; RPA. 44-603

Bellini, Vincenzo. Il pirata di Felice Romani. The pirate; a melo-dramatic opera in two acts as represented at Palmo's New York Opera House, October, 1844. 59 p. MH. 44-604

Bellows, Henry Whitney, 1814-1882. Sermon, November 26, 1843, at the ordination of Dexter Clapp, Savannah, Georgia. New York: 1844. 24 p. MH-AH. 44-605

Bellows, Henry Whitney, 1814-1882. Some of the points of difference between Unitarian and Orthodox Christians. Boston: James Munroe and company, 1844. 54 p. DLC; ICMe; MeB; MH; PPL. 44-606

Bellows, Henry Whitney, 1814-1882. Some of the points of difference between Unitarian and Orthodox Christians. By Rev. Henry W. Bellows. Printed for the American Unitarian Association. Bos-

ton: James Munroe and company, 1844. 24 p. MBAU. 44-607

Belser, James Edwin. Remarks.... in committee of the whole, on the bill to refund the fine imposed on General Jackson, at New Orleans. Delivered in the House of Representatives.... January 8, 1844. Washington: Blair and Rives, 1844. 8 p. A-Ar; GEU. 44-608

Belser, James Edwin. Speech of Mr. Belser, of Alabama, on the right of members to their seats in the House of Representatives. Washington: Globe, 1844. 13 p. GEU; OClWHi. 44-609

Beman, Nathan Sidney Smith, 1785-1871. Christ, the only sacrifice, or the atonement in its relations to God and man. New York: Mark H. Newman, 1844. 171 p. NCH; NjMD; NNUT; PWaybu. 44-610

Beman, Nathan Sidney Smith, 1785-1871. Christ, the only sacrifice, or the atonement in its relations to God and man. Second edition, revised, rewritten, enlarged and improved. New York: Mark H. Newman, 1844. 171 p. IaDL; KWiU; NcMHi; NNUT; PCC. 44-611

Bemis, pseud? Clay and Frelinghuysen. Whig songs for the great mass convention of Boston common, September 19, 1844. Boston: 1844. 18 p. NNC. 44-612

Benedict, George Wyllys, 1796-1871. New England educational institutions in relation to American government.... Burlington: Chauncey Goodrich, 1844. 48 p. CtY; ICN; MH; MPiB; VtHi. 44-613

Benjamin, Asher, 1773-1845. The architect, or practical house carpenter....

Boston: L. Coffin, 1844. 199 p. DLC; MBU-Lin; MiD; NN; NNC. 44-614

Benjamin, Park, 1809-1864. Infatuation: a poem spoken before the Mercantile Library Association of Boston, October 9, 1844. Boston: William D. Ticknor and company, 1844. 31 p. CtY; DLC; MH-AH; MWA; RPB. 44-615

Benner, Enos. Abhandlung uber die rechenkunst 4te Auflage. Sunnytown, Pennsylvania: E.M. Benner, 1844. PPG. 44-616

Bennett, Alfred, 1780-1851. A discourse, embracing the history of the Baptist Church of Christ in Homer, New York, for about thirty years from its commencement. By Rev. Alfred Bennett. Utica: Bennett, Backus and Hawley, 1844. 28 p. MNtcA; MWA; NHC-S; PHi; RPB. 44-617

Bennett, Charles E. Seminary quick step.... Boston: 1844. 3 p. RHi. 44-618

Bennett, John. Letters to a young lady, on a variety of useful and interesting subjects. Calculated to improve the heart, to form the manners and enlighten the understanding... Tenth American edition. Philadelphia: Grigg and Elliot, 1844. 334 p. NcRP. 44-619

Bennett, P.S. A review of Rev. H. Mattison's tract for the times. ....Watertown, New York: press of J. Greene, 1844. 48 p. CSmH; DLC; N; PPPrHi; WHi. 44-620

Bent, Nathaniel Tucker, 1810-1856. A discourse, historical of St. Thomas' Church, Taunton, Massachusetts. Delivered on the afternoon of Easter day, 1844. Taunton, Massachusetts: Hack and Bradbury, printers, 1844. 33 p. CSmH; MBAt; MWA; NN; RPB. 44-621

Bentham, Jeremy, 1748-1832. Benthamiana; or, select extracts from the works of Jeremy Bentham. With an outline of his opinions on the principal subjects discussed in his works. Edited by John Hill Burton.... Philadelphia: Lea and Blanchard, 1844. 446 p. GEU; KTW; MeAug; OClW; PPL-R. 44-622

Bentley, Rensselaer. Introduction to the pictorial reader... New York: 1844. CtHWatk. 44-623

Bentley, Rensselaer. The pictorial spelling book:.... New York: 1844. MH; NNC. 44-624

Benton, Thomas Hart, 1782-1858. Speech of Mr. Benton, of Missouri, on the tariff. Delivered in the Senate of the United States, March, 25, 1844. Washington: printed at the Globe office, 1844. 16 p. CtY; MoShi; TxU. 44-625

Benton, Thomas Hart, 1782-1858. Speech of Mr. Benton, of Missouri; delivered in the Senate of the United States, May 16, 18, and 20, in secret session on the treaty for the annexation of Texas. Washington: 1844. 8 p. CtY; MoHi; OClWHi. 44-626

Benton, Thomas Hart, 1782-1858. Texas annexation bill. Speech of Mr. Benton, of Missouri, in reply to Mr. McDuffie. Delivered in the Senate of the United States, Saturday, June 15, 1844. Washington: Gideon's office, printer, [1844?] 16 p. CLU; ICU; LU; NcD; PHi. 44-627

Benton, Thomas Hart, 1782-1858. Three Speeches. Two delivered in the Senate and on at Boonville, Indiana, on the subject of the annexation of Texas to the United States. New York: 1844. 48 p. CtY; ICN; MWA; Nh; OClWHi. 44-628

Beranger, Pierre Jean de, 1780-1857. The songs of Beranger, in English. With a sketch of the author's life. Philadelphia: Carey and Hart, 1844. 148 p. CtY; OUr; PU; RPA; ScC. 44-629

Berdmore, Thomas. A treatise on the disorders and deformitites of the teeth and gums, explaining the most rational methods of treating their diseases.... Baltimore: American Society of Dental Surgeons, 1844. 87 p. DSG; MBC; MH; PPiU-D; TNN. 44-630

Berg, Joseph Frederick. An open Bible, the peoples safeguard against false prophets and fanatics. Philadelphia: J.B. Lippincott and company, 1844. 96 p. MH-AH; NjPT; PLERC-Hi; PPPrHi. 44-631

Berkshire Medical College. Pittsfield, Massachusetts. Catalogue of the trustees, overseers, faculty and students.... 1844. Pittsfield, Massachusetts: 1844. 12 p. MHi; WU-M. 44-632

Berquin, Arnaud, 1749-1791. The looking glass for the mind, or intellectual mirror.... with elegant engravings on wood by Anderson. Baltimore: Parsons and Preston, 1844. 216 p. MBMu; WaT. 44-633

Berrian, William, 1787-1862. Devotions for the sick room and for times of trouble; compiled from ancient liturgies and the writings of holy men. From the first London edition, with alterations and additions, by the Rev. William Berrian.... New York: J.A. Sparks, 1844. 4 p. MBAt; NjMD; NNG; OSW; OU. 44-634

Berrian, William, 1787-1862. The sailors' and soldiers' manual of devotion. New York: [V. L. Dill, 1844] 120 p. DLC; ICN; MB; NN; NNG. 44-635

Berrian, William, 1787-1862. The sailors' manual of devotion, by William Berrian....New York: Daniel Dana, [1844] DLC; MB; MCET; NjMD. 44-636

Berrien, John MacPherson, 1781-1856. Speech of Mr. Berrien, of Georgia, on the tariff. Delivered in the Senate of the United States on the 9th of April, 1844. Washington: Gales and Seaton, printers, 1844. 23 p. GU; In. 44-637

Berrien, John MacPherson, 1781-1856. Speech.... on the treaty for the annexation of Texas. Delivered in the Senate of the United States.... June 8, 1844. Washington: 1844. CtY; MHi. 44-638

Berry, R.T. A national warning; a sermon preached.... as an improvement of the calamity that occurred on board.... the steam frigate Princeton, etc. ....Philadelphia: 1844. DLC; MB; MHi; NjP. 44-639

The Berkshire jubilee, celebrated at Pittsfield, Massachusetts, August 22 and 23, 1844. Albany, New York: Weare C. Little; Pittsfield: E.P. Little [1844?] [7]-244 p. MWiW; NjP; NUtHi; WBeloC. 44-640

Bethune, George Washington, 1805-1862. The strength of Christian charity; a sermon, preached before the Foreign Evangelical Society, New York, May 5,

1844. Philadelphia: Clark, 1844. 39 p. CtSoP; IEG; MB; NCH; PPL-R. 44-641

Betts, Sarah. A letter to Hugh L. Hodge, on pessaries and the uterine supporter. Philadelphia: 1844. 12 p. DNLM; DSG; MH-M. 44-642

Betts, Sarah. The utility of the "uterine supporter," as invented by Mrs. James Betts of Philadelphia, in the cure of prolapsus uteri, etc. Third edition. Philadelphia: Mrs. James Betts, 1844. DLC; DNLM; DSG; KyLx; MdHi. 44-643

Bible. The acts of the Apostles: with a commentary. Boston: James Munroe and company, 1844. 330 p. ICMe; MeBaT; MNt; NCas; PPM. 44-644

Bible. The acts of the apostles; with notes chiefly explanatory; desinged for teachers in Sabbath schools and Bible classes and as an aid to family instruction. By Henry Ripley. Boston: Gould, Kendall and Lincoln, 1844. 334 p. ICU; DLC; MB; NNH; PPT. 44-645

Bible. Bibel; oder die ganze Heilige Schrift des Alten und Neuen Testaments. Nach dr. Martin Luther's uebersetzung. New York: Amerikanische Bibelgeselischaft, 1844. 2 v. in 1. CtMW; InPerM; NcD; OCH; TxH. 44-646

Bible. Bibel; oder die ganze Heilige Schrift des Alten und Neuen Testaments. Nach dr. Martin Luther's uebersetzung. Philadelphia: Mentz und Rovoudt, 1844-1845. 900, 311 p. MdBJ. 44-647

Bible. The commentary on the New Testament. By Lucius R. Paige. Boston: B.B. Mussey; New York: C.L. Stickney,

1844-. DLC; ICU; MB; MH; OClWHi 44-648

Bible. The complete evangelist; comprising the history of the life, actions, death, resurrection, ascension and doctrine, of Jesus Christ. Intended to embrace every important expression and idea recorded in the writings of Matthew, Mark, Luke and John, in the words of the authorized translation. New London: Bolles and Williams, 1844. 226 p. CtY; ICU. 44-649

Bible. The comprehensive commentary on the Holy Bible, edited by Rev. William Jenks. Brattleboro, Vermont: Brattleboro Typographic company, 1844. 838 p. WAsN. 44-650

Bible. The cottage Bible, and family expositor; containing the Old and New Testaments... Edited by Rev. William Patton... Hartford: Case, Tiffany and Burnham, 1844. 2 v. IEG; MAnA; MiGr; OCl. 44-651

Bible. English version of the Polyglott Bible, containing the Old and New Testaments. Philadelphia: Thomas Cowperthwait and company, 1844. 5-587, 190 p. MB; MHi; MiU; NN. 44-652

Bible. English version of the Polyglott Bible, containing the Old and New Testaments. With marginal readings together with a copious and original selection of references to parallel and illustrative passages, exhibited in a manner hitherto unattended. Cincinnati: Jewett and Mason, 1844. 587, 190 p. MnSM. 44-653

Bible. English version of the Polyglott Bible, containing the Old and New Testaments. With marginal readings together with a copious and original selection of references to parallel and illustrative passages, exhibited in a manner hitherto unattended. Franklin, New Hampshire: Peabody and Daniel, and D. Kimball, 1844. 705, 54, 216, 63, 86 p. CSf; MWinchrHi; PU. 44-654

Bible. English version of the Polyglott Bible, containing the Old and New Testaments. With marginal readings together with a copious and original selection of references to parallel and illustrative passages, exhibited in a manner hitherto unattended. New York: C. Wells, 1844. 587, 190 p. DLC. 44-655

Bible. English version of the Polyglott Bible, containing the Old and New Testaments. With marginal readings together with a copious and original selection of references to parallel and illustrative passages, exhibited in a manner hitherto unattended. Philadelphia: Grigg and Elliot, 1844. 392 p. NoLoc. 44-656

Bible. English version of the Polyglott Bible, containing the Old and New Testaments. With marginal readings together with a copious and original selection of references to parallel and illustrative passages, exhibited in a manner hitherto unattended. Philadelphia: Grigg and Elliot, 1844. 587, 190 p. MHi; WRichM. 44-657

Bible. English version of the Polyglott Bible, containing the Old and New Testaments. With marginal readings together with a copious and original selection of references to parallel and illustrative passages, exhibited in a manner hitherto unattended. Philadelphia:

Thomas, Cowperthwait and company, 1844. 587, 190 p. ABBS; CMtv; MB; PP; TxGR. 44-658

Bible. English version of the Polyglott Bible, containing the Old and New Testaments. With marginal readings together with a copious and original selection of references to parallel and illustrative passages, exhibited in a manner hitherto unattended. Portland: Sanborn and Carter, 1844. 587 p. MHolliHi. 44-659

Bible. English version of the Polyglott Bible, containing the Old and New Testaments. With marginal readings together with a copious and original selection of references to parallel and illustrative passages, exhibited in a manner hitherto unattended. Springfield: G. and C. Merriam, 1844. 254 p. VtMidSM. 44-660

Bible. Explanatory and practical notes on the gospel. By Albert Barnes. New York: Harper and Brothers, 1844. 414 p. 44-661

Bible. Explanatory notes upon the New Testament, by John Wesley... New York: G. Lane and P.P. Sandford, 1844. 734 p. GEU-T; MWA; NcA-S; OrU; TU. 44-662

Bible. Exposition of St. Paul's epistle to the Romans... translated by Rev. Robert Menzies. First American from the second revised and corrected Edinburgh edition. Philadelphia: Sorin and Ball, 1844. 432 p. GAGTh; MBrigStJ; TxGeo-S. 44-663

Bible. The exposition of the Gospels of St. Matthew and St. Mark, and of some other detached parts of Holy Scripture. By the Rev. Richard Watson. New York: G. Lane and P.P. Sandford, 1844. 538 p. DLC; Mi; NcD; NN. 44-664

Bible. The four gospels; with a commentary, by Abiel Abbot Livermore. Fourth edition. Boston: James Monroe and company, 1844. 358 p. ICMe; MBr; NCas; OkHi. 44-665

Bible. The four gospels; with a commentary. New edition. Boston: 1844-1845. DLC. 44-666

Bible. The four gospels; with notes, chiefly explanatory designed for teachers in Sabbath schools and Bible classes, and as an aid to family instruction. By Henry Ripley. Seventh edition. Boston: Gould, Kendall and Lincoln, 1844. 2 v. TJaU. 44-667

Bible. The Gospel according to Matthew, and the Acts of the Apostles; translated into the Potawatomie language by Johnston Lykins. Carefully compared with the Greek text. Louisville, Kentucky: Published by the Board of Managers of the American Indian Mission Association, W.C. Buck, 1844. 240 p. NoLoc. 44-668

Bible. The gospel according to Matthew, and the Acts of the Apostles; translated into the Potawatomie language by Johnson Lykins. Carefully compared with the Greek text. Louisville, Kentucky: American Bible Society, 1844. 240 p. CU; GMM; KyLo; NCH; NN. 44-669

Bible. The Gospel according to Matthew. Translated into the Cherokee language. Fourth edition. Park Hill: Mission Press, 1844. 120 p. DLC; MShM; OkMu; PCC. 44-670

Bible. The gospel according to Matthew. Translated into the Cherokee language. Fourth edition. Park Hill: Mission Press, 1844. 347 p. NoLoc. 44-671

Bible. The gospel according to Matthew. Translated into the Cherokee language. Fourth edition. Park Hill: Mission Press, 1844. 416 p. OkEn. 44-672

Bible. The Greek Testament, with English notes, critical, philological and exegetical... Fifth American from the second London edition. Philadelphia, Perkins and Purves, 1844. 2 v. GEU; ICU; MiD; NBuG; WaWW. 44-673

Bible. The Holy Bible, according to the authorized version; with notes explanatory and practical... Prepared and arranged by G. D'Oyly, and Richard Mant. New York: Stanford and Swaords, 1844. 2 v. MCET; McAS. 44-674

Bible. The Holy Bible, authorized version with explanatory notes, marginal references, by Thomas Scott; from the latest London edition. New York: W.E. Dean, 1844. 3 v. IaDaB; NN; OCoC; WFox. 44-675

Bible. The Holy Bible, containing the Old and New Testaments, according to the authorized version; with explanatory notes, practical observations, and copious marginal references. By Thomas Scott. First American stereotype quarto edition, from the London standard edition. Philadelphia: Jesper Harding, 1844-1848. 5 v. IaHumdt; MiD-MCh; MnAn; NKingS; TNV. 44-676

Bible. The Holy Bible, containing the Old and New Testaments, according to the authorized version; with explanatory notes, practical observations, and copious marginal references. By Thomas Scott. From the fifth London edition. Boston: Crocker and Brewster, 1844. 3 v. LStBA; OrPD. 44-677

Bible. The Holy Bible, containing the Old and New Testaments, according to the authorized version; with explanatory notes, practical observations, and copious marginal references. By Thomas Scott. Philadelphia: J.M. Campbell; New York: Saxton and Miles, 1844-1846. 5 v. DLC. 44-678

Bible. The Holy Bible, containing the Old and New Testaments, according to the authorized version; with the references and marginal readings of the Polyglott Bible... Philadelphia: Lindsay and Blakiston, 1844. 937 p. MiU; NN. 44-679

Bible. The Holy Bible, containing the Old and New Testaments, translated out of the original tongues: and with Cannes marginal notes and references... Hartford: S. Andrus and son, 1844. 811 p. MW; MWA. 44-680

Bible. The Holy Bible, containing the Old and New Testaments, translated out of the original tongues: and with the former translations diligently compared and revised. Cooperstown, New York: H. and E. Phinney, 1844. NN; OCA. 44-681

Bible. The Holy Bible, containing the Old and New Testaments, translated out of the original tongues: and with the former translations diligently compared and revised. Fifty-seventh edition. New York: American Bible Society, 1844. 669 p. MH. 44-682

Bible. The Holy Bible, containing the Old and New Testaments, translated out of the original tongues: and with the former translations diligently compared and revised. Hartford: S. Andrus and son, 1844. 681 p. MAnA; MiD-B. 44-683

Bible. The Holy Bible, containing the Old and New Testaments, translated out of the original tongues: and with the former translations diligently compared and revised. Hartford: S. Andrus and son, 1844. 824, 251 p. Nh; PWmpDS-Hi. 44-684

Bible. The Holy Bible, containing the Old and New Testaments, translated out of the original tongues: and with the former translations diligently compared and revised. New York: American Bible Society, 1844. 669 p. MoSpD; NcC; NcD; NNUT. 44-685

Bible. The Holy Bible, containing the Old and New Testaments, translated out of the original tongues: and with the former translations diligently compared and revised. New York: American Bible Society, 1844. 968, 303 p. MAbD; NBu; NjP; PLERC-HI; PPiW. 44-686

Bible. The Holy Bible, containing the Old and New Testaments, translated out of the original tongues: and with the former translations diligently compared and revised. Portland: Sanborn and Carter, 1844. 1109 p. MeLewB. 44-687

Bible. The Holy Bible, containing the Old and New Testaments, translated out of the original tongues: and with the former translations diligently compared and revised. Troy, New York: W. and H. Merriam, 1844. 733, 224 p. MNoanNP. 44-688

Bible. The Holy Bible, containing the Old and New Testaments, translated out of the original tongues; and with the former translations diligently compared and revised. The references and marginal readings of the Polyglott Bible, with numerous additions from Bagster's comprehensive Bible. New York: Robinson, Pratt and Company, 1844. 773 p. ViLxW. 44-689

Bible. The Holy Bible, containing the Old and New Testaments. The text carefully printed from the most correct copies of the present authorized translation, including the marginal readings... by Adam Clarke. A new edition. New York: G. Lane and C.B. Tippett, 1844-1847. 6 v. MiU. 44-690

Bible. The Holy Bible, containing the Old and New Testaments. Translated out of the original tongues and with the former translations diligently compared and revised. Fifth edition. New York: American Bible Society, 1844. 968, 303 p. MSohG. 44-691

Bible. The Holy Bible, containing the Old and New Testaments. Translated out of the original tongues and with the former translations diligently compared and revised. New York: American Bible Society, 1844. 968, 303 p. MB; NNAB. 44-692

Bible. The Holy Bible, containing the Old and New Testaments... With Canne's marginal notes and references, and a concise table of contents of the books of the Old and New Testaments. Hartford:

S. Andrus and Son, 1844. 619, 109 p. NN. 44-693

Bible. The Holy Bible, containing the Old and New Testaments... with explanatory notes, practical observations, and copious marginal references by Thomas Scott...Stereotype edition from the fifth London edition. Boston: Crocker and Brewster, 1844. 6 v. NN; NjN; ViU-L. 44-694

Bible. The Holy Bible, containing the Old and New Testaments... with explanatory notes, practical observations, and copious marginal references. By Thomas Scott. From the latest London edition... New York: W.E. Dean, 1844. 3 v. NN. 44-695

Bible. The Holy Bible, containing the Old and New Testaments: together with the apocrypha; translated out of the original tongue and with Cannes marginal notes and references. Hartford: Sumner and Goodman, 1844. 768p. MoS; MsJPED. 44-696

Bible. The Holy Bible, containing the Old and New Testaments: translated out of the original tongues; and with the former translations diligently compared and revised. Hartford: S. Andrus and son, 1844. 852, 263 p. CStclU; NN. 44-697

Bible. The Holy Bible, containing the Old and New Testaments: translated out of the original tongues; and with the former translations diligently compared and revised. New York: 1844. 979 p. IU. 44-698

Bible. The Holy Bible, containing the Old and New Testaments: translated out of the original tongues; and with the former translations diligently compared and revised. Philadelphia: Lindsay and Blakiston, 1844. 937 p. MiU. 44-699

Bible. The Holy Bible, containing the Old and New Testaments; together with Apocrypha: translated out of the original tongues, and with the former translations diligently compared and revised. With Canne's marginal notes and references. Cooperstown, New York: H. and E. Phinney, 1844. 576, [4] 99, [577]-768 p. NN; PSt; OCA. 44-700

Bible. The Holy Bible, containing the Old and New Testaments; together with the Apocrypha: translated out of the original tongues, and with the former translations diligently compared and revised. Philadelphia: J. Harding, 1844. 575, 96 [577]-768 p. CtY. 44-701

Bible. The Holy Bible, containing the Old and New Testaments; translated out of the original tongues, and with the former translations diligently compared and revised. Hartford: S. Andrus, 1844. 2 v. in 1. CLSU. 44-702

Bible. The Holy Bible, containing the Old and New Testaments; translated out of the original tongues... Hartford: S. Andrus and Son, 1844. 837, 656-681, 31 p. NN; WaS. 44-703

Bible. The Holy Bible, containing the Old and the New Testaments according to the commonly received version. Seventh edition. New York: Stereotyped by White and Hagar for the American and Foreign Bible Society, 1844. InNovJ. 44-704

Bible. The Holy Bible, containing the Old Testament and the New... Hartford: S. Andrus and Son, 1844. 85f2, 263 p. NN. 44-705

Bible. The Holy Bible, containing the Old Testament and the New... Portland: Samborn and Carter, [1844] 852, 259 p. NN. 44-706

Bible. The Holy Bible, containing the Old Testament and the New: according to the commonly received version. New York: R.G. Valentine, for the American and Foreign Bible Society, 1844. 2 v. ICU. 44-707

Bible. The Holy Bible, translated from the Latin Vulgate: diligently compared with the Hebrew, Greek and other editions, in diverse languages... New York: Dunigan, 1844. 752, 968 p. FOA; LNH; MdBS; NN; OClW. 44-708

Bible. The Holy Bible, translated from the Latin Vulgate: diligently compared with the Hebrew, Greek and other editions, in diverse languages... New York: Kennedy, 1844. 968 p. MdBE; MWel; NN; NNUT; PPiW. 44-709

Bible. The Holy Bible, translated from the Latin Vulgate: diligently compared with the Hebrew, Greek and other editions in diverse languages. The Old Testament, first published by the English College at Douay, and the New Testament, first published by the English College at Rheims... New York: E. Dunigan, 1844. 752, 754-968 p. CtY; ICN; MHi; NN. 44-710

Bible. The Holy Bible, translated from the Latin Vulgate: diligently compared with the Hebrew, Greek and other editions in diverse languages. The Old Testament, first published by the English

College at Douay, and the New Testament, first published by the English College at Rheims... New York: Excelsior Catholic Publishing House, [1844] 968 p. KAs. 44-711

Bible. The Holy Bible, translated from the Latin Vulgate: diligently compared with the Hebrew, Greek and other editions in diverse languages. The Old Testament, first published by the English College at Douay, and the New Testament, first published by the English College at Rheims... New York: P.J. Kenedy, [1844] 968 p. NN; PPiPT; WU. 44-712

Bible. The Holy Bible. New York: American Bible Society, 1844. 1284 p. NNAB. 44-713

Bible. The Holy Bible. New York: American Bible Society, 1844. 824, 251 p. MB. 44-714

Bible. Inspired psalms, selected, and literally translated, on an original plan of verification, with explanations and appropriate music. By Joseph Washington Morton.... Freedom, Pennsylvania: published by the author, 1844. 30 p. DLC; PHi; PPPrHi. 44-715

Bible. Isaiah. A new translation, with a preliminary dissertation and notes by Robert Lowth. From the tenth English edition. Boston: Munroe and Francis, 1844. 414 p. MdBD; OO. 44-716

Bible. Isaiah. A new translation; with a preliminary dissertation, and notes...From the tenth English edition. Boston: Munroe and Francis, 1844. 414 p. MdBD. 44-717

Bible. Isaiah: a new translation; with a

preliminary dissertation and notes, critical philological and explanatory. From the tenth English edition. With an appendix containing the essential variations from the translations of Lowth, by Michael Dodson and Joseph Stock. Boston: Munroe and Francis, 1844. 60, 423, 47 p. CtHC; OO. 44-718

Bible. Iu Otoshki. Kikendiuin au kitogimaminon gai bemajiinung Jesus Krist: ima Ojibue ineuining giizhitong. The New Testament of Our Lord nad Saviour Jesus Christ... New York, Printed by the American Bible Society, 1844. 643, 42 p. CSmH; NjPT; MBGCT; PPAmP; WHi. 44-719

Bible. King James version of 1611. The Holy Bible [Second edition] New York: 1844. MB. 44-720

Bible. The life, doctirne, and sufferings of our Blessed Lord and Saviour Jesus Christ, as recorded by the Four Evangelist. New York: R. Martin and company, 1844. 80 p. CSrD; LNL; MdW; MiD-M; NB. 44-721

Bible. The life, doctrine and sufferings of our Blessed Lord and Saviour Jesus Christ, as recorded by the four Evangelists. By Henry Rutter. New York: Johnson, Fry and company, 1844. 535 p. CLamB. 44-722

Bible. Das Neue Testament unsers herrn und heilandes Jesu Christi, nach der Deutschen Uebersetzung Dr. Martin Luther. Lancaster, Johann Barr, 1844. 536 p. MiU-C; PHi. 44-723

Bible. Das Neue Testament unsers Herrn und Heilandes Jesu Christi. New

York: Amerikanische Bible-Gesellschaft, 1844. GEU. 44-724

Bible. The New Testament, arranged in historical and chronological order; with copious notes on the principle subjects of theology... Boston: Crocker and Brester, 1844. 455, 472 p. CSansS; NGlf. 44-725

Bible. The New Testament, arranged in historical and chronological order; with copious notes on the principle subjects of theology... Boston: Crocker and Brester, 1844. 927 p. IaB. 44-726

Bible. The New Testament of our Lord and Saviour Jesus Christ. Text carefully printed from correct copies of the present authorized translation. New York: J. Collard, 1844. 6 v. MBNMHi. 44-727

Bible. The New Testament of Our Lord and Saviour Jesus Christ, Bible. New Testament of Our Lord and Saviour Jesus Christ, the text carefully printed from the most correct copies of the present authorized version including the marginal readings and parallel texts.... by Adam Clarke. New edition. Philadelphia: Thomas, Cowperthwait and company, 1844. 455 p. ICU; MH-AH. 44-728

Bible. The New Testament of Our Lord and Saviour Jesus Christ, translated from the Latin vulgate.... New York: 1844. MHi. 44-729

Bible. The New Testament of Our Lord and Saviour Jesus Christ, translated out of the original Greek, and with the former translations diligently compared and revised [Ninth edition] New York: American Bible Society, 1844. 371 p. NNAB. 44-730

Bible. The New Testament of Our Lord and Saviour Jesus Christ, translated out of the original Greek, and with the former translations diligently compared and revised. Boston: Ticknor, 1844. 450 p. MB. 44-731

Bible. The New Testament of Our Lord and Saviour Jesus Christ, translated out of the original Greek, and with the former translations diligently compared and revised. Concord, New Hampshire: L. Roby, 1844. 254 p. NN. 44-732

Bible. The New Testament of Our Lord and Saviour Jesus Christ, translated out of the original Greek, and with the former translations diligently compared and revised. Fourth edition. New York: American and Foreign Bible Society, 1844. 236 p. IaPeC. 44-733

Bible. The New Testament of Our Lord and Saviour Jesus Christ, translated out of the original Greek, and with the former translations diligently compared and revised. Fourth edition. New York: American and Foreign Bible Society, 1844. NoLoc. 44-734

Bible. The New Testament of Our Lord and Saviour Jesus Christ, translated out of the original Greek, and with the former translations diligently compared and revised. New York: American Bible Society, 1844. 338 p. WHi. 44-735

Bible. The New Testament of Our Lord and Saviour Jesus Christ, translated out of the original Greek, and with the former translations diligently compared and revised. New York: American Bible Society, 1844. 344 p. DLC; MdBD; NFri; NPalK; OO. 44-736

Bible. The New Testament of Our Lord and Saviour Jesus Christ, translated out of the original Greek, and with the former translations diligently compared and revised. New York: American Bible Society, 1844. 375 p. COCA; RPB. 44-737

Bible. The New Testament of Our Lord and Saviour Jesus Christ, translated out of the original Greek, and with the former translations diligently compared and revised. New York: American Bible Society, 1844. 420 p. DLC; MB; RPB. 44-738

Bible. The New Testament of Our Lord and Saviour Jesus Christ, translated out of the original Greek, and with the former translations diligently compared and revised. New York: American Bible Society, 1844. 431, 112 p. MH; NNUT. 44-739

Bible. The New Testament of Our Lord and Saviour Jesus Christ, translated out of the original Greek, and with the former translations diligently compared and revised. New York: American Bible Society, 1844. 543 p. FDb. 44-740

Bible. The New Testament of Our Lord and Saviour Jesus Christ, translated out of the original Greek, and with the former translations diligently compared and revised. New York: American Bible Society, 1844. 650 p. NoLoc. 44-741

Bible. The New Testament of Our Lord and Saviour Jesus Christ, translated out of the original Greek, and with the former translations diligently compared and revised. New York: J.C. Riker, 1844. 350 p. NNAB. 44-742

Bible. The New Testament of Our Lord and Saviour Jesus Christ, translated out of the original Greek, and with the former translations diligently compared and revised. New York: J.S. Redfield, 1844. 348 p. MoU; NNAB. 44-743

Bible. The New Testament of Our Lord and Saviour Jesus Christ, translated out of the original Greek, and with the former translations diligently compared and revised. New York: White and Hagar, 1844. 236 p. IaPeC. 44-744

Bible. The New Testament of Our Lord and Saviour Jesus Christ, translated out of the original Greek, and with the former translations diligently compared and revised. Newark, New Jersey: Benjamin Olds, 1844. 288 p. IU; MiD-M. 44-745

Bible. The New Testament of Our Lord and Saviour Jesus Christ, translated out of the original Greek, and with the former translations diligently compared and revised. Philadelphia: J. Harding, 1844. 312 p. NNAB. 44-746

Bible. The New Testament of Our Lord and Saviour Jesus Christ, translated out of the original Greek, and with the former translations diligently compared and revised. Tenth edition. New York: American Bible Society, 1844. COCA. 44-747

Bible. The New Testament of Our Lord and Saviour Jesus Christ, translated out of the original Greek, and with the former translations diligently compared and revised. Watertown, New York: Knowlton and Rice, 1844. 237 p. NN. 44-748

Bible. The New Testament of Our Lord and Saviour Jesus Christ, with marginal readings... Cincinnati: Jewett and Mason, 1844. 190 p. MnSM. 44-749

Bible. The New Testament of our Lord and Saviour Jesus Christ: according to the common version. New York: American and Foreign Bible Society, 1844. 362 p. KyLoS. 44-750

Bible. Norrim testamentum ad exemplar millianum, etc. Edited by William Greenfield. Philadelphia: Perkins, 1844. 569 p. OO. 44-751

Bible. Notes, critical and practical, on the book of Exodus; designed as a general help to biblical reading and instruction. Fourth edition. New York: Mark H. Newman, 1844. 299 p. WaPS. 44-752

Bible. Notes, explanatory and practical, on the Acts of the apostles. Designed for Bible classes and Sunday schools. By Albert Barnes. Tenth edition. New York: Harper and Brothers, 1844. 356 p. CU; DLC; KWiF; MnSM; PU. 44-753

Bible. Notes, explanatory and practical, on the first epistle of Paul to the Corinthiams. By Albert Barnes. Third edition. New York: Harper and Brothers, 1844. 357 p. TChFPr. 44-754

Bible. Notes, explanatory and practical, on the Gospels... Seventeenth edition. New York: Harper, 1844. MB; OO; PU. 44-755

Bible. Le Nouveau Testament de norte seigneur Jesus Christ; revu sur les originaux par David Martin... New York: publie par la societe Biblique Americaine, 1844. 444 p. GDecCT; MnSS; MsJPED. 44-756

Bible. Novum Testamentum, cum versione Latina ariae montani auctore Johanne Leusden, Professor. New York: W.E. Dean, printer, 1844. 755 p. GDecCT; IEG; KN; OO. 44-757

Bible. Novum Testamentum ad exemplar millianum cum emendationibus et lectionibus Griesbachii, praecipuis vocibus ellipticis, thematibus onmium vocum difficiloirum, atque locis Scripture parallelis... Philadelphiae: Perkins et Purves, 1844. 281 p. MAnP; MdBMP; NjR; TxH. 44-758

Bible. Novum Testametum ad exemplar millianum cum emendationibus et lectionibus Griesbachii, praecipuis vocibus ellipticis, thematibus onmium vocum difficiloirum, atque locis Scripture parallelis... Philadelphiae: Perkins et Purves, 1844. 371 p. MiU; NIC; NjR; OO. 44-759

Bible. Novum Testametum ad exemplar millianum cum emendationibus et lectionibus Griesbachii, praecipuis vocibus ellipticis, thematibus onmium vocum difficiloirum, atque locis Scripture parallelis... Philadelphiae: Perkins et Purves, 1844. 571 p. CSt; PPPrHi. 44-760

Bible. The Old Testament arranged in historical and chronological order. By Rev. George Townsend. Boston: Crocker and Brewster, 1844. 1188, 24 p. ICU; KKcBT; MA; NE; ScSoB. 44-761

Bible. The pictorial Bible... New York: J.S. Redfield, 1844. 1102, 348 p. MiMus; NN; PP. 44-762

Bible. Practical observations on the New Testament. Arranged for family worship.... Philadelphia: Lindsay and Blakiston, 1844. 532 p. ViU. 44-763

Bible. Psalms in metre, selected from the Psalms of David; with hymns, suited to the feasts and fasts of the church, and other occasions of public worhsip. Philadelphia: Protestant Episcopal Female Prayer Book Society, stereotyped by L. Johnson, 1844. 248 p. GAGTh; MH. 44-764

Bible. The Psalms of David in metre [Hartford: 1844?] 39 p. NN. 44-765

Bible. The Psalms of David in metre [Hartford: 1844?] 81 p. NN. 44-766

Bible. The Psalms of David in metre: allowed by the authority of the Kirk of Scotland, and of several branches of the Presbyterian Church in the United States.... Philadelphia: Hogan, 1844. 424 p. ICN. 44-767

Bible. The Psalms of David in metre: being a new metrical and literal version of the book of Psalms. Rossville: J.M. Christy, 1844. 275 p. DLC. 44-768

Bible. The Psalms of David, imitated in the language of the New Testament and applied to the Christian state and worship. Philadelphia: Thomas, 1844. 272 p. PPLT. 44-769

Bible. The Psalms of David, imitated in the language of the New Testament and applied to the Christian state and worship in the United States. Philadelphia: Thomas, 1844. 272 p. PPLT. 44-770

Bible. The Psalms of David, imitated in the language of the New Testament and applied to the Christian use and worship, by I. Watts. Hartford: Printed by Hudson and Goodwin, 1844. 475 p. Ct. 44-771

Bible. The Psalms of David, in metre: being a new metrical and literal version of the Psalms by John Reynolds. Rossville, Ohio, 1844. IEG. 44-772

Bible. Psalms, in metre, selected from the Psalms of David: with hymns, suited to the feasts and fasts of the church, and other occasions of public worship. Hartford: Robins and S. Smith, 1844. 64 p. NNG. 44-773

Bible. Psalms, in metre, selected from the Psalms of David: with hymns, suited to the feasts and fasts of the church, and other occasions of public worship. Hartford: S. Andrus and son, 1844. 208, 19 p. DLC; NNG. 44-774

Bible. Psalms, in metre, selected from the Psalms of David: with hymns, suited to the feasts and fasts of the church, and other occasions of public worship. New York: Blake, 1844. 112 p. MB. 44-775

Bible. Psalms, in metre, selected from the Psalms of David: with hymns, suited to the feasts and fasts of the church, and other occasions of public worship. New York: New York Bible and Common Prayer Book Society, 1844. 102 p. MBC; NNG. 44-776

Bible. Psalms, in metre, selected from the Psalms of David: with hymns, suited to the feasts and fasts of the church, and other occasions of public worship. Philadelphia: Carey and Hart, 1844. 286 p. NN. 44-777

Bible. Psalms, in metre, selected from the Psalms of David: with hymns, suited to the feasts and fasts of the church, and other occasions of public worship. Philadelphia: George and Wayne, 1844. 141 p. CtHWatk; NNG. 44-778

Bible. Psalms, in metre, selected from the Psalms of David: with hymns, suited to the feasts and fasts of the church, and other occasions of public worship. Philadelphia: King and Baird [1844] 105 p. DLC. 44-779

Bible. Psalms, in metre, selected from the Psalms of David: with hymns, suited to the feasts and fasts of the church, and other occasions of public worship. Philadelphia: Protestant Episcopal Female Prayer Book Society, 1844. WNaE. 44-780

Bible. Psalms, in metre, selected from the Psalms of David: with hymns, suited to the feasts and fasts of the church, and other occasions of public worship. Philadelphia: R.S.H. George, 1844. 244 p. NBuG; NN; NNG. 44-781

Bible. Psalter, Der. Des konigs und propheten David's Verdeutscht von Dr. Martin Luther. Philadelphia: Conrad Zentler, 1844. PPG. 44-782

Bible. Select passages from the Holy Scriptures. [In Cherokee. Park Hill? 1844] DLC; MBAt. 44-783

Bible. Selections from the Psalms of David in metre: with hymns suited to the feasts and fasts of the church and other occasions of public worship. New York: Harper, [1844] 109 p. MB. 44-784

Bible. Thoughts of peace for the Chris-

tian sufferer; a selection of short passages from scripture and sacred poetry. From the fourth London edition. Philadelphia: H. Hooker, 1844. 238 p. NNUT; ViU. 44-785

Bible biography in the form of questions. [By a teacher] Boston: 1844. 98 p. MHi. 44-786

The Bible expositor; confirmations of the truth of the Holy Scriptures, from the observations of recent travellers, illustrating the manners.... Published under the direction of the Society for the Promotion of Christian Knowledge. New York: D. Appleton and company, 1844. 320 p. LN; MBC; MoSpD; ODaB; RPAt. 44-787

Bible gazetteer; containing illustrations of Bible geography. New York: W. Robinson, 1844. 6 v. MMeT. 44-788

Bibliotheca sacra; a religious and sociological quarterly. Andover: Allen, Morrill and Wardell, etc., 1844-. v. 1-. CBPSR; CoU; ICU; KWiU; TxD-T. 44-789

Bickersteth, Edward, 1786-1850. Treatise on prayer, designed to assist in the devout discharge of that duty.... New York: Carter, 1844. 240 p. NjP; OSW. 44-790

Bickersteth, Edward, 1786-1850. Treatise on prayer. New York: 1844. 95 p. NjP. 44-791

Bickersteth, Edward, 1786-1850. Treatise on the Lord's supper, designed as a guide and companion to the holy communion. First New York from the ninth London edition. New York: Stanford, 1844. 368 p. CtHT; MH; MPiB; NCH; ScNC. 44-792

Bidlack, Benjamin Alden. Remarks on the right of petition, in the House of Representatives, January 11-12, 1844. Washington: 1844. 7 p. DHU; MBAt; MH. 44-793

Bidlack, Benjamin Alden. Speech of Mr. Bidlack of Pennsylvania, in reply to the political attacks that had been made upon the nominees of the Democratic convention, and in defence of the young hickory: Jas. K. Polk, Geo. M. Dallas. Washington: printed at the Globe office, 1844. 12 p. MiGr; OClWHi; PPFM. 44-794

Bidlack, Benjamin Alden. Speech on the proposition to reduce the duties on coal and iron, in the House of Representatives, May 1, 1844. Washington: 1844. MBAt; NjR; PWbWHi. 44-795

Bigland, John. A natural history of animals. New edition. Philadelphia: Grigg and Elliot, 1844. 190 p. CoD; IaDaM; MLow; MSaP; PWW. 44-796

Bigland, John. A natural history of birds, fishes, reptiles and insects. Philadelphia: Grigg and Elliot, 1844. 179 p. In; LNDil; MChi. 44-797

Bingley, Thomas. Tales about travellers: their perils, adventures and discoveries. New York: 1844. MBC. 44-798

Binney, Amos, 1802-1878. The theological compend: containing a system of divinity, or a brief view of the evidences, doctrines, morals, and institutions of Christianity. Designed for the benefit of families, Bible classes and Sunday schools. New York: James Collord, printer, 1844. 128 p. IaDL; ICP; InGr. 44-799

Binney, Horace, 1780-1875. Argument of Horace Binney, esq., in the case of Vidal vs. the city of Philadelphia, in the Supreme Court of the United States. February, 1844. Philadelphia: C. Sherman, printer, 1844. 144 p. Ct; ICMe; MH-L; NIC; PHi. 44-800

Binney, Horace, 1780-1875. Arguments of the defendant's counsel and judgment of the Supreme Court of the United States, in the case of Vidal and others vs. the mayor of Philadelphia and others... Philadelphia: Crissy, 1844. 307 p. InID; MH; PPAmP; Or-SC; VtU. 44-801

Bird, Milton. Error unmarked: or a plain statement of defence of some of the doctrines of the Gospel, in familiar lectures. Pittsburg [Pa.] A.A. Anderson, printer, 1844. 180 p. MoMM; NcD; NjPT; PPi; PPPrHi. 44-802

Bird, Robert Montgomery, 1805-1854. Sketch of the life, public services, and character, of Major Thomas Stockton, of New Castle, the candidate of the Whig Party for the office of Governor of Delaware. Wilmington, Delaware: Porter and Naff, 1844. 24 p. DeWi; MdBP; WHi. 44-803

The bird book. Philadelphia: American Sunday School Union, [1844] [9]-152 p. DLC; KyHi; ScCliTO. 44-804

A birthday gift. From the English edition, revised by the committee of publication. Boston: Sabbath School Society, 1844. 48 p. MNF. 44-805

Bishop, Henry Rowley, 1786-1855. With hawk and hound. New York: 1844. 4 p. MB. 44-806

Black, Edward Junius, 1806-1846. Speech of Mr. Black, on the right of members to their seats in the House of Representatives delivered February 12, 1844. Washington: Globe office, 1844. 14 p. GEU. 44-807

Black joke almanac for 1844. New York: [1844?] [24 p.] MBNEH. 44-808

Black River Literary and Religious Institute. Catalogue of the officers and students.... Watertown, New York: J. Green's Press, 1844. 24 p. N. 44-809

Black Sluggard, pseud. The proposed alteration of "the judicial tenure," in South Carolina. Discussed by "the Black Sluggard." Hamburg, [South Carolina]: Republican office, printer, 1844. 30 p. DLC; ICN; MH-L; ScU. 44-810

Blackstone, William, 1723-1780. Commentaries on the laws of England... With an analysis of the works... With a life of the author, and notes by Christian, Chitty, Lee, Hovenden and Ryland; also references to American cases by a member of the New York bar. From the nineteenth London edition. New York: Dean, 1844. 4 v. in 2. CU; DLC; Ia; PAtM; PPP. 44-811

Blain, Wilson. The psalms of David: every way suitable to Christian worship. A discourse. Rossville: Christy, 1844. PPPrHi. 44-812

Blair, David. The parent's assistant; or, mothers catechism; containing common things, necessary to be known by children at an early age. Intended as a first book for primary schools in the United States. By Rev. David Blair. Revised edition with additions and corrections. New Haven: S. Babcock, 1844. 72 p. CtMW; MiHi. 44-813

Blair, Franklin O. A poem.... Boston: 1844. 23 p. RPB. 44-814

Blair, Hugh, 1718-1800. Lectures on rhetoric and Belles lettres. Philadelphia: James Kay, Jun. brother, 1844. 577 p. GAuW; ICT; LNH; NjP; ViRut. 44-815

Blair, Hugh, 1718-1800. Sermons. By Hugh Blair, D.D.F.R.S. Ed. ....to which is prefixed the life and character of the author, by James Finlayson, D.D. New York: John S. Taylor and company, 1844. 622 p. CBB; ICU; NBuG; OCX; ScNC. 44-816

Blake, John Lauris, 1788-1857. The beauties of American history. By the author of Evenings in Boston, etc. New York: A.V. Blake, 1844. 9-252 p. Ct; DLC; MHad; MnHi; MWA. 44-817

Blake, John Lauris, 1788-1857. Conversations on natural philosophy, in which the elements of that science are familiarly explained and adapted to the comprehension of young pupils, [illustrated].... also by illustrative notes, and a dictionary of philosophical terms, by Rev. J.L. Blake, D.D. ....Boston: Gould, Kindall and Lincoln, 1844. 276 p. IaDaM; IGK. 44-818

Blake, John Lauris, 1788-1857. A general biographical dictionary, comprising a summary account of the most distinguished persons of all ages, nations and professions. Including more than one thousand articles of American biography....By the Rev. J.L. Blake, D.D. ....Sixth edition, revised. New York: Alexander V. Blake, 1844. 1096 p. CtY; IaGG; MoSM; OCl. 44-819

Blake, John Lauris, 1788-1857. The young orator; and the New York class book; ....Twelfth edition. New York: 1844. MH. 44-820

Blake, Mortimer. Gethsemane and calvary; or a harmony of the last hours [of the Saviour in the flesh] Boston: 1844. 245 p. MBC; NBLiHi; NN. 44-821

Blake, Mortimer. Proper reflection upon the power of God to prevent afflictions: sermon on the death of Harvey Carey. Boston: 1844. 16 p. MBC. 44-822

Blatch, William. Two lectures on the historical confirmation of the Scriptures; with special references to Jewish and ancient heathen testimony. New York: G. Lane and P.P. Sandford, 1844. 144 p. CtY-D; DLC; IEG; MnSH. 44-823

Blatchford, Thomas Windeatt, 1794-1866. Observations on equivocal generation: prepared as evidence in a suit for slander. ....Albany [New York] J. Munsell, printer, 1844. 14 p. CSmH; MB; MWA; NjR; NNN. 44-824

Blauvelt, Jacob I. A statement of the trials of Rev. Isaac D. Code, before the classis of Paramus in 1838 and 1840, for charges preferred against him by Jacob I. Blauvelt.... New York: J.A. Traetas, printer, 1844. 34 p. NIC-L; NjR. 44-825

Blessington, Marguerite Power Farmer Gardiner, 1789-1849. Etiquette of courtship and marriage. New York: Burgess and Stringer, 1844. 57 p. NIC. 44-826

Blind Celestine of Paturages. Translated from the French; revised by the committee of publication. From the London edition. Boston: Sabbath School Society, 1844. 108 p. IaAt; ViU. 44-827

Bliss Lansingburgh almanac for 1845. Lansingburgh, New York: Luther Bliss, [1844] MWA. 44-828

Bliss, Leonard. A practical grammar of the English language: introductory lessons. Louisville, Kentucky: Morton and Griswold, 1844. 72 p. KEmC. 44-829

Bloomfield, Joseph E. Tarriff and railroad iron. Remarks made.... at a conversational meeting of the American Institute.... New York: W.B. and T. Smith, 1844. 8 p. CSmH. 44-830

Blunt, Edmund, 1799-1866. Chart of the Bahama banks and Gulf of Florida. New York: 1844. PPL; PPULC. 44-831

Blunt, Edmund, 1799-1866. The northeastern coast of North America, from New York to Cape Canso, including Sable Island. New York: 1844. PPL; PPULC. 44-832

Blunt, Henry, 1794-1843. Posthumous sermons. By the Rev. Henry Blunt, A.M., late rector of Streatham; and formerly of Pembroke College, Cambridge. First American edition. Philadelphia: Herman Hooker, 1844. 190 p. CtY; MdBD; NcD; ViRu; TChU. 44-833

Blydenburch, Jeremiah W. A treatise on the law of usury; to which are added the statutes of the several states relating to interest now in force: together with a digest of all the decisions, ...New York: John S. Voorhies, 1844. 322 p. CU; DLC; InCW; OrSC; TU. 44-834

Boardman, George S. An address, delivered in Waterville, before the Oneida County Temperance Society, at their annual meeting, February 22, 1844... Rome: Horace N. Bill, printer, 1844. 18 p. CSmH; DSG; In. 44-835

Boardman, Henry Augustus, 1808-1880. The apostolical succession... being a statement of the doctrine, with reasons for discussing it. Philadelphia: William S. Martien, 1844. 23 p. ICP; MB; MH-AH; NjPT; PHi. 44-836

Boardman, Henry Augustus, 1808-1880. The claims of religion upon medical men. A discourse delivered in the Tenth Presbyterian Church, Philadelphia, on November 24, 1844. Philadelphia: Book and Job Printing office, 1844. 24 p. CSt-L; InID; MWA; NNNAM; PAtM. 44-837

Boardman, Henry Augustus, 1808-1880. The claims of religion upon medical men. A discourse delivered in the Tenth Presbyterian Church, Philadelphia, on November 24, 1844. Second edition. Philadelphia: Book and Job Printing office, 1844. 24 p. MWA; NjPT; NNUT; PLT; PPPrHi. 44-838

Boardman, Henry Augustus, 1808-1880. The claims of religion upon medical men. A discourse delivered in the Tenth Presbyterian Church, Philadelphia, on November 24, 1844. Third edition. Philadelphia: Book and Job Printing office, 1844. 24 p. CtMW; MiU; MoSMed; PPL-R. 44-839

Boardman, Henry Augustus, 1808-1880. The intolerance of the church of Rome ....Philadelphia: Presbyterian Board of Publication, 1844. 96 p. GDecCT; MWiW; NjPT; NNUT; TMeSc. 44-840

Boardman, Henry Augustus, 1808-1880. The prelatical doctrine of the apostolical succession examined with a delineation of the high church system. Philadelphia: Martien, 1844. 348 p. ArBaA; GDecCT; OO; TxShA; ViRut. 44-841

Boardman, John Humphrey. Treatise on the scripture doctrine of original sin; with explanatory notes. By H.A. Boardman. Third edition. Philadelphia: Presbyterian Board of Publication, 1844. 25 p. GDecCT; NcMHi; NNUT; PPLT; PPPrHi. 44-842

Bodnar, A. A collection of colloquial phrases on every topic necessary to maintain conversation; arranged under different heads. A new edition, revised and corrected. Philadephia: Lea, 1844. 208 p. MB; MWA; NN; WKenHi. 44-843

Bokum, Hermann, 1807-1878. The fool of the Bible: a sermon preached in the Presbyterian Church of Lancaster, June 16, 1844. Lancaster, Pennsylvania: 1844. DLC; PPPrHi; PPULC. 44-844

Bolles, Isaac Newton, b. 1812. Directory, and guide book, for the city of Hartford. 1844. With a map of the city and a great variety of useful matter. Compiled and published by Isaac N. Bolles. [Hartford, Connecticut] Isaac N. Bolles, 1844. 136 p. CSmH; DLC; NN. 44-845

Bolles, Isaac Newton, b. 1812. The Whig

glee book, containing a variety of new songs, original and selected; suitable to sing at Whig meetings and conventions, also adapted for Clay clubs. Hartford: [I. N. Bolles] 1844. 37 p. WHi. 44-846

Bolles, James Aaron, 1810-1894. A discourse preached in St. James Church, Batavia, New York November 10, 1844. Batvia, New York: Lucas Seaver, 1844. 16 p. MWA; NGH; NNG. 44-847

Bolles, James Aaron, 1810-1894. The general convention of the Protestant Episcopal Church. A discourse preached in St. James' Church, Batavia, N.Y. Batavia: I. Seaver, 1844. 16 p. NNG. 44-848

Bolles, William. The complete evangelist, comprising the history of the life, actions, death, resurrection, ascension, and doctrine of Jesus Christ.... Edited by William Bolles. New London: Bolles and Williams, 1844. 226 p. CtSoP; MBC; MWA; OO; TJaU. 44-849

Bolmar, Antoine. A book of the French verbs... Containing also numerous notes and directions on the different conjugations... to which is added a complete list of all the irregular verbs. A new edition. Philadelphia: Lea and Blanchard, 1844. 173 p. RPB. 44-850

Bolmar, Antoine. A collection of colloquial phrases, on every topic necessary to maintain conversation; arranged under different heads; with numerous remarks on the peculiar pronounciation and use of various words. A new edition revised and enlarged. Philadelphia: Lea and Blanchard, 1844. 8-208 p. MH; NN; ViU. 44-851

Bolmar, Antoine. A theoretical and practical grammar of the French language... Eleventh edition. Philadelphia: Carey and Hart, 1844. 294, 173 p. CoU; MeB; MeHi; NNF; OUrC. 44-852

Bolton, William. A narrative of the last cruise of the United States steam frigate Missouri.... New York: H. Ludwig, printer, 1844. 31 p. CSmH; MdHi; MoS; PHi; PPL. 44-853

Bolton, William. A narrative of the last cruise of the United States steam frigate Missouri.... Philadelphia: 1844. 32 p. MnHi. 44-854

Bolton, William Jay, 1816?-1884. The harp of Pelham. New York: Windt's printery, 1844. CSmH; ICU; MH; NN; RPB. 44-855

Bommer, George. Bommer method for the manufacture of a superior quality of manure both from vegetable and mineral substances with strict economy and dispatch. Revised and improved. New York: Orange Judd company, [1844?] 90 p. M; NN. 44-856

Bond, Alvan. A discourse delivered to the Second Congregational Society in Norwich, October 13, 1844.... By Alvan Bond.... Norwich: J. Dunham's Press, 1844. 18 p. MeBat. 44-857

Bond, Alvan. The life and death of the believer, a discourse delivered to the Second Congregational Society in Norwich, October 13, 1844. The Sabbath subsequent to the interment of Mrs. Zehetable A. Bond. Norwich: J. Dunham's press, 1844. 18 p. MBC; OClWHi. 44-858

Bonnechose, Francois Paul Emile [Boisnormand] de. ....The reformers before the reformation. The fifteenth century. John Huss on the Council of Constance. By Emile de Bonnechose, librarian to the King of France. New York: Harper and brothers, 1844. 173 p. DLC; KyLoS; MWA; PLFM; WNaE. 44-859

Bonnell, W. Wilson. A history of the German Reformed Church, Chambersburg, Pennsylvania, with an appendix also a sermon on the covenant and its blessings. Chambersburg, Pennsylvania: Printed at the publication office of the German Reformed Church, 1844. 57 p. PLERC-Hi; PLT; PPPrHi. 44-860

Bonnett, Louis, 1805-1892. The family of Bethany; or meditations on the eleventh chapter of the Gospels according to St. John by L. Bannet. Fourth American from the eighth London edition. New York: Robert Carter; Pittsburg: Thomas Carter, 1844. 256 p. NAnge. 44-861

Bonnycastle, John, 1750?-1821. Bonnycastle's introduction to algebra; containing the indeterminate and diophantine analysis, and the application of algebra to geometry. Revised and corrected and enlarged by James Ryan.... To which is added a large collection of problems for exercise, original and selected, by John F. Jenkins.... New York: W.E. Dean, 1844. MeU; MiD-B; MnSS; TNP; ViU. 44-862

Bonnycastle, John, 1750?-1821. Introduction to mensuration and practical geometry.... To which are added, a treatise on guaging; and also the most important problems in mechanics. By

James Ryan... Philadelphia: Kimber and Sharpless, 1844. CtY; LNH; PHi; WStfSF. 44-863

The book of discipline; or heads and conclusions of the policy of the kirk. Pittsburgh: J. M'Millin, 1844. 37 p. GDec-Ct. 44-864

The book of pleasures' containing the pleasures of hope, by Thomas Campbell; the pleasures of memory by Samuel Rogers; and the pleasures of imagination by Mark Akenside. New York: Clark and Austin, 1844. 187 p. MdBS; NN; PBm; PPULC. 44-865

The book of poetry. Prepared for the Presbyterian Board of Publication. Philadelphia: P.T. Jones, publishing agent, 1844. 264 p. IaWel; MWiW; PHi; TxU; ViRut. 44-866

Book of wonders! or marvelous chronicle! Authentic account of extraordinary events and occurrences in nature and art; collected from the writings of historians, travellers, etc. Boston: 1844. 48 p. ICJ; MB; MBAt; MiU; NNC. 44-867

Borden, Simeon, 1798-1856. Account of a trigonometrical survey of Massachusetts, with a comparison of its results with those obtained from astronomical observations. Philadelphia: 1844. 59 p. DN-Ob. 44-868

Borden, Simeon, 1798-1856. Topographical map of Massachusetts. [With special geological map by Edward Hitchcock] Boston: 1844. 6 p. PHi. 44-869

Borne, Ludwig. Menzel, der Franzosenfresser. Bon Ludwig Borne. New York: M.M. Radde, 1844. [5]-132 p. LNH. 44-870

Borrow, George Henry, 1803-1881. The Zincali; or an account of the gypsies of Spain. With an original collection of their songs and poetry. Sixth edition. Philadelphia: James M. Campbell; New York: Saxton and Miles, 1844. 148 p. MDanV; NICLA; PPM. 44-871

Boston, Thomas. The crook in the lot... New York: Robert Carter, 1844. 176 p. RP; VtWinds. 44-872

Boston, Massachusetts. Church of the Disciples. Service book for the use of the Church of the Disciples. Boston: Benjamin Greene, 1844. 183 p. ICMe; MB; NNUT; PPL; RPB. 44-873

Boston, Massachusetts. Church of the Disciples. The Disciples hymn book: a collection of hymns and chants for public and private devotion. Prepared for the use of the Church of the disciples. Boston: Green, 1844. ICMe; MB; RPB. 44-874

Boston, Massachusetts. Federal Street Church. Report of the committee for erecting a monument to Rev. Dr. Channing. Boston: 1844. 10 p. MHi; MW. 44-875

Boston, Massachusetts. Maverick Church. Articles of faith and covenant of the Maverick Church, East Boston, with a list of the members. Boston: press of T.R. Marvin, 1844. 24 p. MHi; WHi. 44-876

Boston, Massachusetts. Mercantile Library Association. Catalogue of books

of the.... together with a history of the institution, constitution, by-laws, etc. Boston: printed for the association by Freeman and Bolles, 1844. 100 p. MB; MH; MHi; PPULC; WHi. 44-877

Boston, Massachusetts. Mount Vernon Congregational Church. The confession of faith and covenant of the Mount Vernon Congregational Church in Boston, Massachusetts, organized June 1, 1842. Boston: press of T.R. Marvin, 1844. 28 p. MHi; MWA; NjR. 44-878

Boston, Massachusetts. Reply to the "Remarks of thirty-one Boston schoolmasters on the seventh annual report of the secretary of the Massachusetts board of education." By Horace Mann, Secretary of the Board [Boston: 1844] 176 p. WHi. 44-879

Boston, Massachusetts. Report of the commissioners appointed under the order of the city council, August 26, 1844, on bringing water of Long Pond into the city. Boston: J.H. Eastburn: city printer, 1844. 30 p. CtY; DLC; NN; PPULC. 44-880

Boston, Massachusetts. Report of the commissioners appointed under the order of the city council, August 26, 1844. To report the best mode and expense of bringing the water of Long Pond into the city of Boston: Boston: John H. Eastburn, city printer, 1844. 32 p. CtY; LNH; MBB; N; NRom. 44-881

Boston, Massachusetts. Report of the special committee of the primary school board, on a portion of the remarks of the grammar masters. Boston: John H. Eastburn, printer, 1844. 13, 15 p. CtHWatk; ICU; MB; MBAt. 44-882

Boston, Massachusetts. Rules and regulations of the Boston school committee for 1844. Boston: John H. Eastburn, 1844. 24 p. MnHi. 44-883

Boston, Massachusetts. Rules and regulations of the House of Correction, for the government of the officers and convicts of the establishment. Boston: 1844. 16 p. MB; MHi; PPL-R; PPULC; WHi. 44-884

Boston, Massachusetts. St. Stephen's chapel. Rep. Boston: 1844-74. MB. 44-885

Boston Academy of Music. The academy's collection of choruses: being a selection from the works of the most eminent composers... Boston: J.H. Wilkins and R.B. Carter, and G.W. Palmer and company, 1844. 263 p. MBAt; MBC; NNUT. 44-886

Boston Academy of Music. The Boston Academy's collection of church music, consisting of the most popular psalms and hymns, tunes, anthems... old and new... Works of Hayden, Mozart, Beethoven... also original compositions by German, English and American authors. Eighth edition. Boston: J.H. Wilkins and R.B. Carter, 1844. 357 p. CtHWatk; IaDaM; IEN; MH-AH; MiHi. 44-887

Boston Academy of Music. The Boston Academy's collection of church music, consisting of the most popular psalms and hymns, tunes, anthems, sentences, chants... Ninth edition. Cincinnati: Jewett and Mason, 1844. 357 p. MB; NjR; WKenHi. 44-888

The Boston almanac for the year 1844.

By S.N. Dickinson. Boston: Thomas Groom and company, [1844] MAnHi; MB; MeB; MPeHi; RNHi. 44-889

Boston and Fitchburg Railway Company. Letter [in behalf of the Boston and Fitchburg Railway Company] to... G. Evans upon the subject of the remission, in certain cases of the duty upon railway iron [Washington? 1844] 12 p. DLC. 44-890

Boston and Maine Railroad Extension Company. Statement of principal facts and points relied upon by the remonstrants, at the hearing before the committee. Boston: 1844. MBAt; MH-BA. 44-891

Boston Athenaeum. Catalogue of the eighteenth exhibition of paintings, and of the sixth exhibition of sculpture in the athenaeum gallery. Boston: Clapp and Son;'s Press, [1844] 16 p. MWA. 44-892

Boston Athenaeum. Circular to the public soliciting subscriptions to a proposed issue of 237 new shares, [Boston: 1844] MBAt. 44-893

Boston Clay Club. Constitution adopted November 27, 1843. Boston: 1844. MBAt. 44-894

Boston Gas Light Company. Report of a committee of the consumers of gas, of the city of Boston, February, 1844. Boston: John H. Eastburn, printer, 1844. 15 p. M; MBAt; MH-BA; NNG. 44-895

Boston Library Society. A catalogue of the books of the Boston Library Society, in Franklin Place. January, 1844. Boston: Press of T.R. Marvin, 1844. 334 p. MLow; MH; MnHi; MoS; MSbo. 44-896

Boston Museum. [Programmes, 1856-7, 1863-94. Boston: 1844-1903] 4 v. MBAt. 44-897

Boston Philharmonic Society. Programmes of concerts. December 21, 1844-April 11, 1863. Boston: 1844-1863. MB. 44-898

Boston register and business directory. Boston: Dickinson, 1844. MS. 44-899

Boston School of Practical Rhetoric and Oratory. Prospectus of the school of practical rhetoric and oratory. Boston: 1844. 24 p. MBC; MH; MHi; NN. 44-900

Boston Society for the Care of Girls. Reminiscences of the Boston Female Asylum. Boston: Eastburn's Press, 1844. 88 p. CtSoP; ICMe; MH; MiU; NbU. 44-901

Boston Society of Natural History. Proceedings of the Boston Society of Natural History, 1841 to 1844. Boston: Printed for the society by Dutton and Wentworth, 1844-. v. 1-. CoD; LU; MeB; OrP; PP. 44-902

Boston Society of Natural History. Proceedings of the Boston Society of Natural History. Boston: the society, 1844-1942. 42 v. CSt; ICJ; MiU; OO; TxU. 44-903

Boston Young Men's Total Abstinence Society. Constitution of the Boston Young Men's Total Abstinence Society. Adopted December 11, 1843. Boston: J.B. Chisholm, 1844. 12 p. MB; MBC. 44-904

Boston Young Men's Whig Club. Constitution... Adopted December 12, 1843,

with a list of officers and members. Boston: White, Lewis and Potter, printers, 1844. 30 p. DLC; MB; MBAt; WHi. 44-905

Boswell, James, 1740-1795. The life of Samuel Johnson, LL.D., including a journal of a tour to the Hebrides. A new edition, with numerous additions and notes by John Wilson Crocker, LL.D., F.R.S. New York: Alexander V. Blake, 1844. 2 v. BMilvC; KyDC; OHi. 44-906

Bosworth, J.S. The forty million debt. Albany: 1844. 11 p. M. 44-907

Botanical Society of Wilmington, Delaware. Catalogue of the phaenogamous and filicord plants of New Castle County. Wilminton, Delaware: 1844. 12 p. DeWi; DNAL; PPULC. 44-908

Both sides heard, or an independent Presbyterian, and a member of Bethel Presbytery. Columbia, South Carolina: Morgan's Letter Press, 1844. ScCliJ. 44-909

Bouchereau, Alcee. Statement of the sugar crop made in Louisiana.... with an appendix. New Orleans: 1844-1846. CSt; IU; NjP; TxU. 44-910

Boucicault, Dion, 1820?-1890. Old heads and young hearts; a comedy in five acts. New York: Samuel French, 1844. 73 p. C; OCl. 44-911

Boughton, Joseph. Edward Morley; or, the reward of perseverance.... New York: [1844] 72 p. CtY. 44-912

The bouquet, containing the language of flowers, and their poetic sentiments.

By a lady. Boston: Oliver L. Perkins, 1844. 128 p. MB; MBAt; MH; MPeHi; PU. 44-913

Bourne, Hugh, 1772-1852. A collection of hymns for camp meeting, revivals, etc., for the use of the primitive Methodists. New York: Am. Presb. Methodists, 1844. AmSSchU. 44-914

Bowditch, Nathaniel, 1773-1838. A new American practical navigator: being an epitome of navigation; ...Fourteenth new stereotype edition. New York: E. and G.W. Blunt, 1844. 449 p. MH; MSaP; NNS; TxU. 44-915

Bowditch, Nathaniel, 1773-1838. Useful tables. Edited by J.I. Bowditch. New York: Blunt, 1844. CtHWatk; MB; MBAt; MCM; MWA. 44-916

Bowdoin College. Brunswich, Maine. Catalogue of the Athenaean Society of Bowdoin College. Instituted 1817. Brunswick: Press of John Griffin, 1844. 39 p. MeB; MeHi. 44-917

Bowdoin College. Brunswick, Maine. Laws of Bowdoin College in the state of Maine. Brunswick: press of J. Griffin, 1844. 30 p. CBPSR; MeB; MeBa; MeHi; OO. 44-918

Bowen, Francis, 1811-1890. Lives of Baron Steuben, and Sebastian Cabot, by Francis Bowen and Cornelius C. Feltn. Conducted by Jared Sparks. New York: Harper and brothers, 1844. 358 p. MVh. 44-919

Bowen, Francis, 1811-1890. The recent contest in Rhode Island: an article from the North American Review for April, 1844. Boston: Otis, Broaders and company, 1844. 69 p. Ct; KyBC; MH; Nh-Hi; RPB. 44-920

Bowen, Henry F. A brief inquiry into the peculiarity of the apostolic office, in which the true doctrine is stated and supported by express declarations of Scripture, and the fallacy of Bishop H.U. Onderdonk's argument on this point. Philadelphia: William S. Martien, 1844. 3-30 p. MBAt; NcMHi; NjPT; PPPrHi. 44-921

Bower, Archibald, 1686-1766. History of the popes, from the foundation of the See of Rome to A.D. 1758. By Archibald Bower.... with an introduction and a continuation to the present time by Rev. Samuel Hanson Cox.... Philadelphia: Griffith and Simon, 1844-45. 3 v. CtY; IaDmU; MoSU; ODaU; WMMU. 44-922

Bowlin, James Butler, 1804-1874. Speech of Mr. Bowlin, of Missouri on the bill making appropriations for certain rivers and harbors in the House of Representatives, April 5, 1844. [Washington: 1844] 7 p. WHi. 44-923

Bowlin, James Butler, 1804-1874. Speech of Mr. Bowlin, of Missouri on the removal of obstructions in the Mississippi River and its tributaries. Delivered in the House of Representatives, January 16, 1844. 15 p. InU; MoHi. 44-924

Bowring, John. Matins and vespers with hymns and occasional devotional pieces. Boston: 228 p. MB; NjP; PPL; ODaB; ViRut. 44-925

Boyd, James Robert, 1804-1890. Elements of rhetoric and literary criticism, with copious practical exercises and examples. For the use of common schools and academies. .... on the basis of the recent works of Alexander Reid and Robert Connel; with large additions from other sources. Compiled and arranged by J.R. Boyd.... New York: Harper and brothers, 1844. 306 p. DLC; LN; MdBS; MH; NN. 44-926

Boyd, James Robert, 1804-1890. Elements of rhetoric and literary criticism for the use of common schools and academies. Compiled and arranged by J.R. Boyd.... Sixth edition. New York: Harper and brothers, 1844. 333 p. COT; MeBa; MoWgW. 44-927

Boyd, James Robert, 1804-1890. Elements of rhetoric and literary criticism, with copious practical exercises and examples, for the use of common schools and academies, compiled and arranged by Rev. James Robert Boyd.... Eighth edition. New York: Harper and brothers, [1844] 333 p. CStclU; KyLoN; NStc; PHC. 44-928

Boyd, Linn, 1800-1859. Condensed speech... in reply to the Hon. John White, relative to the coalition between Adams and Clay in 1825. House of Representatives, April 30, 1844. Washington City: J. Heart, printer, [1844] CSmH; MH. 44-929

Boyd, Linn, 1800-1859. Speech in reply to the Hon. John White, relative to the charge of bargain between Messrs. Adams and Clay, in the presidential election of 1824-1825. Washington: 1844. 23 p. CSmH; DLC; WHi. 44-930

Boyd, William P. History of the Boyd family and descendants... First edition. Conesus, New York: 1844. NoLoc. 44-931

Boyden, John. Review of Rev. M. Hills serman on American Universalism. Providence: Printed by B.F. Moore, 1844. MMeT. 44-932

Boyer, Abel, 1667-1729. Boyer's French dictionary; comprising all the improvements of the latest Paris and London editions.... with a table of French verbs.... Boston: Benjamin B. Mussey, 1844. 250 p. ArAO; KyLx; RPB. 44-933

The boy's own printer. By a friend to youth. Cincinnati: W.T. Truman, 1844. MH. 44-934

Boyton, Charles. The rule of faith. A letter to the Rev. George Scott.... in which certain of his statements respecting the prevailing controversy in the church are considered.... Baltimore: J. Robinson, 1844. 84 p. MBD; MdBD; NNG; TSewU; WNaE. 44-935

Brackenridge, Henry Marie, 1786-1871. History of the late war between the United States and Great Britain: comprising a minute account of the various military and naval operations. Philadelphia: J. Kay, junior, and brother; Pittsburgh: C.H. Kay and company, 1844. CSf; DLC; MoS; NPec; OCY. 44-936

Brackett, Edward Augustus, 1818-1908. Works. Boston: W.D. Ticknor and company, 1844. DLC; MB; MH; MWA. 44-937

Bradbury, Osgood. Louise Kempton: or vice and virtue contrasted. Boston: F. Gleason, 1844. [3]-66 p. MWA. 44-938

Bradbury, Osgood. Metallak: the lone Indian of the Magalloway. Boston: F. Gleason, 1844. 31 p. ICN; MB; NjP; NNC. 44-939

Bradbury, Osgood. The mysteries of Boston; or the woman's temptation. By a member of the Suffolk bar...Boston: J.N. Bradley and company, 1844. 40 p. MHi; MWA. 44-940

Bradbury, Osgood. Mysteries of Lowell... Boston: Edward P. Williams, 1844. 40 p. MWA; RPB. 44-941

Bradbury, Osgood. The mysterious mother; or theory of second love... Boston: F. Gleason, 1844. DLC. 44-942

*Bradbury, William Batchelder, 1816-1868. Bradbury's singing school, for ladies and gentlemen... New York: M.H. Newman, 1844. 64 p. DLC; ICN; MBuG; NNUT; RPB. 44-943

Bradbury, William Batchelder, 1816-1868. School singer, or young choir's companion. Fifth edition. New York: 1844. CtHWatk. 44-944

Bradbury, William Batchelder, 1816-1868. The social singing book; a collection of glees, or part songs, rounds, madrigals, etc., chiefly from European masters; with an introductory course of elementary exercises and solfeggios, designed for singing classes and schools of ladies and gentlemen. By William B. Bradbury. New York: Mark H. Newman, 1844. 88 p. NFri. 44-945

Bradford, Ephraim P. A sermon, preached at Dunbarton, New Hampshire, December 27, 1843.... by Ephraim P. Bradford. Concord: press of Asa McFarland, 1844. 16 p. CSmH; ICU; Mh-AH; Nh; RPB. 44-946

Bradford Junior College. Bradford, Massachusetts. Catalogue of the officers and members of Bradford Academy, Bradford, Massachusetts, for the year ending July 16, 1844. Boston: press of T.R. Marvin, 1844. 12 p. MHa. 44-947

Bradish, Luther. Opening address of the seventeenth annual fair of the American Institute of the City of New York, by the Honorable Luther Bradish. New York: Robert Craighead, 1844. 11 p. NSyHi. 44-948

Bradley, Charles, 1789-1871. Family and parish sermons, preached at Clapham and Glesbery; together with practical sermons for every Sunday and principal holy day in the year. English edition. New York: D. Appleton and company, 1844. 4 v. CU; NjPT; OCo; OrPD; ScCliJ. 44-949

Bradley, Charles, 1789-1871. Family and parish sermons preached, at Clapham and Glasbury; together with practical sermons for every Sunday and principal holy day in the year... Four volumes of the English edition in one. New York, Philadelphia: D. Appleton, 1844. 2 v. in 1. CtY; CU; NjPT; OrPD; OCo. 44-950

Bradley, Charles, 1789-1871. Practical sermons for every Sunday and principal holiday in the year. By the Rev. Charles Bradley.... First American, from the last London edition. New York: D. Appleton and company; Philadelphia: G.S. Appleton, 1844. 288 p. KyLo; MCET; OU; PPM; ScC. 44-951

Bradley, Charles, 1789-1871. Sermons, preached at Glasbury, Brecknockshire, and in St. James's Chapel, Clapham, Surrey. By the Rev. Charles Bradley, vicar of Glasbury, and minister of St. James's Chapel, Clapham, Surrey. First American from the seventh London edition. New York: D. Appleton and company; Philadelphia: George S. Appleton, 1844. 288 p. CoU; CtY-D; MBC; NB; PPL. 44-952

Brande, William Thomas, 1788-1866. Dictionary of science, literature and art: comprising the history, description and scientific principles of every branch of human knowledge.... New York: Harper and brothers, 1844. 1352 p. GEU-M; IaDuC; IEN-M; P; TCh. 44-953

Breckinridge, Robert Jefferson, 1800-1871. The Christian pastor, one of the ascension gifts of Christ. A discourse, to vindicate the divine calling of the pastors of the Christian Church, to illustrate the divinely appointed evidence thereof... Baltimore: D. Owen and son, 1844. 49 p. KyDC; OClWHi. 44-954

Breckenridge, Robert Jefferson, 1800-1871. Review on the rights of ruling elders. From the Princeton review. Princeton, New Jersey: Printed by John T. Robinson, 1844. 32 p. NjP; NjPT; NjR. 44-955

Breeden, Henry. An address to those who read, or a call to holiness and usefulness.... With corrections, and....a discourse on perfect love, by J. Miles. Albany: 1844. 60 p. MB; NAl. 44-956

Breese, Sidney. Speech of Mr. Breese, of Illinois, on the Oregon Territory, delivered in the United States Senate, February 27, 1844. Washington: Globe office, 1844. 23 p. CU-B; MBC; WHi. 44-957

Bremer, Fredrika, 1801-1865. The bondmaid. Translated from the Swedish by M.L. Putnam. Boston: James Munroe and company, 1844. [9]-112 p. CtY; MB; MdBE; MH; RPAt. 44-958

Bremer, Fredrika, 1801-1865. The comforter. Translated from the original by a Swede. Boston: Redding and company, 1844. 16 p. MBAt; MBC; MH; MWA; PPM. 44-959

Bremer, Fredrika, 1801-1865. A diary; with strife and peace; translated by Mary Howitt. New York: 1844. MBAt. 44-960

Bremer, Fredrika, 1801-1865. The H--family: Tralinnan; Alex and Anna; and other tales. By Fredrika Bremer. Translated by Mary Howitt. New York: Harper and brothers, 1844. 136 p. CtMW; MBBC; MeBaT; MH; NNF. 44-961

Bremer, Fredrika, 1801-1865. The H--family; ....and other tales by Fredrika Bremer. New York: Harper and brothers, [1844] 257 p. MWinchr. 44-962

Bremer, Fredrika, 1801-1865. The handmaid. By Fredrika Bremer, translated from the Swedish by M.L. Putnam. Boston: J. Munroe and company, 1844. 112 p. TxU. 44-963

Bremer, Fredrika, 1801-1865. The home: or, family cares and family joys.... Translated from the Swedish by Mary Howitt. New York: Harper and brothers, 1844. 134 p. KyLx; MDeeP; NjR; PU; VtU. 44-964

Bremer, Fredrika, 1801-1865. The midnight sun; a pilgrimage. Translated from the unpublished original by Mary Howitt. New York: Harper and brothers, 1844. NCats. 44-965

Bremer, Fredrika, 1801-1865. The neighbours. A story of every day life. By Fredrika Bermer. Translated from the Swedish by Mary Howitt. New York: Harper and brothers, 1844. 2 v. CtY; LNH; MB; NbOM; PU. 44-966

Bremer, Fredrika, 1801-1865. New sketches of every day life: a diary. Together with strife and peace. By Fredrika Bremer. Translated by Mary Howitt. New York: Harper and brothers, 1844. 134 p. CtY; LNH; MeBaT; NbOM; TxU. 44-967

Brent, John Carroll. Letters on the National Institute, Smithsonian legacy, the fine arts, and other matters... Washington: J. and G.S. Gideon, 1844. 90 p. CSmH; IaU; MBAt; MWA; RPB. 44-968

Brewster, David, 1781-1868. The martyrs of science; or the lives of Galileo, Tycho Brahe, and Kepler...New York: Harper and brothers, 1844. 240 p. MeAu; NCaS; NOg; OCY; OSW. 44-969

Brewster, David, 1781-1868. A treatise on optics. A new edition, with an appendix, containing an elementary view of the application of analysis to reflexion and refraction. Philadelphia: Lea and Blanchard, 1844. 323, 95 p. MdBS; OClW; PPCP; ViU. 44-970

The bridegroom cometh. Philadelphia: 1844. PPL; PPUL 44-971

Bridgeman, Thomas, d. 1850. The florist's guide. A new and improved edition.... Boston: J. Breck and company, 1844. 175 p. CtY; MB; NjR; OHi; RPB. 44-972

Bridgeman, Thomas, d. 1850. The fruit cultivators manual; containing ample directions for the cultivation of the most important fruits, ...New York: 1844. 175 p. MH; NNNBG; WaPS. 44-973

Bridgeman, Thomas, d. 1850. The kitchen gardener's instructor, containing a catalogue of garden and herb seeds. A new and improved edition. New York: the author, etc., etc., 1844. 175 p. IU. 44-974

Bridgeman, Thomas, d. 1850. The young gardener's assistant by Thomas Bridgeman. Tenth edition. New York: George Thornburn and Alexander Smith, 1844. MdB; MoS; NPV; PPL-R. 44-975

Bridgewater, Massachusetts. Catalogue of the normal school at Bridgewater, Massachusetts, 1840-1844. Boston: Samuel N. Dickinson, printer, 1844. 30 p. MWo. 44-976

Brief remarks on the organization and action of the Board of Missions of the Protestant Episcopal Church in the United States, by a member of the society... New York: Burgess, Stringer and company, 1844. 15 p. MB; MH; NNG. 44-977

A brief review of the present position of the Republican party. [n.p.: 1844?] 8 p. NcU. 44-978

Brief review of the question whether

the Baltimore and Ohio Railroad will supersede the necessity of extending the canal beyond Dam no. 6. [n.p.: 1844] 17 p. PHi; PPULC. 44-979

A brief sketch of the character and services of captain Josiah Sturgis, of the United States revenue service. By an old friend and schoolmate. Boston: William White and H.P. Lewis, 1844. 34 p. DLC; ICN; MB; MH; MHi. 44-980

Brief view of the origin and object of the native American party, by a native American. Philadelphia: 1844. 16 p. DLC; InHi; MoS; PHi; PPL. 44-981

Briggs, Charles Frederick, 1804-1877. Bankrupt stories, edited by Harry Franco [pseud.] Second edition. New York: John Allen, 1844. 381 p. CtY. 44-982

Briggs, Charles Frederick, 1804-1877. Working a passage; or, life in a liner. [Published for the benefit of young travellers] By B. C.F. New York: John Allen, 1844. 108 p. MB; MH; MWA; NN. 44-983

Briggs, George Nixon. Address of his excellency George N. Briggs, to the two branches of the legislature of Massachusetts, January 10, 1844. Boston: Dutton and Wentworth, state printers, 1844. 19 p. MBC; MWn; Nh. 44-984

Bright, John W. The mother's guide; a plain practical treatise on midwifery, and the diseases of women and children. In seven parts. Louisville, Kentucky: John W. Bright, 1844. 792 p. KyLoJM. 44-985

Brisbane, Albert, 1809-1890. A concise exposition of the doctrine of association; or plan for a reorganization of society which will secure to the human race, individually and collectively, their happiness and elevation. Seventh edition. New York: J.S. Redfield, 1844. 79 p. MdBJ; MdBP; OC. 44-986

Brisbane, Albert, 1809-1890. A concise exposition of the doctrine of association; or plan for a reorganization of society which will secure to the human race, individually and collectively, their happiness and elevation. Eighth edition. New York: J.S. Redfield, 1844. 79 p. CSmH; CtY; WHi. 44-987

Bristed, Charles Astor, The principles of liberality, an oration, delivered in Trinity College Hall, December 15, 1843....Cambridge: 1844. 12 p. CtY. 44-988

Bristol's free almanac for 1845. Calculations by George R. Perkins. Buffalo, New York: Thomas Newell, [1844] MWA; NRMA; WHi. 44-989

Britton, James B. The source and design of the Christian ministry; a sermon preached.... on the occasion of the ordination of Rev. A.T. McMurphy to the priesthood, and of Alexander M'Cloud, M.D., to the diaconate; by Rev. James B. Britton.... Chillicothe: G.C. Allen, 1844. 17 p. NNG. 44-990

Broaddus, Andrew, 1770-1848. The Virginia selection of Psalms, hymns, and spiritual songs; from the most approved authors.... Selected and arranged by Andrew Broaddus. Richmond, Virginia: Smith, Drinker and Morris; Philadelphia: Thomas, Cowperthwait and company, 1844. 592 p. MidSM; PPL; ViU; Vt. 44-991

Brodhead, John Romeyn, 1814-1873. Address delivered before the New York Historical Society, at its fortieth anniversary, November 20, 1844 [on the recent investigation of the historical agent of the state in European archives] With an account of the subsequent proceedings at the dinner given in the evening... New York: Press of the New York Historical Society, 1844. 107 p. CtY; NjPT; PHi; RPAt; WHi. 44-992

Bronson, Asahel. A plain exhibition of Methodist Episcopacy. In fourteen numbers, by Asahel Bronson, minister of the gospel. Burlington, Vermont: Chauncy and Goodrich, 1844. 259 p. IEG; MWA; NjPT; ODaB; VtU. 44-993

Brook Farm Association for Industry and Education. West Roxbury, Massachusetts. Constitution of the Brook Farm Association for Industry and Education, West Roxbury, Massachusetts, with an introductory statement. Second edition with the by-laws of the association. Boston: I.R. Butts, 1844. 20 p. IHi; MBAt; MHi; NBuU; OClWHi. 44-994

Brooke, John Thompson. What is true peace? A sermon: By J.T. Brooke.... Cincinnati: Kendall and Barnard, 1844. 18 p. CtHT; ICP; MdBD; NNG; OClWHi. 44-995

Brookes, Richard. A new universal gazetteer, containing a description of the principal nation, ..., originally compiled by R. Brookes, M.A. Brought down to the present period by John Marshall. Philadelphia: Butler and Williams, 1844. 816 p. MBAt; MeBa; MiD-B; OClWHi; PPM. 44-996

Brooklyn and Jamaica Railroad Company. Remonstrance to the mayor, aldermen, etc., against tunneling Atlantic Lt. [Brooklyn]: 1844. NBLiHi. 44-997

Brooklyn Association for Improving the Condition of the Poor. Address to the citizens of Brooklyn, with the constitution, by-laws, visitors manual and list of officers of the association. Brooklyn: Stationers' Hall Works, 1844. MH. 44-998

Brooklyn, New York. Brooklyn alphabetical and street directory, and yearly advertiser, for 1843-1844. Compiled and published by Thomas Leslie, Henry R., and William J. Hearne. Brooklyn: Stationers' Hall Works, 1844. 256 p. NNA. 44-999

Brooklyn, New York. Brooklyn Daily Advertiser. Brooklyn: 1844-53. 19 v. NBLiHi. 44-1000

Brooklyn, New York. Brooklyn Institute of Arts and Sciences. Charter and bylaws. 144-45. Brooklyn: 184-45. 2 v. NBLiHi; NSmb. 44-1001

Brooklyn Collegiate Institute for Young Ladies. Catalogue of the officers, pupils and patrons of the Brooklyn Collegiate Institute, an English and classical boarding school. Limited to thirty-five pupils. For the year ending April, 1844. New York: H. and S. Raynor, 1844. 8 p. NoLoc. 44-1002

Brooks, Anson P. Temperance catechism. Rochester: Lady Washington Association, 1844. 12 p. MB. 44-1003

Brooks, Charles, 1795-1872. Introduction of natural history into seminaries. Boston: 1844. MB. 44-1004

Brooks, Charles, 1795-1872. On the introduction of natural history as a regular classic in our seminaries. An address, delivered before the American Institute of Instruction at Portland, Maine, August 31, 1844. Boston: W.D. Ticknor and company, 1844. 24 p. CtY; MBAU; MH. 44-1005

Brooks, Charles T. The way, the truth and the life. First series. No. 205. By Charles T. Brooks. Boston: James Munroe and company, 1844. 19 p. IEG; MeB; MH-AH; PPL; RHi. 44-1006

Brooks, Jonathan, 1767-1848. The paragon. Jonathan Brooks of New London, Connecticut, candidate for the presidency. New London: 1844. 34 p. Ct. 44-1007

Brougham and Vaux, Henry Peter Brougham, 1778-1868. Historical sketches of statesmen, who flourished, in the time of George III, to which are added remarks on the French revolution. Third series.... Philadelphia: Lea and Blanchard, 1844. 294 p. ArCH; KyLx; NhD; PPL-R; RNR. 44-1008

Brower, Frank M. Gwine 'long down. [Song with accompaniment for the pianoforte] Boston: Keith's music publishing house, 1844. 3 p. MB. 44-1009

Brower, Frank M. Old Joe. A plantation refrain. Composed.... by.... F.M. Brower [With accompaniment for the pianoforte] Boston: Keith, 1844 [2] p. MB. 44-1010

Brown, Aaron Venable, 1795-1859. Mr.

A.V. Brown, from the committee on the territories, made the following report... [Washington: Blair and Rives, printer, 1844] 24 p. CU; CU-B. 44-1011

Brown, Aaron Venable, 1795-1859. Speech on the right of the members elected by general ticket to their seats; in the House of Representatives, February 9, 1844. Washington: Printed by Blair and Rives, 1844. 13 p. M; MH. 44-1012

Brown, Aaron Venable, 1795-1859. Speech, against receiving, referring, or reporting on abolition petitions. House, January 10, 1844. MH; TxU. 44-1013

Brown, Charles of Pennsylvania. Polk and Clay on the Tariff. Reply of C.B. of Philadelphia to J.M. Clayton, exposing the misrepresentations of Mr. Clayton, etc. Philadelphia: [1844] MB; PPL. 44-1014

Brown, Charles of Pennsylvania. Reply of Charles Brown of Philadelphia to John M. Clayton of Delaware, exposing the misrepresentations of Mr. Clayton and the Whig party on the subject of the tariff, being the concluding portion of a speech of Mr. Brown, to a mass meeting of the Democrats of Delaware, held at Dover, August 6, 1844. [n.p.: 1844] 16 p. MH-BA. 44-1015

Brown, Francis H. Alethea waltz, composed and arranged for the pianoforte. Second edition. New York: Atwell, 1844. 2 p. WHi. 44-1016

Brown, Francis H. Cappadocia waltz...for pianoforte. New York: 1844. CtY. 44-1017

Brown, Francis H. Cottage galop for

pianoforte. New York: 1844. CtY. 44-1018

Brown, Francis H. L'Esmeralda. Galop for pianoforte. New York: 1844. CtY. 44-1019

Brown, Goold, 1791-1857. The institutes of English grammar.... A key to the oral exercises: to which are added four appendixes.... stereotype edition, revised by the author. New York: Samuel S. and William Wood, 1844. 312 p. MWHi; NjR; OSW; TNT; WaU. 44-1020

Brown, Henry, 1789-1849. The history of Illinois, from its first discovery and settlement to the present time. New York: J. Winchester, 1844. 492 p. ICU; MiD-B; NBuG; OCl; WHi. 44-1021

Brown, J. Newton, 1803-1868. encyclopedia of religious knowledge; or dictionary of the Bible... illustrative of the Holy Scriptures... to which is added a missionary gazetteer. Brattleboro, Vermont: Joseph Steen and Company, 1844. 1275 p. ArBaA; CtY-D; FHa; NbOP; PPM. 44-1022

Brown, J.S. Common schools. An address, delivered before the Bethany Academy, Friday evening, October 25, 1844. [Perry] Wyoming County, New York: Printed by P. Lawrence, 1844. 12 p. CSmH. 44-1023

Brown, James. Oration celebrating the declaration of Independence at the Wesleyan Church in the village of Fulton, Oswegolo, on the 4th of July, 1844. and published pursuant to a resolution of the audience. Syracuse: Tucker and Kenney, [1844?] 15 p. DHU; DLC. 44-1024

Brown, John, 1722-1787. A brief concordance to the Holy Scriptures of the Old and New Testaments: by which all, or most, of the principal texts of scripture may be easily found out... Revised and corrected. Hartford: S. Andrus and son, 1844. 136 p. OFH; NN. 44-1025

Brown, John, 1722-1787. A concordance of the Holy Scriptures of the Old and New Testaments, by the Rev. John Brown, of Haddington. Revised and corrected. New York: Saxton and Miles, 1844. 169 p. MdBD; MdBMC. 44-1026

Brown, John, 1722-1787. A concordance of the Holy Scriptures of the Old and New Testaments, by the Rev. John Brown, of Haddington. Springfield: G. and C. Merriam, 1844. 264 p. MH; MWA; WAsN; ViRut; WaPS. 44-1027

Brown, John, 1722-1787. A concordance to the Holy Scriptures of the Old and New Testaments: by which all, or most, of the principal texts of scripture may be easily found out... Revised and corrected. Boston: Sherburne: 1844. 264 p. ICBB; MH; PU. 44-1028

Brown, John, 1722-1787. A concordance to the Holy Scriptures of the Old and New Testaments: by which all, or most, of the principal texts of scripture may be easily found out... Revised and corrected. Concord, New Hampshire: Luther Roby, 1844. 264 p. MdBD; MH; MH-AH; MMeT-Hi; PU. 44-1029

Brown, John, 1722-1787. A concordance to the Holy Scriptures of the Old and New Testaments: by which all, or most, of the principal texts of scripture may be easily found out... Revised and corrected. Franklin, New Hampshire:

Peabody and Daniell, 1844. 83 p. PPULC; PU. 44-1030

Brown, John, 1722-1787. A dictionary of the Holy Bible... by the Rev. John Brown... From the 12th and latest Edinburgh edition containing the author's last additions and corrections, and further enlarged and corrected by his sons, with a life of the author. New York: Harper, 1844. 534, 20 p. PPPrHi; PPULC. 44-1031

Brown, John, 1722-1787. The shorter catechism. Philadelphia: J. Van Court, 1844. AmSSchU. 44-1032

Brown, John, 1778-1848. The exclusive claims of Puseyite Episcopalians to the Christian ministry indefensible: ....In a series of letters to the Rev. Dr. Pusey. By John Brown, D.D. ....Philadelphia: Presbyterian Board of Publication, 1844. 434 p. KyDC; LNB; NbOP; MeBat; ScU. 44-1033

Brown, John Ball, 1784-1862. Reports of cases in the Boston Orthopedic Institution, or hospital for the cure of deformities of the human frame. Boston: Clapp, 1844. 39 p. CtY; MBAt; MHi; PU; RPB. 44-1034

Brown, W.H. Portrait gallery of distinguished American citizens, with biographical sketches. Hartford, Connecticut: E.B. and E.C. Kellogg, 1844. 11 p. MChiL. 44-1035

Brown, William John. To the people of the fifty congressional district of the state of Indiana... [Washington: 1844] InU; M; NN. 44-1036

Brown County, Wisconsin. The people

of Brown County in Wisconsin Territory: feeling a deep interest in the contemplated improvement of the Fox and Wisconsin Rivers, appointed the undersigned a committee to address a circular to the several members of congress, requesting of each their individual endeavors, in favor of the grant of land to effect that object... Green Bay: 1844. WHi. 44-1037

Brown's almanack for 1845. Concord, New Hampshire: John F. Brown, [1844] MWA; Nh-Hi. 44-1038

Brown's business man's almanac for 1845. Springfield, Massachusetts: Ben F. Brown; Boston: R.H. Sherburne and company, [1844] MWA. 44-1039

Browne, Peter Arrell, 1782-1860. Essay on solid meteors and aerolites or meteoric stone. Philadelphia: 1844. 38 p. CtY; NN; PHi; PPL-R; PU. 44-1040

Browne, Rowland Jay. A practical treatise on actions at law, embracing the subjects of notice of action, limitation of actions, necessary parties to and proper forms of actions, the consequence of mistakes therein, and law of costs with reference to damages. Philadelphia: Little, 1844. 452 p. Ct; LNL-L; Mi-L; Nv; PP. 44-1041

Browne, Thomas, 1605-1682. Religio medici. Its sequel, Christian morals. By Sir Thomas Browne.... With resemblant passages from Cowper's task, and a verbal index. Philadelphia: Lea and Blanchard, 1844. 226 p. IaDuU; MWiW; OSW; RP; ViAl. 44-1042

Browning, Elizabeth Barrett, 1806-1861. Complete poetical works from the twelfth London edition. New York: Crowell and company, 1844. 520 p. PScrM. 44-1043

Browning, Elizabeth Barrett, 1806-1861. Poems by Elizabeth Browning. Aldine edition. [Corrected] Vol. 1-4. New York, New York: James Miller, 1844-1856. 353 p. IAlS; MtStJosC; NcAcP. 44-1044

Browning, Elizabeth Barrett, 1806-1861. The poetical works of E. B. Browning. New York: Thomas Y. Crowell and company, 1844. 528 p. MdBE; NjMD; OkMu. 44-1045

Browning, Elizabeth Barrett, 1806-1861. The poetical works of Elizabeth Browning Barrett. New York, First edition. New York: 1844. 557 p. NcDurC. 44-1046

Brownlee, William Craig, 1784-1860. The Christian youth's book; and manual for young communicants. New York: Carter, 1844. 480 p. NBuG; NNC. 44-1047

Brownlee, William Craig, 1784-1860. The Christian youth's books; and manual for young communicants... New York: Robert Carter: Pittburg: Thomas Carter, 1844. 499 p. MLow; NjMD; OkShB. 44-1048

Brownlow, William Gannaway, 1805-1877. A political register, setting forth the principles of the Whig and Locofoco parties in the United States, with the life and public services of Henry Clay. Also an appendix personal to the author; and a general index. By William G. Brownlow.... Jonesborough, Tennessee: office of the Jonesborough Whig, 1844.

349 p. DLC; GMW; MoSM; TxU; WHi. 44-1049

Brownson, Orestes Augustus, 1803-1876. Social reform: an address before the society of the mystical seven in the Wesleyan University, Middletown, Connecticut, August 7, 1844. Boston: Waite and company, 1844. 42 p. CtMW; MBC; MnHi; NCH; Vi. 44-1050

Brownson's quarterly review. Boston: B.H. Green; New York: E. Dunigan and brothers, 1756-1875. 24 v. CBPac; ICN; KU; MiU; RP. 44-1051

Brownson's quarterly review. Merged into the United States magazine and democratic review. In 1844, Brownson severed his connections with the latter periodical and resumed publication of an independent organ under title: Brownson's quarterly review. This work was suspended from 1865 to 1872, inclusive, and ceased with October, 1875. Boston: B.H. Greene; New York: Dunigan and brother, 1844-1875. DLC; FU; OU; PPPrHi; TxU. 44-1052

Bryan, Edward B. An address before the Philolexian Society, delivered on the anniversary of Washington's birthday, February 22, 1844; published by request of the members. Alexandria, D.C.: printed at the Southern Churchman office, 1844. 13 p. NcU. 44-1053

Bryant, John D. The "dark" ages; a lecture delivered before the Carroll Institute.... Philadelphia: M. Fithian, 1844. 27 p. GAM-R; InNd; MdBLC; MdW; PHi. 44-1054

Bryant, William Cullen, 1794-1878. Tales of Glauber Spa. By several

American authors.... New York: Harper and brothers, 1844. 2 v. MB; NBuG; NN; PPL-R. 44-1055

Bryant, William Cullen, 1794-1878. Thirty poems, by William Cullen Bryant. New York: Appleton and company, 1844. MBBCHS. 44-1056

Bryant, William Cullen, 1794-1878. The white-footed deer, and other poems. New York: I.S. Platt, 1844. 24 p. CSmH; MBAt; MWA; NBuU; RPB. 44-1057

Buchanan, Alan. Apology for promoting Christianity in India. Boston: 1844. PCC; PPULC. 44-1058

Buchanan, Edward Young. The parable of the house holder. An essay.... New York: 1844. DLC; MB. 44-1059

Buchanan, James, 1791-1868. Comfort in affliction. A series of mediation. Second American from the eleventh edition. New York: Robert Carter, 1844. 254 p. IaDuU. 44-1060

Buchanan, James, 1791-1868. Speech.... on the Oregon question, delivered in the Senate of the United States, March 12, 1844. [Washington: 1844] 15 p. OClWHi; WHi. 44-1061

Buck, Charles. A theological dictionary, containing definitions of all religious terms; a comprehensive view of every article in the system of divinity, an impartial account of all the principal denominations.... By the Rev. Charles Buck. New American from the latest London edition. Revised and improved.... By the Rev. George Bush, ...Corrected edition. Philadelphia: J.J.

Woodward, 1844. 479 p. KyDC; MoS; PPP; TJaU; WaPS. 44-1062

Buckingham, Joseph Tinker, 1779-1861. An address to native Americans, together with the declaration and principles of the native Americans of Boston. Second edition. Boston: H.B. Skinner, 1844. 24 p. CSmH; MH. 44-1063

Buckingham, Joseph Tinker, 1779-1861. Devotional exercises for schools and families. New edition, with additions. Boston: Munroe, 1844. 192 p. CBPac; DLC; MBAt; MH. 44-1064

Buckingham, Joseph Tinker, 1779-1861. Golden sentiments; being an address to the native Americans of New York, by J.T. Buckingham... together with the declaration of sentiments of the native Americans of Boston. Boston: H.B. Skinner, 1844. 24 p. CtSoP; FU; M; MBAt; MiD-B. 44-1065

Buckstone, John Baldwin, 1802-1879. The dream at sea; a drama in three acts. Philadelphia: R. Harris, 1844. 59 p. MH; NjR; NN. 44-1066

Buckstone, John Baldwin, 1802-1879. Luke the labourer or the lost son. A domestic melodrama in two acts. New York and Philadelphia: Turner and Fisher, 1844. DLC. 44-1067

Budd, Samuel W. An address read before the Goethean Society of Marshall College, at their anniversary, August 28, 1843. Chambersburg, Pennsylvania: publication office of the German Reformed Church, 1844. 15 p. CtY; DLC; OClWHi; PHi; PLFM. 44-1068

Buddicom, Robert Pedder, d. 1846.

Emanuel on the cross and in the garden. New York: John S. Taylor and company, 1844. 224 p. CtY; MWA; NjPT; PPM; ScSoT. 44-1069

Buel, Jesse, 1778-1839. The farmer's companion; or essays on the principles and practice of American husbandry. With the address prepared to be delivered before the agricultural and horticultural societies of New Haven County, Connecticut, and an appendix, containing tables and other matter useful to the farmer. Boston: Marsh, Capen, Lyon and Webb, 1844. 303 p. LNP; M; MdU. 44-1070

Buel, Jesse, 1778-1839. The farmers' instructor; consisting of essays, practical directions and hints for the management of the farm and the garden, originally published in the cultivator; selected and revised for the school district library. New York: Harper and brothers, 1844. 2 v. IaHi; LNP; MSher; RKi; RWe. 44-1071

Buel, Samuel. The apostolical system of the church defended, in a reply to Dr. Whateley on the kingdom of Christ. Philadelphia: H. Hooker, 1844. 165 p. CtHT; ICBB; NjR; OrPD; PPL. 44-1072

Buell, Charles. Proceedings of a court martial for flogging a private soldier. Washington: 1844. PPL. 44-1073

Buffington, Jos. Speech of Mr. Buffington, of Pennsylvania, on the tariff bill. Delivered in the House of Representatives May 1, 1844. Washington: J. and G.S. Gideon, printers, 1844. 16 p. In; MBAt. 44-1074

Buffum, Arnold, 1782-1859. Lecture, showing the necessity for a liberty party, and setting forth its principles, measures, and subject. Cincinnati: C. Clark, printer, 1844. 15 p. DLC; MB; OClWHi. 44-1075

Bugard, B.F. French practical translator; or easy method of learning to translate French to English. Fifth edition. Boston: Munroe and Francis, 1844. ILM; MH; TxU-T. 44-1076

Buist, Robert, 1805-1880. The rose manual; containing accurate descriptions of all the finest varieties of roses, properly classed in their respective families, their character and mode of culture, with directions for their propagation, and destruction of insects.... By.... Philadelphia: the author, 1844. 182 p. CtY; MPiB; NjN; PHi; RPB. 44-1077

Bulfinch, Stephen Greenleaf, 1809-1870. A discourse suggested by Weir's picture of the embarkation of the pilgrims; delivered in the Unitarian Church, Washington, December 31st, 1843. By S.G. Bulfinch. Published by request. Washington: Gales and Seaton, 1844. 13 p. CtY; DLC; ICMe; MWA; NNG. 44-1078

Bulfinch, Stephen Greenleaf, 1809-1870. Farewell discourse, delivered in the Unitarian Church, Washington, May 12, 1844, by S.G. Bulfinch, on relinquishing his charge as pastor of the society... Washington: Gales and Seaton, 1844. 20 p. CBPac; ICMe; MB; OClWHi; RPB. 44-1079

Bull in caena domini... Philadelphia: 1844. PPL. 44-1080

Bullard, Asa, 1804-1888. A short account of William Abbott Douglass, who died at Waterford, Maine, February 23, 1832. ....Fourth edition. Boston, Massachusetts: Sabbath School Society, 1844. 36 p. DLC; MBC. 44-1081

Bullions, Alexander. In chancery, before the chancellor of the state of New York. William Stevenson and others, complainants vs. Alexander Bullions and others, defendants. Salem: Harkness, 1844. 295 p. MH-L; NIC; NNC-L; PPL; PPPrHi. 44-1082

Bullions, Peter, 1791-1864. Practical lessons in English grammar and composition for young beginners. New York: Pratt, Woodford and company, 1844. MBAt; MDeeP; OKentC. 44-1083

Bullions, Peter, 1791-1864. The principles of English grammar; with copious exercises in parsing and syntax, for the use of academies and common schools. A new edition, revised and corrected; with an appendix of various and useful matter. New York: Published by Pratt, Woodford and company, 1844. 216 p. CtY; DLC; InCW; MBAt; NBuG. 44-1084

Bullions, Peter, 1791-1864. The principles of Greek grammar; comprising the substance of the most approved grammar extant, for the use of colleges and academies. Third edition, revised and corrected.... New York: Pratt, Woodford and company, 1844. 312 p. CSt; CoPu; MBBC; MH; OUrC; TKC. 44-1085

Bullions, Peter, 1791-1864. The principles of Latin grammar. By Rev. Peter Bullions, D.D. New York: Pratt, Woodford and company, 1844. 312 p. CtHWatk; InGr; NjPat; OO; OUrC. 44-1086

Bumstead, Josiah Freeman, b. 1797. Second reading book in the primary school designed to follow the reading lessons of "My first school book." Boston: W.D. Ticknor and company, 1844. 166 p. MEab; PU-Penn. 44-1087

Bumstead, Josiah Freeman, b. 1797. Spelling and thinking. Boston: T.R. Marvin, 1844. MH. 44-1088

Bumstead, Josiah Freeman, b. 1797. Third reading book in the primary school. Boston: William D. Ticknor and company, 1844. MH; NNC. 44-1089

Bunker Hill Monument Association. Views from the Bunker Hill monument. Being directions to find the principal objects to be seen from its summit. Boston: 1844. 8 p. ICN; MWA. 44-1090

Bunyan, John, 1628-1688. Grace abounding to the chief of sinners in a faithful account of the life and death of John Bunyan. New York: Dodd, 1844. 176 p. IaGG; KyDC; MB; PP; PReaA. 44-1091

Bunyan, John, 1628-1688. The heavenly footman; or, a description of the man that gets to heaven.... Sellinsgrove, Pennsylvania: P.H. Fisher, 1844. 88 p. PReaAT. 44-1092

Bunyan, John, 1628-1688. The Holy war made by Shaddai upon Diabolus, for the regaining of the metropolis of the world; or the losing and taking again of the town of Mansoul. Philadelphia: American Baptist Publiscation Society [1844] [13]-304 p. CLCo; ICU; TJaU; WMHi. 44-1093

Bunyan, John, 1628-1688. The little

pilgrim's progress. Philadelphia: Smith and Peck, 1844. 192 p. CtY; NN. 44-1094

Bunyan, John, 1628-1688. The Pilgrim's progress, from this world to that which is to come. Delivered under the similitude of a dream. Baltimore: Parsons and Preston, 184. 249 p. MdHi; OFH. 44-1095

Bunyan, John, 1628-1688. The pilgrim's progress, from this world to that which is to come. Delivered under the similitude of a dream. Hartford: S. Andrus, 1844. 360 p. CtY; NN; PP; PScr; RPE. 44-1096

Bunyan, John, 1628-1688. The pilgrim's progress, in two parts; by John Bunyan: with notes, and a life of the author, by Rev. T. Scott, late chaplain to the Lock Hospital. Hartford: Edwin Hunt, 1844. NTRS. 44-1097

Bunyan, John, 1628-1688. The pilgrim's progress by John Bunyan. Embellished with numerous engravings. Illustrated with five hundred explanatory notes, by Mason, Scott and others. New York: D. Newell, 1844. 350 p. MnStCl. 44-1098

Bunyan, John, 1628-1688. The pilgrim's progress, from this world to that which is to come. Delivered under the similitude of a dream. Philadelphia: American Baptist Publication Society, 1844. 360 p. LU. 44-1099

Bunyan, John, 1628-1688. The pilgrim's progress. Most carefully collated with the edition containing the author's last additions and corrections. With explanatory notes, by Thomas Scott, D.D., and a life of the author by Josiah Conder, esq. Philadelphia: Presbyterian Board of Publication, [1844] 554 p. CPasr; NBuDD; OO; OrPD; PPPrHi. 44-1100

Bunyan, John, 1628-1688. The pilgrim's progress. Most carefully collated with the edition containing the author's last notes....With explanatory notes by T. Scott, D.D., and a life of the author by I. Conder. Second American edition. Philadelphia: Presbyterian Board, 1844. CtY; CU; MNtCA; MdBE. 44-1101

Bunyan, John, 1628-1688. The pilgrim's progress. Most carefully collated with the edition containing the author's last additions and corrections. With explanatory notes by Thomas Scott, and a life of the author by Josiah Conder. Third American edition. Philadelphia: Presbyterian Board of Publication, 1844. 554 p. AU; ICP; MdBP; NRU; PBm. 44-1102

Bunyan, John, 1628-1688. The pilgrim's progress. Most carefully collated with the edition containing the author's last additions and corrections; with explanatory notes by Thomas Scott, and a life of the author by Josiah Conder. Fourth American edition. Philadelphia: Presbyterian Board of Publication, [1844] CtHWatk; GS. 44-1103

Burgess, George, 1809-1866. The strife of brothers: a poem: in two parts. With notes....New York: D. Appleton and company; Philadelphia: G.S. Appleton, 1844. 47 p. CSmH; MdBD; MH; RPB; TxU. 44-1104

Burke, Edmund, 1729?-1797. A philosophical enquiry into the origin of our ideas of the sublime and beautiful; with an introductory discourse concerning taste. By the right honorable Edmund Burke. Adapted to popular use by Abraham Mills.... New York: Harper and brothers, 1844. 219 p. GHi; LNT; MdBS; PU; ViRU. 44-1105

Burke, William A. I ne'er can love again: a Page's romance; arranged for pf. New York: 1844. CtY. 44-1106

Burke, William A. I'll hang my harp on a willow tree... arranged for pf. New York: 1844. CtY. 44-1107

Burkitt, William. Expository notes with practical observations on the New Testament of Our Lord and Saviour Jesus Christ... Philadelphia: Sorin and Ball, 1844. 2 v. ICBB; GEU-T; KyDC; MiDD; NbOP. 44-1108

Burling, William. An address, delivered before the Ontario Agricultural Society, on the second day of its annual meeting, October 12, 1844. Published by order of the Society. Canandaigua: printed by George L. Whitney, 1844. 47 p. N. 44-1109

Burlington, New Jersey. St. Mary's Hall. Catalogue and prospectus of St. Mary's Hall; winter term, MDCCCXLIII-IV. Burlington, New Jersey: J.L. Powell, printer, 1844. 16 p. MiD-B; PU. 44-1110

Burnap, George Washington, 1802-1859. The atonement. Boston: Gould, Kendall and Lincoln, 1844. 24 p. CBPac; MeB; MH-AH; PPL; RPB. 44-1111

Burnap, George Washington, 1802-1859. Church and state: or the privileges and duties of an American citizen. A discourse in the First Independent Church on thanksgiving day, December 12, 1844. Baltimore: Toy, 1844. 24 p. CBPac; DLC; ICMe; MWA; PPL. 44-1112

Burnap, George Washington, 1802-1859. A discourse of the principles involved in the Pusey controversy....

Baltimore: John D. Toy, printer, 1844. 24 p. CBPac; ICMe; MH; NIC; PPLT. 44-1113

Burnap, George Washington, 1802-1859. The duties of the citizen soldier; a discourse in the First Independent Church. Baltimore: 1844. 20 p. DLC; MBAt; MWA; NIC; PPL. 44-1114

Burnap, George Washington, 1802-1859. The end of the world. A discourse suggested by the Miller doctrine. Baltimore: William Wooddy, 1844. 32 p. IU; MdBJ; MdToH; MH; PSC-Hi. 44-1115

Burnap, George Washington, 1802-1859. The life of Leonard Calvert. The Library of American Biography. Boston: Charles C. Little and James Brown, 1844-1846. 398 p. IUr. 44-1116

Burnham, Abraham, 1775-1852. A good minister of Jesus Christ. A discourse, delivered before the Hopkinton Association, May 14, 1844, in the new North Church, Concord, New Hampshire... Concord: Hopkinton Association, 1844. 28 p. CSmH; MiD-B; MWA; PPFM; RPB. 44-1117

Burnham, C.G. A new system of arithmetic. Third edition. Concord: 1844. MB. 44-1118

Burns, Jabez, 1805-1876. The youthful Christian; containing instructions, councils, cautions and examples by J. Burns.... Dover: trustees of the Freewill Baptist Connection, 1844. 224 p. MeLewB; NHC-S; NH-Hi. 44-1119

Burns, John. Christian fragments; or, remarks on the nature, precepts, and comfort of religion. By John Burns,

M.D. F.R.S. New York: Robert Carter; Pittsburg: Thomas Carter, 1844. MBAt; ScOrC. 44-1120

Burns, Robert, 1759-1796. The complete poetical works of Robert Burns: with explanatory and glossarial notes; and a life of the author, by James Currie, M.D. The second complete American edition. New York: D. Appleton and company; Philadelphia: G.S. Appleton, 1844. 60, 575 p. ViU. 44-1121

Burr, Charles Chauncey. The gavel: a monthly periodical devoted to Odd Fellowship and general literature. Rev. C.C. Burr and J. Tanner, editors. Albany: 1844-45. v. 1. CtY; MH. 44-1122

Burr, Charles Chauncey. A review of Rev. Mr. Lane's lectures against Universalism. Troy: Cannon Place Printing office, 1844. 144 p. ICBB; MMeT-Hi. 44-1123

Burr, Charles Chauncey. Substance of an extemporaneous oration on Irish repeal, delivered in Troy, October 23, 1844. Albany: Munsell and Tanner, printers, 1844. 28 p. CtY; MB; MWA; NjR. 44-1124

Burr, Samuel Jones. The peri, or, the enchanted fountain. The grand fairy opera of "the peri," or, the enchanted fountain, to be performed at the Melodeon.... February 10, 1844. The overture and music.... By J.G. Maeder. [Boston: 1844] 15 p. MB. 44-1125

Burr Seminary, Manchester, Vermont. Catalogue of officers and students. Troy: 1844. DLC; MB; VtMidbC. 44-1126

Burritt, Elizah Hinsdale, 1794-1838.

The geography of the heavens, and class book of astronomy, accompanied by a celestial atlas.... Fifth edition. With an introduction by Thomas Dick, LL.D. ....New York: Huntington and Savage, 1844. 305 p. IaDmD; IaHi; MH; MPeHi; NcD. 44-1127

Burrowes, John Freckleton, 1787-1852. The pianoforte primer; containing the rudiments of music.... with an appendix. ....New York: Firth and Hall, 1844. 60 p. CtHWatk; IU; NjR; NN; NNF. 44-1128

Burrows, John Lansing, 1814-1893. Discourse on his resignation of the pastorate of the Fifth Baptist Church, in Philadelphia. Philadelphia: 1844. 29 p. MNtCA; PCC; PPULC. 44-1129

Burt, J. Moral responsibilities of citizenship. A discourse delivered... before the quadrennial meeting for the choice of president and vice president of the United States. Hartford: 1844. IEG. 44-1130

Burton, Warren, 1800-1866. The scenery-shower, with word-paintings of the beautiful, the picturesque, and the grand in nature.... Boston: W.D. Ticknor and company, 1844. 119 p. MBAt; MHi; NhPet; NjP. 44-1131

Bury, Charlotte Campbell, 1775-1861. The wilfulness of woman. By the authoress of "The history of a flirt"... New York: W.H. Colyer, 1844. 121 p. ICU; ViU. 44-1132

Bush, George, 1796-1859. Anastasis: or the doctrine of the resurrection of body. New York: 1844. MB; MiGr. 44-1133

Bush, George, 1796-1859. The

hierophant; or, monthly journal of sacred symbols and prophecy. Conducted by George Bush, complete in one volume. New York: Mark H. Neman, 1844. 288 p. ArCH; CtY; GDecCt; MBAt; NNUT. 44-1134

Bush, George, 1796-1859. The life of Mohammed; founder of the religion of Islam, and of the empire of the Saracens. New York: Harper and brothers, 1844. 261 p. InCW; MeAu; OCX; RP. 44-1135

Bush, George, 1796-1859. The prophecies of Daniel. Nebuchadnezzar's dream of the great image. New York: Harper and Brothers, 1844. 2 pts. MB; MH; MNtCA; NNUT. 44-1136

Bush, George, 1796-1859. The valley of vision; or, the dry bones of Israel revived. An attempted proof from [Ezekiel, chap. xxxvii 1-14] of the restoration and conversion of the Jews. By George Bush. New York: Saxton and Miles, 1844. 60 p. CtMW; ICP; KyDC; PHi; NjPT. 44-1137

Bush, Mary A. Hymns original and selected for maternal meetings. By Mrs. Mary A. Bush. Buffalo: press of A.M. Clapp, 1844. 128 p. IU; NBuHi. 44-1138

Bush, William. Brief account of ... including his correspondence with Daniel Wheeler... Philadelphia: 1844. 48 p. CtHWatk; InRchE; MH; PHi; PSC-Hi. 44-1139

Bushnell, Horace, 1802-1876. Politics under the law of God. A discourse delivered....on the annual fast of 1844. By Horace Bushnell, D.D. Hartford: E. Hunt, 1844. 19 p. CtHWatk; MH; MPiB; MWA; PHi. 44-1140

Bushnell, Horace, 1802-1876. Politics under the law of God. A discourse delivered....on the annual fast of 1844, by Horace Bushnell. Second edition. Hartford: Edwin Hunt, 1844. 19 p. CSmH; CtY; MeHi; NCH-S; RPB. 44-1141

Bushnell, Horace, 1802-1876. Politics under the law of God. A discourse delivered in the North Congregational Church, Hartford, on the annual fast of 1844...Third edition. Hartford: Edwin Hunt, 1844. 23p. CtSoP; IEG; OClWHi; TxH; WHi. 44-1142

Bushnell, Horace, 1802-1876. Politics under the law of God. A discourse delivered in the North Congregational Church, Hartford, on annual fast of 1844. Fourth edition. Hartford: Edwin Hunt, 1844. 23 p. CtMW; CtY; IaGG; MBNMHi; MiD-B. 44-1143

Bushnell, Horace, 1802-1876. Review of the errors of the times: a charge by Rt. Rev. T.C. Brownell. [From the New Englander] Hartford: 1844. 51 p. CtHC; CtSoP; CtY; MBC; MiD-B. 44-1144

Butler, Alban, 1711-1773. Lives of the fathers, martyrs and other principal Saints. Baltimore: Metropolitan press, 1844. 3 v. MdHi; ViPet. 44-1145

Butler, Alban, 1711-1773. Lives of the fathers, martyrs and other principal Saints. Baltimore: Metropolitan press, 1844-1845. 4v. in 2. CMenSP; InND; MdW; PPLT; TNV. 44-1146

Butler, Clement Moore, 1810-1890. Address delivered by Rev. Clement M. Butler, at the President's mansion on the occasion of the funeral of Abel P. Upshur, T.W. Gilmer and others, who lost their lives by the explosion on board the Princeton, February 28, 1844... Washington: printed by J. and G.S. Gideon, 1844. 8 p. DLC; ICMe; MdBd; NN. 44-1147

Butler, Clement Moore, 1810-1890. A sermon delivered at the request of the board of missions in the diocese of Massachusetts, in St. Paul's Church, Boston....June 12, 1844.... Boston: Dutton and Wentworth, 1844. 22 p. ICU; MBD; MWA; NjR; OClWHi. 44-1148

Butler, Clement Moore, 1810-1890. A sermon delivered in Grace Church, Boston, [Massachusetts] Whitsunday, May 26, 1844.... By Rev. C.M. Butler. Boston: Dutton and Wentworth's, printers, 1844. 19 p. InID; MeHi; MiD-B; MHi; MNtCA. 44-1149

Butler, Clement Moore, 1810-1890. A sermon giving a historical account of St. John's Church, Georgetown, D.C., delivered October 17, 1843; and an address on the occasion of the funeral of Abel P. Upshur and others, who lost their lives by the calamity on board the Princeton, February 28, 1844, and also a farewell sermon delivered April 7, 1844, on his resignation of the rectorship of St. John's Church. Washington: J. and G.S. Gideon, printers, 1844. 40 p. CtHT; DLC; MBAt; WHi. 44-1150

Butler, Frances Anne Kemble. Poems. Philadelphia: Pennington, 184. 152 p. NBu; PPL-R; PU; VtMontg. 44-1151

Butler, Joseph, 1692-1752. Butler's analogy of religion, natural and revealed, to the constitution and course of nature, as abridged and arranged in Hobart's

analysis of the work. Being questions with brief answers for examination, and a summary of the whole subject. By George W. Cranfurd, ...Revised, enlarged and adapted to the use of classical and theological students. By Charles E. West.... New York: Alexander V. Blake, 1844. 344 p. CtY; PP; PPULC; TJaU. 44-1152

Butler, Joseph, 1692-1752. Sermons by the right reverend father in God, Joseph Butler, D.C.L., late Lord Bishop of Durham. New York: Robert Carter, 1844. 303 p. DLC; ICU; MTop; NNUT; ScCoB. 44-1153

Butler, Joseph, 1692-1752. The works of the Right Reverend Father in God, Joseph Butler, D.C.L., late Lord Bishop of Durham. To which is prefixed, a preface, giving some account of the character and writings of the author. New York: Robert Carter, 1844-1845. 2 v. in 1. OCl. 44-1154

Butler, Samuel, 1774-1839. An atlas of ancient geography. Philadelphia: Lea and Blanchard, 1844. 34 p. MH; OSW; ScCoB; TxU-T; WHi. 44-1155

Butter, Henry, 1794-1885. The scholar's companion, containing exercises in the orthography, derivation, and classification of English words. Philadelphia: Perkins and Purves, 1844. 299 p. MB; MH; MoSW; PPULC; ViRU. 44-1156

Butterworth, John, 1727-1803. A new concordance of the Holy Scriptures, ...by the Rev. John Butterworth. A new edition. ....Boston: Crocker and Brewster, 1844. 516 p. NIC; OCX; OrPD. 44-1157

Byerly, Stephen. Byerly's new

American spelling book calculated for the use of schools in the United States compiled by Stephen Byerly. Philadelphia: Thomas Davis, 1844. 167 p. NoLoc. 44-1158

Byrd, Ann. Narratives, pious meditations, and religious exercises of Ann Byrd, late of the city of New York, deceased. Second edition. Philadelphia: John Comly, 1844. 138 p. FWh; IaOskW; MH; NNUT; PHC. 44-1159

Byreheidt, A. Hydropathy; or the treatment of diseases by water, adapted to warm climates... New Orleans: n.p., 1844. 114 p. DNLM; LU; MBM. 44-1160

Byron, George Gordon Noel Byron, 1788-1824. Childe Harold's pilgrimage. A Romaunt. Boston: Little, Brown and company, 1844. 279 p. NCats. 44-1161

Byron, George Gordon Noel Byron, 1788-1824. The Hebrew melodies of Lord Byron. By George Gordon Noel Byron, Sixth baron. [New York: Morris, Willis and company, 1844] MB; MWH; NNUT. 44-1162

Byron, George Gordon Noel Byron, 1788-1824. The works of Lord Byron, including the suppressed poems. Also a sketch of his life. By J.W. Lake.... Philadelphia: Grigg and Elliot, 1844. 764 p. DLC; MdBJ; ODaU; TxGR; ViU. 44-1163

C

C., A.M. Willie Grant; or, the little Pharisee. By A.M.C. ....written for the New England Sabbath School Union, and revised by the committee of publication. Boston: New England Sabbath School Union, 1844. 162 p. TxSaWi. 44-1164

Caesar, C. Julius. Caesar's commentaries on the Gallic war; and the first book of the Greek paraphrase; with English notes, critical and explanatory, plans of battles, sieges, etc. By Charles Anthon. New York: Harper and brothers, 1844. 493 p. ArAT; CSt; MoSpD; NNC; OWoC. 44-1165

Caesar, C. Julius. Caesaris commentarii de bello Gallico ad codices Parisinos recensiti A.N.L. Achaintre et N.E. Lemaire. Bostoniae: R.S. Davis, 1844. 220 p. CBPSR; MiD; MiEalC; MH; TxU-T. 44-1166

Caesar, C. Julius. Comentarii De Bello Gallico ad codices parisinos recensiti A. N. L. Achaintre et N. E. Lemaire. Accesserunt Notulae Anglicae atque index historicus et geographicus. F. P. Leavitt, curavit. By Caii Jlii Caesaris. Boston: R. S. Davis, 1844. 244 p. MMhHi. 44-1167

Caesar, C. Julius. The commentaries of Caesar, translated into English. To which is prefixed a discourse concerning the Roman art of war. By William Duncan. Philadelphia: McCarty and Davis, 1844. 366 p. MsCld; OCX; WBeloC. 44-1168

Cahen, S. A catechism of religious and moral instruction, for children of the Hebrew faith; as adopted in the consistorial schools for Israelites at Paris. Translated from the French of M. Cahen. Philadelphia: 1844. 86 p. NN; PPDrop. 44-1169

Cairns, John T., 1805-1854. Recruit; a compilation of exercises and movements of infantry, light infantry, and riflemen... New York: E. Walker, 1844. 160 p. Ct; DLC; MCM; MWA. 44-1170

Calabrella, E.C. de baraness. The ladies' science of etiquette. By an English lady of rank. To which is added, the ladies' handbook of the toilet; a manual of elegance and fashion. New York: Wilson and company, 1844. 64 p. CtHT; MB; Nh-Hi; OClWHi. 44-1171

Calderwood, David. The pastor and the prelate, or, reformation and conformity shortly compared by the word of God, by antiquity and the proceedings of the ancient kirk.... First American edition. Philadelphia: Samuel Agnew, 1844. 124 p. CoU; GDecCT; ICP; NbOP; PPL. 44-1172

Caldwell, Charles, 1772-1853. The replier replied to and reviewer reviewed. A lecture to Lundsford P. Yandell, M.D. Containing strictures and thoughts on the errors and false doctrines of Chemico-physiology. Louisville, Kentucky: 1844. 56 p. DLC. 44-1173

Caldwell, David. Masonry, its own defence: or the Freemasons apology for loving his order. An address before Marshall Lodge, No. 39: delivered at Lynchburg, on St. John's Day, 1844. Lynchburg: Toler, Townley and Statham, printers, 1844. 22 p. LNMas; NcD; PPFM; ViL. 44-1174

Caldwell, George Alfred. Speech of Mr. Caldwell, of Kentucky on the tariff: Delivered in the House of Representatives... Washington: Printed at the Globe office, 1844. 11 p. MiD-B. 44-1175

Calender des Bauern und handwerks mannes fur das jahr 1845... Philadelphia: DeSilver und Muir... King und Baird, Buchdrucker [1844] PReaHi. 44-1176

Calender fur stadt und land for 1845. Philadelphia: W.L.J. Kinderlen [1844] MWA. 44-1177

Calhoun, John Caldwell, 1782-1850. Hon. J.C. Calhoun's letter to the Hon. W.R. King. [Charleston, South Carolina] Printed by Walker and Burke, 1844. 8 p. PPL; ScU. 44-1178

Calvin, Jean, 1509-1564. Calvin, on romish relics: being an inventory of saints' relics, personally seen by him in Spain, Italy, France and Germany. Translated by M.M. Backus. New York: S.W. Benedict and company, 1844. 48 p. ILM; MAnP; NjR; NNC; ViRU. 44-1179

Calvin, Jean, 1509-1564. Institutes of the Christian religion. Translated from the original Latin, and collated with the author's latest edition in French, by John Allen. Fifth American edition, revised and corrected.... Philadelphia: Pres-byterian Board of Publication, 1844. 2 v. CoCsC; KWiU; MiU; NcD; OO. 44-1180

Calvin, Jean, 1509-1564. Institutes of the Christian religion. Translated from the original Latin, and collated with the author's latest edition in French, by John Allen. Sixth American edition, revised and corrected.... Philadelphia: pres-byterian Board of Publication, [1844] 2 v. MoSpD; OSW. 44-1181

Cambridge, Massachusetts. Fifteen pamphlets. Cambridge: 1844-1878. MB. 44-1182

Camp, Charles Whittlesey. A poem, by Charles Whittlesey Camp and the valedictory oration by Oswin Hart Doolittle; ....New Haven: B.L. Hamlen, 1844. 40 p. ICU; MiGr; PPM; RPB; TxU. 44-1183

Camp, Charlotte. A tale of 1774. By a member of the bar. Philadelphia: G.B. Zieber and company, 1844. CSmH; OCHP; WHi. 44-1184

Camp meeting chorister; or a collection of hymns and spiritual songs for the pious of all denominations... Philadelphia: Leary, 1844. 320 p. PPLT. 44-1185

The campaign for 1844. v. 1. April 13, 1844-June 4, 1845. Frankfort, Kentucky: Hodges, Todd and Pruett, 1844-1845. 14 p. NcD; KyU. 44-1186

Campbell, Alexander, 1788-1866. An address to the members of the Union Literary Society, of Miami University, Ohio. Bethany, Virginia: Printed by A. Campbell, 1844. 23 p. CSmH; MH; NCH; OOxM; PPPrHi. 44-1187

Campbell, Alexander, 1788-1866. A debate between Rev. A. Campbell and Rev. N.L. Rice, on the action, subject, design and administration of Christian baptism. Lexington: A.T. Skillman and son, 1844. 11-912 p. CoD; IaU; LNB; NNUT; TxHuT. 44-1188

Campbell, Alexander, 1788-1866. Infidelity refuted by infidels; or the gospel proved by the testimony of unbelieving Jews and Pagans. Bethany, Virginia: Campbell, 1844. 352 p. CMenSP; PPPr-Hi; ViRU; WvU. 44-1189

Campbell, Alexander, 1788-1866. Responsibilities of men of genius. An address to the members of the Union Literary Society of Miami University, Ohio. Bethany, Virginia: Campbell, 1844. 23 p. OO. 44-1190

Campbell, Alexander Augustus, 1789-1845. Scripture baptism defined according to the revealed character of God and the doctrine of justification by faith; its origin, design, make and subject, by Rev. Alexander A. Campbell. Cincinnati: A. Pugh and company, 184. 208 p. GDecCT; KyLoP; OClWHi; PPPrHi; TxD-T. 44-1191

Campbell, George, 1719-1796. The philosophy of rhetoric, ...A new edition, with the author's last addition and corrections. New York: Roe, Lockwood and son, 1844. 291 p. RPB. 44-1192

Campbell, George, 1719-1796. The philosophy of rhetoric, ...A new edition, with the author's last additions and corrections. New York: Harper and brothers, 1844. 435 p. CtY; ICU; MH; OMC; PU. 44-1193

Campbell, John. Considerations and arguments proving the inexpediency of an international copyright law. New York: 1844. MBAt; MH. 44-1194

Campbell, John, d. 1845. Speech on the right of petition, delivered in the House of Representatives, February 17, 1844 [Washington, D.C.: 1844] 7 p. MH; WHi. 44-1195

Campbell, Thomas, 1777-1844. The book of pleasures' containing the pleasures, of hope, by Thomas Campbell; the pleasures of memory, by Samuel Rogers; and the pleasures of imagination, by Mark Akenside. New York: Clark and Austin, 1844. 187 p. NN; PBm; PPULC. 44-1196

Campbell, Thomas, 1777-1844. The complete poetical works of Thomas Campbell, with a memoir of his life. New York: John W. Lovell company, 1844. 300 p. KyCovV; Ok-P. 44-1197

Campbell, Thomas, 1777-1844. The poetical works of Thomas Campbell.... Philadelphia: J. Crissy, 1844. 183, 38 p. CL; KyLoP; MoSpD; OWof; PSC. 44-1198

Campbell, William Henry, 1808-1890. A funeral discourse, occasioned by the death of Rev. Andrew Yates, delivered before the classes of Schenectady, in the Reformed Protestant Dutch Church, Schenectady, on Sabbath, November 17, 1844, by William H. Campbell. Albany, New York: Munsell and Tanner, 1844. 34 p. Ct; ICN; MBAt; MWA; NRHi. 44-1199

Campbell, William W., 1806-1881. A memoir of Mrs. Judith S. Grant, late missionary to Persia. By William W. Campbell.... New York: J. Winchester, 1844. 200 p. CtY; IEG; NjR; PHi; RPB. 44-1200

Canandaigua Academy. Catalogue of the trustees, teachers, and students, of Canandaigua Academy, Canandaigua: printed by George L. Whitney, 1844. 15 p. NCanHi; NGH. 44-1201

Canning, George, 1770-1827. Select speeches of the Right Honourable George Canning. With a preliminary biographical sketch.... Edited by Robert Walsh. Philadelphia: James Crissy, 1844. 583 p. LNh; MB; MeAu; ViRU; WvW. 44-1202

Cannon, Charles James. Mora Carmody; or woman's influence... [anon.] New York: Edward Dunigan, 1844. 140 p. DLC; MdBS; MdW. 44-1203

Canton Male Seminary. Catalogue of the officers and students of the Canton Male Seminary, for the year ending November 1st, 1844. Canton: Printed by John Saxton, 1844. 8 p. WaLHi. 44-1204

Capen, Lemuel. Administration of the Hawes Charity. An exposition of the facts relating to the charity by Lemeuel Capen; and reply of the Hawes Place Congregational Society at South Boston to same by a committee. Boston: 1844. 24 p. CtY; DLC; MB; MH; NN. 44-1205

Capen, Lemuel. An exposition of facts relating to the administration of the Hawes Charity, at South Boston. Boston: Andrews, Prentiss and Studley, 1844. 24 p. CtY; MBB; MH; MiD-B; RPB. 44-1206

Capen, Nahum, 1804-1886. Memorial on the subject of international copyright. Washington: 1844. MB; OO; PPL. 44-1207

Capen, Nahum, 1804-1886. A memorial to Congress on the subject of an international copyright law. Boston: 1844. 12 p. MNF. 44-1208

Captains Dreyton and Sayres; or the way Americans are treated for aiding the cause of liberty at home. Philadelphia: 1844? PPL-R; PPULC. 44-1209

Carden, Allen D. The Missouri harmony; or a collection of psalm and hymn tunes... with an introduction. Cincinnati: Phillips and Reyholds, 1844. 200, 38 p. OClWHi. 44-1210

Carey, Eustace, 1791-1855. Memoir of William Carey. With an introductory essay by Jeremiah Chaplin. Hartford: Robins and Smith, 1844. 468 p. KKcBT; KWiU; MiKC; NHC-S. 44-1211

Carey, John L. Addresses of John L. Carey and John Johnson, members of the late house of delegates of Maryland, to their respective constituencies, upon the subject of the state debt; as published in the Baltimore American, after the adjournment of the legislature of 1843-44. With other matter on the same subject. Baltimore: J.D. Toy, 1844. 56 p. MdBE; MdHi. 44-1212

Carey, William. Memoir of William Carey, D. D. Late missionary to Bengal; professor of Oriental languages in the College of Fort William, Calcutta. Hartford: Robins and Smith, 1844. 468 p. KKcBT; KWiU. 44-1213

Carlen, Emilie Smith, 1807-1892. The rose of Tistelon: a tale of the Swedish coast. New York: William H. Colyer, 1844. 128 p. MH; N; NjR; NN. 44-1214

Carlyle, Thomas, 1795-1881. Past and present. ....Third edition. New York: W.H. Colyer, 1844. 205 p. CLCM; GDecCT; NjMD; OClW; WaU. 44-1215

Carlyle, Thomas, 1795-1881. Sartor resartus; the life and opinions of Herr Teufelsdrockh. In three books. ....From the last London edition, revised and corrected by the author. New York: Saxton and Miles, 1844. 130 p. CtMW; LNT; MB; MeB; MWA. 44-1216

Carmichael, William Miller, 1804-1881. The early Christian fathers; or, memorials of nine distinguished teachers of the Christian faith during the first three centuries: including their testimony to the three-fold ministry of the church.... New York: A.V. Blake, 1844. 406 p. CU; ICU; LNT; NjR; PMA. 44-1217

Carolina and Georgia almanac by Robert Grier. Augusta: T. Richards, 1844. MWA. 44-1218

Carolina and Georgia almanac for 1845. By Robert Grier. Charleston, South Carolina: M'Carter and Allen [1844] MWA. 44-1219

Carolina and Georgia almanac for 1845. By Robert Grier. Macon, Georgia: J.M. Boardman [1844] MWA. 44-1220

Carolina planter: a monthly register for the state and local societies. Columbia, South Carolina: [I.C. Morgan] 1844-1845. 288 p. DLC; ICU. 44-1221

Carolina table book; a new selection of arithmetical tables, with a short and easy explanation of the principal rules, etc., for the use of schools and private tuition. Charleston: Babcock and company, 1844. 24 p. MH. 44-1222

Carpenter, George Washington, 1802-1860. A brief description of Phil-Ellena, the country seat of George W. Carpenter, at Germantown.... Pennsylvania. Philadelphia: Barrington and Haswell, 1844. 36 p. DLC; PHi; PPL-R; PU. 44-1223

Carpenter, Thomas F. A full report of the arguments of Thomas F. Carpenter, Samuel Y. Atwell, and Joseph M. Blake, attorney, in the case of the state vs. John and William Gordon. For the murder of Amasa Sprague. Providence: Printed at the office of the Daily Transcript, 1844. 38 p. MoU; NIC-L. 44-1224

Carpenter, W.M. Sketches from the history of yellow fever; showing its origin, together with facts and circumstances disproving its domestic origin, and demonstrating its transmissibility. New Orleans: J.B. Steel, printer, 1844. 64 p. CSmH; LNOP; MBM: NBMS; NNNAM. 44-1225

Carpenter's annual medical advertiser, for 1844... containing an account of the most popular of the new medicines, surgical instruments, etc. Philadelphia: 1844. 96 p. DSG; MBM; MH; PPCP. 44-1226

The carriers' address of the Mineral Point Free Press. January 1, 1844. Poem of eleven stanzas in two columns. Mineral Point: 1844. WHi. 44-1227

Carriers address to the patrons of the Western Literary Magazine. Pittsburgh: 1844. Broadside. NBuG. 44-1228

Carrique, Richard. An address delivered before Hudson Lodge, No.7... December 27, A.L. 5843. Hudson: P. Dean Carrique, printer, 1844. 24 p. MMFM. 44-1229

Carson, Alexander, 1776-1844. Baptism in its mode and subjects. By Alexander Carson, minister of the gospel. First American edition. Philadelphia: American Baptist Publication Society, 1844. 502 p. IaU; ICBB; KyLoS; PCA; RPB. 44-1230

Carter, A.G. To the freeholders of Rowan and Davie Counties. Salisbury: 1844. Broadside. NcU. 44-1231

Carter, James P. Boston gals: song and chorus [with pf.] Boston: 1844. CtY. 44-1232

Carter, James P. Cynthia Sue: [song and chorus with pf.] Boston: 1844. CtY. 44-1233

Carter, St. Leger Landon. Nugae, by Nugator; or, pieces in prose and verse. By St. Leger L. Carter. Baltimore: Woods and Crane, printers, 1844. 215 p. DLC; ICU; MdHi; PPM; RPB. 44-1234

Carter, William Lorenzo, b. 1813. Miscellaneous poems. Chagrin Falls: 1844. OClWHi. 44-1235

Carvosso, William, 1750-1834. The great efficacy of simple faith in the atonement of Christ, exemplified in a memoir of Mr. William Carvosso, sixty years a class leader in the Wesleyan Methodist

Connection. Written by himself and edited by his son. New York: Lane and Sanford, 1844. [29]-348 p. CtY; NcCJ; NcSalL; PRea; TxU. 44-1236

Cary, Thomas Greaves, 1791-1859. Letter on the suppose failure of a national bank, debts of the states, etc., with an answer to enquiries concerning the books of Captain Marryat and C. Dickens. Third edition. Boston: 1844. MBAt. 44-1237

Cary, Thomas Greaves, 1791-1859. Letter to a lady in France, on the supposed failure of a national bank, the supposed delinquency of the national government, the debts of several states, and repudiation; with answers to enquiries concerning the books of Captain Marryat and Mr. Dickens. [Second edition] Boston: B.H. Greene, 1844. 60 p. CtY; MPiB; MH; NjP; OO. 44-1238

Cary, Thomas Greaves, 1791-1859. Letter to a lady in France, on the supposed failure of a national bank, the supposed delinquency of the national government, the debts of several states, and repudiation; with answers to enquiries concerning the books of Captain Marryat and Mr. Dickens. Third edition. Boston: B.H. Greene, 1844. 60 p. MiU; RPB. 44-1239

The casket: A souvenir for 1845. New York: Edward Kearny [1844] 38 p. MoU; RPB; WU. 44-1240

A casket of four jewels, for young Christians. Boston: Gould, Kendall and Lincoln, 1844. 128 p. CtY; MB; MiU; NNUT; OO. 44-1241

Cass, Lewis, 1782-1866. Correspondence between General Cass and Daniel

Webster, in relation to the Quintuple treaty. Cincinnati: Cincinnait Enquirer office, 1844? 24 p. OClWHi. 44-1242

Cassaway, Stephen G. The voice of the Lord; a sermon preached in Christ Church, Georgetown, D.C. on the Sunday after the late melancholy catastrophe on board the U.S. steam ship Princeton. Washington: Alexander and Barnard, printers, 1844. 16 p. MdBP; OClWHi. 44-1243

Cassels, Samuell J.S. The lord's supper, a sermon preached in the Presbyterian Church, Norfolk, Virginia by the pastor. Norfolk: Printed by T.G. Broughton and company, 1844. 12 p. GDecCT; NjPT; PPPrHi. 44-1244

Castania, Christophoros Plato. An essay on the ancient and modern Greek languages, containing remarks on the accents, pronunciation and versification of the Greek languages, with historical notices, etc. To which is added extracts from modern Greek authors; Christopoulos on versification; an oration delivered before the New York legislature; and a guide to acquire a knowledge of the modern Greek. By Christophorus Plato Castanis.... Andover [Massachusetts] Allen, Morrill and Wardwell, printer, 1844. 80 p. DLC; MB; MWA; OMC; PU. 44-1245

Castania, Christophoros Plato. Interpretations of the attributes of the principal fabulous dieties, with an essay on the history of mythology, and relics of Grecian architecture.... Portland: William Hyde, 1844. 102 p. CBPSR; LNHT; MeHi; NBLiHi; RPAt. 44-1246

Castle, L.G. A treatise on African

colonization. Geneva, New York: Scotten and Van Brunt, 1844. 56 p. TNF. 44-1247

Castleton Medical College, Castleton, Vermont. Announcement of the annual course of lectures for 1844. Albany: 1844. 15 p. CtY. 44-1248

Castleton Medical College, Castleton, Vermont. Announcement of the autumnal course of lectures for 1844, and catalogue of the spring session, 1844. Albany: 1844. 14 p. MHi; N. 44-1249

Castleton Medical College, Castleton, Vermont. Announcement of the spring course...for 1845; and catalogue... of 1844. Albany: Printed by C. Van Benthuysen and company, 1844. 16 p. NN. 44-1250

Catherwood, Frederick. Views of ancient monuments in Central America. Chiapas Yucatan, etc. New York: Bartlett and Welford, 1844. CU-B; DLC; MBAt; NN; RPJCB. 44-1251

Catholic Church. Definitions of faith, and canons of discipline of the six oecumenical [sic] councils with the remaining canons of the code of the universal church. First American edition. New York: James A. Sparks, 1844. 356 p. CtHC; GMM; NNS; PPP; WNaE. 44-1252

Catholic Church. Officia propria foederatis provinens Americae Septentrionalis Concessa. Baltimore, [Maryland]: ex typographia metropolitana, 1844. 143 p. IaDuMtC; MdBS; MiDSH. 44-1253

Catholic Church. Provincial council of

Baltimore. Concilia provincialia, Baltimori habita ab anno 1829, usque ad annum 1869. Fifth edition. 1843. Baltimore: Murphy, 1844. 29 p. CSansS; MdHi; OCX. 44-1254

A Catholic Sunday school hymn book; consisting of hymns contained in the manual of the sodality and a selection of other hymns adapted to children. Philadelphia: W.J. Cunningham, 1844. 85 p. AmSSchU. 44-1255

Catholicism compatible with republican government, and in full accordance with popular institutions: or, reflections upon a premium treatise, issued by the American Protestant Society, under the signature of "Civis." By Fenelon. New York: Edward Dunigan, 1844. 48 p. GAM; InND; MiD-B; MdW; MWA. 44-1256

Catholicism compatible with republican government; letters to Rt. Rev. John Hughes upon the present system of public education, by Fenelon [pseud.] New York and Philadelphia: 1844-45. CtY; InNd; MiD-B; MWA; PPL. 44-1257

Catholicism compatible with republican government; or, reflections upon a premium treatise issued by the American Protestant Society; by Fenelon. New York: Harper and brothers, 1844. 48 p. RPB. 44-1258

Catlin, George, 1796-1872. Letters and notes on the manners, customs, and condition of the North American Indians. Written during eight years travel among the wildest tribes of Indians in North America [1832-1839] Third edition. New York: Wiley and Putnam, 1844. 2 v. CtY; LNH; MnHi; WaSp; ViL. 44-1259

Catlin, George Smith, 1808-1851. Speech of Mr. Catlin of Connecticut, on the right to members to their seats in the House of Representatives, February 10, 1844. Washington: Globe office, 1844. 8 p. MH; OClWHi; PHi. 44-1260

Cattanio, P. A. Rudiments of the German language. Arranged and simplified for beginners. Philadelphia: sold for the author by C. Heyer, 184. 96 p. ICU; MB; MH; TxU-T. 44-1261

Cavender, Thomas S. Tribute to memory of Rudolph Justice delivered before the Euphradian Society of Philadelphia. October 7, 1843, ...Philadelphia: 1844. 334 p. MB; MBNEH; PHi; PSC-Hi. 44-1262

Cecil, Richard. Friendly visit to the house of mourning. By Richard Cecil, M.A.... Boston: Tract committee.... of Massachusetts, 1844. 34 p. MB; MBD; MHi. 44-1263

Celebrated women. Philadelphia: Thomas, 1844. MiKL. 44-1264

Celebration of the fifty-seventh anniversary of the settlement of Ohio, April 8, 1844. Cincinnati: E. Morgan and company, 1844. 23 p. CSmH; OClWHi; OMC; PHi. 44-1265

Central Clay Club of Allegheny County, Pennsylvania. Address of the executive committee of the Central Clay Club to the people of Pennsylvania, 1844. Pittsburgh: printed at the office of the Gazette and Advertiser [1844] 24 p. OO. 44-1266

Cervantes Saavedra, Miguel de, 1547-1616. El ingerioso hidalgo Don Quijote de la Mancha... Y anotada por Don Eugenio de Ochoa. New edition. New York: Appleton, 1844. 695 p. PU. 44-1267

Chadler, Joseph R. The Freemason. Vol. 1. Louisville. July, 1844. Masonic character of Washington. Delivered before Mount Moriah Lodge, Pennsylvania. By Joseph R. Chandler, esq. Louisville, Kentucky: 1844. MH: PPFM. 44-1268

Chahta almanac. Pork Hill: Mission Press, 1844. MWA. 44-1269

Chailly-Honore, Nicolas Charles, 1805-1866. A practical treatise on midwifery. By M. Chailly.... A work adopted by the royal council of public instructions. Translated from the French and edited by Gunning S. Bedford.... New York: Harper and brothers, 1844. 530 p. CSt-L; ICJ; LNT-M; MdBJ-W; PU. 44-1270

Challoner, Richard, 1691-1781. The Catholic Christian instructed in the sacraments, sacrifice, ceremonies, and observances of the church. By way of question and answer...Baltimore: Metropolitan Press, 1844. 247 p. GAM-R; ICU; MdBS; MnSS; NRSB. 44-1271

Challoner, Richard, 1691-1781. The grounds of the old religion: or, some general arguments in favour of the Catholic, Apostolic, Roman, communion: Collected from both ancient and modern controvertists, by the Rt. Rev. and venerable Richard Challoner, D.D., V.A. ....New York: D. Murphy, 1844. 223 p. MiD; MoSU; NStc; WStfSF. 44-1272

Challoner, Richard, 1691-1781. Think well on't; or reflections on the great truths of the Christian religion. Baltimore: Metropolitan Press, 1844. 171 p. NoLoc. 44-1273

Chalmers, Thomas, 1780-1847. On natural theology. By Thomas Chalmers, ... New York: Robert Carter; Pittsburg: Thomas Carter, 1844. 2 v. CSt; KyHe; NbOP; PPWe. 44-1274

Chalmers, Thomas, 1780-1847. Sermons and Discourses. First complete American edition, from the last Glasgow stereotype edition, revised and corrected by the author. New York: Robert Carter; Pittsburg: Thomas Carter, 1844. 2 v. NNUT; PU; ViLxW; ViU. 44-1275

Chalmers, Thomas, 1780-1847. Sermons and Discourses. First complete American edition. Second edition. New York: Robert Carter, 1844. 2 v. ICU; NN; ODW; PU; ViU. 44-1276

Chalmers, Thomas, 1780-1847. The works of Thomas Chalmers. Fifth uniform edition. New York: Robert Carter, 1844. 2 v. KBB; OMC; ViW. 44-1277

Chamberlain, N.B. Catalogue of pneumatic instruments, with experiments. Boston: Butts, 1844. 56 p. CtY; IaDaM; MHi; MoU; NRU. 44-1278

Chamberlain, N.B. A price catalogue of pneumatic apparatus. Compiled by N. B. Chamberlain. Boston: Isaac R. Butts, 1844. 14 p. IaDaM; M; MChiA; MiOC. 44-1279

Chambers, Robert. Cyclopedia of English literature. From the earliest to the present time. Philadelphia: J. B. Lippincott Co., 1844. IaMU; MWA. 44-1280

Chambers, Thomas. Letter of G. Evans, against the repeal of duty on railway iron by the tariff act of 1842. Philadelphia: 1844. 17 p. MBAt; P. 44-1281

Chamerovzow, Louis Alexis. Chronicles of the Bastile, an historical romance, to comprise the secret history of the celebrated "Bastile St. Antoine," from the period of its erection to that of its demolition. Philadelphia: Lea and Blanchard, 1844. PPM. 44-1282

Chamisso, Adelbert von, 1781-1838. The wonderful history of Peter Schlemihl by Adelbert von Chamisso. Translated by William Howitt. Original edition. New York: Burgess and Stringer, 1844. 42 p. CtY; KyDC; MBAt; NjR; PHC. 44-1283

Chandler, Joseph Ripley. Masonic discourses containing an inaugural and valedictory address as grand masters, and addresses on occasions of grand visitations. Philadelphia: Barrington and Geo. D. Haswell, 1844. 223 p. ICN; NIC; OCM; RPMA; TxWFM. 44-1284

Chandler, Peleg Whitman, 1816-1889. American criminal trials. By Peleg W. Chandler, member of the American Antiquarian Society and of the Massachusetts Historical Society.... Boston: Timothy H. Carter and company; London: A. Maxwell, 1844. 2 v. IaU; LU-L; MdHi; MeB; NjP. 44-1285

Chandler, Peleg Whitman, 1816-1889. The morals of freedom; an oration delivered before the authorities of the city of Boston, July 4, 1844. Boston: John

H. Eastburn, 1844. 54 p. CtSoP; ICU; MBC; MeB; NjR. 44-1286

Channing, Walter, 1786-1876. An address delivered before the American Peace Society, at its annual meeting, May 27, 1844. Boston: printed by William S. Damrell, 1844. 38 p. ICU; RHi. 44-1287

Channing, Walter, 1786-1876. A plea for pure water: being a letter to Henry Williams, esq., with an address to the citizens of Boston, by Mr. H. Williams. [Boston: 1844] 39 p. CtY; MBC; MH-M; MWA; OO. 44-1288

Channing, Walter, 1786-1876. Thoughts on peace and war, an address.... before the American Peace Society, at its annual meeting, May 27, 1844. Boston: American Peace Society, 1844. 38 p. ICMe; MBC; NNUT; PHC; RPB. 44-1289

Chapin, Alonzo Bowen, 1808-1858. The state of religion in England and Germany compared; being an examination of a review of "New Englandism not the religion of the Bible," in the New Englander for April, 1844. By Juris Consultus. ....Hartford: Henry S. Parsons, 1844. 40 p. CSmH; CtY; NNG; OO; PPLT. 44-1290

Chapin, Edwin Hubbell. 1814-1880. The catastrophe of the Princeton. A discourse, upon the recent national calamity, preached at the Universalist Church, Charlestown, and at Chardon Street Chapel, Boston, on the afternoon and evening of March 3, 1844. Boston: A. Tompkins... 1844. 16 p. MB; Nh-Hi; MWo; PPL-R. 44-1291

Chapin, Edwin Hubbell, 1814-1880. A

discourse preached in the Universalist Church, Charlestown, on Sunday, May 12, 1844, in reference to the recent riots in Philadelphia. By E.H. Chapin. Boston: A. Tompkins, 1844. 16 p. MB; MeHi; OO. 44-1292

Chapin, Edwin Habbell, 1814-1880. Massachusetts election sermon. January 3, 1844. Boston: 1844. 36 p. MoSpD; PHi. 44-1293

Chapin, Edwin Habbell, 1814-1880. The Philadelphia riots. A discourse preached in the Universalist Church, Charlestown, on Sunday, May 12, 1844.... By E.H. Chapin. Boston: A. Tompkins, 1844. 16 p. MiD-B. 44-1294

Chapin, Edwin Hubbell, 1814-1880. The relation of the individual to the republic. A sermon delivered before his excellency Henry H. Childs, governor.... the honorable council and the legislature of Massachusetts, at the annual election, on Wednesday, January 3, 1844. Boston: Dutton and Wentworth, 1844. 36 p. CBPac; IaHi; MBAt; MH; PCC. 44-1295

Chapin, Edwin Habbell, 1814-1880. A sermon delivered before his excellency Marcus Morton, governor, his honor Henry H. Childs, lieutenant governor, the honorable council.... of Massachusetts, at the annual election, on Wednesday, January 3, 1844. By E.H. Chapin.... Boston: Dutton and Wentworth, printers to the state, 1844. 36 p. MLow; MMeT-Hi; MNe; MTop; Nh. 44-1296

Chapin, Joel. An analytic and philosophical grammar. [Opus minor] By Joel Chapin, ...New York: Collins,

brothers and company, 1844. 108 p. NbU; NNC. 44-1297

Chapin, Joshua Bicknell. Tenotomy: its advantages and disadvantages. By Joshua Bicknell Chapin, M.D. ....Boston: Thomas H. Webb and company, 1844. 22 p. MB; MBM; MH-M; NNC-M. 44-1298

Chapin, William. A complete reference gazetteer of the United States of North America; containing a general view of the United States and of each state and territory and a notice of internal improvements.... New York: T. and E.H. Ensign, 1844. 371 p. NGH; NNA; OClWHi; PLFM; Vi. 44-1299

Chapin, William. Reference gazetteer of the United States of North America. New York: 1844. NNer. 44-1300

Chaplin, Jeremiah, 1813-1886. Tekel: a discourse occasioned by the late calamity on board the United States' ship Princeton. Delivered Sunday, March 10, 1844, by Jeremiah Chaplin, pastor of the First Baptist Church, Bangor, Maine. Bangor: Samuel S. Smith, printer, 1844. 24 p. CSmH; MeBaT; MWA. 44-1301

Chapman, C.C. Scientific amusements; for the old and the young, the grave and the gay. Designed for centre table and fire side recreation. By C.C.C. Philadelphia: stereotyped by S. D. Wyeth, 1844. 29 p. CSmH; DLC; MH; MWA; PHi. 44-1302

Chapman, Edwin. The life of our lord and Saviour Jesus Christ. Written especially for children and youth. Boston: 1844. 159 p. MB; MH; MH-AH. 44-1303

Chapman, F.W. The Chapman family;

or the descendants of Robert Chapman, one of the first settlers of Saybrook, Connecticut, with genealogical notes. Hartford: Printed by Case, Tiffany and company, 413 p. MPiB. 44-1304

Chapman, F.W. The Pratt family; or the descendants of Lieut. William Pratt, on the first settlers of Hartford and Saybrook, with genealogical notes. Hartford: Printed by Case, Lockwood, and company, 1844. 420 p. MPiB. 44-1305

Chapman, George Thomas. Sermons, upon the ministry, worship, and doctrines, of the Protestant Episcopal Church. By G.T. Chapman, D.D......Third edition. Boston: Charles Stimpson, 1844. 312 p. IEG; GMM; MBD; NjR. 44-1306

Chapman, Nathaniel, 1780-1853. Lectures on the more important diseases of the thoracic and abdominal viscera. Delivered in the University of Pennsylvania... Philadelphia: Lea and Blanchard, 1844. [13]-383 p. CtMW; GEU-M; NRAM; PP; ViRA. 44-1307

Chapman, Nathaniel, 1780-1853. Lectures on the more important eruptive fevers, haemorrhages and dropsies, and on gout and rheumatism. Delivered in the University of Pennsylvania... Philadelphia: Lea and Blanchard, 1844. [13]-448 p. CSt-L; DLC; KyLxT; PPCP; RNR. 44-1308

Chapman. The news boy; a new comic song. Boston: 1844. 5 p. MB; MBAt. 44-1309

Chappell, Absalom Harris. Address of Honorable A.H. Chappell, to the people

of Georgia. Washington: J. Heart, printer [1844] CSmH. 44-1310

Character of Romanism as developed in history. "I saw the woman drunken with the blood of the Saints and with the blood of the martyrs of Jesus," New York: American Protestant Society, 1844. 12 p. ICP. 44-1311

Charles, Edmund. Suggestions upon the nature and disadvantages of the present post office tariff, ...New York: the author, 1844. 15 p. MiU. 44-1312

Charles, Thomas. Geiriadur Yagrythyrol; yn cynnwys arwyddocad geiriau anghyfiaith, ynghyd ag enwau ac hanesion yr amrywiol genedloedd, teyrnasoedd, a dinasoedd, y crybwyllir am danynt yn yr ysgrythyrau. Gan y diweddar Barchedig Thomas Charles of Bala. Llyfr I. Utica: Evan E. Roberts, 1844. CSmH; MH. 44-1313

Charles, Thomas. Geiriadur Yagrythyrol....[A dictionary of the Bible in Welsh] Utica: 1844-45. CSmH; CtY; MH. 44-1314

Charles, firm, exchange brokers, New York. Suggestions upon the nature and disadvantages of the present post office tariff showing the injurious effects of the high rates of postage, especially on letter containing enclosures.... By.... Edmund Charles and son....New York: E. Charles and son, 1844. 15 p. DLC. 44-1315

Charles Prindle's almanac. New Haven, 1844. MBC. 44-1316

Charleston, South Carolina. Ordinances, etc. A digest of the ordinances of the city council of Charleston, from the year

1783 to October, 1844. To which are annexed the acts of the legislature which relate exclusively to the city of Charleston. Prepared under resolution of the city council by George B. Eckhard. Charleston: Walker and Burke, printers, 1844. 517 p. CtY; DLC; NcD; ScC; TxU. 44-1317

Charlestown, Massachusetts. List of persons assessed a state, town, and county tax in the town of Charlestown. 1844. ICU. 44-1318

Charlestown, Massachusetts. First Universalist Church. Articles of faith, plan of church government, and covenant, proposed by the general convention of Universalists, in the year of our Lord 1803. Charlestown: 1844. 16 p. M; MHi. 44-1319

Charton, M.S. Methode Chartonnienne, ou Methode naturelle theorisee. Washington: The author, 1844. MH. 44-1320

Chase, Irah, 1793-1864. Remarks on the book of Daniel, in regard to the four kingdoms. Boston: Gould, Kendall and Lincoln, 1844. 84 p. ICU. 44-1321

Chase, Philander, 1775-1852. Bishop Chase's letter; and review of Jubilee College. New York: Alexander V. Blake, 1844 32 p. MWA. 44-1322

Chase, Philander, 1775-1852. A consecration sermon... Preached in Christ Church, Philadelphia, October 20, 1844. New York: James A. Parks, 1844. 22 p. Nh; PPL. 44-1323

Chase, Philander, 1775-1852. The law and the prophets fulfilled in Christ. A

consecration sermon... preached in Christ Theological Church. Phiadelphia, October 24, 1844. New York: James A. Sparks, 1844. 22 p. ICN; MH; OClWHi; PPULC; TxDaM. 44-1324

Chase, Philander, 1775-1852. Letters to his absent friends. New York: 1844. NoLoc. 44-1325

Chase, Philander, 1775-1852. Reminiscences of Bishop Chase. New York: A.V. Blake, 1844. 2 v. DLC; KyU. 44-1326

Chase, Philander, 1775-1852. Sermon. Philadelphia. October 20, 1844. "The law and the prophets fulfilled in Christ." Consecration sermon. New York: 1844. OCHP. 44-1327

Chase, Pliny Earle, 1820-1886. The elements of arithmetic.... in which decimal and integral arithmetic are combined, and taught inductively, on the system of Pestalozzi. Part first. Philadelphia: U. Hunt and son, 1844. 144 p. CSt; DLC; InRchE; MH; PHC. 44-1328

Chateaubriand, Francois Auguste Rene, Viscomte de. Atala; or the love and constancy of two savages in the desert. Translated by M.J. Smead and H.P. Lefebore. New York: 1844. PHC. 44-1329

Chavasse, Pye Henry, 1810-1879. Advice to mother's [sic] on the management of their offspring. During the periods of infancy, childhood, and youth. From the third English edition. New York: D. Appleton and company, [1844] 153 p. MB; MoSpD; MWA; NbG; PP. 44-1330

Cheever, George Barrell, 1807-1890. American commonplace book of prose.

Cooperstown, New York: H. and E. Phinney, 1844. 468 p. ICU; MBAt; MH; NjMD; NSherb. 44-1331

Cheever, George Barrell, 1807-1890. The dream; or the true history of Deacon Giles' Distillery, and Deacon Jones' Drewery... New York: 1844. 48 p. DLC; MH; MnU; NN. 44-1332

Cheever, George Barrell, 1807-1890. A hierarchical despotism. Lectures on the mixture of civil and ecclesiastical power in the governments of the middle ages. In illustration of the despotism in the Romish church. New York: Saxton and Miles, 1844. 418 p. CtY; MoWgT; NjR; PBa; RPAt. 44-1333

Cheever, George Barrell, 1807-1890. Lectures on pilgrims progress and on the life and times of John Bunyan. New York: Wiley and Putnam, 1844. 514 p. ICT; MdBE; MTop; NbOP; RNR. 44-1334

Cheever, George Barrell, 1807-1890. Mr. Cheever's lectures on the Pilgrim's progress and on the life and times of John Bunyan. Number 3. New York: Wiley and Putnam, 1844. 128 p. MdBLC; MWA; NjR. 44-1335

Cheever, George Barrell, 1807-1890. Sophisms of the apostolical succession. Lecture IV. New York: 1844. 120 p. MBAt; ICP. 44-1336

Cheever, George Barrell, 1807-1890. The true history of deacon Giles' distillery. Reported for the benefit of posterity. New York: 1844. 48 p. DLC; MeB; MnU; Nh; RWe. 44-1337

Cheney, Harriet V. Sketches from the

life of Christ. Boston: 1844. 147 p. MWA; NBLIHI; TNM. 44-1338

The Cherokee advocate. Tahlequah, Cherokee Nation: 1844. CtY; DLC; ICN; TxU. 44-1339

Cherokee Messenger. Tsalagi at-sinvsidv. Cherokee Baptist Mission Press, 1844-1846. 192 p. ICN; MH; RPB; WHi. 44-1340

Cherokee Nation. The constitution and laws of the Cherokee Nation: passed at Tah-le-quah Cherokee Nation. Washington: 1844. 44 p. NoLoc. 44-1341

Cherwell, Mary. Happy hours; or, the home story book. By Mary Cherwell. New York: Wiley and Putnam, 1844. 202 p. MBAt; MChiA. 44-1342

Chesapeake and Ohio Canal Company. Communication of the president of the Chesapeake and Ohio Canal Company, enclosing a law passed by the Legislature of Virginia on the twentieth instant, to amend the Charter of said company, and asking the assent of the Legislature of Maryland thereto. Annapolis: William M'Neir, 1844. 8 p. ViU. 44-1343

Chesapeake and Ohio Canal Company. Report of the president... giving a state-ment of the amount expanded on the canal from its eastern teminus to dam no. 5. and thence to Cumberland. [An-napolis? 1844] 16 p. ViU. 44-1344

Chesapeake and Ohio Canal Company. Report of the president relative to ex-aminations and surveys made with reference to a dam or slack water naviga-tion from dam no. 6 to Cumberland, 40. [Annapolis, 1844] 9 p. ViU. 44-1345

Chesapeake and Ohio Canal Company. Some considerations on the question of completion.... Baltimore: Joseph Robinson, printer, 1844. 50 p. DLC; MdHi; MH-BA; NNC. 44-1346

Chesapeake and Ohio Canal Company. Some considerations on the special report of the president and directors of the Chesapeake and Ohio Canal Company, on the subject of completing the canal to Cumberland, made November 16th, 1843, in a series of letters addressed to John Johnson, esq., member of the house of delegates, and published in the "American." Baltimore: Bull and Tuttle, printers, 1844. 24 p. MdHi. 44-1347

The chess player's handbook; containing a full account of the game of chess, and the best mode of playing. Boston: Saxton Pierce and company [etc., etc.] 1844. 8-67 p. MH; MWA; OCl; NjP; PP. 44-1348

Chester, Albert Tracy. God's dealing with the aged: a funeral sermon, occasioned by the death of Mrs. Abigail Davison, mother of G.M. and Clement Davison... Saratoga Springs: printed by G.M. Davison and company, 1844. 24 p. NBLlHI; NCH; VtMidSM. 44-1349

Chesterfield, Philip Dormer Stanhope, 1694-1773. Chesterfield's advice to this son, on men and manners; in which the principles of politeness, and the art of acquiring a knowledge of the world, are laid down. To which are annexed the polite Philosopher: or an essay on the art which makes a man happy in himself and agreeable to others... Portsmouth [New Hampshire] W.B. and T.Q. Lowd, 1844. 223 p. CSmH; DLC; MB. 44-1350

Cheves, Langdon, 1776-1857. Letter of the Hon. Langdon Cheves, to the editors of the Charleston Mercury, September 11, 1844. [Charleston: printed by Walker and Burke, 1844] 15 p. A-Ar; MiD-B; PHi; RPB; ScU. 44-1351

Chicago Medical Journal and Examiner. The Illinois medical and surgical journal. Edited by James V.Z. Blaney. Chicago, Illinois: Ellis and Fergus, 1844. V. 1-. NNNAM. 44-1352

Child, David Lee, 1794-1874. An appeal from David L. Child, editor of the anti-slavery standard, to the abolitionists. Albany: Albany Evening Journal, 1844? 24 p. CtY; MB; OClWHi. 44-1353

Child, Lydia Maria Francis, 1802-1880. American frugal housewife, dedicated to those who are not ashamed of economy. New York: 1844. 130 p. CtHWatk; IaHA; MH; MSa; RWe. 44-1354

Child, Lydia Maria Francis, 1802-1880. Flowers for children. New York: C.S. Francis and company; Boston: J.H. Francis, 1844-1847. 3 v. CtY; MWA; NCD; RPB. 44-1355

Child, Lydia Maria Francis, 1802-1880. Letters from New York. Second edition. New York: C.S. Francis and company; Boston: J. H. Francis, 1844. 2 v. Cty; MWC; PP. 44-1356

Child, Lydia Maria Francis, 1802-1880. Letters from New York. Third edition. New York: C.S. Francis and company; Boston: J. H. Francis, 1844. 288 p. DLC; StTeachC. 44-1357

Child, Lydia Maria Francis, 1802-1880. Letters from New York. Second series...

Fifth edition. New York: C.S. Francis and company; Boston: J. H. Francis, 1844. 287 p.NSyU. 44-1358

Child, Lydia Maria Francis, 1802-1880. The mother's book. Sixth edition with corrections and additions by the author. New York: C.S. Francis and company; Boston: J.H. Francis, 1844. 175 p. DLC; MBAU; MiU; PNt; ViR. 44-1359

The child's cabinet of beasts and birds. Greenfield, Massachusetts: A. Phelps, 1844. NoLoc. 44-1360

The child's friend; designed for families and Sunday schools; edited by Eliza L. Follen. V. 1-2, October, 1843 to September, 1844. Boston: Leonard C. Bowles, 1844. 2 v. in 1. MoSW. 44-1361

The Child's gem for 1845. Boston [1844] MB. 44-1362

The child's instructor improved: consisting of easy lessons for children; on subjects which are familiar to them, in language adapted to their capacities... By a teacher of little children in Philadelphia. Improved by John C. Totten... Newark: 1844. CtY; NN. 44-1363

Child's prayer and hymn book, for the use of Catholic Sunday schools... Baltimore: J. Murphy, 1844. 220 p. DLC; MnSS. 44-1364

The childrens new church magazine... V. 1. Boston: O. Clapp, 1844-. 141 p. DLC; PBa; RPB. 44-1365

Childs, Henry Halsey, 1783-1868. Introductory lecture before the Willoughby University. By Professor H.H. Childs, of

Massachusetts [n.p.: 1844?] 27 p. NN; OClWHi. 44-1366

Childs, Henry Halsey, 1783-1868. Philosophy of general principles: an introductory lecture delivered before the medical class of the Berkshire Medical Institution, August 1, 1844. Pittsfield, Massachusetts: C. Montague, 1844. 32 p. CtY; DNLM; NN; OClW; PBL. 44-1367

Chillingworth, William, 1602-1644. The works of W. Chillingworth, M.A., containing his book, entitled "The religion of Protestants, a safe way to salvation," ....First American from the twelfth English edition, complete in one volume. With life by Birch.... Philadelphia: R. Davis, 1844. 764 p. CtY; GEU; KyDC; NjR; PPLT. 44-1368

Chilton, Thomas. The engineers' text book, and general mechanics' pocket guide: By Thomas Chilton and Paxton Thompson.... Boston: S.N. Dickinson, 1844. 236 p. MB; NNE. 44-1369

Chipman, Samuel, b. 1786. Report of an examination of poorhouses, jails, &c., in the state of New York, and in the counties of Berkshire, Massachusetts; Litchfield, Connecticut; Bennington, Vermont, &c., addressed to Aristarchus Champion, esquire, of Rochester, New York. Albany: executive committee of the New York State Temperance Society, 1844. 96 p. NRHi. 44-1370

Chipman, Samuel, b. 1786. The temperance lecturer: being facts gathered from a personal examination of all the jails and poorhouses of the state of New York, and of numbers in Maine, Pennsylvania, Delaware, Ohio, Indiana, etc., showing the effects of intoxicating drinks in producing taxes, pauperism and crime. Also facts showing the number and proportion of deaths from intemperance....etc., addressed to Aristarchus Champion, esq. By Samuel Chipman. Albany: 1844. 70 p. CU; ICU; MeLewB. 44-1371

Chitty, Joseph, 1776-1841. Pleading and parties to actions with a second volume containing modern precedents of pleadings, and practical notes. Ninth American edition. Springfield: John A. Dunlap, E.D. Ingraham, and J.C. Perkins, 1844. MH-L; PPB; PU-L. 44-1372

Chitty, Joseph, 1776-1841. A practical treatise on the law of contracts.... by Joseph Chitty, junior. ....Sixth American edition from the third London edition. ....By Thompson Chitty.... with notes of American and late English decisions.... By J.C. Perkins.... Springfield: G. and C. Meriam, 1844. 947 p. CtMW; InU; LU; NIC-M; WaU. 44-1373

Choate, Rufus. Speech.... on the question of annulling the convention for the common occupation of the Territory of Oregon; and in reply to Mr. Buchanan. Delivered in the Senate.... March 21, 1844. Washington: 1844. 34 p. MBAt; MWA. 44-1374

Choate, Rufus. Speech upon the subject of protecting American labor, by duties on imports. Delivered in the Senate 12th and 15th of April, 1844. Washington: 1844. 52 p. MH; MiGr; NjR. 44-1375

Choctaw Indians. Memorial of J.T.H. Claiborne praying that the law of 1842, creating the Choctaw Commission, be repeated; and that provision be made to satisfy the just claim of the Choctaw Indians and for their removal from the state of Mississippi, February 19, 1844. Referred to the committee on Indian affairs. Printed by order of the House of Representatives. Washington: Blair and Rives, printers, 1844. 6 p. MsJs. 44-1376

The choice medley; or, "here a little and there a little" by a mother written for the American Sunday School Union, and revised by the committee of publication. Philadelphia: American Sunday School Union, 1844. 123 p. ICartC. 44-1377

Choules, J.O. History of missions. Seventh edition. New York: 1844. 2 v. MB. 44-1378

Christian Home Missionary Society. Quarterly report. Philadelphia: Barrett, 1844. V. 1-. PPULC; PU. 44-1379

Christian instructor. Newburgh, New York: Proudfit, 1844-. v.1-. MnSM; NjR; PPPrHi. 44-1380

Christian life of the early Friends. New Bedford, Massachusetts: Lindsey's press for William C. Taber, 1844. 32 p. MNBedf. 44-1381

The Christian parlor magazine. New York: 1844. V. 1. CSmH; DLC; MBC; OCl; RPB. 44-1382

Christian retirement. New York: 1844. v.1. MdAS. 44-1383

Christians book, containing extracts from Rev. Messrs Wesley, Fletcher, Mahan, Upham, and others... on Christian perfection. Boston: Scott, 1844. 300 p. IEG; OO; TxDaM. 44-1384

Christmas tales. New York: C.S. Francis and company; Boston: J.H. Francis, 1844. [9]-255 p. LNH. 44-1385

The church almanac for the year of our Lord, 1845. New York: Protestant Episcopal Tract Society [1844] 36 p. MWA; WHi. 44-1386

Church of England. Homilies. Certain sermons or homilies appointed to be read in churches in the time of Queen Elizabeth; and reprinted by authority from King James I., A.D. 1623. Third American from the last English edition. Philadelphia: George and Wayne, 1844. 678 p. InID; MiDU; NcAS; Nh; PCA; ViAl. 44-1387

Church of Jesus Christ of Latter-day Saints. Collection of sacred hymns, for the use of the Latter Day Saints. Bellows Falls: Blake and Bailey, 1844. 80 p. MH; Vt. 44-1388

Church psalmist; or psalms and hymns, for the public, social, and private use of Evangelical Christians. New York: Mark H. Newman, 1844. 668 p. NN. 44-1389

Churchill, Fleetwood, 1808-1878. The diseases of females: including those of pregnancy and childbirth. By Fleetwood Churchill.... Third American edition.... With notes by Robert M. Huston.... Philadelphia: Lea and Blanchard, 1844. 571 p. GEU-M; ICJ; LNT; NNN. 44-1390

The churchman armed: containing Palmer's ecclesiastical history and Bishop Hobart's apology. New York: Stanford and Swords, 1844. 273 p. CtY; GDecCT; ICN; MdBD. 44-1391

The churchman's library: a series of publications, original and from the English press, issued in monthly numbers. New York: J.R. Dunham, 1844-1845. 2 v. CtY; ICU; MiDD; OCl; PP. 44-1392

Cicero, Marcus Tullius. Ciceronis orationes of quaedam selectae, notis illustratae. In usum Academiae Exoniensis. Editio stereotypa, tabulis analyticis instructa. Boston: [1844?] CtY. 44-1393

Cicero, Marcus Tullius. The orations, translated by Duncan. The offices by Cockman, and the Cato and Laelius by Melmoth. New York: Harper, 1844. 3 v. MH; MLow; MWiW; ViRU; WU. 44-1394

Cicero, Marcus Tullius. De oratore. ed. Kingsley. M. Tulllii Ciceronis Ad Quintum fratrem dialogi tres de oratore. Cum excerptis ex notis variorum. Ed. 4. Jac. L. Kingsley.... New York: Alexander V. Blake, 1844. CtY; NiP; NRU; ViU. 44-1395

Cicero, Marcus Tullius. Pro Cluentio. ed. Johnson. M. Tullii Ciceronis Oratio pro Cluentio Avito ad judices. Edited by E. A. Johnson.... New York: 1844. 100 p. CSt; CtY; KyBC; TxU; ViU. 44-1396

Cicero, Marcus Tullius. Select orations.... With English notes.... By Charles Anthon.... A new edition.... New York: Harper, 1844. 518 p. CtY; ICU; OOtP; PPWe; ScK. 44-1397

Cincinnati. Memorial of the citizens of Cincinnati, relative to the navigation of the Ohio and Mississippi Rivers. Cincinnati: Printed at the Daily Atlas office,

1844. 53 p. CSmH; KyU; MH; MdBJ; OCHP. 44-1398

Cincinnati. Tabernacle Church. Brief history: together with the standing rules, articles of faith and covenant, and a list of the members. Cincinnati, Ohio: Faulkner, 1844. PPPrHi. 44-1399

Cincinnati. University Medical College of Ohio. Catalogue of students for 1843-1844 and annual announcement for 1844-1845 of the Medical College of Ohio. Cincinnati: Printed by R.P. Brooks, 1844. 16 p. OC. 44-1400

Cincinnati Astronomical Society. The annual address delivered before the Cincinnati Astronomical Society, June 3, 1844, by the Hon. Jacob Burnot, together with the act of incorporation, the constitution and the annual reports, and the catalogue of the stockholders. Cincinnati: Printed at the Daily Atlas office, 1844. 46 p. DLC; MH; OC; OClWHi; OCU. 44-1401

The Cincinnati business directory; as also, the regular city directory with a supplement, containing the changes of firms, residences, etc. Cincinnati, Ohio: R.P. Brooks, 1844. CoD; DLC; MH; KHi. 44-1402

Cincinnati Classical Academy. Catalogue. List of students. Cincinnati: 1844. 7 p. OCHP. 44-1403

Cincinnati Master Carpenters' and Joiners' Society. Book of Prices of the House Carpenters and Joiners of the city of Cincinnati. Cincinnati: 1844. OC. 44-1404

Cincinnati Morning Herald. Cincinnati: 1844-. v. 1-. VtBrt. 44-1405

Cincinnati Type Foundry, Cincinnati, Ohio. Speciments of printing types and ornaments from the Cincinnati Type Foundry, by Horace Wells, agent. Cincinnati: 1844. NNC. 44-1406

Ciocci, Raffaele. A narrative of iniquities and barbarities practised at Rome in the nineteenth century. ....Philadelphia: Jame M. Campbell, 1844. 140 p. CtY; MB; NjPT; NjR; PPL. 44-1407

Circular to the members of the Protestant Episcopal Church in and near Charleston. By the bishop of the Diocese of South Carolina. Charleston: Miller and Browne, 1844. 3 p. WHi. 44-1408

Circumnavigation of the globe. New York: Harper and Brothers, 1844. 366 p. MsU; OCX. 44-1409

The citizen's law book... with notes: together with a large amount of useful and interesting legal information. By a member of the bar. New York: Printed by Henry Ludwig, 1844. 464 p. IaU-L. NNLI; NSchHi. NIC. 44-1410

Citizens and farmer's almanac for 1845. Calculations by Edward Hagerty. Philadelphia: Desilver and Muir [1844] MdHI; MWA. 44-1411

Citizens' Bank of Louisiana, New Orleans. Report to the Senate, February 2, 1844 [New Orleans, 1844] 4 p. LU. 44-1412

Civis, pseud. Romanism incompatible with republican institutions. New York:

American Protestant Society, 1844. 107 p. NNUT; TWcW; VtMidb. 44-1413

Claggett, Rufus. The American expositor,.... designed for the use of schools. By R. Claggett, A.M., ... Stereotype edition. New York: Saxton and Miles; Boston: Saxton and Peirce, 1844. 190 p. MiD-B; NNC. 44-1414

Claiborne, John F.H. Memorial praying that the laws of 1842, creating the Choctaw commission, be repealed and that provision be made for the removal from the state of Mississippi of the Choctaw Indians. Washington: Blair and Rives, printers, 1844. 6 p. MsJS. 44-1415

The claims of the Free Church of Scotland: an article from the Princeton Review, for April, 1844. Princeton: John T. Robinson, 1844. 35 p. ICU; MBC; NjR; NN; PPPrHi. 44-1416

Clairville, Louis Francois Nicolaie. Satan in Paris; or, the mysterious stranger, a drama in 2 acts adapted.... from a vaudeville, by M. Clairville et Damarin. Called Satan; ou, Le. diable a Paris, by Charles Selby.... New York: S. French, [1844] 70 p. C; OCl. 44-1417

Clap, Roger, 1609-1691. Memoirs of Roger Clap. 1630. Boston: D. Clapp, Jr., 1844. [17]-62 p. CtSoP; DLC; IU; MeHi; NcD; RPB. 44-1418

Clark, Davis Wasgatt, bp., 1812-1871. An alarm to Christian patriots. A Thanksgiving sermon, delivered November 30th, 1843, in the Methodist Episcopal Church, in Winsted, Connecticut. By Rev. D. W. Clark.... Published by request. Hartford: Press of E. Geer, 1844.

23 p. CtMW; ICT; MnHi; MWA; PHi. 44-1419

Clark, George W. The liberty minstrel. First edition. New York: Leavitt and Allen, 1844. CtY; GEU; IHi; PPM; TxU. 44-1420

Clark, George W. The liberty minstrel. Seventh edition. New York: Published by the author, [1844] 214 p. DHU; MB; NcU; NjP; OCl. 44-1421

Clark, Joel W. Miniature of Dansville Village: humbly inscribed to the first settlers and their immediate descendants. Dansville, New York: 1844. 72 p. MH; NBLiHi. 44-1422

Clark, John A. Gathered fragments. New York: Robert Carter; Pittsburg: Thomas Carter, 1844. MdBMC. 44-1423

Clark, John Alonzo, 1801-1843. Awake thou sleeper! A series of awakening discourses. New York: Carter, 1844. 244 p. DLC; MBC; NjPT; OrPD; PU. 44-1424

Clark, Nancy M. Triumph of faith or memoir of, destined on a mission to western Asia, under the direction of the American board. Second edition. Boston: 1844. NoLoc. 44-1425

Clark, Willis Gaylord, 1808-1841. The literary remains of the late Willis Gaylord Clak. Including the Ollapodiana papers, the Spirit of life and a selection from his various prose and poetical writings. Edited by Lewis Gaylord Clark. New York: Burgess, Stringer and company, 1844. 480 p. CtMW; DeWi; IaK; RPAt; TxU. 44-1426

Clarke, Adam. A dissertation on the use

and abuse of tobacco wherein the advantages and disadvantages attending the consumption of that entertaining weed are particularly considered. Sixth edition with additions. Baltimore: printed for the publisher by R.J. Matchett, 1844. 31 p. MdHi. 44-1427

Clarke, Calvin. Christian submission. A sermon preached at the funeral of Mrs. Susan Heard Cleaveland, [wife of the Rev. John P. Cleaveland] who died at Marshall, Michigan, October 1st, 1843, by the Rev. Calvin Clarke of Kalamazoo. Cincinnati: Shepard and company, printer, 1844. 32 p. CSmH; MBAt; MWA: OClWHi; PPPrHi. 44-1428

Clarke, Charles C. The little Gardener. Boston: 1844. 168 p. MWA. 44-1429

Clarke, Charlotte. The kingdom of heaven among children, twenty-five narratives of a religious awakening in a school in Pomerania, by Charlotte Clarke; revised by D. P. Kidder. New York: G. Lane and C. B. Tippett, 1844. NjMD. 44-1430

Clarke, James Freeman, 1810-1888. The annexation of Texas. A sermon, delivered in the Masonic temple on fast day. Published in compliance with a vote of the Church of the Disciples. Boston: Office of the Christian World, 1844. 42 p. MBAt; MH-AH; MWA; RPB; TxU. 44-1431

Clarke, James Freeman, 1810-1888. The peculiar doctrine of Christianity. First series. No. 208. Boston: James Munroe and company, 1844. 24 p. ICMe; MeB; MH; NjR; RP. 44-1432

Clarke, James Freeman, 1810-1888.

Sermon delivered in the masonic temple on fast day. [The annexation of Texas] Boston: 1844. 42 p. PHi; TxHuT. 44-1433

Clarke, Julius L. Constitution of the United States, with the amendments. To which is appended a table of comparative statistics showing the division of power and patronage of the general government between the free and slave states. Worcester: Julius L. Clarke, 1844. 34 p. MPiB; MWA. 44-1434

Clarke, M.G. Christian baptism, and church communion. By M.G. Clarke, pastor of the Central Baptist Church, Norwich, Connecticut. Norwich, Connecticut: John G. Cooley, 1844. [13]-141 p. LnB; MBC; NjPT; RPB. 44-1435

Clarke, Walter, 1812-1871. The American Anti-slavery Society at war with the church. A discourse, delivered before the First Congregational Church and Society, in Canterbury, Connecticut, June 30th, 1844. By Walter Clarke.... Hartford: press of E. Geer, 1844. 21 p. CSmH; MH-AH; NcD; OClWHi; PPL. 44-1436

Clarkson, J. G. Report of the discussion at Pottsville, August 10, 1844, between J. G. Clarkson and F.W. Hughes, on the course of Henry Clay and James K. Polk. Philadelphia: 1844. 27 p. PHi. 44-1437

Clarkson, Thomas, 1760-1846. Letter to a friend on the ill-treatment of the people of color in the United States, on account of the color of their skin. By Thomas Clarkson, of England. Boston: J.W. Olden, 1844. 8 p. CU. 44-1438

Clarkson, Thomas, 1760-1846. Letter to a friend on the ill-treatment of the people of color in the United States, on account of the color of their skin. By Thomas Clarkson, of England. [Boston: New England Anti-slavery Tract Association, 1844?] 8 p. MH; OClWHi. 44-1439

Clarkson, Thomas, 1760-1846. Letter to a friend on the ill-treatment of the people of color in the United States, on account of the color of their skin. By Thomas Clarkson, of England [Suffolk, Virginia: Playford Hall, 1844] 8 p. GU; MH; NcD. 44-1440

The class book of nature. Eighth edition. Hartford: Belknap and Hammersley, 1844. 283 p. NPlaK. 44-1441

Clater, Francis. Every man his own cattle doctor: containing the causes, symptoms and treatment of all the diseases incident to oxen, sheep, and swine; and sketch of the anatomy and physiology of meat cattle by Francis Clater. Philadelphia: Lea and Blanchard, 1844. 251 p. ICU; KyDC; LNP; NNNAM; OMC. 44-1442

Clay, Cassius Marcellus, 1810-1903. A letter of Cassius M. Clay, of Lexington, Kentucky, to the mayor of Dayton, O., with a review of it by Gerrit Smith, of Peterboro, New York [Utica, New York] Jackson and Chaplin [1844] 12 p. DLC; KyU; NIC; OClWHi; WHi. 44-1443

Clay, Cassium Marcellus, 1810-1903. Speech at the Tremont Temple on the 19th after the adjournment of the convention on Boston Common. [Boston] 1844] 1 p. MB; MH; MHi. 44-1444

Clay, Cassius Marcellus, 1810-1903. Speech... delivered in a mass meeting of a portion of the citizens of the eighth con-

gressional district, on December 30, 1843, at the White Sulphur Springs, in Scott County, Kentucky, in reply to Col. R.M. Johnson, and others [n.p.: 1844] 8 p. DLC; MiU-C; NIC; PHC; TxU. 44-1445

Clay, Cassius Marcellus, 1810-1903. Speech of Cassius M. Clay, against the annexation of Texas to the United States of America, in reply to Col. R.M. Johnson and others in a mass meeting of citizens of the Eighth Congressional District, at the White Sulphur Springs, Scott County, Kentucky, on Saturday, December 30, 1843. Lexington: printed at the Observer and Reporter office, 1844. 22 p. DLC; IEN; InHi; KyBgW; MB. 44-1446

Clay, Henry, 1777-1852. Ashland text book, being a compendium of Mr. Clay's speeches, on various public measures... Second edition. Boston: 1844. 72 p. N. 44-1447

Clay, Henry, 1777-1852. Ashland text book, being a compendium of Mr. Clay's speeches, on various public measures... Third edition. Boston: Redding and Company; New York: Saxton and Miles [etc.] 1844. 72 p. DLC; KyHi; MnU; OCl; TxU. 44-1448

Clay, Henry, 1777-1852. Ashland text book, being a compendium of Mr. Clay's speeches, on various public measures... Fourth edition. Boston: Redding and Company, 1844. 72 p. PHi; PPL; PPULC. 44-1449

Clay, Henry, 1777-1852. Ashland text book, being a compendium of Mr. Clay's speeches, on various public measures... Fifth edition. Boston: Redding and Company; New York: Saxton and Miles [etc.] 1844. 72 p. DLC; PPL. 44-1450

Clay, Henry, 1777-1852. Christian votes read!. Philadelphia: 1844. PPL. 44-1451

Clay, Henry, 1777-1852. Clay and Freylinghuysen's views on dwelling. Philadelphia: 1844. PHi; PPL; PPULC. 44-1452

Clay, Henry, 1777-1852. Clay code; or text-book of eloquence, a collection of axioms, apothegms, sentiments, and remarkable passages on liberty, government, policical morality and national honor; gathered from the public speeches of Henry Clay. Ed. by G. Vandenhoff... New York: C. Shepard, 1844. [13]-144, 147-149 p. DLC; KyRE; LU; MPiB; RPB. 44-1453

Clay, Henry, 1777-1852. Fifty reasons why H. Clay should not be President. Washington: 1844. PPL. 44-1454

Clay, Henry, 1777-1852. Letters of Messrs. Clay, Benton, and Barrow, on the subject of the annexation of Texas to the United States [Washington?: 1844] 16 p. GEU; MH; PPL. 44-1455

Clay, Henry, 1777-1852. The life and speeches of the Hon. Henry Clay. New York: Greeley and McElrath, 1844. 2 v. InThE; MB; MiU; PMA; ViU. 44-1456

Clay, Henry, 1777-1852. The life and speeches of the Hon. Henry Clay. New York: Van Amringe and Bixby, 1844. 2 v. NcU; NjR; OCU. 44-1457

Clay, Henry, 1777-1852. The life and speeches of the Hon. Henry Clay. Third edition. New York: R.P. Bixby and com-

pany, 1844. 2 v. IGK; KyU; MsV; OU; ViU. 44-1458

Clay, Henry, 1777-1852. The life and speeches of the Hon. Henry Clay. Compiled and edited by Daniel Mallory. Fourth edition. New York: Van Amringe and Bixby, 1844. 2 v. CoU. KyOw; KyHi; MB; OWoC. 44-1459

Clay, Henry, 1777-1852. The life and speeches of the Hon. Henry Clay. Compiled and edited by Daniel Mallory. Fifth edition. Baltimore: 1844. 2 v. PU; PU-L; PPULC. 44-1460

Clay, Henry, 1777-1852. The life and speeches of the Hon. Henry Clay. Compiled and edited by Daniel Mallory. Fifth edition. New York: Van Amringe and Bixby, 1844. 2 v. MeB; NPot; PU-L; OkEn; ScDuE. 44-1461

Clay, Henry, 1777-1852. The life and speeches of the Hon. Henry Clay. Compiled and edited by Daniel Mallory. Sixth edition. New York: Van Amringe and Bixby, 1844. 2 v. KyBgW; MiU; NjN; PRea; WaPS. 44-1462

Clay, Henry, 1777-1852. Mr. Clay's speech, delivered in the city of Raleigh, North Carolina, April 13, 1844 [New York: Greeley and McElrath, 1844] 12p. ICU. 44-1463

Clay, Henry, 1777-1852. Patriotic songs of Clay Glee Club; presidential campaign of 1843. New York: 1844. OCHP. 44-1464

Clay, Henry, 1777-1852. Speech of Henry Clay, on abolition petitions, delivered in the Senate of the United States on February 7, 1839...extract from

Mr. Clay's reply to Mr. Mendenhall, of Richmond, Indiana, October 1, 1840. [Utica? Jackson and Chaplin, 1844] 16 p. NUt. 44-1465

Clay, Henry, 1777-1852. Speeches of the Hon. Henry Clay, at Raleigh, North Carolina, April 13, 1844 and of Hon. John M. Clayton, at Wilmington, Delaware, June 15, 1844. Hartford: Journal office press, 1844. 24 p. Ct. 44-1466

Clay, Henry, 1777-1852. Suppressed letter. New York: 1844. MB. 44-1467

Clay and Frelinghuysen almanac for 1845. Compiled by F.B. Graham. New York, New York: Turner and Fisher [1844] DLC; InU; MWA; PBL; PPULC. 44-1468

Clay and Frelinghuysen songster... New York: 1844. PPL-R; PPULC. 44-1469

Clay and Polk; the difference between them on the tariff question. By a Columbia county man. Philadelphia: The Pennsylvanian [1844] 8 p. NN; PPL; PPULC. 44-1470

The Clay bugle. Ser. 1. no 1-26. May 11-November 2, 1844. Rochester: Strong and Dawson, 1844. 26 no. in 1 v. KU. 44-1471

Clay or Polk. By an adopted citizen during twenty-one years residence in the United States. New York: 1844. 37 p. NjP; NNC; PHi; PPL; TxU. 44-1472

The clay tribune. New York: Greeley and McEbrath, 1844-. No. 1-. NIC. 44-1473

Claybaugh, Joseph. Address on the reasons of the Presbyterian form of church government. To the students of the theological seminary of the Second A.R. synod of the west: at the opening of the session, November 10, 1844... Rossville: J.M. Christy, 1844. 25 p. OClWHi; PPPrHi. 44-1474

Clayton, John M., 1796-1856. Speech of Honorable John M. Clayton, at the Delaware Whig mass convention, held at Wilmington, June 15, 1844. New York: Greely and McElrath [1844?] 12 p. DLC; OClWHi; Vi. 44-1475

Clayton, John M., 1796-1856. Speech of the Hon. John M. Clayton, of Delaware. Delivered at the Massachusetts Whig Convention, held at Wilmington, June 15, 1844. Philadelphia: Printed at the Forum office [1844] 12 p. MoKU; MH; PHi; PPL. 44-1476

The clergyman's orphan...New York: Harper and Brothers, 1844. 200 p. OSW. 44-1477

Cleveland, Anthony Benezet. Academy for young ladies. Baltimore: 1844. 21 p. MH. 44-1478

Cleveland, Charles Dexter. First lessons in Latin, upon a new plan; combining abstract rules with a progressive series of practical exercises. Improved stereotype edition. Philadelphia: H. Hooker, 1844. 238 p. ScCMu. 44-1479

Cleveland, Henry Russell, d. 1843. A selection from the writings of Henry R. Cleveland....[Boston]: printed for private distribution, 1844. 278 p. ICU; MBC; MH; MPiB; Nh. 44-1480

Clingman, Thomas Lanier. Speech on

the principles of the Whig and Democratic parties; March 7, 1844. Washington: 1844. In; MH; NcU. 44-1481

Clinton Seminary. Clinton, New York. Catalogue of the officers and students of Clinton Seminary, at Clinton, Oneida County, New York. For the year ending July, 1844. Utica: H.H. Curtiss, 1844. 16 p. MeLewB. 44-1482

Clodpole, Christopher, pseud. The Clodpole papers, containing... incidents, adventures, wise sayings, shrewd remarks, philosophical disquisitions, political opinions, and theological lectures. Baltimore: Parsons and Preston, 1844. 64 p. DLC; MdBP; MdHi; PHi; PPULC. 44-1483

Coale, Samuel Chase. Address delivered before the Society of Improvement and the Franklin Debating Club, of the Maryland Institute, at their annual commencement, Baltimore, July 23, 1844. Baltimore: printed by Robert Neilson, 1844. 16 p. MdBD; MdHi; PPL. 44-1484

Coates, Reynell. Physiology for schools by Reynell Coates, M.D. Fourth edition revised. Philadelphia: Butler and Williams, 1844. 333 p. IaPeC; LNB; OUrC. 44-1485

Cobb, Alvan. A sermon, preached to the First Church and Society in Dighton, November 26, 1844, occasioned by the death of their pastor, Rev. Joseph H. Bailey, who died at West Newbury, Massachusetts, on the tenth of November, 1844, aged thirty-six. Taunton, Massachusetts: n.p., 1844. 16 p. ICMe; MBC; Nh-Hi; RPB. 44-1486

Cobb, Howell. Speech on the tariff bill, in the House of the United States, May 3, 1844. Washington: Printed by Blair and Rives, 1844. 76 p. M. 44-1487

Cobb, Lyman, 1800-1864. Cobb's juvenile reader, no 1; containing interesting, moral, and instructive reading lessons, composed of easy words of one or two syllables. Designed for the use of small children, in families and schools. Ithaca: Andrus, Woodruff and Gauntlett [1844?] 72 p. NCH; NIC. 44-1488

Cobb, Lyman, 1800-1864. Cobb's new juvenile reader, no. 1; or first reading book, containing interesting, moral and instructive reading lessons, composed of easy words of one and two syllables.... Designed for the use of small children in schools and families. Ithaca: Andrus, Woodruff and Gauntlett, 1844. [11]-98 p. N; NCH; NIC. 44-1489

Cobb, Lyman, 1800-1864. Cobb's new juvenile reader. Philadelphia: Printed by Biddle, 1844. 106 p. PALT. 44-1490

Cobb, Lyman, 1800-1864. Cobb's new juvenile reader, no.3, or third reading book, containing interesting historical, moral and instructive reading lessons. Newark: A.L. Dennis, 1844. 216 p. NjR; MPalK. 44-1491

Cobb, Lyman, 1800-1864. Cobb's new juvenile reader, no.3, or third reading book... Designed for the use of larger children in schools and families. Pulaski, New York: Robinson, Wright and company, 1844. 216 p. NcAS; NCH. 44-1492

Cobb, Lyman, 1800-1864. Cobb's new North American reader; or Fifth reading book... Designed for the use of the highest classes in schools and academies. New York: C. Bartlett, 1844. [19]-384 p. DLC; GGaB; NBuG; NjR; NRivHi. 44-1493

Cobb, Lyman, 1800-1864. Cobb's new spelling book, in six parts... New York: Caleb Bartlett, 1844. 163 p. NjR; PWCHi. 44-1494

Cobb, Lyman, 1800-1864. Cobb's new spelling book, in six parts. Philadelphia and Harrisburg: 1844. BrMus. 44-1495

Cobb, Lyman, 1800-1864. Cobb's spelling book, being a just standard for pronouncing the English language...Newark, New Jersey: Benjamin Olds, 1844. 168 p. NRivHi. 44-1496

Cobb, Lyman, 1800-1864. An introduction to algebra upon the inductive method of instruction. Boston: R. H. Sherburne, 1844. 276 p. MCM; MH; MiU. 44-1497

Cobb, Lyman, 1800-1864. New juvenile reader. Pulaski, New Jersey: Robinson, Wright and company, 1844. PPeSchw. 44-1498

Cobb, Lyman, 1800-1864. New juvenile reader.... No. 2. New York: 1844. CTHWatk. 44-1499

Cobb, Lyman, 1800-1864. New juvenile reader.... No. 2. Philadelphia: 1844. CTHWatk. 44-1500

Cobb, Lyman, 1800-1864. New North American reader or fifth reading book. New York: Caleb Bartlett, 1844. MiD. 44-1501

Cobb, Lyman, 1800-1864. New North

American reader or fifth reading book. Philadelphia: 1844. CtHWatk. 44-1502

Cobb, Lyman, 1800-1864. New sequel or fourth reading book. New York: 1844. CtHWatk. 44-1503

Cobb, Lyman, 1800-1864. New spelling book... Ithaca, New York: Andrus, Woodruff and Gauntlett, 1844. 168 p. N. 44-1504

Cobbett, William, 1763-1835. Advice to young men, and [incidentally] to young women, in the middle and higher rank of life. In a series of letters, addresses to a youth, a bachelor, a lover, a husband, a citizen or a subject. New York: John Dyle, 1844. 268 p. KyHop; RPAt; RPB. 44-1505

Cobbett, William, 1763-1835. Cobbett's legacy to labourers...In six letters, addressed to the working people of England... New York: John Boyle, 1844? 104 p. CSmH; CtY. 44-1506

Cobbett, William, 1763-1835. Cobbett's legacy to parsons; or have the clergy of the established church an equitable right to the tithes, or to any other thing called church property, greater that the dissenters have to the same and ought there, or ought there not, to be a separation of the church from the state. New York: Doyle, 1844. CSmH; CtY; InCW; OC; OrP. 44-1507

Cobbett, William, 1763-1835. French grammar; or plain instructions for the learning of French. In a series of letters. New York: John Doyle, 1844. 368 p. CU; WaPS. 44-1508

Cobbett, William, 1763-1835. A history

of the Protestant reformation in England and Ireland. New York: D. and J. Sadlier, 1844. 2v. in 1. MBrigStJ; MiOC; PLor. 44-1509

Cobbett, William, 1763-1835. Legacy to labourers, or what is the right which the lords, baronets and squires have to the lands of England? New York: 1844. RPAt. 44-1510

Cobbett, William, 1763-1835. Legacy to parsons, or have the clergy of the established church an equitable right to the tithes. New York: 1844. 143 p. CtY; OCX. 44-1511

Cobbett, William, 1763-1835. Paper against gold, or, the history and mystery of the bank of England.... by William Cobbett, M.P. New York: John Doyle, 1844. 432 p. IaB; MS; NjP; O; OrP. 44-1512

Cock, Micajah R. The American poultry book: being a practical treatise on the management of poultry. New York: Harper and Brothers, 1844. 179 p. CtY; RPE; ScGrw. 44-1513

Cockton, Henry, 1807-1853. The life and adventures of Valentine Vox, the ventriloquist... With illustrations by Phiz... Philadelphia: Carey and Hart, 1844. CtY. 44-1514

Cockton, Henry, 1807-1853. The sisters; or England and France. A romance of real life. New York: William H. Colyer, etc., etc., etc., 1844. MWA. 44-1515

Cockton, Henry, 1807-1853. Sylvester Sound, the somnambulist. A humorous novel. Boston: 1844. MB. 44-1516

Cockton, Henry, 1807-1853. Sylvester Sound, the somnambulist. A humorous novel. New York: Burgess, Stringer and company, 1844. 185 p. MH. 44-1517

Coe, David Benton, 1814-1895. Religious formation. A sermon preached at the installation of the Rev. James A. Hawley, as pastor of the First Congregational Church and Society in Ridgefield, Connecticut....New Haven: B. L. Hamlen, printer, 1844. 20 p. CBB; CtSoP; ICT; MH-AH; RPB. 44-1518

Coffin, Charles. The life and services of Major General John Thomas. New York: printed by Egbert, Hovey and King, 1844. 33 p. Ct; DLC; MBBC; MWA; PHi. 44-1519

Cogswell, William, 1787-1850. Theological class book. Boston: 1844. 172 p. MiU; Nh-Hi. 44-1520

Colburn, Warren, 1793-1833. Arithmetic upon the inductive method of instruction. Boston: Reynolds, 1844. 245 p. MB. 44-1521

Colburn, Warren, 1793-1833. First lessons in reading and grammar; chiefly from the works of Miss Edgeworth. Boston: T.H. Webb and company, 1844. 82 p. CtHWatk; MH. 44-1522

Colburn, Warren, 1793-1833. Intellectual arithmetic. Watertown: P. Knowlton and Rice, 1844. 177 p. NcRS; NSYU. 44-1523

Colburn, Warren, 1793-1833. An introduction to algebra upon the inductive method of instruction. Boston: R. H. Sherburns, 1844. MH; MiU. 44-1524

Colburn, Warren.   119

Colburn, Warren, 1793-1833. Second lessons in reading and grammar: chiefly from the works of Miss Edgeworth. Boston: T.H. Webb and company, 1844. 95 p. CtHWatk; MH. 44-1525

Colburn, Warren, 1793-1833. Third lessons in reading and grammar; chiefly from the works of Miss Edgeworth. Boston: T. H. Webb and company, 1844. CtHWatk; MB. 44-1526

Colby, Benjamin. A guide to health; being an exposition of the principles of the Thomsonian system of practice, and their mode of application in the cure of every form of disease. Nashua, New Hampshire: 1844. 144 p. MBM; Nh; RNHi. 44-1527

Cold water fountain. Vol. 1, no. 5. Folio. Gardiner, Maine: 1844. NoLoc. 44-1528

Cole. A letter to professor Edwards A. Park, Bartlett professor, Andover Theological Seminary, touching his late sermon before the Pastoral association of Massachusetts. Boston: Charles Stimpson, 1844. 30 p. GDecCT; MBC; MH-AH; PPL; RPB. 44-1529

Coleman, Lyman, 1796-1882. The apostolical and primitive church, popular in its government and simple in its worship. Boston: Gould, Kendall and Lincoln, 1844. 456 p. GAU; IaK; ICT; MMeT; OSW; 44-1530

Coleman, Lyman, 1796-1882. The apostolical and primitive church, popular in its government, and simple in its worship.... With an introductory essay by Dr. Augustus Neander.... Second edition. Boston: Gould, Kendall and Lincoln, 1844. 456 p. GMM; MeBat; NbOP; TKC; WBeloC. 44-1531

Coleman, Lyman, 1796-1882. A church without a bishop. The apostolical and primitive church, popular in its government, and simple in its worship. Boston: Gould, Kendall and Lincoln, 1844. 432 p. CSansS; IU; LNB; PPM; WNaE. 44-1532

Coleridge, S. Phantasmion, Prince of Palmland. Philadelphia: 1844. 2 v. in 1. MB. 44-1533

Coleridge, Samuel Taylor, 1772-1834. Aids to reflection.... With the author's last corrections. Edited by Henry Nelson Coleridge.... To which is prefixed a preliminary essay by John M'Vickar; Fourth edition revised and corrected. New York: Stanford and Swords, 1844. 324 p. CtMW; MoS; OO. 44-1534

Coleridge, Samuel Taylor, 1772-1834. The poetical works of S. T. Coleridge. Edited by Herman Hooker. Philadelphia: Locken, 1844. 256 p. IaU; MiU. 44-1535

Coleridge and the moral tendency of his writings... New York: Leavitt, Trow and company, 1844. 118 p. CSansS; MB; MWA; OO; VtU. 44-1536

Colgan, William James. Poems by William James Colgan. New York: Leavitt, Trow and company, 1844. 112 p. CtY; MB; MPiB; NjP; TxU. 44-1537

Colgate University. Hamilton, New York. A catalogue of the officers and students of Hamilton Literary and Theological Insittution, 1844-5. Hamilton, New York, 1844. Utica: R.W.

Roberts, [1844] 24 p. A-Ar; PCA. 44-1538

Collamer, Jacob. Speech of Mr. J. Collamer of Vermont; delivered in the House on the constitutional validity of the act of congress... February 8, 1849 [sic] Washington: D.C. Gales and Seaton, 1844. 13 p. IaGG; OClWHi. 44-1539

Collamer, Jacob. Speech of Mr. J. Collamer of Vermont; on wool and woolens; delivered before the House in committee of the whole on the tariff, April 29, 1844. Washington: J.G.S. Gideon, printer, 1844. 16 p. IaGG; MH. 44-1540

A collection of hymns and a liturgy for the use of Evangelical Lutheran churches; to which are added prayers for families and individuals. New York: Henry Ludwig, printer, 1844. 660 p. IEG; MdBD; MeLewB; PAtM. 44-1541

A collection of speeches in the congress of the United States, on the annexation of Texas, the navy, the tariff, the Rhode Island controversy, Oregon... Washington: 1844. PPL; PPULC. 44-1542

College of Physicians of Philadelphia. Charter, ordinances, and by-laws of the ... Philadelphia: W.F. Geddes, 1844. 31 [1] p. DLC. 44-1543

Collier, William, Evangelical instructor; or Gospel treasury. Designed for the use of schools and families. Boston: Sold by N. Willis, 1844. 312 p. NNUT. 44-1544

Collins, George C. Fifty reasons why the Honorable Henry Clay should be elected president of the United States. By an Irish adopted citizen... Baltimore: for the author, 1844. 43 p. CSmH; IaU; OO; PPL, WHi. 44-1545

Collins, John A. A bird's eye view of society as it is, and as it should be... Boston: Printed by J.P. Mendum, 1844. 32 p. OClWHi. 44-1546

Collins, Robert, 1801-1868. A practical treatise on midwifery, containing the result of sixteen thousand, six hundred and fifty four births, occuring in the Dublin Lying-in Hospital during a period of seven years. Boston: W. D. Ticknor, 1844. 320 p. NIC. 44-1547

Collins, William, 1721-1759. The poetical works of Collins, Gray, and Beattie, with a memoir of each. New York: Turner and Hayden, 1844. 308 p. MH; MoS; NcAS; TNP; VtB. 44-1548

Collot, Alexander G., b. 1796. Progressive French anecdotes and questions: intended as a reading, reciting, and question book; and forming a guide.... to conversational French narration. ....Philadelphia: J. Kay, junior and brothers; Pittsburg: C. H. Kay, 1844. 233 p. CoLH; DLC; RPB; ViU. 44-1549

Collot, Alexander G., b. 1796. Progressive French dialogues and phrases, consisting of a systematic collection of conversations on familiar subjects and also of select idioms and proverbs arranged in a progressive order of difficulty. Philadelphia: James Kay, junior and brother, 1844. MH; OO; PHi; RPB. 44-1550

Collot, Alexander G., b. 1796. Progressive French grammar and exercises.... Philadelphia: J. Kay, junior, and brother;

Pittsburgh: C. H. Kay, 1844. 15-227 p.
CtY; DLC; MMal; MoSU; PSC. 44-1551

Collot, Alexander G., b. 1796. Progressive interlinear French reader....
Philadelphia: 1844. CtY; DLC. 44-1552

Collot, Alexander G., b. 1796. Progressive pronouncing French reader: on a plan new, simple and effective: being a course of interesting and instructive lessons selected from the works of the best prose writers and poets, preceded by a collection of easy fables.... Philadelphia: James Kay, junior and brother; Pittsburgh: C. H. Kay, 184. MH; MWHi; PMA; RPB; TxU-T. 44-1553

Collyer, Robert H. Lights and shadows of American life. Boston: Brainard and company, 1844? 40 p. OCl. 44-1554

Collyer, Robert H. Lights and shadows of American life. Boston: Redding and company, etc., etc. [1844?] ICN; MH. 44-1555

Colman, Henry, 1785-1849. Consolatory views of death, addressed to a friend under bereavement; to which are added some prayers in affliction. Boston: A.D. Phelps, 1844. 53 p. MB; MBC; MH; MH-AH. 44-1556

Colman, Henry, 1785-1849. European agriculture and rural economy from personal observation, by Henry Colman.... Boston: A. D. Phelps, 1844-48. 2 v. MdBP. 44-1557

Colman, Henry, 1785-1849. European agriculture and rural economy from personal observation. Second edition. Boston and London: 1844 and 1849. MBHo. 44-1558

Colman, Julia? New stories for little boys. Original and selected. By Miss Colman. Boston: S. Colman, 1844. 91 p. 44-1559

Colman, Julia? New stories for little girls. Boston: T. H. Carter and company, 1844. 96 p. MHa; NHuntHi; WHi. 44-1560

Colman, Lyman, 1796-1862. The apostolical and primitive church, popular in its government and simple in its worship. Second edition. Boston: Gould, 1844. 456 p. AMaJ; GEU-T; OkU; PU; TxAbH. 44-1561

Colman, Pamela. The little keepsake. Boston: T.H. Carter and company, 1844. MH. 44-1562

Colman, S. The child's gem; a holiday gift. Edited by Mrs. S. Colman. Boston: T.H. Carter and company, 1844. 110 p. NjR. 44-1563

Colquhoun, Janet. The world's religion contrasted with Christianity.... By Lady Colquhoun. New York: John S. Taylor, 1844. 207 p. GDecCT. 44-1564

Colt, John Caldwell, 1810-1842. The science of double entry book keeping. Tenth edition. Boston: William Robinson, Nafis and Cornish, 1844. 253 p. MWHi. 44-1565

Colt, Nelson. The devil's hole, with an account of a visit made to it in 1679 by Robert Cavelier de La Salle. To which is added a memoir of the life of La Salle... Lockport, New York: Crandall and Brigham, printers, 1844. 24 p. DLC; MH; NN. 44-1566

Colton, Calvin, 1789-1857. Annexation of Texas. New York: Greeley and McElrath, 1844. 23 p. MiD-B; NjP; Tx; Tx-ComT; TxU. 44-1567

Colton, Calvin, 1789-1857. Democracy, by Junius [pseud.].... New York: Greeley and McElrath, 1844. 16 p. CSmH; CtY; MH; MnU; MWA. 44-1568

Colton, Calvin, 1789-1857. Junius tracts. No. 1. March 1843. Published every second month. The test; or, parties tried by their acts. By Junius.... New York: Greeley and McElrath, 1844. 10 v. in 1. IU; MeBa; NjR; TxDaM. 44-1569

Colton, Calvin, 1789-1857. Labor and capital, by Junius [pseud.] New York: Greeley and McElrath, 1844. 16 p. CtY; MiU-C; MWA; NjPT; OO. 44-1570

Colton, Calvin, 1789-1857. Life of Henry Clay. By Junius [pseud.].... New York: Greeley and McElrath, 1844. 16 p. CtY; ICU; MiD-B; MWA; NjPT. 44-1571

Colton, Calvin, 1789-1857. Political abolition, by Junius [pseud.]....New York: Greeley and McElrath, 1844. 16 p. CtY; MiU-C; MWA; OO; PPL. 44-1572

Colton, Calvin, 1789-1857. The public lands. By Junius [pseud.].... New York: 1844. 16 p. C-S; GEU; MiD-B; NjPT; OO. 44-1573

Colton, Calvin, 1789-1857. The tariff. By Junius [pseud.].... New York: Greeley and McElrath, 1844. 16 p. CSmH; MiGr; OO; PU; TxDaM. 44-1574

Colton, Calvin, 1789-1857. The tariff triumphant. By Junius, psued. ....New York: Greeley and McElrath, 1844. 16 p. CtY; MHi; MiD-B; OO. 44-1575

Colton, Calvin, 1789-1857. A test, or parties tried by their acts. By Junius. New York: Greeley and McElrath, 1844. 16 p. CtY; MiD-B; MnU; NjPT. 44-1576

Colton, Joseph Hutchins. Guide to Illinois... New York: 1844. NoLoc. 44-1577

Colton, Joseph Hutchins. The western tourist, or emigrant's guide through the states of Ohio, Michigan, Indiana, Illinois, and Missouri.... New York: J.H. Colton, 1844. 119 p. ICHi; IGK: MnHi; MoSM; NNF. 44-1578

Colton, Josiah. Woman as maiden, wife, and mother: an epitome of social and domestic enjoyment, to which is added ten minute advice to a lady going to choose a husband. New York: Wilson and company, 1844. 258 p. GMM; LNH. 44-1579

Colton, Walter, 1797-1851. The Bible in public schools.... A reply to the allegations and complaints contained in the letter of Bishop Kenrick to the board of controllers of public schools. By Rev. Walter Colton. Philadelphia: T.K. and P.G. Collins, printers, 1844. 16 p. CtY; MH-AH; MiD-B; NcMHi; PCA. 44-1580

Columbia University. Catalogue of Columbia College, in the city of New York; embracing the names of its trustees, officers, and graduates; ....New York: printed for Columbia College, 1844. 60 p. MdHi; MHi; MiU; NjR; NNC. 44-1581

Columbia University. Catalogue of officers and graduates... from the foundation of King's College in 1754 [5th]-16th edition. [1844-1916] New York: 1844-1916. 12 v. in 9. NjP. 44-1582

Columbia University. Officers and graduates of Columbia University, orginally the college of the province of New York, known as King's College; general catalogue.... New York: n.p., 1844, 57, 64, 67, 70, and 76. IU. 44-1583

Columbian almanac for 1844, being bissextile or leap year... Philadelphia: Jos. McDowell [1844] 34 p. NCH. 44-1584

The Columbian lady's and gentleman's magazine, embracing literature in every department; embellished with the finest steel and mezzotint engravings, music, and colored fashions.... New York: I. Post, 1844-49. 10 v. CtY; IaU; MiU; PU; TxU. 44-1585

Columbus and his times... Albany: Erastus H. Pease, 1844. 186 p. NMuntL. 44-1586

Columbus, Ohio. First Baptist Church. Articles of faith, First Baptist Church.... Columbus, Ohio: 1844. 16 p. CSmH. 44-1587

Colver, Nathaniel, 1794-1870. Three lectures on Odd-Fellowship. By Rev. Nathaniel Colver. With an essay on its practical influence in regard to church discipline. Boston: William S. Damrell, 1844. 32 p. MeBat; MH; MiD-B. 44-1588

Combe, Andrew, 1797-1847. The physiology of digestion considered with relation to the principles of dietetics. From third Edinburgh revised.... edition. New York: W. H. Colyer; Boston: Lewis

and Sampson, 1844. 25-287 p. ANA; MBC; MdBM; NBMS; PPCP. 44-1589

Combe, Andrew, 1797-1847. Physiology of digestion considered with relation to the principles of dietetics. Sixth American edition. Boston: Webb, 1844. 310 p. PPCP. 44-1590

Combe, Andrew, 1797-1847. The principles of physiology applied to the preservation of health, ...by Andrew Combe, M.D. ....New York: Harper and brothers, 1844. 396 p. MB; MBM; MoSpD; NNN; TxxShA. 44-1591

Combe, Andrew, 1797-1847. The principles of physiology applied to the preservation of health, ...By Andrew Combe, M.D. ....Notes....by O. S. Fowler, ...From the seventh Edinburgh edition. ....New York: O.S. Fowler, 1844. 320 p. MdBJ-W; NNN; WU-M. 44-1592

Combe, George, 1788-1858. The constitution of man considered in relation to eternal objects. New York; Harper and brothers, 1844. 382 p. RPE. 44-1593

Combe, George, 1788-1858. The constitution of man considered in relation to eternal objects. Alexandrian edition. Hartford: S. Andrus and son, 1844. 60 p. MH; MH-AH; NBuCC; TxW; WU. 44-1594

Combe, George, 1788-1858. The constitution of man considered in relation to eternal objects. Fifteenth American edition, materially revised and enlarged. Boston: Thomas H. Webb and company, 1844. 450 p. FSar. 44-1595

Combe, George, 1788-1858. The constitution of man considered in relation to eternal objects. From the third enlarged Edinburgh edition. New York: William H. Colyer, 1844. 382 p. KSalW; NGou; PCA; ScDuE; TU. 44-1596

Combe, George, 1788-1858. The constitution of man, essays on decision of character...Hartford: S. Andrus and son, 1844. 6 v. in 1. CU-M; IaMp; KyBgW; WvSh. 44-1597

Combe, George, 1788-1858. The constitution of man. With additional chapter on the harmony between phrenology and revelation. By Joseph A. Warne. Boston: William D. Ticknor and company, 1844. 412 p. MMeT-Hi; NCaS; TxABH. 44-1598

Combe, George, 1788-1858. Elements of phrenology. From the fifth Edinburgh improved and enlarged edition. New York: William H. Colyer, 1844. 256 p. ICRL. 44-1599

Combe, George, 1788-1858. Moral philosophy; or the duties of man; considered in his individual, social and domestic capacities. From the revised and enlarged Edinburgh edition. Cooperstown, New York: H. and E. Phinney, 1844. 372 p. CtY; IaDmD; ICU; MB; MnSS. 44-1600

Combe, George, 1788-1858. A system of phrenology. ....The only complete American edition, being from the fourth and last [revised and enlarged] Edinburgh edition. ....New York: Colyer, 1844. 516 p. CBPac; MWA; NbCrD; NNC-M. 44-1601

Combs, Leslie, 1793-1881. Erwin and Combs controversy in regard to the bank of the United States claims. New Orleans[?] n.p., 1844? 3 v. in 1. IU. 44-1602

Come now, and let us reason together. Philadelphia: 1844. 4 p. PHi; PPULC. 44-1603

Comings, William Freeman, b. 1814. Report of the trial of William F. Comings, on an indictment for the murder of his wife, Mrs. Adeline T. Comings, at Haverhill...Together with his life written by himself. Boston: Printed by S.N. Dickinson, 1844. 158 p. CtY; MB; MoU; N-L; PP. 44-1604

Comly, John, 1773-1850. English grammar, made easy to the teacher and pupil. Fifteenth edition, corrected and much improved. Philadelphia: Kimber and Sharpless, 1844. MH; PHi; PPULC; PSC-Hi. 44-1605

Comly, John, 1773-1850. A new spelling book, compiled with a view to render the arts of spelling and reading easy and pleasant to children, by John Comly; to which is added a variety of useful exercises, so arranged as to familiarize the pupil with the correct spelling, pronunciation and meaning, of about two thousand ambiguous or difficult words. Philadelphia: Kimber and Sharpless, 1844. 180 p. MiU. 44-1606

Commercial Bank of Albany, New York. Articles of Association. Albany: Van Benthuysen, 1844. 16 p. NN. 44-1607

The commercial intercourse of the United States and Great Britain. New York: Greeley and McElrath [1844] 7 p. CtY; ViU. 44-1608

Committee on Consumers of Gas. Boston. Report, February, 1844. Boston: Eastburn, 1844. 15 p. MB. 44-1609

Committee on Horticulture. Reports of the committee at their 15th, 16th, and 17th annual fairs, held at Niblo's Garden, October 1842-1844. New York: D. Mitchell, printer, 1844. 22 p. NNNBG. 44-1610

Common school almanac for the year 1844. Calculated for the meridians of Boston, New York, Baltimore, Charleston, Richmond, etc. New York: Samuel S. and William Wood, 1844. NCH. 44-1611

The common school controversy. The Secretary of the Board of Education of the state of Massachusetts in reply to charges preferred... Boston: Printed by J.N. Bradley and company, 1844. 55 p. CSmH; ICU; MeB; NjR; PPAmp. 44-1612

Common school controversy; consisting of three letters of the secretary of the board of education of the state of Massachusetts in reply to charges preferred against the board; by the editor of the Christian witness, and by Edward A. Newton.... Boston: J. N. Bradley and company, 1844. 55 p. AzU; ICJ; MnHi; Nh; OO. 44-1613

The common school journal of the state of Pennsylvania: published under the supervision of the superintendent of common schools of the commonwealth. Philadelphia: E.C. Biddle; [etc., etc.] 1844. 376 p. CSt; DLC; MH; MnHi; PPAmP. 44-1614

The complete confectioner, pastry-cook and baker; plain and practical directions for making confectionary and pastry, and for baking, with upwards of 500 receipts, consisting of directions for making all sorts of preserves... With additions and alterations by Parkingson, confectioner. Philadelphia: Lea and Blanchard, 1844. MH; NjR; PPL-R. 44-1615

The complete florist; a manual of gardening, containing practical instruction for the management of greenhouse plants, and for the cultivation of the shrubbery, the flower garden and the lawn.... Philadelphia: Lea and Blanchard, 1844. 108 p. MB; MWA; NBuG; OClW; PU. 44-1616

Comstock, Andrew. A system of elocution with special reference to gesture. Philadelphia: Published by Butler and Williams, 1844. 1 v. CtHWatk; MeB; MiU; MPiB; PPeSchw. 44-1617

Comstock, John Lee, 1789-1859. Elements of chemistry, in which the recent discoveries in the science are included and its doctrines familiarly explained. Ilustrated by numerous engravings, and designed for the use of schools and academies. Forty-ninth edition. New York: Pratt, Woodford and company, 1844. 420-[12] p. Ia; MAnP; MdBJ; NNN; PPi. 44-1618

Comstock, John Lee, 1789-1859. An introduction to minerology; adapted to the use of schools and private students; illustrated by nearly two hundred wood cuts. Third edition. New York: Robinson Pratt and company, 1844. 369 p. MH; NBuG; NcElon; NjR. 44-1619

Comstock, John Lee, 1789-1859. Introduction to the study of Botany including a treatise on vegetable physiology. New York: Pratt, Woodford and company, 1844. IaHA; MtBu; ODW. 44-1620

Comstock, John Lee, 1789-1859. Outlines of physiology, both comparative and human, etc. Third edition. [To which is prefixed, report on the method of teaching English grammar, etc. By R.K. Finch] New York: Woodford and company, 1844. CtHWatk; MiKt; MiU; NcU; OClW. 44-1621

Comstock, John Lee, 1789-1859. A system of natural philosophy; in which the principles of mechanics, hydrostatics, hydraulics, pneumatics, acoustics, optics, astronomy, electricity and magnetism, are familiarly explained, and illustrated by more than two hundred engravings... Fifty-third edition. New York: Pratt, Woodford and comapny, 1844. 340 p. CoD; IGK; MdBJ; MiU; MH; PPWa. 44-1622

Concord Railroad. Upham, Nathaniel Gookin. Concord: 1844. DLC. 44-1623

Concordia Parish, Louisiana. Proceedings of the police jury of the parish of Concordia.... November and December, 1844. Vidalia: printed at the Intelligencer office, 1844. CSmH. 44-1624

Condie, David Francis, 1796-1875. A practical treatise on the diseases of children. By D. F. Condie....Philadelphia: Blanchard and Lea, 1844. 651 p. CSt-L; KyLxT; NjP; OrUM; PPAN. 44-1625

Condit, Jonathan Bailey. Christians, fellow helpers to the truth, a sermon delivered in Bath, June 26, 1844, before

the Maine Missionary Society, at its thirty-seventh anniversary, by Rev. J.B. Condit, pastor of the Second Congregational Church, Portland. Portland: Thurston, Ilsley and company, printers, 1844. 52 p. MBC; MeBa; MeBaT; MH-AH; MiD-B. 44-1626

Cone, Spencer H. A summary of the faith and practice with the articles of the covenant of the First Baptist Church in the city of New York. New York: 1844. 23 p. ICU; NHC-S; NjPT. 44-1627

Confessions of a reformed inebriate. An Ower [sic] true tale. New York: American Temperance Union, 1844. 180 p. MLow; NIC; NN. 44-1628

Confessions, trials and biographical sketches of the most cold blooded murderers, who have been executed in this country from its first settlement down to the present time. Compiled entirely from the most authentic sources... Hartford: S. Andrus and son, 1844. 420 p. MNowdHi; NClf; PHi; NBuG. 44-1629

Congdon, James B. An address delivered at the consecration of the Oak Grove Cemetery in New Bedford, October 6th, 1843. ....New Bedford: press of Benjamin Lindsey, 1844. 35 p. ICN; MB; MiD-B; MWA; RPB. 44-1630

Congregational Churches in Connecticut. Congregational Church and Society, Winsted, Connecticut. Minutes of the proceedings in relation to the settlement of Rev. Augustus Pomery as their pastor and the action thereon of the Consociation of Litchfield North. Hartford: 1844. 8 p. MBC. 44-1631

Congregational Churches in Connecticut. Middlesex Consociation. Address to the churches of Middlesex Consociation; with reasons why I an a congregationalist: and the pilgrims legacy. Second Edition. Hartford: Moseley, 1844. 36 p. CtY; ICN; MB. 44-1632

Congregational Churches in Maine. General Conference. Minutes of the general conference of Maine.... Bath, June 25, 1844. Portland: Thurston, Ilsley and company, printers, 1844. 32 p. ICU; IEG; MeBaT. 44-1633

Congregational Churches in Massachusetts. General Association. Minutes of, at their session in Woburn, June, 1844; with the narrative of the state of religion and the pastoral letter. Boston: 1844. 58 p. IEG. 44-1634

Congregational Churches in Massachusetts. General Association. Report of the committee of correspondence with southern ecclesiastical bodies on slavery; to the General Association of Massachusetts. Published by a vote of the association. Salem: J.P. Jewett and company, 1844. 23 p. CSmH; DLC; MB; MnU; NNC. 44-1635

Congregational Churches in Massachusetts. General Association. Minutes of the General Association of Massachusetts, at their session in Woburn, June, 1844, with the narrative of the state of religion, and the pastoral letter. Boston: Press of Crocker and Brewster, 1844. 58 p. MA. 44-1636

Congregational Churches in New Hampshire. General Association. Minutes of the General Association of New Hampshire at their annual meeting held in Concord, August 27, 1844. Con-

cord: press of Asa M'Farland, 1844. 4-12 p. ICN. 44-1637

Congregational Churches in New Hampshire. Piscataqua Asssociation. Articles of faith and form of covenant adopted by the Piscataqua Association of ministers at their meeting July 16, 1834. Portsmouth: C.W. Brewster, printer, 1844. 8 p. ICN; Nh-Hi; NjR. 44-1638

Congregational Churches in New York. Minutes of the annual meeting... Clinton, Oneida County, August 22, 1844. Utica: R. W. Roberts, printer, 1844. 19 p. MiD-B; NN. 44-1639

Congregational Churches in Ohio. Minutes.... June 20, 1844. Cleveland: T.H. Smead, printer, 1844. 23 p. ICP; NN; PPPrHi. 44-1640

Congregational Churches in the United States. New Haven: A.H. Maltby, 1844. 137 p. TxShA. 44-1641

Congregational Conference and Missionary Society of Maine. Sermon and annual report. Portland: Thurston, Ilsley and company, 1844. 52 p. MiD-B. 44-1642

Congregational tracts. No. 1. [Bridgeport: 1844] 15 p. Ct; CtHWatk. 44-1643

The congregational visitor, for parents, church members, and Sabbath school teachers. Edited by the publishing committee of the Massachusetts Sabbath School Society. Boston: Massachusetts Sabbath School Society, 1844-. v. 1-. IaDuU; MB; MBAt; MnHi; NT. 44-1644

Conkling, Margaret Cockburn.

Memoirs of the mother and wife of Washington. Life story of Mary Washington, and Martha Washington. Auburn, New York: Derby, Miller and company, 1844. 248 p. OAk. 44-1645

Connecticut annual register and United States calendar for 1844. To which is prefixed an almanac. No. 54. Hartford: Samuel Green, 1844. 176 p. Ct. 44-1646

Connecticut. The executive journal of the Senate of the state of Connecticut, May session, 1844. Published under the superintendence of the clerk of the Senate. New Haven: Babcock and Wildman, 1844. [3]-8 p. Mi; MiD-B. 44-1647

Connecticut. Journal of the House of Representatives of the state of Connecticut, May session, 1844. Printed by order of the House. New Haven: Babcock and Wildman, printers, 1844. 183 p. Mi; MoU. 44-1648

Connecticut. Journal of the Senate of the state of Connecticut, May session, 1844. Published under the direction of the clerk of the senate. New Haven: Babcock and Wildman, printers to the state, 1844. 190 p. Mi; MiD-B; MoU. 44-1649

Connecticut. Legislative roll: rules of the House of Representatives, joint rules of proceedings; and joint standing committees. May Session, 1844. New Haven: printed by Babcock and Wildman, 1844. 15 p. Ct; MiD-B. 44-1650

Connecticut. Public acts passed by the General Assembly of the state of Connecticut, May session, 1844. New Haven [Connecticut] printed by Babcock and

Wildman, 1844. 48 p. Ar-SC; Ia; Ky; Mo; NNLI. 44-1651

Connecticut. Report of the Bank Commissioners to the General Assembly. May session, 1844. Printed by order of the assembly. New Haven: printed by Babcock and Wildman, 1844. 51 p. Ct; CtHWatk. 44-1652

Connecticut. Report of the Commissioner of the School Fund, to the General Assembly. May session, 1844. Printed by order of the assembly. New Haven: printed by Babcock and Wildman, 1844. 29 p. Ct. 44-1653

Connecticut. Report of the Committee on the punishment and reformation of juvenile offenders. New Haven: 1844. 8 p. CtSoP; NN. 44-1654

Connecticut. Report of the committee on the subject of taxation, to the General Assembly, May session, 1844. Printed by order of the Senate. New Haven: Babcock and Wildman, 1844. 16 p. CtSoP; CtY; NN. 44-1655

Connecticut. Report of the Directors of the Connecticut State Prison, together with the reports of the warden, physician and chaplain. May session, 1844. Printed by order of the assembly. New Haven: Baldwin and Wildman, 1844. 33 p. Ct. 44-1656

Connecticut. Report of the Joint Select Committee, on so much of the governor's message as relates to the insane poor, to the General Assembly, May session, 1844. ... New Haven: printed by Babcock and Wildman, 1844. 12 p. CtSoP; CtY; Mhi; WHi. 44-1657

Connecticut. Report of the Joint Standing Committee on the State Prison, to the General Assembly. May session, 1844. Printed by order of the assembly. New Haven: printed by Babcock and Wildman, 1844. 6 p. Ct. 44-1658

Connecticut. Speech of His Excellency, Roger S. Baldwin... to the legislature of the state, May, 1844. By order of the assembly. New Haven: Babcock and Wildman, printers, 1844. 23 p. CtHWatk; CtY. 44-1659

Connelly, H. Verbal amendments of the metrical version of David's Psalms now used in the Associate Reformed and other churches, proposed by H. Connelly.... Newburgh: Spalding, 1844. PPPrHi. 44-1660

Connery, Edward D. American liberty vindicated, and the right of foreigners to share its blessings, defended. An oration....New York: 1844. CtY. 44-1661

The consoled mourner. Containing "The cypress leaf." Boston [1844?] MB. 44-1662

Conspiracy against the liberties of the United States. "The numbers under signature of Brutus" by the author Samuel F.B. Morse. Sixth edition. New York: 1844. OCHP. 44-1663

Convention of Colleges. Richmond, Virginia. 1844. Memorial of the convention of colleges, recently assembled in the city of Richmond, asking an appropriation from the literary fund. Richmond: Sheperd and Colin, printers, 1844. 13 p. MoFayC; NjR; Vi. 44-1664

Conversations on life in the insect world. Philadelphia: Lindsay and Blakiston, 1844. 241 p. MSaP. 44-1665

Cook, Eliza, 1818-1889. Melaia, and other poems. By Eliza Cook... New York: J. and H.G. Langley, 1844. [3]-352 p. DeWi; LNH; MB; NbU; PSC-Hi; RPAt. 44-1666

Cook, Simeon A. Address... before the Medical Society of New York... Troy, New York: printed at the Budget office, 1844. 31 p. CSmH; MB; MBNMHi; NjR; NNNAM. 44-1667

Cooke, Corbett. The opinions of the Rev. John Wesley, in reference to the relation which Methodism sustains to the established church fully and fairly stated; and its present ecclesiastical position vindicated.... Exeter: W. Balle, 1844. 51 p. TxDaM. 44-1668

Cooke, H. The sacrifice of the mass examined in the light of the words of our Lord Jesus Christ.... report of a sermon preached 15th December, 1844. Philadelphia: Presbyterian Board of Publication, 1844. 45 p. PPPrHi. 44-1669

Cooke, William M. The anniversary address, of the Jefferson Society, of the University of Virginia, delivered on the 13th, April, 1844. Charlottesville: James Alexander, printer, 1844. 20 p. CSmH. 44-1670

Cookman, George C. Speeches delivered on various occasions. By George C. Cookman, Chaplain to the Senate. New York: J. Collard, 1844. 139 p. MBNMHi; NcD; NjPT. 44-1671

Cooley, Timothy Mather. Sketches of the life and character of the Rev. Lemuel

Haynes, A.M. ....By Timothy Mather Cooley, D.D., with some introductory remarks by William B. Sprague, D.D. ....New York: John S. Taylor, 1844. 348 p. MoWgT; OSW; OUrC; WM. 44-1672

Coolidge, George. Anniversary poem delivered before the Mechanic Apprentices' Library Association, in the Masonic Temple, Boston, on its 24th anniversary, February 22, 1844. Boston: published for the association, 1844. 16 p. MB; MWA; PHi; RPB; TxU. 44-1673

Coolidge, George. Poem before mechanic apprentices library association, February 22. Boston: 1844. MBAt. 44-1674

Coolidge and Haskell. Catalogue of 129 modern European paintings for sale at auction April 5, 1844. Now exhibited in the horticultural room. Boston: Dutton and Wentworth, 1844. 8 p. MB. 44-1675

Cooper, Astley Paston, 1768-1841. The anatomy and surgical treatment of abdominal hernia....By Sir Astley Cooper, bart. ...From the second London edition. By C. Aston Key.... Philadelphia: Lea and Blanchard, 1844. 427 p. CU-M; LNOP; PPCP; RNR; WU. 44-1676

Cooper, Astley Paston, 1768-1841. A treatise on dislocation and fractures of the joints. by Sir Astley Paston Cooper, bart. A new edition, much enlarged. Edited by Bransby B. Cooper. Philadelphia: Lea and Blanchard, 1844. 499 p. CtMW; MdBJ; NNU-M; ViRA. 44-1677

Cooper, James Fenimore, 1789-1851. Afloat and ashore; or the adventures of Miles Wallingford. Philadelphia: the author, 1844. 4 v. CtY; DLC; MH; NcD; PPL. 44-1678

Cooper, James Fenimore, 1789-1851. Cruise of the Somers ... Third edition. New York: J. Winchester, 1844. 132 p. DLC; MB; NN. 44-1679

Cooper, James Fenimore, 1789-1851. Jack Tier or the Florida reef by J. Fenimore Cooper. New York: D. Appleton and company, 1844. 510 p. MTop. 44-1680

Cooper, James Fenimore, 1789-1851. John Templar Shuhrick. Philadelphia: 1844. MBAt. 44-1681

Cooper, James Fenimore, 1789-1851. The wept of wish-ton-wish. A tale. Complete in one volume. New York: James G. Gregory, 1844. 483 p. MChesh. 44-1682

Cooper, Joseph T. Answers to questions without answers. Philadelphia: Young, 1844. MB; MBAt; PPPrHi. 44-1683

Cooper, Peter. Galileo the Roman inquisition: a defence of the Catholic Church from the charge of having persecuted Galileo for his philosophical opinions.... From the Dublin review. With an introduction by an American Catholic. Published for the Catholic Book Society. Cincinnati: Montfort and Conahans, 1844. 68 p. CtY; MiDSH; OO; PPL; WStfSF. 44-1684

Cooper, Samuel, 1780-1848. Dictionary of practical surgery; containing a complete exhibition of the present state of the principles and practice of surgery, collected from the best and most original sources of information and illustrated by critical remarks. Revised with a supplementary index.... From seventh London edition. New York: Harper, 1844. 506 p. MB; MBM; NBMS; PPCP. 44-1685

Cooper, Samuel, 1780-1848. The first lines of the theory and practice of surgery.... Fourth American from the seventh London edition. New York: S.S. and W. Wood, 1844. 2 v. ArU-M; CtY; MnU; NBMS; PPHa. 44-1686

Cooper, Samuel, 1798-1876. A concise system of instructions and regulations for the militia and volunteers of the United States.... New edition, with additions and improvements. Philadelphia: R.P. Desilver, 1844. Ct; NcG; PHi; ScCliP. 44-1687

Coote, Charles. MaClaine Mosheims church history. New York: Harper Brothers, 1844. 2 v. ODefC. 44-1688

Copies of the original grant of order of survey, the survey and final grant, granting a tract of land on the White River, lying in the states of Arkansas and Missouri, made in the year 1793, by the Baron de Carondelet.... to Captain Don Joseph Valliere. Also copies of the power of attorney.... to Creed Taylor.... and a deed.... to John Wilson.... New York: 1844. 32 p. CSmH; CtY; MH. 44-1689

Copley, Esther. Profit and honour: or illustrations of humble life. Dodd, New York: 1844. OCo. 44-1690

Cornwall, J.A. A vindication of the doctrine of the final perserverance of the saints.... substance of a sermon preached July 2d, 1843. Pittsburgh: Anderson, 1844. PPPrHi. 44-1691

Corporation for the Relief of the Widows and Children of Clergymen in the communion of the P.W. Church in Pennsylvania. By-laws and members. Philadelphia: 1844. PPL. 44-1692

Coswell, Joseph, 1792-1863. Thirty years passed among the players in England and American: interspersed with anecdotes and reminiscences of a variety of persons, directly or indirectly connected with the drama during the theatrical life of Joe Cowell, comedian. Written by himself.... New York: Harper and brothers, 1844. 103 p. IU; MWA; OC; RHi; ScC. 44-1693

Cotterill, Thomas, 1799-1813. Cotterill's family prayers.... revised by William W. Spear, to which is prefixed a memoir of the author. Philadelphia: Herman Hooker, 1844. 216 p. CBCDS; MBC; MH; NcD; NjP. 44-1694

Court martial case of A.S. Mackenzie and a review of case by J.F. Cooper, New York: Langley, 1844. 3, 344 p. MB; MWCL. 44-1695

Cousin, Victor, 1792-1867. Lectures on the true, the beautiful and the good. New York: 1844. CtY. 44-1696

Covel, James, Jr. A concise dictionary of the Holy Bible. Designed for the use of Sunday school teachers and families. With maps and numerous fine engravings. New York: G. Lane and Scott, 1844. MB. 44-1697

Coverdale, Miles, 1488-1565. Writings and translation; edited for the Parker

Society. Cambridge: University printer, 1844. 544 p. GDecCT; InGrD; KyLo; MBAt; OClW. 44-1698

Covert, Bernard. Covert and Dodge's collection of songs, duets, glees, etc. sung by them and J.B. Gough, at their temperance concerts throughout the Union. Boston: Keith's Music and Publishing House, 1844. 48 p. MH; NBuG. 44-1699

Covington Female Seminary. Covington, Kentucky. Annual catalogue. September, 1844. Covington, Kentucky: Langdon and Munger, printers, 1844. KyHi; MH. 44-1700

Cowen, Esek, 1787-1844. Civil jurisdiction of justices of the peace in the state of New York. Third edition. Albany, 1844. 2 v. MBS; MH-L. 44-1701

Cowen, Esek, 1787-1844. A treatise on the civil jurisdiction of justices of the peace in the state of New York.... Third edition....Albany: W. and A. Gould and company; New York: Gould, Banks and company, 1844. 2 v. CU; ICU-L; MiDU-L; MnU; NNLI. 44-1702

Cowper, William, 1731-1800. The complete poetical works of William Cowper, esq... with a memoir of the author by Rev. H. Stebbing. New York: D. Appleton; Philadelphia: George S. Appleton, 1844. 2 v. in 1. CSmH; IaFairP; MB; NN; PPD. 44-1703

Cowper, William, 1731-1800. John Gilpin: Music by W.A. Nield. Boston: 1844. MB. 44-1704

Cowper, William, 1731-1800. Poems, by William Cowper, esq., together with his posthumous poetry, and a sketch of his life by John Johnson, LL.D. Boston: Lewis and Sampson, 1844. 3 v. InU; TMeSC. 44-1705

Cox, Francis Augustus, 1783-1853. History of the English Baptist Missionary Society, from A.D. 1792 to A.D. 1842. By the Rev. F.A. Cox. Boston: Isaac Tompkins, 1844. 2 v. in 1. CBB; LNB; MBC; NHC-S; PCA. 44-1706

Cox, Samuel H. Introduction to and continuation of Bower's history of the popes. Philadelphia: 1844. MBC. 44-1707

Coxe, Richard Smith. Address before Peithesophian and Philoclean Societies, Rutgers College, July 23, 1844. New York: 1844. 24 p. OClWHi. 44-1708

Coxe, Richard Smith. Address delivered before the Peithessophian and Philoclean Societies of Rutgers College, July 23 , 1844. New York [B. Owen, printer] 1844. 24 p. MH-AH; NjR; PPL; NNG. 44-1709

Coyne, Joseph Stirling, 1803-1868. The signal; a drama, in three acts. New York: Samuel French and son [1844] 40 p. OCl. 44-1710

Coyne, Joseph Stirling, 1803-1868. The trumpeter's daughter; a farce in one act. New York: Samuel French, [1844] 17 p. LNH; OCl. 44-1711

Cozzens, Samuel W. The prominent sins of the times. A sermon, delivered in Milton and Dorchester, on the day of the annual state fast, April 4, 1844. Published by request of the society. Boston: press of

T. R. Marvin, 1844. 21 p. DLC; ICMe; MH-AH; MPiB; NjPT. 44-1712

Cozzens, Samuel W. A sermon occasioned by the death of Honorable William Reed. Delivered February 26, 1837. Boston: Crocker and Brewster, 1844. CtY; MB-FA; MnU; NN; PPL. 44-1713

Crabb, George, 1778-1851. A dictionary of general knowledge; or, an explanation of words and things connected with all the arts and sciences.... Sixth edition.... New York: J.C. Riker, 1844. 368 p. CtY; MLow; MPiB; PBa; ViU. 44-1714

Crabb, George, 1778-1851. English synonyms, with copious illustrations and explanations.... New edition enlarged. New York: Harper and brothers, 1844. 535 p. C-S; CSt; NJam; ScDuE; TBriK. 44-1715

Crabbe, George, 1754-1832. The poetical works of Crabbe, Heber, and Pollok, complete in one volume. Philadelphia: Grigg and Elliot, 1844. 396 p. CoU; LPL; MnS; PHC; ScDuE. 44-1716

Crabbe, George, 1754-1832. The tales of the hall, a poem. By Rev. George Crabbe. New York: Burgess, Stringer and company, 1844. 129 p. CSmH; MLow; MPiB; NjR; OMC. 44-1717

Craik, Diana Maria Mulock. Poems. Boston: 1844. 270 p. TxW. 44-1718

Craik, George Lillie, 1798-1866. Pursuit of knowledge under difficulties, its pleasures and rewards, illustrated by memoirs of eminent men. New York: Harper, 1844. 2 v. MChi; MiThr; MnSM; MoSM; MRP. 44-1719

Craik, James, 1806-1882. A pastoral letter from the rector to the congregation of Christ Church, Louisville, Diocese of Kentucky. Louisville: Morton and Griswold, 1844. 12 p. MdBD. 44-1720

Cram, T.J. Report ...on navigation of the Ohio River, at Louisville. Washington: 1844. NN. 44-1721

Cramp, John Mockett, 1796-1881. The reformation in Europe, with a chronology of the reformation [New York: American Tract Society, 1844? 432 p.] MiGr. 44-1722

Cramp, John Mockett, 1796-1881. The reformation in Europe. By the author of the Covent of Trent, with a chronology of the Reformation. New York: Published by the American Tract Society, D. Fanshaw, printer, 1844. 432 p. PLT. 44-1723

Cranch, Christopher Pearse, 1813-1892. Poems, by Christopher Pearse Cranch. Philadelphia: Carey and Hart, 1844. 116 p. ICU; LU; MoSM; OCHP; TxU. 44-1724

Crandall, Andrew Jackson. An address pronounced before the Philomathesian Society, at the opening of their new room in the Oneida Conference Seminary, Cazenozia, February 8, 1844. Auburn: printed by Henry Oliphant, 1844. 15 p.. CSmH; NCH. 44-1725

Crane, E.B. Brief notices of the life.... of author Rev. F. William Hotchkiss. New York: 1844. 40 p. MB. 44-1726

Crane, E.B. A sermon preached at Saybrook, Connecticut, September 24, 1843, by the late Rev. Frederick William Hotchkiss, senior pastor of the First Congregational Church in that place: to which is appended a brief notice of his life, death, and general character; by Rev. E. B. Crane, junior pastor. New York: S. W. Benedict and company, 1844. 40 p. NUtHi. 44-1727

Cranfield, Richard. Memoir of Thomas Cranfield, of London. By his son, assisted by Rev. Dr. Harris, ...First American edition. Boston: Massachusetts Sabbath School Society, 1844. 276 p. DLC; MeBa; MTop; NjPT; RKi. 44-1728

Cranmer, Thomas. The doctrine of the sacraments maintained by Archbishop Cranmer. Baltimore: Joseph Robinson, 1844. 24 p. MBAt; MdBD; PPL-R; WNaE. 44-1729

Cranmer, Thomas. The works of Thomas Cranmer, archbishop of Canterbury, martyr, 1556. Edited for the Parker Society, by the Rev. John Edmund Cox, M.A., F.S.A., of All Soul's College, Oxford; curate and lecturer of Stepney. Cambridge: University Press, 1844. 2 v. MBC; NcHy; NcMHi; NcU. 44-1730

Crawford, T.C. A man and his hole. A romance. New York: 1844. DLC. 44-1731

Crawford, Thomas G. Description of the Orpheus and other works of sculpture, by Thomas G. Crawford. Boston: Eastburn's press, 1844. 8 p. GDecCT; MBAt; MH; MHi. 44-1732

Creath, Jacob. An address delivered in Quincy, Illinois, at the Masonic celebration of the anniversary of St. John, the Baptist, June 24, 1844, By Jacob Creath, Jr., Quincy, Illinois: Bartlett and Sullivan, printers, 1844. 15 p. IaCrM; MBFM; NNFM. 44-1733

Cresson, Warder. Jerusalem, the centre and joy of the whole earth. Philadelphia: Jesper Harding, 1844. 111 p. PPWe. 44-1734

Cricketer's hand book. The origin of the game. Boston: Saxton, Peirce and company, 1844. 48 p. MB; MWA. 44-1735

The cries of London. Cooperstown: H. and E. Phinney, 1844. [5]-31 p. DLC; MH. 44-1736

The crisis: an appeal to the countrymen, on the subject of foreign influence in the United States. Issued under the sanction of the General Executive Committee of the American Republican Party of the city and county of New York... New York [Joseph F. Atwill] 1844. 80 p. CSmH; ICP; MH-AH; OCl; PU. 44-1737

Crocker, Alvah, 1801-1874. Letter to G. Evans, upon the remission of the duty on railroad iron. Washington: 1844. MBAt. 44-1738

Crocker, Alvah, 1801-1874. Rejoinder to the reply of a committee appointed by the iron trade in Philadelphia, "to enforce upon congress the necessity and propriety of continuing the duty upon railway iron," with the letters of Major General Scott and others, to the Hon. George Evans... by the author of the first letter... Washington: 1844. 32 p. DLC; ICJ; MiD-B; NBu; OClWHi. 44-1739

Croker, Thomas Crofton, 1798-1854. Fairy legends and traditions of the South of Ireland. Philadelphia: Lea and

Blanchard, 1844. 251 p. DLC; MB; PPL. 44-1740

Croker, Thomas Crofton, 1798-1854. Fairy legends and traditions of the South of Ireland; a new edition with numerous illustrations after designs of the author and others. Philadelphia: Lea and Blanchard, 1844. 246 p. LNH; PPL-R. 44-1741

Croly, George, 1780-1860. ....The angel of the world. By Rev. George Croly. [New York: Morris and Willis, 1844] 16 p. CtY; MH; MWH. 44-1742

Cromwell, S.T. Method of chanting explained. Charleston: Miller and Browne, 1844. 18 p. DLC. 44-1743

Crosby, Alpheus, 1810-1874. A grammar of the Greek language. Part first. A practical grammar of the attic and common dialects, with the elements of general grammar. By Alphens Crosby, professor of the Greek language and literature in Dartmouth College.... Boston: James Munroe and company, 1844. 487 p. IJI; MH; PBa; ViU; WBeloC. 44-1744

Crosby, George. Crosby's political record of parliamentary elections in Great Britain and Ireland; with select biographical notices and speeches of distinguished statesmen, etc. New York: 1844. 6, 306 p. NcD; NjPaT. 44-1745

Crosfield, George, 1785-1847. Memoirs of the life and gospel labours of Samuel Fothergill, with selections from his correspondence; also an account of the life and travels of his father, John Fothergill and notice of some of his descendants.

New York: Collins, 1844. 544 p. InRchE; MH; NcD; OClWHi; ScC. 44-1746

Crosland, Camilla Dufour Toulmin, 1812-1895. Memorable women; the story of their lives. Boston: Ticknor and Fields, 1844. 360 p. MPiB. 44-1747

Crossman, Martin L. Geography on a new plan; or, a system of classification, adapted to the latest editions of Olney's, Smith's, Mitchell's, and Malt Brun's maps. Seventh edition. Worcester: H. J. Howland, 1844. 48 p. MH; MiD-B. 44-1748

Crowe, Eyre Evans, 1799-1868. The history of France. New York: Harper and brothers, 1844. 3 v. IGK; MdAN; ScDuE. 44-1749

Crowell, Moses. The counsellor, or, every man his own lawyer: the several modes of commencing and conducting actions in the justices' courts in the state of New York, rendered plain and easy; with a variety of forms for drawing declarations and other instruments of writing used between man and man.... Ithaca, New York: D.D. and A. Spencer, printers, 1844. 192 p. CSmH; InRchE; MB; NIDHi; NRHi. 44-1750

Cruikshank, George. The bottle in eight plates... New York: Wiley and Putnam [1844] MH. 44-1751

The crusade of the children: A story of the middle ages. Translated from the German... Philadelphia: American Sunday School Union, 1844. 101 p. GEU-T; NNF; OO. 44-1752

Crusius, Gottlieb Christian, 1785-1848. A complete Greek and English lexicon of the poems of Homer, and the Homeridae. Composed with constant religious, poetical and military condition of the heroic age... Hartford: H. Huntington, 1844. 542 p. IaGG; MdBJ; OMC; ScCC; WU. 44-1753

Cruveilhier, Jean, 1791-1874. The anatomy of the human body. By Jean Cruveilhier.... The first American, from the last Paris edition. Edited by Granville Sharp Pattison.... New York: Harper and brothers, 1844. 907 p. ArU-M; MeB; OCU-M; RPM; WU-M. 44-1754

Cuba. Notes containing an account of its discovery and early history. Boston: Munroe, 1844. PHatU. 44-1755

Cubi y Soler, Mariano, 1801-1875. A new Spanish grammar, adapted to every class of learners. By Mariano Cubi y Soler. Seventh edition. Baltimore: F. Lucas, junior, 1844. 294 p. AzU; ViU. 44-1756

Cubitt, George. Life of Martin Luther, to which is prefixed an expository essay on the Lutheran Reformation. New York: Lane and Sandford, 1844. 348 p. DAU; InLog; NcD; OO; TCle. 44-1757

Cullom, Alvan. Remarks on the bill making appropriation for certain harbors and rivers in the House of Representatives of the United States, April 20, 1844. Washington: Blair and Rives, printer, 1844. 8 p. M. 44-1758

Cultivator almanac for 1845. By Luther Tucker. Albany, New York: Luther Tucker [1845] MWA. 44-1759

Cultivator almanac for 1845. By Luther

Tucker. Auburn: J.C. Derby and company [1845] 32 p. CtY; MWA. 44-1760

Cultivator almanac for 1845. By Luther Tucker. New York: M.H. Newman [1844] MWA. 44-1761

Cultivator almanac for 1845. By Luther Tucker. Riverhead, Long Island, New York: G.O. Wells [1844] MWA. 44-1762

Cultivator almanac for 1845. By William Tucker. New York: William H. Carey and company [1844] MWA. 44-1763

Cultivator almanac. Albany, New York: S. Tucker, 1844. MWA. 44-1764

Cultivator almanac. By W. Gaylord and Luther Tucker. New York: Beach, 1844. MWA. 44-1765

The cultivator almanac or rural calender, No. 1. By Willis Gaylord and Luther Tucker. Lansingburg, New York: 1844. MBHo. 44-1766

Culverwell, Robert James, 1802-1852. Porneio pathology. A popular treatise on venereal and other diseases, of the male and genital system.... New York: J. S. Redfield, 1844. 215 p. CtY; GU; MBM; NNN; PPCP. 44-1767

Cumberland almanac, for the year of our Lord, 1845. Calculated for the horizon of Nashville, Tennessee. Calculated by William L. Willeford. Nashville: W.F. Bang and company [1844] MWA; T. 44-1768

Cumberland Presbyterian Church. The confession of faith. Pittsburgh: Bird, 1844. 286 p. PPPrHi. 44-1769

Cuming, Francis H. Allegiance to Almighty god. Grand Rapids: J.H. Morse and company, 1844. 15 p. NGH. 44-1770

Cummings, Ariel Ivers. The mourner's pocket companion. Ashburnham, Massachusetts: J.L. Cummings, 1844. 62 p. DLC; MFiHi; MWA. 44-1771

Cummings, J.A. An introduction to ancient and modern geography, on the plan of Goldsmith and Guy, comprising rules for projecting maps. With an atlas. Second edition. Boston: Cummings and Hilliard, 1844. 256 p. MnHi. 44-1772

Cundall, Joseph, 1818-1895. Robin Hood and his merry foresters.... New York: H. G. Langley, 1844. 179 p. MH; N. 44-1773

Cundall, Joseph, 1818-1895. Tales of the kings of England: stories of camps and battlefields, wars and victories; from the old historians. By Stephen Percy [pseud.] Fourth American edition. New York: Wiley and Putnam, 1844. 239 p. ViU. 44-1774

Cunningham, Allan, 1784-1842. The lives of the most Eminent British painters and sculptors. New York: Harper and Brothers, 1844. 5 v. NOg; MeAu; PSew; RWe; WKen. 44-1775

Cunningham, John William. The velvet cushion. Philadelphia: Simon, 1844. MB. 44-1776

Curtis, Benjamin Robbins, 1809-1874. An article on the debts of the states. Boston: Damrell, 1844. 24 p. PU. 44-1777

Curtis, Benjamin Robbins, 1809-1874. An article on the debts of the states.

From the Christian review for March, 1844. Boston: W.S. Damrell, 1844. 24 p. MiU. 44-1778

Curtis, Benjamin Robbins, 1809-1874. An article on the debts of the states. From the Democratic review, for January, 1844. Boston: 1844. 19 p. CtY. 44-1779

Curtis, Benjamin Robbins, 1809-1874. An article on the debts of the states. From the North American Review, for January, 1844. Baltimore: Joseph Robinson, 1844. 47 p. Ct; MdBE; MdHi; NjPT. 44-1780

Curtis, Benjamin Robbins, 1809-1874. An article on the debts of the states. From the North American review, for January, 1844. Boston: T.R. Marvin, 1844. 36 p. CtY; MH; MiU; NN; NNC. 44-1781

Curtis, Benjamin Robbins, 1809-1874. An article on the debts of the states. From the North American Review, for January, 1844. New York: G.F. Nesbitt, 1844. 48 p. CtY; MB; NN; NNC. 44-1782

Curtis, George Ticknor, 1812-1894. American conveyancer; by George T. Curtis. Boston: Charles C. Little and James Brown, 1844. 269 p. MH-L; NCaS. 44-1783

Curtis, George Ticknor, 1812-1894. The merits of Thomas W. Dorr and George Bancroft, as they are politically connected. By a citizen of Massachusetts [pseud.] Boston: John H. Eastburn, [1844] 36 p. M; MBAt; MH; MiD-B; OO. 44-1784

Curtis, George Ticknor, 1812-1894.

The merits of Thomas W. Dorr and George Bancroft, as they are politically connected. Second edition. Boston: J.H. Eastburn, 1844. 41 p. CtY; MB: RPB; RNR. 44-1785

Curtis, George William, 1824-1892. Potiphar papers. Illustrated. New York: Putman, 1844. 250 p. Ia. 44-1786

Curtis, Harvey, 1806-1862. Address before the Union Literary, and Zelomathean Societies of Madison University. Annual exhibition, 1844. Madison: 1844. 16 p. CSmH; InU; OO. 44-1787

Curtis, Harvey, 1806-1862. Address before the Union Literary, and Zelomathean Societies of Madison University... Madison [Indiana] Office of the Republican Banner, 1844. 16 p. CSmH. 44-1788

Curtis, John Harrison, b. 1778. Curtis on the preservation of sight, the diseases of the eye, and the use, abuse, and choice of spectacles, reading glasses, etc. being practical observations for popular use. First American from the second London edition. New York: Burgess and Stringer, 1844. 48 p. DLC; PHC. 44-1789

Curtis, Moses Ashley, 1808-1872. Sacerdotal absolution: a sermon, preached before the convention of the diocese of North Carolina, 1843: by the Reverend M.A. Curtis.... New York: J.A. Sparks, 1844. 33 p. IEG; MBC; MdBD; NcU; NNG. 44-1790

Curtis, S. Voyage by the whale ship of N.B. Boston: 1844. MB. 44-1791

Curtis, Thomas. Bible episcopancy, a Bible constituency of the church, and Bible church ordinances, exhibited, eight lectures, delivered during the spring of 1844. Charleston: Burges and James, 1844. 251 p. GMM; ICU; LNB; NjPT; ScDuE. 44-1792

Curwen, Samuel, 1715-1802. Journal and letters of the late Samuel Curwen, ...a loyalist-refugee in England during the American revolution.... Second edition. By George Atkinson Ward.... London: Wiley and Putnam; New York: Leavitt, Trow and company, 1844. 600 p. MdHi; OClWHi. 44-1793

Cushing, Luther Stearns, 1803-1856. Manual of parliamentary practice. Rules of proceedings and debate in deliberative assemblies. Boston: Thompson, Bigelow and Brown, 1844. 189 [3] p. IaPeC; KGrb; MWC; ScSpW. 44-1794

Cushing, Luther Stearns, 1803-1856. Rules of proceeding and debate in deliberative assemblies. By Luther S. Cushing. Boston: Thompson, Brown and company, 1844. 192 p. IaCf; MoHu. 44-1795

Cushing, Luther Stearns, 1803-1856. Rules of proceeding and debate in deliberative assemblies. By Luther S. Cushing. New York: Hurst and company, [1844] 207 p. OCStR. 44-1796

Cushing, Luther Stearns, 1803-1856. Rules of proceeding and debate in deliberative assemblies. By Luther S. Cushing. Revised by John Freeman Baker, LL.D. New York: Excelsior Publishing House [1844?] 220 p. COT; MBBC; MEab; OCStR. 44-1797

Cushman, Robert Woodward, 1800-

1868. Lives of the twelve apostles. Boston: Perkins, 1844. 180 p. DLC; MB; MH; MWA. 44-1798

Cutler, Benjamin C. Twelve hours on the wreck; or, the stranding of the Sheffield. New York: T.C. Butler, 1844. MB; MiD-B; MSaP; NSmb; RPB. 44-1799

Cutler, Curtis. A discourse delivered in the Congregational Church, Peterboro, New Hampshire, Sunday, December 24, 1843. By Curtis Cutler, Keene: J. and J. Prentiss, 1844. 12 p. MeHi; Nh; NjPT; NN. 44-1800

Cutter, Calvin, 1807-1872. A female guide: containing facts and information upon the effects of masturbation, and the causes, prevention, treatment, and cure of hernia or rupture.... West Brookfield, Massachusetts: Mirick, 1844. 72 p. DNLM. 44-1801

Cutter, Calvin, 1807-1872. Practical physiology: applied to the preservation of health, and removal of disease, designed for schools and families. Boston: R. S. Davis, 1844. 180 p. MB; MBM; MH-M; MWbor; NBMS. 44-1802

Cutter, Calvin, 1807-1872. Practical remards upon the treatment and cure of burns, scalds, sprains, etc. Springfield, Massachusetts: Wood and Rupp, 1844. DLC. 44-1803

Cutter, Edward Francis, 1810-1880. Signs of the times. A series of sermons, by Edward F. Cutter, pastor of the Congregational Church in Warren, Maine. Portland: Thurston, Ilsely and company, printers, 1844. 48 p. MeHi; MeLeB; MWA. 44-1804

Cutting, James A. A short treatise on the care and management of bees, and the construction of the changeable beehive. Newbury, Vermont: L.J. McIndoe, 1844. 12 p. MH. 44-1805

Cuveilhier, J. The anatomy of the human body. The First American from the last Paris edition. Edited by Granville Sharp Pattison. New York: Published by Harper and Brothers, 1844. 907p. ViRMC. 44-1806

Cuyler, Cornelius C., 1783-1850. The evidences of a gracious state. By the Rev. Cornelius C. Cuyler, D.D., pastor of the Second Presbyterian Church, Philadelphia. Philadelphia: Presbyterian Board of Publication, [1844] 24 p. CtHC; GDecCT; MeBat; MnSM; PHi. 44-1807

Cuyler, Cornelius C., 1783-1850. The parity of the Ministry. Philadelphia: Published by the Presbyterian Board of Publication, 1844. 18 p. LNB; MAnP; MeBat; Nh; PPLT. 44-1808

D

D'arusmont, Frances Wright, 1795-1852. Biography, notes, and political letters of Frances Wright D'Arusmont. Dundee: J. Myles, 1844. 48 p. ICU; PHi. 44-1809

D'Arusmont, Frances Wright, 1795-1852. Biography, notes, and political letters of Frances Wright D'Arusmont. From the first British edition. New York: J. Windt, 1844. 2 v. DLC; MH. 44-1810

D'Israeli, Isaac C. Curiosities of literature, and the literary character illustrated. By I.C. D'Israeli, esq., D.C.L. D.S.A. With curiosities of American literature, by Rufus W. Griswold, esq.. Complete in one volume. New York: D. Appleton and company, 1844. 446 p. FWpR; MsU; MWA; NCH; PPL-R. 44-1811

Daboll, Nathan, 1750-1818. Daboll's complete schoolmaster's assistant; being a plain comprehensive system of practical arithmetic, adapted to the use of schools; exemplified and illustrated to engage the minds of youth in their study of practical arithmetic. New London, [Connecticut]: Bolles and Williams, 1844. 249 p. IaDaP; IEN; INormN. 44-1812

Daboll, Nathan, 1750-1818. Daboll's schoolmaster's assistant, improved and enlarged. Being a plain practical system of arithmetick.... With the addition of the farmers' and mechanicks' best method of bookkeeping.... by Samuel Green. Ithaca, New York: Andrus, Woodruff and Gauntlett, 1844. 228 p. CtY; FH; MB; MH. 44-1813

Dadoo, Mar Shimon Ben. The "wise sayings" and "doings" of Ben Evil, the lying prophet.... Translated in the language of the "favored land" by Mar Shimon Ben Dadoo.... Worcester: J.M. Stone, printer, 1844. 27 p. MH; MiD-B; MWA. 44-1814

Daily food for Christians; being a promise and another scriptural portion for every day in the year. Together with a verse of a hymn. Portland: Sanborn and Carter, 1844. MH. 44-1815

The daisy, or, litle rhymes for little readers. New Haven: S. Babcock, 1844. 16 p. CtY; MH: RPB. 44-1816

Dakin, Samuel D. A brief sketch of the plan and advantages of a sectional floating dry dock, combined with a permanent stone basin and platform.... and laying up in ordinary the ships of the United States navy. New York: Jared W. Bell, printer, 1844. 32 p. MBAt; MiD-B; PHi; RPB. 44-1817

Dallam, Jas. W. A brief compilation of the laws of the Republic of Texas, together with a view of their connection with the principles of the common law. By a member of the bar. Matagorda:

James Attwell, 1844. Broadside. TxU. 44-1818

Dallas, George Mifflin, 1792-1864. Mr. Dallas' opinion on annexation. 1844. PPL. 44-1819

Dalzel, Andrew, 1742-1806. Collectanea Graeca Minora; with notes partly compiled, and partly written. Sixth American edition. New York: W.E. Dean, 1844. 299 p. NcMHi; P. 44-1820

Dana, Amasa. Speech of Mr. Dana of New York on the bill making appropriations for the military academy at West Point. Delivered in the House of Representatives, March 6, 1844. Washington: 1844. 6 p. MH. 44-1821

Dana, Charles Anderson. A lecture on association in its connection with religion, delivered before the New England Fourier Society in Boston, March 7, 1844. Boston: B.H. Greene, 1844. 19 p. IU; MBAt; MH. 44-1822

Dana, James Dwight, 1813-1895. A system of mineralogy, comprising the most recent discoveries. With numerous woodcuts and four copper plates. New York: Wiley and Putnam, 1844. 633 p. CU; GAU; MB; TNP. 44-1823

Dana, James Dwight, 1813-1895. A system of mineralogy, comprising the most recent discoveries. With numerous woodcuts and four copper plates. Second edition. New York and London: Wiley and Putnam, 1844. 633 p. LN; MB; MiH; PPL-R; ScC. 44-1824

Dana, James Dwight, 1813-1895. Review of a system of mineralogy. Extracted from the American Journal of Science, V. XLVI. New Haven: Printed by B.L. Hamlen, 1844. 28, 4 p. MCM; MH-Z; MLow; MWA; NjR. 44-1825

Dana, Richard Henry, 1815-1882. Two years before the mast, a personal narrative of life at sea.... New York: Harper and brothers, 1844. 483 p. IaBo; MShM; OCX; PHi. 44-1826

Dana, Samuel Luther. Manures: a prize essay. Lowell: Bixby and Whiting, 1844. 47 p. LNT; MBAt; Nh-Hi; NNC; OCHP. 44-1827

Dandy Jim. Quickstep and song arranged for the pianoforte. [Words by S.S. Steele. Music by Daniel Myers] Boston: Prentiss, 1844. 3 p. CtY; MB. 44-1828

Dante, Alighieri, 1265-1321. Divine comedy. New York: Worthington, 1844. 600 p. ILinC. 44-1829

Dante, Alighiere, 1265-1321. The divne comedy; or vision of hell, purgatory and paradise. Translated by the Rev. Henry Francis Cary, with a life of Dante, chronological view of his age, selected explanatory notes and index. New York: A. L. Burt, 1844. 500 p. KyLoSX; LSH. 44-1830

Dante, Alighieri, 1265-1321. Inferno; translated by Rev. H.F. Cary, with critical and explanatory notes, life of Dante and chronological view of his age. New York: Hurst and company, 1844? 230 p. IaOskW; OMC. 44-1831

Dante, Alighieri, 1265-1321. The vision or Hell, purgatory paradise of Dante Alighieri, by Rev. Henry Francis Cary. New York: Hurst and company, 1844.

600 p. KWel; MdBS; NcD; ScCoB; ViHop. 44-1832

Danvers Eagle. Published every Wednesday morning, by Samuel T. Damon, Danvers, Massachusetts. September 4, 1844. v. 1, no 2, 4 p. MPeaHi. 44-1833

Danville, Kentucky. Centre College. Centre College. Catalogue year ending September 22, 1844. Danville: 1844. OCHP. 44-1834

Darley, W.H.W. Cantus Ecclesiae; or the sacred chorister: being a collection of psalm and hymn tunes, chants, sentences, and anthems. Philadelphia: Thomas, Cowperthwait and company, 1844. 300 p. CtHWatk; MoS; NjHo. 44-1835

Darlington, William. Address delivered before the Philadelphia Society for Promoting Agriculture, at the annual exhibition, held October 17, 1844. [Germantown: printed at the office of the Germantown Telegraph] 1844 8 p. AzU; DLC; NNUT; PHi; TxCsA. 44-1836

Darlington, William. A lecture on the study of botany. Read before the Ladies' Botanical Society. At Wilmington, Delaware, March 2, 1844. [Wilmington?] 1844. 24 p. CtY; DLC; NNC; PPAmP; PPL. 44-1837

Darrach, William, 1796-1865. Drawings of the anatomy of the groin, with anatomical remarks... Philadelphia: Lindsay and Blakiston, 1844. [15]-127 p. CSt-L; DLC; NbU-M; PU; RNR. 44-1838

Darrach, William, 1796-1865. Lecture introductory to the course of theory and practice of medicine in the medical

department of Pennsylvania College, Philadelphia. For the session 1844-1845. Philadelphia: William S. Young, printer, 1844. 16 p. DLC; KyDC; NBMS; PPL; ViU. 44-1839

Darscott, Celestine. The history of Celestine Darscott, the blind woman of Paturages. Translated from the copy published by the Evangelical Society of Belgium. Philadelphia: Presbyterian Board of Publication, 1844. 138 p. GDecCT; NjPT; ViRut. 44-1840

Dartmouth University. A catalogue of the officers and students of Dartmouth College, for the academical year, 1842-43. Concord: press of Asa McFarland, 1844. 26 p. MeB. 44-1841

Dartmouth University. A catalogue of the officers and students of Dartmouth College, for the academical year 1844-45. Hanover: the students, 1844. 22 p. MeB; OC. 44-1842

Dartmouth University. A catalogue of the officers and students of Dartmouth College, for the academical year, 1844-45. Hanover: September; 1844. 24 p. MeB. 44-1843

Davenport, Richard Alfred, 1772?-1852. Perilous adventures; or, remarkable instances of courage, perserverance, and suffering. ....New York: Harper and brothers, 1844. 335 p. AFIT; MB; NbOM; OCX; ViL. 44-1844

Davidson, David. Connection of sacred and profane history, being a review of the principal events in the world, as they bear upon the state of religion from the close of the Old Testament history, till the establishment of Christianity. New York:

Robert Carter, 1844. ICP; NNS; OWoC; ScCoB; WBeloC. 44-1845

Davidson, Robert. Plea for Presbyterianism. Two discourses, delivered in the Presbyterian Church, New Brunswick, March 11, 1844. By Rev. Robert Davidson, ...New York: Robert Carter; Pittsburgh: Thomas Carter, 1844. 35 p. CSansS; DLC; GDecCT; NjPT; PPPrHi. 44-1846

Davies, Charles, 1798-1876. Arithmetic, designed for academies and schools. [with answers] By Charles Davies. Philadelphia: A.S. Barnes and company, 1844. 340 p. InICC; MB; NPV; PRea. 44-1847

Davies, Charles, 1798-1876. Elementary algebra embracing the first principles of science. Philadelphia: A.S. Barnes and company, 1844. 279 p. ICU; MH; MoS; NjR; OMC. 44-1848

Davies, Charles, 1798-1876. Elementary geometry, with applications in mensuration. By Charles Davies, LL.D.... Philadelphia: A.S. Barnes and company, 1844. 216 p. CtHWatk; IGK; MPeHi; PLFM; RPB. 44-1849

Davies, Charles, 1798-1876. Elements of algebra: including Sturms' Theorem. Translated from the French of M. Bourdon. Adapted to the course of Mathematical instruction in the United States. Philadelphia: A.S. Barnes and company; New York: Pratt, Woodford and company, 1844. 368 p. DAU; DLC; ICU; MsY; PU. 44-1850

Davies, Charles, 1798-1876. Elements of analytical geometry; embracing the equations of the point, the straight line,

the conic sections, and surfaces of the first and second order.... revised. Philadelphia: A.S. Barnes and company, 184. 352 p. IaDaM; LNP; MsCliM; NPalk; ViW. 44-1851

Davies, Charles, 1798-1876. Elements of descriptive geometry with their application to spherical trigonometry, spherical projections and warped surfaces. Philadelphia: A.S. Barnes and company, 1844. CtHWatk; MH; OO. 44-1852

Davies, Charles, 1798-1876. Elements of the differential and integral calculus, by Charles Davies. Improved edition. Philadelphia: A.S. Barnes and company, 1844. 283 p. CoDR; MH; NjP; OC; WaPS. 44-1853

Davies, Charles, 1798-1876. First lessons in arithmetic, designed for beginners. ....Philadelphia: A.S. Barnes and company, 1844. 168 p. CtHWatk; ICBB; InU; MPiB; NN. 44-1854

Davies, Charles, 1798-1876. A key containing the statements and solutions of questions in Davies' elementary algebra for the use of teachers only. Philadelphia: A.S. Barnes and company, 1844. 99 p. MH; MiD-B; PV; NRivHi. 44-1855

Davies, Charles, 1798-1876. Key to Davies' arithmetic: with additional examples. For the use of teachers only. Philadelphia: A.S. Barnes and company, 1844. 278 p. CtY; PLFM; WaU. 44-1856

Davies, Charles, 1798-1876. Practical geometry: with selected applications in mensuration, in artificer's work and mechanics. By Charles Davies, LL.D. Philadelphia: A.S. Barnes and company,

1844. 252 p. CtHWatk; MH; ScNC; WMNDC. 44-1857

Davis, Asabel, b. 1791. Discovery of New England by the Northmen, five hundred years before Columbus, with an introduction on the antiquities of America and on the first inhabitants of Central America.... Twelfth edition. Boston: Dutton and Wentworth's, printers, 1844. 24 p. CtHT; DLC; MiD-B; NbO; NjPT. 44-1858

Davis, Charles Augustus. Peter Scriber [pseud.] on protection. [Washington: 1844] MBAt. 44-1859

Davis, Garret. Extract from the speech of Mr. Garret Davis, of Kentucky, exhibiting the expenditures of Mr. Van Buren's administration, ...Delivered in the House.... April 5, 1844. [Washington: printed at Gideon's] 1844. 8 p. ICN; MBAt; MBevHi; OClWHi; PHi. 44-1860

Davis, James M. A plea for new measures in the promotion of revivals.... Pittsburgh: A. Jaynes, printer, 1844. 140 p. In; MeBat; OO. 44-1861

Davis, T. Lecture on American history anterior to Columbus. Boston: 1844. OCHP. 44-1862

Davy Crockett's almanac. Boston: J. Fisher, 1844. MWA. 44-1863

Davy Crockett's almanac. New York: Turner and Fisher, 1844. MWA. 44-1864

Davy Crockett's almanac for 1845. Boston, Massachusetts: James Fisher, [1844] MWA. 44-1865

Davys, George. Village conversations

on the baptismal office and the church catechism. By the Rt. Rev. George Davys, D.D., Bishop of Peterborough. Adapted to the liturgy of the Protestant Episcopal Church. ....Boston: Tract company.... of Massachusetts, 1844. 24 p. MBC; MBD; NjPT; WHi. 44-1866

Dawson, William, 1773-1841. Memoirs of the Rev. David Stoner, containing copious extracts from his diary and epistolary correspondence. New York: G. Sandford, 1844. 286 p. DLC; KBB. 44-1867

Dawson, William, 1773-1841. Memoirs of the Rev. David Stoner: containing copious extracts from his diary and epistolary correspondence.... Second American from the second English edition. New York: G. Lane and P.P. Sandford, 1844. 286 p. CtMW; DLC; MWelC. 44-1868

Day, Charles William. Hints on etiquette and the usages of society; with a glance at bad habits. Adapted to American society, by the author. Boston: Otis, Broaders and company, 1844. 154 p. ICN; MH; NN; ViU. 44-1869

Day, Charles William. Hints on etiquette and the usages of society; with a glance at bad habits. Adapted to American society, by the author. Boston: Ticknor, 1844. 157 p. LNH; MDeeP; MWA; PAtM. 44-1870

Day, Charles William. Hints on etiquette and the usages of society; with a glance at bad habits. New York: A.V. Blake, 1844. 157 p. MWA; NN. 44-1871

Day, Charles William. Maxims, experiences, and observations of Agogos.

Boston: Otis, Broaders and company, 1844. 180 p. DLC; InNd; MBAt; PPL; RPAt. 44-1872

Day, H.W. The vocal school; or, Pestalozzian method of instruction in the elements of vocal music.... illustrated by a great variety of examples and exercises.... Second edition. Boston: Otis, Broaders and company, 1844. 279 p. IaSlB; MWA; RPB. 44-1873

Day, Henry N. The art of elocution, exemplified in a course of exercises. New Haven: A.H. Maltby, 1844. CtY-D; ICP; MHad; OClWHi; WBeloC. 44-1874

Day, Jeremiah, 1773-1867. Elements of algebra, being an abridgment of Day's algebra. Third edition. New Haven: Durrie and Peck, 1844. MH. 44-1875

Day, Jeremiah, 1773-1867. Elements of algebra, being an abridgment of Day's algebra, adapted to the capacities of the young and the method of instruction in schools and academies. Fourth edition. New Haven: Durrie and Peck, 1844. 252 p. MiU; NcHiC. 44-1876

Day, Jeremiah, 1773-1867. Elements of algebra, being an abridgment of Day's algebra, adapted to the capacities of the young and the method of instruction in schools and academies. Fifth edition. New Haven: Durrie and Peck, 1844. 252 p. IaU; KyBC; MH; RPB. 44-1877

Day, Jeremiah, 1773-1867. Introduction to algebra. Forty-ninth edition. New Haven: Durrie and Peck, 1844. 332 p. MeHi. 44-1878

Day, Jeremiah, 1773-1867. Introduc-

tion to algebra. Fiftieth edition. New Haven: 1844. 332 p. MB. 44-1879

Day, Parsons E. District school grammar. The principles of English grammar. Second edition. Ithaca, New York: Andrus, Woodruff and Gauntlett, printers, 1844. 120 p. CtHWatk; NICLA; NRHi. 44-1880

Day, Thomas, 1777-1855. A historical discourse delivered before the Connecticut Historical Society, and the citizens of Hartford, on the evening of the 26th day of December, 1843. Hartford: Case, Tiffany and Burnham, 1844. 36 p. CtSoP; DLC; NjP; OMC; PHi. 44-1881

Day school sketches. Boston: 1844. 111 p. MWA. 44-1882

Dayton, William Lewis, 1807-1864. Speech of Mr. Dayton, of New Jersey, on the subject of Oregon, etc. Delivered in the Senate, February 23 and 26, 1844. Washington: Gales and Seaton, 1844. MHi; MnHi; PPL. 44-1883

Dayton, William Lewis, 1807-1864. Speech of Mr. Dayton, of New Jersey, on the tariff. Delivered in the Senate, April 29, 1844. Washington: Printed at Gideon's [1844] 15 p. In; MH; TxU. 44-1884

Dean, C.C. A child assisted in giving the heart to God... Boston: Massachusetts Sabbath School Society, 1844. 72 p. NPlaK. 44-1885

Dean, Ezra. Speech of Mr. Dean, of Ohio, on the F... on General Jackson: delivered in the House, January, 1844. 8 p. MHi; NNC; OClWHi. 44-1886

Deane, J. On the discovery of fossil footmarks. New Haven: 1844. MB. 44-1887

Death of the prophets Joseph and Hyram Smith, who were murdered while in prison at Carthage, Illinois, on the twenty-seventh day of June, A.D. 1844. Compiled and printed for our venerable brother in Christ, Freeman Nickerson. Boston: Printed by J. Gooch, 1844. 12 p. MH. 44-1888

Dedham, Massachusetts. South Parish. Catalogue of the Social Circulating Library, in Dedham, South Parish, with the proprietors' names, and the constitution of the library. Boston: press of T.R. Marvin, 1844. 16 p. 44-1889

Dedham, Massachusetts. Valuation and tax on the polls and estates of the inhabitants of the town of Dedham. Dedham: 1844. 55 p. MHi. 44-1890

Dedham Village Total Abstinence Association. Report of the executive committee of the Dedham Village Total Abstinence Association, presented July 11, 1844. [Dedham Village: C.B. Ewer, printer] 1844. 15 p. NNUT. 44-1891

A defence of some important doctrines of the Gospel, in twenty-six sermons. Preached at the Lime Street Lecture. Philadelphia: Presbyterian Board of Publication, [printed by William S. Martien] 1844. 472 p. CSansS; ICU; KyLoS; OO; WHi. 44-1892

DeFoe, Daniel, 1661-1731. The life and adventures of Robinson Crusoe; by Daniel DeFoe. ....New York: Alexander V. Blake, 1844. 248 p. CLSU; CtY; MiU; MWA. 44-1893

Defoe, Daniel, 1661-1731. Robinson Crusoe. Adaptations. The little Robinson Crusoe. Philadelphia: Smith and Peck; New Haven: Durrie and Peck, 1844. 191 p. CtY; MWA. 44-1894

Dehon, Theodore. Sermons on confirmation and an address. New York: Stanford and Swords, 1844. 71 p. OrPD. 44-1895

DeKalbe, Pliny. The American wife... Philadelphia: Murray, 1844. 24 p. PPPr-Hi. 44-1896

DeKay, James Ellsworth, 1792-1851. Birds. Albany, New York: Printed by Carroll and Cook, 1844. IaAS; MH-Z. 44-1897

DeLancey, William Heathcote, 1797-1865. Courage in God's service. A sermon, preached at the institution of the Rev. Thomas C. Pitkin, into the rectorship of St. Luke's Church, Rochester, on Sunday, August 11, 1844... Rochester [New York] printed by D. Hoyt, 1844. 24 p. CSmH; MiD; NBuG; NGH; PPL-R. 44-1898

DeLancey, William Heathcote, 1797-1865. Episcopal address to the annual convention of the Diocese of Western New York, August 21, 1844, by the Rt. Rev. William Heathcote DeLancey, D.D., Bishop of the Diocese. Utica, Western New York: H.H. Curtiss, printer, 1844. 29 p. NBuDD. 44-1899

DeLancey, William Heathcote, 1797-1865. The office of a Bishop being part of the sermon preached by the Rev. William DeLancey, at the consecration of the present Bishop of the Diocese of Massachusetts. Boston: The tract com-tee...of Massachusetts, 1844. 30 p. AMob; CtHT; KyLoS; MPiB; MWA. 44-1900

Delaware and Maryland farmer's almanac for 1845. Philadelphia, Pennsylvania: J. M'Dowell, [1844] MWA. 44-1901

Delaware County Institute of Science. Media, Pennsylvania. Report of a committee of the Delaware County Institute of Science, on the great rain storm and flood, which occurred in that county on the fifth of August, 1843. With a map of the county. Read at a special meeting of the institute, January 4th, 1844. Chester, [Pennsylvania]: Y.S. Walter, printer, 1844. 52 p. CSmH; MiD; PHi; PPAmP; PPL-R. 44-1902

Delaware Mutual Safety Insurance Company. Instructions and explanations for the use and direction of the agents of the Delaware Mutual Safety Insurance Company. Philadelphia: H. Evans, printer, 1844. 38 p. PHi; PhInsLib. 44-1903

Dellet, James. Speech of Mr. Dellet, of Alabama, on the motion to recommit the report of the committee on the rules... Delivered in the House, February 22, 1844. Washington: Gales and Seaton, 1844. 15 p. GEU; OClWHi. 44-1904

Delta Kappa Epsilon. Song book. Apud Epsilon edition. Boston: O. Ditson and company, 1844. 168 p. OFH. 44-1905

Democratic almanac for 1844, containing a life of Martin Van Buren and political information. Philadelphia: Democratic Hickory Club, 1844. 8 p. PHi. 44-1906

Democratic almanac for 1844, containing a life of Martin Van Buren and various political information.... Philadelphia: Mifflin and Parry, 1844. 20 p. ArU; MWA; PHi; PPL. 44-1907

Democratic argus. October 31, 1843-January 22, 1844. Philadelphia: 1844-. PHi. 44-1908

Democratic Association, Norwich, Connecticut. Address of the Democratic Association of Norwich. To the people of Connecticut. [Norwich: 1844?] 12 p. Ct; CtHWatk. 44-1909

Democratic Association, Washington, D.C. Address of the... The treaty in favor of American tobacco, cotton, rice and lard, rejected by the Whigs. [Washington: 1844] 4 p. DLC; N. 44-1910

Democratic Association, Washington, D.C. Desperation of Whigery. Lying outright, and forgery to sustain it. [n.p.: 1844?] CSmH. 44-1911

Democratic Association, Washington, D.C. Oregon, published by the Democratic Association of Washington, D. Washington: J. Heart, [1844?] 4 p. CSmH; CtY; CU-B; OClWHi, Or. 44-1912

Democratic Association, Washington, D.C. South in danger. Address of the Democratic Association of Washington, D.C. Washington: J. Heart, [1844] 4 p. DLC; GU; NBuG; NcU. 44-1913

Democratic Association, Washington, D.C. South in danger. Read before you vote. Address of the Democratic Association of Washington, D.C.

[Washington: 1844] 8 p. CtY; DLC; IaGG; MWA; WHi. 44-1914

Democratic Association, Washington, D.C. South in danger; being a document published for circulation at the South, and showing the design of the annexation of Texas to be the security and perpetuation of slavery. [Boston, 1844] 10 p. CtY; MWA; NN; NNC; WHi. 44-1915

Democratic Association, Washington, D.C. Texas; the first duty of Democrats is to preserve our principles. Address of the Washington Democratic Association to the Democracy of the United States. [Washington, 1844] 56 p. MWA; TxU. 44-1916

Democratic Association, Washington, D.C. The Whigs hate and persecute the naturalized citizens. [Washington: 1844] 4 p. N. 44-1917

Democratic Clay Club of the Seventh Ward, New York. Constitution, declaration and by-laws adopted by the Democratic Clay Club of the Seventh Ward. [New York] Joseph W. Harrison [1844?] 16 p. NNC. 44-1918

Democratic Congressional Committee. Shall it be surrendered to Great Britain? Washington: 1844. PPL. 44-1919

Democratic Congressional Committee, 1844. Oregon. American protection to American Pioneers; or shall Oregon be surrendered to Great Britain? [n.p.: 1844] 7 p. OrU. 44-1920

Democratic Hickory Club. Philadelphia. Address of the Democratic Hickory Club, for the city and county of Philadelphia, recommending Martin Van Buren

as the presidential candidate for 1844. Also, the letter of Mr. Van Buren to the state convention of Indiana. [Philadelphia: Mifflin and Parry, printers, 1844] 16 p. DLC; OClWHi; Vi. 44-1921

The democratic mentor: containing political information, documents, proofs, &c., connected with the presidential election of 1844....v. 1, no. 1-34; March 20-November 11, 1844. Tuscaloosa: State Journal and Flat of the Union office, 1844. 1 v. TxU. 44-1922

Democratic Party. Fifty reasons why it should succeed... Washington: 1844. PPL. 44-1923

Democratic Party. Indiana. State Convention. An address in relation to national policy. Indianapolis:, 1844. 16 p. In; InU. 44-1924

Democratic Party. New York. New York City. Central Clay committee. Rules for the organization and government of the Central Clay Committee of the city and county of New York, as revised and amended, April 1, 1844. New York: Harrison, 1844. 30 p. ICN. 44-1925

Democratic Party. Ohio. Convention, 1844. Proceedings and address of the Democratic state convention of the state of Ohio, held in the city of Columbus on the eighth and ninth days of January, 1844. Columbus: S. Medary, printer, 1844. 31 p. DLC; IU; OClWHi; PPFrankI. 44-1926

Democratic Party. Ohio. Young Men's State Central Committee. An address to the electors of Ohio, on the coalition of 1825; or Henry Clay's bargain with John Quincy Adams, through which the latter, in defiance of the will of the people was made president of the United States.... Columbus: Office of the Ohio Statesman, 1844. 15 p. CSmH. 44-1927

Democratic Party. Pennsylvania. Committee of correspondence. Clay and Polk: the difference between them on the tariff question. By a Columbia County man. Philadelphia: printed at the office of the Pennsylvania, [1844] 8 p. MH. 44-1928

Democratic Party. Pennsylvania. Political biography: Polk, Dallas and Shunk. Philadelphia: Mifflin and Parry, 1844. 15 p. NN; OkU; P; PHi; PPL. 44-1929

Democratic Party. Pennsylvania. To the Democratic party of the United States on the presidential election.... Philadelphia: printed for the committee, 1844. 27 p. OkU. 44-1930

Democratic Party. Tennessee. Vindication of the revolutionary character and services of the late Col. Ezekiel Polk of Mecklenburg, North Carolina.... Nashville: 1844. 16 p. DLC; MiGr; NcU; NN; PHi. 44-1931

Democratic Party. Virginia. Democratic electoral ticket for Virginia. For president, James K. Polk, of Tennessee. For vice president, George M. Dallas, of Pennsylvania. [Richmond? 1844] Broadside. PPRF. 44-1932

Democratic Party. Virginia. Fincastle Democratic - Extra. [Fincastle, Virginia? Democratic Republic Central Committee 1844?] Broadside. ViU. 44-1933

Democratic Party. Virginia. Richmond. Democratic meeting, this evening. Seth

Barton, ...[on] the annexation of Texas. Richmond, June 11, 1844. [Richmond: 1844] ViU. 44-1934

Democratic reformer, embodying documents concerning governmental reformation in the state of New York.... [1843-44] Albany: 1844. NNC. 44-1935

The democratic text book. New York: Burgess, Stringer and company; and others; Baltimore: Murphy, printer, [1844] 8 p. ICN; WHi. 44-1936

Demosthenes. The Olynthiac orations, chiefly from the text of Dindorf; with English explanatory notes, chronology, etc. Cambridge: W.P. Grant, 1844. 96 p. MH. 44-1937

Demosthenes. The orations of Demosthenes. Translated by Thomas LeLand. New York: Harper and brothers, 1844. 2 v. MChi; MNBedf; RKi; RPE. 44-1938

Dempster, John. A thanksgiving discourse, delivered in the Second Wesleyan Chapel, New York, Thursday, December 14, 1843. By Rev. John Dempster, A.M. New York: G. Lane and P.P. Sandford, 1844. 24 p. IEG; MB; MBNMHi; Nh; PPL. 44-1939

Dempster, William Richardson. The lonely auld wife, a ballad [Accompaniment for pianoforte] Boston: Ditson, 1844. 7 p. MB. 44-1940

Denig, John. Denigs vs. Nevin! A second reply to Rev. J.W. Nevin, D.D., on the anxious bench. By John Denig, P.P.M. Chambersburg: Thomas J. Wright, printer, 1844. 20 p. DLC; PLERC-Hi. 44-1941

Denison University. Granville, Ohio. Annual catalogue. 1844-46. Granville: 1844-1901. ICN. 44-1942

Dennis, Rodney Gove. Review of Christ seen by every eye... Springfield: 1844. 22 p. MBC. 44-1943

Dennison, Charles. Illustration of the signs, tokens, passwords and grips belonging to the I.O.O.F. together with the form of initiation and the fire degrees. Fourth edition. Boston: 1844. IaCrM; MB. 44-1944

The denominations and the Church, their principles and differences considered. In a letter to a deacon. Philadelphia: R.S.H. George, 1844. 34 p. MdBD. 44-1945

DePauw University. Sixth annual catalogue of the officers and students.... Greencastle, Indiana: 1844. 16 p. In; InGDU; OCHP. 44-1946

DeQuincey, Thomas. The logic of political economy. Boston: Ticknor, 1844. 387 p. MnM. 44-1947

DeQuincey, Thomas. Theological essays, and other papers. Boston: Ticknor, Reed, and Fields, 1844. 2 v. PEdg; PU. 44-1948

Derby, Elias Hasket, 1803-1880. Two months abroad: or, a trip to England, France, Baden, Prussia, and Belgium. In August and September, 1843. By a railroad director of Massachusetts. Boston: Redding and company, 1844. 64 p. ICJ; MiU; MWA; Nh; RPAt. 44-1949

Dermit? The Christian companion, being a summary of the most select devo-

tions.... New York: 1844. 380 p. DLC. 44-1950

Description of statuary executed by Mrs. W. Pelby. Boston: Hooton and Upton, 1844. 8 p. MB. 44-1951

Description of the grand historical picture of Belshazzar's feast, painted by Allston, and now exhibiting at the Corinthian Gallery, Federal Street. Second edition. Boston: Eastburn's Press, 1844. [8] p. MH; MHi. 44-1952

Description of the grand historical picture of Belshazzar's feast, painted by Allston, and now exhibiting at the Corinthian Gallery. Fourth edition. Boston: 1844. MB; MBC; MH. 44-1953

Description of Washington's monument, and the public buildings in Baltimore. Baltimore: Printed by J. Murphy, 1844. 12 p. MB; MdBJ. 44-1954

Detection of the errors of Dr. J. Prescott.... Augusta: William T. Johnson, printer, 1844. 16 p. MeLewB. 44-1955

The detriments of civilization and benefits of association; also, pledges and rules for the integral phalanx.... with objections to the common property system of Owen, Rapp and others. Cincinnati: 1844. 36 p. RPB; WHi. 44-1956

DeVeaux, Samuel, 1789-1852. The traveler's own book, to Saratoga Springs, Niagara Falls and Canada. A complete guide for the valetudinarian and the tourist. Fifth edition. Buffalo: Faxon and company, 1844. 251 p. DLC; LU; MB; MnHi; RNR. 44-1957

Devinne, Daniel, 1793-1883. The

church and slavery. A historical survey of the Methodist Episcopal Church in its relation to slavery. Boston: 1844. 106 p. CtY; MB; MBNMHi; PHi. 44-1958

Dewey, Orville, 1794-1882. An appeal of religion to men in power. A sermon on occasion of the late calamity at Washington. New York: C.S. Francis and company, 1844. 20 p. DLC; ICMe; MBC; MHi; MNtCA. 44-1959

Dewey, Orville, 1794-1882. A discourse on slavery and the annexation of Texas.... New York: C.S. Francis and company, 1844. 18 p. CSmH; NNC; OClWHi; TxU; WHi. 44-1960

Dewey, Orville, 1794-1882. On American morals and manners. Boston: William Crosby, 1844. 34 p. CtY; MH; MnHi; NNC; PU. 44-1961

Dewey, Orville, 1794-1882. A sermon, preached in the Church of the Messiah, November 24, 1844, on the character and claims of seamen. [New York: American Seamen's Friend Society] 1844. 19 p. OO. 44-1962

Dewey, William. Black river journal... Suggestions, urging the construction of a railroad, from Rome to Watertown, and Cape Vincent. Watertown, New York: from the press of J. Greene, 1844. 32 p. NNE. 44-1963

Dewey, William. Suggestions, urging the construction of a railroad from Rome to Watertown, and Cape Vincent. By William Dewey, esq. ....Watertown, New York: press of J. Greene, 1844. 32 p. N; NN. 44-1964

DeWitt, W.R. The spiritual wants of Pennsylvania, and the duty and importance of supplying them: a sermon, preached before the Philadelphia Home Missionary Society.... May 22, 1844. By W. R. DeWitt.... Philadelphia: Isaac Ashmead, printer, 1844. 22 p. KyDC; MH-AH; NjR; PLT; PPPrHi. 44-1965

Dialogue between the devil, and a teetotaler. Philadelphia: Brown, Bicking and Guilbert, 1844. 23 p. DLC; PU. 44-1966

Dialogue on democracy, in which the democratic principle is defined and applied as a touchstone to party-men and measures. New York: 1844. 28 p. MH; NNC; OClWHi. 44-1967

Dibble, Sheldon. Thoughts on missions. By the late Rev. Sheldon Dibble, missionary in the Sandwich Islands. ....New York: American Tract Society, 1844. IaMP; ICNBT; KWiU; MChiA; OSW. 44-1968

Dibdin, Charles, 1745-1814. The songs and ballads of Charles Dibdin. [New York: 1844] 16 p. CtY; DLC; MB; NN. 44-1969

Dick, John, 1764-1833. Lectures on the Acts of the apostles. By the late John Dick... First American from the second Glasgow edition. New York: Robert Carter; Pittsburg: Thomas Carter, 1844. 407 p. CtY; IaMP; KyDC; MeBaT; MoS. 44-1970

Dick, John, 1764-1833. Lectures on theology... published under the superintendence of his son, with a preface, memoir, ect., by the American editor... Philadelphia: W.G. Wardle, 1844. 2 v.

CtY; GMM; ODaB; PPLT; TxShA. 44-1971

Dick, Thomas, 1774-1857. Christian philosopher; or the connection of science and philosophy with religion. Cooperstown, New York: H.E. Phinney, 1844. 350 p. IaK; NN. 44-1972

Dick, Thomas, 1774-1857. Christian philosopher; or the connection of science and philosophy with religion. Philadelphia: Biddle, 1844. 350 p. IaK; NN; PPA; OU; WS. 44-1973

Dick, Thomas, 1774-1857. On the improvement of society by the diffusion of knowledge. Hartford: Sumner and Goodman, 1844. 191 p. RJa. 44-1974

Dick, Thomas, 1774-1857. On the improvement of society by the diffusion of knowledge; or an illustration of the advantages which would result from a more general dissemination of rational and scientific information among all ranks. New York: Harper, 1844. 442 p. MChi; OCY. 44-1975

Dick, Thomas, 1774-1857. The sidereal heavens and other subjects connected with astronomy. New York: Harper and brothers, 1844. 432 p. CtY; GAuY; OCX; RPE; WaPS. 44-1976

Dick, Thomas, 1774-1857. The works of Thomas Dick. An essay on the improvement of society; the philosophy of a future state; the philosophy of religion.... Hartford: Sumner and Goodman, 1844. 4 v. in 1. IaLaw; KyLo; NbK; RJa; ScCoB. 44-1977

Dickens, Charles, 1812-1870. A Christmas carol. In prose. Being a ghost story of Christmas. New York: Harper and Brothers, 1844. [5]-31 p. CSmH; DLC; MeB; OClWHi; PPL. 44-1978

Dickens, Charles, 1812-1870. A Christmas carol. In prose. Being a ghost story of Christmas. Philadelphia: Carey and Hart, 1844. 156 p. MBL; MH; MWA; NNP; PPL-R. 44-1979

Dickens, Charles, 1812-1870. The chimes!... New York [1844] 32 p. MHi. 44-1980

Dickens, Charles, 1812-1870. The life and adventures of Martin Chuzzlewit by Charles Dickens, with illustrations by Phiz. New York: Harper and brothers, 1844. [6]-312 p. CtHT; MH; OUrC; RBr; TNP. 44-1981

Dickens, Charles, 1812-1870. Oliver Twist. By Charles Dickens, author of "Pickwick papers," "Nicholas Nickleby." With illustrations by George Cruikshank. Fourth edition. Boston: Lewis and Sampson, 1844. 314 p. MdBJ; PHC. 44-1982

Dickens, Charles, 1812-1870. The posthumous papers of the Pickwick Club. By Charles Dickens, with illustrations by Crowquill. Fifth edition. Boston: Lewis and Sampson, 1844. 609 p. MNe; OU. 44-1983

Dickey, Mr. Speech of Mr. Dickey, of Pennsylvania, on the tariff bill. Delivered in the House of Representatives, May 4, 1844. Washington: J. and G.S. Gideon, printers, 1844. 16 p. MH; NUtHi; OClWHi. 44-1984

Dickinson, Austin, 1791-1849. Sermon by Dickinson... Story of David Rouge.

[text in Cherokee] Park Hill: 1844? 24 p. NN. 44-1985

Dickinson, David. Speech...of Tennessee, on the report and resolutions of the committee on elections, relative to the elections by general ticket, in the states of New Hampshire, Georgia, Mississippi, and Missouri. Delivered in the House, February 12, 1844. Washington: Printed by Gales and Seaton, 1844. 16 p. NNC; T. 44-1986

Dickinson College. Register 1844/5, 1852/53. Carlisle, Pennsylvania: 1844-1852. MBAt. 44-1987

Dickinson College. Register, for the academical year, 1844-5. Carlisle, Pennsylvania: John D. Fay, printer, 1844. 24 p. MBAt; PPL; PWW. 44-1988

Diefenbach, Daniel. Des deutschen Mannes Geschaftshelfer, enthaltend die nutzlichsten und gebrauchlichsten Vorschriften, um mehrere Arten von Geschaftsschriften, Johne Kulfe eines Anwalts oder Notarius gesetzmassig in deutscher Sprache selbst zuschreiben. Baltimore: gedruckt in der Buchhandlung der Evang. Luth. Kirche, 1844. MH; PPG. 44-1989

Dike, Samuel Fuller. Doctrines of the New Jerusalem; sermon at the dedication of the New Jerusalem Temple, Bath, Maine. Boston: James Munroe, 1844. 64 p. CtHT; MBAt; MeB; NNG; RPB. 44-1990

Dike, Samuel Fuller. A sermon delivered at the dedication of the New Jerusalem Temple in Bath, Maine. January 11, 1844. By Samuel Dike.... Bos-

ton: T. Harrington and company, 1844. 64 p. MeB; MH; MH-AH. 44-1991

Dillard, Ryland Thompson. Address of Rev. R.T. Dillard, delivered by request, on the fourth of July, 1844, before a numerous assemblage of the citizens of several counties. Near Chilesburg, Fayette County, Kentucky. Lexington: Inquirer office, printer, 1844. 12 p. ICU; KyLx; MBAt; MWA. 44-1992

Dillingham, J.R. Explanation on the use and abuse of dental surgery. Lynn: 1844. MBAt. 44-1993

Dillon, Charles. The mysteries of Paris; a drama, in three acts. London, New York: Samuel French, [1844?] 37 p. OCl. 44-1994

Dinsmore's and Appleton's railroad and steam navigation guide. New York: 1844. PPL. 44-1995

A directory and gazetteer of the city of Rochester, for 1844... Rochester: Printed by Canfield and Warren, 1844. 306 p. CSmH; IaGG; MWA; NRHi; NRU. 44-1996

Directory of the city of Mobile. Directory and register for 1844.... with a variety of.... statistical matter, etc. By E.E. Wood. 1844. AMob; MBNEH. 44-1997

A directory to the age of the world, by Scripture testimony and an exposition of part of the book of Daniel. Boston: Howes Press, 1844. 16 p. DLC. 44-1998

District of Columbia. Laws of the corporation of the city of Washington, passed by the forty first council.

Washington: printed by J. and G.S. Gideon, 1844. 143 p. IaU-L. 44-1999

Disturnell, John, 1801-1877. The northern and western traveller. New York: 1844. MB. 44-2000

Disturnell, John, 1801-1877. The northern traveller; containing the Hudson River guide, and tour to the Springs, Lake George and Canada, passing through Lake Champlain. New York: J. Disturnell, 1844. 84 p. DLC; MWA; NBU; NcD; PPAmP. 44-2001

Disturnell, John, 1801-1877. The western traveller; embracing the canal and railroad routes, from Albany and Troy to Buffalo and Niagara Falls. Also, the steamboat route from Buffalo to Detroit and Chicago. New York: J. Disturnell, 1844. 90 p. CSt; DLC; MH; NGH; OClWHi. 44-2002

The divine right of church government: wherein it is proved that the Presbyterian government, by preaching and ruling elders, in sessional, presbyterial, and synodical assemblies, may lay the only lawful claim to a divine right according to the Holy Scriptures. A new edition, corrected and amended.... to which is added an appendix.... together with an abstract.... New York: R. Martin and company, 1844. GDecCT; ICN; KyLOP; NbOP; PPi. 44-2003

Dix, Dorothea Lynde, 1802-1887. An address by a recent female visitor to the prisoners in the eastern penitentiary of Pennsylvania. Philadelphia: Joseph and William Kite, printers, 1844. 12 p. MB; MBAU; MH; PHC. 44-2004

Dix, Dorothea Lynde, 1802-1887. Con-

versations on common things or guide to knowledge. For the use of schools and families. By a teacher. Boston: Monroe and Francis, 1844. 288 p. CtHWatk. 44-2005

Dix, Dorothea Lynde, 1802-1887. Memorial. To the legislature of New York [concerning the condition of indigent and pauper insane persons in the county houses of this state. Albany: 1844] 59 p. MB; MBAt; MBM; MH; PPL. 44-2006

Dix, William Giles, d. 1898. An imaginary conversation between William Shakespeare and his friend, Henry Wriothesley, Earl of Southampton. Also, an imaginary conversation between the same Mr. Shakespeare, and Mr. Richard Quyner, an old associate of his, at Stratford-upon-Avon. Boston: Jordan and company, 1844. 40 p. DLC; MBC; MH; NN. 44-2007

Dixon, John. A key to the prophecies; ....the chronology of the Bible....by John Dixon, junior. Boston: printed for the author, 1844. 342 p. DLC; MH-AH; NbLU. 44-2008

Dixon, John. The twin brothers: being the lives of John and James Dixon. Thirtieth edition. By John and James Dixon. Albany: 1844. 72 p. MWA. 44-2009

Dixon, John. The twin brothers; being the lives of John and James Dixon. Thirty-first edition. Albany: J. Munsell, 1844. 72 p. OClWHi. 44-2010

Doane, George Washington, 1799-1859. Ancient charity, the rule and the reproof of modern: a sermon in St. Mary's.

Burlington: 1844? 16 p. MB; PHi. 44-2011

Doane, George Washington, 1799-1859. Christian pastor. Burlington: 1844. CtHT. 44-2012

Doane, George Washington, 1799-1859. A pastoral for the season of confirmation; baptism; confirmation; the supper of the Lord. Burlington, New Jersey: 1844. 12 p. CtHT; MdBD; NNG; PPLT. 44-2013

Doane, George Washington, 1799-1859. A shepherd of the sheep: a sermon, in St. John's Church, Salem, commemorative of Rev. Edward Gordon [!] Prescott, ...10 July, 1844....Burlington: Missionary Press, 1844. 31 p. CtY; MdBP; MWA; NGH; PHi. 44-2014

Dobb, Alexander F. Christ the corner stone. A sermon delivered on the occasion of laying the corner stone of St. Peter's Church, Delaware, Ohio, on July 10, 1844. By the Rev. Alexander F. Dobb, rector of Trinity Church, Columbus, Ohio... Columbus, Ohio: Tribune office, 1844. 17 p. CSmH. 44-2015

Dod, William Armstrong, d. 1872. History of the college of New Jersey, from its commencement, A.D. 1746, to 1783. [Prepared originally for the Princeton Whig, February, 1844] By a graduate. Princeton, New Jersey: J.T. Robinson, 1844. 50 p. CtHC; MH; NjP; O; PU. 44-2016

Dodd, Mary Ann Hamner. Poems. By Mary Ann H. Dodd.... Hartford: Case, Tiffany and Burnham, 1844. 184 p. CtY; DLC; MB; OCl; RPB. 44-2017

Doddridge, Philip, 1702-1751. The family expositor, a version of the New Testament... [Fourteenth edition] Amhurst: Published by J.S. and C. Adams, 1844. 1006 p. IaHoL; MAJ. 44-2018

Doddridge, Philip, 1702-1751. The rise and progress of religion in the soul; a sermon on the care of the soul. Philadelphia: W.A. Leary, 1844. 326 p. IU; PAtM. 44-2019

Dodson, Elder E. A refutation of some of the errors, inconsistencies, and misrepresentations, of the Rev. Wm. Jerome, on the mode of Baptism... Winchester: J.M. Ruggles, printer, 1844. 16 p. IAlS; IEdS. 44-2020

Dodson, Obadiah. Moral instructor and guide to youth, a book containing answers to eleven biblical questions; also, seventeen propositions upon the training of children. Jackson, Tennessee: Gates and Parker, printers, 1844. 250 p. OClWHi; T; TJaU. 44-2021

Dodworth, Allen. Ferris quick step.... New York: 1844. 5 p. NN. 44-2022

The doer of the word; a missionary. Boston: Crocker and Brewster, 1844. 1-200 p. ICT; MBC; MWiW; VtWemo. 44-2023

Doggett, David Seth. The responsibility of talent. An address delivered before the Franklin Literary Society of Randolph Macon College, on the evening of the 11th of June last. By Rev. Professor Doggett.... Richmond, [Virginia]: Christian advocate office, 1844. 14 p. A-Ar; CSmH. 44-2024

Doggett, John. The case of John Doggett vs. William Emerson and others, in equity, in the Circuit Court of the United States First circuit district of Maine. Boston: Freeman and Balles, 1844. 212 p. MH-L; NIC-L; N-L. 44-2025

Doggett, John. The New York city directory, for 1844-1845. Third publication. New York: John Doggett, junior, [1844] 432 p. CtSoP. 44-2026

The doing of good works. A letter to a Sunday class. New York: 1844. 24 p. DLC. 44-2027

The dollar globe, a paper for the presidential canvass of 1844, advocating the claims of James K. Polk and George M. Dallas to the presidency and vice presidency of the United States. Blair and Rives, editors. No. 1-52; June 8, 1844-February 13, 1845. Washington: for the editors, 1844. 423 p. CtHWatk; DLC; LNH; NhD; TxU. 44-2028

Donaldson, John William. The theatre of the Greeks, a series of papers relating to the history and criticism of the Greek drama. With a new introduction and other alterations by John William Donaldson. Fifth edition. Cambridge: J. and J.J. Deighton, T. Stevenson, and R. Newby, 1844. 597 p. CStclU; GHi; TNV. 44-2029

Donaldson, Peter. The life of Sir William Wallace. The governor general of Scotland... Rochester: William Alling, 1844. 132 p. C; NP; NR. 44-2030

Donizetti, Gaetano. By that consuming, quenchless flame. Per questa fiamma indomita sung in the opera Anna Boleyn... Philadelphia: Fiat, 1844. 9 p. MB. 44-2031

Donizetti, Gaetano. Oh! Bear me to my own sweet native hamlet. Cavatina... Boston: Distson, 1844. MB. 44-2032

Donnegan, James. A new Greek and English lexicon.... alphabetically arranged.... by James Donnegan, M.D. Boston: J.H. Wilkins and R.B. Carter, and Little and Brown, 1844. 1413 p. IU; NcU; PU. 44-2033

Doolittle, N. Address delivered by Rev. N. Doolittle at the public installation of the officers of King Solomon's Lodge, Akron, January 16, A.L. 5844. Massillon [Ohio] Luce and Worstell, 1844. 16 p. IaCrM. 44-2034

Doolittle, Oswin Hart. Idolatry of intellect valedictory oration before the senior class in Yale College. New Haven: 1844. 22 p. Ia; MBC. 44-2035

Dorchester, Massachusetts. Constitution of the fire department. Boston: 1844. MB. 44-2036

Dorchester, Massachusetts. Fire Department. Constitution of the Board of Firewards. Boston: Tarrey, 1844. DLC; MB. 44-2037

Dorchester Antiquarian and Historical Society, Dorchester, Massachusetts. Collections of the Dorchester Antiquarian and Historical Society. Boston: D. Clapp, 1844-1850. 3 v. CtY; IU; MH; MiU; RPB. 44-2038

Dorchester Washington Total Abstinence Society. Appeal of the Dorchester Washington Total Abstinence Society, to the inhabitants, to which is added the semi-annual report of the society, January 26, 1844. Boston:

printed at the Washingtonian office, 1844. 20 p. M. 44-2039

Dorr, Benjamin, 1796-1869. An address to young persons about to be confirmed. Second edition. Philadelphia: R.S.H. George, 1844. PPeSchw. 44-2040

Dorr, Benjamin, 1796-1869. The history of a pocket prayer book. Written by itself.... New edition. Philadelphia: R.S.H. George, 1844. 184 p. CSmH; CtY; DLC. 44-2041

Dorr, Thomas Wilson, 1805-1854. Dorr Liberation Stock. I hereby certify that... has contributed ten cents to the Dorr Liberation Fund, for the purpose of carrying the case of the state of Rhode Island against Thomas Wilson Dorr to the Supreme Court of the United States. Providence, Rhode Island: 1844. MH. 44-2042

Dorr, Thomas Wilson, 1805-1854. Report of the trial of Thomas Wilson Dorr, for treason against the state of Rhode Island, containing the arguments of counsel, and the charge of Chief Justice Durfee. By Joseph S. Pitman, attorney and counsellor at law. Boston: Tappan and Dennet, 1844. 131 p. CtY; IU; MH; OClWHi; PP. 44-2043

Dorr, Thomas Wilson, 1805-1854. Report of the trial of Thomas Wilson Dorr, for treason: including the testimony at length... together with the sentence of the court, and the speech of Mr. Dorr before sentence. From notes taken at the trial. Providence: B.F. Moore, printer, 1844. 115 p. CSmH; MnU; PP; RWe; WHi. 44-2044

Dorr, Thomas Wilson, 1805-1854.

Speech of Governor Dorr, in answer to the question by the court, why sentence should not be pronounced against him. Newport: 1844. Broadside. MHi; WHi. 44-2045

Dorr Liberation Society of Rhode Island. Constitution... instituted November 5, 1844. Providence: 1844. 8 p. RHi; RPB. 44-2046

Dougherty, Peter. A Chippewa primer. Compiled by the Rev. Peter Dougherty... New York: J. Westall, printer, 1844. 84 p. CtHWatk; DLC; MBAt; NjPT; PWW. 44-2047

Dougherty, Peter. The first initiatory catechism, by James Gall; with the ten Commandments, and the Lords Prayer, translated in Ojibwa, by the Rev. P. Dougherty. New York: Printed for the Board of Foreign Missions of the Presbyterian Church, 1844. MBAt. 44-2048

Douglas, Stephen Arnold, 1813-1861. A collection of speeches by Senator Douglas of Illinois delivered between 1844-1855. Washington: 1844-1859. 8 v. in 1. ICHi; NN; OClW. 44-2049

Douglas, Stephen Arnold, 1813-1861. Speech on the bill to refund General Jackson's fine. January 7, 1844. Washington: Globe office, 1844. 8 p. MH; MnHi; OClWHi. 44-2050

Douglass, David Bates, 1790-1849. Reply of the trustees of Kenyon College, Gambier, Ohio, to statement of D.B. Douglass, etc. Philadelphia, Pennsylvania: 1844. OCHP; WHi. 44-2051

Douglass, David Bates, 1790-1849. Statement of facts and circumstances connected with the removal of the author from the presidency of Kenyon College. By D.B. Douglass, LL.D. [Gambier?, Ohio]: printed for private circulation, 1844. 37 p. NjR; NN; NNG; OClWHi; RPB. 44-2052

Douglass, David Bates, 1790-1849. Statement of facts and circumstances connected with the removal of the author from the presidency of Kenyon College. By D.B. Douglass, LL.D. Second edition. New York: D. Appleton and company; Philadelphia: G.S. Appleton, 1844. 30 p. CtY; DLC; MiD-B; OClWHi; WHi. 44-2053

Dover, George James Welbore Agar-Ellis, 1797-1833. Lives of the most eminent sovereigns of modern Europe. From the second London edition. New York: A.V. Blake, 1844. 252 p. MVh; NLew; RNR; RPAt; WaS. 44-2054

Downing, Andrew Jackson, 1815-1852. Cottage residences, or a series of designs for rural cottages and cottage villas, and their gardens and grounds, adapted to North America. Second edition. New York: Wiley and Putnam, 1844. 2 v. DLC; ICJ; MWA; OO; ScU. 44-2055

Downing, Andrew Jackson, 1815-1852. Landscape gardening, adapted to North America, with a view to the improvement of country residences.... with remarks on rural architecture. Second edition.... New York and London: Wiley and Putnam, 1844. 497 p. LN; MB; NPV; WBelo-C. 44-2056

Downing, Andrew Jackson, 1815-1852. A treatise on the theory and practice of landscape gardening, adopted to North America; with a view to the improvement

of country residences. Second edition enlarged, revised. New York and London: Wiley and Putnam, 1844. 497 p. CtB; ICN; MH; Nh; OCY. 44-2057

Downs, Soloman Weathersbee, 1801-1854. Speech... before a public meeting of the people of the parish of Union, on the annexation of Texas, delivered at Farmersville, on June 19, 1844. New Orleans: J.A. Noble, 1844. 64 p. L-M; MH; PHi; TxU. 44-2058

Dr. Cleveland's Academy of Young Ladies. Baltimore: Printed by John D. Toy, 1844. 21 p. MdHi. 44-2059

Drake, Benjamin, 1794-1841. The life and adventures of Black Hawk: with sketches of Keokuk, the Sac and Fox Indians, and the late Black Hawk war. Seventh edition, improved. Cincinnati: G. Conclin, 1844. 288 p. KyU; LNT; MB; NN; OHi. 44-2060

Drake, Daniel. Analytical report of a series of experiments in mesmeric somniloquism, performed by an association of gentlemen; with speculations on the production of its phenomena. Louisville: F.W. Prescott and company, 1844. 56 p. CtY; LNT-M; MH; NN; PPi. 44-2061

Drake, Daniel. Introductory lecture on the means of promoting the intellectual improvement of the students and physicians of the valley of the Mississippi. Delivered in the medical institute of Louisville. Second edition. Louisville, Kentucky: Prentice, 1844. 24 p. CSmH; MB; NNN; OClM; WU-M. 44-2062

Drake, Joseph Rodman, 1795-1820. The Culprit Fay, by Joseph Rodman

Drake [New York: Morris and Willis, 1844] 10 p. MB; MH; MWH. 44-2063

Drake, Joseph Rodman, 1795-1820. The Culprit Fay. The Rococo; containing the Culprit Fay, by Joseph Rodman Drake; Lillian, By William Mackworth Praed; and the Eve of St. Agnes by N.P. Willis. New York: Morris, Willis, 1844. 16 p. CtY; TxU. 44-2064

Draper, John William, 1811-1882. Organization of plants. New York: Harper and brothers, 1844. MdAN; OCN. 44-2065

Draper, John William, 1811-1882. A treatise on the forces which produce the organization of plants. With an appendix, ... by John William Draper, M.D. ....New York: Harper and brothers, 1844. 216 p. GU; KyLxT; LU; NNN; ScU. 44-2066

The drawing room library. Various authors. New York, 1844. 8 parts in 1 v. MB. 44-2067

Drieude, E.S. Lorenzo, or the empire of religion. By a Scotch nonconformist, a convert to the Catholic faith. Translated from the French, by a lady of Philadelphia. Baltimore: J. Murphy, 1844. [9]-311 p. DLC; MdHi; MoS; MtH; NBuDC. 44-2068

Dromgoole, George C. Speech of Mr. Dromgoole, of Virginia, on the right of members to their seats in the House. Delivered in the House, February 13, 1844. Washington: 1844. 14 p. MHi. 44-2069

Drown, Simeon De Witt. The Peoria directory, for 1844: containing an account of the early discovery of the country, with a history of the town, down to the present time.... and much other statistical information.... Peoria: printed for the author, 1844. 124 p. DLC; IHi; NN; WHi. 44-2070

Druitt, Robert, 1814-1883. The principles and practice of modern surgery. By Robert Druitt.... From the third London edition. Illustrated with one hundred and fifty-three wood engravings. With notes and comments by Joshua B. Flint.... Philadelphia: Lea and Blanchard, 1844. 568 p. CSt-L; MoSW; OSW; PPHa; RPM. 44-2071

Dryden, John. The poetical works of John Dryden, with illustrations. n.p.: George Routledge and sons, 1844. 532 p. ViRVMI; WvF. 44-2072

Dryden, John. The works of John Dryden in verse and prose, with a life by Rev. John Milford. New York: Harper and brothers, 1844. 2 v. KyDC; Me; MH; NN; RPB. 44-2073

Duane, William, 1807-1882. A view of the relation of landlord and tenant in Pennsylvania, as affected by acts of assembly and judicial decisions. Pittsburgh: C.H. Kay, 1844. 136 p. CtY; NjP; PP; PPiU; PU-L. 44-2074

DuCygne, R.P. Marino. Ars rhetorica, auctore R.P. Maratino DuCygne, audomarensi, societatis Jesu. Editio Postrema Emendatior. Baltimore: Joannis Murphy, 1844. 200 p. MBrigStJ; MdBLC; MdW; MWH. 44-2075

Dudgeon, Thomas. Lectures on a litteral transcript of ancient prophets. New York: Bell, 1844. NN. 44-2076

Duer, John, 1782-1858. A lecture on the law of representations in marine insurance, with notes and illustrations; and a preliminary lecture on the question whether marine insurance was known to the ancients. New York: J.S. Voorhies, 1844. 239 p. DLC; MeBat; MnU; PU-L; RPB. 44-2077

Duer, William Alexander, 1780-1853. Lectures on the constitutional jurisprudence of the United States. New York: 1844. 419 p. Ia; InRch; MB; MH-L; PU-L. 44-2078

Dukes, Joseph H. Oration, before the firemen of Charleston, on the fourth of July, 1844. Charleston: Walker and Burke, 1844. 16 p. MH; ScHi. 44-2079

Dumanoir, Philippe Francois Pinel, 1806-1865. Don Caesar de Bazan, a drama in three acts by G.A. A'Beckett and Mark Lemon. New York: Samuel French [1844] 47 p. C; OCl. 44-2080

Dumas, Jean Baptiste Andre, 1800-1884. The chemical and physiological balance of organic nature: an essay...From the third edition with new documents. New York: Saxton and Miles; Boston: Saxton, Peirce and company, 1844. 15-174 p. MCM; MeU; MH; NcU; OHi. 44-2081

Dummer Academy. Byfield, Massachusetts. Catalogue of the officers and students of Dummer Academy. Instituted 1763. Salem, Massachusetts: printed at the Salem Gazette office, 1844. 53 p. IaHi; ICN; MB; MNe. 44-2082

Duncan, Alexander, d. 1852. Remarks of Mr. Duncan, of Ohio, on the right of

petition: delivered in the House, January 6, 1844. Washington: Globe office, 1844. 8 p. MiD-B; OClWHi; OO; PU. 44-2083

Duncan, Alexander, d. 1852. Speech on the tariff? delivered in the House, May 6, 1844. Washington: Globe office, 1844. 16 p. KyDC; MBAt; MiD-B; OclWHi; TxDaM. 44-2084

Dunglison, Robley, 1798-1869. The dictionary of medical science; containing a concise account of the various subjects and terms; with the French and other synonyms; notices of climate, and of celebrated mineral waters; formulae for various officinal and empirical preparations. Fourth edition, modified and enlarged. Philadelphia: 1844. 771 p. CU-M; ICJ; MB; MoS; PPCP. 44-2085

Dunglison, Robley, 1798-1869. Human health; or the influence of atmosphere and locality; change of air and climate; seasons; food; clothing; bathing and mineral springs; exercise; sleep; corporeal and intellectual pursuits, etc., etc. on healthy man; constituting elements of Hygiene. A new edition, with many modifications and additions. Philadelphia: Lea and Blanchard, 1844. [13]-464 p. C-S; DLC; OO; PPA; TxU-M. 44-2086

Dunglison, Robley, 1798-1869. Human Physiology. With upwards of three hundred illustrations... Fifth edition, greatly modified and improved. Philadelphia: Lea and Blanchard, 1844. 2 v. ABBS; CoCsC; KyU; NcDaD; PPCP; WaPS. 44-2087

Dunglison, Robley, 1798-1869. An introductory lecture to the course of institutes of medicine, &c., in Jefferson Medical College, delivered November 4,

1844. By Professor Dunglison. Published by the class. Philadelphia: B.E. Smith, 1844. 31 p. DLC; ICJ; GMW; MBAt; PPM. 44-2088

Dunglison, Robley, 1798-1869. The medical student; or aids to the study of medicine. A revised and modified edittion. Philadelphia: Lea and Blanchard, 1844. 312 p. CU-M; ICU; PPAmP; OClM; WaU. 44-2089

Dunglison, Robley, 1798-1869. A new dictionary of medical science and literature, containing a concise account of the various subjects and terms; and formulae for various official and empirical preparations. Fourth edition. Philadelphia: 1844. DSG; MBM. 44-2090

Dunglison, Robley, 1798-1869. The practice of medicine: a treatise on special pathology and therapeutics. Second edition.... Philadelphia: Lea and Blanchard, 1844. 2 v. DLC; ICJ; OSW; PPiU; TCh. 44-2091

Dunglison, Robley, 1798-1869. A public discourse in commemoration of Peter S. Du Ponceau, LL.D., late president of the American Philosophical Society, delivered before the society pursuant to appointment, on the 25th of October, 1844, Philadelphia: printed for the American Philosophical Society, 1844. 44 p. CSmH; ICN; MiGr; PPL; TxHR. 44-2092

Dunham, Samuel Astley, d. 1858. History of Spain and Portugal. New York: Harper and brothers, 1844. 5 v. Mi; MSbo; PWWJS; RPE; ScDuE. 44-2093

Dunlap, George W. The atonement.... Printed for the American Unitarian As-

sociation. Boston: James Munroe and company, 1844. 24 p. IaHi. 44-2094

Dunlap, Robert Pinckney, 1796-1859. Speech on the tariff; delivered in the House of Representatives, May 1, 1844. Washington: Printed at the Globe office, 1844. 8 p. NNUT; WHi. 44-2095

Dunlap, William. History of New York. New York: Harper and brothers, 1844. GAuY; MiD-B; MSbo; RPE; ScGrw. 44-2096

Dunton, Joseph. The scholar's guide to a practical knowledge of sacred geography. Ithaca: Andrus, Woodruff and Gauntlett, 1844. 46 p. MCH; MH; NCH; NlC; Vt. 44-2097

DuPonceau, Peter Stephen, 1760-1844. Catalogue of valuable law and miscellaneous books, from the library of the late Peter S. Du Ponceau, to be sold by order of executors... October 16, 1844... at M. Thomas and son's auction store... Philadelphia: E.G. Dorsey, printer, 1844. 66 p. DLC; NN; PPAmP; PPL. 44-2098

Durbin, John Price, 1800-1876. A letter to Rev. William H. Norris... on the indemnity of fundamental doctrines in the Church of England, the Protestant Episcopal Church and Methodist Episcopal Church. Philadelphia: Sorin, 1844. 40 p. LU; MBNMHi; NNG; PPL; PPPrHi. 44-2099

Durbin, John Price, 1800-1876. Observations in Europe, principally in France and Great Britain. New York: Harper and brothers, 1844. 2 v. CtMW; IU; MBBC; ODaB; TxHR. 44-2100

Durriot, Risdon. Scripture marks of salvation; drawn up to help Christians to know the true state of their souls. From the third American and sixty-second Edinburgh edition.... Boston: Oliver L. Perkins, 1844. 128 p. MPeHi. 44-2101

Dwight, John Sullivan. Lecture on association in its connection with education, delivered before the New England Fourier Society, in Boston, February 20, 1844. Boston: George Coolidge, printer, 1844. 22 p. ICJ; IU; MBAU; MH; RPB. 44-2102

Dwight, John Sullivan. Lecture on association, in its connection with education; delivered before the New England Fourier Society, in Boston, February 29, 1844. Boston: Benjamin H. Greene, for the society, 1844. 41 p. MBAt; MBC; MWA; MNotnW; Nh. 44-2103

Dwight, T.M. A farewell discourse to the Congregational Church and Society of Winsted.... Hartford: D.B. Mosely, 1844. 16 p. Ct; CtHWatk; CtY; RPB. 44-2104

Dwight, Theodore William, 1822-1892. Mnemonics; or the new science of artificial memory; explained in its application to the study of numbers, the sciences; and the useful occupations of life. New York: J. Mowatt and company, 1844. ICN; MH; NN; PPL; PU. 44-2105

Dwight, William Theodore, 1795-1865. An address delivered before the Association of Alumni of Yale College: August 14, 1844.... Portland, Maine. Published by request of the association. New Haven: printed by B.L. Hamlen, 1844. 36 p. CBPSR; MeB; MWA; PHi; Vt. 44-2106

Dwyer, John Hanbury. An essay on elocution, with elucidatory passages from various authors, to which are added remarks on reading prose and verse with suggestions to instructors of the art. Fifth edition, with additions. Albany: Weare C. Little, 1844. 300 p. GU; MH; MWA; NN; PPA. 44-2107

Dymond, Jonathan, 1796-1828. Essays on the principles of morality and on the private and political rights and obligations of mankind, by Jonathan Dymond. New York: Collins, Brothers and company, 1844. 576 p. MoS; NNUT; OCl; PHi; RNHS. 44-2108

Dymond, Jonathan, 1796-1828. An inquiry into the accordancy of war with the principles of Christianity, and an examination of the philosophical reasoning by which it is defended. With observations on some of the causes of ware and some of its effects. Fourth edition, corrected and enlarged. New York: 1844. DLC; ICU; NN. 44-2109

E

Earle, Thomas. The systematic speller. Philadelphia: Biddle, 1844. 72 p. DLC. 44-2110

Earnings entertainments, or, the country visit. Embellished with fourteen engravings. Philadelphia: Presbyterian Board of Publication and Sabbath School work, 1844. 222 p. MnLer. 44-2111

East, John. My Saviour, or devotional meditation, in prose and verse, on the names and titles of the Lord Jesus Christ. Ninth edition. Boston: J.B. Dorr, 1844. IaFayU; MH; NPlak; ViAl. 44-2112

East Boston. Maverick Church. The articles of faith and covenant of the Maverick Church, East Boston, with a list of the members. Boston: 1844. 24 p. CtY. 44-2113

East Tennessee University, Knoxville. Catalogue of the officers, alumni and students of East Tennessee University, 1844. Knoxville: E.G. Eastman, 1844. 19 p. TU. 44-2114

Eastburn, Manton, 1801-1872. A few pages for the information of inquiries respecting the Protestant Episcopal Church in the United States of America.... Boston: Tract committee of the Diocese of Massachusetts, 1844. 18 p. MB; MBD; NjR; PPPD; RPB. 44-2115

Easton, Massachusetts. Reports of the town officers. Taunton: n.p., 1844-[76] M. 44-2116

Easy nat: or, Boston bars and Boston boys. A tale of home trials. By one who knows them. Boston: 1844. 48 p. CtY; MB; MBAt; MH; NIC. 44-2117

Easy nat; or, Boston bars and Boston boys. A tale of home trials, by one who knows them. Third edition. Boston: Redding and company, 1844. 48 p. MB. 44-2118

Eaton, Peter. A discourse delivered at the dedication of a new house of worship, at West Boxford, November 22, 1843.... Andover: Allen, Morrill and Wardwell, printers, 1844. 24 p. CtSoP; MH-AH; MiD-B; MWA; RPB. 44-2119

Eberle, John. A treatise on the disease and physical education of children, by John Eberle.... Third edition. Philadelphia, Pennsylvania: Grigg and Elliot, 1844. 543 p. CtY; MdBM; MoSW-M; PPiAM. 44-2120

The eccaleobion. A treatise on artifical incubation, and the general management of poultry. Philadelphia: 1844. PHi. 44-2121

Eckard, James Read. A personal narrative of residence as a missionary in Ceylon and southern Hindoostan.... By James Read Eckard, late missionary of Ceylon. Philadelphia: Perkins and Purves; Boston: Benjamin Perkins, 1844. 254 p. MB; MNe; NjPT; PPL-R; TKc. 44-2122

Eclectic magazine. v. 1-148, No. 6; January 1844-June 1907. New York: 1844-. 149 v. AU; DLC; MH; PHC; WaS. 44-2123

Eclectic magazine of foreign literature. v. 1-148. New York: 1844-1907. DLC; MH. 44-2124

Eclectic magazine of foreign literature. Science and art. New York: J.H. Bidwell, 1844. DLC; IaU; OU. 44-2125

Eddy, Robert Henry, 1812-1887. Plan of East Boston exhibiting the land and water lots and other improvements. Boston: John Noble, 1844. MB; MH. 44-2126

Edes, Richard Sullivan. Discourse preached March 21st, 1844, at the funeral of the late Reverend Isaac Allen.... Worcester: Jonathan L. Esty, 1844. 20 p. MB; MBAU; MiD-B; MWA. 44-2127

Edgarton, Sarah C. The Rose of Sharon, a religious souvenir. Boston: A. Tompkins and B. B. Mussey, 1844. KU; MBC; MHa; PHi; WHi. 44-2128

Edgeworth, Maria. Parent's assistant; or, stories for children.... New edition. New York: Harper and brothers, 1844. 455 p. GU-M; MBL; NNG; PHC. 44-2129

Edgeworth, Maria. Rosamond: with other tales. By Maria Edgeworth, complete in one volume. New York: Harper and brothers, 1844. 373 p. MAcc; NNCo-Ci. 44-2130

Edmands, Benjamin Franklin. The Boston school atlas, ...Fifteenth edition; stereotyped.... Boston: Robert S. Davis, 1844. 78 p. NNC. 44-2131

Edson, Theodore, 1793-1883. The rector's library. A lecture preached in St. Anne's Church, Lowell, on the evening of November 24, 1844. By Rev. Theodore Edson. Published by request. Lowell: Stearns and Taylor, printer, 1844. 23 p. CtHT; InID; MB; MH-AH; OClWHi. 44-2132

Edwards, Jonathan, 1703-1758. Thoughts on the revival of religion. New York: American Tract Society, 1844. IaPeC. 44-2133

Edwards, Jonathan, 1703-1758. The works of President Edwards. A reprint of the Worcester edition, with valuable additions and a copious general index. New York: Leavitt Trow and company, 1844. 4 v. CU; OOxM; ScU; TxDaM; WHi. 44-2134

Edwards, Jonathan, 1703-1758. The works of President Edwards.... a reprint of the Worcester edition, with valuable additions and a copious general index.... New York: Leavitt, Trow and company, 1844-47. 6 v. ICU; MiU; MnU. 44-2135

Edwards, Justin, 1787-1853. Permanent Sabbath documents, no. 1. Boston, 1844? 60 p. IU. 44-2136

Edwards, Justin, 1787-1853. Permanent sabbath documents. By the reverend Justin Edwards, D.D. Philadelphia: 1844. 54 p. MiD-B; NcWsM; PHi; PPAmP; PPL. 44-2137

Edwards, Justin, 1787-1853. A plea for

the Sabbath enforced by facts. By Rev. Justin Edwards, D.D. Philadelphia: Presbyterian Board of Publication, 1844. 54 p. MeBat; PPPrHi. 44-2138

Edwards, Peter. Candid reasons for renouncing the principles of antipaedobaptism... Seventh American edition. Rossville: 1844. ICU. 44-2139

Edwards, Tryon, 1809-1894. Self cultivation. New York: John S. Taylor and company, 1844. 43 p. MBC. 44-2140

Eighth National Guard. By-laws of the Eighth National Guard. Adopted 1827, revised 1844.... New York: Burroughs and company, 1844. 32 p. CtMMHi. 44-2141

Einige wenige und Einfache Thatsachen fur das Pennsylvanische Volk. Philadelphia: 1844. PPL. 44-2142

Eldridge, Joseph, 1804-1875. Reform and reformers. A sermon delivered at Norfolk, Connecticut, November 30, 1843. By Joseph Eldridge, pastor of the Congregational Church. New Haven: B.L. Hamlen, printer, 1844. 27 p. CtY; MBC; MPiB. 44-2143

Election handbill against William B. Reed. Philadelphia: 1844. PPL. 44-2144

The elements of social disorder; a plea for the working classes in the United States. by a mechanic. Providence: B.F. Moore, 1844. 96 p. CSmH; ICU; MBAt; MH; PU. 44-2145

The elephant, as he exists in a wild state; and as he has been made subservient in peace and in war, to the purposes of man,

New York: Harper, 1844. InRch; MAm; NcWfC; RPB. 44-2146

Elkington, John A. Lecture on capital punishment. Philadelphia: 1844. PPL. 44-2147

Ellen Merton, the belle of Lowell; or the confessions of the "G.F.K. Club." Boston: Brainard and company, 1844. 32 p. NN. 44-2148

Ellen Woodville; or life in the west... New York: Henry G. Langley, 1844. 160 p. CtY; NcD; IHi; MdBP; Tx. 44-2149

Ellet, Charles, 1810-1862. Canals and railroads. Letter of Mr. Ellet to the president of the Chesapeake and Ohio Canal Company [Alexandria, Virginia: Printed at the Alexandria Gazette office, 1844?] CSmH. 44-2150

Ellet, Charles, 1810-1862. Coast of transportation on railroads. Philadelphia: 1844. 2, 1, 24, 34 p. DLC; ICU; PPL. 44-2151

Ellet, Elizabeth Fries, 1818-1877. Biographical notice of Francis Liszt. New York: 1844. PPL. 44-2152

Elliot, Samuel Hayes. The sequel to rolling ridge. By the author of the latter, assisted by the worthy Mr. Fory.... [anon.] Boston: Crocker and Brewster, 1844. 248 p. DLC. 44-2153

Elliotson, John. The principles and practice of medicine. By John Elliotson.... Edited by Nathaniel Rogers.... and Alexander Cooper Lee. First American, from the second London edition, greatly enlarged and improved. With notes and additions by Thomas Stewardson....

Philadelphia, Pennsylvania: Carey and Hart, 1844. 1046 p. GEU-M; IEN; PPCP; TxHR; VtBrt. 44-2154

Elliott, Charles W. Catalogue of fruit trees, etc., cultivated and for sale at the Walnut Hill Nursery. Cincinnati: 1844. OCHP. 44-2155

Elliott, Charles, 1792-1869. The life of the Rev. Robert R. Roberts, one of the bishops of the Methodist Episcopal Church. Cincinnati: J.F. Wright and L. Swormstedt, 1844. 407 p. GEU; IU; LNH; TJaL; WHi. 44-2156

Elliott, Ebenezer, 1781-1849. The poems of Ebenezer Elliott, with introduction, by Rufus W. Griswold. Philadelphia: J. Locken, 1844. 288 p. CtMW; MB; MiD; OC; ScNC. 44-2157

Elliott, Jesse Duncan. Address of Com. Jesse D. Elliott, U.S.N. delivered in Washington County, Maryland, to his early companions, at their request on November 24, 1843. Philadelphia: G.B. Zieber and company, 1844. InHi; MBC; MiGr; OCHP; PPL. 44-2158

Elliott, Jesse Duncan. Speech of Com. Jesse Duncan Elliott, delivered in Hagerstown, Maryland, on November 14, 1843. Published by the committee of arrangement of Washington County, Maryland. Philadelphia: G.B. Zieber and company, 1844. [4] 82 p. MNBedf; MnHi; NBLiHi; OCl; WHi. 44-2159

Elliott, Stephen. A high civilization, the moral duty of Georgians. A discourse delivered before the Georgia Historical Society, on the occasion of its fifth anniversary.... 12th February, 1844. Savannah: the society, 1844. 21 p. ICU; MWA; PHi; PPL; RPB. 44-2160

Elliott, Stephen. Sermon, in St. Peter's Church, Philadelphia, October 26, 1844, on consecration of William J. Boone, George W. Freeman, and Horatio Southgate. New York: 1844. 15 p. IEG; NGH; RPB. 44-2161

Elliott, Stephen. The sword of the Lord in the land, and proud boasting our besetting sin as a nation: two sermons preached in Christ Church and St. John's, Savannah, on the 2d and 3d Sundays in Lent, in connexion [sic] with the awful catastrophe on board the Princeton. By the Rt. Rev. Stephen Elliott, junior, D.D. Published at the request of the vestry of St. John's. Savannah: W.T. Williams, 1844. 24 p. A-Ar; CSmH; MBC; NeWsM; TSewU. 44-2162

Ellis, A.J. Colloquy on writing and printing reformation. Bath: 1844. MB. 44-2163

Ellis, G.E. Tract, relative obligations of Christians to the heathen. Boston: American Unitarian Association, 1844. MDeeP. 44-2164

Ellis, George Edward, 1814-1894. The relative obligations of Christians to the heathen. Boston: Munroe and company, 1844. ICMe; MeBat; MH; MnHi; RNR. 44-2165

Ellis, George Edward, 1814-1894. Sketches of Bunker Hill battle and monument; with illustrative documents. Fourth Edition. Charlestown, Massachusetts: C.P. Emmons, 1844. 172 p. CtMW; DLC; ICJ; NNC; PWbo. 44-2166

Ellis, George W. A poem of the awful catastrophe on board the U.S. steam frigate Princeton. Together with a full description of the terrible calamity, the proceedings at Washington, and the funeral obsequies. Boston: A.J. Wright, 1844. 72 p. MH; MMeT-Hi; MWA; RPB. 44-2167

Ellis, George W. Synopsis of phrenology: presenting general principles of the science, a brief description of the mental organs and their location; also a combination, showing the manner in which they assist or counteract each other. Third edition. Boston, 1844. 48 p. MH. 44-2168

Ellis, Samuel. An address delivered at the Tremont Temple on the anniversary of the Washington Division N. 1 of the Sons of Temperance of the state of Massachusetts. Boston: R.K. Potter, 1844. 22 p. MH. 44-2169

Ellis, Sarah Stickney, 1812-1872. The brother and sister, and other tales. New York: James Langley, 1844. 216 p. MBAt; MH; RPE. 44-2170

Ellis, Sarah Stickney, 1812-1872. The daughters of England: their position in society, character, and responsibilities. By Mrs. Ellis.... Uniform edition, complete in one volume. New York: Langley, 184. CoCsC; MH; NhPet; OO; PHi. 44-2171

Ellis, Sarah Stickney, 1812-1872. The family monitor and domestic guide. By Mrs. Ellis... Comprising the women of England, the daughters of England, the wives of England, the mothers of England. New York: Henry G. Langley, 1844. 4 v. in 1. MB; MoS; NbU; OO; PPi. 44-2172

Ellis, Sarah Stickney, 1812-1872. Irish girl and other poems. New York: James Langley; Philadelphia: Thomas, Cowperthwait and company, 1844. 263 p. DLC; IaU; KU; NjR; OC. 44-2173

Ellis, Sarah Stickney, 1812-1872. The minister's family. New York: D. Appleton and company; Philadelphia: George S. Appleton, [1844] 174 p. CtY; NGos. 44-2174

Ellis, Sarah Stickney, 1812-1872. The mothers of England; their influence and responsibility. New York: D. Appleton and company; Philadelphia: G.S. Appleton, 1844. 226 p. CtY; MiU; NjN; OSW; RNR. 44-2175

Ellis, Sarah Stickney, 1812-1872. The mothers of England; their influence and responsibility. New York: J. and H. Langley, 1844. 148 p. MChi. 44-2176

Ellis, Sarah Stickney, 1812-1872. The mothers of England; their influence and responsibility. New York: J. and H.G. Langley, 1844. 122 p. LNH; NNG; OO; P; RShaw. 44-2177

Ellis, Sarah Stickney, 1812-1872. The mothers of England; their influence and responsibility. New York: J. and H.G. Langley, 1844. 125 p. NjR. 44-2178

Ellis, Sarah Stickney, 1812-1872. The mothers of England; their influence and responsibility. New York: J. and H.G. Langley, 1844. 470 p. ICham. 44-2179

Ellis, Sarah Stickney, 1812-1872. Pictures of private life. By Mrs. Ellis.... New

York: J. and H.C. Langley, 1844. 2 v. in 1. LNH; NFred; PU; RPAt; TxDaM. 44-2180

Ellis, Sarah Stickney, 1812-1872. Prose works. New York: Langley, 1844. 2 v. CtSoP; MB-W; MH; MNan; MoK. 44-2181

Ellis, Sarah Stickney, 1812-1872. The select works of Mrs. Ellis: comprising "The Women of England," "Wives of England," "Daughters of England," "Poetry of life," etc. ....Authorized edition. New York: J. and H.G. Langley, 1844. MBev; NcAS; PP; ScC; TBriK. 44-2182

Ellis, Sarah Stickney, 1812-1872. Temper and temperament. New York? J. and H.G. Langley? 1844? 32 p. MH. 44-2183

Ellis, Sarah Stickney, 1812-1872. The wives of England, their relative duties, domestic influence, and social obligations. By Mrs. Ellis.... Author's edition, complete in one volume. New York: Langley, 1844. 116 p. MH; OO. 44-2184

Ellis, Sarah Stickney, 1812-1872. The women of England; their social duties, and domestic habits. By Mrs. Ellis, author of "The Poetry of Life," "Pictures of Private Life," etc. etc. Uniform edition, complete in one volume. New York: Henry G. Langley, 107 p. CtY; MH; Nh; OO; PPi. 44-2185

Ellms, Charles. Shipwrecks and disasters at sea, or, historical narratives of the most noted calamities, and providential deliverances from fire and famine, on the ocean. Compiled by Charles Ellms. New York: Robert P. Bixby and com-pany, 1844. 427 p. MH; MNBedf. 44-2186

Ellwood, Thomas. Sacred history; or, the historical part of the Old and New Testaments. From the first American, compared with the last London edition. Mount Pleasant, Ohio: republished by Enoch and Emily M. Harris, 1844. 2 v. OkEnS. 44-2187

Ellyson's business directory, and almanac...for ... 1845... Richmond: H.K. Ellyson [1844?] CSmH; DLC. 44-2188

Elmer, Lucius Quinties Cincinnatus. Speech on the right of members to their seats in the House [delivered] in the House, February 6 and 7, 1844. [n.p.: 1844] 8p. M; MHi; WHi. 44-2189

Elton, Romeo. A memoir of the life of Jonathan Maxcy. New York: 1844. IEG. 44-2190

Elton's comic all-my-nack, 1845. New York: [1844] MWA. 44-2191

Elworth, Thomas. Sketches of incidents and adventures in the life of Thomas Elworth, the American pedestrian. Boston: Brainard and company, 1844. 60 p. MB. 44-2192

Elworth, Thomas. Sketches of incidents and adventures in the life of Thomas Elworth, the American pedestrian; written by himself. Boston: Redding and company, 1844. 68 p. CSmH; LNH; NcD; PHi; RBr. 44-2193

Ely, Caroline T. Holmes. Memoir of Harriet Ann Holmes. Phildelphia: Perkins and Purves, 1844. 108 p. MH. 44-2194

Embury, Emma Catherine. American wild flowers in their native haunts; by Emma Embury.... New York: D. Appleton and company, 1844. 256 p. ICJ; NNNBG; NRivHi. 44-2195

Emerson, Benjamin Dudley, 1781-1872. Emerson's progressive primer, and fourth class reader; a first book for children, to be used as an introductory to his spelling book and third class reader, or similar books. Claremont, N.H.: Claremont Manufacturing Company, 1844. 64 p. CtY. 44-2196

Emerson, Benjamin Dudley, 1781-1872. The first class reader: a selection for exercises in reading from standard British and American authors, in prose and verse; for the use of schools in the United States. Claremont, New Hampshire: Claremont Manufacturing Company, 1844. 276 p. ICMeHi; MH; MiHi; NNC. 44-2197

Emerson, Benjamin Dudley, 1781-1872. Second-class reader. Claremont: 1844. 168 p. MH; Nh-Hi; Nhu. 44-2198

Emerson, Frederick, 1788-1857. Key to the North American arithmetic, part second and part third for the use of teachers. Boston: Jenks and Palmer, 1844. 70 p. MH; MScitHi; PPF. 44-2199

Emerson, Frederick, 1788-1857. Key to the North American arithmetic, part second and part third for the use of teachers. Philadelphia: Hogan and Thompson, 1844. MH; PPM. 44-2200

Emerson, Frederick, 1788-1857. The North American arithmetic. Part second, uniting oral and wirtten exercises. Bos-

ton: Jenks and Palmer, 1844. 216 p. MB; MH. 44-2201

Emerson, Frederick, 1788-1857. The North American arithmetic. Part second, uniting oral and written exercises, in corresponding chapters. Windsor, Vermont: N.C. Goddard, [1844?] MH. 44-2202

Emerson, Frederick, 1788-1857. The North American arithmetic. Part third, for advanced scholars. Cincinnati: Published by Jewett and Mason, 1844. 288 p. KyBC. 44-2203

Emerson, George Barrell, 1797-1881. The advancement of the common schools, an address delivered on the 23rd of August, 1843, before the pupils and alumni of the normal school at Bridgewater, Massachusetts. Boston: W.D. Ticknor and company, 1844. 38 p. MBAt; MeB; MH; MWA; O. 44-2204

Emerson, George Barrell, 1797-1881. Observations on a pamphlet, entitled "Remarks on the seventh annual report of the Hon. Horace Mann... Boston: S.N. Dickinson, printer, 1844. CtY; IaU; MB; OU; RPB. 44-2205

Emerson, Joseph, 1777-1833. The evangelical primer, containing a minor doctrinal catechism and a minor historical catechism; added, Westminster Assembly's shorter catechism. Boston: Crocker, [1844] 72 p. CtSoP; MHa; MNt; MWA; NNC. 44-2206

Emerson, Joseph, 1777-1833. Questions adapted to Whelpley's compend of history, Twelfth edition. New York: Collins brothers and company, 1844. 69 p. MnHi; ViU. 44-2207

Emerson, Joseph, 1777-1833. Questions and supplement to Goodrich's history of the Untied States. A new edition, revised, and adapted to the enlarged edition of the history. Boston: Jenks and Palmer, 1844. 192 p. MH; NNC. 44-2208

Emerson, Ralph Waldo, 1803-1882. An address delivered in the courthouse in Concord, Massachusetts, on August 1, 1844, on the anniversary of the emancipation of the negroes in the British West Indies. Boston: J. Munroe and company, 1844. 34 p. CSmH; ICN; KyBC; PU; WHi. 44-2209

Emerson, Ralph Waldo, 1803-1882. Essays: second series. ...Boston: J. Munroe and company, 1844. 313 p. CSt; MeAug; NhD; RPAt; ViU. 44-2210

Emery's Manchester, Amoskeag and Piscataquog directory and annual advertiser: containing historical and statistical information; names, places of business, and residences of the inhabitants; Brown's almanac, pocket memorandum and account book. Manchester, New Hampshire: J.P. Emery, 1844. 1 v. CSmH; MB. 44-2211

Emma Mortimer, the cottage girl. Cincinnati: 1844. FU. 44-2212

Emmons, Ebenezar, 1799-1863. The taconic system; based on observations in New York, Massachusetts, Maine, Vermont, and Rhode Island. By Ebenezar Emmons, M.D. ....Albany: Carroll and Conk, printers, 1844. 65 p. IGK; MoRM; MWiW; OkU; PPAN. 44-2213

Emmons, Henry. Sermon preached in the Unitarian Church, Vernon, New York, May 27, 1844, at the funeral of Abraham Van Eps. Printed by request. Utica: John F. Kittle, printer, [1844] 15 p. MH; NCH; NNMHi; NUt; RPB. 44-2214

Emmons, Samuel Bulfinch. Book of promises; or Universalist's daily pocket companion. Boston: 1844. 128 p. MWA. 44-2215

Emmons, Samuel Bulfinch. The family physician, containing the description and cure of different diseases, including those of children, together with one hundred fifty valuable recipes. Boston: E. Cutting, 1844. 79 p. DNLM; MBCo; MH. 44-2216

Emmons, William, b. 1792. Biographies of Martin Van Buren and Richard M. Johnson. New York, 1844. PPL. 44-2217

Emory, Robert, 1814-1848. History of the discipline of the Methodist Episcopal Church. New York: G. Lane and P.P. Sandford, 1844. 350 p. CoDI; IaMp; LNL; NNG; PU. 44-2218

Emory, William Helmsley. Map of Texas and the countries adjacent, comp, in the Bureau of the Corps of topographical engineers from the best authorities for the state department under the direction of Colonel J.J. Abert Washington, 1844. NIC; RPAt. 44-2219

Encyclical letter of Gregory XVI.... Philadelphia: 1844. PP. 44-2220

Encyclopaedia Americana.... A new edition.... Edited by Francis Lieber, assisted by E. Wigglesworth. Supplementary volume, by Henry Vethake, [XIV] Philadelphia: Lea and Blanchard, 1844 [-1847] 14 v. NNA; PPPrHi. 44-2221

End of the world: an original painting....
by F. Anelli. New York: 1844. 8 p. CtY.
44-2222

Engelbrecht, J.C. Good bye or farewell
is a lonely sound. A ballad. Composed by
J.C. Engelbrecht. Baltimore: Frederick
D. Benteen, 1844. 5 p. KU; MB; ViU;
WHi. 44-2223

England, John, 1786-1842. Letters of
the late Bishop England to the Hon. John
Forsyth, on the subject of domestic
slavery: to which are prefixed copies in
Latin and English, of the pope's apostolic
letter, concerning the African slave
trade. Baltimore: J. Murphy, 1844. [13]-
156 p. CtY; DLC; ICJ; MBBC; PHi. 44-
2224

Engles, William Morrison, 1797-1867.
Evenings' entertainment, or the country
visit. Philadelphia: Presbyterian board of
publication, [1844] 222 p. DLC; NNUN-
W. 44-2225

Episcopal Recorder. Remarks on Mr.
Barnes' inquiry into the position of the
Evangelical Party in the Episcopal
Church. Philadelphia: R.S.H. George,
1844. 54 p. CSansS; MAnP; MWA; NNC;
PHi. 44-2226

Equitable Life Assurance Society of
Boston. An act to incorporate the....
[Boston: 1844] 3 p. MHi. 44-2227

Ermengarde of the Rhine and the
diamond king. A German tale. Published
at the May day collation by the ladies of
the South Congregational Society.
Lowell: printed by Stearns and Taylor,
1844. MB; MLow. 44-2228

Erskine, Ralph, 1685-1752. Gospel son-
nets; or, spiritual songs. Aberdeen: G.
and R. King, 1844. 326 p. DLC; ICN. 44-
2229

Erskine, Ralph, 1685-1752. Life and
practical works of the Reverend Ralph
Erskine. From the Glasgow edition,
1777. Xenia: Published by the Board of
the Calvinistic Book Concern, 1844. 592
p. KEmC; MoU. 44-2230

Eschenburg, Johann Joachim, 1743-
1820. Manual of classical literature.
From the German of J.J. Eschenburg,
....with additions....by N.W. Fiske....
Fourth edition. Philadelphia: Edward C.
Biddle, 1844. 690 p. DLC; KyLoP;
MWA; RNR; WaS. 44-2231

An essay on the American system; or,
reasons why the productive classes
should not support Henry Clay for the
presidency. Washington: printed at the
Spectator office, 1844. 14 p. MBAt; MiD-
B; NcD; NNUT. 44-2232

Essex County, Massachusetts. Rules
and regulations of the House of Correction. Salem: 1844. 8 p. MHi. 44-2233

Euripides. Tragedies. Translated by R.
Potter. New York: 1844. 3 v. MB; MdAN.
44-2234

Eustace Willoughby: or, the confessions of an apostate. By the author of
"Felix De Lisle." Baltimore: Armstrong
and Berry, 1844. 123 p. ICBB. 44-2235

Evangelical Congregational Association. Declaration of sentiment, constitution, confession of faith, and address to
the Christian public of the Evangelical
Congregational Association. New York:

G.B. Maigne, 1844. 23 p. MiMarqN. 44-2236

Evangelical Congregational Association. New York. Declaration of sentiment, constitution, confession of faith.... New York: 1844. 23 p. MBC. 44-2237

Evangelical Lutheran Church. A liturgy for the use of Evangelical Lutheran Churches. New and enlarged edition. New York: Henry Ludwig, 1844. 172 p. MdBD. 44-2238

Evangelical Lutheran Church. Proceedings of the convention held by representatives from various Evangelical Lutheran synods. Pittsburgh, Pennsylvania: Bakewell and Marthens, 1844. 4 v. MdBLF. 44-2239

Evangelical Lutheran Ministerium of New York. Minutes of the forty-ninth synod, Valatie, August 31-September 4. Baltimore: 1844. 24p. ICartC; MBAt. 44-2240

Evangelical Lutheran Ministerium of Pennsylvania and Adjacent States. Minutes of the 96th meeting of the New Evangelical Lutheran Ministerium of Pennsylvania and adjacent states convened at Pottstown, Pennsylvania during Trinity week. Pittsburgh: printed by Johnson and Stockton, 1844. 44 p. ICartC. 44-2241

Evangelical Lutheran Synod of Virginia. Fourteenth session. Minutes.... held in Winchester, May 11-16, 1844. Baltimore: printed at the publication rooms of the Evangelical Lutheran Church, 1844. 42 p. ICartC; ScCoT. 44-2242

Evans, Estwick, 1787-1866. Essay on state rights. [The first of a series] The object of which is to define and illustrate the spirit of our institutions and of liberty, and to renovate our political elements. By Estwick Evans of the North. Washington City: William Greer, printer, 1844. 40 p. A-Ar; CtY; LNH; MdHi; Nh-Hi. 44-2243

Evans, Estwick, 1787-1866. Essay on state rights. [The first of a series] The object of which is to define and illustrate the spirit of our institutions and of liberty....By Estwick Evans, of the North. Second edition. Washington: W. Greer, printer, 1844. 40 p. NNC; NP; P; PHi; TxH. 44-2244

Evans, George, 1797-1867. Discussion on the tariff. Reply of Mr. Evans, of Maine, to Mr. McDuffie's second speech on the tariff. Delivered in the Senate of the United States, February 6 and 7, 1844. Washington: Gales and Seaton, 1844. 40 p. CtY; IaGG; MWA; NjR; TxH. 44-2245

Evans, George, 1797-1867. The tariff of 1842 vindicated. Speech... in reply to....Mr. McDuffie, ...on the tariff. Delivered in the Senate.... January 22 and 23, 1844. Washington: 1844. 40 p. CtY; ICN; MdHi; MWA; OClWHi. 44-2246

Evans, George, 1797-1867. The tariff of 1842 vindicated; speech... in reply to the Hon. McDuffie, of South Carolina, on the tariff, delivered in the Senate, January 22 and 23, 1844. Washington: Printed by Gales and Seaton, 1844. 16 p. MeLewB; NcD; PHi; WHi. 44-2247

Evans, Hugh Davey. Essays to prove the

validity of Anglican ordinations: in answer to Reverend Peter Richard Kenrick. By a layman. Baltimore: J. Robinson, 1844. 328 p. CtHT; IES; LU; MdHi; PPi. 44-2248

Evans, John, 1767-1827. History of all christian sects and denominations; their origin, peculiar tenets and present condition. From the 15th London edition, revised and enlarged with the addition of the most recent statistics relating to religious sects in the U.S. Second edition. New York: James Mowatt and company, 1844. 288 p. ICN; MB; NjMD; OClWHi; OrP. 44-2249

Evans, Robert Wilson. The rectory of Valehead. By the Rev. Robert Wilson Evans.... from the twelfth English edition. New York: D. Appleton and company, 1844. 259 p. CoD; IES; MdBD; WaPS. 44-2250

Everest, Charles William, 1814-1877. The poets of Connecticut; with biographical sketches.... Edited by Rev. Charles W. Everest. Hartford: Case, Tiffany and Burnham, 1844. 468 p. AzT; CSt; MNF; NCh; TxU. 44-2251

Everett, Alexander Hill, 1790-1847. A letter on the Texas question. [New York: 1844] 23 p. CU; PPL. 44-2252

Everett, Alexander Hill, 1790-1847. A letter on the Texas question. [Springfield: 1844] 23 p. TxU. 44-2253

Everett, Edward, 1794-1865. Importance of practical education and useful knowledge... Boston: Marsh, Copen, Lyon and Webb, 1844. 419 p. M. 44-2254

Everett, Edward, 1794-1865. Impor-

tance of practical education and useful knowledge... Boston: Thomas H. Webb and company, 1844. 396 p. CtY; IGK; MFai; MSbo; NIC. 44-2255

The evergreen, or church offering for all seasons; a repository of religious, literature, and entertaining knowledge, for the Christian family. Edited by Joseph Salkeld. New Haven: J. Salkeld, 1844. [63] p. InU; MBAt; PHi; RPB; TSewU. 44-2256

The evergreen; or, monthly church magazine, a repository of religious, literary and entertaining reading for the Christian family. [January, 1844-December, 1853] New York: 1844-53. 10 v. CtY; ICN; NjR; OO; PHi. 44-2257

The evergreen; or, stories for childhood and youth. Edited by Walter West [illustrated by engravings] Boston: Munroe and Francis, 1844. 160 p. MNF. 44-2258

The evil of intoxicating liquor, and the remedy. Second editon. Park Hill [Ind. Territory] mission press: J. Candy, printer, 1844. 24 p. DLC; MHi; NN. 44-2259

Ewbank, Thomas, 1792-1870. Transactions of the Society of Literary and Scientific Chiffonniers. The spoon, with upwards of 100 illustrations. Primitive, Egyptian, etc. New York: Harper and brothers, 1844. 72 p. NBu; P; PHi. 44-2260

Ewing, John D. A sermon preached at the opening of the first semi-annual meeting of Montgomery Presbytery April 17, 1844, by the moderator, the Rev. John D. Ewing. [Published by order of the Presbytery] Lexington: printed at

the Gazette office, 1844. 21 p. NcMHi.
44-2261

Examiner, pseud. The Reading Railroad Company: their policy and
prospects. Being a series of articles
published in the Pennsylvanian in
January, February and March, 1844.
Philadelphia: C. Sherman, printer, 1844.
70 p. CtY; IU; MB; NNE; PHi. 44-2262

Exeter, New Hampshire. First Congregational Church. Celebrated trial of
Rev. Joy Hamlet Fairchild, together with
his own defence before the council. Exeter: 1844. 32 p. MBC. 44-2263

Experience of several eminent
Methodist preachers: with an account of
their call to and success in the ministry.
In a series of letters, written by themsel-
ves, to the Rev. John Wesley. Published
for the Methodist Episcopal Church.

New York: G. Lane and C.B. Tippett,
1844. 354 p. ICartC; GHi; TNMPH. 44-
2264

An explanation and history of the book
of common prayer, to which are added
the articles of religion, as established by
the bishops, clergy and laity of the Protestant Episcopal Church in the United
States. Philadelphia: George, 1844.
MnHi. 44-2265

Explanation of the national game of the
star spangled banner, or, geographical
and historical tourist through the United
States and Canada. Philadelphia: L.I.
Cohen and company, [1844] 15 p.
OClWHi. 44-2266

Eyre, John. Man's ruin and recovery.
New York: Piercy, 1844. ICBB; MWiW.
44-2267

F

Fables for boys and girls, by the author of popular lessons. Newark, New Jersey: author, 1844. 96 p. WaPS. 44-2268

The factory girl's garland. Vol. 1, No. 11. Exeter, New Hampshire: [1844] MH. 44-2269

Facts and arguments on the transmission of intellectual and moral qualities from parents to offspring. Second edition. New York: J. Winchester, 1844. 191 p. IU; MBM; NjR; OO; RNR. 44-2270

Facts and estimates relative to the business on the route of the contemplated Providence and Worcester Railroad. Providence: Knowles and Vose, 1844. 30 p. CSt; ICU; MH; OClWHi; RP. 44-2271

Facts for farmers and mechanics. The commercial intercourse of the United States and Great Britain. New York: Greeley and McElrath, 1844. 8 p. MBAt; MH-BA; OO; PU; TxU. 44-2272

Facts relative to the brief statement of proposed railroad from Fitchburg to Brattleborough.... Boston: Dutton and Wentworth, 1844. 24 p. MB. 44-2273

Fairchild, Hamlet, 1790-1859. Iniquity unfolded. An account of the treatment of Mr. Fairchild by the deacons in South Boston, and others. Written by himself. Third edition. Exeter, New Hampshire: published for the author, 1844. 84 p. NjR; OO. 44-2274

Fairchild, Joy Hamlet, 1790-1859. Celebrated trial of Rev. Joy Hamlet, for the alleged seduction of Miss Rhoda Davidson, together with his own defence before the council... Exeter, New Hampshire, Daily Mail, 1844. 32 p. MBC; MBNEH; MoU; OCLaw; WaU. 44-2275

Fairchild, Joy Hamlet, 1790-1859. Iniquity unfolded! An account of the treatment of Mr. Fairchild by the Deacons in South Boston, and others. Written by himself. Exeter: published for the author, 1844. 84 p. MBC; MoU; NjR; RPB; WaU. 44-2276

Fairchild, Joy Hamlet, 1790-1859. Iniquity unfolded! An account of the treatment of Mr. Fairchild by the Deacons in South Boston, and others. Written by himself. Second edition. Exeter: published for the author, 1844. 84 p. DLC; M; MB; MBNEH. 44-2277

Fairchild, Joy Hamlet, 1790-1859. Iniquity unfolded. An account of the treatment of Mr. Fairchild by the Deacons in South Boston, and others. Third edition. Exeter: Published for the author, 1844. 84 p. DLC; ICU; MnU; OO. 44-2278

Fairchild, Joy Hamlet, 1790-1859. Trial for seduction, ecclesiastical council, Exeter, New Hampshire, 1844; reported by W.B. English. Exeter: 1844. 32 p. MH-L. 44-2279

Fairchild, Joy Hamlet, 1790-1859. Trial

of Rev. Joy Hamlet Fairchild for the alleged seduction of Miss Rhoda Davidson. Boston: 1844. 32 p. MBC; MH-L. 44-2280

Fairhaven, Massachusetts. Statutes in relation to the public schools and the report of the school committee of Fairhaven for the year 1843-1844. New Bedford, [Massachusetts] H. Tilden's Press, 1844. 45 p. MNBedf. 44-2281

Falkner, Frederic. The farmer's treasure, a practical treatise of the nature and value of manures, with a brief account of all the most recent discoveries in agricultural chemistry. New York: D. Appleton and company, 1844. 8-153, 8-138, 1-14 p. ICU; NhPet; NIC; NRU. 44-2282

Fall River, Massachusetts. An authentic account of the value of property destroyed by the great fire in Fall River, July 2, 1843. Boston: 1844. MF; NN. 44-2283

The family altar; or the duty, benefits, and mode of conducting family worship, with remarks on the various parts of prayer. Boston: Gould, Kendall and Lincoln, [1844] 128 p. CSmH; ICN; MB; NNU-W; ViU. 44-2284

The family instructor; or a manual of the duties of domestic life. New York: Harper and brothers, 1844. 300 p. LN; MMh; RKi; RPE. 44-2285

Family medical almanac for 1845. New York: Comstock and company, 1844. NoLoc. 44-2286

The family of the Seisers: A satirical tale of the city of New York... New York:

printed for the author, by J.M. Elliott, 1844. 2 pts. CSmH; DLC; MH. 44-2287

Farmer, George O. Summer night waltz, arranged for the pianoforte. Boston: G.P. Reed, 1844. 2 p. WHi. 44-2288

Farmer's almanac. By David Young. New York: Collins brothers, 1844. MWA. 44-2289

Farmer's almanac. By David Young. Plattsburgh: Vilas and Edsall, 1844. MWA. 44-2290

Farmer's almanac. New Brunswick: John Terhune, 1844. MWA. 44-2291

Farmer's almanac. New York: Greeley and McElrath, 1844. MWA. 44-2292

Farmer's almanac. Trenton: Charles Scott, 1844. MWA. 44-2293

The farmer's almanac.... 1845.... by Robert B. Thomas.... Boston: Jenks and Palmer. 47 p. MDovC. 44-2294

Farmer's almanac for 1845. By David Young. New York, New York: H. and S. Raynor, [1844] MWA. 44-2295

Farmer's almanac for 1845. By Robert B. Thomas. Boston, Massachusetts: Jenks and Palmer, [1844] MWA; MWinchrHi; PPM. 44-2296

Farmer's almanac for 1845. By Robert B. Thomas. Boston, Massachusetts: Jenks and Palmer; Nashua, New Hampshire: J. Buffum, [1844] MWA. 44-2297

Farmer's almanac for 1845. Calculations by John Ward. Philadelphia, Pennsylvania: Thomas Davies, [1844] MWA. 44-2298

Farmer's almanac for 1845. New York, New York: William K. Cornwell, [1844] MWHi; MWA. 44-2299

Farmer's almanac, for the year 1844, by Thomas Spofford. Boston: Thomas Groom and company, 1844. 34 p. RNHi. 44-2300

Farmer's almanack 1845. Burlington, Vermont: Chauncy Goodrich, [1844] MWA. 44-2301

Farmer's almanack for 1845. By David Young. Ithaca, New York: Andrus, Woodruff and Gauntlett [1844] MWA; NIC; WHi. 44-2302

Farmer's almanack for 1845. By Robert B. Thomas. Portland, Maine: Sanborn and Carter [1844] MeHi; MWA. 44-2303

The farmer's almanack, ...for the year of our Lord 1845; by Robert B. Thomas.... Boston: Jenks and Palmer, [1844] 48 p. MeHi; MHaHi; MWA; RPE. 44-2304

The farmer's almanack, calculated on a new and improved plan, for the year of our Lord 1845; ....by Robert B. Thomas. ....Boston: Jenks and Palmer, [1844] 48 p. MHa. 44-2305

Farmer's almanack. By David Young. New York: H. and S. Raynor, 1844. MWA. 44-2306

The farmer's almanack. Calculated on a new and improved plan, new, useful, and entertaining matter, by Robert B.

Thomas. Boston: Jenks and Palmer, 1844[-76] 48 p. MDanV. 44-2307

Farmer's almanack, calculated on a new and improved plan, for the year of our Lord 1844.... By Robert B. Thomas. Boston: Jenks and Palmer, 1844. 48 p. CoU. 44-2308

The farmer's almanack, calculated on a new and improved plan, for the year of our Lord 1844.... No. 52.... Established in 1793 by Robert B. Thomas.... Boston: Carter, Hendee and company, [1844] CU. 44-2309

The farmer's almanack, calculated on a new and improved plan, for the year of our Lord 1845.... Number fifty-three.... By Robert B. Thomas. Boston: Jenks and Palmer, [1844] 47 p. MPeHi. 44-2310

The farmer's almanack, calculated on a new and improved plan, for.... 1845.... Boston: Carter, Hendee and company, 1844. CU. 44-2311

The farmers' almanack, calculated on a new and improved plan for the year 1845.... By Robert B. Thomas.... Boston: Jenks and Palmer, [1844] 48 p. MWA; NjR. 44-2312

The farmer's almanack.... 1845.... By Robert B. Thomas.... Boston: Jenks and Palmer. 46 p. MeBa. 44-2313

The farmers' almanack, ...for the year....1845; ....by Robert B. Thomas. Boston: Jenks and Palmer, [1844] 48 p. MBevHi. 44-2314

Farmer's and mechanic's almanac for 1845. Calculations by John Armstrong.

Wheeling, West Virginia: William J. Robb, [1844] MWA. 44-2315

The farmers and mechanics almanack for the year of our Lord 1845.... by Charles Frederick Egelmann.... Philadelphia: Mentz and Rovoudt, [1844] 34 p. MWA; WHi. 44-2316

The farmers' calendar for the year 1845... By Edward Hagerty, M.D. Philadelphia: Grigg and Elliot [1844] MWA; NjR. 44-2317

Farnham, Thomas Jefferson, 1804-1848. History of Oregon Territory, it being a demonstration of the title of these United States of North America, to the same. Accompanied by a map. By Thomas J. Farnham, esq. New York: J. Winchester, 1844. 80 p. Ct; MoSM; OrHi; RPB; ViU. 44-2318

Farnham, Thomas Jefferson, 1804-1848. History of Oregon Territory, it being a demonstration of the title of these United States of North America, to the same. Second edition. New York: W. Taylor, 1844. 38 p. OrU; PHi. 44-2319

Farnham, Thomas Jefferson, 1804-1848. Travels in the Californias and scenes in the Pacific Ocean. New York: Saxton and Miles, 1844. 96 p. CU-B; DLC; MoU; NNC; ViU. 44-2320

Farnham, Thomas Jefferson, 1804-1848. Travels in the Californias, and scenes in the Pacific Ocean. New York: Saxton and Miles, 1844. 416 p. CoD; ICN; OrU; PPL; RPAt. 44-2321

Farnum, Caleb. Practical grammar. A grammar of the English language. Providence: 1844. 124 p. RHi. 44-2322

Farr, R.A. Phrenological chart, and synopsis of the mental faculties, in seven degrees of development, systematically arranged in orders, genera and species, with the temperaments. R.A. Farr, practical phrenologist. Buffalo: 1844. 35 p. NBu. 44-2323

Farrar, Eliza Ware Rotch, 1791-1870. The young lady's friend. By Mrs. John Farrar... New York: Samuel S. and William Wood, 1844. 432 p. MHi. 44-2324

Fauvel-Gouraud, Francois. First fundamental basis of phreno-mnemotechnic principles, consisting in a philosophical decomposition of all the human languages.... New York: 1844. 60, 80-82, [8] p. CtY; RPB. 44-2325

Fauvel-Gouraud, Francois. First fundamental basis of phreno-mnemotechnic principles, New York: The author, 1844. 90 p. MH. 44-2326

Fauvel-Gouraud, Francois. Phreno-mnemotechnic dictionary: a classification of all the homophonic words of the English language; part 1. New York: Howell and Macoy, 1844. 197 p. CtMW; MnHi; NNNAM; PPAmP; RPB. 44-2327

Fay, Theodore Sedgwick. Robert rueful; or, a lesson to valetudinarians.... Philadelphia: Louis A. Godey, 1844. 69 p. CtY; MWA. 44-2328

Fear of God and human respect. Philadelphia: Fithian, 1844. 35 p. LN. 44-2329

Featherstonhaugh, George William, 1780-1866. Excursion through the slave states, from Washington on the Potomac, to the frontier of Mexico: with sketches of popular manners and geological notices.... New York: Harper and brothers, 1844. 168 p. DeWi; LNX; MoS; NNA; OO. 44-2330

Feijo, Diogo Antonio. Demonstration of the necessity of abolishing a constrained clerical celibacy; exhibiting the evils of that institution, and the remedy. Translated with introduction and appendix by D.P. Kidder. Philadelphia: Sorin and Ball, 1844. 128 p. CtMW; IEG; MH; NjPT; PPPrHi; WHi. 44-2331

Fellows, Henry Parker. Boating trips on New England rivers. Illustrated by Willis H. Beals. Boston: Cupples, Upham and company, 1844. 176 p. NhD. 44-2332

Felton, Cornelius Conway, 1807-1862. A Greek reader, for the use of schools.... with English notes and a lexicon. Adapted particularly to the Greek grammar of E.A. Sophocles. Third edition, revised by C.C. Felton. Hartford, [Connecticut]: H. Huntington, junior, 1844. CoU; MB; OU; TxDaM; WLac. 44-2333

The female student.... Wilmington, Delaware: 1844-. OO. 44-2334

Fenelon, Francois de Salignac de La Mothe, 1651-1715. Les aventures de Telemaque, fils d'Ulysse. Nouv. ed... revised and cor. sur l'edition de Didot a Paris par A. Bolmar. Philadelphia: Lea and Blanchard, 1844. 323 p. OOxM; PWcHi. 44-2335

Fenelon, Francois de Salignac de la Mothe, 1651-1715. Lives of the ancient philosophers; Translated with notes, and a life of the author by...John Cormack.

New York: Harper, 1844. 299 p. InRch; MeAu; MMat; NcWfC; OCX. 44-2336

Fenelon, Francois de Salignac de la Mothe, 1651-1715. Pious thoughts concerning the knowledge and love of God, translated from the French.... by Mrs. Mant, with a life of the author. New York: C. Shepard, 1844. 219 p. CtY; InCW; MoSU; NCH; NNG. 44-2337

Fenelon, Francois de Salignac de la Mothe, 1651-1715. Selections from the writings of Fenelon: with a memoir of his life. By Mrs. Follen. Fifth edition. Revised and enlarged. Boston: Samuel G. Simpkins, 1844. 329 p. InGrD; MB; MMe; Nh-Hi; TxH. 44-2338

Fenelon, Francois de Salignac de la Mothe, 1651-1715. On the use of the Bible, by Fenelon. New York: Published by Cosserly and sons, 1844. 112, 43 p. ArLSJ; NStBA. 44-2339

Ferguson, Adam, 1724-1816. The history of the progress and termination of the Roman Republic. By Adam Ferguson.... A new edition, abridged. New York: Harper and brothers, 1844. 598 p. OClW; OCY; RKi; RPE. 44-2340

Fernald, Woodbury M. Universalism against partialism: in a series of lectures delivered in Newburyport, Massachusetts. By Woodbury M. Fernald. Second edition. Philadelphia: John H. Gihon, 1844. 68 p. MH; MMeT-Hi; MWA. 44-2341

Ferretti, Giovanni. La cenerentola, osiala bonta in trionof Cinderella, or the triumph of goodness, a melo-dramatic opera, in two acts. New York: Houel and

Macoy, printers, 1844. 71 p. MH; RNR.
44-2342

Feval, Paul Henri Corentin, 1817-1887.
Les Mysteres de Londres. Troisieme par-
tie, La Grande Famille. New York:
Bureau du Courrier des Etats-Unis,
1844. MB; PPL-R. 44-2343

A few plain facts, addressed to the
people of Pennsylvania. By a citizen of
Pennsylvania. Philadelphia: J. Crissy,
printer, 1844. 16 p. CtY; CU; ICU; NjR;
PHi. 44-2344

A few plain facts, addressed to the
people of Pennsylaniva. By a citizen of
Pennsylvania. Third edition. Philadelphia: 1844. 14 p. MBAt; PHi. 44-2345

Few plain facts, addressed to the people
of Pennsylvania. By a citizen of Pennsylvania. Fourth edition enlarged. Philadelphia: 1844. 14 p. PHi. 44-2346

A few remarks in behalf of the tariff and
currency, with a brief comparison of the
merits of the two candidates for the
presidency, by a mechanic. Philadelphia:
1844. 16 p. OClWHi. 44-2347

Ficklin, Orlando Bell, 1808-1886.
Remarks in the House of Representatives of the United States, January 10,
1844, on the improvement of the western
lakes and rivers. n.p.: 1844. 8 p. M. 44-
2348

Ficklin, Orlando Bell, 1808-1886.
Speech on the public land bill, delivered
in the House, December 19, 1844,
Washington: Printed at the Globe office,
1844. 7 p. DLC; MBAt; MH; NBU. 44-
2349

Field, Barnum, 1786-1846. American
school geography. With an atlas. Fourteenth edition. Boston: Otis, Broaders
and company, 1844. MH. 44-2350

Field, Barnum, 1786-1846. Samuel
Taylor Coleridge and the moral tenden-
cy of his writings. New York: 1844. 118 p.
MWA. 44-2351

Field, David Dudley, 1781-1867. A his-
tory of the town of Pittsfield, in Berkshire
County, Massachusetts. With a map of
the county. Hartford: Case, Tiffany and
Burnham, 1844. 80 p. CtSoP; MH;
NNUT; OCHP; PHi. 44-2352

Field, S.J. Some opinions and papers of
S.J. Field. New York: Appleton, 1844. 6
v. MWiW. 44-2353

Fisher, E. Burke, 1799?-1859? Wars of
the Barnburners, of Cuyahoga County.
An epic extraordinary. Cleveland: The
author, 1844. 38 p. OClWHi; RPB. 44-
2354

Fisher, Samuel Reed, 1810-1881. Exercises on the Heidelbergh catechism,
adapted to the use of Sabbath schools
and catechetical classes. Chambersburg,
Pennsylvania: printed at the publication
office of the German Reform Church,
1844. 352 p. ICU; MoWgT; OSW; PAtM;
PPPrHi. 44-2355

Fisher, Samuel Ware, 1814-1874. Our
country, its position, obligation, and
power. A sermon. Albany: Erastus H.
Pease, J. Munsell, printers, 1844. CtY;
MB; NCH; NjR; PPPrHi. 44-2356

Fisher, Samuel Ware, 1814-1874. The
supermacy of mind: a lecture, introductory to the eleventh annual course of lec-

tures before the Young Men's Association of the City of Albany. By Rev. Samuel W. Fisher. Albany: Munsell and Tanner, printers, 1844. 49 p. MB; NjR; OO; PPPrHi. 44-2357

Fisher's comic almanac for 1845. Boston, Massachusetts: James Fisher, [1844] MWA. 44-2358

Fisk, Benjamin Franklin, d. 1832. Fisk's Greek exercises, sixteenth stereotype edition. Adapted to the author's Greek grammar. Boston: Robert S. Davis; New York: Robinson, Pratt and company, and Collins, brothers and company; Philadelphia: Thomas, Cowperthwait and company; Baltimore: Cushing and brothers, 1844. MH; ViU. 44-2359

Fisk, Benjamin Franklin, d. 1832. Grammar of the Greek language. Twenty-sixth stereotyped edition. Boston: Robert S. Davis, 1844. 263 p. IaPeC; MH; MsCliM; NB; OMC. 44-2360

Fisk, Benjamin Franklin, d. 1832. Greek exercises; containing the substance of the Greek syntax. Sixteenth stereotyped edition. Boston: 1844. 171 p. MBC; MH; ViU. 44-2361

Fisk, Gordon M. Story of the female captive and the Indian leap, or great cove; poems. Palmer, Massachusetts: 1844. ICN; MDeeP; NN. 44-2362

Fiske, Nathan Welby, 1798-1847. Supplemental plates to the "Manual of classical literature." Philadelphia: Edward C. Biddle, 1844. 64 p. CSansS; PBa. 44-2363

Fiske, Nathan Welby, 1798-1847. Supplemental plates to the "Manual of classical literature." Fourth edition.

Philadelphia: E.C. Biddle, 1844. 32 p. LNT. 44-2364

Fitchburg Railroad Company. Annual report. Boston: Dutton and Wentworth's Printer, 1844-. V. 1. No. 1. DLC; WU. 44-2365

Fitchburg Railroad Company. Report to the stockholders on the affairs of the Fitchburg Railroad Company.... 1844. Boston: Dutton and Wentworth's, printers, 1844. 15 p. CtY; MeHi; MH-BA; MHi. 44-2366

Fitts, John. Second advent hymns, designed for the saints. Westminister: William Wiswall, 1844. 23 p. CSmH; MB; NNUt. 44-2367

Fitz, Asa. The American school song book, improved. By Asa Fitz. Boston: William B. Fowle and N. Cape, 1844. 128 p. MB; MHi. 44-2368

Fitz, Asa. The primary school song book. Boston: W.B. Fowle and N. Capen, 1844. 30 p. MH; RPB. 44-2369

Fitzball, Edward, 1792-1873. Home again; or, the lieutenant's daughter; a domestic drama, in three acts. New York: Samuel French, [1844?] 34 p. OCl. 44-2370

Fitzball, Edward, 1792-1873. Jonathan Bradford: or, the murder at the roadside inn; a drama, in two acts.... New York: Samuel French, [1844] 30 p. C; OCl. 44-2371

Fitzball, Edward, 1792-1873. The momentous question; an original domestic drama, in two acts... New York:

Samuel French [1844?] 22 p. C; OCl. 44-2372

Flagg, Wilson. The tailor's shop; or, crowns of thorns and coats of thistles.... By Wilson Flagg. Boston: Hotchkiss and company, 1844. 58 p. MB; RPB. 44-2373

Flake, Jacob. The Christian miscellany; containing memoirs of my own life, the church of God in America, three years in Lancaster, Pennsylvania, the first and second advent, the prophecies and various other pieces. No. 1.-1844. Philadelphia: [John C. Clark] 1844. 106 p. FTa; MH; OClWHi. 44-2374

Flanders, Charles W. Divine beneficence. A discourse delivered February 4, 1844.... published by request. Salem: printed at the Gazette office, 1844. 24 p. MBAt; MNtcA; MWelC; NHC-S. 44-2375

Flavel, John. The fountain of life; or display of Christ in his essential and mediatorial glory. Revised and somewhat abridged. New York: American Tract Society, [1844] [3]-558 p. CSansS; IaSlB. 44-2376

Fleetwood, John. The life of Our Lord and Saviour Jesus Christ; containing a full and accurate history from His taking upon Himself our nature to His crucifixion, resurrection, and ascension; together with the lives, transaction and sufferings of His holy evangelist apostles and other primitive martyrs. To which is added the history of the Jews. New Haven: John Galpin, 1844. 606 p. DLC; ICartC. 44-2377

Fleissige Amerikaner. Ein Calender fur stadt und land. Philadelphia: W.L.J.

Kiderlen, 1844. MWA; PPeSchw. 44-2378

Fleming, A. Lessons in geography and astronomy on the globes, supplementary to the text books generally used on these subjects. Boston: Eayrs and Fairbanks, 1844. 106 p. KHi; MH; MiOC; NIC; VtU. 44-2379

Fleming, Charles. A new and complete French and English and English and French dictionary, on the basis of the royal dictionary.... Philadelphia: Carey and Hart, 1844. IaDt; InEvW; MNowo; PRosC; ScCliP. 44-2380

Fleming, John Ambrose. Electric lamps and electric lighting, a course of four lectures on electric illumination delivered at the Royal Institution of Great Britain. New York: D. Van Nostrand company, 1844. 228 p. IaDm. 44-2381

Fleming, L.D. A brief history of that old serpent called the Devil and Satan. Newark, New Jersey: James and Cox, 1844. 46 p. MBC. 44-2382

Fleming, L.D. First principles of the second advent faith, with scripture proofs. Boston: 1844. 36 p. IEG; MBC. 44-2383

Fletcher, John. Christian perfection; being an extract from the Rev. John Fletcher's treatise on that subject. New York: J. Collord, 1844. 141 p. CtY; NN. 44-2384

Fletcher, Silas S. A sermon on the fanaticism of the present age. Delivered in the Universalist Church, New Bedford, Massachusetts, October 27th, 1844. By Silas S. Fletcher. New Bedford: press of Benjamin Lindsey, 1844. 16 p. MNBedf. 44-2385

Flint, Abel, 1765-1825. System of geometry and trigonometry: together with a treatise on surveying. With additional tables by George Gillet. Stereotype edition, enlarged. Hartford: Belknap and Hammersley, 1844. 160 p. MDeeP; MeB; MH; NCH; TxU-T. 44-2386

Flint, Austin. The reciprocal duties and obligations of the medical profession and the public: Chicago: Z. Eastman, printer, 1844. 24 p. DLC; ICJ; MBAt; NBMS; WMAM. 44-2387

Flint, James, 1781-1855. Historical address and poem delivered at the bicentennial celebration of the incorporation of the old town of Reading, May 29, 1844. With an appendix. Boston: printed by Samuel N. Dickinson, 1844. 131 p. CtHC; ICN; MiD-B; RPB; TxU. 44-2388

Flint, James, 1781-1855. A present from a pastor to his young parishioners: in ten discourses; urging upon them an early and earnest attention to religion. Boston: William Crosby, 1844. 328 p. MBC; MFiHi; MH; MNotn; WHi. 44-2389

Flint, James, 1781-1855. The vanity and unsatisfactory nature of earthly possessions, pursuits and pleasures. A discourse delivered in the North Church, January 6, 1833.... By James Flint.... Salem: Francis Putnam, 1844. 18 p. CtSoP; MH-AH; MHi; NjR. 44-2390

Flint, Timothy, 1780-1840. Biographical memoir of Daniel Boone the first settler of Kentucky: interspersed with incidents in the early annals of the country., By Timothy Flint. Cincinnati: G. Conclin, 1844. 252 p. IaFayU; ICU; OC; MoSU; Vi. 44-2391

Florian, Jean Pierre Claris de, 1755-1794. History of the Moors of Spain. Translated from the French original of M. Florian. To which is added a brief note of Islamism. New York: Harper and brothers, 1844. 296 p. OCY; PAtM; RWe; ScGrw; WNaE. 44-2392

Flowers by the way side. Written for the American Sunday School Union and revised by the committee of publication. Philadelphia: American Sunday School Union, 1844. 187 p. MA. 44-2393

Follen, Charles Theodore Christian. A practical grammar of the German language. Stereotype edition. Boston: S.G. Simpkins, 1844. 238 p. ICU; MH; MiU; MtU; NjP. 44-2394

Follen, Eliza Lee Cabot, 1787-1860. The life of Charles Follen. Boston: Thomas H. Webb and company, 1844. 386 p. NNUT; OO; PP; RPB; TxU. 44-2395

Foot, Samuel Augustus, 1780-1846. Speech of Mr. Foot, delivered at the mass meeting at Millstone, New Jersey, August 7, 1844. Somerville: S.L.B. Baldwin, printer, 1844. 16 p. MBAt; NN. 44-2396

Foot, Solomon, 1802-1866. Speech of Mr. Foot, of Vermont on the Oregon question. Washington: 1844. PPL. 44-2397

Forbes, Robert Bennet, 1804-1889. Remarks on China and the China trade. Boston: Samuel N. Dickenson, printer,

1844. 80 p. ICMe; MdAN; MSaP; MWA; WHi. 44-2398

Forget-me-not; a Christmas, New Year's and birthday present, for 1844.... edited by Frederic Shoberl. New York: D. Appleton and company, 1844. 363 p. NjR. 44-2399

Forman, Jacob Gilbert. Elements of phrenology applied to the human character. Cincinnati: Printed by W.L. Mendenhall, 1844. 50 p. InU-M; KAStB; MH; NB; OC. 44-2400

Forrey, Samuel. On the position of man in the scale of organic creation. New York: J.F. Trow and company, 1844. NN; PPL. 44-2401

Forstall, Edmund J. Memorial of Edmund J. Forstall in behalf of Hope and company of Amsterdam. New Orleans, 1844. AU. 44-2402

The forty acre boy. August 12, 1844. Batesville, Arkansas: 1844. NoLoc. 44-2403

The forty-two children at Mount Bethel. By a Sabbath school teacher. Revised by the editor, D.P. Kidder. New York: G. Lane and C.B. Tippett, for the Sunday School Union of the Methodist Episcopal Church, 1844. 47 p. DLC; MBC; TNT. 44-2404

Foster, B. Wood. A practical system of book-keeping, by double and single entry. Third edition. Boston: J. French, 1844. MBC; MH. 44-2405

Foster, B. Wood. A practical system of book-keeping, by double and single entry....With the most approved forms of exchanges, calculations, &c. ....Fourth edition. Boston: James French, 1844. 150 p. MH; MMae; NNC. 44-2406

Foster, Eden B. The scriptural authority and propriety of sprinkling and infant baptism. Preached at Henniker, New Hampshire....By E. B. Foster, ...Concord: press of Asa McFarland, 1844. 48 p. Nh. 44-2407

Foster, Eden B. Four sermons on baptism; the scriptural authority and propriety of sprinkling and infant baptism at Henniker, New Hampshire, October 29, and November 19, 1843. Concord: 1844. MBAt; MiD-B; MnHi; MWA; NHCS. 44-2408

Foster, John, 1770-1843. Biographical, literary and philosophical essays; contributed to the eclectic review. With an index of the principal subjects, prepared for this edition. New York: D. Appleton and company; Philadelphia: G.S. Appleton, 1844. 419 p. GU; KyLoP; MPiB; OWoC; OAU. 44-2409

Foster, John, 1770-1843. Essays in a series of letters on the following subjects: on a monk's writing memoirs of himself.... by which evangelical religion has been rendered less acceptable to persons of cultivated taste. Eighteenth edition. Hartford: S. Andrus and son, 1844. 133 p. MH; NBuCC; PPAN; TxW. 44-2410

Foster, John, 1770-1843. Miscellaneous essays on Christian morals; experimental and practical. New York: D. Appleton and company; Philadelphia: George S. Appleton, 1844. 252 p. ICMe; LNB; MBC; PCA; VtU. 44-2411

Foster, Stephen Symonds, 1809-1881.

The brotherhood of thieves, or a true picture of the American church and clergy.... Boston: Anti-slavery office, 1844. 72 p. CBPac; MBAt; MiD-B; NcD; PPL. 44-2412

Foster and Dickinson's Oneida almanac for 1845. By George R. Perkins. Utica, New York: R.W. Roberts, [1844] MWA; NUtHi. 44-2413

Fourier, Francois Marie Charles, 1772-1837. Fourier's theory of society. Translated for the London phalanx from Abel Transon. New York, 1844. 28 p. CtY. 44-2414

Fowle, William Bentley, 1795-1865. The child's arithmetic; or the elements of calculation, in the spirit of Pestalozzi's method, for the use of children between the ages of three and seven years. Boston: W.B. Fowle and N. Capen, 1844. 52 p. CtHWatk; MH; NNC; OCl. 44-2415

Fowle, William Bentley, 1795-1865. The common school speaker; a new collection of original and selected pieces, for reading and recitation... New Haven: S. Babcock; Boston: Fowle and Capen, 1844. CtHWatk; ICU; MH; MiU; TxU. 44-2416

Fowle, William Bentley, 1795-1865. The common school speller. Boston: William B. Fowle and N. Capen, 1844. 204 p. MBevHi; MH; NNC. 44-2417

Fowle, William Bentley, 1795-1865. Familiar dialogues, and popular discussions, for exhibition in schools and academies of either sex. Boston: Tappan and Dennet, 1844. 286 p. MH; MsWJ; MVh. 44-2418

Fowle, William Bentley, 1795-1865. French first class book; being a new selection of reading lessons: ....By William B. Fowle, principal of the Monitorial school, Boston. Third edition. Boston: 1844. 288 p. MH; MHi; WPre. 44-2419

Fowle, William Bentley, 1795-1865. A practical French accidence; being a comprehensive grammar of the French language; ....Boston: William B. Fowle and N. Capen, 1844. 286 p. MB; MHi; MPeHi; PU; WaPS. 44-2420

Fowler, Orson Squire, 1809-1887. Education and self improvement founded upon physiology and phrenology. New York: O.S. and L.N. Fowler, 1844-1846. 3 v. in 2. CtY; DLC; WaU. 44-2421

Fowler, Orson Squire, 1809-1887. Education and self improvement. Second edition, enlarged and improved. New York: O.S. and L.N. Fowler, 1844. 118 p. CtY-M; KyBC; NLac; WaU. 44-2422

Fowler, Orson Squire, 1809-1887. Fowler on matrimony: ....New York: O.S. and L.N. Fowler, 1844. 32 p. NNNAM. 44-2423

Fowler, Orson Squire, 1809-1887. Love and parentage, applied to the improvement of offspring, including important directions and suggestions to lovers and the married, concerning the strongest ties and the most momentous relations of life. Fourtieth edition. New York: Fowler and Wells, 1844. 144 p. DLC; ICJ; PU; RPM; TxAbH. 44-2424

Fowler, Orson Squire, 1809-1887.

Phrenology proved, illustrated, and applied, accompanied by a chart; embracing an analysis of the primary mental powers in their various degrees of development, etc. by O.S. and L.N. Fowler, assisted by Samuel Kirkham. Thirteenth edition enlarged and improved. New York: O.S. and L.N. Fowler, 1844. 430 p. MH. 44-2425

Fowler, Orson Squire, 1809-1887. Practical phrenology; giving a concise elementary view of phrenology, presenting some new and important remarks upon the temperaments: and describing the primary mental powers in seven different degrees of development. Tenth edition enlarged and improved. New York: O.S. and L.N. Fowler, 1844. 430 p. DCU; MdBM; MH; MiU. 44-2426

Fowler, Orson Squire, 1809-1887. Religion; natural and revealed: or, the natural theology and moral bearings of phrenology and physiology: including the doctrines taught and the duties inculcated thereby, compared with those enjoined in the scriptures.... Second edition. New York: O.S. Fowler, 1844. 176 p. DLC; MU; NNUT; OrU; PLF. 44-2427

Fowler, Orson Squire, 1809-1887. Religion; natural and revealed, or, the natural theology and moral bearings of phrenology and physiology, including the doctrines taught and the duties inculcated thereby, compared with those enjoined in the scriptures.... Third edition enlarged and improved. New York: O.S. Fowler, 1844. 176 p. MH; NcD; OkHi; TNDL; TNL. 44-2428

Fowler, Orson Squire, 1809-1887. Religion, natural and revealed.... Tenth

edition enlarged. New York: Fowler and Wells, 1844. InU. 44-2429

Fowler, Orson Squire, 1809-1887. Tight-lacing, ...New York: O.S. and L.N. Fowler, [1844] 16 p. CtY; DNLM; MdBP; NNNAM; TxU. 44-2430

Fowler, Orson Squire, 1809-1887. Works. New York: 1844. MH. 44-2431

Fownes, George, 1815-1849. Chemistry, as exemplifying the wisdom and beneficence of God. New York: Wiley and Putnam; Philadelphia: J.W. Moore, 1844. 158 p. AMaJ; InNd; KyLo; PPA; TNV. 44-2432

Fox, Charles James, 1811-1846. The New Hampshire book. Being specimens of the literature of the granite state. Nashville: Charles T. Gill, 1844. 391 p. KyHi; MHi; MnHi; RPB; WHi. 44-2433

Fox, John. A history of the lives, sufferings, and triumphant deaths of the primitive as well as the Protestant martyrs.... New edition. Philadelphia: James M. Campbell, 1844. 627 p. MBoxf; PPWe; WBeloC. 44-2434

Foxcroft, Thomas, 1697-1769. An apology in behalf of the Rev. Mr. Whitefield. Boston: 1844? MDeeP. 44-2435

Francis, Convers, 1795-1863. Life of John Eliot, the apostle to the Indians. New York: Harper, 1844. CSmH; CSfCW; MChi; MCli. 44-2436

Francis and companys little libr. New York and Boston: 1844-47. NoLoc. 44-2437

Franklin, Benjamin, 1706-1790. The life

of Benjamin Franklin; containing the autobiography, with notes and a continuation by Jared Sparks. Boston: Tappan and Dermet, 1844. 612 p. ICHi; MH; NNUT; OWoC; ViPet. 44-2438

Franklin, Benjamin, 1706-1790. The works of Benjamin Franklin; containing several political and historical tracts not included in any former edition, and many letters official and private, not hitherto published; with notes and a life of the author. By Jared Sparks. Boston: Tappan, 1844-47. 10 v. ICU; MB; OrU; OSW. 44-2439

Franklin, Benjamin, 1706-1790. The works of Benjamin Franklin; by Jared Sparks. Boston: Tappan and Whittemore, [1844] 10 v. CtY; DLC; InU; NjP; PHi. 44-2440

Franklin, Benjamin, 1706-1790. The works of Benjamin Franklin; containing political and historical tracts not included in any former edition, and many letters official and private not hitherto published; with notes and a life of the author. By Jared Sparks. Eighth edition. Boston: Tappan and Dennett, 1844. 10 v. RWe; TMeSC. 44-2441

Franklin, Benjamin, 1706-1790. The writings of Benjamin Franklin; collected and edited by Jared Sparks. New York: Tappan, 1844. DLC; ScCliP. 44-2442

Franklin, New Hampshire. Town schools. The undersigned having been regularly appointed the superintending school committee for the town of Franklin, hereby present from the statute book, ...a statement of the duties imposed by the laws of the state.... [signed] Elijah Shaw, Isaac Knight, David Kim-

ball. Franklin: Franklin printing office, 1844. MH. 44-2443

Franklin almanac for 1845. Calculations by John Armstrong. Pittsburgh, Pennsylvania: Johnston and Stockton, [1844] MWA. 44-2444

Franklin and Marshall College. Lancaster, Pennsylvania. Catalogue of the members and library of the Gothean Literary Society of Marshall College, Mercersburg, Pennsylvania from 1835 to 1844. Chambersburg, Pennsylvania: Weekly Messenger, 1844. 300 p. MB; MoWgT; PLT. 44-2445

Franklin and Marshall College. Lancaster, Pennsylvania. Catalogue of the members. Chambersburg, Pennsylvania: Weekly Messenger, 1844. 22 p. CSmH. 44-2446

Franklin and Marshall College. Lancaster, Pennsylvania. Catalogue of...Marshall College, Mercersburg, Pennsylvania, 1843-1844. Chambersburg, Pennsylvania: Printed at the office of the Weekly Messenger, 1844. 32 p. PWW. 44-2447

Franklin College, Elm Crag, Tennessee. Outlines of the system of education proposed to be adopted in Franklin College at Elm Crag, five miles from Nashville, Tennessee. Nashville: printed by Cameron and Fall; Office of the Tennessee Agriculturist, 1844. 12 p. OCHP. 44-2448

Franklin County Benevolent Societies. Annual report of the Benevolent Societies of Franklin County, for the year 1844. Greenfield: L. Merriam and company, printer, 1844. 12 p. MWA. 44-2449

Franklin Institute, Philadelphia. Constitution and by-laws for the promotion of the mechanic arts with the act of incorporation. Philadelphia: King and Baird, 1844. 32 p. DLC; PPFrankI. 44-2450

Franklin Typographical Association. New York. Constitution and by-laws of the Franklin Typographical Association of New York, with the scale of prices adopted March 30, 1844; to which is added a list of members. New York: Kimber and Kraft, printers, 1844. 26 p. MiD; NNC. 44-2451

Fraser, Lieutenant Col. Sweet home of my childhood. I bid thee farewell, a ballad sung by Mr. Dempster, at his public concerts. New York: William DuBois, 1844. 7 p. IaDuPrC. 44-2452

Frazee, Bradford. An appeal to the Methodist Episcopal Church, North and South, on the course of the Christian Advocate and Journal. New York, 1844. 20 p. NoLoc. 44-2453

Frazee, Bradford. An improved grammar of the English language, on the inductive system; with which elementary and progressive lessons in composition are combined. For the use of Schools and academies. Philadelphia and New York: 1844. 192 p. CtY; ICBB; NbOM; McWsM; NNC. 44-2454

Fredet, Peter. A treatise on the eucharistic mystery; or, defense of the Catholic dogma of the eucharist against the recent attacks of adversaries. By Peter Fredet, D.D. ....Baltimore: Metropolitan press, 1844. 156 p. CtHT; MBAt; NBuDC; ODaU; PPP. 44-2455

Fredonia Academy. Chautauqua County, New York. Annual catalogue of the officers and students of Fredonia Academy, at Fredonia, Chautauque [sic] County, New York, for the year 1844. Fredonia Censor office, printer, 1844. 22 p. NFred. 44-2456

The freeman's almanac. 1844. Cincinnati: 1844. IU. 44-2457

Freemasons. September 1844- Lousiville: 1844-. v. 1-. MH. 44-2458

Freemasons. Alabama. Proceedings of the most worshipful Grand Lodge of free and accepted Masons in the state of Alabama, at the annual communication, December A.L. 1844. Tuscaloosa: printed by R.A. Eaton, 1844. 44 p. NNFM. 44-2459

Freemasons. Arkansas. Proceedings of the annual communication of the Grand Lodge of the state of Arkansas begun and held in the Masonic Hall in the city of Little Rock, on Monday, the sixth day of November, A.L. 5843. Little Rock: Printed at the Times and Advocate office, 1844. 22 p. ArLFM; MDFM. 44-2460

Freemasons. Georgia. Proceedings of the most worshipful Grand Lodge of the state of Georgia at an annual communication held at Milledgeville, from the 5th to the 8th November A.A. 5844. Macon: S. Rose and Company, 1844. 39 p. NNFM. 44-2461

Freemasons. Illinois. Proceedings of the Grand Lodge of Illinois, at a grand annual communication, in the town of Jacksonville, commencing October 7, 5844. Jacksonville: William C. Swett, printer,

1844. 48 p. IaCrM; DSC; NNFM; PPFM. 44-2462

Freemasons. Indiana. Proceedings of a grand communication of the Grand Lodge of Indiana, begun and held in the city of Indianapolis, on Monday, the 27th day of May, A.L. 5844. Indianapolis: G.A. and J.P. Chapman, 1844. 71 p. MBFM; NNFM; OCM. 44-2463

Freemasons. Iowa. By-laws of the Dubuque Lodge, no. 3. by authority of the most worshipful Grand Lodge of Iowa. Dubuque, Iowa: A. Keesecker, printer, 1844. 10 p. IaCrM 44-2464

Freemasons. Iowa. By-laws of Iowa City Lodge, Number 4. Chartered by the Grand Lodge of Iowa, January 8, 1844; adopted June 5, 1844. Iowa City: Jesse Williams, 1844. 8 p. IaCrM. 44-2465

Freemasons. Iowa. The constitution and code of the Grand Lodge of Iowa. By-laws masonic code. Edition 1. Burlington, Iowa, 1844. 8 p. IaCrM. 44-2466

Freemasons. Iowa. The Constitutions and code of the Grand Lodge of Iowa, ancient, free and accepted Masons. Adopted in convention, at Iowa City, Iowa, January 3 A.D. 1844. Bloomington: Johm B. Russell, 1844. 8 p. IaCrM. 44-2467

Freemasons. Kentucky. Proceedings of the Grand Lodge of Kentucky, at a grand annual communication, in the city of Lexington, commencing August twenty-sixth, A.L. 5844. Frankfort: Hodges, Todd and Pruett, 1844. 80 p. NNFM. 44-2468

Freemasons. Louisiana. General regulations of the Grand Lodge of the state of Louisiana. New Orleans: printed by Gaux and company, 1844. 20 p. DLC; PPFM. 44-2469

Freemasons. Louisiana. Reglements generaux de la Grande Loge de l'etat de la Louisiane. Nouvelle-Orleans: Imprime par A. Gaux and company, 1844. 20 p. DLC. 44-2470

Freemasons. Maine. Grand Lodge of the most ancient and honorable fraternity of free and accepted Masons of the state of Maine. Augusta: Severance and Dorr, printers, 1844. 20 p. NNFM. 44-2471

Freemasons. Maine. The act of incorporation and by-laws, for the government and management of the master, wardens, and members of the Grand Lodge of Maine. Incorporated June 16, 1820, and adopted January 11, 1821. Augusta: Severence and Dorr, Printers, 1844. 22 p. IaCrM; PPFM. 44-2472

Freemasons. Maryland. Proceedings of the Grand Lodge of Masonic Lodge in Maryland; meeting held in 1844. Baltimore: Joseph Robinson, 1844. IaCrM; PPFM. 44-2473

Freemasons. Maryland. Proceedings of the Grand Royal Arch Chapter of the state of Maryland... in the city of Baltimore, on the 20th November, 1843. Baltimore: Printed by Jos. Robinson, 1844. 25 p. NNFM. 44-2474

Freemasons. Massachusetts. By-laws of St. John's Lodge. Boston: Tuttle and Dennett, 1844. 9 p. NjR. 44-2475

Freemasons. Massachusetts. Grand

lodge of the most ancient and honorable fraternity of free and accepted Masons of the commonwealth of Massachusetts. Boston: printed at the office of the Freemasons' magazine. 1844. 36 p. NjR; NNFM. 44-2476

Freemasons. Massachusetts. Proceedings of the most worshipful Grand Lodge of ancient and accepted masons of the commonwealth of Massachusetts for the years 1826 to 1844 inclusive. Boston: Caustic and Clafin Company, 1844? 801 p. OCM. 44-2477

Freemasons. Mississippi. Extracts from the proceedings of the Grand Lodge of the state of Mississippi, at the grand annual communication, held at the Masonic hall in the city of Natchez, January, A.D. 1844. Natchez: printed at the Natchez Daily Courier Office, 1844. 104 p. NNFM. 44-2478

Freemasons. Missouri. Proceedings of the Grand Lodge of Missouri; meeting held in 1844. Bloomington [Il?] Jno. B. Russell, 1844. 24 p. IaCrM. 44-2479

Freemasons. New Hampshire. A journal of the proceedings of the Grand Lodge of New Hampshire at an adjourned meeting in Portsmouth, December 13, A.D. 1843. and of the annual communication in Concord. Exeter: Charles E. Folsom, 1844. 32 p. LNMas. 44-2480

Freemasons. New Hampshire. A Journal of the proceedings of the Grand Royal Arch Chapter of the state of New Hampshire. Concord, June 14, 1843 and June 12, 1844. Concord: Asa M'Farland, 1844. 10 p. NNFM. 44-2481

Freemasons. New York. By-laws of Syracuse Lodge Number 102 of free and accepted Masons, adopted, September, 1844. Syracuse: J. Barber, 1844. 16 p. NNFM. 44-2482

Freemasons. New York. Transactions of the Grand Lodge of free and accepted Masons of the state of New York. New York: J.M. Marsh, printer, 1844. 72 p. OCM. 44-2483

Freemasons. North Carolina. Proceedings of the Grand Lodge of Ancient York Masons, of North Carolina, A.L. 5843. Raleigh: Thomas Loring, printer, 1844. 84 p. IaCrM; NNFM. 44-2484

Freemasons. Ohio. Proceedings of Grand Commandery of Masonic Lodge in Ohio; meeting held in 1844. Columbus: C. Scott and company, 1844. 16 p. IaCrM. 44-2485

Freemasons. Ohio. Proceedings of the grand encampment of Knights Templar of the state of Ohio, at its second session, held at the city of Columbus, October 26, 1844. Columbus: printed by C. Scott and company, 1844. 25 p. NNFM. 44-2486

Freemasons. Ohio. Proceedings of the Grand Royal Arch Chapter of the state of Ohio. Columbus: printed by C. Scott and company, 1844. 23 p. IaCrM; NNFM. 44-2487

Freemasons. Pennsylvania. By-laws and rules of order of Lodge Number 3. Philadelphia: printed for Lodge Number 3 by P.G. Collins, 1844. 40 p. NjR; PPFM. 44-2488

Freemasons. Pennsylvania. By-laws of Lodge Number 2, ancient York Masons, held in the city of Philadelphia, under the sanction of the Grand Lodge of Pennsylvania, finally adopted by the Lodge, May 8th, 1843, and approved in Grand Lodge, at a grand quarterly communication, March 4th, 1844. Philadelphia: Desilver and Muir, 1844. 8 p. IaCrM; PPFM. 44-2489

Freemasons. Pennsylvania. Epistle of caution and advice from the meeting for sufferings in Philadelphia. Philadelphia: Joseph and William Kite, 1844. 8 p. IEG; NjR. 44-2490

Freemasons. Rhode Island. A journal of the proceedings of the Grand Lodge of Rhode Island for the year ending June 24, A.L. 5844. Providence: 1844. 24 p. RHi. 44-2491

Freemasons. Tennessee. Proceedings of the Grand Lodge of the state of Tennessee at a grand annual communication, held at the Masonic Hall in the city of Nashville, on Monday, October 7, A.L. 5844. Nashville: Printed by Cameron and Fall, 1844. 32 p. DSC; IaCrM; NNFM. 44-2492

Freemasons. Texas. Proceedings of the Grand Lodge of Texas at its seventh grand annual communication. Washington: 1844. 30 p. PHi. 44-2493

Freemasons. Virginia. Proceedings of a grand annual communication of the Grand Lodge of Virginia, begun and held in the Mason's Hall in the city of Richmond, December A.D. 1844. Richmond: printed by John Warrock, 1844. 35 p. NNFM. 44-2494

The freewill Baptist register, for the year of our Lord, 1844.... Dover: trustees of the Freewill Baptist Connection, 1844. 76 p. MHa; MWA; NhHi; PCA. 44-2495

Freiligrath, F.F. Freiligrath's epistle and Audabon nebst einer Antwort aus Amerika an Freiligrath. Philadelphia: 1844. MB; PPG; PPL-R. 44-2496

Fremont, John Charles, 1813-1890. Map of an exploring expedition to the Rocky Mountains in the year 1842, and to Oregon and North California in the years 1843-4. Mounted in section on linen. Baltimore, 1844. OMC; PHi. 44-2497

French, Benjamin Brown, 1800-1870. Fitz Clarence: a poem. By B.B. French. Washington: Blair and Rives, printers, 1844. 31 p. ICU; MWA; NhPoA; RPB. 44-2498

French, James. Penmanship, or the beauties of writing, exemplified in a variety of specimens, practical and ornamental. Boston: J. French, 1844. NhD. 44-2499

French, Jonathan. The true republican: containing the inaugural addresses, together with the first annual addresses and messages of all the presidents of the United States, from 1789 to 1845; with their farewell addresses.... To which is annexed the Declaration of Independence and Constitution of the United States.... Philadelphia: Richardson, 1844. 456 p. ScCleA. 44-2500

French, Richard. Speech of Mr. French of Kentucky, on the right of members to their seats in the House, February 12, 1844. MHi; MoS; NNC. 44-2501

Fresenius, Carl Remigius, 1818-1897.

Elementary instruction of chemical analysis. With a preface by Professor Liebig. Edited by J. Lloyd Bullock.... New York: D. Appleton and company, 1844. 288 p. CtY; IaMP; KyLxT; MH; NcD. 44-2502

Frey, Joseph Samuel. A course of lectures on the Messiahship of Christ. By the Rev. Joseph Samuel C.F. Frey... New York: printed for the author, 1844. 300 p. GDecCT; ICP; InIBU; ScDuE; TChU. 44-2503

Frey, Joseph Samuel. The messiahship of Jesus, a course of lectures by Joseph Samuel; C.F. Frey, author of a Hebrew grammar, Hebrew dictionary, the Scripture types, etc. ....Revised by the committee of publication. Philadelphia: American Baptist Publication Society, 1844. 299 p. IaPeC; InR; LNB; MiU; OrPWB. 44-2504

Friends' intelligencer. Philadelphia: Friends' Intelligencer Association Limited, 1844. V. 1-. DLC; MoSU; NcD; TxU; WaPS. 44-2505

Friends of Literary, Benevolent and Religious Associations of Virginia. An Appeal to the legislature of Virginia, by the Friends of Literary, Benevolent and Religious Associations in Virginia, for the passage of a law authorizing them to receive and hold bequests. Richmond: H.K. Ellyson's Press, 1844. 14 p. DLC; MB; NcMHi; NjPT. 44-2506

Friends, Society of. Anti-Slavery. Indiana Yearly Meeting. Address, of Indiana yearly meeting of Anti-slavery Friends held at Newport, Wayne County, Indiana, from the 2nd of the 9th month to the 7th of the same, inclusive. 1844. [Newport? 1844] 20 p. In. 44-2507

Friends, Society of. Anti-Slavery. Indiana Yearly Meeting. Minutes of Indiana yearly meeting of Anti-slavery Friends, held at Newport, Wayne County, Indiana 9th month 2nd 1844. [Newport? 1844] 30 p. In. 44-2508

Friends, Society of. Baltimore Yearly Meeting. Rules of discipline of the yearly meeting of Friends. Held in Baltimore. Baltimore: William Wooddy, printer, 1844. 115 p. CtY; DLC; InRchE; MWA; NcD. 44-2509

Friends, Society of. Hicksite. Ohio Yearly Meeting. Minutes of the yearly meeting. St. Clairsville: 1844. OHi. 44-2510

Friends, Society of. London Yearly Meeting. An appeal on the iniquity of slavery and the slave trade: issued by the yearly meeting of the religious Society of Friends, held in London, 1844; republished for general circulation, by Indiana Yearly Meeting of Friends, held at Whitewater, in Wayne County, Indiana, 1844. Cincinnati [Ohio] A. Pugh and company, 1844. 9 p. CtY; KyLx; MBAt; OCHP; WHi. 44-2511

Friends, Society of. Memorials of deceased Friends of New England yearly meeting. Published by the meeting for sufferings. Providence: Knowles and Vose, printers, 1844. 16 p. PPM. 44-2512

Friends, Society of. New England Yearly Meeting. Memorials of deceased Friends of New England Yearly meeting. Published by the Meeting for sufferings, 1844. Providence: Knowles and Vose, printer, 1844. 16 p. DLC; MH; MiD-B; PHC; RPB. 44-2513

Friends, Society of. New England Yearly Meeting for Sufferings. To the preparative, monthly and quarterly meetings of Friends within the limits of New England Yearly Meeting. [Providence, Rhode Island?] [1844] 2 p. MH; PHC. 44-2514

Friends, Society of. New York Yearly Meeting. An address of Friends of the yearly meeting of New York to the citizens of the United States, especially to those of the southern states, upon the subject of slavery. New York: press of Mahlon Day and company, 1844. 16 p. KyLx; MB; NcGu; NNUT; PHC. 44-2515

Friends, Society of. Ohio Yearly Meeting. Minutes... held at Mountpleasant, September 2-6, 1844. Mountpleasant: 1844. OU. 44-2516

Friends, Society of. Philadelphia Yearly Meeting. The ancient testimony of the Religious Society of Friends, commonly called Quakers, respecting some of their Christian doctrines and practices reviewed and given forth by the Yearly Meeting held in Philadelphia, in the fourth month, 1843. Manchester: W. Harrison, 1844. 84 p. InRE; PHC. 44-2517

Friends, Society of. Philadelphia Yearly Meeting. Epistle of caution and advice from the meeting for sufferings in Philadelphia. Philadelphia: Joseph and William Kite, printers, 1844. 8 p. IEG; NjR. 44-2518

Friends, Society of. Philadelphia Yearly Meeting. Report of the committee on

education to the yearly meeting. Philadelphia: Joseph and William Kite, printers, 1844. 12 p. InRchE; NjR; PHC. 44-2519

Friendship's offering and winter's wreath; a christmas and new year's presentation for 1843-1855. Boston: Lewis and Sampson [1844] 4 v. MnU. 44-2520

Froissart, Jean, 1338?-1410? Chronicles of England, France, Spain, and the adjoining countries, from the latter part of the reign of Edward II to the coronation of Henry IV; by Sir John Froissart. Translated from the French, with variations and additions, from many celebrated mss. by Thomas Johnes, esq. To which are prefixed a life of the author, an essay on his works, and a criticism on his history. With an original introductory essay on the character and society of the middle ages, by Rev. John Lord. First American edition. New York: J. Winchester, 1844? CL; CtHWatk; MsGW; OCU; TMeSC. 44-2521

Frost, Anna P. An address written for the Ladies Literary Society of Newbury Seminary, in commemoration of the sudden removal by death of their beloved President Miss R. Smith. Published by request. Newbury, Vermont: L.J. McIndoe, 1844. 8 p. MH; Nh; Vt. 44-2522

Frost, J. American speaker containing numerous rules, observations and exercises on pronunciations, pauses, inflections.... Philadelphia: Thomas, Cowperthwait and company, 1844. 448 p. ICU; MH. 44-2523

Frost, John, 1800-1859. American naval biography, comprising lives of the commodores, and other commanders distinguished in the history of the American navy. Compiled from the best authorities. Philadelphia: E.H. Butler, 1844. 400 p. LNH; MeHi; OClWHi; PU; TJoT. 44-2524

Frost, John, 1800-1859. The beauties of French history. By the author of the Beauties of English history [,] American history, etc. New York: Alexander V. Blake, 1844. 252 p. MBC; NbBla. 44-2525

Frost, John, 1800-1859. City scenes; by Robert Ramble [pseud.] Boston: J.H. Francis, 1844. MH. 44-2526

Frost, John, 1800-1859. Heroes of the revolution: comprising lives of officers who were distinguished in the war of independence. Edited by J. Frost. New York: Saxton and Miles, 1844. 240 p. Ct; MBC; NAlf; TxDa; Vi. 44-2527

Frost, John, 1800-1859. Heroes of the revolution: comprising lives of officers who were distinguished in the war of independence. Edited by J. Frost. Third edition. New York: Saxton and Miles, 1844. 240 p. Ct; DLC; NBuG; RP. 44-2528

Frost, John, 1800-1859. Lives of American merchants, eminent for integrity, enterprise and public spirit.... New York: Saxton and Miles, 1844. 240 p. MBC; MBedf; PPL-R; PU; ScNC. 44-2529

Frost, John, 1800-1859. Lives of American merchants, eminent for integrity, enterprise and public spirit.... Second edition. New York: Saxton and Miles, 1844. 240 p. DLC; MBedf; OC; PU; RPB. 44-2530

Frost, John, 1800-1859. Pictorial history of the United States of America from the discovery by the Northmen in the tenth century to the present time. Philadelphia: S. Collins, 1844. 4 v. in 2. CtMW; DeWi; OCY; PSC; RHi. 44-2531

Frost, John, 1800-1859. Pictorial history of the United States of America, from the discovery by the Northmen in the tenth century to the present time.... Philadelphia: Walker, 1844. 4 v. in 2. IaPeC; NcNb; PHatU; PPLT; RP. 44-2532

Frost, John, 1800-1859. Robert Ramble's scenes in the country. Boston: J.H. Francis, etc, etc, 1844. LU; MH; MLex. 44-2533

Frost, John, 1800-1859. The wonders of history, comprising remarkable battles, seiges, feats of arms and instances of courage.... New York: Nafis and Cornish, 1844. 567 p. IaK; LNH; MH; OCY; PPM. 44-2534

Frothingham, Nathaniel Langdon, 1793-1870. Discourse before the Alumni of the Divinity School at Harvard University. Boston: Printed by William Crosby, 1844. 38 p. MBC. 44-2535

Frothingham, Nathaniel Langdon, 1793-1870. The duty of the citizen to the law. A sermon. Boston: Leonard C. Bowles, 1844. 14 p. MB; MBAt; MHi; MiD-B. 44-2536

Frothingham, Nathaniel Langdon, 1793-1870. Our religious times. An address delivered before the Association of the Alumni of the Cambridge Theological School, July 12, 1844. Boston: William Crosby, 1844. 23 p. ICMe; MBC; MnHi; MWA; RPB. 44-2537

Fry, Caroline. The listener. Sixth edition from the last London edition revised. Philadelphia: George and Wayne, 1844. 2 v. KyHi; MiD; NjR. 44-2538

Full and complete account of the late awful riots in Philadelphia. Philadelphia: John B. Perry and Henry Jordan; New York: Nafis and Cornish, [1844] 36 p. DLC; ICU; MBBC; MWA; WHi. 44-2539

Full particulars of the late riots, with a view of the burning of the Catholic Churches; St. Michaels and St. Augustines. [Sic.] Philadelphia: 1844. 24 p. DLC; PHi; PV. 44-2540

Fuller, Robert W. A sermon preached at the funeral of Nathaniel Grant, esq., Acworth, New Hampshire, February 17, 1844. By Robert W. Fuller. Claremont, New Hampshire: N.W. Goddard, printer, 1844. 15 p. MHi. 44-2541

Fuller, Sarah Margaret, 1810-1850. Summer on the lakes, in 1843. Boston: Charles C. Little and James Brown; New York: Charles S. Francis and company, 1844. 256 p. IGK; NBu. 44-2542

Furness, William Henry, 1802-1896. Domestic worship. ....Third edition. Boston: William Crosby, 1844. 272 p. GAGTh; IGK; MBAU; RP. 44-2543

Furness, William Henry, 1802-1896. Religion, a principle, not a form. A discourse, delivered on the Lord's day, March 17, 1844, in the First Congregational Unitarian Church, in reference to the question concerning the use of the Bible in the public schools. Philadelphia: J. Crissy, 1844. 16 p. CtY; ICMe; LNB; MiD-B; PPPrHi. 44-2544

G

G., G.P. Tockwotton waltz. The subject from "we met." For pianoforte. Boston: Reed, 1844. 3 p. MB. 44-2545

Gallaudet, Thomas Hopkins. School and family dictionary.... New York: 1844. CTHWatk. 44-2546

Galloupe, Daniel P. Some of the dangers of teachers; an address delivered before the American Institute of Instruction at Portland, Maine, August 30, 1844. Boston: W.D. Ticknor and company, 1844. 39 p. MH. 44-2547

Galt, John, 1779-1839. All the voyages round the world; from the first, by Magellan, in 1520, to that of Freycinet, in 1820. Now first collected by Captain Samuel Prior. New York: William H. Colyer, 1844. 418 p. IaAt; NICLA. 44-2548

Galt, John, 1779-1839. Voyages round the world, from the first of Magellan, 1520 to Freycinet, 1820. New York: William H. Colyer, 1844. 418 p. OCX. 44-2549

Galusha, Elon. Address, of Elder Elon Galusha, with reasons for believing Christ's second coming, at hand. Rochester: Printed by Erastus Shepard, 1844. 24 p. MH; MWA. 44-2550

Gammell, William, 1812-1889. Address delivered before the Rhode Island Historical Society, at the opening of their cabinet on Wednesday, November 20, 1844. Providence: B. Cranston and company, 1844. 30 p. ICN; MeHi; MWA; OCHP; PPAmP. 44-2551

Gannett, Ezra Stiles, 1801-1871. The rejected article, in reply to Parker's review of "Hennell on the origin of Christianity." Offered first to the Dial; then to the Christian Examiner. By a Unitarian minister. Boston: Benjamin H. Greene, 1844. 32 p. CBPac; ICMe; MBAU; Nh-Hi; OO. 44-2552

Gardner, Daniel. A treatise on international law, and a short explanation of the jurisdiction and duty of the government of the republic of the United States. Troy: N. Tuttle, printer, 1844. 315 p. CU; ICN; MiU; NjR; RLa. 44-2553

Gardner, Francis. A dictionary of the Latin language, particularly adapted to the classics usually studied perparatory to a colllegiate course. Boston: J.H. Wilkins and R.B. Carter, etc., etc., 1844. 419 p. MHi; MsH; NbU; NIC; OO. 44-2554

Gardner, James. Memoirs of eminent Christian females; with an essay on the influences of female piety. By the Rev. James Gardner. Philadelphia: Lindsay and Blakeston, 1844. 5-311 p. MiD; MoK; NCH; PPL. 44-2555

Garrison, William Lloyd. Letter to N.A. Foster, regarding an anti-slavery lecturer for Portland, dated March 22, 1844. Boston: 1844. 1 p. MW. 44-2556

Gates, Jeremiah. In the court for the correction of errors. The Madison County Mutual Insurance Company, plantiffs in error vs. Jeremiah Gates, and Abner P. Downer, defendants in error. Cazenovia: 1844. N. 44-2557

Gaussen, Louis, 1790-1863. Theopneusty; or, the plenary inspiration of the Holy scriptures, by S. R. L. Gaussen.... Translated by Edward Norris Kirk. Second American from the second French edition, enlarged and improved by the author. New York: John S. Taylor and company, 1844. 410 p. NbOP; OTifH; TxHR. 44-2558

Gaussen, Samuel Robert Louis. Geneva and Rome. Rome papal as portrayed by S.R.L. Gaussen.... with an introduction by the Rev. E. Bickersteth.... New York: J.S. Taylor and company, 1844. 66 p. KyLoP; NcAS; NjMD; OSW; PPPrHi. 44-2559

Gebahnte Pilgerstrasse nach dem Berge Zion. Baltimore, Maryland: J.F. Zetztener, 1844. PPeSchw; PPG. 44-2560

Geer's Hartford city directory, for 1844; with a complete stage, railroad, steamboat, packet, and a freight boat register, &c., &c., and a map of the city with engravings of four churches. Published on the 1st of May, annually. No. 7; May, 1844 to May, 1845. Hartford: Elihu Geer, 1844. 168 p. Ct. 44-2561

The gem or fashionable business directory for the city of New York. New York: 1844. 108 p. DLC; NBLIHI. 44-2562

Das Gemeinschaftliche Gesangbuch zum Gottesdienstlichen Gebrauch der Lutherischen und Reformirten Gemeinden in Nord Amerika... Philadelphia: Mentz und sohn, 1844. 372 p. PReaHi. 44-2563

Gems of poetry; containing the poems of Samuel Woodworth, the biography and poetry of "Amelia," the western poetess... Lancaster: James H. Bryson, 1844. 232 p. LNH; PHi; RPB. 44-2564

Gems of sacred poetry. Boston: Saxton, Peirce and Company, 1844. 9-128 p. DLC; NBuG; TxU. 44-2565

General Association of Connecticut. Minutes of the General Association of Connecticut, at their meeting in New London, June, 1844. With an appendix, containing the report on the state of religion, etc. New Haven: printed by J. Hall Benham, 1844. 50 p. MoWgT. 44-2566

General Association of New York. Minutes of the General Association of New York at their meeting in Clinton, Oneida County, August 22, 1844. With an appendix containing the narrative of the state of religion.... Utica, New York: R. W. Roberts, 1844. 28 p. MoWgT. 44-2567

General family directory for 1845. New York: Comstock and company [1844] MWA. 44-2568

General Protestant Episcopal Sunday School Union. Sixth triennial meeting, Philadelphia, Fourth October, 1844. New York: Church Depository, 1844. 48 p. M; MdBD; NjR. 44-2569

Genesee Wesleyan Seminary. Lima,

New York. Catalogue of the officers and students of the Genesee Wesleyan Seminary, Lima, New York. 1844. Rochester: David Hoyt, printer, 1844. 32 p. NLG. 44-2570

Geneva Courier. Carriers address of the Geneva Courier. January 1, 1845. [Geneva: 1844] Broadside. NHi. 44-2571

Geneva Medical College. Geneva, New York. Annual circular of the medical institution of Geneva College. June, 1844. Geneva: Ira Merrell, printer, 1844. 14 p. DSG. 44-2572

Geneva Medical College. Geneva, New York. Catalogue of the medical institution of Geneva College. Session of 1843-4. Geneva, New York: Ira Merrell, printer, 1844. 15 p. MBC; MH; MiU; N; NGH. 44-2573

Georgetown College. Georgetown, Kentucky. The laws of Georgetown College. Cincinnati: 1844. MH. 44-2574

Georgia. Bill of equity. Copies of contracts for building the Monroe Railroad and Banking Company and temporary injunction of the Court. Macon? 1844. Broadside. ViU. 44-2575

Georgia. Journal of the Senate of the state of Georgia, at an annual session of the General Assembly, begun and held in Milledgeville, the seat of government, in November and December, 1843. Milledgeville: S. Rogers, 1844. 440 p. G-Ar; NcU. 44-2576

Georgia Railroad and Banking Company. Reports of the directors, and engineer-in-chief to the stockholders in conventions, May 14, 1844, May 17, 1845,

May 13, 1846. Augusta, Georgia: Chronicle and Sentinel office, 1844-1846. 3 v. DLC; MB. 44-2577

Gesenius, Friedrich Heinrich Wilhelm, 1786-1842. A Hebrew and English lexicon of the Old Testament, including the biblical Chaldee. From the Latin of William Gesenius. By Edward Robinson. A new edition. Boston: Crocker and Brewster, 1844. 1144 p. CtY; IU; MWiW; NbOP; ViU. 44-2578

Gesta romanorium. Select tales, translated from the Latin by C. Swan. Folklore, New York: G.P. Putnam's sons, 1844. MGa. 44-2579

Gettysburg College. The library record and journal of the Linnaean Association of Pennsylvania College. Gettysburg: Printed by H.C. Neinstedt, 1844. v.1-. ICJ; MdBP; PAtM. 44-2580

Gibbon, Edward. The history of the decline and fall of the Roman empire. By Edward Gibbon, esq., with notes, by the Rev. H. H. Milman, prebendary of St. Peters and Vicar of St. Margaret's Westminster. With maps. New York: Harper and brothers, 1844. 4 v. CoLas; GFtv; TxSaWi. 44-2581

Gibbon, Edward. History of the decline and fall of the Roman empire. By Edward Gibbon, esq. A new edition, revised and corrected.... preceeded by a preface, ...notes, critical and historical.... By M.F. Guizot.... In two volumes. Cincinnati: J.A. James, 1844. 2 v. CEu; CoCra; IaSC; MNBedf; NIC. 44-2582

Gibbons, J.V. A brief and dispassionate review of a lecture delivered by the Rev. J.T.A. Henderson, in the Cumberland

Presbyterian Church, Uniontown, on the evening of January 3, 1844. Uniontown: 1844. 11 p. WHi. 44-2583

Gibbs, Antony and sons, firm. London. Peruvian and Bolivian Guano; its nature, properties and results, with an account of authentic experiments made with it in Great Britain, France and America, etc. Baltimore: 1844. 32 p. MBHo; NSchHi. 44-2584

Gibson, William. Introductory lecture before the medical class of the University of Pennsylvania, delivered November 4, 1844. By William Gibson, M.D., professor of surgery. Philadelphia: Isaac Ashmead, printer, 1844. 25 p. MBAt; MBM; MdBM; NBuU-M; PU. 44-2585

Giddings, Joshua Reed, 1795-1864. A letter from Hon. J.R. Giddings, upon the duty of anti-slavery men in the present crisis. Ravenna, Ohio: printed by W. Wadsworth, 1844. 16 p. MiD-B; MoKU; OClWHi; OO. 44-2586

Giddings, Joshua Reed, 1795-1864. Speech of Mr. J.R. Giddings, of Ohio, upon the annexation of Texas delivered in the House of Representatives, United States, May 21, 1844. Washington: Gideon, [1844] 15 p. MH; NBU; PHi; TxU; WHi. 44-2587

Giddings, Joshua Reed, 1795-1864. Speech.... on the motion of Mr. C.T. Ingersoll.... in favor of paying for the Negroes on board the schooner Amistad. Delivered in the House.... April 18, 1844. Washington: 1844. 11 p. OClWHi. 44-2588

Giddings, Joshua Reed, 1795-1864. Speech.... upon the improvement of the

harbors on the lakes;....January 12, 1844. [Washington: 1844] 8 p. MBAt; MHi; OClWHi. 44-2589

Gifford, George P. An address... before the Bunker Hill Native American Association in the town hall, Charlestown, September 17, 1844. [Charlestown] 1844. 12 p. M. 44-2590

The gift for all seasons. Philadelphia: 1844. MB. 44-2591

Gilbert, Ann Taylor, 1782-1866. Original poems for infant minds by the Taylor family. From the 1212 London edition. New York: Saxton and Miles, 1844. 174 p. MH; MnS; NUt. 44-2592

Gilbert, David. Lecture introductory to the course of principles and practice of surgery in the medical department of Pennsylvania College for the session, 1844-1845. Philadelphia: Young, 1844. 12 p. MdBM; NjPT; NNAm; PHi; PU. 44-2593

Gilbert, John S., 1801-1891. An argument in favor of the iron balance dock of John S. Gilbert. New York: Tribune Power Press Printing Establishment, 1844. 22 p. DLC; MWA; NNE; PPAN. 44-2594

Giles, Charles, b. 1783. Pioneer: a narrative of the nativity, experience, travels, and ministerial labors of Rev. Charles Giles.... With incidents, observations, and reflections. New York: G. Lane and P. P. Sandford, 1844. 333 p. CU; MPiB; OO; PPL; WHi. 44-2595

Gillette, Abram Dunn, 1807-1882. Address delivered at the great Protestant meeting in Independent Square...

Philadelphia: 1844. 12 p. NHC-S. 44-2596

Gilman, Charles, d. 1849. Digest of the decisions of the Supreme Courts of the states of Indiana and Illinois, and the circuit court of the United States, for the seventh circuit. Columbus: Henry W. Darby, 1844. 321 p. CtY; DLC; ICarbS; NN; PPb. 44-2597

Gilmanton Academy, Gilmanton, New Hampshire. Catalogue of the trustees, instructors and students of Gilmanton Academy at Gilmanton, N. H. for the year ending August 14, 1844. Gilmanton: Printed by A. Prescott, 1844. 16 p. MBC; MeHi. 44-2598

Gilmanton Theological Seminary. Circular in behalf of the library. Gilmanton: 1844. 2 p. Nh-Hi. 44-2599

Gilmanton Theological Seminary. Constitution and laws of Gilmantown Theological Seminary. Gilmantown: Alfred Prescott, 1844. 24 p. CBPSR; MWA; NjR. 44-2600

Gilmanton Theological Seminary. Map showing congregationalism in New Hampshire at the beginning of the Gilmanton Institution. n.p.: 1844. 4 p. Nh-Hi. 44-2601

Gilmanton Theological Seminary. Triennial catalogue, 1844. Gilmanton: 1844. Nh-Hi. 44-2602

Gilpin, Henry Dilworth, 1801-1860. Life of Martin Van Buren. Philadelphia, 1844. PPL; TU. 44-2603

Gilpin, Thomas. On the representation of minorities of electors to act with the majority in elected assemblies. Philadelphia: John C. Clark, 1844. 15 p. MdHi; MH; PPAmP; PHi. 44-2604

Gilroy, Clinton G. The art of weaving, by hand and by power, with an introductory account of its rise and progress in ancient and modern times. New York: G.D. Baldwin, 1844. 574 p. KyLo; MiD; NcD; RWe; VtU. 44-2605

The Gipsie's festival, or come to the old oak tree. Philadelphia: Lee and Walker, 1844. 3 p. PHrD 44-2606

Girard, A. Essay on natural philosophy and astronomy. Mobile: Printed by Dade and Thompson, 1844. 19 p. DLC; MH. 44-2607

Girard almanac for 1845. By Joseph Foulke. Philadelphia, Pennsylvania: Thomas L. Bonsal [1844] MWA. 44-2608

Girard College, Philadelphia. Extraordinary magnetic observations. Philadelphia, 1844. MWiW. 44-2609

Giraud, Jacob Post, 1811-1870. The birds of Long Island. New York: Wiley and Putnam, 1844. DLC; ICJ; KU; MdBP; PPL. 44-2610

Girault, Arsene Napoleon. Colloquial and grammatical exercises. Philadelphia: Perkins and Purves, 1844. MH. 44-2611

Girault, Arsene Napoleon. French guide; or, an introduction to the study of the French language. By A.N. Girault.... Sixth edition. Philadelphia: Perkins and Purves, 1844. 324 p. CtY; MH; ScU. 44-2612

The girl's token. Philadelphia [1844] MBAt. 44-2613

Glaubenslehre und kirchen zucht ordnung der evan gelishen gemeinschaft... New Berlin, Pennsylvania: J. Reiszner, 1844. 146 p. PPEschw; PReaAT. 44-2614

Gleig, Goerge Robert. The history of the Bible. New York: Harper and brothers, 1844. 2 v. FDef; MeAu; MLanc; NcU; OCo. 44-2615

Glenn, James. The real nature of the electric fluid; explained and illustrated by numerous facts, and a cause assigned for the polarity of the magnet. A new edition improved. To which is annexed a theory of the tides and currents of the ocean....New York: [1844?] CtY; IU: NNC. 44-2616

Glennie, Alexander. Sermons preached on plantations to congregations of negroes. By the Rev. Alexander Glennie, pastor of All Saints Parish, Waccamaw, South Carolina. Charleston: A.E. Miller, 1844. 161 p. DLC; ICN; NjN; OClWHi; WHi. 44-2617

Glorious triumph of the truth, in the trial and conviction of the Pope and the Puseyites, etc. New York: 1844. 43 p. DLC; IES; MBAt. 44-2618

Glover, E.B. An explanation of the prayers and ceremonies of the Holy sacrifice of the Mass. Derby: Richardson and son, 1844. [6]-131 p. MnSS. 44-2619

Glynn, William C. Bayeaux quick step, composed and arranged for the pianoforte. Boston: Keith, 1844. 2 p. MB. 44-2620

Glynn, William C. Manual of arms No. 1. Arranged for the pianoforte. Boston: Prentiss, 1844. 3 p. MB. 44-2621

Gnadenhuetten Monument Society. True history of the massacre of 96 Christian Indians at Guadenhuetten, Ohio; March 8, 1782. New Philadelphia [O] printed at the Lutheran Standard office, 1844. 11 p. 11 p. DLC; OHi; PHi; PPRF. 44-2622

Goadby, John. The pre-eminent importance of the study of the Scriptures. A discourse delivered before the Education Society of the Saratoga Baptist Association, at the fortieth annual session, held at Ballston Spa, June 26th, 1844. ....Schenectady: printed at the Reflector office, [1844] IEG; MiD-B; N; NHC-S; RPB. 44-2623

Goddard, Kingston. A sermon delivered in Emmanuel Church, Brooklyn, Long Island, on resigning the charge of said parish, Sunday, May 27, 1844. New York: Gray, 1844. 16 p. NBLIHi; NCH. 44-2624

Goddard, Paul Beck, 1811-1866. The anatomy, physiology and pathology of the human teeth; with the most improved methods of treatment; including operations, and the method of making and setting artificial teeth.... by Paul B. Goddard.... aided in the practical part by Joseph E. Parker.... Philadelphia: Carey and Hart, 1844. 227 p. CU-M; IaU; LNOP; NBMS; PP. 44-2625

Goddell, William, 1792-1878. Letter from the missionaries of Constantinople in reply to charges by Rev. Haratio Southgate. Boston: Crocker and

Brewster, 1844. 51 p. CtHT; MB; MeBat; OMC; PHi. 44-2626

Godolphin, Gregory. The unique, a book of its own kind: containing a variety of hints, thrown out in a variety of ways, for evangelical ministers, churches, and Christians, by Gregory Godolphin. Boston: John Putnam, 1844. 234 p. KyLoS; MB; MH-AH; NjMD; PU; RLa. 44-2627

Godwin, Parke, 1816-1904. Democracy, constructive and pacific... New York: J. Winchester, 1844. 55 p. DLC; MiU-C; NjP; NN; WHi. 44-2628

Godwin, Parke, 1816-1904. The popular view of the doctrines of Charles Fourier. ....New York: J. S. Redfield, 1844. 120 p. CtY; ICN; MMeT-Hi; OMC; RPB. 44-2629

Godwin, Parke, 1816-1904. Popular view of the doctrines of C. Fourier. Second edition. New York: J.S. Redfield, 1844. 120 p. DLC; ICJ; MHi; NcD; PU. 44-2630

Goff, William. Julia Glenroy. A narrative of crime. Newport: 1844. 34 p. RPB. 44-2631

The golden rule. Albany: Troy and Lansingburgh, 1844-1846. 3 v. in 1. NN. 44-2632

Goldsbury, John. The American common school reader and speaker: being a selection of pieces in prose and verse, with rules for reading and speaking... Boston: Charles Tappan, 1844. MNowd-Hi. 44-2633

Goldsbury, John. The American common school reader and speaker; being a selection of pieces in prose and verse, with rules for reading and speaking. Boston: James Munroe [1844] 13-428 p. RPB. 44-2634

Goldsbury, John. The American common school reader and speaker; being a selection of pieces in prose and verse, with rules for reading and speaking. Boston: Whittemore, Niles and Hall, 1844. 338 p. MFai; MH; MNS. 44-2635

Goldsbury, John. The American common school reader and speaker; being a selection of pieces in prose and verse, with rules for reading and speaking. Improved edition. Boston: Tappan and Whittemore [1844] 432 p. CtNwchA. 44-2636

Goldsmith, Oliver, 1728-1774. Goldsmith's Roman history, for the use of schools. Revised and corrected, and a vocabulary of proper names appended. Improved edition. Philadelphia: Grigg and Elliot, 1844. 235 p. GAU; IGK; MH; OClWHi. 44-2637

Goldsmith, Oliver, 1728-1774. The miscellaneous works of Oliver Goldsmith, with an account of his life and writings. Stereotyped from the Paris edition. Edited by Washington Irving. Philadelphia: J. Crissy, and Thomas, Cowperthwait and company, 1844. 527 p. AMob; MLow; MPax; ODaU. 44-2638

Goldsmith, Oliver, 1728-1774. Natural history. Philadelphia: Thomas, Cowperthwait and company, 1844. 427 p. RLa. 44-2639

Goldsmith, Oliver, 1728-1774. Pinnock's improved edition of Dr. Goldsmith's abridgement of the history of Rome. Illustrated. First American from the twelfth English edition. Philadelphia: Thomas, Cowperthwait and company, 1844. 384 p. KyU. 44-2640

Goldsmith, Oliver, 1728-1774. Pinnock's improved edition of Dr. Goldsmith's history of England from the invasion of Julius Caesar to the death of George II with a continuation to the year 1832. Philadelphia: Thomas, Cowperthwait, 1844. 468 p. PPCC; TSewU. 44-2641

Goldsmith, Oliver, 1728-1774. Poems, plays, and essays, with an account of his life and writings; to which is added a critical dissertation on his poetry. By J. Aiken, M.D. New York: Turner and Hayden, 1844. 384 p. CtHWatk; MiD-U; NIC; OCX; PBm. 44-2642

Goldsmith, Oliver, 1728-1774. Poetical works, prefaced by a brief memoir of the author. Concord, New Hampshire: J.F. Brown, 1844. 88 p. MH. 44-2643

Goldsmith, Oliver, 1728-1774. The vicar of Wakefield. A tale. New York: Harper and brothers, 1844. 190 p. RPE. 44-2644

Goldsmith, Oliver, 1728-1774. The vicar of Wakefield. A tale. New York: Piercy and Reed, 1844. 143 p. CtHWatk; CtY; MnU; PWbo. 44-2645

The good boy. Greenfield [Massachusetts] A. Phelps, 1844. 18 p. CtY; MNF. 44-2646

Good, John Mason. The book of nature. From the last London edition... Hartford: Belknap and Hamersley, 1844.

467 p. KyLoP; LNT; MeBat; PCA; TxU. 44-2647

Goodell, William, 1792-1867. Mr. Southgate and the missionaries at Constantinople. A letter from the missionaries [W. Goodell, H.G.C. Dwight, W.G. Schauffler, Henry A. Homes, C. Hamlin, G.W. Wood, H.J. Van Lennep] at Constantinpole, in reply to charges by Rev. Horatio Southgate. Boston: Crocker and Brewster, 1844. 44 p. CBB; ICT; MB; MiD-B; MWA. 44-2648

Goodell, William, 1792-1878. Views of American constitutional law in its bearing upon American slavery. Utica, New York: Jackson and Chaplin, 1844. 160 p. DLC; MoS; NcU; OO; PU-L. 44-2649

Goodrich, Charles Augustus, 1790-1862. The child's history of the United States, Designed as a first book of history... Philadelphia: Thomas, Cowperthwait and company, 1844. 150 p. MFiHi; MPri. 44-2650

Goodrich, Charles Augustus, 1790-1862. The history of the United States of America from the discovery of the continent to the present time. Hartford: J. Seymour, Brown, 1844. 654 p. OUr; WaWW. 44-2651

Goodrich, Charles Augustus, 1790-1862. History of the United States of America on a plan enlarged from the 100th edition. Boston: Jenks and Palmer, 1844. 384 p. CtHWatk; MH; MPeaHi; NNC. 44-2652

Goodrich, Charles Augustus, 1790-1862. The pictorial and descriptive view of all religions. Embracing the forms of worship practiced by the several nations of the known world, from the earliest records to the present time.... By Rev. Charles A. Goodrich, A.M. Hartford: Sumner and Goodman, 1844. 576 p. IaHoL; LNX. 44-2653

Goodrich, Charles Augustus, 1790-1862. The universal traveller; designed to introduce readers at home to an acquaintance with the arts, customs, and manners, of the principal modern nations on the globe. Hartford: Robins and Smith, 1844. 504 p. IaHA; OCASH; OClWHi. 44-2654

Goodrich, Chauncey Allen, 1790-1860. Can I conscientiously vote for Henry Clay? New Haven: 1844. 4 p. CtY. 44-2655

Goodrich, Chauncey Allen, 1790-1860. Lessons in Greek parsing; or, outlines of the Greek grammar, divided into short portions and illustrated by appropriate exercises in parsing. Nineteenth edition. New Haven: Durrie and Peck, 1844. 142 p. IaHi; MNS; VtU. 44-2656

Goodrich, Chauncey Allen, 1790-1860. Lessons in Latin parsing; containing the outlines of the Latin grammar, divided into short portions. Twentieth edition. New Haven: Durrie and Peck, 1844. 214 p. DLC; IU; MNBedf. 44-2657

Goodrich, Samuel Griswold, 1793-1860. Asia. Lights and shadows of Asiatic history. Boston: Thompson, Brown and company, 1844. 320 p. Mi. 44-2658

Goodrich, Samuel Griswold, 1793-1860. Book of quadruped for youth. Illustrated by 200 engravings. Brattleboro, Vermont: George H. Salisbury, 1844. 324p. MNF; MoKU. 44-2659

Goodrich, Samuel Griswold, 1793-1860. Celebrated American Indians. Indians of North American biography. Indians of South America. Indians of Mexico biography. Boston: Thompson, 1844. 315 p. CoD; MdBE; Mi; MiCal; ODaMSJ. 44-2660

Goodrich, Samuel Griswold, 1793-1860. Common school history,... Stereotype edition. Philadelphia: Butler and Williams, 1844. 309 p. OTifH. 44-2661

Goodrich, Samuel Griswold, 1793-1860. Curiosities of human nature; by the author of Peter Parley's tales. Boston: Bradbury, Soden and company, 1844. 320 p. DLC; NNC. 44-2662

Goodrich, Samuel Griswold, 1793-1860. The every day book for youth. Philadelphia: James M. Campbell, 1844. 359 p. PMA. 44-2663

Goodrich, Samuel Griswold, 1793-1860. Fairy land, and other sketches for youth. Boston: J. Munroe and company, 1844. 167 p. RPB. 44-2664

Goodrich, Samuel Griswold, 1793-1860. Famous men of ancient times: by the author of Peter Parley's tales. Boston: Bradbury, Soden and company, 1844. [7]-310 p. CtY; MBL; MdBE; Mi; VtBrt. 44-2665

Goodrich, Samuel Griswold, 1793-1860. Famous men of modern times. Boston: Bradbury, Soden and company, 1844. [3]-315 p. MBevHi; MBU-A; MiD-B; MH; MSha. 44-2666

Goodrich, Samuel Griswold, 1793-1860. Famous men of modern times.

Boston: Thompson, Brown and company, 1844. 2 v. MBevHi; MBL; MiCal. 44-2667

Goodrich, Samuel Griswold, 1793-1860. First book of history: for children and youth. Cincinnati: 1844. OCHi. 44-2668

Goodrich, Samuel Griswold, 1793-1860. First book of history, for children and youth, by the author of Peter Parley's tales with sixty engravings and sixteen maps. Revised edition. Boston: Charles J. Hendee and Jenks and Palmer, 1844. 179, [180]-181, 182-183 p. MAshl; MH; NBuG; PPeSchw; WPta. 44-2669

Goodrich, Samuel Griswold, 1793-1860. The fourth reader for the use of schools. Boston: Otis, Broaders and company, 1844. NoLoc. 44-2670

Goodrich, Samuel Griswold, 1793-1860. A glance at the physical sciences; or the wonders of nature...Boston: Bradbury, Soden and company, 1844. 352 p. CtY; DLC; NBuCC; OClW; ViR. 44-2671

Goodrich, Samuel Griswold, 1793-1860. A glance at the physical sciences...By the author of Peter Parley's tales. Boston: J.E. Hickman [1844] 352 p. LNT. 44-2672

Goodrich, Samuel Griswold, 1793-1860. A glance at the physical sciences; of the wonders of nature in earth, air and sky. Boston: W.A. Hall and company, printers, 1844. 291 p. REd. 44-2673

Goodrich, Samuel Griswold, 1793-1860. A glance at the physical sciences; or, the wonders of nature, in earth, air, and sky: by the author of Peter Parley's tales. New York: J. Allen, 1844. 352 p. NbU; NcU; ViU. 44-2674

Goodrich, Samuel Griswold, 1793-1860. History of the Indians of North and South America. Boston: Bradbury, Soden and company, 1844. [5]-320 p. AB; CoD; MiD-B; MPiB; TMeC. 44-2675

Goodrich, Samuel Griswold, 1793-1860. History of the Indians of North and South America. Boston: Hickman, 1844. [5]-320 p. LN; NjN. 44-2676

Goodrich, Samuel Griswold, 1793-1860. History of the Indians, of North and South America. New York: J. Allen, 1844. 320 p. CtSoP; DLC; NcU; PPFr. 44-2677

Goodrich, Samuel Griswold, 1793-1860. History of the Indians of North and South America. By the author of Peter Parley's tales. Philadelphia: Thomas, Cowperthwait and company, 1844. 5-320 p. MnHi; PHi; RJa. 44-2678

Goodrich, Samuel Griswold, 1793-1860. Lights and shadows of African history: by the author of Peter Parley's tales. Boston: Bradbury, Soden and company, 1844. [5]-336 p. IaDmD; MeBa; MH; OCl; ViU. 44-2679

Goodrich, Samuel Griswold, 1793-1860. Lights and shadows of African history: by the author of Peter Parley's tales. Boston: J.E. Hickman [1844] 336 p. LNT. 44-2680

Goodrich, Samuel Griswold, 1793-1860. Lights and shadows of African history: by the author of Peter Parley's tales.

Boston: Thompson, Biglow and Brown, 1844. 336 p. InElk. 44-2681

Goodrich, Samuel Griswold, 1793-1860. Lights and shadows of American history: by the author of Peter Parley's tales. Boston: Bradbury, Soden and company, 1844. 320 p. CtY; IU; KWiU; MBBC; NHem. 44-2682

Goodrich, Samuel Griswold, 1793-1860. Lights and shadows of American history: by the author of Peter Parley's tales. Boston: J.E. Hickman [1844] 320 p. DLC; LNT; MiD; NjR; ViU. 44-2683

Goodrich, Samuel Griswold, 1793-1860. Lights and shadows of American history: by the author of Peter Parley's tales. Boston: Thompson, Brown and company, 1844. 320 p. MB-HP; MoSAV; WM. 44-2684

Goodrich, Samuel Griswold, 1793-1860. Lights and shadows of American history: by the author of Peter Parley's tales. Boston: Wlliam A. Hall and company, 1844. 320 p. MTai; REd; RLal RPaw, 44-2685

Goodrich, Samuel Griswold, 1793-1860. Lights and shadows of American history: by the author of Peter Parley's tales. New York: J. Allen, 1844. 320 p. Ct; MBevHi; MFai; NcU; ViU. 44-2686

Goodrich, Samuel Griswold, 1793-1860. Lights and shadows of Asiatic history: by the author of Peter Parley's tales. Boston: Bradbury, Soden and company, 1844. 320 p. CtY; MiU; MOx; NhM; ViU. 44-2687

Goodrich, Samuel Griswold, 1793-1860. Lights and shadows of European history: by the author of Peter Parley's tales. Boston: Bradbury, Soden and company, 1844. 320 p. CtY; Cu; GMar; MLanC; MWA. 44-2688

Goodrich, Samuel Griswold, 1793-1860. Lights and shadows of European history: by the author of Peter Parley's tales. Boston: J.E. Hickman, 1844. 320 p. LNT; NjR; RSaw. 44-2689

Goodrich, Samuel Griswold, 1793-1860. Lights and shadows of European history: by the author of Peter Parley's tales. Boston: Thomas Bigelow and Brown, 1844? 320 p. IaFayU; MiGr; MoSAV; WHi. 44-2690

Goodrich, Samuel Griswold, 1793-1860. Lights and shadows of European history: by the author of Peter Parley's tales. New York: J. Allen, 1844. 320 p. MBelc; ViU. 44-2691

Goodrich, Samuel Griswold, 1793-1860. Lives of benefactors: by the author of Peter Parley's tales. Boston: Bradbury, Soden and company, 1844. CtY; KWiU; MB; OCl; ViU. 44-2692

Goodrich, Samuel Griswold, 1793-1860. Lives of benefactors; by the author of Peter Parley's tales. Boston: J.E. Hickman, 1844. 320 p. ViU. 44-2693

Goodrich, Samuel Griswold, 1793-1860. Lives of benefactors 1844. Boston: Thompson, Brown and company, 1844. 320 p. CSmH; DLC; MB; OU; ViU. 44-2694

Goodrich, Samuel Griswold, 1793-1860. Lives of benefactors; by the author of Peter Parley's tales. New York: J.M.

Allen, 1844. 320 p. CtY; MH; ViU. 44-2695

Goodrich, Samuel Griswold, 1793-1860. Lives of celebrated American Indians: by the author of Peter Parley's tales. New York: J.M. Allen, 1844. 315 p. MH; MiD-B; MiU; MBarn; WBeloC. 44-2696

Goodrich, Samuel Griswold, 1793-1860. Lives of celebrated women: by the author of Peter Parley's tales. Boston: Bradbury, Soden and company, 1844. 352 p. LN; MeBa; MH; PPi; OClWHi. 44-2697

Goodrich, Samuel Griswold, 1793-1860. Lives of celebrated women: by the author of Peter Parley's tales. Boston: J.E. Hickman [1844] 352 p. MWA; NjR; ViU. 44-2698

Goodrich, Samuel Griswold, 1793-1860. Lives of celebrated women: by the author of Peter Parley's tales. New York: J. Allen, 1844. 352 p. In; InPen; MiU; NcU; OO. 44-2699

Goodrich, Samuel Griswold, 1793-1860. Lives of celebrated women: by the author of Peter Parley's tales. Philadelphia: Thomas, Cowperthwait and company, 1844. 352 p. CtY; DLC; IG; PKit; PRea. 44-2700

Goodrich, Samuel Griswold, 1793-1860. Manners and customs of the principal nations of the globe. Boston: Thompson, Bigelow and Brown, 1844. 352 p. IaFayU; LNT; MeAug; NjR. 44-2701

Goodrich, Samuel Griswold, 1793-1860. Manners, customs, and antiquities of the Indians of North and South America; by the author of Peter Parley's tales. Boston: J.C. Hickman, 1844. 336 p. GColu; LNX; OkU; RShaw. 44-2702

Goodrich, Samuel Griswold, 1793-1860. Manners, customs, and antiquities of the Indians of North and South America; by the author of Peter Parley's tales. Boston: Soden and company, 1844. 336 p. DLC; LNH; MNBedf; OC; WaS. 44-2703

Goodrich, Samuel Griswold, 1793-1860. Manners, customs, and antiquities of the Indians of North and South America; by the author of Peter Parley's tales. New York: J. Allen, 1844. 336 p. GMar; MBev; NcU; PU; ViU. 44-2704

Goodrich, Samuel Griswold, 1793-1860. Peter Parley's Bible gazetteer; containing illustrations of Bible geography. New York, 1844. 208 p. IU. 44-2705

Goodrich, Samuel Griswold, 1793-1860. Peter Parley's book of Bible stories for children and youth. Boston: Munroe and Francis, 1844. 256 p. KWiU; NP. 44-2706

Goodrich, Samuel Griswold, 1793-1860. Peter Parley's common school history. Illustrated by engravings. A new edition, revised and brought down to the present time. Philadelphia: E.H. Butler and company, 1844. 309 p. CtY; MoWgT; OHi. 44-2707

Goodrich, Samuel Griswold, 1793-1860. Peter Parley's farewell. Philadelphia: R.S.H. George, 1844. 324 p. MoSU; NUt. 44-2708

Goodrich, Samuel Griswold, 1793-

1860. Peter Parley's illustrations of astronomy. New York: 1844. 160 p. CtSoP. 44-2709

Goodrich, Samuel Griswold, 1793-1860. Peter Parley's illustrations of the animal kingdom; beasts, birds, fishes, reptiles and insects. New York: 1844. 199 p. CtSoP. 44-2710

Goodrich, Samuel Griswold, 1793-1860. Peter Parley's illustrations of the vegetable kingdom: trees, plants and shrubs. New York: W. Robinson, 1844. 330 p. FDeS. 44-2711

Goodrich, Samuel Griswold, 1793-1860. Peter Parley's method of telling about geography to children... Principally for the use of schools. New York: Huntington and Savage, 1844. CtY; MFiT; MNowdHi; OClWHi. 44-2712

Goodrich, Samuel Griswold, 1793-1860. Peter Parley's second book of history. New York: 1844. CtHWatk. 44-2713

Goodrich, Samuel Griswold, 1793-1860. Peter Parley's short stories for long nights. Boston: William D. Ticknor and company, 1844. 140 p. MHi. 44-2714

Goodrich, Samuel Griswold, 1793-1860. Pictorial history of America; embracing both the northern portions of the new world. Hartford: E. Strong, 1844. CtHT-W; DLC; MFalm; MB; MWA. 44-2715

Goodrich, Samuel Griswold, 1793-1860. Pictorial history of the United States, with notices of other portions of America. Philadelphia: Sorin and Ball, etc., 1844. CSt; MH; NSmb. 44-2716

Goodrich, Samuel Griswold, 1793-1860. Present from Peter Parley to all his little friends. Cooperstown: H. and E. Phinney, 1844. 168 p. PMA. 44-2717

Goodrich, Samuel Griswold, 1793-1860. Second book of history. Thirty-fifth edition. Boston: Jenks and Palmer, etc., etc., 1844. CtY; MH; ViU. 44-2718

Goodrich, Samuel Griswold, 1793-1860. Second book of history including the modern history of Europe, Africa, and Asia. Illustrated by engravings and sixteen maps, and designed as a sequel to the "First book of history, by the author of Peter Parley's tales." Fifty-fifth edition. Boston: C.J. Hendee, and Jenks and Palmer, 1844. 180 p. CtHC; CtY; MH; MPiB. 44-2719

Goodrich, Samuel Griswold, 1793-1860. Second reader for schools. Boston: Otis, Broaders and company, 1844. 144 p. Ct. 44-2720

Goodrich, Samuel Griswold, 1793-1860. Tale of adventure, or the Siberian Sable hunter. New York: Wiley and Putnam, 1844. CtHWatk; ViU. 44-2721

Goodrich, Samuel Griswold, 1793-1860. What to do, and how to do it; or morals and manners. New York: Wiley, 1844. 172 p. CtY; LU; NRU; TNP; TxU. 44-2722

Goodrich, Samuel Griswold, 1793-1860. Wit bought; or the life and adventures of Robert Merry, by Peter Parley [pseud.] New edition. New York: Lamport, 1844. OCl. 44-2723

Goodrich, Samuel Griswold, 1793-1860. Wit bought; or the life and adventures of Robert Merry, by Peter Parley [pseud.] New York: Wiley and Putnam, 1844. 171 p. DLC; OCl; PU; WHi. 44-2724

Goodrich, Samuel Griswold, 1793-1860. Wonders of geology. By the author Peter Parley's tales. Boston: J.E. Hickman [1844] 291 p. CU-I; DI-GS; NcU; NjR. 44-2725

Goodrich, Samuel Griswold, 1793-1860. Young American: or, book of government and law; showing their history, nature and necessity. For the use of schools. Fourth edition. ....Baltimore: Parsons and Preston, 1844. 282 p. MdHi; MiU; NT; OSW; ScNC. 44-2726

Goodwin, Frederic Jordan, 1812-1872. Parting counsels: a farewell sermon, on resignation the parochial charge of St. George's Church, Flushing, Long Island; delivered on the second Sunday after the Epiphany, January 14, 1844. Flushing, Long Island: 1844. 14 p. CtMW; CtY; IEG; NNG; NNQ. 44-2727

Goody Two Shoes. The history of Goody Two Shoes. New York: E. Dunigan [1844?] 15 p. DLC; InGoP. 44-2728

Gorden, Thomas F. A collection of the laws of the United States relating to revenue, navigation and commerce and light houses, etc., up to March 4, 1843, including the treatise with foreign powers. Philadelphia: Isaac Ashmead and company, 1844. 1292 p. LNT-L; PU-L. 44-2729

Gordon, Alexander, 1692-1754. The lives of Pope Alexander VI and his son Caesar Borgia. Philadelphia: James M.

Campbell and company; New York: Saxton and Miles, 1844. 232 p. CSansS; ICP; LNH; NGH; PU. 44-2730

Gordon, John. A full report of the trial of John Gordon and William Gordon, charged with the murder of Amasa Sprague; before the supreme court of Rhode Island, March term, 1844. Reported by E. C. Larend and William Knowles. Providence: printed at the office of the Daily Transcript, 1844. 38 p. MBAt; MdBB; MH-L; RPL. 44-2731

Gordon, John. A full report of the trial of John Gordon and William Gordon, charged with the murder of Amasa Sprague. Second edition. Providence: 1844. 45 p. MHi. 44-2732

Gordon, John. The trial of John Gordon and William Gordon. Charged with the murder of Amara Sprague. Reported by E. C. Larned and W. Knowles. Providence: Daily Transcript, 1844. 153 p. NIC. 44-2733

Gordon, William Robert, b. 1811. A rebuke to high churchism as exhibited in Dr. Carmichael's book on the Christian fathers. Flushing: Flushing Journal, printer, 1844. 32 p. NCH; NjPT; NjR; NNUT; PPPrHi. 44-2734

Goshen, Wilmington and Columbus Turnpike Company. Report. Wilmington: 1844. OClWHi. 44-2735

Gospel missionary. Marietta, Pennsylvania: 1844-. v. 1-. PCA. 44-2736

Goudy's Illinois farmer's almanac for 1845. Springfield, Illinois: Robert Goudy, [1844] IHI; MWA. 44-2737

Gould, Adeline Eunice Abbot. The two half dollars and other tales; a gift for children. Boston: Charles Tappan, 1844. MH. 44-2738

Gould, Hannah Flagg. The golden vase; a gift for the young. Second edition. Boston: Benjamin B. Mussey, 1844. [9]-224 p. ICU; MB; NcWsS. 44-2739

Gould, Marcus Tullius Cicero, 1793-1860. The art of short-hand writing.... Compiled from the latest European publication with sundry improvements, adapted to the present state of literature in the United States.... Revised stereotyped edition, with new engravings. Philadelphia: U. Hunt and son, 1844. 60 p. CU; LNH; NIC; NjR; PP. 44-2740

Gould, Nathaniel Duren, 1781-1864. Companion for the psalmist; original music arranged for hymns. Boston: Gould, Kendall and Lincoln, 1844. 32 p. KyLoS. 44-2741

Gould, Nathaniel Duren, 1781-1864. The Sabbath school harmony.... hymns and music, for Sabbath schools, juvenile singing schools, and family devotion, by N. D. Gould.... Boston: Gould, Kendall and Lincoln, 1844. 48 p. CtHWatk; ViRU. 44-2742

Gourlay, Robert Fleming, 1778-1863. Plans for beautifying New York, and for enlarging and improving the city of Boston. Boston: Crocker and Brewster, printers, 1844. 384 p. CtY; MHi; MWA; NBuG; OCHP. 44-2743

Government of the thoughts for young men. Boston: Sunday School Society, 1844. 168 p. OO. 44-2744

Govett, R. Not water baptism, but the gifts of the Holy Spirit; the baptism of Christ. By R. Govett, junior. Norwich: [n.p.] 1844. 58 p. NjPT. 44-2745

Graeter, Francis. Hydriatics; or manual of the water cure, especially as practiced by Vincent Priessnitz in Graefenberg... Fourth edition. New York: W. Radde, 1844. CU-M; ICJ; MoKJM; NNN; OCl. 44-2746

Graham, A.E. Looking glass for the benefit of families, and churches of all denominations, executed upon the old plan. Columbus: 1844. ViU. 44-2747

Graham, John, 1776-1844. A history of the siege of Londonderry, and defence of Enniskellen, in 1688 and 1689.... Philadelphia: J. M. Campbell; New York: Saxton and Miles, 1844. 247 p. GEU; MiD; OO; RPAt; WHi. 44-2748

Graham, Sylvester, 1794-1851. A lecture to young men, on chasity interested also for the serious consideration of parents and guardians. Eighth stereotype edition. Boston: Waitt, Pierce and company, 1844. Nc. 44-2749

Graham, William, 1798-1854. The contrast; or the Bible and abolitionism: an exegetical argument, by Rev. William Graham... Cincinnati: printed at the Daily Cincinnati Atlas office, 1844. 48 p. KyLxT; NcD; OCHP; TxU; WHi. 44-2750

Grandma's book of rhymes for the nursery. Boston: Gould, Kendall and Lincoln, 1844. 56 p. RPB. 44-2751

Grandma's book of rhymes for the nursery. Boston: T.H. Carter and company, 1844. 56 p. MiD-B. 44-2752

Grandy, Moses, b. 1786?. Narrative of the life of Moses Grandy; late a slave in the United States of America....First American from the last London edition. ....Boston: O. Johnson, 1844. 45 p. MBNEH; MdHi; OO; PHi; TNF. 44-2753

Grandy, Moses, b. 1786?. Narrative of the life of Moses Grandy; formerly a slave in the United States of America....Second American from the last London edition. ....Boston: O. Johnson, 1844. 45 p. CtY; MdBJ; MiD-B; MWA; RPB. 44-2754

Grant, Anne MacVicar, 1755-1838. Memoirs of an American lady with sketches of manners and scenery in America, as they existed previous to the Revolution. New York: D. Appleton and company, 1844. 295 p. MiKL; NhM. 44-2755

Grant, Horace. Drawing for young children, containing 150 drawing copies. New York: Joseph H. Francis, 1844. RPB. 44-2756

Grant, Jedediah M. A collection of facts, relative to the course taken by Elder Sidney Rigdon, in the states of Ohio, Missouri, Illinois, and Pennsylvania.... Philadelphia: Brown, Bicking and Guilbert, printers, 1844. 46 p. USlC. 44-2757

A graphic account of the alarming riots at St. Mary's Church, in April of 1822, together with the most important extracts from the decisions of chief justices Tilghman, Duncan and Gibson, relative to the charter of said church, including letters from J.R. Ingersol and Thos. Kittera. Compiled by a reporter, June, 1844 [New York: 1844] 16 p. MH. 44-2758

Grattan, Thomas Colley. Case of T.C. Grattan, administrator of the estate of the late Sir John Caldwell, vs. Wm. Appleton etal. Boston: 1844. 13 p. MBAt; MH-L. 44-2759

Graves, A.J. Girlhood and womanhood: or sketches of my schoolmates. Boston: T.H. Carter and company and Benjamin B. Mussey, 1844. 216 p. CSfA; CtY; LNT; OClWHi; PPA. 44-2760

Graves, A.J. Girlhood and womanhood. Second edition. Boston: 1844. MB. 44-2761

Graves, J. Truth against error; a defence of slavery; being a review of a letter written by the Rev. Charles T. Torrey, now confined in the Baltimore jail, upon the charges of abducting slaves from their masters, in Maryland and Virginia. Baltimore: Woods and Crane, printers, 1844. 32 p. MB; MdHi; WHi. 44-2762

Gray, James. A dissertation on the coincidence between the priesthoods of Jesus Christ and Melchisedec.... Hagerstown, Maryland: W. Stewart; Baltimore: Cushing and brothers, 1844. 158 p. ICP; MiU; NNUT; ScDuE; TNT. 44-2763

Gray, John Henry. An address delivered on the ... 27th December, 1843-before the Vicksburg Lodge, No. 26, of Free and accepted Masons. Vicksburg: Published by order of the Lodge, 1844. 14 p. NNFM. 44-2764

Gray, John Henry. Information upon

the theory and practice of the celebrated cold water cure of Germany. Boston: 1844. 15 p. MB; MBM. 44-2765

Great Barrington, Massachusetts. First Congregational Church. Manual. Barrington: 1844. 16 p. MBC. 44-2766

Great Britain. Reports of cases argued and determined in the high court of chancery, during the time of Lord Chancellor Thurlow, and of the several Lords commissioners of the great seal, and Lord Chancellor Loughborough, from 1778 to 1794 by William Brown, Esq. First American from the fifth London edition. Boston: Charles C. Little and James Brown, 1844. 4 v. KyLoU-L; MiDu-L; MWiW; Nj; PP. 44-2767

Great Britain. Reports of cases argued and determined in the High Court of Chancery... By Francis Vesey. From the last London edition. With the notes of Francis Vesey. Boston: Charles C. Little and James Brown, 1844. 20 v. Co-SC; MH-L; NTSC; NjR; PU-L; ViU. 44-2768

Great Britain. Reports of cases in chancery, argued and determined in the Rolls court during the time of Lord Langdale, master of the rolls. By Benjamin Keen, with notes and references, to both English and American decisions. By John A. Dunlap. New York: Gould, Banks, and company, 1844. 4 v. Ia; NNLI; MoKB; PP. 44-2769

Great Polk meeting of Rockingham!!! At Exeter, New Hampshire, October 15, 1844. 20,000 freemen in the field! - The democracy of New Hampshire invincible!! - The granite state safe!!! Broadside. MH. 44-2770

The great western almanac for 1844. Philadelphia: Jos. McDowell, 1844. NCH. 44-2771

Greek ecclesiastical historians of the first six centuries of the Christian era. Boston: 1844-1847. 6 v. NBLiHi. 44-2772

Greeley, Horace, 1811-1872. An address before the literary societies of Hamilton College, July 23, 1844. ....New York: William...., 1844. 40 p. CtY; MB; MMet-Hi; NUt; OO. 44-2773

Greeley, Horace, 1811-1872. Protection and free trade. The question stated and considered. [New York: Greeley and McElrath, 1844?] CtY; NCH; NIC; OO. 44-2774

Greeley, Horace, 1811-1872. The tariff as it is, compared with the substitute proposed by its adversaries in the bill reported to the United States House of Representatives by General McKay of North Carolina, from the Committee of Ways and Means [New York: Greeley and McElrath, 1844?] CtY; In; NCH; OO; PPL. 44-2775

Greeley, Horace, 1811-1872. The tariff question: protection and free trade considered.... [New York: Tribune office, 1844?] 24 p. CU; WHi. 44-2776

Green, Beriah, 1795-1874. Belief without confession. A sermon preached at Whitesboro, New York. "I am opposed to slavery; but am not an abolitionist." Published by request. Utica: printed by R.W. Roberts, 1844. 15 p. A-Ar; NCH; NUtHi. OCHP; PHi. 44-2777

Green, Beriah, 1795-1874. Memorial of Ann Parker Green Hough. Utica: R.W.

Roberts, 1844. 40 p. Ct; CtHC; DLC; N. 44-2778

Green, Beriah, 1805-1874. A sermon, preached at Whitesboro, New York. By Beriah Green.... Utica: J.C. Jackson, 1844. 15 p. Ct; MBC; MeBat; NCanHi; NUt. 44-2779

Green, Beriah, 1805-1874. Sketches of the life and writings of James Gillespie Birney. By Beriah Green. Utica, New York: Jackson and Chaplin, 1844. 119 p. KHi; MWA; NCaS; RPB; WHi. 44-2780

Green, J. W. Satan conquered; or, the son of God victorious. A poem; in five books. Albany: C. Van Benthuysen and company, 1844. 166 p. MB; NjP; NNC; NNUT; RPB. 44-2781

Green, James. Catalogue of mathematical and optical instruments, philosophical and chemical apparatus, constructed and sold by James Green. Baltimore: Printed by John D. Toy, 1844. 12 p. DLC; LLNT; MdHi. 44-2782

Green, Jonathan H. Gambling unmasked! or, the personal experience of the reformed gambler, J.H. Green; designed as a warning to the young men of this country; written by himself. New York: Burgess, Stringer and company, 1844. 193 p. MBAt; MH; Nh-Hi; NjR; TJoT. 44-2783

Green, Lewis Warner, 1806-1863. Popery and puseyism; being two discourses prepared agreeable to a resolution of the synod of Pittsburgh of 1843 and preached at Pittsburgh. September, 1844. Pittsburgh: Lormes, 1844. CSansS; KyLoP; MoMM; NjPT; PPi. 44-2784

Green, Lewis Warner, 1806-1863. The right of judgement; or freedom of individual opinion and belief, a sermon. [Pittsburg: Published by order of the synod, 1844] 103 p. CSansS; InUpT; PPL. 44-2785

Green, Willis. Address before the Alexandria [D.C.] Clay Club, July 19, 1844. n.p. [1844] MBAt; NIC. 44-2786

Green, Willis. The sub-treasury: a tract for the times: prepared by order of Willis Green, chairman of the executive committee of the Whig members of Congress. Washington: John T. Towers, printer, 1844. 14 p. GEU; MoS; NN; NIC; TxDaM. 44-2787

Greenfield, William, 1799-1831. Polymicrian Greek lexicon to the New Testament, etc. Philadelphia: Perkins, 1844. 281 p. CSt; OO; PPPrHi; PU. 44-2788

Greenhow, Robert, 1800-1854. The history of Oregon and California and the other territories on the northwest coast of North America; accompanied by a geographical view and map of those countries and a number of documents. Boston: C.C. Little and J. Brown, 1844. 482 p. CtMW; ICN; OrCA; PPAmP; RHi. 44-2789

Greenleaf, Benjamin, 1786-1864. A key to the national arithmetic for the use of teachers only. Boston: Davis, 1844. 206 p. OO. 44-2790

Greenleaf, Benjamin, 1786-1864. Introduction to the national arithmetic.... Boston: R.S. Davis and Gould, Kendall and Lincoln; New York: Robinson, Pratt and company, and Collins brothers and com-

pany, 1844. 184 p. DAU; MiU; PBL; PU.
44-2791

Greenleaf, Benjamin, 1786-1864. The
national arithmetic on the inductive system; combining the analytic and syn-
thetic methods....practical systems of
mensuration, gauging, geometry, and
book-keeping; with an appendix, comprising the cancelling method....designed
for common schools and academies.
....Boston: Robert S. Davis, and Gould,
Kendall and Lincoln; New York: Pratt,
Woodford and company, and Collins,
brother and company, 1844. MH; TxU-T.
44-2792

Greenleaf, Jeremiah, 1791-1864.
Grammar simplified, or an ocular
analysis of the English language. Edition
20. New York, 1844. ODW. 44-2793

Greenleaf, Moses, 1777-1834. Map of
the state of Maine with province of New
Brunswick. Philadelphia: 1844. Nh-Hi.
44-2794

Greenleaf, Simon, 1783-1853. Greenleaf on evidence, No. 1: a treatise on the
laws... Second edition. Boston: Charles
Little and James Brown, 1844. 3 v. DLC;
ICRL; NcD; TxU; ViU-L. 44-2795

Greenleaf, Simon, 1783-1853. A
treatise on the law of evidence by Simon
Greenleaf....Second edition. Boston:
Charles C. Little and James Brown,
1844-1853. 3 v. DLC; LNL-L; NcD; TxU;
ViU. 44-2796

Greenwood, Benjamin. Key to the national arithmetic. Boston: R.S. Davis,
1844. MWbor; OO. 44-2797

Greenwood, Francis William Pitt,

1797-1843. Collection of psalms and
hymns for Christian worship. Thirty-
seventh edition. Boston: Carter, Hendee
and company, 1844. MB; MH-AH;
Mlanc; RHi. 44-2798

Greenwood, Francis William Pitt,
1797-1843. Collection of psalms and
hymns for Christian worship. Thirty-
ninth edition. Boston: Charles J. Hendee, and Jenks and Palmer, 1844. 609 p.
CtY; MB; MBeHi. 44-2799

Greenwood, Francis William Pitt.
1797-1843. Sermons by Rev. F.W.P.
Greenwood, D.D. ....Boston: Charles C.
Little and James Brown, 1844. 2 v.
CBPac; GMM; MBAU; NCaS; PPLT.
44-2800

Greenwood, Francis William Pitt.
1797-1843. Sermons of consolation.
Second edition. Boston: Charles C. Little
and James Brown, 1844. 312 p. CtHC;
MNan; MWA; NCaS; RPB. 44-2801

Greenwood Cemetery, Brooklyn.
Report of the vice president, made to the
Board of Trustees, December 4, 1843.
New York: 1844. NBHi; NBLiHi; NN.
44-2802

Gregg, Josiah, 1806-1850? Commerce
of the prairies; or the journal of a Santa
Fe Trader, during eight expeditions
across the great western prairies, and a
residence of nearly nine years in northern Mexico. New York: H.G. Langley,
1844. 2 v. GEU; LU; NNA; OrHi; ScC.
44-2803

Gregg, Josiah, 1806-1850? Gregg's
commerce of the prairies, or, the journal
of a Santa Fe trader, 1831-1839.... New

York: H.G. Langley, 1844. 2 v. CU; DLC; IU; UU; ViU. 44-2804

Gregg, Josiah, 1806-1850? A map of the Indian Territory, Northern Texas and New Mexico. Showing the Great Western Prairies map of Mexico, Central America and Yucatan. New York: 1844. 1 p. PHi. 44-2805

Gregory, John, 1724-1773. A father's legacy to his daughters and trials and temptations of women. New York: 1844. 16 p. CLU; CtY; LNH; MH; NcC. 44-2806

Greiner, M. Civil practice. New Orleans: J.B. Steel, 1844. 240 p. OrSC. 44-2807

Gresley, William, 1801-1876. Church Clavering; or the schoolmaster. Flemington, New York: J.R. Dunham, 1844. 85 p. CtMW; MH; NjR; NBuDD; TSewU. 44-2808

Gresley, William, 1801-1876. Ecclesiastes Anglicanus being a treatise on preaching by William Gresley. New York: D. Appleton and company, 1844. 340 p. IEG; NcD; MiU; OClW; OOxM. 44-2809

Grew, Henry, 1781-1862. Argument for the perpetuity of the Sabbath. Rev. H. Grew of Phelps. Philadelphia: 1844. MB. 44-2810

Grew, Henry, 1781-1862. An examination of the divine testimony, concerning the character of the son of God. By Henry Grew, minister of the gospel. Second edition. Philadelphia: Merrihew and Thompson, printers, 1844. 72 p. MWA. 44-2811

Grew, Henry, 1781-1862. The intermediate state. Philadelphia: 1844. 24 p. MHi; NIC; PPL. 44-2812

Grew, Henry, 1781-1862. A review of Phelps' argument for the perpetuity of the Sabbath. By Henry Grew. Philadelphia: Merrihew and Thompson, printers, 1844. 24 p. MBrZ; MH; MNBedf; MWA; PPL. 44-2813

Grew, Henry, 1781-1862. Six tracts. Philadelphia: 1844-1845. MNtCA. 44-2814

Grider, Henry. Remarks of Mr. Grider of Kentucky, as to the right of certain members elected by general ticket to retain their seats in the House, against the law providing for the elections by single districts. Washington: Gales and Seaton, 1844. 13 p. M; OClWHi. 44-2815

Grier, James. A lecture on the subject of the use of intoxicating liquors. By Rev. J. Grier... Pittsburgh, Pennsylvania: printed at the Franklin office, 1844. 236 p. IaMp; PPi; PPiHi; PPPrHi. 44-2816

Griffin, Edward Dorr, 1770-1837. Sermons, not before published, on various practical subjects. By the late Edward Dorr Griffin.... New York: M.W. Dodd, 1844. 328 p. CBB; NjP; ODaB; OClWHi; PPiW. 44-2817

Griffiths, John W. Marine and naval architecture, or the science of ship building, condensed into a single lecture, and delivered before the shipwrights of the city of New York. New York: 1844. MdAN; MWA. 44-2818

Grigg, John, 1792-1864. A first reader.

Philadelphia: Grigg and Elliot, 1844.
MH. 44-2819

Grigg, John, 1792-1864. Grigg's southern and western songster: being a choice collection of the most fashionable songs, ...New edition, greatly enlarged. Philadelphia: Grigg and Elliot, 1844.3 24 p. MiD-B; MoSM; MoK. 44-2820

Grimshaw, William, 1782-1852. History of England from the first invasion by Julius Caesar to the accession of William the Fourth, in 1830. Philadelphia: Published by Grigg and Elliot, 1844. 318 p. IGK; KPar; LN; TNT. 44-2821

Grimshaw, William, 1782-1852. History of the United States from their first settlement as colonies to the period of the fifth census in 1830... Philadelphia: Grigg and Elliot, 1844. 326 p. NIC; PPeSchw. 44-2822

Grimshaw, William, 1782-1852. Life of Napoleon: with the history of France, from the death of Louis XVI to the year 1821. Philadelphia: Grigg and Elliott, 1844. 285 p. NoLoc. 44-2823

Grimshaw, William, 1782-1852. United States from their first settlement as colonies, to the period of the fifth census, in 1830. Accompanied by a book of questions and a key. Philadelphia: Grigg and Elliot, 1844. 324 p. MH; PBa; PPeSchw. 44-2824

Grimshawe, Thomas Shuttleworth, 1778-1850. A memoir of the Rev. Legh [sic] Richmond. Seventh American from the last London edition. New York: M.W. Dodd, 1844. 362 p. KyLoP; NjP; OCl; RPB; TxBrdD. 44-2825

Grinnell, Joseph. Speech of Mr. Grinnell, of Massachusetts, on the tariff, with statistical tables of the whale fishery of the United States. Washington: Gales and Seaton, 1844. 16 p. Lu; MBAt; MH; MNBedf. 44-2826

Griswold, Alexander Viets, 1766-1843. The apostolic office: being some brief remarks on the different orders of the Christian ministry. Philadelphia: Caxton Press, 1844. 16 p. NNG. 44-2827

Griswold, Alexander Viets, 1766-1843. The doctrine of justification: being part of a pastoral letter to the clergy and other members of the Protestant Episcopal Church in the United States written by the late Rt. Rev. Alexander V. Griswold. Boston: Published by the Tract Committee, Diocese of Massachusetts, 1844. 22 p. MBC; MBD; MWA; PPPL-R; RHi. 44-2828

Griswold, Rufus Wilmot, 1815-1857. Cypress wreath; a book of consolation for those who mourn. By R.F. Griswold. Boston: Gould, Kendall and Lincoln, 1844. 128 p. CtHC; ICN; MWA; NjP; ScC. 44-2829

Griswold, Rufus Wilmot, 1815-1857. Gems from the American poets, with brief biographical notices. Philadelphia: H. Hooker, 1844. 120 p. IU; MB; MH; MHa; RPB. 44-2830

Griswold, Rufus Wilmot, 1815-1857. The illustrated book of Christian ballads and other poems. Philadelphia: Lindsay and Blakiston, 1844. 164 p. CtY; MB; MnSS; OMC; RPB. 44-2831

Griswold, Rufus Wilmot, 1815-1857. The poetry of flowers, original and selected; edited by Rufus W. Griswold. Philadelphia: John Locken, 1844. 287 p. MB; NjP; PPWa; WGrNM. 44-2832

Griswold, Rufus Wilmot, 1815-1857. The poetry of love. Edited by R. W. Griswold. Boston: Gould, Kendall and Lincoln, 1844. 128 p. MB; NhRo; OO; RPB. 44-2833

Groton, Massachusetts. Parish Library. A catalogue of the First Parish Library, Groton. Instituted 1841. Lowell: Stearns and Taylor, printers, 1844. 12 p. MeHi; PPL-R. 44-2834

Groton and Nashua Railroad. Groton and Nashua Railroad; a history of the origin, progress, and objects of the scheme discussed and exposed. Nashville: 1844. 23 p. MH-BA; Nh-Hi. 44-2835

Grouard, George M. A practical printer's answer to Mr. Kendall's tract no. 5, on the public printing. Addressed to himself. [Washington?: 1844] 8 p. M; MH; PPL; TxU. 44-2836

Groves, John. A Greek and English dictionary. With corrections and additional matter, by the American editor. Boston: J.H. Wilkins and R.B. Carter, and B.B. Mussey, 1844. 616, 102 p. CoDR; IaMc; IEN; ODaB; NjP. 44-2837

Growlund, Laurence. The cooperative commonwealth in its outlines. Boston: Lee and Shepard, 1844. 278 p. OTU. 44-2838

Guernsey, Alfred Hudson, 1825-1902. The world's opportunities and how to use them, by Alfred H. Guernsey, Ph.D. A view of the industrial progress of our country, a consideration of its future development, a study of the sphere of woman's work, and estimates of the rewards which art and science, invention and discovery, have in store for human endeavor, with an analysis of the conditions of present and prospective prosperity. New York: Harper and brothers, 1844. 600 p. NIC. 44-2839

Guide book to West Point and vicinity; containing descriptive, historical and statistical sketches of the United States Military Academy and of other objects of interest. New York: J.H. Colton, 1844. 112 p. DLC; DNW; PP. 44-2840

Guild, E.E. The Universalist's book of reference: containing all the principal facts and arguments and scripture texts pro and con, on the great controversy between Limitarians and Universalists. Utica: Grosh and Walker, 1844. 412 p. NRC-R; NUt. 44-2841

Guizot, Elizabeth Charlotte Pauline. Young student; or, Ralph and Victor, from the French by Samuel Jackson. New York: 1844. 3 v. in 1. CtHT; FTU; MWA; OUrC; RPAt. 44-2842

Guizot, Francois Pierre Guillaume, 1787-1874. The history of civilization, from the fall of the Roman Empire to the French revolution.... translated by William Hazlett.... [Third edition] New York: Appleton, 1844. 4 v. Nv; OT. 44-2843

Gully, Robert. Journals kept by Mr. Gully and Capt..Denham during a captivity in China in the year 1842. Edited by a barrister. New York: J.L. Linney, 1844. 198 p. CSt; IaU; MH; NIC; PU. 44-2844

Gummere, Samuel R., 1789-1866. The progressive spelling-book, in two parts; containing a great variety of useful exercises in spelling, pronunciation, and derivation; including extensive tables of words deducted from their Greek and Latin roots. The second part enlarged on the basis of Butter's etymological spelling book. Philadelphia: Published by Kimber and Sharpless, 1844. 156 p. NbOM; OO; PPM; PSC-Hi. 44-2845

Gunn, John C. Gunn's domestic medicine or poor man's friend in the hours of affliction, pain, and sickness. First revised edition enlarged. Philadelphia: B.J. Webb and Brothers, 1844. 893 p. DNLM; FTaSU; PPPH. 44-2846

Gunn, John C. Gunn's domestic medicine or poor man's friend in the hours of affliction, pain, and sickness. New revised edition, improved and enlarged. New York: Saxton, 1844. 893 p. CtY; PaHosp. 44-2847

Gunn, Lewis C. The age to come: the present organization of matter, called earth, to be destroyed by fire at the end of this age or dispensation. Also, before the event, Christians may know about the time when it shall occur. Boston: Joshua V. Hines, 1844. 65 p. CLamb; MBNMHi; MH. 44-2848

Gurley, Ralph Randolph, 1797-1872. Life and eloquence of the Rev. Sylvester Larned, first pastor of the First Presbyterian Church in New Orleans. New York: Wiley and Putnam, 1844. [13]-412 p. DLC; IaGG; MWA; OO; TChU. 44-2849

Gwynn, Walter. The reply of the president of the Portsmouth and Roanoke Railroad Company to the address of Captain Francis E. Rives to the public. Norfolk: T.G. Broughton and company, 1844. 23 p. DLC; NcU. 44-2850

H

Haddock, Charles Brickett, 1796-1861. Address delivered before the railroad convention at Montpelier, Vermont, January 8, 1844. Montpelier [Vermont] E.P. Walton and Son, 1844. 24 p. CSmH; MiU; NNC; Vt; VtMidbC. 44-2851

Hagerstown town and country almanack for 1845. By John F. Egelmann. Hagerstown, Maryland: J. Gruber, [1844] MWA. 44-2852

Hale, Salma, 1787-1866. History of the United States, from their first settlement as colonies, to the close of the war with Great Britain in 1815 to which are added questions, adapted to the use of schools. Cooperstown: H. and E. Phinney, 1844. 298 p. ALT; ICU; MH; NUtHi; WaSN 44-2853

Hale, Sarah Josepha Buell, 1788-1879. The good housekeeper, or the way to live well, and to be well while we live; containing directions for choosing and preparing food, in regard to health, economy, and taste. Seventh edition. Boston: Otis, Broaders, and company, 1844. 144 p. CtY; GU; IU; MH; MWA. 44-2854

Hale, Sarah Josepha Buell, 1788-1879. The little boy's and girl's library of amusement and instruction... New York: Edwd. Dunigan [1844?] 4 parts in 1 v. CtY. 44-2855

Haliburton, Thomas Chandler, 1796-1865. The attache, or Sam Slick in England. By the author of the "clockmaker, or, sayings and doings of Sam Slick." Revised second and last series. New York: W.H. Colyer, 1844. 68 p. ICU; LNH; MH; RNHi. 44-2856

Haliburton, Thomas Chandler, 1796-1865. The attache, or Sam Slick in England. By the author of the "clockmaker, or, sayings and doings of Sam Slick." Revised second and last series. Philadelphia: Lea and Blanchard, 1844. CSmH; MBL; MH; PPL. 44-2857

Haliburton, Thomas Chandler, 1796-1865. Judge Haliburton's Yankee stories. By Judge J.C. Haliburton. Philadelphia: 1844. 2 v. in 1. CU; IU; PPL-R. 44-2858

Hall, Anna Maria Fielding, 1800-1881. Turns of fortune and other tales. New York: C.S. Francis and company, 1844. 195 p. MHi; MVh. 44-2859

Hall, Edward Brooks, 1800-1866. Christians forbidden to fight; an address before the Rhode Island Peace Society, at its 27th annual meeting, June 30, 1844. Providence: H.H. Brown, printer, 1844. 24 p. ICMe; MBAt; NNC; WHi. 44-2860

Hall, J.B. The stranger's guide; or information about Boston and vicinity... Boston: J.B. Hall, 1844. 8 p. M; MB; MNF. 44-2861

Hall, James. Report of a reconnaissance of a route for a railroad from Portland to Montreal. Portland, Maine: printed by order of the city council, 1844. 16 p. DLC; MBAt; MH; RPB. 44-2862

Hall, James, 1811-1898. An address delivered before the Society of Natural History of the Auburn Theological Seminary, on their anniversary, August 15, 1843. Published by request of the society. Auburn: printed by Henry Oliphant, 1844. 20 p. IaPeC; ICP; MB; MWA; NAuT. 44-2863

Hall, James, 1811-1898. Niagara falls; their physical charges, and the geology and topography of the surrounding country. Boston: [1844] 30 p. DLC. 44-2864

Hall, John. The readers manual designed for the use of common schools in the U.S. Hartford: Robins and Smith, 1844. 312 p. Ct; CtHWatk; NNF. 44-2865

Hall, John. The scriptures the only rule of faith: an exposition of the second answer of the shorter catechism. By the Rev. John Hall. Philadelphia: Presbyterian Board of Publication, 1844. 108 p. CSansS; GDecCT; MWiW; NNUT; PPPrHi. 44-2866

Hall, Joseph G. Intemperance. A wickedness of the commonwealth. A sermon preached on fast day, April 4, 1844. At the Congregational Church, South Egremont, Massachusetts.... Great Barrington, Massachusetts: 1844. 15 p. CtY. 44-2867

Hall, Louisa Jane Park, 1802-1892. The cross and anchor [and other poems] written for the fair, in aid of the Mariner's

Church, Providence, Rhode Island, April, 1844. Providence: B. Cranston and company, 1844. 31 p. CtY; MBC; MH; MWA; OO. 44-2868

Hall, Louisa Jane Park, 1802-1892. Memoir of Miss Elizabeth Carter; illustrating the union of learning and piety. Boston: T.H. Carter and company, 1844. 68 p. ICBB; MB; MBC; MWA; PPL. 44-2869

Hall, Nathaniel. The Christian ministry. A sermon preached at the ordination of Mr. Hiram Withington, as pastor of the First Congregational Church in Leominster, December 25, 1844. By Nathaniel Hall, minister of the First Church in Dorchester. With the charge, right hand of fellowship, and the address to the society. Boston: William Crosby and H.P. Nichols, 1844. 30 p. MHi. 44-2870

Hall, Robert, 1764-1831. The works of.... with a memoir of his life, by Dr. Gregory; reminiscences, by John Greene, esq. and his character as a preacher, by the Rev. John Foster.... New York: Harper and brothers, 1844. 4 v. IaPeC; KEmC; NjPT; ViU. 44-2871

Hall, Samuel. A revelation from God, out of the scriptures, to settle the long disputed doctrines which hinder Christians from working together in love. Boston: printed by S.N. Dickinson, 1844. 32 p. MB. 44-2872

Hall, Samuel Carter, 1800-1889. The book of British ballads, edited by S.C. Hall. With illustrations after designs by Creswick, Gilbert, and others. New York: G.P. Putnam's Sons [1844?] 368 p. NcU; NN; OClW; PBm; PP. 44-2873

Hall, Samuel Carter, 1800-1889. The book of British ballads. Edited by S.C. Hall, esq. With preliminary remarks to each ballad, and an introduction by Park Benjamin. New York: Douglas, printer, 1844. 153 p. CoD; DLC; IU; MWiW; TxU. 44-2874

Hall, Samuel Read, 1795-1877. The child's book of geography.... with outlines of countries, cuts and ten maps. Sixth edition. New York: Pratt, Woodford and company, 1844. 112 p. MnS. 44-2875

Hall, Samuel Read, 1795-1877. The child's book of geography.... with outlines of countries, cuts and ten maps. Fifteenth edition. New York: Pratt, Woodford and company, 1844. 112 p. MnS. 44-2876

Hall, Willis, 1801-1868. An address delivered August 14, 1844, before the Society of Phi Beta Kappa in Yale College. By Hon. Willis Hall, of Albany, New York. New Haven: printed by B.L. Hamlen, 1844. 32 p. CtY; KHi; MWA; NHC-S; Vt. 44-2877

Hallett, Benjamin Franklin. Speech of the Hon. B.F. Hallett, of Boston, on Bunker Hill, July 4th, 1844. 12 p. RHi. 44-2878

Halpine, Charles Graham, 1829-1868. The life and adventures, songs, services, and speeches of Private Miles O'Reilly... New York: Carleton, 1844. 12-237 p. NhPet. 44-2879

Halsted, Caroline Amelia, d. 1851. Richard III, as duke of Gloucester and king of England. ....Philadelphia: Carey, 1844. 472 p. LNH; OHi; PPA; RWoH; WvU. 44-2880

Halsted, Oliver Spencer, 1792-1877. Address upon the character of the late, the Hon. Isaac H. Williamson, delivered before the bar of New Jersey. Newark: Aaron Gust, printer, 1844. 23 p. MWA; Nj; PHi; PPL; RPB. 44-2881

Hamden. pseud. Letter to John C. Calhoun on the annexation of Texas. Cooperstown: 1844. 34 p. NIC. 44-2882

Hamilton Academy. Hamilton, New York. Annual catalogue. 1844-45. MH. 44-2883

Hamilton, James. Address on the agriculture and husbandry of the south.... Charleston: Miller and Browne, 1844. 14 p. ScCC. 44-2884

Hamilton, James, 1814-1867. Farewell to Egypt, or the departure of the Free Church of Scotland out of the Erastian establishment by the Rev. James Hamilton of London. New York: Robert Carter, 1844. 23 p. NcMHi; NN; PHi; PPPrHi. 44-2885

Hamilton, James, 1814-1867. The harp on the willows, remembering Zion, farewell to Egypt.... From the forty-fifth London edition. New York: Robert Carter; Pittsburg: Thomas Carter, 1844. 178 p. ICP; LNT; MnDu; NjP; NN. 44-2886

Hamilton, Robert. Silent love and other poems illustrative of that feeling of the heart. Edited by Robert Hamilton. Boston: Saxton Peirce and company, 1844. 128 p. MB; MHolliHi. 44-2887

Hamilton, W. Delano. Ask why: song [with pianoforte] New York: 1844. CtY. 44-2888

Hamilton, William Thomas, 1796-1884. Lecture: on the indebtedness of modern literature to the Bible. Delivered before the citizens of Mobile, in the lecture room of the Government Street Church, Mobile, Tuesday, December 26, 1843. Mobile [Alabama] F.H. Brooks, 1844. 24 p. DLC; InFtwL; MB; NjPT; PPPrHi. 44-2889

Hamilton College, Clinton, New York. Catalogue of the corporation, officers, and students of Hamilton college. 1844-45. Utica, New York: R.W. Roberts, [1844] 20 p. MWA; NN. 44-2890

Hamilton College, Clinton, New York. Catalogue of the corporation, officers, and students, of Hamilton college. 1844-45. [Utica: 1844] 23 p. NN; NUt. 44-2891

Hamilton College, Clinton, New York. Catalogue of the officers and students of Hamilton Literary and Theological Institution, 1844-1845. Hamilton: 1844. 24 p. A-Ar. 44-2892

Hamilton College. Clinton, New York. Phoenix Society. Triennial catalogue of the Phoenix Society, Hamilton College, Clinton, November, 1844. Studia et artes colimus. Utica: R.W. Roberts, printer, 1844. 48 p. NCH; NN. 44-2893

Hamilton College, Clinton, New York. Union Society. Triennial catalogue of the Union Society of Hamilton College. Clinton, June, 1844. Utica: R.W. Roberts, printer, 1844. 22 p. NUt. 44-2894

Hamilton County Agricultural Society. Proceedings of the Hamilton County Agricultural Society, and report of the annual exhibition.... held.... on the 19th and 20th of September, [1844] ....Cincinnati: office of the Plow Boy, 1844. 32 p. CSmH; OClWHi. 44-2895

Hamilton County Medical club. Medical ethics; or principles and rules by which medical practioners should be regulated: including a fee bill. Cincinnati: 1844. OC. 44-2896

Hamilton's Boarding and Day School. Prospectus of Mr. and Mrs. Hamilton's Boarding and Day School for Young Ladies. Baltimore: John D. Toy, 1844. 13 p. MdBD; NjP. 44-2897

Hamlin, Hannibal. Speech of Mr. Hamlin of Maine, on the army appropriation bill, and reply to Mr. Morse upon the professions, practices, and principles of the Federal party, delivered in the House, April 15, 1844. Washington: 1844. 12 p. M; MeHi; NNC. 44-2898

Hammond, Jabez Delano, 1778-1855. History of the political parties of the state of New York from the ratification of the federal constitution in December, 1840. New York: H. and E. Phinney, 1844. 3 v. CtHT; MiDW; NRU; PHC; WaS. 44-2899

Hammond, Jabez Delano, 1778-1855. history of the political parties in the state of New York from the ratification of the federal Constitution to December, 1840. Third edition revised. Cooperstown: Published by H. and E. Phinney, 1844. 2 v. NRU; WaS; WvU. 44-2900

Hammond, Jabez Delano, 1778-1855.

History of the political parties in New York to 1840. Fourth edition, corrected and enlarged to which is added notes by General Root. Cooperstown, 1844-1846. 2 v. MiDW; NRU; NKings; NLock; WaS. 44-2901

Hammond, Jabez Delano, 1778-1855. Letter to the Hon. John C. Calhoun, on the annexation of Texas. Cooperstown: Printed by H. and E. Phinney, 1844. 34 p. CtY; DLC; MB; MWA; TxU. 44-2902

Hammond, James Henry, 1807-1864. Letter of his excellency, Governor Hammond, to the Free Church of Glasgow, on the subject of slavery. Columbia: W.D. Temberton, 1844. 7 p. CSmH; MH; OClWHi; PPL; TxU. 44-2903

Hammond, John. A tabular view of the financial affairs of Pennsylvania, from the commencement of her public works to the present time; in which are included the cost, revenue and expenditures of the several lines of canals and railroads, &c. The whole prepared from the official records. ....Philadelphia: E.C. Biddle, 1844. 60 p. CtY; ICJ; OSW; PPB; PU. 44-2904

Hammond, William Andrew. Canon law, patriotic - the definitions of faith and canons of discipline of the six ecumenical councils. New York: James A. Sparks, 1844. IES. 44-2905

Hampden, Renn Dickson. Christ "the way" a sermon preached before the University of Oxford... Baltimore: Publication rooms of the Evangelical Luthern Church, 1844. 20 p. ICN; MdBD; NNC; PPL. 44-2906

Hampden-Sidney College. Virginia.

Catalogue of the officers and students of the medical department of Hampden-Sidney College, in Richmond, Virginia, session 1843-44. Richmond: P.D. Bernard, 1844. 20 p. GEU. 44-2907

Hanby, William. The Church harp: Or latest compilation of sacred songs, designed for all denominations. Circleville, Ohio: Conference office of the United Brethren in Christ, 1844. 138 p. IaHA; OHi; ODaB; OWervO; PReaAT. 44-2908

Hancorn, James Richard. Medical guide for mothers in pregnancy, accouchements, suckling, weaning, etc. and in most of the important diseases of children. From the second London edition. New York: Saxton and Miles; Philadelphia: G.B. Zeiber and company, 1844. 117 p. PPCP; ViRMC. 44-2909

The hand book of manners; or, rules for the regulations of conduct; "The history of manners, the history of common life." [Dr. Johnson] New York: James Langley, 1844. 60 p. VtMorr. 44-2910

Haney, John. Address to the people by the original, John Haney, the independent candidate. Philadelphia: 1844. PPL. 44-2911

Hanna, John Smith. A history of the life and services of Captain Samuel Dewees, a native of Pennsylvania, and soldier of the revolutionary and last wars. Baltimore: printed by R. Neilson, 1844. 360 p. CtY; ICN; MB; OCHP; PHi. 44-2912

Hanna, John Smith. Lectures on the glory of Columbia; embracing a succinct account of numerous events from the landing of Christopher Columbus up to

the present time. Baltimore: printed by
Robert Neilson, 1844. 56 p. DLC; MdHi.
44-2913

Hannam, John. Economy of waste
manures, a treatise on the nature and use
of neglected fertilizers. Written for the
Yorkshire Agricultural Society, and
published by permission of the council.
By John Hannam, honorary member of
the New York State Agricultural Society,
Philadelphia: Carey and Hart, 1844. 94 p.
MWA; PPL-R. 44-2914

Hannegan, Edward Allen, 1807-1859.
Remarks of Mr. Hannegan, of Indiana,
on the Oregan Territory, delivered in the
Senate of the United States, February 23,
1844. Washington: printed at the Globe
office, 1844. 8 p. CU; In; InU; MBAt. 44-
2915

Hanover College. Hanover, Indiana.
Catalogue of Hanover Academy, Indiana. For 1844. Madison: Rolla Doolittle, printer, 1844. 12 p. CSmH; DLC; In;
InHC. 44-2916

Hanson, Emma Cole. The life and sufferings of Miss Emma Cole: being a faithful narrative of her life, written by
herself. Second edition. Boston: M.
Aurelius, 1844. 36 p. DLC; IU; MBAt;
MWA; WHi. 44-2917

Hanson, Emma Cole. The life and sufferings of Miss Emma Cole: being a faithful narrative of her life, written by
herself. Fifth edition. Boston: M.
Aurelius, 1844. 36 p. MH. 44-2918

Happiness and misery: being the history
of a few days in the lives of two persons
....Boston: Tract Committee, 1844. 30 p.
MBD. 44-2919

Hardin, John J. Speech of Mr. J.J. Hardin, of Illinois, reviewing the principles
of James K. Polk and the leaders of
modern democracy. Delivered in the
House of Representatives, June 3, 1844.
Washington: Gideon, 1844. 16 p. MH;
NjR; OClWHi; PPL; Tx. 44-2920

Hardin, John J. Speech of Mr. J.J. Hardin, of Illinois, reviewing the public life
and political principles of Mr. Van
Buren, delivered in the House of
Representatives, March 21, 1844.
Washington: Printed at Gideon's, 1844.
32 p. MHi; OClWHi; TxU; WHi. 44-
2921

Hardy, John?. Startling developments
of crim. con! [sic] or, two Mormon
apostles exposed, in practicing the
spiritual wife system in Boston. Boston:
Conway and company, 1844. 12 p. ICN;
MB; MH; OC. 44-2922

Hare, Joseph Thompson. The life of the
celebrated mail robber and daring highwayman Joseph Thompson Hare....
Philadelphia: J.B. Perry; New York:
Mafis and Cornish, 1844. 44-2923

Hare bell; a token of friendship.
Hartford: Gurdon Robins, Junior, 1844.
192 p. CtHWatk; DLC; ICU; MH; NNC.
44-2924

The hare bell; a token of friendship.
Edited by Rev. C.W. Everest....Hartford:
H.S. Parsons and company, 1844. 192 p.
IU. 44-2925

The hare bell; a token of friendship.
Edited by Rev. C.W. Everest....New
York: J. Winchester, 1844. 192 p. DLC;
IU; MiU; PPi. 44-2926

The hare bell; a token of friendship. Edited by Rev. C.W. Everest. Second edition. Hartford: 1844. NN. 44-2927

Hargrave, Richard. Treatise upon the Lord's supper and baptism, with a specific argument deduced from the significetion [sic] of baptism.... with strictures throughout upon Cambellism. Lafayette: 1844. 60 p. In; NjPT. 44-2928

Harkey, Simeon Walcher, 1811-1889. Daily prayer book, containing hymns, exhortations or scripture lessons, and prayers, for the use of families and individuals.... compiled from the German of John Frederick Starck.... Frederick: Thomas Haller, printer, 1844. 408 p. MdHi; MdU. 44-2929

The harmonist. A collection of tunes from the most approved authors, adapted to every variety of metre in the Methodist hymn book. And for particular occasions. A selection of anthems, pieces, and sentences. New edition, in patent notes, revised and greatly enlarged. New York: G. Lane and C.B. Tippett, 1844. 384 p. GU. 44-2930

Harper, plaintiff and appellee. Supreme Court of Louisiana. Harper vs. Moore. Brief for Plaintiff and Appellee. T.H. Howard and Lockett and Goold, Counsel for the Plaintiff. New Orleans: Crescent, printer, 1844. 11 p. LNSCR. 44-2931

Harring, Harro Paul, 1798-1880. Harro-Harring's werke. New York: 1844-1846. ICU; MB; OCU; PPG; WU. 44-2932

Harris, Isaac. Harris' business directory of the cities of Pittsburgh and Al-leghany.... Pittsburgh: A.A. Anderson, 1844. 105 p. MB; OClWHi. 44-2933

Harris, John, 1802-1856. The active Christian. From the writings of John Harris, D.D. ....Boston: Gould, Kendall and Lincoln, 1844. 128 p. CtHC; MB; Nh; OO; ViU. 44-2934

Harris, John, 1802-1856. Mammon: or, couvetousness, the sin of the Christian Church.... New York: G. Lane and C.B. Tippett, 1844. 208 p. DLC; NN. 44-2935

Harris, John, 1802-1856. Miscellanies, consisting principally of sermons and essays... with introduction and notes by Joseph Belcher. Boston: Gould, Kendall and Lincoln, 1844. [17]-287 p. GDecCT; IaMp; OWoC; TxShA. 44-2936

Harris, John, 1802-1856. Sermons and essays. Boston: Gould and Lincoln, 1844. 287 p. IaPeC; PPWe. 44-2937

Harris, Robert. A treatise on the laws of propelling powers and a new system of millwrighting; with tables and illustrations for practical use. Philadelphia: Printed by Merrihew and Thompson, 1844. 152 p. MB; NBu. 44-2938

Harris, Thaddeus William, 1795-1856. Description of an African beetle; allied to Scarabaeus polyphemus. [Boston] 1844. 10 p. DLC; MH-Z. 44-2939

Harris, William Cornwallis, 1807-1848. The highlands of Ethiopia described, during eighteen months' residence of a British embassy at the Christian court of Shoa. By Major W.C. Harris. With illustrations. New York: J. Winchester [1844] 392 p. DLC; ICU; MoS; OClW; WKen. 44-2940

Harrison, John Hoffman, 1808-1849. An essay towards a correct theory of the nervous system. By John Harrison, M.D. Philadelphia: Lea and Blanchard, 1844. 292 p. A-Ar; CSt-L; GEU-M; MH-M; TxU. 44-2941

Harrison, John Pollard, 1796-1849. Lecture November 4, 1844, on the formation of professional character. Cincinnati: 1844. OCHP. 44-2942

Harrison, John Pollard, 1796-1849. Medical ethics, a lecture, delivered December 23, 1843 before the Ohio Medical Lyceum. Cincinnati: Enquirer and Message, 1844. 20 p. DLC; OClWHi; PPAN. 44-2943

Harrison, John Pollard, 1796-1849. Medical ethics. A lecture delivered December 23, 1843, before the Ohio Medical Lyceum. Enquirer and Message, printer, 1844. 20 p. NNNAM; OC; OCGHM; OClWHi. 44-2944

Harrison, John Pollard, 1796-1849. On the formation of professional character. An introductory lecture, delivered November 4th, 1844. Cincinnati: Printed by R.P. Donogh, 1844. 15 p. CSmH; DLC; NBMS; OHi. 44-2945

Harrison, William, 1811-1882. The tongue of time: or, the language of a church clock. By William Harrison.... From the second London edition. Boston: Saxton, Peirce and company; New York: Saxton and Miles, 1844. 108 p. CtHC; DLC; IU; MB; NjMD. 44-2946

Hart, Cyrus Wadsworth. Selections from [his] philosophical, polemical, amatory, moral, and other works. Partly in prose and partly in verse. Cincinnati:

S.W. Johns, 1844. 344 p. CtY; MH; PPi; RPB; TxU. 44-2947

Hart, I.A. A farewell sermon preached in the First Congregational Church of Sandusky.... April 28, 1844. Sandusky: Campbell, 1844. 12 p. OClW. 44-2948

Hart, I.A. A sermon on the seventh commandment, being one of a series upon the ten, preached in Medina, by Rev. I.A. Hart. [Published by request] Medina, Ohio: Speer and Bennett, printers, 1844. 15 p. MWA. 44-2949

Hartford, Connecticut. Booksellers and publishers. Books and engravings. Hartford: Henry Benton, 1844. 2 p. CtHWatk. 44-2950

Hartford, Connecticut. Ordinances. The by-laws of the city of Hartford. Hartford: Case, Tiffany and Burnham, 1844. 123 p. NN. 44-2951

Hartford, Connecticut. Public library. Catalogue of the library and reading room of the young men's institute, Hartford. Hartford: press of Case, Tiffany and Burnham, 1844. 359 p. CtY; DLC; MH; NN; RPAt. 44-2952

Hartford, Connecticut. Young Men's Institute. Catalogue of the library and reading room of the young men's institute, Hartford. Hartford: 1844. CtHC; MBAt; PPL-R. 44-2953

Hartford and New Haven Railroad Company. [Petition of the company to the honorable court to be holden at Hartford, for erecting a toll bridge from Enfield to Suffield] [n.p.]: 1844. 23 p. CSt. 44-2954

Hartford Theological Seminary. Hartford, Connecticut. Laws of the theological institute of Connecticut. Hartford: press of Elihu Geer, 1844. 8 p. Ct; MH-AH. 44-2955

Hartley, Oliver Cromwell, 1823-1859. An address delivered before the soldiers and citizens of Bedford, Pennsylvania, July 4, 1844. By O.C. Hartley, esq. Chambersburg, Pennsylvania: publication office of the German Reformed Church, printer, 1844. 19 p. DLC; MWA; NjR; PHi. 44-2956

Hartshorn, Charles Warren, 1814-1893. New England sheriff: being a digest of the laws of Massachusetts relating to sheriffs, jailers, coroners, and constables. With copious forms. ....Worcester: W. Lazell, 1844. 372 p. DLC; MH-L; MMe; MWHi. 44-2957

Hartzel, Jonas. Dissertation on Christian baptism. Negative arguments on infant baptism. Difficulties lying at the basis of the system; and a few authorities and remarks on the right and scriptural action. Warren, Ohio: A.W. Parker, printer, 1844. 16 p. CSmH; DLC; OClWHi. 44-2958

Harvard University. A catalogue of the officers and students of Harvard University, for the academical year 1844-45. Cambridge: Metcalf and company, printers to the university, 1844. 62 p. MiD-B; NbHi; OC. 44-2959

Harvard University. Divinity School. Catalogue of the alumni of the divinity school of the university in Cambridge. Metcalf and company, printers to the university, 1844. 18 p. DLC; MA; MB; MBC; MH. 44-2960

Harvard University. [Votes on the panorama of Athens] 27th January, 1844. [Cambridge: 1844] MBAt. 44-2961

Haskel, Daniel, 1784-1848. A complete descriptive and statistical gazetter of the United States of America, containing a particular description of the states, territories... New York: Sherman and Smith, 1844. 752 p. CU-B; ICU; LNB; MoS; VtU. 44-2962

Haskel, Daniel, 1784-1848. Gazetteer of the United States of America. New York: Sherman and Smith, 1844. 752 p. IaDuCM; MB; O; PHi. 44-2963

Haskell, D.H. Woodland quick step. Composed and arranged for the pianoforte. Boston: Reed, 1844 [2] p. MB. 44-2964

Haskins, Roswell Wilson. The arts, sciences and civilization, anterior to Greece and Rome... Buffalo: A.W. Wilgus, 1844. 32 p. DLC; ICU; MBAt; NBu; TxU. 44-2965

Hassler, Ferdinand Rudolph, 1770-1843. Logarithmic and trigonometric tables; to seven places of decimals, in a pocket form. A new edition, with introductions in the English and French Languages. New York: E. Hassler and F.E. Hassler, 1844. 10 [314] p. DLC; MWA; NWM; PPAmP; ViAl. 44-2966

Hastings, Thomas, 1784-1872. Christian psalmist; or Watts' psalms and hymns, with copious selections from other sources. The whole carefully revised and arranged, with directions for musical expression. New York: D. Fanshaw, 1844. CoCs; DLC; ICN; OrAlc; PPLT. 44-2967

Hastings, Thomas, 1784-1872. The psalmodist; a choice collection of psalm and hymn tunes, chiefly new; adapted to the very numerous metres now in use, together with chants, anthems, motets, and various other pieces.... New York: E. Collier, 1844. 352 p. NjPT; NNUT; OCY; VtMidSM. 44-2968

Haswell, Charles Haynes, 1809-1907. Engineers' and mechanics' pocket book. New York: Harper and brothers, 1844. 264 p. DLC; MiU; NN; TxHR. 44-2969

Hatch, Julius Wells, 1801-1882. Arithmetic on the German plan of cancellation. By J.W. Hatch. Syracuse: S.F. Smith, printer, 1844. 60 p. DAU; DLC; NCH; NjR. 44-2970

Hatfield, Robert Griffith, 1815-1879. The American house carpenter: a treatise upon architecture, cornices and mouldings, framing doors, windows, and stairs. Together with the most important principles of practical geometry. By R.G. Hatfield, architect. Illustrated by more than three hundred engravings. New York and London: Wiley and Putnam, 1844. 254 p. DLC; LNP; MBL; PPCC; RPAt. 44-2971

Haven, John. Presidential and statistical chart. 1790, 1800, 1810, 1820, 1830, 1840. New York: 1844. MB. 44-2972

Haverford College. The budget. Haverford: 1844-. v. 1-. PHC. 44-2973

Haweis, Thomas, 1734-1820. The communicant's spiritual companion; or, an evangelical preparation for the Lord's supper, with meditation and helps for prayer suitable to the subject, by Rev. T. Haweis, LL.D. With an introductory essay by Rev. John Forsyth, junior, D.D. Newburgh, New York: David L. Proudfit, 1844. 192 p. NN; NSchU. 44-2974

Hawes, Joel, 1789-1867. Collected writings. Hartford, 1844-1859. 4 v. in 1. RPB. 44-2975

Hawes, Joel, 1789-1867. Discourse on the death of Mrs. Mary E. Van Lennep, his daughter.... Hartford: D.B. Moseley, printer, 1844. 28 p. CtHC; MBAt; MBC; PHi. 44-2976

Hawes, Joel, 1789-1867. A father's memorial of an only daughter: A discourse delivered in the First Church in Hartford, December 9, 1844, on the death of Mrs. Mary E. Van Lennep, wife of Rev. Henry J. Van Lennep, missionary to Turkey; who died in Constantinople, September 27, 1844. [Hartford] D.B. Moseley, 1844. 28 p. CtSoP; MH-AH; RPB; TxU; VtU. 44-2977

Hawes, Joel, 1789-1867. Memoir of Normand Smith; or, the Christian serving God in his business. By Rev. Joel Hawes, D.D. Springfield: G. and C. Merriam, 1844. 72 p. IEG; PCA. 44-2978

Hawes, Joel, 1789-1867. A prosperous journey by the will of God. A discourse delivered in the First Church in Hartford, on Sabbath evening, July 7th, 1844. Hartford: 1844. 24 p. CtY; ICT; MDeeP; OClWHi; RPB. 44-2979

Hawes, Joel, 1789-1867. Saviour's legacy to his disciples. Sermon occasioned by the death of Miss Frances C. Webb, delivered August 11th, 1844, being the Sabbath after her interment. Hartford: D.B. Moseley, 1844. CtHC; CtSoP; MB; MBC; RPB. 44-2980

Hawes Place Congregational Society. The reply of the Hawes Place Congregational Society, at South Boston, to a pamphlet entitled "an exposition of facts relating to the administration of the Hawes Charity, by Lemuel Capen, former minister of the Hawes Place Society." Boston: Andrews, Prentiss and Studley, 1844. 26 p. DLC; ICMe; MH-AH; MHi; MiD-B. 44-2981

Hawkes, Julia S. Conversations on Italy; in English and French. By Miss Julia S. Hawkes. Philadelphia: Grigg and Elliot, 1844. 260 p. IaMp; MdW; MH; NCH; NjP. 44-2982

Hawkins, Christopher, 1764-1837. Adventures, containing details of the captivity and escape from the Jersey prison ship. Written by himself. New York, 1844. 314 p. PHi. 44-2983

Hawkins, Edward. The ministry of men in the economy of Grace and the danger of overvaluing it. A sermon preached before the University of Oxford. New York: D. Appleton and company; Philadelphia: George S. Appleton, 1844. 41 p. CSansS; DLC; MiD-B; Nh; RPB. 44-2984

Hawkins, John H.W. The new impulse: or, Hawkins and reform. Boston: 1844. MWA. 44-2985

Hawks, Francis Lister, 1798-1866. The adventures of Daniel Boone, the Kentucky rifleman by the author of "Uncle Philip's conversations" ....New York: D. Appleton and company, 1844. 174 p. DLC; ICM; NNS; TxU; WHi. 44-2986

Hawks, Francis Lister, 1798-1866. The early history of the southern states: Virginia, North and South Carolina, and Georgia. Illustrated by tales, sketches, anecdotes, and adventures, with numerous engravings. By Lambert Lilly, schoolmaster [pseud.] Boston: W.D. Ticknor and company, 1844. 192 p. DLC; MiU-C; MWH; NcAs; NUt. 44-2987

Hawks, Francis Lister, 1798-1866. Evidences of Christianity; or, Uncle Philip's conversations with the children about the truth of the Christian religion. New York: Harper and brothers, 1844. 209 p. NcU. 44-2988

Hawks, Francis Lister, 1798-1866. The history of New England. Illustrated by tales, sketches, and anecdotes... By Lambert Lily, schoolmaster. Boston: W.D. Ticknor, 1844. 184 p. NcA-S. 44-2989

Hawks, Francis Lister, 1798-1866. The history of the Middle states, illustrated by tales, sketches and anecdotes.... By Lambert Lilly, school master [pseud.] Boston: W.D. Ticknor and company, 1844. 167 p. DLC; NcU; NUt; PBa; PPi. 44-2990

Hawks, Francis Lister, 1798-1866. History of the United States, or conversations with the children about New Hampshire. New York: Harper and brothers, 1844. 2 v. IaDuMtC; MeAu; MSbo; NcA-S. 44-2991

Hawks, Francis Lister, 1798-1866. History of the United States: no. 1. Or, Uncle Philip's conversations with the children about Virginia. New York: Harper and brothers, 1844. 232 p. DLC; LN; NcD; OSW; ScGrw. 44-2992

Hawks, Francis Lister, 1798-1866. History of the United States: No. 11; or, Uncle Philips' conversations with the children about New York.... New York: Harper and brothers, 1844. 2 v. CSmH; NcAs; NN; OSW. 44-2993

Hawks, Francis Lister, 1798-1866. History of the United States: no. III, or, Uncle Philip's conversations with the children about Massachusetts. New York: Harper and brothers, 1844. 2 v. COT; MH; MPiB; NcA-S; NN. 44-2994

Hawks, Francis Lister, 1798-1866. History of the western states, illustrated by tales, sketches and anecdotes... By Lambert Lily, schoolmaster [pseud.] Boston: W.D. Ticknor, 1844. 167 p. InU; MBuU: NcAs; OClWHi. 44-2995

Hawks, Francis Lister, 1798-1866. The lost Greenland; or Uncle Philip's conversations with the children about the lost colonies of Greenland. New York: Harper and Brothers, 1844. 180p. MiGr; OSO; RJa; RPE. 44-2996

Hawks, Francis Lister, 1798-1866. Natural history: or, Uncle Philip's conversations with the children about tools and trades among inferior animals. New York: 1844. 213 p. OSW; RPE. 44-2997

Hawks, Francis Lister, 1798-1866. A story of the American revolution, illustrated by tales, sketches, and anecdotes... by Lambert Lilly, schoolmaster. Boston: W.D. Ticknor and company, 1844. 204 p. RPB. 44-2998

Hawks, Francis Lister, 1798-1866. Uncle Philip's history of the United States No. VI. or Uncle Philip's conversation with the children about New Hampshire. New York: Harper and brothers, 1844. 2 v. NcA-S; OCh. 44-2999

Hawthorne, Nathaniel. A good man's miracle; the child's friend, designed for families and Sunday schools. Edited by Eliza L. Follen. Boston: Leonard C. Bowles, 1844. 2v. in 1. MoSW. 44-3000

Hawthorne, Nathaniel. A visit to the celestial city. Revised by the committee of publication of the American Sunday School Union. Philadelphia, Pennsylvania: American Sunday School Union, [1844] 54 p. MB; MH; MWA. 44-3001

Hayes, George E. Organization and diseases of the teeth: with familiar directions for preserving their health and beauty. Buffalo: Steele's press, 1844. 80 p. NBuHi. 44-3002

Hayes, John Lord, 1812-1887. The probable influence of icebergs upon drift. Read before the Association of American Geologists and Naturalists, May 4, 1843. [Boston: 1844] 28 p. CtY; DLC; MWA; OClWHi; VtU. 44-3003

Haynes, Daniel. Poems by Daniel Haynes of North Adams, Massachusetts. North Adams: 1844. 12 p. MDeeP; RPB. 44-3004

Haynes, Lemuel. Universalism exposed! Being a discourse in answer to one by Hosea Ballou, delivered by Lemuel Haynes, A.M., pastor of the Presbyterian Church, Rutland, Vermont. Utica: Potter, 1844. MBAt; PPPrHi. 44-3005

Hayward, George, 1791-1863. Outlines of human physiology, designed for the use of the higher classes in common schools. By George Hayward, M.D., professor of the principles of surgery and clinical surgery in Harvard Univeristy.

Fifth edition. Boston: Thomas H. Webb and company, 1844. 216 p. ICBB: KyBC; MH. 44-3006

Hazen, Edward. Popular technology; or, professions and trades. New York: Harper, 1844. 2 v. MNoboro, OAsht; PHatU. 44-3007

Hazen, Edward. A practical grammar of the English language; or, an introduction to composition. ....A.M. New York: Huntington and Savage, 1844. 240 p. CtHWatk; MH; NNC; OMC; OSW. 44-3008

Head, Francis Bond, 1793-1875. life and adventures of Bruce, the African traveller. From the last London edition. New York: Harper and brothers, 1844. 382 p. IEG; InCW; MsU; OCX; RWe. 44-3009

Head, Francis Bond, 1793-1875. Life in Germany; or, a visit to the springs of Germany by "an old man in search of health." [New York: Leavitt and Allen, 1844] 228 p. MB; NN; OCl. 44-3010

Headley, Joel Tyler. Italy and the Italians, in a series of letters. By J.T. Headley. New York: I.S. Platt, 1844. 64 p. DLC; LNH; MPiB. 44-3011

Heads of the people; drawn by Kenny Meadows. With original essays by Douglas Jerrold, William Howitt, Nimrod, W. Thackeray, &c., &c. Philadelphia: Carey and Hart, 1844. 48 p. MH; MWA; TxHuT. 44-3012

Health almanac. New York: Saxton and Miller, 1844. MWA. 44-3013

Hedge, Frederic Henry, 1805-1890.

Christianity confined to no sect. A sermon preached at the dedication of the Church, presented to the town of Stetson, by the hon. Amasa Stetson of Dorchester, Massachusetts, February 22, 1844, Bangor: 1844. 16 p. DLC; MHi; NN; RPB. 44-3014

Hedge, Frederic Henry, 1805-1890. A sermon preached before the ancient and honorable artillery company on their 196th anniversary, June 2, 1844. Boston: 1844. 30 p. MH-AH. 44-3015

Hedge, Levi, 1766-1844. Elements of logick; or, a summary of the general principles and different modes of reasoning. By Levi Hedge, LL.D., professor of natural religion, moral philosophy, and civil polity in Harvard University. Stereotype edition. Cooperstown: H. and E. Phinney, 1844. 178 p. IaGG; MoHi; NCaS; ViU; VtMidSM. 44-3016

Heidelberg catechism. Der Heidelberg Katechismus. Chambersburg, Pennsylvania: in der Druckerei der Deutsch Reform Kirche, 1844. 57 p. PLERC-Hi. 44-3017

Heidelberg catechism. Der Heidelberg Katechismus oder Unterrichtsweise in der Christliche Religion. Chambersburg, Pennsylvania: in der Drucherei der Deutsch-Reform Kirche, 1844. 69 p. PLERC-Hi. 44-3018

Heidelberg catechism. The Heidelberg catechism; or, method of instruction in the Christian religion as the same is taught in the reformed churches and schools of the United States and Europe; translated from the German. Philadelphia: Mentz and Rovoudt, 1844. 71 p. MiPon; NCH. 44-3019

Hemans, Felicia Dorothea [Browne] 1793-1835. The poetical works of Mrs. Felicia Hemans. Complete in one volume. New edition with a critical preface and a biographical memoir. Philadelphia: Grigg and Elliot, 1844. 559 p. FStP; MH; MWelD; NjP. 44-3020

Hemans, Felicia Dorothea [Browne] 1793-1835. The sacred poems of Mrs. Hemans [and the Hebrew melodies of Lord Byron] [New York: 1844] 16 p. CtY; DLC; LNH; MWH; NN. 44-3021

Hemans, Felicia Dorothea [Browne] 1793-1835. The works of Mrs. Hemans, with a memoir by her sister, and an essay on her genius, by Mrs. Sigourney. Philadelphia: Lea and Blanchard, 1844. 7 v. KyLo; NBu; PPL-R; Vi; Vt. 44-3022

Henderson, W.A. Modern domestic cookery and useful receipt book, adapted for families... Boston: William J. Reynolds, 1844. 360, 61 p. MB; MWA; WHi. 44-3023

Hendrick, J.L. A grammatical manual; or an outline of English grammar, designed for the use of students of Onondaga Academy. Syracuse: L.W. Hall and company, 1844. 105 p. CtHWatk; NNC. 44-3024

Henkel, M.M. An address delivered before the Grand Lodge of Kentucky, in the city of Lexington, August 30, 1844....n.p.: 1844. 8 p. IaCrM. 44-3025

Henkle, M.M. An address delivered at Shelbyville, upon laying the corner stone of the court-house, June 11, 1844. Frankfort, Kentucky: Hodges, Todd and Pruett, printers, 1844. 12 p. NNFM. 44-3026

Henry, John Joseph, 1758-1811. Accurate and interesting account of the hardships of that band of heroes, who traversed the wilderness in the campaign against Quebec in 1775. Revised edition. Watertown, New York: 1844. CtHWatk. 44-3027

Henry, John Joseph, 1758-1811. Campaign against Quebec: being an accurate and interesting account of the hardships and sufferings of that band of heroes who traversed the widerness. Watertown, New York: Knowlton and Rice, 1844. [13]-312 p. MH; NBuG; PHi; RHi; WHi. 44-3028

Henry, John Joseph, 1758-1811. Campaign against Quebec; an account of the sufferings of that band of heroes who traversed the wilderness to Quebec in 1775. Revised edition. Watertown: 1844. 212 p. M; MoSM; NBuG; OFH; PHi. 44-3029

Henry, John Joseph, 1758-1811. Campaign against Quebec...Second revised edition. Watertown, New York: Knowlton and Rice, 1844. NN. 44-3030

Henry Clay almanac for 1843; Philadelphia: T.K. and P.G. Collins, 1844. MB; PHi. 44-3031

The Henry Clay almanac, containing songs and anecdotes. New York: 1844. PPL-R. 44-3032

Henshaw, David, 1791-1852. A refutation ... of the calumnies against David Henshaw in relation to the failure of the Commonwealth bank and the transfer of South Boston lands to the United States. Boston: Beals and Greene, 1844. 60p. MBAt; NjR; PPL. 44-3033

Henshaw, John Prentiss Kewley. Duties suggested by the signs of the times; triennial sermon before the Board of Missions in Philadelphia, October 3, 1844. New York: Daniel Dana, 1844. 18 p. MHi; MWA; PHi; RHi; RPB. 44-3034

Henshaw, John Prentiss Kewley. Sermon before the board of missions. Baltimore: 1844. PPL. 44-3035

Hentz, Caroline Lee Whiting, 1800-1856. Human and divine philosophy: A poem, written for the Erosophic Society of the University of Alabama by Caroline L. Hentz, and recited by A.W. Richardson, December 12th, 1843. Tuscaloosa: Journal and Flagg office, 1844. 16 p. NcD; NjP; TxU. 44-3036

Herald, James. Hand book of universal receipts carefully prepared and compiled from original sources. New York: G.C. Moore, 1844. 64 p. DLC. 44-3037

Herbert, Henry William, 1807-1858. Guarica, the Charib bride. A legend of Hispaniola.... Philadelphia: A.J. Rockafellar, 1844. 66 p. MB; MMA. 44-3038

Herbert, Henry William, 1807-1858. Lord of the Manor; or, Rose Castleton's temptation. An old English story. Philadelphia: A.J. Rockafellar, 1844. 64 p. CtY; CU; ViU. 44-3039

Herbert, Henry William, 1807-1858. The magnolia. New York: Robert P. Bixby and company, 1844. 300 p. AzPrHi; IaL-B; IEN. 44-3040

Herbert, Henry William, 1807-1858. The revolt of Boston, a continuation of Ruth Whaley; or, The fair puritan. A

romance of the Bay. Boston: 1844. 48 p. RPB. 44-3041

Herbert, Henry William, 1807-1858. Ruth Whalley; or The fair Puritan. A romance of the Bay province. Boston: Henry L. Williams, 1844. 72 p. NoLoc. 44-3042

Hering, Constantine, 1800-1880. The homeopathist; or, domestic physician. Second American from fourth German edition. Philadelphia: Behlert, 1844. 217 p. Cty; MH; NNNAM; PPHa; PU. 44-3043

Herodotus. Herodotus, translated from the Greek, with notes and life of the author. By Rev. William Beloe. A new edition, corrected and revised. Philadelphia: M'Carty and Davis, 1844. 489 p. IaLamG: NjMD. 44-3044

Herodotus. Herodotus. Translated by the Rev. William Beloe. New York: Harper and brothers, 1844. 2 v. AMOb; CoU; IaK; NN; PP. 44-3045

Herodotus. Herodotus. Translated by the Rev. William Beloe.... New York: Harper and brothers, 1844-1859. 3 v. ODa. 44-3046

Herodotus. Works translated by....William Beloe. New York: Harper and brothers, 1844[-1846] 3 v. NcU; PP; WBeloC. 44-3047

Herrick, Edward Claudius, 1811-1862. An answer to the "Bible reader, No. II, of Henry Jones, New York" or Northern lights, shooting stars, and other meteoric phenomena, proved to be not of modern origin. New Haven: 1844. CtY; ICN; MH; MWA; NjR. 44-3048

Herschel, John Frederick William, 1792-1871. Treatise on astronomy. A new edition with a preface and a series of questions for the examination of students by S.C. Walker. Philadelphia: Lea and Blanchard, 1844. 417 p. CtY; ICBB; MdBG; MH; PFal. 44-3049

Hershberger, Henry R. The horseman, a work on horsemanship; containing plain practical rules for riding, and hints to the reader on the selection of horses... added, a sabre exercise from mounted and dismounted service... New York: Langley, 1844. 141 p. CtY; MdBE; MiU; NjP; PPL-R. 44-3050

Hervey, Henry. A series of lectures on Old Testament miracles. Springfield, Ohio: office of the Presbyterian of the West, 1844. 301 p. DLC; ICP; OClWHi. 44-3051

Hervey, James, 1714-1758. Reflections on flowers by Rev. James Hervey. New York: John S. Taylor and company, 1844. 140 p. ICNBT. 44-3052

Hervey, N. Witness of the spirit in the work of sanctification. Baptism of the Holy Ghost. Second edition. Boston: Dow and Jackson's power press, 1844. 94 p. MB; MBC. 44-3053

Hetherington, William Maxwell, 1803-1865. History of the Church of Scotland from the introduction of Christianity to the period of the disruption in 1843, by the Rev. W.M. Hetherington, A.M. First American from the third Edinburgh edition. New York: Robert Carter; Pittsburg: Thomas Carter, 1844. 500 p. CtY; KyHe; MH; MNtCA; PPL. 44-3054

Hetherington, William Maxwell, 1803-

1865. History of the Church of Scotland from the introduction of Christianity to the period of the disruption in 1843. Third American from the third Edinburgh edition. New York: Robert Carter, 1844. CBPSR; CSd; MHi; NcHil; OAU. 44-3055

Hetherington, William Maxwell, 1803-1865. History of the Church of Scotland from the introduction of Christianity to the period of the disruption in 1843. Seventh edition. New York: Carter, 1844. 2 v. PPPrHi. 44-3056

Heuberer, Charles F. The mosquito: a popular comic song. Boston: Prentiss, [1844] MB. 44-3057

Hewett, William. The history and antiquities of the hundred of Compton, Berks, being a topographical, statistical and arechaeological description of the parishes of Aldworth... Reading: J. Snare, 1844. 164 p. CtY; ICN; MB; MH; NcD. 44-3058

Hewitt, John Hill. Kentucky gentleman. A ballad, written, composed, and respectfully dedicated to Henry Clay, the farmer of Ashland, by John H. Hewitt. New York: John F. Nunns, 1844. 7 p. CSt; ViU. 44-3059

Hewitt, John Hill. Singer not long: [Song accompaniment for pianoforte] Baltimore: Benteen, 1844] 2 p. MB; NN. 44-3060

Hewitt, Mary C. Sleeping, I dreamed of love. New York: Firth, Hall and Pond, 1844. 5 p. KU; MB; MNe; ViU. 44-3061

Hews, George. The cot where I was born: ballad; melody by L. Heath. Sung by the Hutchinson family; arranged for the pianoforte by George Hews. New York: William Hall and Son, 1844. 5 p. WHi. 44-3062

Heyde, Charles Louis. Louie and Marie; a tale of the heart: and other poems... New York: R.P. Bixby and company, 1844. 88 p. CtY; DLC; MB; RPB. 44-3063

Hickey, John. The democratic lute, and Polk and Dallas minstrel.... Philadelphia: H.B. Pierson, 1844. 36 p. DLC; MH; PPL; RPB. 44-3064

Hickman, George H. The life and public services of the Honorable James Knox Polk, with a compendium of his speech on various public measures. Baltimore: N. Hickman, 1844. 47 p. DLC; IaHi; OO; PPL; TxDaM. 44-3065

Hickman, George H. The life and public services of James Knox Polk. With compendium of speeches. Also, life of George Mifflin Dallas. Edition 2. Baltimore: N. Hickman, 1844. 48 p. DLC; MH; MiD-B; MoK; NN; PHi. 44-3066

Hickman, George H. The life and public services of the Honorable James Knox Polk, with a compendium of his speeches on various public measures. Also, a sketch of the life of the Honorable George Mifflin Dallas. Third edition. Baltimore: N. Hickman, 1844. 47 p. DLC; NcD. 44-3067

The hierophant, Monthly journal of sacred symbols and prophecy; conducted by G. Bush, 1842-1843. New York: M.H. Newman, 1844. 288 p. DLC; MBAt; NjR; NN; PPPrHi. 44-3068

Higgins, W. Mulinger. The earth: its physical conditions and most remarkable phenomena. By W. Mulinger Higgins, fellow of the geographical society, and lecturer on natural philosophy at Guy's hospital. New York: Harper and brothers, 1844. 408 p. MChi; OCo; OWoC; PCC; WWaN. 44-3069

Hildreth, Richard, 1807-1865. A joint letter to Orestes A. Brownson and the editor of the North American Review: in which the editor of the North American Review is proved to be no Christian, and little better than an atheist [Boston? 1844] 34 p. CtY; MH-AH. 44-3070

Hildreth, Richard, 1807-1865. Theory of morals: an inquiry concerning the law of moral distinctions and the variations and contradictions of ethical codes. ....Boston: C.C. Little and J. Brown, 1844. 272 p. CtY; IEG; NNUT; RPAt; WHi. 44-3071

Hildreth, Richard, 1807-1865. What can I do for the abolition of slavery? [Boston: J.W. Alden, 1844] 7 p. CtHWatk; MH. 44-3072

Hildreth, Samuel Prescott, 1783-1863. Original contributions to the American pioneer. Cincinnati: J.S. Williams, 1844. 144 p. AU; DLC; InHi; MH; OClWHi. 44-3073

Hill, Anne. Drawing book of flowers and fruit with beautifully colored illustrations for the use of seminaries, private pupils and amateurs. Philadelphia: E.C. Biddle, 1844. 6 p. NNF. 44-3074

Hill, George, 1750-1819. Lectures in divinity. By the late George Hill, D.D. principal of St. Mary's College, St.

Andrews. Edited from his manuscript, by his son, the Rev. Alexander Hill, minister of Dailly. Philadelphia: Herman Hooker, 1844. 781 p. ArBaA; ICP; KyLoS; ScCoB; WNaE. 44-3075

Hill, George, 1750-1819. What is the church of Christ? Second American edition. Baltimore: Daniel Brunner, 1844. 156 p. CBCDS; GDecCT; MdHi; NNG; PPPrHi. 44-3076

Hill, M. The system of American Universalism exhibited and exposed in a sermon. By Rev. M. Hill,.... Second edition. Portland: Thurston, Illsley and company, printers, 1844. 24 p. CtW; DLC; MeHi. 44-3077

Hill, M. The system of American Universalism exhibited and exposed in a sermon. By Rev. M. Hill.... Third edition. Portland: Thurston, Illsley and company, printers, 1844. 24 p. CSmH; IEG; MBC; MeHi. 44-3078

Hill, M. The system of American Universalism exhibited and exposed, in a sermon by Rev. M. Hill.... Fourth edition. Portland: Thurston Ilsley and company, printers, 1844. 24 p. MeHi; MMeT; NNUT. 44-3079

Hill, Robert W. Protestant churches defended. By Robert W. Hill. New York: M.W. Dodd, 1844. 112 p. PReaAt. 44-3080

Hillard, George Stillman, 1808-1879. Six months in Italy. Boston, 1844. 455 p. PHC. 44-3081

Hilliard, Francis. Law of mortgages of real and personal property. Third edition. Boston: 1844. 2 v. NjP. 44-3082

Hillsborough Mutual Fire Assurance Association. Constitution, by-laws and conditions of insurance. Somerville: S.L.B. Baldwin, 1844. 8 p. CSmH. 44-3083

Hinton, John Howard, 1791-1873. History and topography of the United States.... Additions and corrections by Samuel L. Knapp and John O. Choules. Second edition. Illustrated with numerous engravings. Boston: Samuel Walker, 1844. 2 v. AMob; CSf; MiD-B; NN; OClW. 44-3084

Hiram Elwood, the banker: or, "like father, like son." New York: 1844. 93 p. CtHWatk; RPB. 44-3085

An historical account of the circumnavigation of the globe, and of the progress of discovery in the Pacific Ocean; from the voyage of Magellan to the death of Cook. Illustrated with numerous engravings. New York: Harper and brothers, 1844. 366 p. Ia; MB. 44-3086

The history and mystery of puffing; or a few fragrant whiffs of the weed, evolving... hints touching the poetry of smoking, etc. New York: 1844. MH; NN. 44-3087

History of beasts and birds. Cooperstown: H. and E. Phinney, 1844. 32 p. MiHi. 44-3088

History of popedom. New York: 1844. 243 p. DLC. 44-3089

A history of Texas, or, the emigrant's guide to the new republic, by a resident emigrant, late from the United States. With a brief introduction by the Rev.

A.H. Lawrence. New York: Nafis and Cornish, 1844. 275 p. ICN; NcD; PMA; TxU; WHi. 44-3090

History of the Baptist churches composing the Sturbridge Association, from their origin to 1843. Prepared by a committee of the association. New York: J.R. Bigelow, 1844. 54 p. Ct; MiD-B; MWA; NHC-S. 44-3091

History of the erection of the monument on the grave of Myron Holley. Utica, New York: H.H. Curtiss, printer, 1844. 20 p. CSmH; MBAt; MWA; NcD; OCHP. 44-3092

History of the Huguenots. Written for the American Sunday School Union, and revised by the committee of publication. Philadelphia: American Sunday School Union, 1844. 300 p. InRch; MBC; NPlaK; TxDaTS; WvSh. 44-3093

History of the Indian king Matamors, the last of the Wampanoags. Philadelphia: Turner and Fisher, 1844. 36 p. NN; RPB. 44-3094

The history of the Pilgrims. New York: Harper and brothers, 1844. 2v. NKeuC. 44-3095

Hitchcock, David K. Vindication of Russia and the emperor Nicholas.....Boston: Saxton, Peirce and company, 1844. 276 p. CtY; MeLewB; MH; NNS; PPL-R. 44-3096

Hitchcock, Edward, 1793-1864. Elementary geology. Third edition revised and improved. New York: Printed by Newman, 1844. 348 p. CU; ICJ; MoS; NCH; RPB. 44-3097

Hitchcock, Edward, 1793-1864. Elementary geology.... Third edition, revised and improved. New York: M.H. Newman, 1844. 352 p. A-GS; MSaP; OCY; PPi; TxU-T. 44-3098

Hitchcock, Edward, 1793-1864. Explanation of the geological map attached to the topographical map of Massachusetts. Prepared by Edward Hitchcock.... Boston: C. Hickling, 1844. 22 p. ICJ; MH; MSaP; MWA; NjR. 44-3099

Hitchcock, Ira Irvine. A new method of teaching book-keeping. Boston: Benjamin B. Mussey, 1844. 40 p. MB; MH; RPB. 44-3100

Hitchcock, Ira Irvine. A new method of teaching book-keeping.... stereotype edition. Hartford: Belknap and Hamersley, [1844] MH. 44-3101

Hobart, John Henry, 1775-1830. An apology for apostolic order and its advocates. In a series of letters addressed to Rev. John M. Mason. New York: Stanford and Swords; Philadelphia: G.S. Appleton, 1844. 273 p. DLC; LNB; MB; NNG; PWW. 44-3102

Hobart, John Henry, 1775-1830. An apology for apostolic order and its advocates. In a series of letters addressed to Rev. John M. Mason. Second edition. New York: Stanford and Swords; Philadelphia: G.S. Appleton, 1844. 273 p. CtHt; CtMw; IEG; MiU; WM. 44-3103

Hobart, John Henry, 1775-1830. An apology for apostolic order and its advocates. In a series of letters addressed to Rev. John M. Mason. Third edition. New York: Stanford and Swords; Philadelphia: G.S. Appleton, 1844. 273 p. CtMW; KyLo; NCH; OrP; TJaL. 44-3104

Hobart, John Henry, 1775-1830. Christian's manual of faith and devotion: containing dialogues and prayers suited to the various exercises of the Christian life, and an exhortation to ejaculatory and other prayers. Sixth edition. New York: Stanford and Swords, 1844. 442 p. MB; MH-AH; NN. 44-3105

Hobart, John Henry, 1775-1830. A companion for the festivals and fasts of the Protestant Episcopal Church in the United States of America. New York: Sanford and Swords, 1844. 331 p. LNH; MB; MdBD; PPLT; PPWe. 44-3106

Hobart, M. Ballard. Arithmetical calculator; containing a variety of abridged methods for computing numbers. Designed for the use of teachers, merchants, farmers, mechanics, etc. New York: published by the author, 1844. 96 p. DLC; NSyHi. 44-3107

Hodge, Charles, 1797-1878. A discourse delivered at the funeral of Mrs. Martha Rice, March 7, 1844. By Charles Hodge. Princeton: printed for private distribution, 1844. 16 p. ICU; MBAt; NjP; NjR; PPPrHi. 44-3108

Hodges, Richard Manning, 1794-1878. Address at the laying of the cornerstone of the First Congregational Society. Somerville, September 28, 1844. Cambridge: Metcalf and company, 1844. 19 p. MBC: MBNEH; MHi; NIC; RPB. 44-3109

Hodges, Richard Manning, 1794-1878. A collection of orders of exercises, etc. in church celebrations, mostly in the neigh-

borhood of Cambridge, Mass. 1844-1877. With the order of exercises at the dedication of the soldiers' lot by the Cambridge City government. [1844-1877] MH. 44-3110

Hodges, William. Infant baptism tested by scripture and history. Or the infant's claim to church membership defended and established, on testimony scriptural and historical. Philadelphia: Stavely and M'Calla; New York: Stanford and Swords; Alexandria: Bell and Entwisle, 1844. 252 p. CtHT; MBC; NcAS; ViRU. 44-3111

Hodgson, William. Select historical memoirs of the religious Society of Friends, commonly called Quakers. By William Hodgson, junior. Philadelphia: Joseph and William Kite, printers, 1844. 420 p. InRchE; NNUF; PPF; ViL. 44-3112

Hodgson, William Brown, 1800-1871. Notes on Northern Africa, the Sahara and Soudan, in relation to the ethnography, languages, history, political and social conditions, of the nations of those countries. New York: Wiley and Putnam, 1844. 107 p. CtY; DLC; MB; NIC. 44-3113

Hoffman, Charles Fenno, 1806-1884. The administration of Jacob Leisster, a chapter in American history. By Charles F. Hoffman. Boston: C.C. Little and J. Brown, 1844. 238 p. DLC; OClWHi; OOC. 44-3114

Hoffman, Charles Fenno, 1806-1884. An echo; or, borrowed notes for home circulation.... Philadelphia: Lindsay and Blakiston, 1844. 48 p. CSmH; ICU; MnU; PCA; RPB. 44-3115

Hoffman, David. Circular to students at law in the United States. Philadelphia: 1844. 11 p. MH-L. 44-3116

Hoffman's Albany directory and city register, for the years 1844-1845. Compiled and published by L.G. Hoffman. Albany: 1844. 41-356 p. MHi; NAl; NN. 44-3117

Hofland, Barbara Wreaks Hoole, 1770-1844. Farewell tales. Boston, 1844. MBAt. 44-3118

Hofland, Barbara Wreaks Hoole, 1770-1844. Integrity. A tale. Boston: T.H. Carter and company, and Benjamin B. Mussey, 1844. 155 p. MeBaT. 44-3119

Hofland, Barbara Wreaks Hoole, 1770-1844. Moderation, a tale. Boston: J.H. Carter and company, and Benjamin B. Mussey, 1844. 148 p. MMedHi. 44-3120

Hofland, Barbara Wreaks Hoole, 1770-1884. The unloved one, a domestic story. New York: 1844. 160 p. CSto; DLC; IaDu; ViU. 44-3121

Hogg, James, 1770-1835. Winter evening tales. Hartford: S. Andrus and son, 1844. 2 v. CtY; IaMp. 44-3122

Holdich, Joseph, 1804-1893. Questions on historical parts of the Old Testament for Bible classes by Rev. J. Holdich. New York: J. Collord, 1844. 194 p. MBNMHi. 44-3123

Holland, J.G. Bitter-sweet, a poem, by J.G. Holland. New York: Charles Scribner, 1844. 220 p. NNebg. 44-3124

Holland, John, 1794-1872. Memoirs of the life and ministry of the Rev. John Summerfield.... With an introductory letter by James Montgomery.... Sixth edition. New York: D. Mead, 1844. 460 p. CtMW; GEU; IEG; LNB; MdBD. 44-3125

Holland Patent. Church of Christ. The articles of faith and covenant, of the Church of Christ, Holland Patent. Adopted May 3, 1844. Utica: R.W. Roberts, printers, 1844. 10 p. NUt-Hi. 44-3126

Holley, Orville Luther, 1791-1861. The picturesque tourist; being a guide through the northern and eastern states and Canada: ....New York: J. Disturnell, 1844. 336 p. IU; MWA; PU; RPB; WHi. 44-3127

Holley, Platt Tyler. Death, the Christian's pain. A sermon delivered at the funeral of Deacon Samuel Wilcox. Hartford: press of Case, Tiffany and Burnham, 1844. 16 p. ICT; MBC; NN; RPB. 44-3128

Hollis, New Hampshire. Annual report 1844, 1849, 1857-1859, 1861-. Nashua: 1844-. Nh-Hi. 44-3129

Holmes, Oliver Wendell, 1809-1894. The position and prospects of the medical student. An address delivered before the Boylston Medical Society of Harvard University, January 12, 1844. First edition. Boston: J. Putnam, printer, 1844. 28 p. CSt; DLC; NhD; PU; WMAM. 44-3130

Holthaus, Peter Diedrich. Wanderings of a journey-man tailor through Europe and the east, during the years 1824 to 1840. By P.D. Holthaus.... Translated from the third German edition, by William Howitt.... New York: J. Winchester, [1844?] 97 p. CtY; NNS; WHi. 44-3131

Homans, John. The character and qualifications of the good physician. Read before the Massachusetts Medical Society at their annual meeting, May 29, 1844. Boston: Willian S. Damrell, 1844. 36 p. MBAt; MDeep; MH-M; MWA. 44-3132

Homerus. The first three books of Homer's Iliad to which are appended English notes, critical and explanatory, a metrical index and Homeric glossary. By Charles Anthon. New York: Harper and brothers, 1844. 599 p. CtY; NjP OWoC; TSewU; ViU. 44-3133

Homerus. Homer. Translated by Alexander Pope, esq. New York: Harper and brothers, 1844. 3 v. MBBC: Mlow; NCoh. 44-3134

Homerus. The Illiad of Homer, from the text of Wolf, with English notes. Edited by C.C. Felton. Boston: Munroe, 1844. 476 p. ArU; GEU; NjMD; PWW; TxU-T. 44-3135

Homerus. The odyssey of Homer, according to the text of Wolf; with notes, for the use of schools and colleges. Sixteenth edition. New York: Leavitt and Allen, 1844-1859. 568 p. NTRS. 44-3136

Honesdale, Pennsylvania. Presbyterian Church. Church manual for the use of the Presbyterian Church in Honesdale, Pennsylvania. Prepared by Henry A. Rowland, pastor, and printed by order of the session, October, 1844. New York: J.F. Trow and company, printer, 1844. 23 p. NNUT. 44-3137

An honest appeal to every voter. The Bible in the school. New York: 1844. KyLx; MB; NjR; NN; PPL. 44-3138

Honker, Edward William. Duties to the aged. Sermon delivered... in Bennington, Vermont, December 14, 1843. Bennington, Vermont: Haswell and Bushnell, 1844. MB; MWiW; NBLIHI; VtHi. 44-3139

Honorable A. Porter. Brief notice of his life [Nashville?] 1844. 10 p. T. 44-3140

Hood, Samuel, 1800?-1875. A brief account of the society of the Friendly Sons of St. Patrick. Philadelphia: By order of the Hibernain Society, 1844. 112 p. IaCrM; MB; NjP; PPA. 44-3141

Hood, Thomas, 1799-1845. A plea of the midsummer fairies [and miscellaneous poems] ....[New York: 1844] 16 p. CtY; DLC; MH; MWH; OO. 44-3142

Hood, Thomas, 1799-1845. Tylney hall. By T. Hood. Philadelphia: Farrett and company, 1844. 151 p. CtY; NjP; NN; RPB. 44-3143

Hood, Thomas, 1799-1845. Whims and oddities; in prose and verse. New edition. Philadelphia: Lea, 1844. MB; MBL; MNotnW. 44-3144

Hook, Theodore Edward, 1788-1841. Merton; or, "there's many a slip 'twixt the cup and the lip." A novel. By Theodore Hook.... Complete in one volume. Philadelphia: Carey and Hart, 1844. 106 p. MBL. 44-3145

Hook, Theodore Edward, 1788-1841. Peregrine Bunce or Settled at last, a novel. First American edition. Philadelphia: Lea and Blanchard, 1844. 140 p. CtY; MdBP; MnU; PBm. 44-3146

Hooker, Edward William. Duties to the aged: a sermon delivered at the funeral of General David Robinson, Bennington, Vermont, December 14, 1843.... Published by request. Bennington, [Vermont]: Haswell and Bushnell, 1844. 16 p. MB; MWiW; NBLiHi; Vt; VtHi. 44-3147

Hooker, Edward William. Memoir of Mrs. Sarah Lanman Smith, late of the mission in Syria, under the direction of the American Board of Commissioners for Foreign Missions. Second edition. Boston: T.R. Marvin, 1844. 306 p. MBAt; MPiB; NNMr; OO; PP. 44-3148

Hooker, Edward William. A sermon occasioned by the catastrophe on board the United States ship of war Princeton. Troy, New York: press of N. Tuttle, 1844. 24 p. CtHC; ICN; MBC; MnHi; NjPT. 44-3149

Hooker, Herman, 1804-1865. The philosophy of unbelief in moral and religion, as discoverable in the faith and character of men. By the Rev. Herman Hooker, M.A. Hartford: S. Andrus and son, 1844. 286 p. InID; LN; MeBa; OCel; RNR. 44-3150

Hooker, Richard, 1553 or 4-1600. The works of Mr. Richard Hooker: with an account of his life and death. By Isaac Walton. First American from the last Oxford edition. New York: D. Appleton and company, 1844. 2 v. DLC; InCW; LNB; MiD; PPL-R. 44-3151

Hooker, Richard, 1553 or 4-1600. The works of that learned and judicious divine, Mr. Richard Hooker: with an ac-

count of his life and death, by Isaac Walton. Arranged by the Rev. John Kebble.... First American from the last Oxford edition. New York: Appleton, 1844. 2 v. CtHT; ICT; RP; RPAt; WBelo-C. 44-3152

Hooker, Worthington, 1806-1867. Dissertation on the respect due to the medical profession, and the reasons that it is not awarded by the community. Norwich: Cooley, 1844. 28 p. CtSoP; MB; MWA; NNN. 44-3153

Hooksett, [New Hampshire] Annual report, 1844-64, 1866. Manchester: 1844. Nh-Hi. 44-3154

Hooper, Robert, 1773-1835. Lexicon medicum: or medical dictionary: containing an explanation of terms...Thirteenth American edition from the last London edition with additions. By Samuel Akerly. New York: Harper and brothers, 1844. 2v. in 1. CBPSR; MH-M; MoSU-M; OCGHM. 44-3155

Hope, J. Principles and illustrations of pathological anatomy; being a complete series of colored lithographic drawings. First American edition. Edited by L. M. Lawson. Cincinnati: Desilver and Burr; Lexington: Skillman and son, 1844. KyLoJM; KyLxT; MoSw-M; NBMS; NNN. 44-3156

Hopkins, Asa T. Trial of the Rev. Asa T. Hopkins pastor of the First Presbyterian Church, Buffalo before a special meeting of the Buffalo Presbytery commencing October 29 and ending October 31, 1844. Buffalo, 1844. DLC; MBC; NIC-L. 44-3157

Hopkins, John Henry, 1792-1868. The

novelties which disturb our peace. A letter addressed to the bishops, clergy and laity of the Protestant Episcopal Church. Philadelphia: H. Hooker, 1844. 4 v. in 1. CtY; ICU; IEG; MB. 44-3158

Hopkins, John Henry, 1792-1868. The novelties which disturb our peace. A letter addressed to the bishops, clergy and laity of the Protestant Episcopal Church. Philadelphia: H. Hooker, 1844. 71 p. DLC; IEG; MH; NcD; PPL. 44-3159

Hopkins, John Henry, 1792-1868. The novelties which disturb our peace. A letter addressed to the bishops, clergy and laity of the Protestant Episcopal Church. Philadelphia: James M. Campbell and company; New York: Saxton and Miles, 1844. NjNbT; PPRETS; ViU. 44-3160

Hopkins, John Henry, 1792-1868. Sixteen lectures on the causes, principles, and results of the British reformation. By John Henry Hopkins, D.D. ....Philadelphia: J. M. Campbell and company; New York: Saxton and Miles, 1844. 387 p. InID; MdBD; NNUT; PPLT; TxShA. 44-3161

Hopkins, Mark. The law of progress of the race: an address. New York: 1844. PPL. 44-3162

Hopkinton, Massachusetts. An account of the state of the treasury and report of the expenses of the town of Hopkinton, February 20, 1844. West Brookfield: C.A. Mirick, 1844. 12 p. MAshlHi. 44-3163

Hopkinton, [New Hampshire] Superintending School Committee. Annual report, 1843/4, '58/9, '59/60, '68/9. Concord: 1844-69. Nh; Nh-Hi. 44-3164

Hopper, Isaac Tatem. New York Association of Friends. Testimony for the relief of those held in slavery, etc., concerning Charles Marriott, deceased. New York: 1844. 15 p. DeWi; MH; PSC-Hi. 44-3165

Hoppin, Frederic, 1815-1873. Escape of Captain Wharton [New York, 1844] RPB. 44-3166

Horace. The works of Horace, with English notes, critical and explanatory. By Charles Anthon, LL.D. ....A new edition, with corrections and improvements. New York: Harper and brothers, 1844. 681 p. ScCliP. 44-3167

Horatius Flaccus, Quintus. Works of Horace, translated by Philip Francis, D.D. To which is prefixed the life of the translator....New York: Harper, 1844. 2 v. CLSU; OHi. 44-3168

Horatius Flaccus, Quintus. Works of Horace, with English notes, critical and explanatory, by Charles Anthon. New edition. New York: Harper, 1844. 681 p. NJam; PLT; PU; TJaL; ViU. 44-3169

Horne, Richard Henry, 1803-1844. A new spirit of the age....New York: Harper and brothers, 1844. 365 p. CU; IaDmD; RLa. 44-3170

Horne, Richard Henry, 1803-1884. A new spirit of the age. Edited by R.H. Horne....New York: J.C. Riker, 1844. 364 p. ArU; GAuY; Mi; PEal; TSewU. 44-3171

Horne, Thomas Hartwell, 1780-1862. An introduction to the critical study and knowledge of the Holy Scriptures. New York: Published by Robert Carter, 1844.

2 v. MBNEB; Nh; OO; OrU; PPWe. 44-3172

Horne, Thomas Hartwell, 1780-1862. An introduction to the critical study and knowledge of the Holy Scriptures.... New edition, from the eighth London edition, corrected and enlarged. New York: Robert Carter, 1844. 2 v. ArCH; CBPac; KyLoS; NbCrD; PV. 44-3173

Horne, Thomas Hartwell, 1780-1862. Protestant memorial; comprising 1. A concise history of the reformation. 2. The antiquity of the religion of Protestants demonstrated. 3. The safety of continuing in the Protesant Church. 4. Romanism contradictory to the Bible. New York: 1844. 149 p. ICBB; ICP; MWA; OCMtSM; PPL-R. 44-3174

Horne, Thomas Hartwell, 1780-1862. Mariolatry: or, Facts and evidences demonstrating the worship of the Blessed Virgin Mary. Hartford: H.S. Parsons, 1844. 98 p. CtY; NBuG; NN; PPPrHi; RPB. 44-3175

Horne, Thomas Hartwell, 1780-1862. Mariolatry; or facts and evidences demonstrating the worship of the blessed Virgin Mary by the Church of Rome. First American, corrected and enlarged by the Rev. Samuel Farmer Jarvis. Hartford: Parsons, 1844. [13]-98 p. CtHT; DLC; NjR; NNG; PPL. 44-3176

Horne, Thomas Hartwell, 1780-1862. Protestant memorial.... From the ninth London edition. New York: 1844. 148 p. CtY; MWA. 44-3177

Horner, James M. Rights of adopted citizens and the claims of the "natives" il-lustrated and set forth. New York, 1844. 24 p. NN; NNC; RPB. 44-3178

Hoshour, Samuel Klinefetter, 1803-1883. Letters to Esq. Pedant, in the East, by Lorenzo Altisonant [pseud.] an emigrant to the West. Published for the benefit of youth, by a lover of the studious. Canbridge City, Iowa: D.K. Winder, printer, 1844. 64 p. CtY; IU; MiU-C; OC; WHi. 44-3179

Hosmer, William Henry Cuyler, 1814-1877. Yonnondio, or warriors of the Genesee: a tale of the seventeenth century. ....New York: Wiley and Putnam; Rochester [New York]: D.M. Dewey, 1844. 239 p. CU; DLC; MnU; RPB; WHi. 44-3180

Hotchkiss, Frederick William, 1763?-1844. Contemplations of an aged pastor on completing the sixtieth year of his ministry. A sermon preached at Saybrook, Connecticut, September 24, 1843... Senior Pastor of the First Congregational Church in that place to which is appended a brief notice of his life, death and general character. New York: S.W. Benedict and company, 1844. 40 p. CtY; ICT; MH; NjPT; PPPrHi. 44-3181

Hough, Franklin B. Results of a series of meteorological observations made in obedience to instructions from the regents of the University at sundry academies in the state of New York from 1826 to 1850 incl. Compiled by Franklin B. Hough. Albany: 1844? 3 v. PPAN. 44-3182

Houghton, D.C. A discourse, delivered on occasion of Thanksgiving, at Honeoye Falls, New York, December 14, 1843, by Rev. D.C. Houghton, M.A. Rochester:

David Hoyt, printer, 1844. 16 p. IEG; MnHi; Nh; NjPT; OO. 44-3183

House, E.G. Botanic family friend. Being a complete guide to the new system of thomsonian medical practice, explained and enlarged. Boston: 1844. 300 p. DSG; MBP. 44-3184

Housekeeper's almanac, or, young wife's oracle for 1845. New York: [1844] MWA. 44-3185

Housekeeper's annual and ladies' register for 1845. Boston, Massachusetts: T.H. Carter and company, [1844] MWA. 44-3186

Houston, George Smith, 1811-1879. Speech on the civil and diplomatic appropriation bill, in the House, June 4, 1844. Washington: Printed at the Globe office, 1844. 16 p. M; TxU. 44-3187

Houston, James Alexander. An address, explanatory of the principles and objects of the United Brothers of Temperance... New York: Herald Book and Job Printing office, 1844. 10 p. CtY; DLC; MH-AH; PPPrHi. 44-3188

Houston, Thomas. Divine commendation of Abraham, or, parental duties and the blessings resulting from their faithful performance.... Philadelphia: Presbyterian board of publication, 1844. 224 p. ICP; PU; ScCliTO; ViRut. 44-3189

Hovey and Company. Boston. Catalogue of Hovey and company: fruits. Boston: 1844-5. MHi. 44-3190

Hovey and Company. Boston. A descriptive catalogue of fruits cultivated and for sale by Hovey and Company at their Cambridge nurseries. Boston: Hovey and company, 1844. 17 p. MB; MWA. 44-3191

Hovey and company, Boston. Hovey and company's descriptive catalogue of roses; ....at the Cambridge nurseries. For the autumn of 1843 and spring of 1844. In two divisions. Boston: Hovey and company, [1844] MB; VtMidb. 44-3192

Howard, John. Capital punishment unjust and inexpedient. New York: published at the Sun office, 1844. 36 p. CtHT; NjR. 44-3193

Howard, O.O. Major General Howard's address. Philadelphia: 1844. MB. 44-3194

Howard, Roger S. A few of the "hows" of school-keeping; a lecture delivered before the American Institute of Instruction, at their fourteenth anniversary, at Pittsfield, Massachusetts. Boston: W.D. Ticknor and company, 1844. 28 p. MH; NjR. 44-3195

Howe, George. A discourse on theological education; delivered on the dicentenary of the Westminister Assembly of Divines, July, 1843. New York: Trow and company, 1844. 243 p. CtHC; GDecCT; MBC; NNUT; TxAuPT. 44-3196

Howe, George. Theological education. New York: Leavitt, Trow and company, and M. W. Dodd, 1844. 243 p. NcMHi. 44-3197

Howe, Henry, 1816-1893. Memoirs of the most eminent American mechanics: also, lives of distinguished European mechanics; together with a collection of anecdotes, descriptions, &c., &c. Relating to the mechanic arts.... New York: Alexander V. Blake, 1844. 482 p. CSfCW; DLC; MiU; MoSM; Nh-Hi. 44-3198

Howe, Leonard and Company. A catalogue of the most curious, interesting and valuable library.... [Boston: 1844] 40 p. DLC. 44-3199

Howitt, Mary Botham, 1799-1888. child's poetry book... New York: J. Mowatt and company, 1844. 60 p. CtY; MNHi. 44-3200

Howitt, Mary Botham, 1799-1888. The favorite scholar by Mary Howitt and other tales by Mr. S.C. Hall, Charles Cowden Clark, and James D. Haas. New York: C.S. Francis and company; Boston: J.H. Francis, 1844. 175 p. NNU-W. 44-3201

Howitt, Mary Botham, 1799-1888. Love and money, an everyday tale. New York: Appleton, 1844. 173 p. MDux; NNC; NN; OO. 44-3202

Howitt, Mary Botham, 1799-1888. Lowing and reaping; or what will come of it. New York: 1844. 3 p. RPAt. 44-3203

Howitt, Mary Botham, 1799-1888. Marien's pilgrimage. A poem... [New York: 1844] 16 p. MB; NN. 44-3204

Howitt, Mary Botham, 1799-1888. My own story; or autobiography of a child. New York: D. Appleton and company, 1844. MBL; MH; PSC-Hi. 44-3205

Howitt, Mary Botham, 1799-1888. The poems of Mary Howitt. With a memoir....

Philadelphia: J. Locken, 184. 303 p. CtY; KyDC; MH; NJam; NNUT. 44-3206

Howitt, Mary Botham, 1799-1888. Sowing and reaping, or, what will come of it. Boston: J. Munroe and company, 1844. MF; MH. 44-3207

Howitt, William, 1792-1879. The life and adventures of Jack of the Mill: commonly called Lord Othmill, created for his eminent services, Baron Waldeck and Knight of Kitcottie, a fireside story by William Howitt. New York: Harper and brothers, 1844. MH; NN; NRSB; PU; RPB. 44-3208

Howland, G. and E. Howland's Albany almanac for 1845, being [till July 4] the sixty-ninth year of American independence. Calculated for the meridian of Albany.... Sandy Hill, New York: G. and E. Howland, [1844] 36 p. NGlf. 44-3209

Howland, Mary W. The infant school manual, or teacher's assistant. Containing a view of the system of infant schools. Also a variety of useful lessons; for the use of teachers. Eleventh edition. Worcester: Warren Lazell, 1844. 274 p. ICU; MH-Ed; MWHi. 44-3210

Hoyle, Edmund, 1672-1769. Hoyle's games: containing the established rules and practice of whist, quadrille, piquet, quinze, ...revised edition. Philadelphia: Henry F. Anners, 1844. 256 p. MWiW; NNS. 44-3211

Hoyt, Nathan, 1793-1866. History of a church in the south. Philadelphia: Presbyterian Board of Publication, 1844. 11 p. CU; DLC; MeBat; NcD. 44-3212

Hoyt, Ralph, 1806-1878. A chaunt of

life, and other poems, with sketches and essays. In six parts. New York: Piercy and Reed, 1844. 6 v. CtY; IU; MB; NBuG; TxU. 44-3213

Hubard, Edward W. Speech of Mr. Hubard, of Virginia, on the tariff, delivered in the House of Representatives, May 1, 1844. 15 p. MH; MHi; NcHic; NBu; Vi. 44-3214

Hubbell, William Wheeler. Remarks of the subject of his patent on fire arms and his explosive destructive concussion shell. Philadelphia: 1844. 14 p. DLC; MnHi; NN. 44-3215

Hudson, Charles. Letters on the Vermont and Massachusetts Railroad, addressed to Hon. Thomas H. Perkins. Boston: 1844. 23 p. MB; MHi. 44-3216

Hudson, David. Memoir of Jemima Wilkinson, a preacheress of the eighteenth century; containing an authentic narrative of her life and character, and of the rise, progress and conclusion of her ministry. Bath, New York: R.L. Underhill and company, 1844. 288 p. CtY; DLC; IaU; MiU-C; PHi. 44-3217

Hudson, New York. Presbytery. [Presbyterian Church in the United States of America] The support due to the Christian ministry. A pastoral letter from the Presbytery of Hudson to the churches under their care. Goshen, New York: Mead, printer, 1844. PPPrHi. 44-3218

Hudson River. The northern traveller... Hudson River guide... New York: 1844. 84 p. MWA. 44-3219

Hufeland, Christopher William, 1762-1836. Enchiridion medicum; or, the prac-

tice of medicine.... by C.W. Hufeland.... from the sixth German edition. Translated by Caspar Bruchhausen.... Revised.... by Robert Nelson, M.D. Second edition. New York: William Radde; London: H. Balliere, 1844. 630, 79 p. DLC; NhD; NNNAM; PPCP; PPiAM. 44-3220

Hufeland, Christopher Wilhelm, 1762-1836. The three cardinal means of the art of healing. ....New York: W. Radde, [1844] 79 p. CSt-L; DLC; PPiAM. 44-3221

Hughes, F.W. Report of the discussion at Pottsville, August 19, 1844, between F.W.H. and J.L. Clarkson on course of H. Clay and Jas. K. Polk, relative to Protective System. Philadelphia: 1844. 27 p. PHi. 44-3222

Hughes, George W. Report relative to the working of copper ore. Washington: U.S. War Department, 1844. 58 p. NNC; PPFrankI. 44-3223

Hughes, John, 1794-1864. Importance of a Christian basis for the science of political economy, 1844. 27 p. MBC. 44-3224

Hughes, John, 1794-1864. A lecture on the importance of a Christian basis for the science of political economy, and its application to the affairs of life. New York: J. Winchester, [1844] 27 p. ICU; MoSU; NjR; PU; TxU. 44-3225

Hughes, John, 1794-1864. A lecture on the importance of a Christian basis for the science of political economy, and its application to the affairs of life. Delivered before the Calvert Institute, Baltimore, and the Carroll Institute,

Philadelphia, on the 17th and 18th, January, 1844, by Rt. Rev. Dr. Hughes, Bishop of New York. New York: J. Winchester, [1844] 27 p. ICLoy; MdHi. 44-3226

Hughes, John, 1797-1864. Letter including a vindication of the author from the infamous charges made against him by James Gordon Bennett, William Stone and others. New York: 1844. PPL. 44-3227

Hughes, John, 1797-1864. A letter on the moral causes that have produced the evil spirit of the times; addressed to the Hon. James Harper, mayor of New York, including a vindication of the author, from the infamous charges made against him, by Jame Gordon Bennet, William L. Stone, and others, by the Right Rev. Dr. Hughes.... New York: J. Winchester, 1844. 23 p. MB; MWA; NN; OCLaw; PPL; PU. 44-3228

Hughes, John, 1797-1864. Second letter on the moral causes that have produced the evil spirit of the times.... By the Right Rev. Dr. Hughes, bishop of New York. New York: J. Winchester, [1844?] 24 p. MdBLC; MdHi; MiD-B; OClWHi; PPL. 44-3229

Hughs, Mary. The ornaments discovered: A story founded on facts. New York: Harper and brothers, 1844. 194 p. OSW; ScGrw. 44-3230

Hugo, Victor Marie, 1802-1885. Bug-Jargal; or a tale of the massacre in St. Domingo, 1791. Translated from the sixteenth French edition. New York: J. Morvatt and company, 1844. 80 p. DLC; KyU. 44-3231

Hugo, Victor Marie, 1802-1885. The hunchback of Notre Dame. A romance of the time of Louis XI. Translated by Frederic Shoberl... Philadelphia: Lea and Blanchard, 1844. 154 p. DLC; KSalW; OU; PPL. 44-3232

Huie, James A. The history of the Jews, from the taking of Jerusalem by Titus, to the present time, comprising a narrative of their wanderings... Third American from the Edinburgh edition. Greatly enlarged by the publisher... Preface by William Jenks. Boston: M.A. Berk, 1844. 400 p. FSar; MeBa; MnHi; NNUT; OCl. 44-3233

Hulett, Thomas G. Every man his own guide to the falls of Niagara, or the whole story in few words... to which is added a chronological table, containing the principal events of the late war between the United States and Great Britain. Fourth edition. Buffalo: Printed by Faxon and company, 1844. 128 p. DLC; KyHi; MH; NN; PHi. 44-3234

Hulett, W.E. Every stranger; his own guide to Niagara Falls. The latest and most comprehensive work yet before the public. Containing a table of distances, and the intermediate places on the five principal routes leading from Niagara Falls to Albany, via Montreal, Quebec and Saratoga Springs, Buffalo: Steele's Press, 1844. [4] [5]-32 p. MB; MH; MWA; OClWHi. 44-3235

Humboldt, Alexander Von, 1769-1859. Kosmos Entwurf einer physichen weltberchreibung. Philadelphia [1844] 636 p. MH-Z. 44-3236

Hume, David, 1711-1776. The history of England, from the invasion of Julius

Caesar, to the revolution in 1688. By David Hume, esq. ....Philadelphia: Thomas Davis, 1844. 4 v. NbOC. 44-3237

Hume, David, 1711-1776. The history of England, from the invasion of Julius Caesar, to the revolution in 1688. By David Hume, esq. With notes and references, exhibiting the most important differences between this author and Dr. Lingard. Philadelphia: Davis, 184. 2 v. MFi; MNan; OC; OWerv; TxU. 44-3238

Humphrey, Heman, 1779-1861. Revival conversations. Boston: Samuel N. Dickinson, printer, 1844. 168 p. IaMp; ICP; KyLo; MPiB; NNUT. 44-3239

Humphrey, Heman, 1779-1861. Woman that feareth the Lord. A discourse delivered at the funeral of Mrs. D.W.V. Fiske, February 21, 1844. By Rev. Heman Humphrey, D.D. ....Amherst, [Massachusetts]: J. S. and C. Adams, 1844. 48 p. CtHC; IaMp; MH-AH; MWA. 44-3240

Hunt, James H. A history of the Mormon war, with a prefix, embracing the rise, progress, and peculiar tenets of Mormom doctrine; with an examination of the Book of Mormon. St Louis: Printed by Ustick and Davies, 1844. 304 p. CtY; CU; DLC; IHi; MB. 44-3241

Hunt, James H. Mormonism: embracing the origin, rise and progress of the sect, with an examination of the Book of Mormon; also their troubles in Missouri, and final expulsion from the state by James H. Hunt. With an appendix, giving an account of the late disturbance in Illinois, which resulted in the death of Joseph and Hyrum Smith, by G.W.

Westbrook. St Louis: Printed by Ustick and Davis, 1844. 304 p. ICU; NjP; NN; OCX; UU. 44-3242

Hunt, James Henry Leigh, 1784-1859. The indicator. New York: Wiley and Putnam, 1844. 236, 257 p. PPP. 44-3243

Hunt, James Henry Leigh, 1784-1859. Rimini, and other poems, by Leigh Hunt. Boston: W.D. Ticknor and company, 1844. 123 p. IaU; NUt; OCl; PU; RP. 44-3244

Hunt, Washington. Remarks [of Mr. Hunt, of New York] in the House of Representatives, February 9, 1844. On the resolution of the majority of the committee on elections, declaring that the representatives from New Hampshire, Georgia, Mississippi, and Missouri, elected by general ticket, are entitled to their seats. [Washington: 1844] 8 p. MH. 44-3245

Hunter, Henry. Sacred biography; or, the history of the patriarchs. To which is added the history of Deborah, Ruth, and Hannah, and also the history of Jesus Christ. New York: Harper and brothers, 1844. 596 p. CoDI; IaCrC; KyDC; PWW; ViRU. 44-3246

Hunter, William, 1811-1877. Select melodies; comprising the best of those hymns and spiritual songs in common use, not to be found in the standard Methodist Episcopal hymn book, as also a number of original pieces. Cincinnati: the Methodist Book Concern, 1844. 320 p. MiU; RPB. 44-3247

Huntington, Frederic Dan, 1819-1904. Christian doctrine of charity. Sermon delivered before the Howard

Benevolent Society on their 32nd anniversary, at the Old South Church, Boston, January 15, 1844. Boston: Crosby, 1844. 26 p. CBPac; DLC; ICMe; MH-AH; MiD-B. 44-3248

Huntington, Frederic Dan, 1819-1904. The signification and value of "a good life." Printed for the American Unitarian Association. Boston: J. Munroe and company, 1844. 14 p. ICMe; MeBat; MH-AH; MW; PPL. 44-3249

Huntington, Frederic Dan, 1819-1904. Tract, signification and value of a good life. Boston: American Unitarian Association, 1844. MDeeP. 44-3250

Huntington, Gurdon. The guests of Brazil, or, the martyrdom of Frederick. A tragedy. New York: Burgess, Stringer and company, 1844. 70 p. ICU; MBAt; MH; MWA; RPB. 44-3251

Hunt's almanack for 1845. Philadelphia: Uriah Hunt, [1844] MWA. 44-3252

Hurd, John Russell. Hyponia; or thoughts on a spiritual understanding... of the Apocalypce, or book of revelations; with some remarks upon the Parousia, or second coming of the Lord Jesus Christ. New York: Leavitt, Trow and company, 1844. 707 p. IaGG; MBC; MiU; NBu; ViAl. 44-3253

Hurlbut, E.P. Civil office and political ethics for the use of citizens and schools. New York: Wells, 1844. 216 p. MoSU. 44-3254

Huron Institute, Milan, Ohio. Catalogue of the officers and students of Huron Institute, July, 1844. Milan: Clark

Waggoner, printer, 1844. 8 p. OClWHi. 44-3255

Hussey, Ebenezer. The religion of slavery. Boston: New England Antislavery Tract Association, [1844] 4 p. MH. 44-3256

Huston, Felix, 1800-1857. Gen. Huston's letter to a committee of the Democratic Association of Clairborne County, Mississippi giving his reasons for desiring the immediate annexation of Texas. [Natches: Mississippi Free Trader, 1844] 8 p. DLC; NcD. 44-3257

Huston, Robert. Scripture characters: letters in the distinguishing excellencies of remarkable scripture passages, by Rev. Robert Huston. New York: G. Lane and C.B. Trippett, 1844. 245 p. DLC; KBB. 44-3258

Hutchins improved almanac... for the year of our Lord 1845, being the first after bissextile, or leap year, and [until July 4th] the 69th year of American independence... By David Young... New York: H. and S. Raynor [1844] 35 p. NjMo; WHi; NjMo. 44-3259

Hutchins improved almanack. By David Young. New Brunswick: John Techeme [sic] 1844. MWA. 44-3260

Hutchins' improved for 1845. By David Young. New York: printed for the booksellers by Mahlon Day and company [1844] MB; MWA. 44-3261

Hutchins improved for 1845. By David Young. New York: Upper Aquebogue, Long Island: G.I. Wells, [1844] MWA. 44-3262

Hutchinson, Jesse, Jr. "Get off the track!" A song for emancipation, sung by the Hutchinsons. Boston: 1844. 5 p. MHi; MNF. 44-3263

Hutchinson Family. Programme of concert, November 11, 1844. Albany: 1844. MHi. 44-3264

The hyacinth; or affection's gift. A Christmas, New Year, and birthday present for 1845-54. Philadelphia: H. F. Anners, 1844-1853. 10 v. ICN; ICU; PHi; TxU; WU. 44-3265

Hydropathy: Water cure for ladies. New York: 1844. 156 p. MWA. 44-3266

Hymns for Sabbath schools. Selected from various works. Revised, with alterations and additions. Racine: 1844. WHi. 44-3267

Hymns for Sunday schools, selected from various authors. New York: G. Lane C.B. Tippett, 1844. 208 p. RPB. 44-3268

Hymns in the Cherokee language. Park Hill: 1844. NN. 44-3269

Hymns in the Ojibway language. Boston: 1844. NN. 44-3270

Hymns of zion, with appropriate music... Eighth edition... Philadelphia: Gihon, Fairchild and company, 1844. 216 p. IGK; MMeT-HI. 44-3271

The hypocrite, or sketches of American society from a residence of forty years. By Oesop [pseud.] New York: T. Fox and company, 1844. MB; MH; N. 44-3272

I

Illinois and Michigan Canal. Documents relating to the negotiation which has been carried on with the foreign creditors of Illinois, for the purpose of raising funds to complete this work: consisting of certain publications contained in the Journal of Commerce... and the reply of Governor Davis to the statements of Mr. Ryan. Boston: 1844. 44 p. CtY; DLC; ICN; MiD; N. 44-3273

Illinois. Eighth annual report of the acting commissioner of the Illinois and Michigan Canal, to the general assembly. December 18, 1844. Springfield: Walter and Weber, Public printers, 1844. 98 p. IaHi. 44-3274

Illinois. Journal of the House of Representatives of the 14th General Assembly of the State of Illinois at their regular session held at Springfield, December 2, 1844. Springfield: Walters and Weber, 1844. 633 p. IHi. 44-3275

Illinois. Journal of the Senate of the fourteenth general assembly of the state of Illinois at their regular session, begun and held at Springfield, December 2, 1844. Springfield: Walters and Weber, Public printers, 1844. 469 p. IAIS; IHi; Mi. 44-3276

Illinois. Message [of the Governor] in relation to the disturbances in Hancock County, December 23, 1844. Springfield, 1844. MBAt. 44-3277

Illinois. Report of the Auditor of Public Accounts, of the state of Illinois, transmitted to both houses of the general assembly, December 6, 1844. Springfield: Walters and Weber, Public printers, 1844. 32 p. L; R; W. 44-3278

Illinois. Report of the Commissioner of the State Bank of Illinois, in relation to the affairs of the bank. December 20, 1844. Springfield, 1844. 7 p. WHi. 44-3279

Illinois. Reports of cases argued and determined in the Supreme Court of the state of Illinois. by J. Young Scammon, Counsellor at Law. Chicago: Stephen F. Gale and company; Galena: Augustus H. Burley, 1844. CoU; F-SC; Ia. 44-3280

Illinois College, Jacksonville, Illinois. Catalogue of the officers and students... year ending June, 1844. Alton: printed at the Telegraph Office, 1844. 24 p. IHi; OCHP. 44-3281

The illuminated American primer, being an introduction to Mrs. Sigourney's pictorial reader: for the use of schools. New York: Turner and Hayden, 1844. 36 p. Mh; NhD; NN. 44-3282

The illuminated American primer, being an introduction to Mrs. Sigourney's pictorial reader: for the use of schools. Fifth edition. Claremont,

New Hampshire: Claremont Manufacturing Company, 1844. MH. 44-3283

Illustrated astronomy; a pictorial display of the astronomical phenomena of the universe, with sixty-three colored plates, illustrating a series of familiar discourses on astronomy. New edition. New York: R.W. Barnard and company, 1844. 99 p. MWHi; NN. 44-3284

Illustrated Christian almanack for 1845. By David Young. New York, New York: American Tract Society [1844] MWA. 44-3285

Illustrations of the prayer book by a layman... Philadelphia: George and Wayne, 1844. 187 p. NNG. 44-3286

Imitatio Christi. The imitation of Christ... By Thomas A Kempis. Rendered into English from the original Latin by John Payne. With an introductory essay by Thomas Chalmers, of Glasgow. New York: Collins, brother and company, 1844. 229 p. MiU; MWA; NNC; OO; PPAmP. 44-3287

Imitatio Christi. The imitation of Christ in four books. By Thomas A Kempis. New York: D. Appleton, 1844. 324 p. CtHT; IU; MWA; OrSaW; UU. 44-3288

Imitatio Christi. The imitation of Christ in four books. By Thomas A Kempis. Translated from the original Latin by the R. Rev. Challoner. To which is added the life of the author. New York: Edward Dunnigan, 1844. 8-312 p. IaDuMtC; MsY; TxBry. 44-3289

Imitatio Christi. The imitation of Christ in three books. By Thomas A Kempis. Rendered into English from the original

Latin by John Payne. With an introductory essay by Thomas Chalmers, of Glasgow. A new edition; edited by Howard Malcolm. Boston: Gould, Kendall and Lincoln, 1844. [11]-228 p. KWS; NHC-S; PCA; ScCoB. 44-3290

The improved housewife, or book of receipts; with engravings. By a married lady... Hartford: 1844. 213 p. DLC; MU; NNT-C; ViSwc. 44-3291

The improved housewife, or book of receipts; with engravings. By a married lady... Second edition, revised. Hartford: 1844. 214 p. MeHi; MH. 44-3292

The improved housewife, or book of receipts; with engravings. By a married lady... Fourth edition, revised. Hartford: 1844. NT. 44-3293

The improved housewife, or book of receipts; with engravings. By a married lady... Fifth edition, revised. Hartford: 1844. NPlaK. 44-3294

Independent democrat, January 13, 1844. Springfield, Massachusetts, 1844. MBAt. 44-3295

Independent Mutual Fire Insurance Company of Bucks, Montgomery and Philadelphia Counties. Charter and by-laws. Germantown, Pennsylvania: Printed by P.R. Freas and company, 1844. 12 p. PP. 44-3296

Independent order of Rechabites. The regulations and general laws.... Order of Rechabites.... Portland: A. Shirley and sons, 1844. 52 p. MBAt; MeHi; NN. 44-3297

Index of fees under the new fee bill,

passed May 4, 1844, so arranged that all charges relating to any head are brought together. By R.M.T. New York: H. Anstice, 1844. 24 p. CtY; MH; RPB. 44-3298

Index to bibliotheca Sacra and American biblical repository.... Andover: Wiley and Putnam, 1844-76. IaGG. 44-3299

Index to Braithwaite's retrospect of practical medicine and surgery. Parts 1 to 8, inclusive. Uniform American edition. New York: Daniel Adee, 1844. 229 p. OMC. 44-3300

Indian anecdotes and barbarities. Being a description of their customs and deeds of cruelty, with an account of the captivity, sufferings and heroic conduct of those who have fallen into their hands, illustrating the general traits of Indian character. Palmer, Massachusetts: Printed for M. Baldwin [1844?] 29 p. NN. 44-3301

The Indian bride's farewell. An admired ballad, arranged for the guitar. Baltimore: Benteen: 1844. 2 p. CtY; MB. 44-3302

The Indian queen of Chenango, a poem in four cantos, by a student. Oxford, [New York] Printed by La. J. Leal, 1844. 64 p. CSmH; MH; NBuG; NN; NOx. 44-3303

Indiana. Communication from Silas Wood, esq., enclosing the petition of sundry creditors of the state of Indiana, on the subject of state bonds and unpaid interest [Indianapolis: 1844] 5 p. WHi. 44-3304

Indiana. Laws of a local nature, passed and published at the twenty-eighth session of the General Assembly of the state of Indiana, held at Indianapolis on the first Monday in December, 1843. By authority. Indianapolis: Dowling and Cole, State printers, 1844. 196 p. L; MdBB; Ms; Wa-L; WHi. 44-3305

Indiana. Message and executive correspondence and contract for building the new state prison. Indianapolis: J.P. Chapman, state printer, 1844. InU. 44-3306

Indiana. Report of the Department of Public Instruction. Indianapolis: Dowling and Cole, 1844. InU; WHi. 44-3307

Indiana. Report of the examiners of the new state prison, to the General Assembly, January 31, 1844. Indianapolis, 1844. 7 p. WHi. 44-3308

Indiana. Report of the president of the state bank to the General Assembly. Indianapolis: J.P. Chapman, 1844. 8 p. MH-BA; WHi. 44-3309

Indiana. Reports of cases argued and determined in the Supreme Court of judicature of the state of Indiana, with tables of the cases and principal matters. Containing the cases from November term, 1838 to May term, 1841, both inclusive. Indianapolis: Printed by Cutler and Chamberlain, 1844. 647 p. IaHi; LU-L; MdUL; NdU-L; WvW-L. 44-3310

Indiana. School laws of the state of Indiana, with forms appended thereto, designed to aid county auditors, school commissioners, township and district trustees, and others connected with common schools and the trust funds, in the discharge of their respective duties;

prepared by the Superintendent of common schools. Indianapolis, 1844. 105 p. DE; InU; WHi. 44-3311

Indiana annual register and pocket manual for 1845. Edited by C.W. Cady. Indianapolis: 1844. DLC; InU: MiD-B; NN; WHi. 44-3312

Influence of religious parents. Boston: Massachusetts Sabbath society, 1844. 88 p. MWHi. 44-3313

Ingersoll, Charles Jared, 1782-1862. Mr. C.J. Ingersoll's view of the Texas question. [Washington: 1844] 15 p. CSmH; CtY; TxDaM; TxU. 44-3314

Ingersoll, Charles Jared, 1782-1862. Speech on the Oregon Territory, House of Representatives, March 18, 1844. Washington: 1844. 8 p. MH; TxU; WHi. 44-3315

Ingersoll, Charles Jared, 1782-1862. View of the Texas question. Washington, 1844. 15 p. CtY; MBAt; NNC; PPL; RPBN. 44-3316

Ingersoll, George Goldthwait, 1796-1863. A farewell address to the First Congregational Society, in Burlington, Vermont, delivered June 2, 1844... Burlington: Stillman Fletcher, 1844. 48 p. CBPac; DLC; MB; MH; NN. 44-3317

Ingraham, Ira. Democracy; sermon, Presbyterian church, Lyons, Thanksgiving Day, December 14, 1843. Lyons: Western Arguss Press, 1844. 19 p. RPB. 44-3318

Ingraham, Joseph Holt, 1809-1860. Arnold; or the British spy. A tale of treason and treachery. By Professor J.H. In-graham... Boston: published at the Yankee office, 1844. 39 p. CtY; DLC; MB; NjR; RPB. 44-3319

Ingraham, Joseph Holt, 1809-1860. Frank Rivers [Boston] E.P. Williams, 1844. 47 p. ICU. 44-3320

Ingraham, Joseph Holt, 1809-1860. The beautiful unknown; or Massey Finke. Boston: Published at the Yankee office, 1844. 61 p. CtY. 44-3321

Ingraham, Joseph Holt, 1809-1860. Biddy Woodhull; or the pretty haymaker. Boston: E.P. Williams, 1844. 44 p. CtY; MWA; NjP; RPB; ViU. 44-3322

Ingraham, Joseph Holt, 1809-1860. Black Ralph; or the helmsman of Hurlgate... Boston: Edward P. Williams, 1844. 35 p. CtY; ICN; MH; PU; ViU. 44-3323

Ingraham, Joseph Holt, 1809-1860. Caroline Archer, or the Milliner's apprentice. Boston: Edward P. Williams, 1844. 38 p. MeB. 44-3324

Ingraham, Joseph Holt, 1809-1860. The corsair of Casco Bay; or the pilot's daughter.... Gardiner, Maine: G.M. Atwood, 1844. 58 p. DLC; MB; MH; MHa; OClWHi. 44-3325

Ingraham, Joseph Holt, 1809-1860. The dancing feather; or the amateur freebooters. A romance of New York... Boston: Yankee office, 184. 63 p. DLC; ICU; MH; NN. 44-3326

Ingraham, Joseph Holt, 1809-1860. The diary of a hackney coachman. Boston: 'Yankee' office, 1844. [3]-42 p. CtY; ICU; ViU. 44-3327

Ingraham, Joseph Holt, 1809-1860. Eleanor Sherwood, the beautiful temptress. Boston: 'Yankee' office, 1844. CtY. 44-3328

Ingraham, Joseph Holt, 1809-1860. Ellen Hart: or the forger's daughter. Boston: Yankee office, 1844. 46 p. CU; MWA; ViU. 44-3329

Ingraham, Joseph Holt, 1809-1860. Herman De Ruyter: or the mystery unveiled. A sequel to the beautiful cigar vender. Boston: H.L. Williams at the Yankee office, 1844. 47 p. MoKU; NN. 44-3330

Ingraham, Joseph Holt, 1809-1860. The midshipman; or, the corvette and brigantine. A tale of sea and land.... Boston: F. Gleason, 1844. 64 p. DLC; ICU; MeU; MsU; MWA. 44-3331

Ingraham, Joseph Holt, 1809-1860. The miseries of New York: or the burglar and counsellor... Boston: Yankee office, 1844. 48 p. CU; DLC; NN. 44-3332

Ingraham, Joseph Holt, 1809-1860. Rafael; or the twice condemned. A tale of the West. Boston: H.L. Williams, 1844. 47 p. DLC; ICN; NcD; ViU. 44-3333

Ingraham, Joseph Holt, 1809-1860. Rodolphe in Boston.... Boston: Williams, 1844. 48 p. CU; ICN; MB; PU; RPB. 44-3334

Ingraham, Joseph Holt, 1809-1860. Santa Claus: or, the merry king of Christmas. A tale for the holidays.... Boston: H.L. Williams, 1844. 34 p. CtHT; MeU; RPB. 44-3335

Ingraham, Joseph Holt, 1809-1860. The silver bottle; or, the adventures of "Little Marlboro" in search of his father.... [Boston: 1844] 2 pts. CtY; CU; RPB; ViU. 44-3336

Ingraham, Joseph Holt, 1809-1860. Spanish galleon; or, the pirate of the Mediterranean. A romance of the Corsair Kidd.... Boston: F. Gleason, 1844. 64 p. CSmH; MeB; MnU; NjR; NN. 44-3337

Ingraham, Joseph Holt, 1809-1860. Steel belt; or, the three masted goleta. A tale of Boston Bay.... Boston: "Yankee" office, 1844. 48 p. CtY; CU; MH. 44-3338

Ingraham, Joseph Holt, 1809-1860. Theodore; or, the "Child of the Sea." Being a sequel to the novel of "Lafitte, the pirate of the gulf" ....Boston: Edward P. Williams, 1844. 36 p. CtY; LNH; MWA. 44-3339

The injustice of the tariff on protective principles.... New York: Levi D. Slamm, 1844. 15 p. DLC; MBevHi; NN; Vi; WHi. 44-3340

An inquiry into the causes and origin of slavery in the United States, and a plan suggested for its extinction. By an American citizen.... Philadelphia: William S. Young, printer, 1844. 8 p. NIC. 44-3341

Instructions for the.... sliding rule. New York: 1844. CtHWatk. 44-3342

Instructive and entertaining conversations, for Sunday school children. Revised by the editor. New York: G. Lane and C.B. Tippett, 1844. 16 p. NNMuCN. 44-3343

Insurance company of the state of Pennsylvania. Circular and report of the committee.... appointed at the meeting of the stockholders. Philadelphia: 1844. 7 p. NNC; PHi; PP. 44-3344

Insurance company of the state of Pennsylvania. Report on the advisability of continuing to write marine insurance. Philadelphia: 1844. 7 p. PHi; PhInsLib; PP. 44-3345

Insurance company of the state of Pennsylvania. Selected statements. Philadelphia: 1844. 12 p. PHi. 44-3346

The interpreter. An aid to the study of modern languages. Containing extracts from French, Spanish, Italian and German writers, with word for word translations. Edited by B. Jenkins. Charleston, South Carolina: John W. Stoy, 1844. 192 p. ScHi. 44-3347

Introits: or, ante-communion psalms for the Sundays and holidays throughout the year. Philadelphia: Lindsay and Blakiston, 1844. 186 p. CBCDS; MdHi; NNG; PPL; TxU. 44-3348

Iowa. Constitutions adopted in conventions, November 1, 1844. Iowa City, 1844. CtHWatk; IaHi; IaU-L; MB; MH-L. 44-3349

Iowa. Journal of the House of Representatives, of the sixth legislative assembly of the territory of Iowa. Begun and held at Iowa City on the first Monday of December, 1843. Dubuque: Wilson Keesecker, 1844. 316 p. Ia; IaHi. 44-3350

Iowa. Laws of Iowa passed at the session of the Legislative Assembly which commenced on the 4th of December, 1843.

John Chambers, governor Francis Springer, President pro tem of the Council until the 11th day of January, and Thomas Cox, president thereafter. James P. Carleton, speaker of the House of Representatives. Published by authority. Burlington: James Clark, printer, 1844. 227 p. CSmH; Nj; NNLI; T; Wa-L. 44-3351

Irby, Richard. History of Randolph-Macon College, Virginia; the oldest incorporated Methodist college in America. First edition. Published and printed by Whittet and Shepperson. Richmond, Virginia: 1844. 331 p. NcDaD. 44-3352

The Iris; or, annual visiter [sic] for 1844. By Daniel Mallory. New York: Robert P. Bixby and company, 1844. 2 v. CtY; LNH; MH; NjR; OCh. 44-3353

Iron and Coal Trade Committee, Philadelphia. Letter of a committee, appointed at a meeting of the iron and coal trade, in Philadelphia, to the Hon. George Evans, against the repeal of the duty upon railway iron, imposed by tariff act of 1842. Philadelphia: J. Harding, 1844. 17 p. DLC. 44-3354

Irving, Christopher. Catechism of universal history; containing a concise account of the most striking events from the earliest ages to the present time. Second American edition revised and improved. New York: Collins, 1844. 103 p. PPWI. 44-3355

Irving, Washington, 1783-1859. The life and voyages of Christopher Columbus. Abridged and arranged by the author expressly for the use of schools. Bath, New

York: Richardson and Dow, 1844. 202 p. IaBo; MiToC. 44-3356

Irving, Washington, 1783-1859. The life of Oliver Goldsmith, with selections from his writings. New York: Harper and brothers, 1844. 2 v. GFtvN; InCW; MChi; NCaS; OCX. 44-3357

Isabella: or the pride of Palermo. New York: 1844. MB. 44-3358

Ithaca, New York Glee Club. A new collection of Democratic songs. [Ithaca: 1844] CtY. 44-3359

Ithaca, New York. Glee club. The Ithaca glee club's collection. A new collection of Democratic songs. Ithaca: Andrus, Woodruff and company, [1844] [2] p. CtY. 44-3360

Ithaca Academy. Ithaca, New York. Catalogue of the trustees, teachers and students, of the Ithaca academy, for the year ending August 7, 1844. Ithaca: Andrus, Woodruff and Gauntett [sic] printers, 1844. 18 p. NIC; NIDHi. 44-3361

Ivers, William. Reply to Mr. Brownley of New York; and a rejoinder to Rev. Dowling of Providence, on the relative merits of the Protestant and Catholic Bibles. Providence: 1844. 120 p. MdBLC; MdW; RHi. 44-3362

Ives, Elam, 1802-1864. The Beethoven collection of sacred music to which is prefixed a new method of instruction in the rudiments of music, and the art of reading with intonation. By E. Ives, Jr., W. Alpers, and H.C. Timm. New York: 1844. 192 p. CtY; MH; NNG; OCl; PPM. 44-3363

Ives, Elam, 1802-1864. The musical album; a collection of concerted vocal pieces for soprano voices. New York: J. Winchester, 1844. 3 nos. in 1 v. NN. 44-3364

Ives, Levi Silliman, 1797-1867. The apostles' doctrine and fellowship; five sermons preached in the principal churches of his diocese, during his spring visitation, 1844. New York: Appleton, 1844. 189 p. CtHT; DLC; MBC; NN; TChU. 44-3365

Ives, Levi Silliman, 1797-1867. An introductory address of the historical society of the University of North Carolina, delivered in the university chapel, June 5th, 1844, by L. Silliman Ives.... Raleigh: T. Loring, printer, 1844. 18 p. CtHT; DLC; MH; RHi; WHi. 44-3366

Ives, Levi Silliman, 1797-1867. Sermon before the convention, October 2, 1844. ....Philadelphia: 1844. 44-3367

Ives, Levi Silliman, 1797-1867. The struggle of sense against faith. The sermon at the opening of the triennial convention of the Protestant Episcopal Church.... By the Rt. Rev. L. Silliman Ives.... Philadelphia: George and Wayne, 1844. 24 p. CtHT; InID; MiD-B; NcU; PHi. 44-3368

Izard, Ralph, 1742-1804. Correspondence of Mr. Izard of South Carolina, from the year 1774 to 1804; with a short memoir. New York: C.S. Francis and company, 1844. 2 v. CU; InU; MdBJ; NcAS; PPM. 44-3369

J

Jack, Charles J. Speech of Charles J. Jack, at the meeting in favor of the re-annexation of Texas to the United States, Friday evening, April 5, 1844. Philadelphia: 1844. 12 p. CtY. 44-3370

Jackson, Andrew. Life of Andrew Jackson, private, military, and civil, with illustrations. By Amos Kendall. New York: Harper and Brothers, 1844. 208 p. A-Ar. 44-3371

Jackson, Andrew. Opinions of General Andrew Jackson, on the annexation of Texas. n.p., n.p., 1844. 8 p. CU; DLC; MB; MiD-B. 44-3372

Jackson, Francis. Letter from Francis Jackson to his excellency George N. Briggs. Boston: Printed by Andres, Prentiss and Studley, 1844. 8 p. MeB. 44-3373

Jackson, Francis. Memorial respecting slavery. Boston: 1844. Nh. 44-3374

Jackson, Joseph H. A narrative of the adventures and experience of Joseph H. Jackson, in Nauvoo, disclosing the depths of Mormon Villany. Warsaw, Illinois: 1844. 32 p. ICN. 44-3375

Jackson, Samuel. Lecture, introductory to a course on the Institutes of medicine in the University of Pennsylvania. Delivered November 5, 1844. Philadelphia: King and Baird, printers, 1844. 28 p. MBAt; MdBJ; NNNAM; OC; PPL. 44-3376

Jackson, Thomas, 1579-1640. A treatise of the Holy Catholic faith and church divided into three books. Philadelphia: H. Hooker, 1844. IES. 44-3377

Jackson, Thomas, 1579-1640. Two treatises on the church. The first by Thomas Jackson.... the second by Robert Sanderson.... To which is added a letter of Bishop Cosin, on the validity of the orders of the reformed churches. Edited, with introductory remarks, by William Goode. Philadelphia: Hooker, 1844. 238 p. CBPSR; ICMe; MdBD; PWmp; ScU. 44-3378

Jackson, Thomas, 1783-1873. The life of the Rev. Charles Wesley... comprising a review of his poetry... with notices of contemporary events and characters. New York: G. Lane and P.P. Sandford, 1844. 797 p. MBC; NcD; NN; OClWHi. 44-3379

Jackson, William, b. 1794. Christian's legacy. By William Jackson. Eighth edition. Philadelphia: author, 1844. MWiW; ODW. 44-3380

Jackson, William, b. 1794. The man of sorrows, or, the providence of God displayed; as exemplified in the life of William Jackson. Sixth edition. Philadelphia: William Jackson, 1844. ODefC; ViLxW. 44-3381

Jackson, William H. Life and confession of Sophia Hamilton, who was tried, condemned, and sentenced to be hung at Montreal, L.C., on the 25th of November, 1844, for the perpetration of the most shocking murders and daring robberies perhaps recorded in the annals of crime. Carefully selected by the author, William H. Jackson. New York: printed for the publisher, 1844. 24 p. NIC. 44-3382

Jacobs, Enoch. The doctrine of a thousand years millennium, and the return of the Jews to Palestine, before the second advent of our Saviour, without foundation in the Bible; to which is added a paraphrase of Romans 9th, 10th, and 11th chapters.... Cincinnati: Kendall, 1844. 75 p. IEG; NN; OC. 44-3383

Jacobs, Frederich, 1764-1847. The Greek reader, by Frederich Jacobs.... Boston: J. Munroe and company, 1844. 516 p. M; MiD; NN; PReaAt. 44-3384

Jacobs, Frederich, 1764-1847. The Greek reader, by Frederich Jacobs.... with improvements, additional notes, and corrections, by David Patterson, A.M. New York: W.E. Dean, 1844. ICMcHi; MdMwM; NcU. 44-3385

Jacobs, Frederich, 1764-1847. A Greek reader, selected principally from the work of Frederich Jacobs.... With English notes, critical and explanatory, a metrical index to Homer and Anacreon, and a copious lexicon. By Charles Anthon.... New York: Harper and brothers, 1844. 613 p. AFIT; DLC; MoSMa; NCH; PP. 44-3386

Jacobs, Frederich, 1764-1847. The Latin reader, by Frederich Jacobs and Frederich William Doring. With notes and illustrations, partly translated from the German and partly drawn from other sources, by John D. Ogilby, principal of the grammar school of Columbia College, New York.... From the seventh German edition. Eighth New York edition. New York: W.E. Dean, printer, 1844. CSt; LN; MChi; PPAN. 44-3387

Jacobs, Thomas Jefferson. Scenes, incidents and adventures in the Pacific Ocean, or the islands of the Australian Seas, during the cruise of the clipper Margaret Oakeley under Captain Benjamin Morrell. ....Illustrated by numerous engravings. New York: Harper and brothers, 1844. 372 p. CoU; MSaP; PFal; RPA; WHi. 44-3388

James, Augustus. In Chancery: Before the chancellor. John Townsend and Abba, his wife, and Augustus James and Elizabeth his wife, vs. James McBride and Hannah his wife, William James and others. Bill for partition of land, etc., at Syracuse. Pruyn and Martin, Solicitors. Albany: printed by C. Van Benthuysen and company, 1844-1846. 2 v. in 1. MiD-B; NSy. 44-3389

James, Charles T. A lecture on the comparative cost of steam and water power, delivered at Hartford, Connecticut, February, 1844. Newburyport: printed by Morss and Brewster, 1844. 26 p. MiD-B; MNe; MHi; RPB. 44-3390

James, George Payne Rainsford, 1801?-1860. Abram Neil; on times of old; a romance. New York: Harper, 1844. 139 p. PLFM. 44-3391

James, George Payne Rainsford, 1801?-1860. Agincourt. A romance. New

York: Harper and brothers, 1844. 157 p. OCl; ViU. 44-3392

James, George Payne Rainsford, 1801?-1860. Arabella Stuart; romance from Englsih history. New York: Harper and brothers, 1844. 143 p. MH; NRMA; RPB; ViU. 44-3393

James, George Payne Rainsford, 1801?-1860. Arrah Neil: or times of old. A romance... New York: Harper and brothers, 1844. [5]-139 p. CtY; MBL; NjR; PPL; TxShA. 44-3394

James, George Payne Rainsford, 1801?-1860. The false heir. New York: Harper and brothers, 1844. 157 p. MBL; PPFM; TxShA; ViAl. 44-3395

James, George Payne Rainsford, 1801?-1860. Forest days. By G.P.R. James, esq. ....New York: Harper and brothers, 1844. 145 p. TxShA. 44-3396

James, George Payne Rainsford, 1801?-1860. Rose d'Albret; or, troublous times. A romance. By G.P.R. James, esq. ....New York: Harper and brothers, 1844. 152 p. KyU; NjR; PLMF; TxShA; ViAl. 44-3397

James, J.A. A pattern for Sunday school teachers and tract distributors, and a word for all. .... New York: John S. Taylor and company, 1844. 87 p. MLow. 44-3398

James, John Angell. Anxious enquirer after salvation, directed and encouraged. New York: D. Appleton and company: Philadelphia: George S. Appleton, 1844. 12, 176 p. GMM; LN; NbOM; ScCMu. 44-3399

James, John Angell. The church member's guide. Edited by J.O. Choules. Boston: Gould, Kendall and Lincoln, 1844. 196, 36 p. GDecCT; GMM; ViRU. 44-3400

James, John Angell. The widow directed to the widow's God. By John Angell James.... New York: D. Appleton and company; Philadelphia: George S. Appleton, 1844. 205 p. MLow. 44-3401

James, John Angell. The young man from home. New York: D. Appleton and company, 1844. 187 p. MHolliHi; MLow. 44-3402

Jameson, Anna Brownell Murphy, 1794-1860. Memoirs of celebrated female sovereigns. By Mrs. Jameson.... New York: Harper and brothers, 1844. 2 v. LN; MPeaI; MWA; NCaS; PSew. 44-3403

Jameson, Anna Brownell Murphy, 1794-1860. Memoirs of the loves of the poets. Biographical sketches of women celebrated in ancient and modern poetry. By Mrs. Jameson.... From the last London edition. Philadelphia: Lea, 1844. 376 p. ArL; KyLxT; MB; RPA; WHi. 44-3404

Jameson, Robert, 1774-1854. Narrative of discovery and adventure in Africa, from the earliest ages to the present time; with illustrations of geology, mineralogy, and zoology. By Professor Jameson, James Wilson.... and Hugh Murray.... New York: J.J. Harper, 1844. 359 p. LNP; MdAN; OCo; PPFr; RWe. 44-3405

Jamieson, Alexander. A grammar of rhetoric and polite literature; comprehending the principles of language and style, the elements of taste and criticism; with rules for the study of composition and eloquence. Twenty-fourth edition. New Haven: A.H. Maltby, 1844. [19]-306 p. CU; MH; OSW; OC; TMeC. 44-3406

Janeway, Jacob Jones. Unlawful marriage, an answer to "the Puritan" and "Omricon," who hale [!] advocated in a pamphlet, the lawfulness of the marriage of a man with his deceased wife's sister.... By J.J. Janeway. New York: Carter, 1844. 215 p. GDecCT; ICP; NjP; PPL; ViRut. 44-3407

Janin, Jules Gabriel, 1804-1874. The American in Paris, during the summer. By Jules Janin. New York: Burgess, Stringer and company, 1844. 117 p. DLC; KHi; NNQ; PP; TxU. 44-3408

Janin, Jules Gabriel, 1804-1874. The American in Paris, during the winter. By Jules Janin. New York: Burgess, Stringer and company, 1844. 120 p. ICU; NNQ; PU; RPB; WU. 44-3409

Jarnagin, Spencer, 1793-1851. Speech of Mr. Jarnagin, of Tennessee, on the treaty for the annexation of Texas. Delivered in the Senate in executive session, June 6, 1844. [Washington: 1844] 32 p. GEU; MBAt; MH; Nj; TxU. 44-3410

Jarves, James Jackson, 1820-1888. History of the Hawaiian or Sandwich Islands, embracing their antiquities, mythology, legends, discovery by Europeans in the sixteenth century, rediscovery by Cook.... with their civil, religious, and political history.... Second edition. Boston: J. Munroe and company, 1844. 407 p. CL; IaB; MH; NhPet; PPiW. 44-3411

Jarves, James Jackson, 1820-1888. Scenes and scenery in the Sandwich Islands, and a trip through Central America: being observations from my note-book during the years 1837-1842. Boston: J. Munroe and company, 1844. 341 p. DLC; InRch; KyLo; NNMr; RP. 44-3412

Jarvis, Edward, 1803-1884. Insanity among the coloured population of the free states.... Philadelphia: T.K. and P.G. Collins, printers, 1844. 15 p. DLC; MBAt; MiD-B; MWA; NN. 44-3413

Jarvis, George Ogelvie, 1795-1875. To the medical profession. Remarks on the advantages of Dr. Jarvis's surgical adjuster, in the treatment of fractures and dislocations. New York: J. Meakim, agent, 1844. 12 p. DLC. 44-3414

Jay, John, Abolitionist. An address in behalf of the colored orphan asylum, delivered at their seventh anniversary. New York: 1844. 13 p. NN. 44-3415

Jay, William, 1769-1853. Evening exercises for the closet, for every day in the year. New York: Carter, 1844. 2v. in 1. NjP; OO. 44-3416

Jay, William, 1769-1853. The works of the Rev. William Jay....comprising matter not heretofore presented to the American public....New York: Harper and brothers, 1844. 3 v. ArAT; IGK; NN; PPL-R; TJoT. 44-3417

Jay, William, 1789-1858. Comprising matter not heretofore presented to the American public. Containing morning and evening exercises. New York: Harper and brothers, 1844. 431 p. IaFd. 44-3418

Jay, William, 1789-1858. Letter on the

honorable William Jay, to the Hon. Theo. Frelinghuysen. New York: 1844. 8 p. MiD-B; NjR; NN; PPL; TxH. 44-3419

Jay, William, 1789-1858. A view of the action of the federal government, in behalf of slavery. Utica: J.C. Jackson, 1844. 112 p. CtY; DLC; MWA; PHi; TNF. 44-3420

Jayne, David. Jayne's medical almanac and guide to health, 1844. By David Jayne, M.D. Philadelphia: Dr. D. Jayne and son, printers, 1844. 45 p. MsJS. 44-3421

Jefferson Brick vs. Delirium tremens.... New York: 1844. 19 p. NN; PPL. 44-3422

Jefferson College. Cannonsburg, Pennsylvania. Catalogue of members of the Philo. Literary Society of Jefferson College, Cannonsburg, Pennsylvania, from its formation August 23, 1797 to August 23, 1844. Pittsburgh: Printed by A. James, 1844. 34 p. MH; PWW. 44-3423

Jefferson College. Cannonsburg, Pennsylvania. Catalogue of the officers and students of Jefferson College, July, 1844. Pittsburgh: John Grant, 1844. 16 p. PWW. 44-3424

Jefferson College. Cannonsburg, Pennsylvania. Philo. Literary Society. Catalogue of members of the Philo Literary Society of Jefferson College, Cannonsburg, Pennsylvania, from its formation, August 23d, 1797, to August 23d, 1844. Pittsburgh: A. Jaynes, printer, 1844. 34 p. DLC; PWW. 44-3425

Jefferson Medical College. Philadelphia, Pennsylvania. Catalogue of the faculty and students of Jefferson Medical College of Philadelphia for the session 1843-44. With a list of graduates of March 10, 1843. Philadelphia: Merrihew and Thompson, printers, 1844. 12 p. CSansS; MOSMed; PPL-R; PWW. 44-3426

Jerram, Charles. A tribute of parental affection, to the memory of my beloved and only daughter, Hanna Jerram; with a short account of the last illness and death of her elder brother, Charles Stranger Jerram. Third American from the Fifth London edition. New York: R. Carter, 1844. 171 p. InU; MLow; PPM. 44-3427

Jerrold, Douglas William, 1803-1857. Complete letter writer, with illustrations by Leech and others. Philadelphia: Carey and Hart, 1844. 13-65 p. MdBP; MH; NN. 44-3428

Jerrold, Douglas William, 1803-1857. The natural history of courtship. By "Punch." With illustrations by Leech and others. Philadelphia: Carey and Hart, 1844. 62 p. MoKU; PHatU; RPA. 44-3429

Jersey City, New Jersey. Charters and acts... Jersey City: 1844. 92 p. IU; MH. 44-3430

Jersey City, New Jersey. Ordinances published by order of the common cuncil. Jersey City: 1844. 80 p. CSmH; PPL. 44-3431

Jesse, William. Beaux and Belles of England, by Captain William Jesse. New York: Athenaeum Press, 1844. 2 v. NNQ; NWM. 44-3432

Jesse, William. The life of George Brummel, commonly called Beau Brummel. Philadelphia: Carey and Hart, 1844. 164 p. LN; MWA; PPA; RNR; ScSoh. 44-3433

The Jew, among all nations.... New York: G. Lane and C.B. Tippett, 1844. PPAmS. 44-3434

The jewel, or, token of friendship, an annual for 1844. New York: R.P. Bixby and company, 1844. 248 p. IU; MHi; NcAS; NNC; TxU. 44-3435

Jewett, John P. Jewett's economical writing book. Each book contains three sheets of foolscap paper, ruled and manufactured in the best manner. In 12 numbers, with a port. and sketch of the life of each of the presidents of the United States. Salem: John P. Jewett and company, 1844. [12] p. MWA; MWbor-Hi. 44-3436

Jewett, Milo Parker. The mode and subjects of baptism. Eight thousand. Stereotyped edition. Philadelphia: American Baptism Publication Society, 1844. 108 p. CtY; ICNBT. 44-3437

Jewish chronicle. New York: 1844-. Vol. 1. ICP; MBC; NjR; NN. 44-3438

Jobson, David Wemyss. A treatise on the physiology of the teeth, &c., &c. their diseases and treatment, with practical observations on artificial teeth, and rules for their construction.... Baltimore: American Society of Dental Surgeons, 1844. 132 p. MdBM; MH; NNN; PPCP. 44-3439

Johnson, Andrew. Speech of Mr. Andrew Johnson of Tennessee on the right of petition: delivered in the House of Representatives, January 31, 1844. Washington: Printed at the Globe office, 1844. 8 p. FC; M. 44-3440

Johnson, Artemas Nixon, b. 1817. Instructions in thorough base; being a new and easy method for learning to play church music upon the pianoforte or organ. Boston: G.P. Reed, [1844] 120 p. DLC; MBC; MHi; MLanc; NNebg. 44-3441

Johnson, Charles P. A treatise on animal magnetism. New York: Burgess and Stringer, 1844. 96 p. MdBM; MWA; NN; WHi. 44-3442

Johnson, Cuthbert William, 1799-1878. The farmer's encyclopaedia, and dictionary of rural affairs; embracing all the most recent discoveries in agricultural chemistry. Adapted to the comprehension of unscientific readers... Adapted to the United States by Gouverneur Emerson. Philadelphia: Carey and Hart, 1844. 1165 p. ArU-M; CU; DLC; MWA; TxGR. 44-3443

Johnson, E.M. Pastoral address to the members of the congregation of St. John's Church. Brooklyn: I. Van Anden, printer, 1844. 12 p. MBD; MWA. 44-3444

Johnson, James C. The May festival. A musical recreation for flower time. Boston: Ditson, [1844] 36 p. MB. 44-3445

Johnson, James Finlay Weir. Applications of chemistry and geology to agriculture with an appendix. New York: Wiley and Putnam, 1844. 4, 89, 619 p. NP. 44-3446

Johnson, Jane. Early impressions: or, evidences of the secret operation of the divine witness.... compiled by Jane Johnson. Philadelphia: T.E. Chapman, 1844. 144 p. InRchE; MH; NBu; NcGu; NNUT. 44-3447

Johnson, John. Speech of John Johnson, esq., of Anne Arundel County, on the bill to provide for completing the Chesapeake and Ohio Canal from the revenues of the work. Delivered in the House of Delegates of Maryland, on Tuesday, 27th, and Wednesday, 28th, February. Annapolis: Riley and Davis, printers, 1844. 19 p. MdHi. 44-3448

Johnson, Lawrence. Specimen of printing types and ornaments cast by L. Johnson, successor to Johnson and Smith. Philadelphia: 1844. NNC-Atf. 44-3449

Johnson, Louisa. Every lady her own flower gardener, by Louisa Johnson.... New Haven: S. Babcock, 1844. 142 p. AzU; MSaP; NBuG; OC; WU-A. 44-3450

Johnson, Samuel, 1709-1784. Johnson's English dictionary, as improved by Todd, and abridged by Chalmers; with Walker's pronouncing dictionary combined: to which is added Walker's key to the classical pronunciation of Greek, Latin and scripture proper names. Philadelphia: Griffith and Simon, 1844. 1156 p. DLC; NFred; NjP; TxU. 44-3451

Johnson, Samuel, 1709-1784. The life and writings of Samuel Johnson, LL.D., selected and arranged by William P. Page. New York: Harper, 1844. GAuY; MsU; NcWfC; PAnL; RWe. 44-3452

Johnson, Samuel, 1709-1784. The life and writings [essays] of Samuel Johnson, LL.D. Selected and arranged by Rev. W.P. Page. New York: Harper and brothers, 1844. 2 v. OCX. 44-3453

Johnson, Samuel, 1709-1784. Rasselas, prince of Abyssinia. A tale. By Dr. Johnson. Boston: T.H. Carter and company, 1844. 124 p. IaMpI; IEG; MB; MH; WGr. 44-3454

Johnson, Samuel, 1709-1784. Works. ....With an essay on his life and genius by Arthur Murphy. Second complete American edition. New York: Blake, 1844. 2 v. GU; IGK; NHudH; ScDuE. 44-3455

Johnson, Samuel, 1763-1843? The triple wreath: poems on various subjects by Samuel Johnson....Newton, Pennsylvania: S.J. and E.M. Paxson; Philadelphia: T.E. Chapman, 1844. 162 p. DLC; NjR; PP; RPB; ViRut. 44-3456

Johnson, Walter Rogers, 1794-1852. A memoir of the scientific character and researches of the late James Smithson, esq. Read before the National Institute, Washington, April 6, 1844. Philadelphia: Barrett and Jones, printers, 1844. 25 p. CtY; In; MiD-B; MWA; PHi. 44-3457

Johnson, Walter Rogers, 1794-1852. Report of experiments on the evaporative power and other properties of coals. Washington: Government Printing Office, 1844. 221 p. MH-BA. 44-3458

Johnson, Walter Rogers, 1794-1852. Report of experiments on the evaporative power and other properties of coals. Washington: Government Printing Office, 1844. 606 p. NTRPI. 44-3459

Johnson, Walter Rogers, 1794-1852. A

report to the navy department of the United States, on American coals applicable to steam navigation.... Washington: Gales and Seaton, 1844. 607 p. A-GS; DLC; OCY; PEaL; RPA. 44-3460

Johnson, William Lupton. Christ's agony in the garden; the rector's offering for 1844, being a pastoral... to the parishioners of Grace Church, Jamaica, L.I. Jamaica: 1844. 27 p. NB; NBLIHI; NNQ; NSmb; TSewU. 44-3461

Johnson's pocket almanac for 1845. [Philadelphia] Pennsylvania: [W. Johnson 1844] MWA. 44-3462

Johnston, George. The morning and evening prayer, translated from the Book of Common Prayer of the Protestant Episcopal Church in the United States of America, together with a selection of hymns. Detroit: Geiger and Christian, printers, 1844. 59 p. MBAt. 44-3463

Johnston, James Finlay Weir, 1796-1855. Lectures on the applications of chemistry and geology to agriculture... With an appendix, containing suggestions for experiments in practical agriculture. New York: Wiley and Putnam, 1844. [11]-619 p. DLC; MiU; OClW; RPB; ViU. 44-3464

Johnston, John, 1806-1879. Manual of chemistry, on the basis of Dr. Turner's elements of chemistry; containing, in a condensed form, all the most important facts and principles of the science. New edition. Philadelphia: Thomas, 1844. 480 p. ICJ; KyU; MB; Nh; NNNAM. 44-3465

Johnstone, Christian Isobel, 1781-1857. Lives and voyages of Drake Cavendish,

and Dampier; including an introductory view of the earlier discoveries in the South Sea, and the history of the buccaniers... New York: Harper and Brothers, 1844. DLC; NCaS; NNS; PSew; MWar. 44-3466

Joinville, Francois Ferdinand Philippe Louis Marie d' Orleans, 1818-1900. Remarks on the state of the naval forces of France, with an appendix and notes. Translated from the French, with a few preliminary remarks, by an officer of the United States navy. Boston: 1844. 30 p. MH; MHi; NBLiHi; PPL; WHi. 44-3467

Jones, Charles Colcock. A catechism, of scripture doctrine and practice, for families and Sabbath schools, designed also, for the oral instruction of colored persons. Third edition. Savannah: T. Purse and company, 1844. 154 p. MdBP; NcD; KyLoP. 44-3468

Jones, Charles Colcock. Sketch of the life and character of Miss Anne Clay; delivered at her funeral services in Bryan Church, Georgia, the Second Sabbath in January, 1843. Boston: Crocker, 1844. 23 p. CtY; MBC; MW; MWA; RPB. 44-3469

Jones, George, 1810-1879. Tecumseh and the prophet of the west, an historical Israel-Indian tragedy, in five acts. London: Longman, Brown, Green and Longmans; New York: Harper and brothers, 1844. InG; MoSHi; NBuG; O; OkU. 44-3470

Jones, John Taylor. Outlines of Old Testament biography. Bangor: Mission Press, 1844. 68 p. MB. 44-3471

Jones, Justin. The belle of Boston: or

the rival students of Cambridge. By Harry Hazel [pseud.] Boston: F. Gleason, 1844 [7]-58 p. CtY; IUC; MWA; NNS; RPB. 44-3472

Jones, Justin. The burglars; or the mysteries of the League of Honor. An American tale, by Harry Hazel [pseud.] Boston: Hatch and company, 1844. DLC. 44-3473

Jones, Norris M. A letter to a Methodist. By a Presbyter of the Diocese of Maryland. Baltimore: D. Brunner, 1844. 49 p. CtY; KyLx; NjPT; NN; PHi. 44-3474

Jones, Peter, 1802-1856. Ojibue nvgvmouinvn. Geaiouajin igiu anishinabeg envmiajig. Boston: American borad of commissioners for foreign missions, 1844. 212 p. CtHWatk; DLC; MBGCT; MH-AH; WHi. 44-3475

Jones, Thomas P., 1774-1848. New conversations on chemistry adapted to the present state of that science.... on the foundation of Mrs. Marcet's conversations on chemistry. Philadelphia: Grigg and Elliot, 1844. 332 p. ILM; MdBM; PPAN. 44-3476

Jones, William Basil, 1822-1897. Wonderful curiosity; or a correct narrative of the celebrated mammoth cave of Kentucky. Russellville: 1844. 67 p. DLC. 44-3477

Jonson, Ben. To William Camden, [etc., etc.] ....Philadelphia: T. Wardle, 1844. 4 p. MdBJ. 44-3478

Josephus, Flavius. The genuine works of Flavius Josephus: translated by Wil-

liam Whiston.... New York: 1844. 6 v. CtY; InNdS; PPi. 44-3479

Josephus, Flavius. The works of Flavius Josephus, the learned and authentic Jewish historian and celebrated warrior, containing twenty books of the Jewish antiquities, seven books of the Jewish war, and the life of Josephus, written by himself.... By the late William Whiston.... Complete in two volumes.... Philadelphia: Grigg and Elliot, 1844. 2 v. RPB. 44-3480

Josephus, Flavius. The works of Flavius Josephus, the learned and authentic Jewish historian and celebrated warrior: with three dissertations, concerning Jesus Christ, John the Baptist, James the Just, God's command to Abraham, etc., and explanatory notes and observations. Translated by William Whiston, with portrait and engravings. Cincinnati: E. Morgan and company, 1844. 1 v. CtY; MoMob; NKings; OC. 44-3481

Josse, Augustin Louis. Grammar of the Spanish language, with practical exercises; revised by F. Sales.... Eleventh American edition. Boston: James Munroe and company; Cambridge: Metcalf and company, 1844. 468 p. CtY; MeLewB; PPi. 44-3482

Jourdain, Silvester, d. 1650. A plaine description of the Barmvdas, now called Sommer Islands. With the manner of their discouerie anno 1609, by the shipwrack and admirable deliuerance of Sir Thomas Gates, and Sir George Sommers.... [Washington: Peter Force, 1844] 24 p. MnHi. 44-3483

Journal of health. Cincinnati, July, 1844-. V. 1-. No. 1-. DNLM; NN. 44-3484

A journey to my grandfather's, written for the Massachusetts Sabbath School Society, and revised by the committee of publication. Boston: Massachusetts Sabbath School Society Depository, 1844. 68 p. MHolliHi. 44-3485

Journeymen Shoemakers Society. Woburn, Massachusetts. Constitution and by-laws of the Journeymen Shoemakers Society of Woburn, May 18, 1844. Woburn: William White, printer, 1844. 8 p. MWo. 44-3486

Journeymen Tailors of Indianapolis. Bill of prices established by the Journeymen Tailors of Indianapolis, Indiana, March 23, 1844. Indianapolis: State Sentinel, 1844. Broadside. In. 44-3487

Joy, Henry. On the evidence of accomplices. By the Right Honorable Henry Joy, Lord Chief Baron of His Majesty's Court of Exchequer in Ireland. Philadelphia: John S. Littell, 1844. 48 p. CoU; In-SC; MdBB; Nj; PP. 44-3488

Joyce, John. Brief hints to parents on the subject of education by John Joyce. Pittsburgh: 1844. CSmH; IEG; NN. 44-3489

Joyce, John. A sermon on the duty of obedience to parents. Pittsburgh: A. Jaynes, 1844. 22 p. CSmH. 44-3490

Joynes, William T. An essay upon the act of the general assembly of Virginia, passed April 3, 1838, entitled "an act amending the statute of limitations"....By William T. Joynes, ...Richmond, Virginia: Drinker and Morris; Philadelphia: Thomas, Cowperthwait and company, 1844. 311 p. NjR; NNLI; OCLaw; PU-L; RPL. 44-3491

Jubilee College, Illinois. View of Jubilee College, New York: 1844. PPL. 44-3492

Judah, Samuel Benjamin Herbert, 1799-1876. The mystical craft, the most crafty of all crafts, and the most delusive of all delusions, as exemplified by our modern mercuries, or missionaries and others engaged in the great measures for proselytizing the world, and for hastening on the glorious millenium of ecclesiastical supremacy in this favoured land of liberty. New York: G. Vale; Philadelphia: H. Young, 1844. 24 p. DLC; MB; NN; PPM. 44-3493

Judson, Emily Chubbock. Allen Lucas; the self-made man. By the author of "Charles Linn"... Utica: Bennett, Backus and Hawley, 1844. 180 p. NUt. 44-3494

Julia: or, reminiscences of a western friend. Written for the Massachusetts Sabbath School Society and revised by the committee of publication. Boston: Massachusetts Sabbath School Society, 1844. 32 p. DLC. 44-3495

Jullien. The prima donna waltzes composed by Jullien. Boston: Oliver Ditson, 1844. 7 p. KU. 44-3496

Jung-Stilling, Johann Heinrich, 1740-1817. The autobiography of Heinrich Stilling... Translated from the German of S. Jackson. New York: Harper and brothers, 1844. 187 p. DLC; IaB; MBL; PPL; WHi. 44-3497

Junius. Five articles on the Schuylkill Navigation Company. [n.p.] 1844. 16 p. PHi. 44-3498

Junkin, D.H. The good steward; or systematic beneficence an essential element of Christianity. Philadelphia: Presbyterian Board... 1844. 119 p. PPM. 44-3499

Junkin, David Xavier, 1808-1880. Superiority of the Calvinistic faith, and the Presbyterian government. A discourse commemorative of the meeting of the Westminster Assembly, delivered upon the occasion of the two hundredth anniversary thereof. By Rev. D.X. Junkin, A.M. Easton: Hetrich and Maxwell, printers, 1844. 31 p. CtHWatk; ICP; MB; NjPT; PPPrHi. 44-3500

Junkin, George, 1790-1868. The little stone and the great image; or lectures on the prophesies symbolized in Nebuchadnezzar's vision of the golden headed monster. Philadelphia: Campbell, 1844. 318 p. KyLoP; OO; PWW; ScDuE; WHi. 44-3501

Junkin, George, 1790-1868. On decision of character. The baccalaureate in Miami Unviersity, delivered August 8th. Rossville, Ohio: J.M. Christy, 1844. 32 p. CSmH; IU; MBAt; NCH; RPB. 44-3502

Juvenalis, Decimus Junius. Decimi juni juvenalis et auli persii flacci satirae ex-

purgatae notes illustratae. Bostoniae: J.H. Wilkins and R.B. Carter, 1844. 252 p. CSr; ILM; NAlf. 44-3503

Juvenalis, Decimus Junius. Juvenal tr. by Charles Badhans.... New edition, with an appendix containing imitations of the third and tenth satires. By Dr. Samuel Johnson. To which are added the satires of Persius. New York: Harper brothers, 1844. 58 p. CLSU; LNP; MoSM; RWe; ViU. 44-3504

Juvenalis, Decimus Junius. Satires, translated by Charles Badham. New edition. New York: Harper, 1844. 310 p. Ia-Corn; ODa; OHi. 44-3505

A juvenile guide; or, manual of good manners. Consisting of counsels, instructions and rules of deportment, for the young. By lovers of youth. In two parts.... Canterbury, New Hampshire: printed in the United Society, 1844. 131 p. DLC; ICMe; MH; OClWHi; WHi. 44-3506

The Juvenile Wesleyan. Published semimonthly at the office of the true Wesleyan, for the Wesleyan method connection. L. Lee, editor. New York: O. Scott, 1844-. v. 1-. OClWHi. 44-3507

K

Kalloch, Amariah. A sermon, preached to the Baptist Church and Society, in East Thomaston, July 7, 1844. By Rev. A. Kalloch.... on the characteristics of the present generation.... Portland: Charles Day and company, printers, 1844. 24 p. MWA. 44-3508

Kames, Henry Home, 1698-1782. Elements of criticism, with analyses, and translations of ancient and foreign illustrations. By Henry Home, Lord Kames, judge of the court of sessions in Scotland, &c., &c. Edited by Abraham Mills, A.M. New edition. New York: Huntington and Savage, 1844. 504 p. KyLoS; MDux; MNe; NcGB; PPins. 44-3509

Kane, John Kintzing, 1795-1858. The annexation of Texas. Philadelphia: 1844. PPL. 44-3510

Kane, Patrick. Key to the Rev. A. Atwood's commentary on tract no. 4, for the people, by Patrick Kane. Philadelphia: M. Fithian, 1844. 24 p. GAM-R; MdBLC; MdW. 44-3511

Kane, Robert John, 1809-1890. Elements of chemistry, including the most recent discoveries and applications of the science to medicine and pharmacy and to the arts. American edition, with additions and corrections.... by J.W. Draper. New York: Harper and brothers, 1844. 704 p. ArU-M; CSt; ICP; WU. 44-3512

Kanhouse, Peter. An historical sermon; designed as a memorial to the inhabitants of Wantage, Sussex County, New Jersey.... New York: M.W. Dodd, 1844. 66 p. MWA; Nj. 44-3513

Katechismus. Doylestown: J. Jung, 1844. PPeSchw. 44-3514

Kavanaugh, B.T. Masonic oration at Platteville, June 24, 1844. Platteville: 1844. 15 p. WHi. 44-3515

Kearny, Philip, 1815-1862. Service with the French troops in Africa. By an officer in the United States army. ....New York: 1844. 100 p. FOA; InGrD; MnHi; Nj; Wv. 44-3516

Keats, John, 1795-1821. The eve of St. Agnes. The rococo; containing the culprit Fay, by Joseph Rodman Drake; Lillian, by William Mackworth Praed; and the eve of St. Agnes, by John Keats.... with original notes by N.P. Willis. New York: Morris, Willis, 1844. 16 p. MWH; TxU. 44-3517

Keats, John, 1795-1821. Poetical works. Philadelphia: Thomas, Cowperthwait and company, 1844. 75 p. IaDa. 44-3518

Keble, John, 1792-1866. The Christian year; thoughts in verse for the Sundays and holy days throughout the year. By the Rev. John Keble, professor of poetry in the university of Oxford. ....A new

American edition. Edited with an introduction by the Right Rev. George W. Doane, bishop of New Jersey. Philadelphia: Lea and Blanchard, 1844. 331 p. CtMMH; OCX; OO; VtMidSM. 44-3519

Keefe, N.J. Caroline Henson; or, The pious orphan girl. Philadelphia: Henry McGrath, 1844. 77 p. NoLoc. 44-3520

Keese, John, 1805-1856. The mourner's chaplet: an offering of sympathy for bereaved friends. Selected from American poets.... Boston: Gould, Kendall and Lincoln, 1844. 128 p. MB; MBC; NjP; RPB; WU. 44-3521

Keese, John, 1805-1856. The wintergreen, a perennial gift for 1844.... edited by John Keese.... New York: Charles Wells and company, 1844. 260 p. NjR. 44-3522

Keightley, Thomas, 1789-1872. The history of England, by Thomas Keightley. Revised edition. By Joshua Toulmin Smith. New York: Turner and Hayden, 1844. 2 v. InGrD; MCli; MoWgW; Vi; WHi. 44-3523

Keightley, Thomas, 1789-1872. The history of Greece. To which is added a chronological table of contemporary history. New York: Turner and Hayden, 1844. 490 p. IaDuC; LNL; MPiB; OCY. 44-3524

Keightley, Thomas, 1789-1872. The history of Rome, to which is added a chronological table of contemporary history by J.T. Smith. New York: Turner and Hayden, 1844. 2 v. CoDR; IaGG; OCX; ScCC. 44-3525

Keith, Alexander, 1791-1880.

Demonstration of the truth of the Christian religion by Alexander Keith.... From the second Edinburgh edition. New York: Harper and brothers, 1844. 336 p. IaMuC; KyBgW; ScCliJ; TChU; WM. 44-3526

Keith, Alexander, 1791-1880. Evidence of the truth of the Christian religion, derived from the literal fulfilment of prophecy; particularly as illustrated by the history of the Jews, and by the discoveries of recent travellers. ....Philadelphia: Presbyterian Board of Publication, 1844. 395 p. CtHC; NIC; OO; PP; TxAbH. 44-3527

Keith, Alexander, 1791-1880. The land of Israel, according to the covenant with Abraham, with Isaac, and with Jacob. New York: Harper and brothers, 1844. 388 p. CtY; ICP; LNB; OCY; PPi. 44-3528

Keller, Ezra 1812-1848. An address delivered before the alumni and students of the Theological Seminary of the Lutheran Church, at Gettysburg, Pennsylvania, April 16, 1844. Baltimore: printed at the publication rooms of the Evangelical Lutheran Church... 1844. 10 p. IU; MoKU; NjPT; OSW; RPB. 44-3529

Kellogg, Edward, 1790-1858. Currency: the evil and the remedy. By Godek Gardwell [pseud.] Fourth edition, improved [New York: 1844?] 43 p. CtHC; DLC; MB; PPTU; WHi. 44-3530

Kellogg, Edward, 1790-1858. Currency; the evil and the remedy. Fifth edition. New York: 1844. 48 p. CtY; MB; MBAt; MH-BA. 44-3531

Kelty, Mary Ann, 1789-1873. Address to the Society of Friends. [n.p.] 1844. 15 p. PPFr. 44-3532

Kemble, Francis Anne, 1809-1893. Journal of a residence on a Georgian plantation in 1838-1839. New York: Harper and brothers, 1844. 337 p. MWbri. 44-3533

Kemble, Francis Anne, 1809-1893. Poems. By Frances Anne Butler. Philadelphia: J. Penington, 1844. 152 p. CSt; DLC; NNC; OO; PHi. 44-3534

Kendall, Amos, 1789-1869. Mr. Clay against the frontier settlers; Mr. Clay and the laboring millions. Washington: 1844. PPL. 44-3535

Kendall, Amos, 1789-1869. Providential dispensation... Washington: 1844. PPL. 44-3536

Kendall, Edward Augustus, 1776-1842. Keeper's travels in search of his master. Boston: 1844. MBAt. 44-3537

Kendall, Ezra Otis, 1818-1899. Uranography; or, a description of the heavens; designed for academies and schools; accompanied by an atlas of the heavens, showing the places of the principal stars, clusters, and nebulae. By E. Otis Kendall. Philadelphia: Butler and Williams, 1844. 365 p. ICJ; OCX; PU; RPB; WBeloC. 44-3538

Kendall, George Wilkins, 1809-1867. Narrative of the Texan Santa Fe expedition, comprising a description of a tour through Texas and across the great southwestern prairies, the Camanche and Caygua hunting-grounds, with an account of the sufferings from want of food, losses from hostile Indians, and final capture of the Texans, and their march, as prisoners, to the city of Mexico.... New York: Harper and brothers, 1844. 2 v. DLC; MTop; NGH; ScC; TxD-T. 44-3539

Kenly, John R. Our republic: a lecture delivered before the Eagle artillery, February 22d, 1844. Published by request. Baltimore: Printed by John Murphy [1844] 32 p. MdHi. 44-3540

Kennaday, John, 1800-1863. Address delivered before the Theological Society of Union College. Albany: C. Van Benthuysen and company, 1844. 16 p. MnHi; NvCrD; NcD; NN; PPL. 44-3541

Kennaday, John, 1800-1863. The work and spirit of the ministry. A sermon preached by appointment before the Philadelphia annual conference, April 4, 1844. By.... John Kennaday.... Philadelphia: Sorin and Hall, 1844. 26 p. KyLx; NNUT; PCA; PHi; ScSpW. 44-3542

Kennebec County Agricultural Society, Maine. Order of exercises for the second day of the twelfth annual show and fair of the Kennebec County Agricultural Society, Augusta, October 10, 1844. By Rev. John H. Ingraham. Address, by Elihu Burritt, of Worcester, Massachusetts. [....] [Augusta, Maine? 1844?] WHi. 44-3543

Kennedy, Andrew, 1810-1847. Remarks of Andrew Kennedy on the removal of obstructions in the Mississippi River and its tributaries. Delivered in the House of Representatives, etc. [Washington: 1844] 4 p. DLC; TxHU. 44-3544

Kennedy, Andrew, 1810-1847. Remarks.... in the House of Representatives, December 20, 1844.... in answer to Mr. C.B. Smith's remarks on the bill to regulate the collection, safe-keeping, and disbursement of the public moneys. [Washington] 1844. 4 p. DLC; WHi. 44-3545

Kennedy, Andrew, 1810-1847. Speech on the bill to refund General Jackson's fine, in the House January 2, 1844. Washington: Printed by Blair and Rives, 1844. 7 p. M; PHi. PU. 44-3546

Kennedy, Andrew, 1810-1847. Speech on the resolution authorizing the committee on the Rhode Island controversy to send persons and papers, delivered in the House of Representatives, March 13, 1844. Washington: Globe, 1844. 8 p. MH; OC; RHi. 44-3547

Kennedy, John Pendleton, 1795-1870. Defence of the Whigs. By a member of the twenty-seventh congress. New York: Harper and brothers, 1844. 152 p. DLC; ICN; MnU; NjP; RPA. 44-3548

Kennedy, John Pendleton, 1795-1870. Letter of John Kennedy in the congress of the United States on the proposition to transfer the stock held by the federal government in the Chesapeake and Ohio Canal to the state of Maryland... Washington: J. and G.S. Gideon, printers, 1844. 20 p. MBAt; MdBP; MdHi; MnHi. 44-3549

Kennedy, John Pendleton, 1795-1870. To the Whigs of Baltimore [letter, January 25, 1844] 6 p. MdHi; MHi; NcD. 44-3550

Kennedy, William, 1799-1871. Texas: its geography, natural history and topography.... New York: Benjamin and Young; Boston: Redding and company, 1844. 118 p. CtY; LNH; MH; OClWHi; TxU. 44-3551

Kenney, Joel. Historical sketches of the Baptist Church in Sturbridge, Massachusetts, from 1740-1843. New York: 1844. NoLoc. 44-3552

Kenrick, William, 1789-1872. The new American orchardist; or, an account of the most valuable varieties of fruit, of all climates, adapted to cultivation in the United States; with their history, modes of culture, management, uses, &c. With an appendix on vegetables, ornamental trees, shrubs, and flowers, the agricultural resources of America, and on silk, &c. Seventh edition, enlarged and improved. With a supplement. Boston: Otis, Broaders, and company, 1844. 450 p. CU; DLC; MWA; PPWa; Vi. 44-3553

Kent, James, 1763-1847. Commentaries on American law. New York: J. Van Worden and company, 1844. 4 v. ArCH; GDecCT; LNT; OMC; WaU. 44-3554

Kent, James, 1763-1847. Commentaries on American law. Fifth edition. New York: The author, 1844. CtY; DLC; IaU-L; MdBJ; NjR. 44-3555

Kentish, John. The Christian's offering in the house of prayer. A sermon... By John Kentish. [n.p.] Printed by James Belcher and son, 1844. 18 p. ICMe. 44-3556

The Kentucky minstrel and Jersey warbler: being a choice selection of coon melodies. Philadelphia: Robinson and

Peterson, 1844. 64 p. MB; NN; RPB. 44-3557

Kentucky. Acts of the General Assembly of the Commonwealth of Kentucky: passed at December session, 1843. Published by authority. Frankfort: A.G. Hodges, State printer, 1844. 300 p. Ar-Sc; Wa-L. 44-3558

Kentucky. Biennial report of the school for the deaf at Danville. Frankfort, Kentucky: 1844-1876. 19 v. M. 44-3559

Kentucky. Documents accompanying the Governor's annual message in relation to the penitentiary. December 23, 1844. Frankfort, 1844. 24 p. WHi. 44-3560

Kentucky. Journal of the House of Representatives of the Commonwealth of Kentucky: begun and held in the town of Frankfort: on Tuesday the thirty-first day of December. Frankfort: A.G. Hodges, State printer, 1844. 401 p. InU; Ky; KyDC. 44-3561

Kentucky. Journal of the Senate of the Commonwealth of Kentucky, begun and held in the town of Frankfort on the thirty first day of December in the year of our Lord, 1844. Frankfort: A.G. Hodges, State printer, 1844. 323 p. Ky; KyU-L; WHi. 44-3562

Kentucky. Report of the Second Auditor, October, 1844; also the balance sheets, receipts, expenditures, etc. Frankfort: State printer, 1844. M. 44-3563

Kentucky. Reports communicated to both branches of the Legislature of Kentucky at the December session 1844.

Frankfort: A.G. Hodges, State printer, 1844. InU. 44-3564

Kentucky. Reports of cases at common law and in equity decided in the Court of Appeals of Kentucky. Frankfort: Printed for the reporter by William M. Todd, 1844. KyLa; NcS; N-L; Vi-L; W. 44-3565

Kentucky. Special Report of the Board of Internal Improvement of the state of Kentucky in relation to claims, etc. Frankfort: 1844. 60 p. ICU; WHi. 44-3566

Kenyon College. Gambier, Ohio. Gambier catalogue and calender, for 1843-4; Comprising the theological seminary of the diocese of Ohio, Kenyon College and Kenyon grammar schools. Corrected to December, 1843. Gambier, Ohio: G.W. Meyers, [1844] 34 p. CSmH. 44-3567

Kenyon College. Gambier, Ohio. Reply of trustees of Kenyon College, Ohio, to the statement of D.B. Douglass, LL.D., of facts and circumstances connected with his recent removal from the presidency of same. Philadelphia: Stavely and McCalla, 1844. 48 p. CtY; InID; MH; NNG; OClWHi. 44-3568

Kenyon College, Gambier, Ohio. Reply to the trustees to statement of D.B. Douglas, etc. Philadelphia: 1844. WHi. 44-3569

Kerr, James, 1805-1855. A treatise on the mode of baptism, showing the unfounded nature of the assumption that immersion is the only proper mode of administering the ordinance; and that pouring or sprinkling is the most scriptural and siginificant, and by far the preferable mode of its administration. By Rev.

James Kerr.... steubenville, [Ohio]: A.L. Frazer, 1844. 196 p. DLC; KyLoP; MoHi; OClWHi; TxHuT. 44-3570

Keteltas, Caroline M. The last of the plantagenets; a tragic drama in three acts, founded on the romance of that name by William Heseltine. New York: R. Craighead, 1844. 56 p. CSmH; DLC; ICU; MH; PU. 44-3571

Ketley, Joseph. The two liturgies, A.D. 1549, and A.D. 1552: with other documents set forth by authority in the reign of King Edward VI.... Edited for the Parker Society by the Rev. Joseph Ketley. Cambridge: University Press, 1844. 582 p. GDecCT; MiGr; NjR; OClW; TSewU. 44-3572

Kidder, Daniel Parish, 1815-1891. Mormonism and the Mormons; a historical view of the rise and progress of the sect self-styled Latter Day Saints. New York: G. Lane and C.B. Tippett, for the Methodist Episcopal Church, 1844. 342 p. CSmH; ICU; MiD-B; NcD; OSW. 44-3573

Kidwell, J. The alpha and omega. Part 2. A key to the Apocalypse. Philomath: Printed by George W. Matchett, 1844. 94 p. MMeT; NNC. 44-3574

Kilbourn, Austin. A treatise on agriculture, being a complete system or body of husbandry compiled from various authors with notes by a practical agriculturalist. Hartford: Wells and Willard, 1844. 1 v. Ct. 44-3575

Kilbourn, Byron. To the people of Milwaukee County. Your fellow citizens, Byron Kilbourn. Milwaukee, October 19, 1844 [Milwaukee: 1844] WHi. 44-3576

Kilpatrick, J.H.T. The reviewer, reviewed; or a rejoinder to the Rev. J.J. Triggs' 'Revies,' of the controversy on baptism. Augusta: McCafferty, 1844. 63 p. PPPrHi; RPB. 44-3577

Kimball and James business directory, for the Mississippi Valley, 1844.... Cincinnati: Kendall and Barnard, 1844. 546 p. ICHi; MoK; OC; PPL-R; WHi. 44-3578

Kimball, Alba. Review of the objections to a railroad in Broadway; in a letter addressed to the mayor, aldermen, and commonalty of the city of New York. New York: G. Ambrose and company, 1844. 21 p. DLC; NNC. 44-3579

Kimball, Richard Burleigh, 1816-1892. The true life of the scholar: an address delivered before the literary societies of Dartmouth College, Hanover, New Hampshire, July 24, 1844. New York: George Ambrose and company, 1844. 18 p. IU; MH; NhD; NjP; PHi. 44-3580

Kind words. For his young friends. By Uncle William.... Philadelphia: Presbyterian Board of Publication, 1844. 137 p. IaDuU; MNS; NjPT. 44-3581

King, Alonzo, 1796-1835. Memoir of George Dana Boardman, late missionary to Burmah. Containing much intelligence relative to the Burman Mission.... With an introductory essay. New and improved stereotype edition. Boston: Gould, Kendall and Lincoln, 1844. 319 p. GCarr; KyLoS; MnU; PCA; TJaU. 44-3582

King, Preston, 1806-1865. Speech of Preston King on the tariff, delivered in the House of Representatives, April 30,

1844. Washington: Globe office, 1844. 7 p. MiD-B; WHi. 44-3583

King, Thomas Butler, 1800-1864. Address to the voters of the first district of Georgia. [Savannah, Georgia: printed at the Republican Press, 1844] 16 p. MH. 44-3584

Kingsley, George. The harp of David: a collection of church music.... with a system of elementary instruction for pupils. Philadelphia: 1844. MBC; MNF; MWA; NNUT; PPL. 44-3585

Kinne, Asa. General index to the first, second and third volumes, of Kinne's law compendiums. New York: Published for the author, 1844. 529 p. GAWW; OCoSc; WMMU-L. 44-3586

Kinne, Asa. Kinne's digest of the United States criminal code. Questions and answers on law, alphabetically arranged, with references to the most approved authorities by Asa Kine. Fourth edition. New York: Published for the author, 1844. 616 p. CoU; MWiW; WMMU. 44-3587

Kinne, Asa. Law compendium. Questions and answers on law. Alphabetically arranged. Third edition. New York: Published for the author, 1844. 512 p. Md; OCoSc. 44-3588

Kinne, Asa. The most important parts of Blackstone's commentaries. Fourth Edition. New York: 1844. 266 p. MWA. 44-3589

Kinne, Asa. Questions and answers on law, alphabetically arranged, with reference to the most approved authorities. Fourth edition. New York:

Published for the author, 1844. WMMU. 44-3590

King, Thomas Butler, 1800-1864. Address to the voters of the first district of Georgia [Savannah, Georgia, printed at the "Republican Press,"] 1844. 16 p. MH. 44-3591

Kinzie, Juliette Augusta McGill, 1806-1870. Narrative of the massacre at Chicago, August 15, 1812, and of some preceding events. Chicago: Ellis and Fergus, printers, 1844. 34 p. ICHi; MB; NNC; OCHP; PPiU. 44-3592

Kip, William Ingraham, 1811-1893. The double witness of the church. By the Rev. William Ingraham Kip. Second edition, revised. New York: D. Appleton and company, 1844. 256 p. CSansS; GDecCT; MdBP; NBuDD; PPLT. 44-3593

Kip, William Ingraham, 1811-1893. The history, object, and proper observance of the holy season of Lent: by the Rev. William Ingraham Kip.... Second edition. Albany: E.H. Pease, 1844. 228 p. GDecCT; MdBD; MoS; NGlf; PP. 44-3594

Kippis, Andrew, 1725-1795. A narrative of the voyages round the world, performed by Captain James Cook; with an account of his life during the previous and intervening periods. New York: Harper and brothers, 1844. 445 p. CtHC; OMC; ScCC. 44-3595

Kippis, Andrew, 1725-1795. A narrative of the voyages round the world, performed by Captain James Cook. With an account of his life during the previous and intervening periods. Philadelphia: Henry F. Anners, 1844. 2 v. in 1. MdBD; MiD; MWA; OClWHi; PPM. 44-3596

Kippis, Andrew, 1725-1795. Voyages round the world, from the death of Captain Cook to the present time.... New York: Harper and brothers, 1844. 395 p. CtY; MB; MiD; NBuCC; RPE. 44-3597

Kippis, Andrew, 1725-1795. Voyages round the world, from the death of Captain Cook to the present time; including remarks on the social condition of the inhabitants in the recently discovered countries; their progress in the arts; and more especially their advancement in religious knowledge. New York: Harper and brothrs, 1844. 401 p. CtY; CSmH; KyHi; MnU; PSC. 44-3598

Kirchain, Ferdinand. The little lamb, or virtues reward. Boston: 1844. MBC. 44-3599

Kirk, Edward Norris, 1802-1874. Address to the Ladies Grande Ligne Missionary Society... Delivered in the Mount Vernon Chapel... Boston: John B. Hall, printer, 1844. 12 p. MBAt; MBC; PHi; NjR; RPB. 44-3600

Kirk, Edward Norris, 1802-1874. The greatness of the human soul. An address delivered at the seventh anniversary of the Mount Holyoke Female Seminary, South Hadley, Massachusetts, August 1, 1844. Boston: T.R. Marvin, 1844. 27 p. CtSoP; MWA; NCH; RPB. 44-3601

Kirk, Edward Norris, 1802-1874. The unrivalled glory of the cross. A sermon delivered at the dedication of the church belonging to the Mount Vernon Congregational Society. Boston: Tappan and Dennet, 1844. 34 p. CtHC; ICN; MWA; NjR; OClWHi. 44-3602

Kirkham, Samuel. English grammar in familiar lectures. Sixteenth edition, enlarged and improved. Rochester: William Alling, 1844. 228 p. ICRL; MH; WU. 44-3603

Kirkham, Samuel. English grammar in familiar lectures; accompanied by a compendium, embracing a new systematic order of parsing...One hundred and seventh edition, enlarged and improved. New York: Collins, brothers and company, 1844. 228 p. Fstar; MH; NE; ViU; ViW. 44-3604

Kirkham, Samuel. English grammar in familiar lectures; accompanied by a compendium, embracing a systematic order of parsing... Latest edition, enlarged and improved. Cincinnati: E. Morgan and company, 1844. 228 p. CtY; IaBo; ICU. 44-3605

Kirkham, Samuel. An essay on elocution, designed for the use of schools and private learners. Third edition, improved and enlarged. New York: Pratt, Woodford, 1844. 357 p. LU. 44-3606

Kirkland, Caroline Matilda Stansbury, 1801-1864. Forest life. By the author of "a new home"....New York: C.S. Francis and, company; Boston: J.H. Francis, 1844. 2 v. CtY; DLC; IU; MiU. 44-3607

Kirkpatrick, David Shields. The wisdom of Moses, the Hebrew prophet, historian and lawgiver.... Wheeling: Hall, 1844. 16 p. Wv. 44-3608

Kirkwood, or, "The Blue Hen's chickens," a romance of the American revolution.... Wilmington, Delaware: Harker and Johnson, printers, 1844. 40 p. DLC. 44-3609

Kirschner, Lula. Our own set, a novel. Translated from the German by Clara Bell. New York: Gottsberger, 1844. KyLo. 44-3610

Kitchel, Harvey Denison, 1812-1895. Nature and source of ministerial authority: sermon at the ordination of J.C. Dickinson, Northfield, February, 1844. Hartford: J. Paine, 1844. CtHC. 44-3611

Kitchel, Harvey Denison, 1812-1895. Who gave thee this authority? The nature and source of ministerial authority: a scriptural and congregational view of the Christian ministry. A sermon preached at the ordination of Rev. Joel L. Dickinson.... By H.D. Kitchell.... Hartford: John Paine, 1844. 16 p. CBB; CtHC; ICT; MBC; NHC-S. 44-3612

The kitchen and fruit gardener. A select manual of kitchen gardening, and culture of fruits; containing familiar directions for the most approved practice in each department, descriptions of many valuable fruits, and a calendar of work to be performed each month in the year. The whole adapted to the climate of the United States. Philadelphia: Lea and Blanchard, 1844. 108 p. CtY; MiGr; NcCJ; NIC. 44-3613

The kitchen companion, and housekeeper's own book, containing all the modern and most approved methods in cookery, pastry, and confectionary, with an excellent collection of valuable recipes, to which is added the whole art of carving, illustrated. Philadelphia: Turner and Fisher, 1844. 36 p. MH. 44-3614

The kitchen directory, and American housewife: containing the most valuable and original receipts in all the various branches of cookery; together with a collection of miscellaneous receipts, and directions relative to housewifery. New York: M.H. Newman, 1844. 144 p. KMK; MH; NN; PP. 44-3615

Kitto, John, 1804-1854. The history of Palestine, from the patriarchal age to the present time. New York: [Benjamin and Young] 1844. 223 p. ICMe; MiGr; ODa. 44-3616

Kittridge [of Concord] Report of the case Kittridge vs. Emerson decided in the superior court of Judicature... July term. 1844. Concord: Asa McFarland, 1844. 52 p. CtHWatk; DLC; IU; MB; N-L. 44-3617

Kleine Lieder-Sammlung, oder Auszug aus dem Psalterspiel der Kiknder Zion's.... Eighth edition. Poland, Ohio: H. Kurtz, 1844. 256 p. OClWHi. 44-3618

Knapp, William Henry. Reforms fellow laborers of Christ; a sermon delivered to the Second Congregational Society at Nantucket, Sunday, 26, 1844. Boston: James Munroe and company, 1844. 20 p. MMeT-Hi; RPB. 44-3619

Kneass, Samuel H. Report of an examination of the coal mines, lands and estate of the Lykens Valley Coal Company. Philadelphia: 1844. 23 p. M; PHi; PPAN. 44-3620

Knickerbocker almanac for 1845. By David Young. New York, New York: H. and S. Raynor, [1844] MWA. 44-3621

Knight, Charles, 1791-1873. Natural history. The elephant as he exists in a wild state, and as he has been made subservient, in peace and in war, to the purposes of man. New York: Harper and brothers, 1844. 300 p. CtY; MeB; MsU; NOg; RKi. 44-3622

Knight, Charles, 1791-1873. Old England: a pictorial museum of regal ecclesiastical... and popular antiquities. Boston: Samuel Walker and company, 1844. InLPU. 44-3623

Knight, Helen Cross, 1814-1906. Reuben Kent at school; or influence as it should be... Philadelphia [1844?] 87 p. CtY; MB; NN; OrP; PReaAT. 44-3624

Knight, Helen Cross, 1814-1906. What shall I do? or, the Cauderts [sic] first prestion. [sic] Boston: 1844. 71 p. DLC; MB. 44-3625

Knight, Nehemia Rice, 1780-1854. Address to the people of the United States. Suffrage troubles in Rhode Island [Providence: 1844] 15 p. MB; MH; NN. 44-3626

Know Nothing Party. New York [City] Address...New York: 1844. MH. 44-3627

Knowlan, James. The mysteries of Wesleyanism, no fiction; or the British Conference an unjust and tyrannical... Despotism... New York: 1844. 80 p. CtY; PPL. 44-3628

Knowles, James Davis, 1798-1838. Memoir of Ann H. Judson, late missionary to Burmah; including a history of the American Baptist Mission in the Burman empire. A new edition, with a continuation of the history of the mission to the present time. Boston: Gould, Lincoln

and Kendall, 1844. 392 p. CU; MH; MWA; RPA; WHi. 44-3629

Knowles, James Sheridan, 1784-1862. Knowles's elocutionist; a first-class rhetorical reader and recitation book. Altered and adapted to the purposes of instruction in the United States by Epes Sargent. New York: J. Mowatt and company, 1844. 322 p. DLC; IaU; MH; NBuG; OO. 44-3630

Knowles, James Sheridan, 1784-1862. Knowles's elocutionist; a first-class rhetorical reader and recitation book, containing the only essential principles of elocution, directions for managing the voice, etc., simplified and explained on a novel plan, with numerous pieces for reading and declamation. Designed for the use of schools and colleges. Fifth edition. New York: Saxton, 1844. 322 p. CtHWatk; DLC; MB; NBuG; OO. 44-3631

Knox College, Galesburg, Illinois. Catalogue of the officers and students of Knox Manual Labor College, Galesburg, Illinois... July 10, 1844. Peoria: S.H. Davis, printers, 1844. 12 p. MH. 44-3632

Kock, Charles Paul de, 1798-1871. Comic almanac. New York: 1844. CtHWatk. 44-3633

Kohl, Johann Georg, 1808-1878. Austria, Vienna, Prague, etc., etc., By J.G. Kohl. Philadelphia: Carey and Hart, 1844. 104 p. MPiB; OCY; PPA; RNR; WU. 44-3634

Kohl, Johann Georg, 1808-1878. Ireland. Dublin, the Shannon, Limerick, Cork, and the Kilkenny races, the round towers, the lakes of Killarney, the county of Wicklow.... and the Giant's causeway. New York: Harper and brothers, 1844. 115 p. DLC; MB; OO; PPM; RPA. 44-3635

Kohl, Johann Georg, 1808-1878. Scotland, Glasgow, the Clyde, Edinburgh; the forth, Stirling; Drummond Castle, Perth, and Taymouth castle; the lakes. By J.G. Kohl. Philadelphia: Carey and Hart, 1844. 52 p. InNd; MPiB; PPM; RNR; WHi. 44-3636

Krummacher, Friedrich Wilhelm, 1796-1868. Elias der Thisbiter, nach seinem aussern und innern leben dargestellt von F.W. Krummacher. New York: Herausgegeben von der Amerikanischen traktat-gesellschaft, [1844] 707 p. DLC; ViU. 44-3637

Krummacher, G.D. Jacob wresting with the angel. By Rev. G.D. Krummacher. Solomon and Shulamite. By F.W. Krummacher, D.D. ....Translated from the German. Second American edition. New York: John S. Taylor, 1844. 288 p. IGK; NbOP. 44-3638

Kuhner, Raphael, 1802-1878. Grammar of the Greek language for the use of high schools and colleges. Translated from the German by B.B. Edwards... and S.H. Taylor... Andover: Allen, Morrill and Wardwell; New York: M.H. Newman; [etc., etc.] 1844. [13]-603 p. CtHC; DLC; KyLoS; TxU; WU. 44-3639

Kurtz, Benjamin, 1795-1865. The year book of the reformation. Edited by B. Kurtz and J. G. Morris.... Baltimore: printed at publication rooms, 1844. 416 p. IaDL; MdBP; OCoC; PPLT; ScNC. 44-3640

L

Labagh, Isaac P., 1804-1879. The mediatorial reign of Christ on the earth revealed in a series of essays, compiled from eminent authors; to which is added a letter from Charlotte Elizabeth to the bishop of Jerusalem, on the perpetuity of Israel's ordinances. New York: I.P. Labagh, 1844. 123 p. PPL; ViRU. 44-3641

Labitzky, Joseph. Ole Bull's waltzes, as performed at the American Institute, with enthusiatic applause, by Ole Bull. Composed by Labitzky. New York: Firth and Hall [1844?] 5 p. MB; ViU. 44-3642

Ladies handbook of fancy needlework and embroidery containing plain and simple directions... Edited by an American lady. New York: J.S. Redfield, 1844. 60 p. CtMMHi; NN. 44-3643

The ladies scrapbook.... Hartford: S. Andrus and son [1844?] [7]-336 p. MB; MTemNHi. 44-3644

The ladies' handbook of baby linen: containing plain and ample instructions for the preparation of an infant's wardrobe, with additions by an American lady. New York: J.S. Redfield, 1844. 60 p. NcGU. 44-3645

Ladies' handbook of embroidery on muslin, lacework, and tatting; containing plain directions for the working leaves, flowers, and other ornamental devices. Edited by an American lady. New York:

J.S. Redfield, 1844. 60 p. CtHWatk; CtY. 44-3646

The ladies' handbook of letter-writing; containing original letters relative to business, duty, friendship, love and marriage, written in a modern style, and adapted to all subjects of general correspondence. New York: James Langley, 1844. 64 p. NbHi. 44-3647

The ladies' handbook of millinery and dressmaking, with plain instructions for making the most useful articles of dress and attire. With additions by the American lady. New York: J.S. Redfield [1844] 60 [4] p. CtMMHi; NN. 44-3648

Ladies' handbook of plain needlework... Edited by an American lady. New York: Redfield, 1844. 60 p. MBC; PU. 44-3649

The ladies' work table book; containing clear and practical instructions in plain and fancy needlework... New York: J. Winchester, 1844. 168 p. N; NjR; NRU-W; OC. 44-3650

Ladreyt, Casimir, 1797-1877. The study of French simplified: or, new elements of the French language, methodically displayed in a complete course of progressive practical lessons.... New York: H. and S. Raynor, 1844. 163 p. CtMW; DLC; MdBS; PPi; PPM. 44-3651

Lady Alice; or a tale of the reformation.

By the author of Mabel, the actress. New York: W. Applegate, 1844. 48 p. NN. 44-3652

The lady's handbook of the toilette, of fashion, health and beauty. By a lady of New York. From the second London edition. New York: Burgess, Stringer and company, 1844. 64 p. MBC; NN. 44-3653

The lady's self-instructor in millinery, mantua making and all branches of plain sewing... By an American lady. New York: Burgess, Stringer and compnay, 1844. [7]-48 p. LNH; NN. 44-3654

Lady's work-box companion: being instructions in all varieties of canvas work. New York; Burgess, Stringer and company, 1844. 45 p. MWA; Nh-Hi. 44-3655

The lady's wreath, a monthly miscellany of religion, literature, science and art. Boston: 1844. V. 4. No. 4-5. WHi. 44-3656

Lahm, Samuel. Speech of Mr. Lahm, of Stark, on the bill to amend the charter of the Bank of Wooster. Columbus: 1844. OClWHi . 44-3657

Laicus. The testimony of the fathers. By Laicus. Albany: J. Munsell, printer, 1844. 16 p. CtY; MB: MdBD; NGH; NjR. 44-3658

Lake Ontario and Hudson River Company. Sackett's Harbor and Saratoga Railroad. Report of A.E. Edwards.... New York: 1844. MB. 44-3659

Lamar, Mirabeau Buonaparte, 1798-1859. Letter of General Mirabeau B. Lamar, expresident of Texas, on the subject of annexation, addressed to several citizens of Macon, Georgia. Savannah: printed by T. Purse, 1844. 48 p. DLC; GMW; TxU; ViU; WHi. 44-3660

Lamb, Charles, 1775-1834. Mrs. Leicester's school; or the history of several young ladies... By Charles Lamb and sister. New York: Henry M. Onderdonk, 1844. 165 p. CtY; MB; MoSU. 44-3661

Lamb, Charles, 1775-1834. Mrs. Leicester's school; or the history of several young ladies... Philadelphia: 1844. 165 p. GColu; PU. 44-3662

Lamb, Jonathan. The practical spelling book, and child's instructor: or second book for primary schools. Boston, [Massachusetts]: Webb, 1844. 144 p. DLC. 44-3663

Lamborn, Thomas. A legacy of counsel and advice, from Thomas Lamborn, late of New Garden, Chester County, Pennsylvania, deceased to his children. Philadelphia: Printed for his relatives, 1844. 34 p. InRchE; PPFr; PSC-Hi. 44-3664

Lamson, Alvan, 1792-1864. What is Unitarianism? or, a statement of the views of the Unitarian Congregationalists of the United States; with some historical and statistical notices of the denomination. Boston: James, Munroe, 1844. 32 p. CtY; LU; MBC; MiGr; PPM. 44-3665

Lancaster, James W. An oration on the anniversary of American independence, delivered in Nashville, North Carolina. Raleigh: Signal, 1844. 9 p. NcU. 44-3666

Lander, Richard. Journal of an expedition to explore the course and termination of the Niger: with a narrative of a voyage down that river to its termination. By Richard and John Lander. Illustrated with engravings and maps.... New York: Harper and brothers, 1844. 2 v. IU; RPE; ScGrw. 44-3667

Landing of the pilgrims at Plymouth, December 22, 1620. Anniversary celebration in Cincinnati, on Monday, December 23, 1844. Cincinnati: 1844. OCHP. 44-3668

Landis, Robert Wharton. Rabbah taken: or, the theological system of Rev. Alexander Campbell, examined and refuted. By Robert W. Landis, pastor of the Presbyterian church, Bethlehem, New Jersey.... Cincinnati: William H. Moore and company, 1844. 135 p. KyLo; OC; PPPrHi; TxDaM; TxHuT. 44-3669

Landis, Robert Wharton. Rabbah taken; or, the theological system of Rev. Alexander Campbell, examined and refuted. By Robert W. landis....New York: Mark H. Newman, 1844. 135 p. CtHT; KyDC; NjPT; NNUT; PCA. 44-3670

Landon, Letitia Elizabeth, 1802-1838. The improvisatrice [sic.] New York: Morris and Willis, 1844. 32 p. MB. 44-3671

Landon, Letitia Elizabeth, 1802-1838. The passion flower. [New York: 1844] 32 p. CtY; DLC; LNH; MWH. 44-3672

Landon, Letitia Elizabeth, 1802-1838. Works. Philadelphia: Carey and Hart, 1844. 2 v. MBBC; PPL. 44-3673

Lane, Benjamin Ingersoll. Sabbath eve-

ning lectures; or, the refuge of lies and the covert from the storm, ...a series of thirteen lectures on.... future punishment. Troy, New York: Young and Hartt, 1844. 331 p. GDecCT; LNB; MWA; PAtM; RPB. 44-3674

Lane, John F.W. Human anatomy and physiology, for the use of common schools... Boston: William B. Fowle and Nahum Capen, 1844. 223 p. MB; MH; NBMS; NNUT; RPB. 44-3675

Lane Theological Seminary. Cincinnati, Ohio. Catalogue of the officers and students of Lane Theological Seminary, Cincinnati, Ohio, 1834-'44. Cincinnati: George L. Weed, 1844. 22 p. IaPeC; OClWHi. 44-3676

Lane Theological Seminary. Cicinnaati, Ohio. Order of exercises at the anniversary of Lane Theological Seminary. June 12th, 1844. Sparhawk, [printer] 1844. OMC. 44-3677

Lang, William. Animal magnetism, or Mesmerism; its history, phenomena, and present condition; containing practical instructions with the latest discoveries in the science. With a supplement containing new and important facts. By Rev. Chauncy Hare Townsed. New York: J. Mowatt and company, 1844. 109 p. DNLM; NBMS; NNC. 44-3678

Lape, Thomas. Kleines handbuch der christlichen taufe, kinder-taufe und er tauf-art; in zwei predigtne, uebersetzt von der 2. engl. auf. Baltimore: Buchhandlung der Ev. Luth. kirche, 1844. 90 p. NjPT; PPG; PPLT; PPL-R. 44-3679

Lape, Thomas. Manual of Christian baptism; two discourses. Fourth edition.

Baltimore: 1844. MBAt; MBC; NjPT. 44-3680

Lapham, Increase Allen, 1811-1875. Wisconsin; its geography and topography, history, geology, and mineralogy. Milwaukee, 1844. NoLoc. 44-3681

LaPorte, Theodore Charles, comte de. A French grammar; containing besides the rules of the language, a complete treatise on prepositions. By Count de La-Porte.... Boston: Otis, Broaders and company, 1844. 782 p. MB; NNC; PU; RPA; ViU. 44-3682

Lardner, Dionysius, 1793-1859. Investigation of the causes of the explosion of the locomotive engine, "Richmond," near Reading, Pennsylvania, on the 2d September, 1844, made at the request of messrs. Norris, brothers.... [New York] Herald Book and Job Printing office, 1844. 22 p. CSt; DBRE; MH-BA; NjP; PHi. 44-3683

Lardner, Dionysius, 1793-1859. Lardner's outlines of universal history: embracing a concise history of the world from the earliest period to the present time. Arranged so that the whole may be studied. Philadelphia: Hogan and Thompson, 1844. 514 p. MW; NEaa; ViL; WJan. 44-3684

The last supper.... Our Saviour and His apostles are represented in statuary the size of life, designed from Leonardo de Vinci's celebrated painting and executed by an American lady of extraordinary talent. Portland: Thurston, Ilsley and company, printers, 1844. 12 p. MPeaHi. 44-3685

Lathbury, Thomas. Protestantism the

old religion, popery the new. New York: 1844. 20 p. MBC; MDeeP. 44-3686

Lathrop, Joseph. Christ's warning to the churches; with an appendix of the Apostolic succession, with an introductory notice by the Rev. J.M. Wainwright. New York: Alexander V. Blake, 1844. [3]-120, [1]-18 p. CtHC; ICU; MdBD; NBuG; RNR. 44-3687

Lathrop, Leonard E. The way of safety, lectures to young men, delivered in the Second Presbyterian Church, Auburn. New York: 1844. IEG; InCW. 44-3688

Latimer, Hugh, 1490-1555. Sermons by Hugh Latimer, sometime bishop of Worchester, martyr, 1555. Edited for the Parker Society by the Rev. George Elwes Corrie, B.D., fellow and tutor of Catharine Hall, Cambridge, and Norrisian professor of divinity in that university. Cambridge: printed at the University Press, 1844. 551 p. CBB; GEU; KEmC; MiGr; NjMD. 44-3689

The Latin poets of the decline. New York: Langley, 1844. 598 p. MB. 44-3690

Latta, S.A. Constitutional claims and powers of Methodist Episcopacy; being a review of the discussion of the late general conference and an appeal to the North and South in favor of union. Cincinnati: 1844. 43 p. ICU; NcD; OClWHi; OCX. 44-3691

Laughlin, H.A. Laughlin's political register, containing the popular vote since 1828. Map. Philadelphia: 1844. PPL. 44-3692

Launsbury, Thomas. The touchstone truth applied to modern abolition; or seven lectures in answer to the question; what do the scriptures teach on the subject of slavery. Geneva, New York: Scotter and Van Brunt, 1844. 155 p. NcD. 44-3693

Laurel Hill Cemetery. Philadelphia. Guide to Laurel Hill cemetery, near Philadelphia. Philadelphia: C. Sherman, printer, 1844. 160 p. LNH; MB; MnHi; MWA; RHi. 44-3694

Laurel Hill Cemetery. Philadelphia. Guide to Laurel Hill cemetery, near Philadelphia. Philadelphia: Sherman, 1844. 137 p. PPL-R; PPPrHi. 44-3695

Laurel wreath; or, affections keepsake. Second edition. Philadelphia: 1844. 176 p. MW; NjR. 44-3696

Law among the birds, in three parts, to which is added "the sparrow's ball." Boston: 1844? 68 p. MH. 44-3697

Law, Samuel Warren. Fragments: or, miscellaneous sketches. New York: Published by the author, 1844. CtHC; CtY; NN; RPB. 44-3698

Law, William, 1686-1761. Remarks on the fable of the bees, by William Law....with an introduction by the Rev. F.D. Maurice.... with an appendix containing.... Cambridge: printed at the University Press, for D. and A. MacMillan, 1844. 130 p. CU; ICU; MdBJ; MH-AH; RPB. 44-3699

Law, William, 1686-1761. The spirit of prayer; or, the soul-rising out of the vanity of time into the riches of eternity. New York: [n.p.] 1844. 2 v. in 1. MH; NjPT; WNaE. 44-3700

Law, William, 1686-1761. The true way of turning to God, etc. Prefixed a short account of the author. Peekskill, [New York]: G.K. Lymon, printer, 1844. 32 p. CSmH. 44-3701

The laws of etiquette; or short rules and reflections for conduct in society. By a gentleman... Philadelphia: Lindsay, 1844. 224 p. CtHT. 44-3702

Lawson, George, 1749-1820. Reflections on the illness and death of a beloved daughter. By the late Rev. George Lawson. Philadelphia: Presbyterian Board of Publication, 1844. [3]-115 p. GDecCT; NjR; PPPrHi. 44-3703

Lawson, Henry, 1774-1855. Paper on the arrangment of an observatory. Bath, New York, 1844. 20 p. DAS; NjP. 44-3704

Lawson, L.M. Physician to the St. Mary-Le-Bone infirmary; hon. mem. de la societe de statistique universelle; extraord mem. and formerly pres. of the reg. med. soc. ed., etc. First American edition. Edited by L.M. Lawson, M.D., editor of the western lancet; lecturer on the theory and practice of medicine. Cincinnati: Desilner and Burr, 1844 [46] p. KyLoSiU. 44-3705

Lawyer, John D. A scripture guide to the mode of baptism. Albany: 1844. 67 p. NjPT. 44-3706

Lazhechnickov, Ivan Ivanovich, 1792-1869. The heretic, translated from Russian of Lazhecknikov by Thomas B. Shaw. New York: 1844. 150 p. CU; MBAt; NN; PPL; RPB. 44-3707

Leach, Sanford. Bible baptism

defended... New York: 1844. 57 p. NjPT; NHCS; PCA; RPB. 44-3708

Leaflets of memory; an illuminated annual. Philadelphia: E.H. Butler and company, 1844-1855. 11 v. ICN; KyHop; MnU; MWA; NNF. 44-3709

Leavitt, Joshua. The great duellist. [Utica: Jackson and Chaplin, 1844] 15 p. N. 44-3710

Lebannon Liberal Institute. A catalogue of the officers and students... Concord: Asa McFarland, 1844. 10 p. MBC; MiD-B. 44-3711

LeConte, John Lawrence, 1825-1883. Descriptions of some new and interesting insects, inhabiting the United States. Boston, 1844. 7 p. CtY; PPAmE. 44-3712

Lecraw, J.B. Sketch of the life, travels, and sufferings of a reformed man: showing the misery to which intemperance brought him.... Written by himself. Pawtucket: 1844. 36 p. MWA; WHi. 44-3713

Lee, Charles Alfred, 1801-1872. The elements of geology, for popular use; containing a description of the geological formations and mineral resources of the United States. New York: Harper and Brothers, 1844. 375 p. DLC; MiD; OSW; PPM; ViL. 44-3714

Lee, Charles Alfred, 1801-1872. An introductory discourse on medical education, delivered to the students of Geneva Medical College, October 1, 1844.... Geneva, New York: I. Merrell, 1844. 40 p. DLC; MH-M; MiU; NBuU-M; NNN. 44-3715

Lee, Daniel, 1806-1895. Ten years in Oregon, by [D.] Lee and [J.H.] Frost, late of the Oregon Mission of the Methodist Episcopal Church. New York: the authors, 1844. 344 p. CtHWatk. 44-3716

Lee, Daniel, 1806-1895. Ten years in Oregon. By D. Lee and J.H. Frost. New York: J. Collord, printer, 1844. ICN; MWA; PHi; OCl; WaU. 44-3717

Lee, Daniel, 1806-1895. Ten years in Oregon. By D. Lee and J.H. Frost.... New York: for the authors, 1844. 344 p. CSt; CU; IaU; MiD-B; PHi. 44-3718

Lee, George Alexander. I met him in the happy throng. Ballad. New York: Firth and Hall, 1844. 3 p. NN. 44-3719

Lee, Hannah Farnham Sawyer. The log cabin; or the world before you... Philadelphia: George S. Appleton, 1844. 207 p. CtY; ICHi; MWA; PPL-R; RPA. 44-3720

Lee, Henry. Letters to the cotton manufacturers of Massachusetts [on the condition of the cotton market as affected by the policy of the government with regard to banking, currency, and taxation] n.p. [1844] MBAt; MH. 44-3721

Lee, Henry Washington, 1815-1874. A short story about little Daniel the good boy: who died in Springfield, Massachusetts, August 4, 1844. By Henry Washington Lee. Boston: Tract com., 1844. 10 p. MBD; MHi; MPiB; MSHi. 44-3722

Lee, Leroy M. Methodist ministers, true ministers of Christ. A discourse delivered in the centenary church, Richmond, ...17th of November, 1843, under the appointment of the Virginia annual conference of the Methodist Episcopal Church. Richmond: Christian Advocate office, 1844. 36 p. MB; MBNMHi. 44-3723

Lee, Robert, 1793-1877. Lectures on the theory and practice of midwifery. Delivered in the theatre of St. George's Hospital... Philadelphia: E. Barrington and G.D. Haswell, 1844. 540 p. ArU-L; CSt-L; LNT-M; PPA; WMAM. 44-3724

Leech, Samuel, 1798-1848. Thirty years from home, or a voice from the main deck, being the experience of Samuel Leech. Boston: published by Charles Tappan, 1844. 305 p. CtY; DLC; InU; MH; MSaP. 44-3725

Leech, Samuel, 1798-1848. Thirty years from home, or a voice from the main deck; being the experience of Samuel Leech. Fifteenth edition. Boston: 1844. CtY; MW. 44-3726

Leech, Samuel, 1798-1848. Thirty years from home; or, A voice from the main deck; being the experience of Samuel Leech. Boston, 1844. 305 p. NIC. 44-3727

Lefevre, George William, 1798-1848. Keep warm! Thermal comfort: or, possible hints for preservation from colds, coughs and consumption.... New York: Mowatt Company, 1844. 68 p. MB. 44-3728

Lefoulin, Pierre Joachim. A new treatise on the theory and practice of dental surgery. By Pierre Joachim Lefoulin. Translated by Thomas E. Bond. Baltimore: Amerian Society of Dental Surgeons, 1844. 295 p. DSG; InU-D; NNN; PPCP; TNV. 44-3729

Legal protection of dogs from the increasing evil by dog stealers and receivers. n.p.: 1844. 31 p. MH. 44-3730

Legendre, Adrien Marie, 1752-1833. Elements of geometry and trigonometry. Translated from the French of A.M. Legendre. Revised and adapted to the course of mathematical instruction in the United States, by Charles Davies. Philadelphia: A.S. Barnes and company, 1844. 297 p. CtHWatk; DLC; InKoHi; NcD; NIDHi. 44-3731

Legendre, Adrien Marie, 1752-1833. Elements of geometry and trigonometry. Translated from the French of A.M. Legendre. Revised and adapted to the course of mathematical instruction in the United States, by Charles Davies. Philadelphia: A.S. Barnes and company, 1844. 291, 150, 62 p. DLC; NcD. 44-3732

Legendre, Adrien Marie, 1752-1833. Elements of geometry: on the basis of Dr. Brewster's Legendre. New Haven: Durrie, 1844. 237. CtHT-W; CtHWatk; PU. 44-3733

The legends of Lampidosa, or the seven heroines. New York: 1844. 39 p. CU; MHi; NN. 44-3734

The legion of liberty! and force of truth, containing the thoughts, words, and deeds, of some prominent apostles, champions and martyrs. Pictures and poetry... Illustrated with engravings. New York: sold at the office of the American Anti-slavery Society, 1844. 140 p. ICN; MiU-C; NhD. 44-3735

Legion of liberty! and force of truth, containing the thoughts, words, and deeds, of some prominent apostles, champions and martyrs. Pictures and poetry... New York: American Sunday School Society, 1844. 72 p. PHi; PU. 44-3736

The legion of liberty! and force of truth.... New York: 1844. 126 p. NjR. 44-3737

Lehigh Coal and Navigation Company. Report of the board of managers, of the Lehigh Coal and Navigation Company, to the stockholders, January 8, 1844. Philadelphia: William S. Young, printer, 1844. 35 p. DLC; NN; PPM. 44-3738

Leidy, S. Snyder. Leidy's business academy, near Franklin Square by... Philadelphia: 1844. 12 p. PHi. 44-3739

Leighton, Robert, 1611-1684. Life and works of Robert Leighton, D.D., to which is prefixed a life of the author, by John Norman Pearson.... New York: J.C. Riker; Philadelphia: George S. Appleton, 1844. 800 p. MTop. 44-3740

Leighton, Robert, 1611-1684. The whole works of Robert Leighton, D.D., ...to which is prefixed a life of the author by John Norman Pearson, M.A. ....New York: J.C. Riker, 1844. 800 p. CtHT; InID; KKcBT; MH; ViU. 44-3741

Leighton, Robert, 1611-1684. The whole works. To which is prefixed, a life of the author, by J.N. Pearson. New York: J.C. Riker; Philadelphia: G.S. Appleton, 1844. 800 p. DLC; MH; OO; PPL; Wa. 44-3742

Leonard and Company. Auction catalogue of books. Boston, 1844-1868. 2 v. MB. 44-3743

Leonard, Levi Washburn, 1790?-1864. Modes of instruction in common schools; adapted particularly to summer schools with prefatory remarks, by L.W. Leonard. Keene: G. Tilden, 1844. 24 p. MBC; MWHi; Nh; NhHi. 44-3744

Leonard, Levi Washburn, 1790?-1864. The North American spelling book, conformed to Worcester's dictionary, with a progressive series of easy reading lessons. Twentieth revised edition. Keene, New Hampshire: G. Tilden; Boston: Gould, Kendall, and Lincoln, 1844. 180 p. NNC. 44-3745

Leonard, Moses G. Speech on the tariff, in the House of Representatives, April 1, 1844. n.p. [1844] 8 p. In; M; MBAt; MBU; MHi. 44-3746

LeSage, Alain Rene, 1668-1747. The adventures of Gil Blas of Santillane. Translated from the French of Le Sage. By T. Smollett. To which are prefixed memoirs of the author. Hartford: S. Andrus and Son, 1844. 3 v. IGK; LNB; MWA; NNN; PWW. 44-3747

Leslie, Eliza, 1787-1858. The house book; or, a manual of domestic economy for town and country.... Seventh edition. Philadelphia: Carey and Hart, 1844. 436 p. ICU; NNNAM. 44-3748

Leslie, Eliza, 1787-1858. Directions for cookery in its various branches. Nineteenth edition, with improvements. Philadelphia: Carey, 1844. 468 p. MB; MBeHi; NN; PP. 44-3749

Leslie, Eliza, 1787-1858. Directions for cookery in its various branches. Twentieth edition, with improvements.

Philadelphia: Carey, 1844. 511 p. DLC; PP. 44-3750

Leslie, John, 1766-1832. Narrative of discovery and adventure in the polar seas and regions ....By Professor Leslie, Professor Jameson and Hugh Murray.... New York: Harper and brothers, 1844. 373 p. DLC; InCW; OCo; RJa. 44-3751

Leslie's museum of foreign literature. New York: J.W. Leslie and Company, 1844. V. 1. No. 1. 64 p. NjR. 44-3752

Lessons from the scriptures, with a familiar catechism. Boston: Massachusetts Sabbath School Society, 1844. 54 p. DLC. 44-3753

A letter addressed to the bishops, clergy, and laity of the Protestant Episcopal Church, by the presbyter. Philadelphia: 1844. 69 p. PHi. 44-3754

Letter concerning imputations of dishonor upon the United States. Boston: 1844. MB. 44-3755

A letter on the subject of the vice presidency, in favor of the claims of J.K. Polk, of Tennessee, to the nomination of the Democratic National Convention. By a Tennesseean. Washington: printed at the Globe office, 1844. 7 p. DLC; MBC; MoS; NcU; PPL. 44-3756

Letter on the supposed failure of a national bank, the supposed delinquent of the national government the debts of the several states... Boston: 1844. PPL. 44-3757

Letter to Honorable George Evans against the repeal of the duty upon rail-

way.... Philadelphia: J. Harding, 1844. 17 p. CSmH. 44-3758

A letter to the Rev. John N. Campbell, suggesting some reasons for the publication of his late lectures against the Protestant Episcopal Church. Albany: 1844. 8 p. MB; MdBD; NCH; NjR. 44-3759

Letters on the moral and religious duties of parents. By a clergyman. Second edition. Boston: B.B. Mussey, 1844. [7]-156 p. CBPac; MMeT-Hi. 44-3760

Lever, Charles James, 1806-1872. Arthur O'Leary, his wanderings and ponderings. Philadelphia: Carey and Hart, 1844. 221 p. IU; MH; NN. 44-3761

Lever, Charles James, 1806-1872. The confessions of Harry Lorrequer. A biography. Third American edition. Philadelphia: Carey and Hart, 1844. 16, 402 p. NoLoc. 44-3762

Lever, Charles James, 1806-1872. Tom Burke, "of ours." By Charles Lever.... New York: William H. Colyer, 1844. MDeeP. 44-3763

Lever, Charles James, 1806-1872. Tom Burke of "ours." Philadelphia: Carey and Hart, 1844. 310 p. MBAt; MH. 44-3764

Lever, Charles James, 1806-1872. Tom Burke "of ours." By Charles Lever.... Philadelphia: Carey and Hart, 1844. LNH; MsNF; MWA; OrAL. 44-3765

Leverett, Frederick Percival, 1803-1836. A new and copious lexicon of the Latin language; ....Boston: J.H. Wilkins and R.B. Carter, and C.C. Little and

James Brown, 1844. 2 v. in 1. MH; NbCrD; NjP; NNN; GCoStM. 44-3766

Levering, Robert E.H. Kingdom of slavery; or, the ark of liberty in the Phillistian hands of the 250,000 slaveholders. Also an appeal to the American churches. Circleville, Ohio: 1844. 16 p. MBAt; MdBP. 44-3767

Levin, Lewis Charles, 1808-1860. A lecture on Irish repeal in elucidation of the fallacy of its principles, and in proof of its pernicious tendency, in its moral, religious and political aspects. Philadelphia: 1844. 24 p. MiD-B; MHi; PPPrHi. 44-3768

Levizac, Jean Pons Victor Lacoutz de, d. 1813. A theoretical and practical grammar of the French language. Revised and corrected by Mr. Stephen Pasquier. Fifteenth American edition. To which have been added several tables on the formation of verbs, and the construction of pronouns, from the synoptical French grammar. New York: W.E. Dean, 1844. 446 p. CL; MB; MH; MiU; ViU. 44-3769

Levizac, Jean Pons Victor Lecoutz de, d. 1813. Theoretical and practical grammar of the French tongue...Fifteenth edition. New York: W.E. Dean, printer, 1844. MH; MiU. 44-3770

Levy, David. Speech of David Levy on the tenth article of the Treaty of Washington and certain fugitive criminals from Florida, ...House of Representatives, March 5, 1844. Washington: 1844. 31 p. MH; MHi; NBu; TxDaM. 44-3771

Levy, Jonas P. Speech of Jonas P. Levy, of Florida, on the tenth article of the

treaty of Washington and certain fugitive criminals from Florida. Washington: 1844. 31 p. FS; PHi. 44-3772

Lewis, Alonzo, 1794-1861. The history of Lynn... including Nahant.... Second edition. Boston: S.N. Dickinson, 1844. 278 p. CtY; MAbD; MWA; OHi; PHi. 44-3773

Lewis, Enoch, 1776-1856. A treatise on plane and spherical trigonometry; including the construction of the auxiliary tables; a concise tract on the conic sections, and the principles of spherical projection. Philadelphia: H. Orr, 1844. 228 p. CtHT; MH; MoS; NCH; PHi. 44-3774

Lewis, Estelle Anna Blanche Robinson, 1824-1880. Records of the heart. New York: D. Appleton and company, 1844. DLC; MH; PPL-R; RPB; ScNC. 44-3775

Lewis, F. The sinners guide, in two books; Book 1, containing a full and ample exhortation to the pursuit of virtue; with instructions and directions on how to become virtuous. Book II, the doctrine of virtue; Necessary instructions and advice for making a man virtuous, by the Rev. F. Lewis, ...translated from the Spanish. Philadelphia: Henry McGrath [1844] 402 p. COHN; IaDuC; InStmaS; MGIStA. 44-3776

Lewis, James Otto, 1799-1858. The North American aboriginal port-folio. [No. 1.] From the London edition. New York: J.O. Lewis, 1844. 16 p. DLC; InHi. 44-3777

Lewis, Robert Benjamin. Light and truth; collected from the Bible and ancient and modern history, containing the universal history of the world to the present times. By R.B. Lewis. Boston: Published by a committee of colored gentlemen, 1844. [9]-400 p. ICMe; MiOC; MWA; NcU; TxU. 44-3778

Lewis, William H. The early called; a gift for bereaved parents. ....Second edition, revised. New York: General Protestant Episcopal Sunday School Union, 1844. 84 p. DLC; MdBD; NBLIHI; NNG. 44-3779

Lewiston, Maine. Lewiston Falls Academy. The annual catalogue of Lewiston Falls Academy, for the year ending August 20, 1844. Portland: Thurston, Illsley and company, 1844. 16 p. MeAu. 44-3780

The librarian: a book for the parlor and the school district library. New York: Charles S. Francis and company. Boston: 1844. [13]-288 p. MMae; MoSMa; NNiaD. 44-3781

Liddle, W.E. Aunt Milly. A popular Virginia melody. Boston: Prentiss, 1844. 4 p. MB. 44-3782

The life and writings of James Gordon Bennett, editor of the New York Herald. New York: 1844. 64 p. DLC; LNH; NBuG; NNC; ScHi. 44-3783

Life in the insect world: or conversations upon insects, between an aunt and her nieces. Philadelphia: Lindsay and Blakiston, 1844. 241 p. KHi; MH; MSaP; OCN; PPL-R. 44-3784

Life in town, or, the Boston spy; being a series of sketches illustrative of whims and women in the Athens of America; by an Athenian. Boston: Redding and company, 1844. 40 p. MB; RNHi. 44-3785

Life in town: or, The Boston spy; being a series of sketches illustrative of whims and women in the Athens of America; by an Athenian. Boston: Redding and company; New York: Burgess and Stringer [etc., etc.] 1844. 24 p.CU; DLC; MB; NjP; ViU. 44-3786

Life in town, or, the Boston spy; being a series of sketches illustrative of whims and women in the Athens of America; by an Athenian. Boston: Redding and company; [Third edition] New York: Burgess and Stringer [etc., etc.] 1844. 56 p.MB; MWA. 44-3787

The life of Andrew Hellman, alias Adam Horn... with an account of his trial and sentence, is added a full account of the Staten Island murders. Philadelphia: Perry, 1844. 67 p. DLC; ICU; MdBE; NIC; PP. 44-3788

The life of Benjamin Franklin. Illustrated by tales, sketches, and anecdotes...Philadelphia: Thomas, Cowperthwait and company, 1844. 180 p. CtY; MWA; PHC; ViU. 44-3789

The life of Christopher Columbus, illustrated by tales, sketches and anecdotes. Philadelphia: 1844. CtY; OCl. 44-3790

The life of Father Matthew, the great apostle of temerance. Boston: 1844. 46 p. NN. 44-3791

The life of General Joseph Markly. Philadelphia: 1844. 12 p. PPL. 44-3792

The life of George Washington. Illustrated by tales, sketches and anecdotes. Adapted to the use of schools. With engravings. [By Peter Parley, Pseud.] Philadelphia: 1844. 174 p. CSmH; DLC; KWiW; MWA; PPM. 44-3793

Life of Hellman, alias Adam Horn, with account of his trial for murder. Baltimore County Court, 1843. Philadelphia: 1844. 67 p. MH-L; PPB. 44-3794

Life of Henry Clay. [Washington: Kendall's expositor, 1844?] [81]-88 p. DLC; OClWHi. 44-3795

Life of John Tyler, president of the United States, up to the close of the second session of the twenty-seventh congress; including some of his most important speeches. New York: Harper and Brothers, 1844. 256 p. DLC; LNH; NjN; OrU; ViU. 44-3796

Life of Lucian Hall and crimes. New Haven: 1844. 16 p. PHi. 44-3797

The life of Miss Marion Smith, being a faithful narrative, written by her niece. Boston: 1844. 12 p. CU; DLC; KEmT. 44-3798

The life of Saint Patrick, Apostle of Ireland. New York: J. McLoughlin, 1844. 107 p. MBrigStJ. 44-3799

The life of the Rt. Rev. Dr. Doyle. Compiled from authentic documents. New York: D. and J. Sadlier and company, 1844. 288 p. MBC; MBrigStJ; MoSCBC; NRSB. 44-3800

The life, trial, and conversations, of Robert Emmet, esq., leader of the Irish insurrection of 1803; also, the celebrated speech made by him on the occasion. First American, from the last Dublin edition. New York: Wm. M. Christy, 1844. 124 p. IaDuU; MdBS. 44-3801

Lighton, William Beeby. Narrative of [his] life and sufferings; his early life, enlistment into the British army, experience in the service, etc., written by himself. New revised edition. Boston: 1844. MBAt; NNUT; NStc; NWM. 44-3802

Lily of the valley. A present from father. Cincinnati: 1844. OClWHi. 44-3803

Lime Street Lecture. A defence of some important doctrines of the Gospel, in 26 sermons. Most of which were preached at the Lime Street Lecture by several eminent ministers. Philadelphia: Presbyterian Board of Publication, 1844. IaFairP; IaHoL; MdW; PPPrHi. 44-3804

Lincoln, Ensign, 1779-1832. Aids to devotion including Beckersteth on prayer and Watt's guide to prayer and select devotion exercises by Ensign Lincoln. Third edition. Boston: Gould, Kendall and Lincoln, 1844. 324 p. MoSpD; NjPT; RPB; ScDuE; ViU. 44-3805

Lincoln, Ensign, 1779-1832. Aids to devotion including Beckersteth on prayer and Watt's guide to prayer and select devotion exercises by Ensign Lincoln, Fifth edition. Philadelphia: American Baptist Publishers Society, 1844. 318 p. MiU; PPABP; RPB. 44-3806

Lincoln, Ensign, 1779-1832. Aids to devotion: including Bickersteth on prayer, Watts's guide to prayer and select devotional exercises. Fifth edition. Philadelphia: American Baptist publication society, [1844] 324 p. CBPSR; InAnd; MiU; OkMc; RPB. 44-3807

Lincoln, Frederic W. An address, delivered before the Mechanic Apprentices' Library Association, in the Masonic Temple, Boston, on its twenty-fourth anniversary, February 22, 1844. By Frederic W. Lincoln, Jr. Honorary member of the association. Boston: Published for the association, 1844. 34, 16 p. MiD-B; NBu; NCH; WHi. 44-3808

Lincoln, Robert W. Lives of the presidents of the United States; with biographical notices of the signers of the Declaration of Independence... New York: Edward Kearny, 1844. 420, 167 p. CMiC; MiPaw; NjP; RWoH. 44-3809

Lincoln, Robert W. Lives of the presidents of the United States; with biographical notices of the signers of the Declaration of Independence... New York: Kearny, 1844. 578 p. CtHT. 44-3810

Lingard, John, 1771-1851. A history of England, from the first invasion by the Romans to the commencement of the reign of William the Third. New edition, corrected and considerably enlarged in thirteen volumes. New York: Edward Dunigan and brother, 1844-1845. IMunS; MdU; MiD; OOxM; MWelC. 44-3811

Lippard, George, 1822-1854. Herbert Tracy, or, the legend of the black rangers, a romance of the battlefield of Germantown, by George Lippard, esq. ....Philadelphia: R.G. Berford, 1844. 117 p. CtY; MdBJ; MH; MWH. 44-3812

Lippard, George, 1822-1854. The lady Annabel; or the doom of the poisoner. A romance by an unknown author. Philadelphia: R.G. Berford, 1844. 133 p. CtY; MdBP; OClW; PHi; ViU. 44-3813

Lippard, George, 1822-1854. The Quaker City; or the monks of Monk Hall. A romance of Philadelphia life, mystery, and crime. Philadelphia: G.B. Zeiber and company, 1844. 494 p. PHi; StTeach-C. 44-3814

Lipscomb, Andrew Adgate, 1816-1890. Our country; its danger and duty. New York: American Protestant Society, 1844. 135 p. GDecCT; MBC; NNC; OClWHi; PPL. 44-3815

Listen to the voice of [Mormon] truth. New York: Printed by Brannan and company, 1844. V.1. no. 1. NoLoc. 44-3816

Litchfield County, Connecticut. North Consociation. Action of the consociation in relation to the settlement of Rev. Augustus Pomeroy at Winsted. Hartford: 1844. 8 p. MBC. 44-3817

The literary museum, an annual volume of the useful and entertaining, including the wonders of nature and art; tales of all countries and all ages... Boston: J.B. Hall and company, 1844-1847. 4 v. in 2. CtY; DLC; MB. 44-3818

Littell, John Stockton, 1806-1875. The Clay minstrel; or national songster... New York: Greeley and M'Elrath; Philadelphia: Thomas, Cowperthwait and company, 1844. 288 p. DLC; NcD; OClWHi; PHi; TxU. 44-3819

Littell, John Stockton, 1806-1875. The Clay minstrel... to which is prefixed a sketch of the life, public services, and character of Henry Clay. Second edition, enlarged. New York: Greeley and M'Elrath, 1844. 384 p. IaU; MdHi; LU; MnU; RNHi. 44-3820

Littell, John Stockton, 1806-1875. The clay minstrel; or, National songster. Sixth edition without biography. New York, 1844. 288 p. PHi. 44-3821

Littell's living age. Boston: Littell, son and company, 1844-. v.1-. CoU; IaB; KyLoS; MBC; WvU. 44-3822

The little girls' missionary meeting. From the London edition, revised by the committee of publication. Boston: Massachusetts Sabbath School Society, 1844. 70 p. MNowdHi. 44-3823

Little Mary; or the infant school child. Philadelphia: Presbyterian Board of Publication, 1844. 11 p. ViRVal. 44-3824

Little Miami Railroad. Annual Report. Cincinnati: 1844-1857. DLC; OCHP; WU. 44-3825

Little miss why-why. Revised by the Committee of Publication. From the London edition. Boston: Sabbath School Society Depository, 1844. 32 p. MH. 44-3826

Little pilgrim's progress. Philadelphia: Smith and Peck, 1844. 192 p. MH; MPlyA; NICLA. 44-3827

Little poems for little folks. Philadelphia: Smith and Peck, 1844. MH; NN; NUt. 44-3828

The little primer, or first lessons for children. Newark, New Jersey: B. Olds, 1844. 24 p. MH; OrU. 44-3829

Little story book for little folks. New York: Howe and Perry [1844] 88 p. OKentU. 44-3830

Little, G. Parker. Duties of educated men. An address delivered before the Alumni Association of Marshall College at its annual celebration September 25th, 1844. Chambersburg: Printed at the Publication office of the German Reformed Church, 1844. 31 p. PHi; PLERC-Hi; PLFM; PPM; PPPrHi. 44-3831

Little, George, b. 1791. Life on the ocean, or twenty years at sea: being the personal adventures of the author. Second edition. Boston: 1844. CSmH; MH; PPL-R; NBellp. 44-3832

Livermore, Harriet, 1788-1868. Counsel of God, immutable and everlasting. Philadelphia: L.R. Bailey, 1844. 6-317 p. IP; MH; OO; ScCoT. 44-3833

Livermore, Harriet, 1788-1868. Counsel of God. Immutable and everlasting. Philadelphia: L.R. Bailey, 1844. 317 p. IP; MHi. 44-3834

Lives of John Sullivan, Jacob Leisler, Nathaniel Bacon, and John Mason. Boston: Charles C. Little and James Brown, 1844. 438 p. MAbD; RLa. 44-3835

Lives of Robert Cavalier de la Salle. Boston: C.C. Little and J. Brown, 1844. MCli. 44-3836

Lives of Robert Cavelier De La Salle and Patrick Henry. Boston: Charles C. Little and James Brown, 1844. 398 p. CSmH; DLC; ICN; RLa. 44-3837

Lives of William Pinkney, William Ellery, and Cotton Mather. New York: Harper and brothers, 1844. 350 p. FPalo; RKi; RPE. 44-3838

The living age. New York: the Living Age company, 1844. CSt; IaDuC; LNH; MiU; NbU. 44-3839

Livins, Titus. The history of Rome by Titus Livins, translated from the original with notes and illustrations by George Baker. A new edition, carefully corrected and revised. Philadelphia: M'Carty and Davis, 1844. 2 v. CU; InFtw; KyDC; MdW; NjP. 44-3840

Livius Patavinus, Titus. Historiarum liber primus et selecta quaedam capita; curavit... C. Folsom... By C. Folsom; Fourteenth edition. Boston: Simpkins, 1844. 286 p. NjP; PPL-R; OrP. 44-3841

Livius, Titus. Livy. Translated. New York: Harper and Brothers, 1844. 5 v. CoU; OHi; PCC; TxD-T. 44-3842

Livius, Titus. Titi Livii patavini historiarum liber primus et selectae quaedam capita. Boston: 1844. MBC. 44-3843

Locke, John, 1632-1704. An essay concerning human understanding and a treatise on the conduct of the understanding, by John Locke, gentleman. Philadelphia: James Kay, Jun, and brother, 1844. 524 p. AFIT; KyLoS; NNUT; ScNC; ViLC. 44-3844

Locke, John, 1632-1704. Philosophical beauties selected from the works of John Locke, esq. Containing the conduct of the understanding; elements of natural philosophy.... to which is prefixed some account of his life. First American edition. Cooperstown: H. and E. Phinney, 1844. 258 p. MH; MiU. 44-3845

Locke, John, 1637-1704. A treatise on the conduct of the understanding. ....To which is now added a sketch of his life. A new edition. Boston: T. H. Carter and company, 1844. 216 p. KWiU; MeBa; NTRS; OMC; TxH. 44-3846

Logan, Cornelius Ambrosius, 1806-1853. Vermont wool dealer; a farce in one act. New York: Samuel French and son; London: Samuel French, [1844?] 18 p. OCl. 44-3847

Longfellow, Henry Wadsworth, 1807-1882. The Spanish student. A play in three acts. Fifth edition. Cambridge: J. Owen, 1844. 183 p. MB; MC; MPly; NNC; TxU. 44-3848

Longfellow, Henry Wadsworth, 1807-1882. The Spanish student. A play in three acts. Sixth edition. Cambridge: J. Owen, 1844. 183 p. CSmH; MB; MH. 44-3849

Longfellow, Henry Wadsworth, 1807-1882. Voices in the night. By Henry Wadsworth Longfellow. Ninth editon. Cambridge: John Owen, 1844. 144 p. Ct; DLC; MWH; NjP; OOC. 44-3850

Longfellow, Henry Wadsworth, 1807-1882. Voices in the night. By Henry Wadsworth Longfellow. Tenth edition. Cambridge: John Owen, 1844. 144 p. MB; MWH; PPL; TxU. 44-3851

Longfellow, Henry Wadsworth, 1807-1882. The waif: a collection of poems.... Cambridge: [1844] MH. 44-3852

Loomis' magazine almanac for 1845. Pittsburgh: [1844] MWA. 44-3853

Loomis' Pittsburgh almanac for 1845. Calculations by Sanford C. Hill. Pittsburgh, Pennsylvania: Luke Loomis, [1844] MWA. 44-3854

Loomis, S.C. A phrenological chart; containing demonstrations of the organs of the brain.... Philadelphia: 1844. 48 p. WHi. 44-3855

Lord, John King. An address before the Gamma Sigma Society of Dartmouth College, July 24, 1844. Boston: 1844. 32 p. DG; MH-AH; Nh. 44-3856

Lord, John King. The dangers of the scholar. An address delivered before the Gamma Sigma Society of Dartmouth College, July 24, 1844. Boston: James Munroe and company, 1844. 32 p. CSans-S; KWiU; MBC; MH; MnHi. 44-3857

Lord, John Perkins, 1786-1877. Maine townsman; or laws for the regulation of towns, with forms and judicial decisions adapted to the revised statutes of Maine; by J.P. Lord. Boston: 1844. 13-300 p. MH-L; OO. 44-3858

Loring, John Greeley, An address delivered before the First Christian Church in Boston, on Sabbath afternoon, June 30, 1844. It being the fortieth anniversary of the organization of said church. Boston: Published by a committee of the church, 1844. 26 p. ICMe; MB; MWA; RPB, WHi. 44-3859

Loss of the Kent East Indiaman. Boston: Tract Committee of the Diocese of Massachusetts, 1844. 39 p. IEG; MBC; MBD. 44-3860

Louisiana. Acts passed at the second session of the sixteenth legislature of the state of Louisiana begun and held in the city of New Orleans, January 1, 1844. New Orleans: Printed by Alexander C. Bullitt, 1844. 106 p. IaU-L; LNA;Nj; OCLaw; Wa-L. 44-3861

Louisiana. Code of practice of the state of Louisiana, containing rules of procedure in civil actions; with notes of and references to, the decisions of the Supreme Court of the state of Louisiana, and also the statutory law relative to practice. New Orleans: J.B. Steel, 1844. 392 p. CLSU; ICLaw; LNT-L; Wa-L. 44-3862

Louisiana. University. Medical Department. Annual circulars. New Orleans: 1844--. PPCP. 44-3863

Louisiana almanac for 1845. By S.S. Steele. New Orleans: S. Woodall [1844] MWA. 44-3864

Louisiana Convention, 1811-1812. Journal de la convention d'Orleans de 1811-1812. Imprime pour l'usage de la convention de 1844. Jackson: Imprime par Jerome Bayon, 1844. 19 p. M. 44-3865

Louisiana merchant's and planter's almanac for the year of our Lord and Saviour, 1845. New York: David Felt and company, 1844. 34 p. NcU. 44-3866

Louisville, Kentucky. Medical Institute. Catalogue of the officers and students of the Medical Institute of the city of Louisville, January, 1844. Louisville, Kentucky: Prentice and Weissinger, 1844. 12 p. NNNAM. 44-3867

Lounsbury, Thomas. The touchstone of the Bible applied to modern abolition. Geneva: Scotten and Van Brunt, 1844. 155 p. OClWHi. 44-3868

Lounsbury, Thomas. The touchstone of truth. Applied to modern abolition; or seven lectures in answer to the question What do the scriptures teach on the subject of slavery. Geneva: Scotten and Van Brunt, 1844. 155 p. CtY; LNH; MWeA; NCH; WBeloC. 44-3869

Love, Thomas N. On hereditary transmission, inaugural dissertation. Charleston: Nixon, 1844. 22 p. PPCP. 44-3870

Lovejoy, J.C. Funeral sermon for Rev. John Wilder, at Cambridgeport, March 8, 1844. Boston: 1844. MDeeP. 44-3871

Lovejoy, J.C. Sermon at the interment of J. Wilder, March 8, 1844. Boston: 1844. 16 p. L-RM. 44-3872

Lovejoy, J.C. Sermon, alliance of Jehoshaphat and Ahab, annual fast, April 4, 1844, Cambridgeport. Boston: 1844. MDeeP. 44-3873

Lovejoy, J.C. A sermon, preached at the interment of Rev. John Wilder, at Cambridgeport, March 8, 1844. ....Boston: Wilder and company, 1844. 16 p. MBNEH; MeBat; MW; NjR; PHi. 44-3874

Lovejoy, Joseph Cammet, 1805-1871. The alliance of Jehoshaphat and Ahab. A sermon, preached on the annual fast, April 4, 1844, at Cambridgeport. Boston: Leavitt and Alden, printer, 1844. 8 p. MH; MHi; TNF. 44-3875

Lovejoy, Joseph Cammet, 1805-1871.

The victory over death. A sermon preached at the interment of Rev. John Wilder, at Cambridgeport, March 8, 1844. By J.C. Lovejoy, pastor of the Second Evangelical Congregational Church, Cambridgeport. Boston: 1844. 16 p. CBPSR; MBC; MnHi; RPB; WHi. 44-3876

Lovell, John Epy, 1795-1892. Rhetorical dialogue; or, dramatic selections for the use of schools, academies, and families; designed to furnish exercises, either for reading, recitation, or exhibition.... Second edition.... New Haven: S. Babcock, 1844. 408 p. ICU; MH; NcAS; WBeloC. 44-3877

Lovell, John Epy, 1795-1892. The United States speaker: A copious selection of exercises in elocution... New Haven: S. Babcock, 1844. 504 p. InI; InPerM; MdCatS; MiU. 44-3878

Lovell, John Epy, 1795-1892. The young pupil's second book. Third edition. New Haven: 1844. CtHWatk. 44-3879

Lovell, John Epy, 1795-1892. The young pupil's second book. Fourth edition. New Haven, Connecticut: 1844. NoLoc. 44-3880

Lover, Samuel, 1797-1868. Barny O'Reirdon, the navigation and tales of Ireland. With the Dowerless. Philadelphia: Carey and Hart, 1844. 118 p. MBL; MiD; PPM. 44-3881

Lover, Samuel, 1797-1868. S.D.; or accounts of Irish heirs. Furnished to the public monthly. New York: J. Winchester, 1844. 80 p. NNC. 44-3882

Lover, Samuel, 1797-1868. Treasure

trove; a tale. New York: D. Appleton and company, 1844. 173 p. GU; MdHi; MoSp; PPL-R; PULowell, James Russell, 1819-1891. A fable for critics. Boston: Ticknor and Fields, 1844. TxSaU. 44-3883

Lowell, Anna Cabot Jackson. Edwards' first lessons in geometry. Boston: W.D. Ticknor and company, 1844. 150 p. MB; MH. 44-3884

Lowell, James Russell, 1819-1891. Poems by James Russell Lowell. Cambridge: John Owen, 1844. 279 p. ICN; LN; MH; NBuU; RNR. 44-3885

Lowell, James Russell, 1819-1891. Poems by James Russell Lowell. Second edition. Cambridge: J. Owen, 1844. 279 p. MB; OCHP; PV; TxU; ViU. 44-3886

Lowell, James Russell, 1819-1891. Poems by James Russell Lowell. Third edition. Cambridge: J. Owen, 1844. 279 p. DLC; MBAt; MH; MWH; RPB. 44-3887

Lowell, Massachusetts. Rules and orders of the city council and a list of the government officers of the city of Lowell. Lowell: Stearns and Taylor, 1844. 20 p. MLow. 44-3888

Lucas, George Washington. Remarks on the musical conventions in Boston, and C. Northampton: the author, 1844. 27 p. M; MB; MH. 44-3889

Ludlow, John Livingston, 1819-1888. A manual of examinations upon the anatomy and physiology, surgery, practice of medicine, chemistry, materia medica, obstetrics, etc. Designed for the use of students of medicine throughout the United States. Philadelphia: E. Barrington and G.D. Haswell, 1844. [9]-615 p. GEU-M; ICU-R; MBM; NNN; PU. 44-3890

Lunt, George. An address, delivered before the Massachusetts Charitable Mechanic Association, September 26, 1844, on occasion of their fourth exhibition. Boston: Crocker and Brewster, 1844. 24 p. MdBJ; MWA; NNC; PHi; RPB. 44-3891

Lunt, William Parsons, 1805-1857. The Christian psalter; a collection of psalms and hymns for social and private worship. Third edition. Boston: Little and Brown, 1844. MB; MB-FA; MWHi; NNUT. 44-3892

Luther, Martin, 1483-1546. A commentary on Saint Paul's epistle to the Galatians. New York: Robert Carter, 1844. 575 [8] p. InU; KyLoP; MeBat; TxAuPT; WHi. 44-3893

Luther, Martin, 1483-1546. Commentary upon the epistle of Paul to the Galatians, to which is prefixed an account of the life of the author. New York: Ezra Collier, 1844. 527 p. IaCrC; CtHC. 44-3894

Luther, Martin, 1483-1746. Der kleine catechismus; nebst den gewohnlichen morgen- abend- und tisch-gebeten, welchem die ordnung des heils in einem liede, in.... satzen, in frag und antwort und in einer tabelle.... auch.... Das wurtembergische kurze kinder-examen.... beygefuget und.... lieder, Freylinghausens ordnung des heils, das guldene A.B.C. ....New York: Ludwing, 1844. 132 p. PPLT. 44-3895

Luther, Martin, 1483-1746. Luther's shorter catechism. by John G. Morris. Baltimore: Printed at the Publication Rooms of the Evangelical Lutheran Church, 1844. 105 p. PAtM; PPLT. 44-3896

Der Lutheraner...St. Louis, Missouri: Gedrudt bei Weber und Dishaufen, 1844. 32 v. CSt; IaDL; MH-AH; MoSC. 44-3897

Lykens Valley Coal Company. Report... Philadelphia: 1844. PPL. 44-3898

Lyman, Azel S. Historical chart presenting at one view the history of the world from the earliest times to the present day.... Cincinnati: T.S. Butler, 1844. MBC; MH-AH; MiU; NIC; OClWHi. 44-3899

Lyme, Connecticut. First Congregational Church. Manual for the communicants of the Congregational Church in North Lyme, Connecticut. n.p.: 1844. 8 p. Ct. 44-3900

Lyne, Thomas A. A true and descriptive account of the assassination of Joseph and Hiram Smith, the Mormon prophet and patriarch. At Carthage, Illinois, June 27, 1844, by an eye witness. New York: Calhoun, 1844. 17 p. CtY; IU; MB; NN; PHi. 44-3901

Lyons, James Gilborne, d. 1868. Twelve Christian songs. Philadelphia: [between 1844 and 1848] 24 p. NNUT. 44-3902

Lyons, New York. Village ordinance. An ordinance in relation to the side walks in the village of Lyons. ....Passed June 25th, 1844. Lyons, New York. NN. 44-3903

Lyra apostolica. First American from the fifth English edition. New York: D. Appleton, 1844. 262 p. MH; NcAS; OCX; ViU. 44-3904

Lyra apostoica...First American from the fifth English edition. New York: D. Appleton and company; Philadelphia: George S. Appleton, 1844. 8, 262 p. CtHWatk; MBC; MH; MNt; OrPD. 44-3905

Lytton, Edward Bulwer Earle Lytton Bulwer-Lytton, 1803-1873. The last days of Pompeii; a dramatic spectacle, taken from Bulwer's celebrated novel of the same title.... New York, London: Samuel French, [1844] 31 p. OCL. 44-3906

Lytton, Edward George Earle Lytton Bulwer-Lytton, 1803-1873. Richelieu, or the conspiracy, a play in five acts, by Sir Edward Lytton Bulwer. New York: James Mowatt and company, 1844. 96 p. MA; MH; NN. 44-3907

Lytton, Edward George Earle Lytton Bulwer-Lytton, 1803-1873. Rienzi, the last of the tribunes; or the life of Nicholas Rienzi, a tribune of the Roman people, who was on the morning he appeared in scarlet furred with ermine. Hartford: Printed by David B. Moseley, 1844. 16 p. CSmH; DLC. 44-3908

Lytton, Edward George Earle Lytton Bulwer-Lytton, 1803-1873. The lady of Lyons; or, Love and pride. A play. In five acts. From the author's latest edition. With stage directions, costumes, etc. New York: J. Mowatt and company, 1844. [9]-61 p. DLC; MB; MH; NIC. 44-3909

M

Macaulay, Thomas Babington Macaulay, 1800-1859. Essays, critical and miscellaneous, by T. Babington Macaulay. Philadelphia: Carey and Hart, 1844. 707 p. CU; MB; NcU; OMC; PCC. 44-3910

McCall, John G. The new English spelling book, and child's first reading book; designed for schools and private families where the English language is spoken. Norwich: 1844. 160 p. CtHWatk; CtY. 44-3911

M'Cartney, Washington, 1812-1856. The principles of the differential and integral calculus; and their application to geometry. Philadelphia: E.C. Biddle, 1844. 340 p. LNT; MiU; NjP; OOxM; PEaL. 44-3912

McCheyne, Robert Murray, 1813-1843. Another lily gathered; conversion of James Laing, who died age fourteen. Philadelphia: 1844. 57 p. MBC; NjPT. 44-3913

McCheyne, Robert Murray, 1813-1843. Children coming to Christ, and the lambs of the flock. Philadelphia: Presbyterian Board of Publication, 1844. 38 p. NNUT; NRHi. 44-3914

McCheyne, Robert Murray, 1813-1843. Memoir and remains of the Rev. Robert Murray McCheyne... By the Rev. Andrew A Bonar... With an introductory letter by the Rev. Samuel Miller...

Philadelphia: Presbyterian Board of Publication, 1844. 386 p. CU; NcDaD; OWoC; PPP; ViRut. 44-3915

McClelland, John Alexander. Speech on the civil and diplomatic appropriation bill, delivered in the House, June 4, 1844. Washington: 1844. 13 p. NNC; T. 44-3916

McClelland, Robert. Speech...on the bill making appropriations for certain rivers and harbors: delivered in the House, April 17, 1844. Washington: printed at the Globe office, 1844. 8 p. Mi; MiD-B; MiU-C. 44-3917

M'Clung, John Alexander, 1804-1859. Sketches of western adventure: containing an account of the most interesting incidents connected with the settlement of the west from 1755 to 1794: by John A. M'Clung. Dayton, Ohio: Ellis and Claflin, 1844. 315 p. InThE; KyDC; MoSU; MWA; ODa. 44-3918

McCollum, John. John McCullom vs. Thomas Fitzsimons; tried in the city court of Charleston, July term, 1844. Charleston: Miller, 1844. 12 p. NcU. 44-3919

M'Conaughy, David. "A sermon on the necessity of a high tone of piety in the gospel ministry." ....Pittsburgh: Presbyterian Advocate office, 1844. 15 p. NbOP; PPPrHi; PWW. 44-3920

McCulloch, J.R. A dictionary,

geographical, statistical, and historical of various counties and places.... New York: Harper and brothers, 1844. 2 v. CSmH. 44-3921

McCulloch, John Ramsay, 1789-1864. A dictionary, geographical, statistical and historical, of the various countries, places, and principal natural objects in the world; in which the articles relating to the United States have been greatly multiplied and extended, and adapted to the present condition of the country and to the wants of its citizens, by Daniel Haskel. New York: Harper and brothers, 1844. 2 v. CBPSR; LNH; MsAb; MWA. 44-3922

McCulloch, John Ramsay, 1789-1864. A dictionary, geographical, statistical and historical, of the various countries, places, and principal natural objects in the world; in which the articles relating to the United States have been greatly multiplied and extended, and adapted to the present condition of the country and to the wants of its citizens, by Daniel Haskel. New York: Harper and brothers, 1844-1846. 2 v. MH-BA. 44-3923

McCulloch, John Ramsay, 1789-1864. A dictionary, geographical, statistical and historical of the world. New York: Harper, 1844-1845. 2 v. MWA; PAnL. 44-3924

McCulloch, John Ramsay, 1789-1864. M'Culloch's universal gazetteer. A dictionary, geographical, statistical and historical, of the various countries, places, and principal natural objects in the world. In which the articles relating to the United States have been greatly multiplied and extended... By Daniel Haskel... Illustrated with seven larger maps... New York: Harper and brothers, 1844-1845. 2 v. DLC; MoKU; OCl; ViU; WvC. 44-3925

MacCulloh, Richard S. Plan of organization for the naval observatory submitted by request to the secretary of the navy, November 17, 1843. Washington: 1844. MBAt; MH. 44-3926

McCullough, John W. The faith of the saints. A sermon in two parts... The true catholic faith. By J.W. McCullough. Wilmington, Delaware: Porter and Naff, 1844. [9]-34 p. CtHT; IEG; MdBD; NcU; PHi. 44-3927

McCurdy, Dennis. An essay on geometry in education. Washington: 1844. PPL. 44-3928

MacDougall, Frances Harriet [Whipple] Greene, 1805-1878. Might and right: by a Rhode Islander.... Providence: A.H. Stillwell, 184. 324 p. CoD; CtSoP; ICN; MiU; Nh-Hi; RP. 44-3929

McDowell, Andrew. A treatise on the subject of baptism designed principally to guide the serious inquirer after truth against the sophistry of Campbellism. Richmond: P.D. Bernard, printer, 1844. 101 p. MdBD; MoFayO; NcD; ViRU; ViU. 44-3930

McDowell, William Adair, 1795-1853. Answer to a review of McDowell's treatise on consumption [by Dr. Yandell] Louisville: 1844. 3 p. CSt-L; DSG; MB; MBM; NNNAM. 44-3931

McDowell, William Adair, 1795-1853. Reply of William A. McDowell to Dr. Yandell's rejoiner in a controversy relative to the cure of consumption. Louisville, Kentucky: Prentice and Weissinger, 1844. 30 p. CSt-L; IEN-M; MH; NNC; NNNAM. 44-3932

McDuffie, George, 1790-1851. Speech of Mr. McDuffie, of South Carolina, in executive session, on the treaty for the reannexation of Texas to the United States: delivered in the Senate May 23, 1844 [n.p.: 1844] 8 p. DLC; NcD. 44-3933

McDuffie, George, 1790-1851. Speech on the traffic in reply to Messrs. Evans and Huntington: delivered in the Senate of the United States, January 19, 1844. Washington: Globe office, 1844. 15 p. DLC; GU; ICN; MiD; TxU. 44-3934

McDuffie, George, 1790-1851. Speech... on the treaty for the re-annexation of Texas to the United States... in the Senate... May 23, 1844. [Washington: 1844] NcD; Tx. 44-3935

McDuffie, George, 1790-1851. Speech...on the tariff, in reply to messrs. Evans and Huntington: delivered in the Senate of the United States, January 19, 1844. Washington: Globe office, 1844. 15 p. In; MBAt; MH; NcD; OClWHi. 44-3936

McElrath, T.L. Relations with the Harpers. New York, 1844. MB. 44-3937

McElroy's Philadelphia directory for 1844; containing names of inhabitants, their occupations, places of business and dwelling houses; besides a list of streets.... Seventh edition. Philadelphia: Edward C. Biddle, 1844. [4] 410 p. KHi. 44-3938

McEwen, Matthew H. Expose of the case of the commonwealth; by M.H. McEwen. [Seduction trial] Philadelphia: 1844. 34 p. CtHWatk; MH-L; PPL. 44-3939

McGee, Thomas D. Hray. Eva Macdonald, a tale of the United Irishmen and their times. Boston: C.H. Brainard, 1844. 47 p. NN. 44-3940

MacGillivary, W. The travels and researches of Alexander von Humboldt; being a condensed narrative of his journeys in the equinoctial regions of America, and in Asiatic Russia. New York: Published by Harper and Brothers, 1844. 368 p. InCW; LNH; MeAu; OCX; PHi. 44-3941

McGrindell, Rachel. English governess: a tale of real life. First American edition. Philadelphia: Hooker, 1844. 264 p. KyBgW; PU; TJoT. 44-3942

McGuffey, Alexander Hamilton, 1816-1896. Newly revised fourth reader.... Cincinnati: Winthrop Smith, 1844. CtHWatk; DLC; NN. 44-3943

McGuffey, Alexander Hamilton, 1816-1896. McGuffey's rhetorical guide; or fifth reader of the eclectic series. Containing elegant extracts in prose and poetry: with copious rules and rhetorical exercises. Cincinnati: Withrop B. Smith and company, 1844. 480 p. ArU; ILM; OAU; OOxM; PAlt. 44-3944

McGuffey, Alexander Hamilton, 1816-1896. McGuffey's rhetorical guide; or fifth reader of the eclectic series. Containing elegant extracts in prose and poetry: with copious rules and rhetorical exercises. New York: Clark, Austin and Smith [1844] ViU. 44-3945

McGuffey, William Holmes, 1800-1873. Eclectic series, newly improved McGuffey's fourth reader, newly revised. Containing elegant extracts in prose and poetry, from the best American and English writers. Enlarged and greatly improved. Cincinnati: Winthrop B. Smith, 1844. 336 p. KyStjM; ScMit. 44-3946

McGuffey, William Holmes, 1800-1873. Eclectic series, newly improved McGuffey's rhetorical guide; or, Fifth reader of the Eclectic series; containing elegant extracts in prose and poetry. With copious rules and rhetorical exercises. Compiled by A.D. McGuffey. Cincinnati: Winthrop B. Smith and company, 1844. 480 p. WWaHi. 44-3947

McGuffey, William Holmes, 1800-1873. First [-sixth] eclectic reader. Cincinnati: Winthrop...., 1844. WaPS. 44-3948

McGuffey, William Holmes, 1800-1873. McGuffey's newly revised first reader: the eclectic first reader for young children. Cincinnati: W.R. Smith and company, 1844. 488 p. CSaT; OOxM. 44-3949

McGuffey, William Holmes, 1800-1873. Newly revised second reader. Enlarged and greatly improved. Cincinnati: Winthrop B. Smith and company, [1844] DLC; MH; OClWHi; OOxM. 44-3950

McGuffey, William Holmes, 1800-1873. McGuffey's newly revised fourth reader. The fourth reader containing elegant extracts in prose and poetry, from the best American and English writers, with copious rules for reading and direction for avoiding common errors, enlarged and greatly improved. Cincinnati:

Smith, 1844. 336 p. InBrB; MH; OClWHi; PPi. 44-3951

McGuffey, William Holmes, 1800-1873. McGuffey's rhetorical guide or fifth reader of the eclectic series. Stereotype edition. New York: Clark, Austin and Smith; Cincinnati: W.B. Smith and company, [1844] 480 p. MnS; NjR; OClWHi; PPi; ViU. 44-3952

McIlvaine, Charles Pettit, 1799-1873. The evidences of Christianity, in their external, or historical, division: exhibited in a course of lectures, by Charles Pettit M'Ilvaine.... Sixth edition, revised and improved by the author. New York: Harper and brothers, 1844. 408 p. CtHC; IaPeC; KyLx; NR; PPA. 44-3953

McIlvaine, Charles Pettit, 1799-1873. The Holy Catholic Church... A sermon, preached in the Church of the Epiphany, in the city of Philadelphia, on Sunday, September 6, 1844. Published by request. Philadelphia: H. Hooker, 1844. 114 p. IU; MBC; NGH; PU; OCl; WHi. 44-3954

McIlvaine, Charles Pettit, 1799-1873. Oxford divinity, compared with that of the Romish and Anglican churches. Philadelphia: Joseph Whetham and son, 1844. 546 p. OCX. 44-3955

McIlvaine, William. Perpetual calendar, civil and ecclesiastical.... Burlington, New Jersey: 1844. PPAmP; PPL. 44-3956

McIntosh, John. The origin of the North American Indians; with a description of their manners and customs, religions, languages, dress, and ornaments. New York: Nafis, 1844. 311 p. MH; NNC; PEaL; RPB. 44-3957

McIntosh, Maria J. The lofty and the lowly; or good in all and none all good. New York: D. Appleton and company, 1844. 2 v. NjR. 44-3958

Mack, Ebenezer. The character and importance of agriculture, and the means and efforts which are and should be directed to its improvement; an address delivered before the Tompkins County Agriculture and Horticulture Society, October 5, 1844. Ithaca: 1844. 16 p. MB; N; NjR; MoS; NIC. 44-3959

MacKellar, Thomas. Droppings from the heart; or occasional poems... Philadelphia: Sorin and Ball, 1844. [9]-144 p. ICU; KyWA; PHi;RPB; TxU. 44-3960

Mackenzie, Alexander Slidell, 1803-1848. Proceedings of the naval court martial in the case of Alexander Slidell Mackenzie, a commander in the navy of the United States, &c., including the charges and specifications of charges, preferred against him by the secretary of the navy. New York: H. J. Langley, 1844. 344 p. GU; NcD; PP; TxU; WaU. 44-3961

Mackenzie, William Lyon. The sons of the Emerald Isle; or, lives of one thousand remarkable Irishmen, including memoirs of noted characters of Irish parentage or descent.... New York: Burgess, Stringer and company, 1844. 60 p. CSmH; M; NjR; PHi; PPL. 44-3962

Mackintosh, John, d. 1837. Principles of pathology and practice of medicine. ....Fourth American, from the last London edition. With notes and additions by Samuel George Morton..... Philadelphia:

Lindsay and Blakiston, 1844. 892 p. GU-M; IEN-M; MdToH; PU; ViU. 44-3963

McLallen, Robert L. A new and interesting arithmetic, in which is explained the method that Zerah Colburn must have pursued in answering the very difficult questions proposed to him by a rapid calculation of the head. ....To which is added, the surveyor's art.... abridged; whereby the contents and mensuration of land is made without the use of trigonometry. North Adams, [Massachusetts]: John R. Briggs, junior, printer, 1844. 210 p. CtHWatk; DLC; NNC. 44-3964

McLane, Louis. Accidents upon railroads: their causes and the mode of prevention; discussed in communications addressed to the Baltimore American. Baltimore: John Murphy, printer, 1844. 23 p. MnHi. 44-3965

McLaren, Donald Campbell, 1794-1882. Boa constrictor, or, fourier association self-exposed as to its principles and aims.... Rochester: Canfield and Warren, printers, 1844. 32 p. DLC; MBC; MH; NIC; PPPrHi. 44-3966

McLaughlin, John T. An examination of the report of the honorable John R. Redding, of the House of Representatives, upon the expenditures of the Florida squadron, by John T. McLaughlin, Lieutenant, United States navy, late commander of that squadron. Washington: C. Alexander, printer, 1844. 20 p. DLC; MdBP; NcHiC; PPL. 44-3967

Maclean, John, 1800-1886. Letters on the elder question. [Princeton, New Jersey] J.T. Robinson, 1844. 55 p. MB; NjR; OO; PPPrHi; T. 44-3968

MacMaster, Erasmus Darwin, 1806-1866. Speech of Mr. MacMaster in the synod of Indiana, October 4, 1844, in relation to Madison University. Madison: Jones and Lodge, 1844. 39 p. DLC; In; OClWHi; PPiU; PPiW. 44-3969

Macnish, Robert. The philosophy of sleep. [To which is appended his "anatomy of drunkenness." Second edition from the fifth Glasgow edition] Hartford: S. Andrus and son, 1844. 53 p. MH; NBuCC; NN; TxW. 44-3970

Macpherson, James, 1736-1796. The poems of Ossian, translated by James Macpherson, esq. To which are prefixed a preliminary discourse and dissertations on the aera and poems of Ossian. New York: Kearny, [1844?] 492 p. NNC. 44-3971

Macy, John B. To the honorable, the legislature of the state of Ohio. Columbus: 1844. 8 p. OClWHi. 44-3972

Madison and Indianapolis Railroad Company. Report of a committee appointed by the directors... to procure the publication, in pamphlet form.... [Indianapolis: 1844] 18 p. NN. 44-3973

Madison County Mutual Insurance Company. In the Court for the correction of errors. The Madison County Mutual Insurance Company, Pl'tffs in error vs. Jeremiah Gates, and Abner P. Downer, Def'ts in error. Cazenovia: W.H. Phillips, printers, 1844. 38 p. N. 44-3974

Madison, James, 1749-1812. A discourse on the death of General Washington, late president of the United States: delivered on the 22d of February, 1800, in the church in Williamsburgh.... Fourth edition, with additions. Richmond: J.B. Martin and company, printers, 1844. 30 p. DLC; MH-AH; NjR; WHi. 44-3975

The madisonian pamphlet. [Washington: 1844] 15 p. DLC; ICN; NN; OClW. 44-3976

The magazine for the million and weekly review of current literature. February 17-April 27, 1844? New York: 1844-. v. 1. IaAS; ICRL; MH; NN; NNC. 44-3977

Magendie, Francois, 1783-1855. An elementary treatise on human physiology, on the basis of the Precis elementaire de physiologie. New York: Harper and brothers, 1844. 539 p. DLC; KyU; NBuG; OClW-H; TNN. 44-3978

Magendie, Francois, 1783-1855. An elementary treatise on human physiology, on the basis of the Precis elementaire de physiologie. Par F. Magendie.... Fifth edition, 1838. Translated, enlarged.... by John Revere.... New York: Harper and brothers, 1844. [13]-539 p. CtMW; DLC; MeB; NNU-M; ViU. 44-3979

Magnetic telegraph, letter from the secretary of the treasury transmitting a letter from Samuel F.B. Morse. December 23, 1844. Washington: 1844. 18 p. PHi. 44-3980

Maguire, Thomas. A series of the controversial sermons of the Rev. T. Maguire.... exposing the fallacy, contradictions, and errors of the thirty-nine articles of the Church of England.... New York: Robert Coddington, 1844. 120 p. MdBLC; MoFloSS; NNF. 44-3981

Mahan, Asa. Scripture doctrine of Christian perfection; discourses designed to throw light on the way of holiness. Seventh edition. Boston: 1844. 193 p. MPiB; MW; MWA; NcU. 44-3982

Mahoney, S.I. Six years in the monasteries of Italy, and two years in the islands of the Mediterranean and in Asia Minor: ....with anecdotes and remarks. Hartford: S. Andrus and son, 1844. 321 p. InCW; MLow; OSW; WRichM. 44-3983

Mahoney, S.I. Six years in the monasteries of Italy, and two years in the islands of the Mediterranean and in Asia Minor: containing a view of the manners and customs of the popish clergy in Ireland, France, etc. Second edition. Hartford: 1844. LNH; MdBE. 44-3984

The maiden aunt. Boston: office of the living age, [1844] 88 p. RJPHL. 44-3985

Maine. An abstract of the return of corporations, 1843. Augusta: William R. Smith and company, Printers to the state, 1844. 31 p. MeB; MeLewB; MeU. 44-3986

Maine. Acts and resolves passed by the twenty-fourth Legislature of the state of Maine, 1844. Published by the Secretary of State, agreeably to resolves of June 28, 1820, February 26, 1840, and March 16, 1842. Augusta: William R. Smith and company, Printers to the state, 1844. 382 p. Ia; Me-LR; T; TxUL; W. 44-3987

Maine. Annual report of the Bank Commissioners, December 31, 1844. Published agreeably to resolve of March 22, 1836. Augusta: Wm. T. Johnson, printer, 1844. 23 p. MeHi. 44-3988

Maine. Communication of Governor Kavanagh to the Legislature of Maine, relating to the Town Court Bill. Augusta: William R. Smith and company, Printers to the state, 1844. 7 p. MeB. 44-3989

Maine. Communication of Governor Kavanagh to the legislature of Maine, transmitting report of the agent of the state at Washington and other documents relating to the north eastern frontier of Maine together with the message of the governor relating to the town court bill. Published agreeably to resolve of March 22, 1836. Augusta: William R. Smith and company, printers to the state, 1844. 5. p. MeLR. 44-3990

Maine. Documents printed by order of the Legislature of the state of Maine, during its session, 1844. Augusta: William R. Smith and company, printers, 1844. 492 p. MBAt; MeU. 44-3991

Maine. Insane Hospital. Reports of the trustees, steward and treasurer, and superintendent of the Insane Hospital, 1844. Augusta: William T. Johnson, printer, 1844. 47 p. MH. 44-3992

Maine. List of stockholders, with amount of stock held by each January 1, 1844, in the banks of Maine. Augusta: William R. Smith and Company, Printers to the state, 1844. 68 p. MeB; MeLewB; MeU. 44-3993

Maine. Private and special laws passed by the twenty fourth legislature of the state of Maine. Augusta: Published by the Secretary of State, 1844. 240 p. CSf-Law. 44-3994

Maine. Report of the Adjutant General of the state of Maine, December 30,

1843. Augusta: William R. Smith and company, Printers to the state, 1844. 18 p. MeU. 44-3995

Maine. Report of the treasurer of Maine, on the state of the treasury, December 30, 1843. Augusta: William R. Smith and company, Printers to the state, 1844. 18 p. MeLewB; MeU. 44-3996

Maine. Rules and orders of the House of Representatives of the state of Maine, 1844. Augusta: William R. Smith and Company, Printers to the state, 1844. 149 p. MeLewB; MeHi. 44-3997

Maine. Rules and orders of the House of Representatives of the state of Maine... Augusta: William R. Smith and company, printers to the state, 1844. 298 p. MeU. 44-3998

Maine. Rules and orders of the Senate of Maine, 1844. Augusta: William R. Smith, Printers to the state, 1844. 149 p. MeB. 44-3999

Maine. Rules of practice for the Supreme Court and of the courts of the state of Maine. Portland: Thurston, Ilsley, and company, printers, 1844. 125 p. MeHi. 44-4000

Maine. Tax for the year 1844. State of Maine, James White, Treasurer of said state. Augusta, 1844. Broadside. MeWebr. 44-4001

Maine. Twenty-Fourth legislature, 1844. First quarterly report of the superintendent and instructor of schools in Madawaska Settlement. Augusta: William R. Smith and company, Printers to the state, 1844. 9 p. MeB. 44-4002

Maine farmers almanack for 1845. By Daniel Robinson. Hallowell, Maine: Glazier, Masters and Smith, [1844] MeBa; MWA. 44-4003

Maine farmers' almanack for 1845. By Daniel Robinson. Portland, Maine: William Hyde, [1844] MWA. 44-4004

Mair, John, 1702 or 3-1769. Introduction to Latin syntax; from the Edinburgh stereotype edition revised and corrected by A.R. Carson.... New York: Dean, 1844. MA; NGH. 44-4005

Mair, John, 1702 or 3-1769. Mair's introduction to Latin syntax. From the Edinburgh stereotype edition. Revised and corrected by A.R. Carson... to which is added copious exercises upon the declinable parts of speech and an exemplification of the several moods and tenses. By David Patterson. New York: W.E. Dean, 1844. 248 p. DCUH; FL; LNL; NcHil. 44-4006

Malan, Caesar. Can I join the church of Rome while my rule of faith is the Bible? An inquiry presented to the conscience of the Christian reader. Translated from the second French edition. New York: Harper and brothers, 1844. 134, 3 p. MNTCA. 44-4007

Malan, Caesar. An inquiry presented to the conscience of the church reader. By the Rev. Caesar Malan, D.D. Translated from the second French edition by Rev. Dr. Baird. New York: Harper and brothers, 1844. 134 p. CSfCW; MEao; OCHP. 44-4008

Malan, Solomon Caesar, 1812-1894. Can I join the Church of Rome while my rule of faith is the Bible? An inquiry presented to the conscience of the Christian reader... translated from the second French edition with an introduction by Rev. Dr. Baird. New York: Harper and brothers, 1844. 134 p. CtMW; GDecCT; MBC; NjR; PPM. 44-4009

Malcom, Howard, 1799-1879. A dictionary of the most important names, objects, and terms, found in the Holy Scriptures. Intended principally for Sunday school teachers and Bible classes. Boston: Gould, Kendall and Lincoln. 1844. 309 p. MiU; TJaU. 44-4010

Malcom, Howard. 1799-1879. Travels in south eastern Asia in two volumes. Seventh edition. Boston: Gould, Kendall and Lincoln, 1844. 321 p. NAlbi; PPiW; TNT; TxH. 44-4011

Malden, Jonas. Education; the substance of an address, delivered before the members of the Worcester Literary and Scientific Institution... in 1841... Worcester: 1844. 20 p. NNC. 44-4012

Maltby, John. Impulses of piety. A discourse preached to the Hammond Street Church and Society, in Bangor, February 18, 1844. Bangor: E.F. Duren, 1844. 16 p. CBPSR; MeBa; MeBaT; MH-AH; MnDu. 44-4013

Malte-Brun, Conrad, 1775-1826. System of geography; edited by J.G. Percival. Boston: 1844-45. 3 v. CtY; MW. 44-4014

Malte-Brun, Conrad, 1775-1826. A system of universal geography. Boston: Printed by Samuel Walker, 1844. 3 v. MH; MoS; NcAS; RPaw; RWoH. 44-4015

Management of the sick-room, with rules for diet, etc. by a lady of New York. New York: 1844. 103 p. MBC. 44-4016

Manchester and Salford Advertiser. June 8, 1844-. Manchester, New Hampshire? 1844-. PPL-R. 44-4017

Manchester, New Hampshire. Annual report of the receipts and expenditures. Manchester, New Hampshire: 1844-1938. 38 v. NhD. 44-4018

Manchester, New Hampshire. Constitution and by-laws...Manchester, New Hampshire: Wetmore and Wallace, printers, 1844. 11 p. Nh. 44-4019

Manchester, New Jersey. Presbyterian Church. Register... compiled by the pastor of the Presbyterian Church, Manchester, New Jersey. New York: 1844. 21 p. NjPT; NNUT. 44-4020

Mancur, John H. Tales of the revolution... New York: William H. Colyer, 1844. 317 p. CtY; DLC; ViU. 44-4021

Mann, A.M. The scriptural and appropriate qualifications of the civil magistrate. The funeral sermon of the Hon. Smith Thompson.... Poughkeepsie: Platt and Schram, 1844. 24 p. MBC; NjR; NP. 44-4022

Mann, Horace, 1796-1859. Controversies, reports, and correspondence. Boston: 1844-1845. 2 v. RPB. 44-4023

Mann, Horace, 1796-1859. Reply to the remarks of thirty-one Boston schoolmasters on the seventh annual report of the secretary of the Massachusetts Board of Education. Boston: W.B. Fowle and

Nahum Capen, 1844. 176 p. ILM; MWA; PPAmP; RHi; TxU. 44-4024

Manning, Anne, 1807-1879. The maiden and married life of Mary Powell. .... Boston: E. Little and company, [1844?] 37 p. MB; NN. 44-4025

Manning, Henry Edward, 1808-1892. The unity of the church. By Henry Edward Manning, M.A., archdeacon of Chichester. New York: D. Appleton and company; Philadelphia: George S. Appleton, 1844. 305 p. CtHT; ICU; NBuDD; OrPD; PPM. 44-4026

Manning, Mississippi. Thoughts suggested on a Thanksgiving Day passed at the State Lunatic Asylum, Worcester, Mass. by a patient. Worcester: printed by request of patients, 1844. 7 p. MWA. 44-4027

Manning, Robert, 1784-1842. Book of fruits: being a descriptive catalogue of the most valuable varieties of the pear, apple, peach, etc.... Second edition, enlarged. Salem and Boston: 1844. 133 p. MBHo; MWA. 44-4028

Manning, Robert, 1784-1842. New England fruit book. Being a descriptive catalogue.... Second edition, enlarged. Salem, Massachusetts: W. and S.B. Ives, 1844. 133 p. IaGG; MB; MoSB; MSa; OClW. 44-4029

Mansfield, Daniel. The sanctuary a blessing, a sermon delivered at the dedication of the new meeting house erected by the Congregational Society in Wenham, December 20, 1843. ....Andover: press of Allen, Morrill and Wardwell, 1844. 24 p. CSmH; MiD-B; MWA; NjR; WHi. 44-4030

Manual alphabet for the deaf and dumb. Philadelphia: 1844. PPL. 44-4031

Manual of the sodality of the Blessed Virgin Mary. Fifteenth revised edition. Baltimore: J. Murphy and company, 1844. 204 p. MBBC. 44-4032

Manzoni, Alessandro. The betrothed. [I promessi sposi] By Alessandro Manzoni. New York: George Munroe [1844?] CoDR; NbH; WStFSF. 44-4033

Manzoni, Alessandro. I promessi sposi. The betrothed. By Alessandro Manzoni. A new translation. Reprinted entirely from the last English edition. New York: D. Appleton and company; Philadelphia: George S. Appleton, 1844. 336 p. Mi; NHem. 44-4034

March, Henry. The early life of Christ. An example to youth. New York: J.S. Redfield, 1844. 140 p. In-CW; TNP. 44-4035

March, John, 1788-1864?. Hannah Hawkins, the reformed drunkard's daughter, New York: American Temperance Union, 1844. 72 p. DLC; MBAt; MH; NCH; PAtM. 44-4036

Marion Academy, Marion, Ohio. Annual catalogue of the officers and students of Marion Academy. Marion: 1844. OClWHi. 44-4037

Mark H. Newman's almanac. New York: M.H. Newman, 1844. MH. 44-4038

Markle, Joseph. Life of Joseph Markle. Philadelphia: 1844. 12 p. PHi. 44-4039

Marks, Richard. Danger and duty, or, a

few words on popery, Puseyism, and the present state of the times in connection with truth, righteousness and peace. First American from the ninth London edition. New York: J.S. Taylor and company, 1844. MH; NcSalL; PPM. 44-4040

Marrant, John. Narrative of.... [his] life.... with an account of the conversion of the king of the Cherokees and his daughter, authenticated by.... Aldridge.... Fourth edition. Manchester: 1844. 23 p. NNC. 44-4041

Marryat, Frederick, 1792-1848. Settlers in Canada written for young people. New York: George Routledge and sons, 1844. 2 v. KyCov. 44-4042

Marsh, Christopher Columbus, b. 1806. The art of single entry book keeping improved by the introduction of the proof or balance. Fourth edition, revised and corrected. New York: J.C. Riker, 1844. 128 p. MiDT; NNAIA; TxU-T. 44-4043

Marsh, Christopher Columbus, b. 1806. The science of double entry book keeping, simplified by the introduction of an infallable rule for dr. and cr.... Inproved edition, revised by the author. Philadelphia: Hogan and Thompson, 1844. 199 p. NNC. 44-4044

Marsh, John, 1788-1864?. An epitome of general ecclesiastical history from the earliest period to the present time with an appendix giving a condensed history of the Jews from the destruction of Jerusalem to the present day. Illustrated by maps and engravings. Eighth edition. New York: J. Tilden and company, 1844. 462 p. InID; MTop; TxFTC. 44-4045

Marsh, John, 1788-1864?. Hannah Hawkins, the reformed drunkard's daughter. Second edition. New York: Piercy and Reed, 1844. 72 p. CtHWatk; DLC. 44-4046

Marsh, John, 1788-1868?. Temperance hymn book and minstrel; a collection of hymns, songs and odes, for temperance meetings and festivals. By Rev. John Marsh. New York: American Temperance Union, 1844. 122 p. NBu. 44-4047

Marsh, Samuel. A message from God unto thee, renouncing heresy a sovereign remedy for divisions among Christians. Montpelier: 1844. 16 p. MWA; VtU. 44-4048

Marsh-Caldwell, Anne Caldwell. The triumphs of time. By the author of "two old men's tales." New York: Harper and brothers, 1844. MBAt; MBL; MH; PPL. 44-4049

Marshall, George. Interesting trials; case of Rev. George Marshall charged with seduction as investigated by the Ohio Presbytery... Pittsburgh: Foster, M'Millin and Gamble, 1844. 16 p. NjR. 44-4050

Marshall, John, 1755-1835. The life of George Washington, written for the use of schools, by John Marshall, late chief justice of the Supreme Court of the United States. Tenth edition. Philadelphia: James Crissy, 1844. 378 p. CSmH; InU; MAm; MB; MPiB. 44-4051

Marshall, Thomas William, 1818-1877. Notes on the Episcopal polity of the Holy Catholic Church; with some account of the development of the modern religious systems. Edited by Jonathan M.

Wainwright. With a preface, and a new complete index of the subjects of the texts of scripture. New York: D. Appleton and company, 1844. 372 p. CtW; ICU; NcD; OO; RP. 44-4052

Marshall, Warren W. Views of the origin, nature, symptoms, and progress of cancer, fistula, etc., derived from practical knowledge. Together with certificates of some of the cures perfected. Richmond: 1844. NcD. 44-4053

Martin, Joseph Hamilton. The influence, bearing, and effects, of Romanism on the civil and religious liberties of our country. New York: Printed by H. Ludwig, 1844. 47 p. DLC; MAnP; NNUT; PPM; RPB. 44-4054

Martineau, Harriet, 1802-1876. The Crofton boys; a tale. New York: 1844. MBAt; MHi; NBuG. 44-4055

Martineau, Harriet, 1802-1876. The hamlets, a tale. Boston: Munroe, 1844. 181 p. CtHT. 44-4056

Martineau, Harriet, 1802-1876. Life in the sick room. Essays by Harriet Martineau. Boston: C. Bowles and William Crosby, 1844. 204 p. MH; MiOC; NjP; OUrC; RNR. 44-4057

Martineau, James. Endeavors after the Christian life. Boston: Munroe and company, 1844-48. 2 v. MB. 44-4058

Martineau, James. Endeavors after the Christian life, a volume of discourses. Boston: James Munroe and company, 1844. 291 p. FDeS; ICN; MH; NN; RNPL. 44-4059

Maryland. Communication from James Hepburn, Esq., President of the Susquehanna and Tide Water Canal Company. n.p., 1844. Mi. 44-4060

Maryland. Communications, transmitted to the Governor of Maryland, enclosing resolutions from the states of Maine, Missouri, New Jersey, Alabama, and Massachusetts. n.p.: 1844. Mi. 44-4061

Maryland. Hospital. Report of the president and board of visiters [sic] of the Maryland Hospital and resident physician's report. For 1843. Baltimore: Printed by John D. Toy, 1844. 24 p. MdBD; MdHi. 44-4062

Maryland. Hospital for the Insane at Spring Grove near Catonsville, Baltimore County. Annual and biannual reports. Baltimore, 1844-. DLC; DSG; M-B. 44-4063

Maryland. House of Delegates. Select committee on assumption of state debts by the general government. Annapolis? 1844. 28 p. DLC. 44-4064

Maryland. Journal of proceedings of the Senate of Maryland, at December session, 1843. Annapolis: William M'Neir, printer [1844] 186 p. MdBB; MdHi; NcU. 44-4065

Maryland. Journal of the proceedings of the House of Delegates. December session, 1843. Annapolis: Riley and Davis, printers, 1843 [i.e. 1844] 695 p. MdBB; MdHi; NcU. 44-4066

Maryland. Laws made and passed by the general assembly of the state of Maryland, at a session begun and held at Annapolis, on Monday, the 25th day of

December, 1843, and ended on Saturday the 9th day of March, 1844. Annapolis: William M'Neir, printer, 1844. 596 p. IaU-L; MdHi; Mi-L; NNLI; R. 44-4067

Maryland. Report from the select committee to who was referred the subject of the removal of the free colored population from Charles County. [Annapolis, 1844] 51 p. NoLoc. 44-4068

Maryland. Report of Mr. Carey on his own behalf on so much of the Governor's message as relates to the finances of the state. Annapolis: Riley and Davis, 1844. 15 p. MdLR; MH. 44-4069

Maryland. Report of the Colonization Society, in answer to an order of the House of Delegates. n.p., 1844. Mi. 44-4070

Maryland. Report of the Committee on Agriculture, relative to the application of lime to the different qualities of soil, and use of calcareous matter for agricultural purposes. Annapolis: Riley and Davis, printers, 1844. 15 p. NoLoc. 44-4071

Maryland. Report of the treasurer of the western shore, relative to the tobacco warehouses, under order of the House of Delegates. n.p., 1844. Mi. 44-4072

Maryland. Report whether the Pennsylvania, Delaware and Maryland Steam Navigation Company and the Chesapeake and Delaware Canal Company have not forfeited their charters. Annapolis, 1844. PPL. 44-4073

Maryland. University. Catalogue of students attending lectures in the medical department; session of 1843-1844. Baltimore, 1844. 5 p. MBC. 44-4074

Maryland Historical Society. Constitution, by-laws, charter, circular and members of the Maryland Historical Society. Baltimore: Printed by J. Murphy, 1844. 19 p. DLC; NN; RHi; RNR; TxU. 44-4075

Mason, Archibald. Observations, doctrinal and practical, on saving faith. First American from the Glasgow edition of 1829. Pittsburgh: printed by A. Jaynes, 1844. 227 p. ICP; PPiRPr; PPiW; PPPrHi; TKC. 44-4076

Mason, John, 1706-1763. A treatise on self-knowledge; showing the nature and benefit of that important science, and the way to attain it. Hartford: Andrus and son, 1844. 41 p. MH-AH; NBuCC; PPAN; TxW. 44-4077

Mason, John Mitchell, 1770-1829. Essays on episcopacy and the apology for apostolic order and its advocates reviewed. Edited by the Rev. Ebenezer Mason. New York: Robert Carter, 1844. 301 p. GDecCT; ICU; KyLoS; MBC; RPB. 44-4078

Mason, Lowell, 1792-1872. Book of chants: consisting mostly of selections from the sacred scriptures, adapted to appropriate music, and arranging for chanting. Designed for congregational use in public or social worship. Boston: J.H. Wilkins and R.B. Carter, 1844. 180 p. IEG; MBC; MH; OO; WNaE. 44-4079

Mason, Lowell, 1792-1872. Boston anthem book. Second edition. Boston: 1844. CtHWatk; MBAt; MH. 44-4080

Mason, Lowell, 1792-1872. The Boston glee Book, consisting of an extensive collection of glees, madrigals and rounds;

selected from the works of the most admired composers.... Boston: J.H. Wilkins and R.B. Carter, 1844. 264 p. CtY; DLC; ICN; NNUT; PLF. 44-4081

Mason, Lowell, 1792-1872. Church psalmody a collection of psalm and hymns adapted to public worship selected from Dr. Watts and other authors. Boston: T.R. Marvin, 1844. 598 p. DLC; GSTA; ICT; MAnP; RPB. 44-4082

Mason, Lowell, 1792-1872. Germina sacra: or, Boston collection of church music, comprising the most popular psalm and hymn tunes in general use. Second edition. Boston: Wilkins, 1844. 348 p. In; MB; MoSpD; NjPT; PPPrHi. 44-4083

Mason, Lowell, 1792-1872. Juvenile singing school. Boston: J.H. Wilkins and R.B. Carter, 1844. 128 p. CtHWatk; DLC; MH; NN; OClWHi. 44-4084

Mason, Lowell, 1792-1872. Manual of Christian psalmody. By Lowell Mason and D. Greene. Boston: 1844. MBAt. 44-4085

Mason, Lowell, 1792-1872. Manual of the Boston Academy of Music, for instruction in the elements of vocal music, on the system of Pestalozzi. Fifth edition. Boston: Wilkins, 1844. 252 p. MBC; MMedHi; OAkU. 44-4086

Mason, Lowell, 1792-1872. The sacred harp; or eclectic harmony; a collection of church music... By Lowell Mason and Timothy B. Mason. Cincinnati: 1844. 238 p. NjPT. 44-4087

Mason, Lowell, 1792-1872. Twenty-one

madrigals, glees and part songs... Boston: J.H. Wilkins and R.B. Carter, 1844. 72 p. NNUT. 44-4088

Mason, Lowell, 1792-1872. The vocalist: consisting of short and easy glees, or songs, in parts. Arranged for soprano, alto and tenor, and bass voices, by Lowell Mason and George James Webb.... Boston: J.H. Wilkins and R.B. Carter, 1844. 200 p. CtHC; MH-AH; NN; NNUT; ViU. 44-4089

Mason, Richard. The gentleman's new pocket farrier, comprising a general description of the noble and useful animal, the horse. Eighth edition, with additions to which is added a prize essay on mules; and an appendix. Philadelphia: Grigg and Elliott, 1844. 419p. NOg. 44-4090

Mason, Timothy Battelle, 1801-1861. The sacred harp; or beauties of church music. Boston: Kidder and Wright, 1844. 352 p. MiU; WaU. 44-4091

Massachusetts. Address to the people of the commonwealth, at the close of the session, 1844. Boston: Wright and Ballow, 1844. 12 p. M. 44-4092

Massachusetts. Adjutant General's Office. General order. September 19, 1844.... Boston: 1844. 12 p. NN. 44-4093

Massachusetts. Charitable Mechanic Association. The fourth exhibition of the Massachusetts Charitable Mechanic Association, at Quincy Hall, in the city of Boston, September 16, 1844. Boston: Crocker and Brewster, 1844. 152 p. KHi; NbHi; RP. 44-4094

Massachusetts. Committee on Railways

and Canals. The Boston and Maine Railroad Extension Company. Statement of principal facts.... Boston: Dickinson, 1844. 10 p. DLC; MB. 44-4095

Massachusetts. Committee on reducing to a written code the common law. Report of one of the committee.... Boston: 1844. 48 p. MB. 44-4096

Massachusetts. Committee on returns of votes for governor and lieutenant governor. Report.... Boston: 1844. 6 p. DLC. 44-4097

Massachusetts. District attorney for the southern district. Memorial respecting salary. Boston: 1844. Nh. 44-4098

Massachusetts. General Association. Minutes of the General Association of Massachusetts at their session in Woburn. With the narrative of the state of religion and pastoral letter. Boston: Press of Crocker and Brewster, 1844. 58 p. NjR. 44-4099

Massachusetts. General Court. Topographical map of Massachusetts.... Boston: G.G. Smith, 1844. DGS. 44-4100

Massachusetts. General Hospital. Boston. The trustees of the Massachusetts general hospital to the public.... Boston: Eastburn's press, 1844. 14 p. DLC; MBM: MHi; MWA. 44-4101

Massachusetts. Governor. Message to the general court respecting the treatment of citizens of the state in other states. Boston: 1844. Nh. 44-4102

Massachusetts. Governor. Message to the general court respecting treatment of colored citizens of Massachusetts in South Carolina and Louisiana. Boston: 1844. Nh. 44-4103

Massachusetts. Governor. Message to the general court....Boston: 1844. Nh. 44-4104

Massachusetts. Governor. To the House of Representatives. [Message transmitting documents relating to the treatment of free negroes....] Boston: 1844. 8 p. MB. 44-4105

Massachusetts. Governor. [George N. Briggs].... Message. To the Senate.... [Boston: 1844] 8 p. MB. 44-4106

Massachusetts. Governor. [Marcus Morton] To the House of Representatives. [Message transmitting documents....] Boston: 1844. 8 p. MB. 44-4107

Massachusetts. House of Representatives. Committee on the Judiciary. [Report on so much of the address of his excellency.... Boston: 1844] 38 p. DLC. 44-4108

Massachusetts. House of Representatives. Report and bill on the organization of the House of Representatives.... Boston: 1844. Nh. 44-4109

Massachusetts. House of Representatives. Report on the alleged bribery.... Boston: 1844. Nh. 44-4110

Massachusetts. House of Representatives. Report on the debt of the state.... Boston: 1844. Nh. 44-4111

Massachusetts. House of Representatives. Report on the expediency of amending the laws relating to seduction. Boston: 1844. Nh. 44-4112

Massachusetts. House of Representatives. Report on the salaries of the judges of the supreme court. Boston: 1844. Nh. 44-4113

Massachusetts. House of Representatives. Special committee on the subject of the abolition of capital punishment. Report. [Boston: 1844] 68 p. M; PP. 44-4114

Massachusetts. House of Representatives. Special committee on petition of Mary W. Healy. House of Representatives, February 23, 1844. ....[Boston: 1844] 2 p. MB. 44-4115

Massachusetts. Joint special committee on so much of the governor's address as relates to slavery. ....The joint special committee, ...[Boston: 1844] 18 p. MB. 44-4116

Massachusetts. Laws regulating the fire department in the town of Roxbury. [March 9, 1830] Boston: 1844. MB. 44-4117

Massachusetts. Minority report on the resolution of the legislature of Massachusetts of 23d March, 1843, proposing to Congress to recommend, according to the provisions of the 5th article of the constitution of the United States, an ammendment to the said constitution [viz., that "representatives and direct taxes shall be apportioned among the several states.... Washington: 1844] 23 p. MH. 44-4118

Massachusetts. Report of the committee of both branches of the legislature, appointed to examine the returns made to the office of the secretary of the commonwealth, of the votes for governor and lieutenant governor for the year 1844. Boston: 1844. 6 p. DLC. 44-4119

Massachusetts. Report of the committee on public charitable institutions, 1844, '49. Boston: 1844-9. Nh. 44-4120

Massachusetts. Report of the committee on the Charlestown prison, 1844. Boston: 1844. Nh. 44-4121

Massachusetts. Report of the joint standing committee on prisions, 1844, '49-50. Boston: 1844-50. Nh. 44-4122

Massachusetts. Report of the penal code of Massachusetts prepared under a resolve of the legislature, passed on the 10th of February 1837, authorizing the appointment of commissioners to reduce so much of the common law as relates to crimes and punishments to a written and systematic code. Boston: Dutton and Wentworth, 1844. DLC; IaHi; Nb; OCLaw; WaU. 44-4123

Massachusetts. Senate. Committee on returns of votes for Senators. [Report on returns of votes.... Boston: 1844] 10 p. DLC. 44-4124

Massachusetts. Senate. Report and bill relating to the salaries of certain officers. Boston: 1844. Nh. 44-4125

Massachusetts. Senate. Report and resolution respecting the disputed territory fund. Boston: 1844. Nh. 44-4126

Massachusetts. Senate. Report and resolution respecting the petition of Church Gray. Boston: 1844. Nh. 44-4127

Massachusetts. Senate. Report and resolution respecting the revolutionary rolls of Massachusetts. Boston: 1844. Nh. 44-4128

Massachusetts. Senate. Report concerning the military stores.... Boston: 1844. Nh. 44-4129

Massachusetts. Senate. Report concerning the withdrawal of troops.... Boston: 1844. Nh. 44-4130

Massachusetts. Senate. Report on the time of service of the judges.... Boston: 1844. Nh. 44-4131

Massachusetts. Senate. [Report of] the joint special committee, to whom was referred so much of the message of the governor as relates to slaves; also, certain petition of Jasper Stone and others; also, the resolutions of South Carolina, recommending the annexation of Texas to the United States. [Boston: 1844] 18 p. MH. 44-4132

Massachusetts. Supplements to the revised statutes. Laws of the commonwealth of Massachusetts, passed frequently to the revised statutes: to which are prefixed.... By Theron Metcalf, and the residue of the volume by Luther S. Cushing. Boston: Dutton and Wentworth, state printers, 1844. 353 p. M; MBC; MLow; R. 44-4133

Massachusetts. Topographical map of Massachusetts; compiled from astronomical, trigonometrical and various local surveys made by order of the Legislature.... Boston: 1844. DSG; MB; Nh; PHi. 44-4134

Massachusetts. Treasury Department. Report transmitting statement of amount paid the lieutenant governor. Boston: 1844. Nh. 44-4135

Massachusetts Charitable Mechanic Association. The fourth exhibition of the Massachusetts charitable mechanic association, at Quincy hall, ...September 16, 1844. Boston: Crocker and Brewster, 1844. 149 p. MBB. 44-4136

Massachusetts Medical Society. Address to the members [by the committee appointed to consider the resolution adopted by the society at its annual meeting, relative to the registration of diseases and their co-existing circumstances and results] Boston: 1844. 16 p. MBM; MH-M. 44-4137

The Massachusetts register and business directory. Boston: James Loring, 1844. 250 p. MeBat; MoSpD; MWHi; NjMD. 44-4138

Massachusetts Society for Promoting Christian Knowledge. Constitution.... 1844. Boston: Marvin, 1844. MB. 44-4139

Massachusetts Temperance Union. The union temperance song book. A collection of songs for picnics and temperance meetings. Boston: Tompkins, 1844. 72 p. DLC; MB; MHi. 44-4140

Massachusetts Temperance Union. The union temperance song book. A collection of songs for picnics, temperance meetings, social gatherings, and the family circle. Boston: Ditson and company, [1844?] [78] p. MB. 44-4141

Massingberd, Francis Charles, 1800-1872. The English reformation. By Francis Charles Massingberd, M.A. Flemington, New Jersey: J.R. Dunham, 1844. 124 p. CSansS; ICU; MdBD; NBuDD; PP. 44-4142

Massingberd, Francis Charles, 1800-1872. A history of the English reformation, by F.C. Massingberd. Flemington, New Jersey: J.R. Dunham, 1844. 126 p. CtY; ICU; PP; RPB. 44-4143

Master Carpenters' and Joiners Society of Cincinnati. The book of prices of the house carpenters and joiners of the city of Cincinnati: Adopted, Monday, January 4, 1819. Carefully revised and enlarged. February, 1844. By Louis H. Shally. Cincinnati: L'Hommedieu and company, printers, 1844. 94 p. DLC; InHi; MH; MiU-C; OCHP. 44-4144

Mather, William Williams, 1804-1859. Elements of geology, for the use of schools and academies by William W. Mather. Fifth edition. New York: Turner, Hughes, and Hayden, 1844. 286 p. MiH; MiHM; OHi. 44-4145

Mather, William Williams, 1804-1859. Report of the Coal Grove Company, Lawrence County, Ohio. Cincinnati: Printed at the Daily Atlas office, 1844. 10 p. DLC; OClWHi. 44-4146

Mathew, Theobald. Life of Theobald Mathew, the great apostle of temperance. Boston: 1844. 46 p. MH. 44-4147

Mathews, Thomas. The whist player's hand-book, containing most of the maxims of the old school, and several new ones. [With] observations on short whist. Also the games of Boston and euchre.

Philadelphia: Isaac M. Mass, 1844. 96 p. MH; TxH. 44-4148

Matthews, B. This picture and that. New York: 1844. MB. 44-4149

Mattison, Hiram, 1811-1868. Articles of the Methodist Episcopal Church, with Scripture proofs. Watertown, New York: Printed and sold by Knowlton and Rice, 1844. 36 p. DLC; NNMHi. 44-4150

Mattison, Hiram, 1811-1868. The church, the ministry and the gospel, the best means for promoting moral reformation.... Troy, New York: press of N. Tuttle, 1844. 40 p. MB. 44-4151

Mattison, Hiram, 1811-1868. A tract for the times; or the church, the ministry and the gospel, the best means for promoting moral reformation. Troy, New York: Tuttle, 1844. 40 p. DLC; MWA; NCaS; NN; PPPrHi. 44-4152

Maull, W.H. The Methodist Episcopal church exposed: in a discourse delivered in Cincinnati, Ohio, January 18, 1844. Cincinnati, Ohio: Gazette office, printer, 1844. 47 p. OClWHi. 44-4153

Maury, Matthew Fontaine, 1806-1873. Paper on the gulf stream and currents of the sea. Read before the national institute at its annual meeting, April 2, 1844. [Richmond: 1844] 16 p. DLC; PPAmP; Vi; ViL. 44-4154

Maverick Church. East Boston. Manual. Boston: 1844. 24 p. MBC. 44-4155

Maxcy, Jonathan, 1768-1820. The literary remains of the Rev. Jonathan Maxcy, Second president of Brown

University, R.I.... With a memoir of his life, by Romeo Elton. New York: A.V. Blake, 1844. 452 p. CSmH; LNB; MWA; NcD; WHi. 44-4156

May, Enoch. Whig melodies, containing original and selected songs, set to popular airs, and embellished with engravings. Indianapolis, Indiana: state journal office, printer, 1844. 32 p. In. 44-4157

May, James. The proper office and spirit of the ministry.... A sermon preached before the society of the alumni of the Theological Seminary of Virginia, and published by request of the society. By the Rev. James May, D.D. Washington: William W. Force, 1844. 20 p. DLC; MdBD; NNG; PHi; RPB. 44-4158

Mayer, Brantz, 1809-1879. Mexico as it was and as it is, By Brantz Mayer... With numerous illustrations on wood, engraved by Butler from drawings by the author. New York: J. Winchester, 1844. 390 p. CtMW; IaU; OCY; PPiW; TxDaM. 44-4159

Mayer, Charles Frederick. First discussed before the Maryland Historical Society delivered on June 20, 1844. Baltimore: Published by the society, 1844. 32 p. MeHi; NcU; Nh-Hi; PPi; RHi. 44-4160

Maygrier, Jacques Pierre, 1771-1835. Midwifery illustrated. Translated from the French with notes by A. Sidney Doane. Fourth Edition. New York: J. S. Redfield, 1844. 180 p. NBMS; NNN; OClCF; PPCP; RPM. 44-4161

Mayo, Sarah Carter Edgarton, 1819-

1848. The flower vase; containing the language of flowers and their poetic sentiments.... Lowell: Powers and Bagley; Boston: B.B. Mussey, 1844. 157 p. DLC; MH; NcD; NjR; OO. 44-4162

Mayo, Sarah Carter Edgarton, 1819-1848. The rose of Sharon; a religious souvenir for 1844. Boston: A. Tompkins, 1844. 304 p. DLC; PHi. 44-4163

Mayo, Sarah Carter Edgarton, 1819-1848. Tables of flora. Lowell: 1844. MB. 44-4164

Meade, William, 1789-1862. The doctrines of the Episcopal Church not Romish, an address of the Right Rev. William Meade, to the convention of the Episcopal Church of Virginia, at the close of the annual report.... Washington: J. and G.S. Gideon, 1844. 36 p. CtHT; DLC; InU; NcD; PPM. 44-4165

Meadows, F.C. New French and English pronouncing dictionary, on the basis of Nugent's, with many new words in general use, in two parts, 1, French and English; 2, English and French, ...to which are prefixed principles of French pronounciation and an abridged grammar, by F.C. Meadows, M.A. Fourth American edition, corrected and improved with a selection of idiomatic phrases, by George Folsom, M.A. New York: Alexander V. Blake, 1844. 729 p. WBur. 44-4166

Means, John Hugh, 1812-1862. An oration on the influence of Odd Fellowship upon society, delivered before De Kalb Lodge, Number 6, in the Presbyterian Church, Winnsboro; on the 6th of March, 1844. Columbia: issued from Morgan's

Letter Press, 1844. 28 p. ScSP; ScU. 44-4167

Mechanic's and Laboring Men's Association of Painesville and its Vicinity. Constitution . Painesville: 1844. OClWHi. 44-4168

Med Vapor Bath Establishment and Asylum.... Boston: Jordon, 1844. 18 p. MB. 44-4169

Medical ethics; or principles and rules by which medical practitioners should be regulated... Cincinnati: Printed by R.P. Donagh, 1844. 11 p. OC. 44-4170

The medium of salvation. Tract No. XI. For the New Church in the United States. Boston: Otis Clapp, 1844. 8 p. DLC; VtMidSM. 44-4171

Meek, Alexander B. Americanism in literature. An oration before the Phi Kappa and Demosthenian Societies of the University of Georgia, at Athens, August 8, 1844. Charleston: Burges and James, printer, 1844. 39 p. AB; CSmH; NcD; ScU; ScCC. 44-4172

Meier, J. Parney's syllabaire Francais; or French spelling book, revised, corrected and improved... Eleventh edition. Philadelphia: Thomas, Cowperthwait and company, 1844. 196 p. NjR. 44-4173

Meigs, Mary Noel [Bleeker] Poems, by Mrs. Mary Noel McDonald.... New York: [Pudney, Hooker and Russell, printers] 1844. 208 p. CtMW; InU; NBuG; NRU; RPB. 44-4174

Melvill, Henry, 1788-1871. Sermons by Henry Melvill, ...Comprising all the discourses published by consent of the author. Edited by the Right Rev. C.P. McIlvaine, ...Third edition, enlarged. New York: Stanford and Swords; Philadelphia: George S. Appleton, 1844. 561 p. CSansS; IaPeC; MBC; OO; TJaU. 44-4175

Melvill, Henry, 1798-1871. Sermons on certain of the less prominent facts and references in sacred story. By Henry Melvill, edited by the Right Rev. C.P. McIlvaine. New York: Stanford and Swords; Philadelphia: George S. Appleton, 1844-1845. 2 v. NNG. 44-4176

Melvill, Henry, 1798-1871. Sermons on certain of the less prominent facts and references in sacred story. By Henry Melvill, edited by the Right Rev. C.P. McIlvaine. Third edition. New York: Stanford and Swords; Philadelphia: George S. Appleton, 1844. 561 p. ICRL; MBC; KKeBT; NjPT; VtU. 44-4177

Melville, Gansevoort. The eloquent champion of democracy, at Ithaca on Monday, October 14, at 12 o'clock M... Ithaca: 1844. NN. 44-4178

Melville, Gansevoort. Speech... in the tabernacle, New York City, at the celebration of the birthday of the hero of New Orleans. Columbus: 1844. OClWHi. 44-4179

Memes, John Smythe. Memoirs of the Empress Josephine. By John S. Memes, LL.D. .... New York: Harper and brothers, 1844. 396 p. CoT; MBradJ; MeAu; PSew; OCX. 44-4180

Memoir of Hannah B. Cook. Boston: Massachusetts Sabbath School Society, 1844. MBC. 44-4181

Memoir of Jemima Wilkinson, a preacheress of the eighteenth century; containing an authentic account of her life and character, and of the rise, progress and conclusion of her ministry.... Bath, New York: R.L. Underhill and company, 1844. 288 p. CSmH; ICU; MWA; NNUT; RHi. 44-4182

A memoir of John Huss. Translated from the German. New York: Robert Carter; Pittsburg: Thomas Carter, 1844. 106 p. ICMe; LNB; LNH; OCh; PWWJS. 44-4183

Memoir of Sarah Atwood Jackson. Chicago: J.A. Horsington, 1844. NBLi-Hi; NCRC; NN. 44-4184

Memorial on slavery in America, from ministers and office bearers in the county of Lancaster, etc., to churches in America. Manchester: Printed at the Gazette Office, [1844] 12 p. DHU; MBAt. 44-4185

Men of different countries. Cooperstown: printed and sold by H. and E. Phinney, 1844. 31 p. NN. 44-4186

Mendenhall, George. The medical student's vade-mecum, containing examinations upon anatomy, chemistry, materia medica, surgery... Cincinnati: Jacob Ernst; Philadelphia: Lindsay and Blakiston, 1844. 328 p. MiKa; OC; OClM; PPHa. 44-4187

Menteith, Alexander H. A course of lessons in the Italian language on the Robertsonian method. First American edition. New York: Wilson and company, 1844. 64 p. GDecCT; MdBP; MdW; MH; OCU. 44-4188

Mercantile Library Association of Boston. Catalogue of books, with a history of the institution. Constitution, by-laws, etc. Boston: 1844. MBAt. 44-4189

Merchant's and seaman's expeditious measurer; containing a set of tables which show at one view, the solid contents of all kinds of packages and casks. New York: Blunt, 1844. 196 p. MS. 44-4190

The merchant's sketch book and guide to New York City.... Particularly intended for the merchant visiting New York. A western merchant. New York: 1844. N. 44-4191

Mercury. Charleston, South Carolina: 1844-. PCA. 44-4192

Mercy Disborough; a tale of New England witchcraft. Bath, New York: R.L. Underhill and company, 1844. 98 p. MH. 44-4193

Merle d'Aubigne, Jean Henri, 1794-1872. Faith and knowledge. Translated from the French by M.M. Baskies. New York; Taylor, 1844. 53 p. GDecCT; MoSpD; MPiB; PPins; OO. 44-4194

Merle d'Aubigne, Jean Henri, 1794-1872. History of the great reformation of the sixteenth century in Germany, Switzerland, etc. New York: Carter, 1844. 4 v. MB-FA. 44-4195

Merle d'Aubigne, Jean Henri, 1794-1872. History of the great reformation of the sixteenth century in Germany, Switzerland, etc. Philadelphia: James M. Campbell, 1844. 608 p. TxShA. 44-4196

Merle d'Aubigne, Jean Henri, 1794-

1872. History of the great reformation. Twenty-fifth edition. Philadelphia: James M. Campbell, 1844. 482 p. ICMBI; MFiHi; MMed; OMC. 44-4197

Merle D'Aubigne, Jean Henri, 1794-1872. The study of the history of christianity, and its adaptation to the present age. A discourse at the opening of a course of lectures on the history of the Reformation. New York: Saxton and Miles, 1844. 36 p. MBC; MH-AH; MWiW; PPM. 44-4198

Merle d'Aubigne, Jean Henri, 1794-1872. The voice from antiuity [sic] to the men of the nineteenth century: or, read the book. By J.H. Merle d'Aubigne.... New York: J.S. Taylor and company, 1844. 69 p. GDecCT; IEG; OO; PEaL; ViU. 44-4199

Merle d'Aubigne, Jean Henri, 1794-1872. A voice of the church one, under the successive forms of Christianity; a discourse pronounced at the opening of the Theological School at Geneva. New York: J.S. Taylor and company, 1844. 63 p. GDecCT; MH; NCH; OO; RNR. 44-4200

Merriam, Charles, 1806-1887. The intelligent reader: designed as a sequel to the child's guide.... Springfield: G. and C. Merriam, 1844. Ct. 44-4201

Merriam, George, 1803-1880. The village reader: designed for the use of schools. By the compilers of the easy primer, child's guide and intelligent reader. Springfield: G. and C. Merriam, 1844. 300 p. CtHWatk; KM; MAm; MShM; OC. 44-4202

Merrill, Joseph Warren. The peoples

cabinet: containing a compendium upon the subjects of natural history; natural philosophy; astronomy; constitution, organization, and functions of the human body... Boston: Joseph W. Merrill, 1844. ICBB; IU; MdBP; MoSpD; TNS. 44-4203

Merrimack, [New Hampshire] Annual report 1844.... Nashua: 1844. Nh-Hi. 44-4204

Messia, Alonso, 1665-1732. The devotion of the three hours agony, in honor of our Lord Jesus Christ, on the cross. Composed originally in the Spanish language, at Lime in Peru. Baltimore: John Murphy, 1844. 52 p. MdHi. 44-4205

Methodist almanac for the year 1845.... By David Young, philom.... New York: G. Lane and C.B. Tippett, [1844] 24 p. MBNMHi; MWA; NjR; PPL; TxGeoS. 44-4206

Methodist Episcopal Church. Address of the bishops of the Methodist Episcopal General Conference held in New York, May, 1844. New York: Conference office, 1844. 23 p. KyLx; PPPrHi. 44-4207

Methodist Episcopal Church. A collection of hymns, for the use of the church. New York: G. Lane and C.B. Tippet, 1844. 616 p. IEG; MiU. 44-4208

Methodist Episcopal Church. A collection of hymns, for the use of the Methodist Episcopal Church; principally from the collection of Rev. John Wesley.... Revised and corrected with a supplement and an index. New York: G. Lane and C.B. Tippett, 1844. 635 p. CBPSR. 44-4209

Methodist Episcopal Church. General Conference. 1844. Report of debates in the general conference of the Methodist Episcopal Church, held in the city of New York, 1844. By Robert Athow West.... New York: G. Lane and C.B. Tippett, for the Methodist Episcopal Church, 1844. 240 p. ArU; CtMW; NcU; PHi; TNS. 44-4210

Methodist Episcopal Church. Journal of the general conference of the Methodist Episcopal Church held in Baltimore. 1840. Published by order of the conference. New York: G. Lane and C.B. Tippett, 1844. 240 p. IaMp; MiD-B; MnSM; MoBolS. 44-4211

Methodist Episcopal Church. Journal of the general conference of the Methodist Episcopal Church, held in the City of Baltimore, 1840. New York: G. Lane and C.B. Tippett, 1844. 172 p. IaMP; MiD-B; NcU; OrLaw; TU. 44-4212

Methodist Episcopal Church. Journal of the General Conference of the Methodist Episcopal Church held in the city of New York, 1844. New York: G. Lane and C.B. Tippett, for the the Methodist Episcopal Church, 1844. 4-210 p. CoDI; IC; ILM; NcU; ScSpW. 44-4213

Methodist Episcopal Church. Minutes of the annual conferences of the Methodist Episcopal Church, for the year 1843. Cincinnati: J.F. Wright and L. Swormstedt... at the Western Book Concern, 1844. 321-427 p. KyLx; NNMHi. 44-4214

Methodist Episcopal Church. Minutes of the... session of the New Hampshire annual conference... 1844. Concord, New Hampshire: 1844. 24 p. CtMW; NNMHi. 44-4215

Methodist Episcopal Church. Report of debates of the general conference of the Methodist Episcopal Church... New York: G. Lane and C.B. Tippett, 1844. 240 p. IEG; Mi; NjR; PU; TxHuT. 44-4216

Methodist Episcopal Church. The doctrines and discipline of the Evangelical Association, together with the design of their union. Translated from the German. New Berlin: J.C. Reisner, for the Evangelical Association, 1844. 118 p. MA. 44-4217

Methodist Episcopal Church. The doctrines and discipline of the Methodist Episcopal Church. Cincinnati: L. Swormstedt and J.T. Mitchell, for the Methodist Episcopal Church, 1844. 213 p. CtHT; InID; MnHi; NbYC; TNS. 44-4218

Methodist Episcopal Church. The doctrines and discipline of the Methodist Episcopal Church. New York: G. Lane and C. B. Triplett, for the Methodist Episcopal Church, 1844. 221 p. CStclU; TJaL; WaPS. 44-4219

Methodist Episcopal Church. The doctrines and discipline of the Methodist Episcopal Church. New York: G. Lane and C.B. Tippett, for the Methodist Episcopal Church, 1844. 213 p. PWmpDS-Hi. 44-4220

Methodist Episcopal Church. The doctrines and discipline.... Cincinnati: J.F. Wright, 1844. 206 p. MBC. 44-4221

The Methodist Episcopal Church and Protestant Episcopal Church compared. In a dialogue between Rev. Mr. Smith and Rev. Mr. Townley. Philadelphia: R.S.H. George, 1844. 36 p. MdBD; PPL; TxDam. 44-4222

Methodist Episcopal Church Conference. Wisconsin. Mr ____ is invited to attend a donation at the house of the Rev. O.F. Curtis on the afternoon or evening of Wednesday, the 28th inst. V. Tichenor, Chairman of the Committee: Prairieville, February 22, 1844. Prairieville, Wisconsin, 1844. Broadside. WHi. 44-4223

Methodist Female Collegiate Institute. Cincinnati. Catalogue of the officers and students for the year 1843-44. Cincinnati: 1844. 24 p. OCHP. 44-4224

Methodist preacher, or lights and shadows in the life of an itinerant. Philadelphia: J. Harmstead, 1844. 31 p. DLC; MH; NN; NNUT. 44-4225

Methodist Protestant Church. Conference. Illinois. Minutes. 1844-1938. 94 v. IEG. 44-4226

Metropolitan Tract Society. On the promises of Christ to his church from Bossnet... Baltimore: Metropolitan Tract Society, 1844. 16 p. MdBS. 44-4227

Metropolitan Tract Society. The catholicity of the church, from the United States magazine... Baltimore: Metropolitan Tract Society, 1844. 24 p. MdBS; MdBS; MdCatS; MoSU. 44-4228

Metropolitan Tract Society. The doctrine of exclusive salvation explained and proved. Baltimore: Metropolitan Tract Society, 1844. 12 p. MdCatS. 44-4229

Metropolitan Tract Society. On religious intolerance. A tract for the times... Balatimore: Metropolitan Tract Society [1844] 12 p. MdBS. 44-4230

Metropolitan Tract Society. On the invocation of saints, compiled from the works of Bossnet... Baltimore: Metropoitan Press, 1844. 24 p. MdBS. 44-4231

Metropolitan Tract Society. Tract number one. On the invocation of the saints. Compiled from the works of Bossuet. Baltimore: Metropolitan Press, 1844. 12 p. MdBLC; MoFloSS; NNF. 44-4232

Michigan. Acts of the legislature of the state of Michigan, passed at the annual session of 1844; with an appendix, containing the treasurer's annual report. By authority. Detroit: Bagg and Harmon, Printers to the state, 1844. 213 p. CtHWatk; Wa-L. 44-4233

Middlebrook's New England almanac for 1845. By Elijah Middlebrook. Bridgeport, Connecticut: John B. Sanford, [1844] MWA. 44-4234

Middlebrook's New England almanac for 1845. By Elijah Middlebrook. Norwalk, Connecticut: W.E. and H.M. Bissell, [1844] MWA; WHi. 44-4235

Middlebury College, Middlebury, Vermont. Alphabetical catalogue of the library of the Philomathesian Society of Middlebury College. Middlebury: Printed by Ephraim Mapham [sic] 1844. NNC. 44-4236

Middlesex Consociation. Address to the churches of the Middlesex Consociation, with reasons why I am a Congregationalist. Second edition. Hartford: printed by D.B. Moseley, 1844. 36 p. Ct; CtSoP; MB; MBC. 44-4237

Middlesex Sunday School Society. Second report of the Middlesex Sunday School Society, made at the third annual meeting, held at Lexington, October 9, 1844. Concord: Charles C. Hazewell, printer, 1844. 16 p. MLexHi. 44-4238

Middleton, Henry, Junior. The government and the currency. Part 1. By Henry Middleton, Junior. Philadelphia: printed for the author, 1844. 69 p. A-Ar; MdBP; NcU; PHi. 44-4239

Middleton, Massachusetts. Report of the town officers. Salem, Massachusetts: Milo A. Newhall and company, 1844-1940. 86 v. M. 44-4240

Miles, Henry Adolphus, 1809-1895. A glance at our history, prospects, and duties. A thanksgiving discourse preached in the South Congregational Church, Lowell. Lowell: printed by Stearns and Taylor, 1844. 16 p. ICMe; IEG; MBAt; OClWHi; WHi. 44-4241

Miles, Pliny. The picture gallery; a series of portraits and plates, from various designs engraved on steel by the best artists... New York: 1844. MnCollS. 44-4242

Milford, Connecticut. First Congregational Church. Manual for the communicants of the First Congregational Church in Milford, Connecticut. New Haven; printed by B.L. Hamlen, 1844. 23 p. Ct; CtHT; NjR. 44-4243

Military despotism in a republic: report of the board... August 30, 1841, to examine into the condition and management of Springfield Armory. Springfield: Springfield Republican, 1844. 32 p. MSHi. 44-4244

Military directory of both banks of the Mississippi... Nouvelle Orleans: Henry and H. De La Roche, 1844. 39 p. LU. 44-4245

Miller, Adam. Incidents in the origin and progress of the Congregational Church, and the settlement of the township of Hartford, Pennsylvania: A discourse delivered on the first Sabbath in 1844. Montrose, Pennsylvania: Printed by Fuller and Turrell, 1844. 24 p. MAtt; PPPrHi. 44-4246

Miller, Ferdinand H. Ready grammarian: to abridge labor, refresh the memory and prepare classes for thorough instruction. Second edition. Ithaca: Andrus, 1844. 32 p. OO. 44-4247

Miller, Ferdinand H. The ready grammarian: to abridge labor, refresh the memory, and prepare classes for thorough instruction. Third edition. Rochester: David Hoyt, 1844. 82 p. NIDHi; NNC. 44-4248

Miller, Georg. Das thatige christenthum, oder kurze und dentliche lehren zur beforderung wahrer gottseligkeit. Von Georg Miller zweite und verbesserte auflage. New Berlin, Pennsylvania: Verlegt von J. C. Reiszner fur die Evangelische gemeinschaft, 1844. 180 p. OBerB; PReaAT. 44-4249

Miller, J.R. The history of Great Britain from the death of George II, to the coronation of George IV. Designed as a continuation of Hume and Smollett by J.R. Miller. Philadelphia: T. Davis, 1844. 724 p. IaFd; NcC; OCo; TSewU; WvW. 44-4250

Miller, Jacob. Leichenrede des.. Heinrich, A. Muhlenberg, gehalten am 15en August, 1844 in der Deutsch Evangelisch Lutherischen Kirche, in Reading. Reading [Pennsylvania] Ritter, 1844. 12 p. PPLT. 44-4251

Miller, Jacob Welsh, 1800-1862. Speech on the treaty for annexing Texas to the United States, delivered in the Senate of the United States, May 23, 1844 [Washington? 1844?] MH; MiD-B; OCl; TxDaM; WHi. 44-4252

Miller, S.G. Der geschwinde interessen-Rechner. Baltimore: Buch-Handlung der Evang. Luth. Kirche: 1844. PPG. 44-4253

Miller, S.G. The ready interest reckoner; or, the computation of interest on 25 cents up to 1000 dollars, at 6 percent, from one day up to a whole year. Baltimore: 1844. 20 p. PPM. 44-4254

Miller, Samuel, 1769-1850. History of the early rise of prelacy. By the Rev. Samuel Miller, D.D., professor in the theological seminary at Princeton. Philadelphia: Presbyterian Board of Publication, 1844. 46 p. NcMHi; NjR; PPPrHi; TSewU; WHi. 44-4255

Miller, Samuel, 1769-1850. The primitive and apostolical order of the church of Christ vindicated. Philadelphia, Pennsylvania: Presbyterian Board of Publication, printer, 1844. 384 p. NcCJ; NcMHi; OO; PPWe. 44-4256

Miller, Samuel, 1769-1850. The warrant, nature, and duties of the office of the ruling elder in the Presbyterian Church: with an appendix. By Samuel Miller, D.D. Philadelphia: William S. Martien, 1844. 166 p. GDecCT; NjP; PPPrHi. 44-4257

Miller, William, 1782-1849. Remarks on Revelations, thirteenth, seventeenth and eighteenth. Boston: Joshua V. Himes, 1844? 47 p. MH; ViU. 44-4258

Millerites. Clerical quackery unmasked and the true doctrine of the second advent vindicated. Philadelphia: 1844. PPL. 44-4259

Miller's planters' and merchants' almanac for 1845. Second edition. Charleston, South Carolina: A.E. Miller, [1844] MWA. 44-4260

Miller's planters' and merchants' almanac for 1845. Third edition. Charleston, South Carolina: A.E. Miller, [1844] MWA. 44-4261

Miller's theory annihilated. Clerical quackery unmasked, and the doctrine of the second advent as taught in the New Testament vindicated, by an ex-editor. Philadelphia: published by the author, 1844. 16 p. CSansS; PPL. 44-4262

Mills, Charles, 1788-1825. The history of chivalry; or, knighthood and its times.... Philadelphia: Lea and Blanchard, 1844. 247 p. GAuY; IaCrM; MH; OSW; ScC. 44-4263

Mills, Charles, 1788-1826. The history of the crusades, for the recovery and possession of the Holy Land. Philadelphia:

Lea and Blanchard, 1844. 2 v. in 1. MW; NNUT; OSW; ScDuE; Wv. 44-4264

Mills, J. The horse keepers guide. New York: 1844. MB. 44-4265

Milman, Henry Hart, 1791-1868. Fazio, or the Italian wife. A tragedy in five acts. From the author's latest edition, with the stage directions. New York: 1844. 60 p. MH; MMal; RPB. 44-4266

Milman, Henry Hart, 1791-1868. The history of Christianity from the birth of Christ to the abolition of paganism in the Roman empire. By Rev. H.H. Milman, with a preface and notes by James Murdock, D.D. New York: Harper and brothers, 1844. 526 p. GMM; KyLoP; MB; NhD; PPiW. 44-4267

Milman, Henry Hart, 1791-1868. The history of the Jews.... Third American, from the Edinburgh edition. By William Jenks, D.D. Boston: M.A. Berk, 1844. 400 p. MeAu. 44-4268

Milner, John, 1752-1826. The end of religions controversy, in a friendly correspondence between a religious society of Protestants and a Catholic divine. By the Right Reverend John Milner. Baltimore: Metropolitan Press, 1844. 326 p. ILM; MB; MH; MiDSH; MoFloSS. 44-4269

Milner, John, 1752-1826. The end of religious controversy, in a friendly correspondence between a religious society of Protestants and a Catholic divine. In three parts. New York: Edward Dunigan, 1844. 318 p. MdCatS; MdBS; NNF; OCh. 44-4270

Milner, John, 1752-1826. The end of religious controversy, in a friendly correspondence between a religious society of Protestants and a Roman Catholic divine. New York: Bookbinders and Catholic Booksellers, 1844. 352 p. LNX. 44-4271

Milner, John, 1752-1826. The end of religious controversy, in a friendly correspondence between a religious society of Protestants and a Roman Catholic divine. New York: D. and J. Sadlier, 1844. 352 p. LNL; NBuDC; NNUT; RNR; WM. 44-4272

Milner, Joseph. The history of the Church of Christ. By the late Rev. Joseph Milner, A.M. With additions and corrections by the late Rev. Isaac Milner, D.D. T.R.S. From the last London edition. Philadelphia: Hogan and Thompson, 1844. 2 v. LN; MBC; NcCJ; PU; ScCoT. 44-4273

Milner, Thomas, d. 1832. The gallery of nature; a pictorial and descriptive tour through creation, illustrative of the wonders of astronomy, physical geography, and geology. New York: Wiley, 1844. 803 p. DLC; LN. 44-4274

Milton, John, 1608-1674. The complete poetical works of John Milton with explanatory notes, and a life of the author by Rev. H. Stebbing, to which is prefixed Dr. Channing's essay on the poetical genius of Milton. New York: D. Appleton and company, 1844. 552 p. CtHC; CtHwchA; NNF; PPL; WM. 44-4275

Milton, John, 1608-1674. Paradise lost: a poem in twelve books. New York: Edward Kearney, 1844. 283 p. IEG; InPer; NjP; OClW; RBa. 44-4276

Milton, John, 1608-1674. Paradise lost. A poem in twelve books, with a life of the author by the Rev. H. Stebbing, A.M. Philadelphia: John Locken, 1844. 356 p. OUr; OUrC. 44-4277

Milton, John, 1608-1674. Paradise regained; and other poems. New York: Kearney, [1844] 215 p. NjP. 44-4278

Milwaukee County, Wisconsin. Fee-bill of the bar of Milwaukee County, Wisconsin. Adopted March 12, 1844. The prices in all cases being stated at the minimum.... Milwaukee, Wisconsin: Franklin Job office, 1844? Broadside. WHi. 44-4279

Milwaukee Courier, Milwaukee, Wisconsin. Milwaukee Courier Extra. Friday Noon, November 15, 1844. Second edition By Steamboat Cleveland. All Hail New York. [Milwaukee, 1844] Broadside. WHi. 44-4280

Milwaukee, Wisconsin. Fire Department. Fireman's annual ball. The members of the Neptune Fire Engine Company respectfully solicit your attendence at the Milwaukee House, February 22, 1844. [Milwaukee: 1844] WHi. 44-4281

Milwaukee, Wisconsin. List of lots to be sold at auction on Thursday August 15th, 1844 at Ragne's auction room near the Cottage Inn. Milwaukee, 1844. Broadside. WHi. 44-4282

Minor, Franklin, 1812-1867. An oration delivered before the Society of alumni, of the University of Virginia, at its seventh annual meeting, held in the rotunda, on the 4th of July, 1844. Charlottesville:

printed at the office of the Intelligencer, 1844. 16 p. DLC; MBC; ViU. 44-4283

Minot, George. Digest of the decision of the Supreme Judicial Court of Massachusetts, reported in the 17th volume of Massachusetts reports, the 24 volumes of Pickering's reports and the first four volumes of Metcalf's reports 1804-1842. Boston: C.C. Little and J. Brown, 1844. 804 p. CtHT; DLC; Md; NcD; PU-L. 44-4284

Miscellanies. [Philadelphia: etc.,1844-1878] 4 v. ICU. 44-4285

Miscellany. Boston: 1844-1877. 10 pphs. MB. 44-4286

Mississippi. A digest of the laws of Mississippi, defining the jurisdiction, duties and powers of the boards of police. Digested and arranged by order of the Board of police of Adams County, Ral. North. Natchez: Natchez Daily Courier, printer, 1844. 48 p. LU; MH-L. 44-4287

Mississippi. Reports of cases argued and determined in the High Court of Errors and Appeals of the state of Mississippi. By Volney E. Howard, reporter to the state. Containing cases for the January term, 1843. Cincinnati: E. Morgan and comapny, 1844. ABCC; CSjo; LNBA; MdBB; NV. 44-4288

Mississippi. Reports of cases decided in the superior court of Chancery, of the state of Mississippi. By John D. Freeman. Containing a series of cases decided between December term 1839, and July term, 1843. Cincinnati: E. Morgan and company, 1844. 183 p. DLC; MdBB; MoU; MsJS; OCLaw. 44-4289

Mitchell, C.L. Introductory lecture to the fall session of lectures in Castleton Medical College. Albany: Printed by C. Van Benthuysen and company, 1844. 16 p. MAnP; NNNAM. 44-4290

Mitchell, Isaac. The asylum; or, Alonzo and Melissa. An American tale founded on fact.... Hartford: S. Andrus and son, 1844. 253 p. MWA. 44-4291

Mitchell, Samuel Augustus, 1792-1868. An accompaniment to Mitchell's map of the world, on Mercator's projection: containing an index to the various countries, cities... Philadelphia: Mitchell, 1844. 572 p. MH; NSton; OClWHi. 44-4292

Mitchell, Samuel Augustus, 1792-1868. Ancient atlas, classical and sacred, containing maps illustrating the geography of the ancient world.... Philadelphia: E.H. Butler and company, 1844? 12 p. IaU; LNL; MdBJ; NBuDC; PP. 44-4293

Mitchell, Samuel Augustus, 1792-1868. A general view of the world, comprising a physical, political and statistical account of its grand divisions, America, Europe, Asia... Philadelphia: Thomas, 1844. 612 p. OClW. 44-4294

Mitchell, Samuel Augustus, 1792-1868. An introduction to the study of geography designed for the instruction of children in schools and families. Illustrated by one hundred and twenty engravings and fourteen maps. Philadelphia: Thomas, Cowperthwait and company, 1844. 178 p. PAtM. 44-4295

Mitchell, Samuel Augustus, 1792-1868. Key for exercise on Mitchell's series of outline maps for the use of academies and schools. Hartford: Mather, Case, Tiffany and Burnham, 1844. CtHWatk; MH. 44-4296

Mitchell, Samuel Augustus, 1792-1868. Map of the states of Missouri and Arkansas, and the Indian Territory, compiled from the latest authorities. Philadelphia: S.A. Mitchell, 1844. IU. 44-4297

Mitchell, Samuel Augustus, 1792-1868. Map of the states of Ohio, Indiana and Illinois, with the settled parts of Michigan and Wisconsin. Philadelphia: S.A. Mitchell, 1844. MdBP; MnSJ. 44-4298

Mitchell, Samuel Augustus, 1792-1868. Mitchell's primary geography, an easy introduction to the study of geography; designs for the instruction of children in schools and families. Philadelphia: Thomas, Cowperthwait and company, 1844. 176 p. MPiB. 44-4299

Mitchell, Samuel Augustus, 1792-1868. Mitchell's school geography. Philadelphia: Thomas, Cowperthwait and company, 1844. 336 p. CtB; MA; MB. 44-4300

Mitchell, Samuel Augustus, 1792-1868. Mitchell's school geography. Second revised edition. A system of modern geography, comprising a description of the present world and its five great divisions, America, Europe, Asia, Africa, and Oceanica.... Illustrated by an atlas of eighteen maps.... Philadelphia: Thomas, Cowperthwait and company, 1844. 336 p. MNF. 44-4301

Mitchell, Samuel Augustus, 1792-1868. A system of modern geography.... illustrated by an atlas of eighteen maps, Philadelphia: Thomas, Cowperthwait and company, 1844. 336 p. MNBedf; NcRSh; PAnL. 44-4302

Mitchell, Samuel Augustus, 1792-1868. A system of modern geography. Philadelphia: Thomas, Cowperthwait and company, 1844. 82 p. PAnL. 44-4303

Mitchell, Samuel Augustus, 1792-1868. A system of modern geography.... Revised edition. Philadelphia: Thomas, Cowperthwait and company, 1844. 88 p. PAnL. 44-4304

Mitchell, Samuel Augustus, 1792-1868. Mitchell's reference and distance map of the United States.... also, an accurate synopsis of the population of the Union, according to the census of 1840.... Philadelphia: S.A. Mitchell, 1844. 208 p. IaK; MiD-B; MnHi; NjR; NNA. 44-4305

The modern British essayists... Philadelphia: Carey and Hart, 1844-1845. 4 v. CBPSR. 44-4306

Modern eleusinia; or, the principles of odd fellowship explained; by a brother of the order. Nashua, [New Hampshire] 1844. 91 p. NBLiHi. 44-4307

Moffat, Robert, 1795-1883. Missionary labours and scenes in Southern Africa by Robert Moffat, twenty three years an agent of the London Missionary Society in that continent. Sixth edition. New York: Robert Carter; Pittsburgh: Thomas Carter, 1844. 406 p. ICP; IP; NcCJ; O; ScCoB. 44-4308

Moffat, Robert, 1795-1883. Scenes and adventures in Africa, collected from Moffat's missionary labours in Africa. Philadelphia: Presbyterian Board of Publication, 1844. 112 p. CSt; GDecCT; ICP; MWiW; PPiW. 44-4309

Moffat's agricultural almanac for 1845.

New York: Dr. William B. Moffat, [1844] MeHi; MWA; WHi. 44-4310

Mogridge, George, 1787-1854. Ephraim Holding's homely hints, chiefly addressed to Sunday School teachers. New York: Robert Carter, 1844. 241 p. MBC; MH-AH; PPL-R. 44-4311

Mogridge, George, 1787-1854. Old Humphrey's country strolls, by the author of "Old Humphrey's observations," [etc.] New York: R. Carter; Pittsburg: T. Carter, 1844. 243 p. NGlo; NNS; RPA; TxU. 44-4312

Mogridge, George, 1787-1854. Old Humphrey's observations. By the author of "Old Humphrey's addresses," "thoughts for the thoughtful," and "walks about London." Fifth edition. New York: R. Carter; Pittsburg: T. Carter, 1844. 258 p. TxU. 44-4313

Mogridge, George, 1787-1854. Old Humphrey's walks in London and its neighbourhood. Third edition. New York: Robert Carter; Pittsburg: Thomas Carter, 1844. 286 p. IGK; MA; MH; MHaHi; PU. 44-4314

Mogridge, George, 1787-1854. Thoughts for the thoughtful, by Old Humphrey [pseud.] ....Fourth edition. New York: R. Carter; Pittsburg: T. Carter, 1844. 240 p. PPWa; TxU. 44-4315

Mohler, Johann Adam, 1796-1838. Symbolism; or, exposition of the doctrinal differences between Catholics and Protestants, as evidenced by their symbolical writings, by Johann Adam Mohler.... Translated from the German with a memoir of the author.... by James Burton Robertson.... New York: Edward

Dunigan, 1844. 575 p. IaB; MdBS; NBuG; OO; PPA. 44-4316

Moliere, Jean Baptiste Poquelin, 1622-1673. Oeuvres choisies de Jean Racine, nouvelle edition Americaine, revue et corrigee. New York: Librarie francaise et etrangere. De. F.G. Berteau, 1844. 326 p. IaDa; MdAS; PPM; TSewU; ViRVal. 44-4317

Mollary, Charles Dutton, 1801-1864. Memoirs of Elder Jesse Mercer... New York: printed by J. Gray, 1844. 455 p. ICU; GU; MWA; NcU; PCA. 44-4318

Mondat, Vincent Marie. On sterility in the male and female; its causes and treatment. Translated from the Fifth edition. New York: Redfield; Boston: Saxton, Pierce and company, 1844. 248 p. DLC; DNLM; MiU; NIC-M. 44-4319

Monita Secreta Societatis Jesu. Secret instructions of the Jesuits: with an appendix, containing a short historical account of the Society of Jesus, their maxims, etc. Philadelphia: F. C. Wilson, 1844. 72 p. LNH; MH; PPL; WHi. 44-4320

Monod, Adolphe, 1802-1856. The inspiration of the Bible. Boston: Sabbath School Society, 1844. 137 p. CBPSR; DLC; MHoly. 44-4321

Monson Academy, Monson, Massachusetts. Catalogue of the trustees, instructors and students of Monson Academy, for the year ending August 14, 1844. Springfield: printed by Wood and Rupp. 1844. 12 p. MMonsA. 44-4322

Montalembert, Charles Forbes Rene de Tryon comte de. Speech of the Count Montalembert on the subject of national education in France; delivered in the Chamber of Peers, in the sittting of April 16, 1844. Translated from the French by Professor Walter. Philadelphia: Wm. J. Cunningham, 1844. 16 p. MdW; Mi; NNUT; PHi; PPL; 44-4323

Monteith, Alexander H. Robertsonian method. Course of lessons in the German language, intended for the use of persons studying the language without a master. By A.H. Monteith, esq.... New York: Wilson and company, 1844. 64 p. MBC; MdHi; MH; NNC; NStC. 44-4324

Montgomery, George Washington. Illustrations of the law of kindness.... Stereotype edition. New York: C.L. Stickney, 1844. 252 p. KyLo; MB; MNowl; NCaS. 44-4325

Montgomery, James, 1774-1854. Lectures on general literature, poetry, etc. Delivered at the Royal Institution in 1830 and 1831. Complete in one volume. New York: Harper and brothers, 1844. [4] 322 [2] p. IGK; InCW; MLaw; NbOC; OCY. 44-4326

Montgomery, James, 1774-1854. The world before the flood, a poem in ten cantos; with other occasional pieces, by James Montgomery. New York: Eastburn, Kirk and company, 1844. 281 p. MWH. 44-4327

The monthly Baptist record. Philadelphia: American Baptist Publication and Sunday School Society, 1844-. V. 1-. NjR; PCA; ViRU. 44-4328

The monthly religious magazine and theological review. Boston: L.C. Bowles, 1844-1874. 51 v. in 34. CBPac; ICU; MBAt; PPI; OCl. 44-4329

Monticello College. Godfrey, Illinois. Catalogue of the officers and members... for the year ending March, 1844. Alton: Telegraph office, 1844. [3] 16 p. IHi; MH. 44-4330

Moore, Amasa C. An address on the battle of Plattsburgh, delivered at the celebration of the anniversary, September 11, 1843. Plattsburgh: J.W. Tuttle, printer, 1844. 12 p. CSmH; MiU-C; NTi; NNG; WHi. 44-4331

Moore, Benjamin. Sermon, by Benjamin Moore, D.D. ....New York: Stanford and Swords, 1844. 2 v. NNG. 44-4332

Moore, Benjamin F. The Providence almanac: embracing a business directory of Providence, Newport, Warren, Bristol, Pawtucket and Woonsocket, Rhode Island. Also of Fall River, Massachusetts. Providence: B.F. Moore, [1844] 134 p. RPE. 44-4333

Moore, Charles K. A book of tracts containing the origin and process; cruelties; frauds; superstitions; miracles, ceremonies... With a succinct account of the rise and progress of the Jesuits. New York: Charles K. Moore, 1844. 8-206 p. GDecCT; ICU; KyBC; KyLoP. 44-4334

Moore, Charles K. Tracts on popery with account of the rise of the Jesuits etc. New York: Charles K. Moore, 1844. CtHC; MBC. 44-4335

Moore, Clement Clarke, 1779-1863. Poems. New York: Bartlett and Welford, 1844. [15]-216 p. DLC; IU; MiD; NBuG; RPB. 44-4336

Moore, Clement Clarke, 1781-1863.

Poems by Clement C. Moore, ...New York: Bartlett and Welford, 1844. 216 p. ICU; MH; NjP; NNC; RPA. 44-4337

Moore, Francis, junior. Map and description of Texas, containing sketches of its history, geology, geography and statistics: ....and some brief remarks upon the character and customs of its inhabitants.... Second edition. New York: Tanner and Disturnell, 1844. 143 p. DLC. 44-4338

Moore, John Stethem. The oracle of Delphos, and other poems. Washington: Alexander and Barnard, printers, 1844. 87 p. DLC; MH; NcD; OO; RPB. 44-4339

Moore, Justus E. The warning of Thomas Jefferson: or, a brief exposition of the dangers to be apprehended to our civil and religious liberties, from Presbyterianism. By Justus E. Moore. Philadelphia: William J. Cunningham, 1844. 35 p. GAM-R; MBC; MdHi; NNC; PHi. 44-4340

Moore, Nathaniel Fish, 1782-1872. Short introduction to universal grammar; compiled for the use of the freshman class in Columbia College, New York. New York: Wiley, 1844. 43 p. InGrD; MH; NB; NNC. 44-4341

Moore, Thomas, 1779-1852. Evenings in Greece. New York: Morris and Willis, 1844. 32 p. DLC; MWH; NNC. 44-4342

Moore, Thomas, 1779-1852. Irish melodies, by Thomas Moore. [New York: Morris and Willis, 1844?] 32 p. MWH; OLak; PPi. 44-4343

Moore, Thomas, 1779-1852. Lalla

Rookh [New York: 1844] 56 p. DLC; MB; MWH; NNC; TxU. 44-4344

Moore, Thomas, 1779-1852. The loves of the angels; a poem. Boston: Saxton, Peirce and company, 1844. 9-128 p. MWH; NjP; NSyHi; OFH. 44-4345

Moore, Thomas, 1779-1852. National airs, by Thomas Moore. [New York: Morris and Willis, 1844?] 32 p. MWH. 44-4346

Moore, Thomas, 1779-1852. Poetical works of Thomas Moore. Complete in one volume, illustrated with engravings from drawings by eminent artists. New York: D. Appleton and company, 1844. 747 p. GASH; IaK; MHi; ViL. 44-4347

Moore, Thomas, 1779-1852. Sacred songs, by Thomas Moore. Hebrew melodies by Lord Byron. Palestine, by Reginald Heber, late bishop of Calcutta. Boston: Saxton and Pierce and company; New York: Saxton and Miles, 1844. 127 p. MoSpD; MPeHi; NHunt; NNUt. 44-4348

Moore, Thomas, 1779-1852. Travels of an Irish gentleman in search of a religion; with notes and illustrations by the editor of Captain Rock's Memoirs. Baltimore: John Murphy, 1844. 264 p. MBC; MdBS; NB; PLor; WM. 44-4349

Moore, William V. Pictorial life of Napoleon Bonaparte, emperor of the French. With numerous illustrative anecdotes of his court and times; compiled from the best authorities, by William V. Moore. Philadelphia: Lindsay and Blakiston, 1844. 222 p. KyHi; MdBD. 44-4350

Moorman, John Jennings. Mineral waters in general White Sulphur Springs. White Sulphur Springs: 1844. 16 p. MH-M. 44-4351

The moral almanac, for the year 1845... Philadelphia: Tract Association of Friends [1844] 36 p. MBNEH; PPM; WHi. 44-4352

Moravian Church. Wisconsin. Psalter. Harpen en samling of aeldre og nyere kristelige psalmer til brug ved broderkirkens gudstjenester i den Nord-Americans pe provinds femte oplag. Fifth edition. Ephraim, Wisconsin, 1844. NoLoc. 44-4353

Mordecai, Alfred. Report of experiments on gunpowder made at Washington Arsenal in 1843 and 1844. Washington: 1844. PPL-R. 44-4354

More, Hannah, 1745-1833. The book of private devotion; a series of prayers and meditations; with an introductory essay on prayer. Chiefly from the writings of Hannah More. Revised and enlarged. Baltimore: Parsons and Preston, 1844. [9]-252 p. ViU. 44-4355

More, Hannah, 1745-1833. The book of private devotion, a series of progress and meditation, with an introductory essay on prayer, chiefly from the writings of Hannah More. Revised and enlarged. New York: Robinson, 1844. 252 p. ICU; KyBgB; MB; MdW; ODaB. 44-4356

More, Hannah, 1745-1833. Domestic tales and allegories; illustrating human life. New York: D. Appleton and company, 1844. 180 p. MH; MWA; PPL-R; TxSaWi. 44-4357

More, Hannah, 1745-1833. Rural tales, portraying social life, by Hannah More.... New York: D. Appleton and company, 1844. 180 p. DLC; MWA; NIC; TxCsA; ViHop. 44-4358

More, Hannah, 1745-1833. The works of Hannah More. First complete American edition. New York: Harper and brothers, 1844-1846. 2 v. CtY; MH. 44-4359

More, Hannah, 1745-1833. Works, first complete American edition. New York: Harper and brothers, 1844-46. 2 v. MH; ScAnC. 44-4360

Moreau, Francois Joseph, 1789-1862. A practical treatise on midwifery: exhibiting the present advanced state of the science. By F. J. Moreau.... Translated from the French by Thomas F. Betton.... and edited by Paul B. Goddard.... With 80 plates, comprising numerous separate illustrations. Philadelphia: Carey and Hart, 1844. 235 p. ICU; MeB; NcD; PAtM; TU-M. 44-4361

Morey, Amos C. Charlotte Corday; a tragedy in five acts. New York: Fraetas, 1844. 48 p. MB; NNC. 44-4362

Morgan, Jonathan. Elements of English grammar. With a postscript analysis, and an appendix. Second edition, revised and corrected. Portland, Maine: Thurston, Ilsley and company, 1844. 180 p. MeHi; MH; MHi; MSwan; NNC. 44-4363

Morgan, Thomas Jefferson. A glance at Texas: being a brief sketch of the history, government, population, climate, soil, productions, and extent of territory to which are added.... Columbus: printed at the Statesman office, 1844. 14 p. OClWHi; P. 44-4364

Mormons and Mormonism. Nauvoo expositor. V. 1, No. 1, June 7, 1844. Nauvoo, Illinois: 1844. MoSHi; NbHi. 44-4365

Morris, Edmund, 1804-1874. Ten acres enough: a practical experience, showing how a very small farm may be made to keep a very large family, etc., etc. New York: 1844. 255 p. MBHo; MeBat; MoU. 44-4366

Morris, Edward Joy. Speech of Edward Morris, of Pennsylvania, in defence of the American navy delivered in the House of Representatives... Washington: Powers Sr., 1844. 80 p. PPFrankI. 44-4367

Morris, Edward Joy. Speech of Edward Morris, of Pennsylvania, in defence of the tariff of 1842, and the protective policy and American labor. Delivered in the House of Representatives, April 24, 1844. Washington: Printed at the office of the Whig Standard, 1844. In; MBAt; MH; P; WHi. 44-4368

Morris, George Pope, 1802-1864. Little Frenchman and his water lots, and other tales of the times. New York: Morris, 1844. MH; MnU; PU. 44-4369

Morris, George Pope, 1802-1864. Songs and ballads: by George P. Morris. [New York: 1844] 16 p. ICU; LNH; MB; RPB; TxU. 44-4370

Morris, Thomas. Speech of Thomas Morris, of Ohio, in the Senate, February 9, 1839. Utica [Jackson and Chaplin, 1844] 16 p. DLC; MHi; N. 44-4371

Morrison, Robert Hall. Funeral sermon of the Rev. John Robinson preached February 22, 1844. Charlotte: Journal, 1844. 15 p. PPPrHi. 44-4372

Morrison's strangers' guide to the city of Washington and its vicinity. Second edition. Washington: Morrison, 1844. 108 p. ICN; MB; MPiB; PPL. 44-4373

Morse, S.F.B. Electro-magnetic telegraph [several congressional papers] also reports of Paris exposition commos. Washington: Government Printing Office, 1844. MdAN. 44-4374

Morse, Samuel Finley Breese, 1791-1872. Foreign conspiracy against the liberties of the United States. The numbers under the signature of Brutus, originally published in the New York Observer. Revised and corrected, with notes by the author, Samuel F.B. Morse.... Fourth edition. New York: American Protestant Society, 1844. 191 p. DLC; Vi. 44-4375

Morse, Samuel Finley Breese, 1791-1872. Foreign conspiracy against the liberties of the United States. The numbers under the signature of Brutus, originally published in the New York Observer. Revised and corrected, with notes by the author, Samuel F.B. Morse.... Sixth edition. New York: American Protestant Society, 1844. 191 p. CBCDS; MBAt; MnHi; OClWHi; TxU. 44-4376

Morse, Sidney Edwards, 1794-1871. A system of geography, for the use of schools. Illustrated with more than fifty cerographic maps, and numerous wood cut engravings. New York: Harper and brothers, 1844. 72. CSt; MH; OHi; PPi; RPA. 44-4377

Morse, Sidney Edwards, 1794-1871. The cerographic Bible atlas. New York: Morse, 1844. CtSoP; OC. 44-4378

Mortimer, Favell Lee Bevan, 1802-1878. Iu pitabvn; gema gaie okikinoamaguziuinuia igiu abinojivg. The peep of day; or, a series of the earliest religious instruction the infant mind is capable of receiving. Boston: T.R. Marvin, printer, 1844. 144 p. CtHWatk; DLC; MB. 44-4379

Mortimer, Favell Lee Bevan, 1802-1878. Line upon line, or a second series of the earliest religous instruction the infant mind is capable of receiving with verses illustrative of the subjects by the "Peep of Day." New York: John S. Taylor company, 1844. 258 p. MChi; OCHP. 44-4380

Morton, Joseph Washington. Inspired Psalms, selected and literally translated.... Freedom, Pennsylvania: the author, 1844. PHi; PPPrHi. 44-4381

Morton, Samuel George, 1799-1851. Crania aegyptiaca; or observations on Egyptian ethnology, derived from anatomy, history and the monuments. Philadelphia: J. Pennington, 1844. 67 p. MdBJ; MiU; OC; PPL-R; ScU. 44-4382

Morton, Samuel George, 1799-1851. The inquiry into the distinctive characteristics of the aboriginal race of America. Second edition. Philadelphia: J. Penington, 1844. 48 p. IaDaP; MdHi; MoSHi; PPAmP; WHi. 44-4383

Morton, Samuel George, 1799-1851. A

memoir of William Maclure, esq., late president of the Academy of Natural Sciences of Philadelphia, read July 1, 1841.... Philadelphia: Merrihew and Thompson, printers, 1844. 33 p. CtHT; LNH; MoSB; NNNAM. 44-4384

Morton, Samuel George, 1799-1851. A memoir of William Maclure, esq., late president of the Academy of Natural Sciences of Philadephia. By Samuel George Morton, M.D., one of the vice presidents of the institution. Read July 1, 1841, and published by direction of the academy. Second edition. Philadelphia: Merrihew and Thompson, printers, 1844. 33 p. CSt; InLPU; MH; NhD; PPAmP. 44-4385

Morton, Samuel George, 1799-1851. On a supposed new species of hippopotamus. Philadelphia: 1844. 10 p. PPAmP; PPL. 44-4386

Morton, Thomas, 1764?-1838. A cure for the heartache; a comedy in five acts. New York, London: Samuel French, [1844] OCl. 44-4387

Moseley, Henry. Illustrations of mechanics. New York: Harper and brothers, 1844. 332 p. MB; NCaS; OSW; PHi; RPE. 44-4388

Mosheim, Johan Lorenz, 1694-1755. An ecclesiastical history, ancient and modern by John Lawrence Mosheim. Translated from the original Latin. By Archibald Maclaine. A new edition, continued to the year 1826. By Charles Coote. New York: Harper and brothers, 1844. 2 v. ICU; MikC; NSchU; PWW; OUrC. 44-4389

Mosheim, Johan Lorenz, 1694-1755. In-

stitutes of ecclesiastical history, ancient and modern....By Johan Lorenz Von Mosheim, D.D. ....A new and literal translation from the original Latin.... by James Murdock, D.D. Second edition revised and enlarged. New York: Harper and brothers, 1844. 3 v. CLSU; GMM; KWiU; MaIn. 44-4390

Mosheim, Johan Lorenz, 1694-1755. Institutes of ecclesiastical history, ancient and modern, in four books, much corrected, enlarged and improved from the primary authorities. By Johan Lorenz von Mosheim, D.D. ....A new and literal translation from the original Latin, with copious additional notes.... by James Murdock, D.D. ....Third edition revised and enlarged. New York: Harper and brothers, 1844. 3 v. ICT; Nh; OZAN; PPEB; PMA. 44-4391

The mother's assistant and young ladies friend. Boston: 1844. 12 v. in 3. VtU. 44-4392

Motherwell, William, 1797-1835. Poems, narrative and lyrical, by William Motherwell. Third edition. Boston: W.D. Ticknor and company, 1844. 216 p. InGrD; MdBJ; MeB; NNUT; ODa. 44-4393

Motley, John Lothrop, 1814-1877. Merry-mount. Boston and Cambridge: 1844. 2 v. in 1. CtHWatk. 44-4394

Motley, John Lothrop, 1814-1877. The rise of the Dutch Republic. A history. New York: A.L. Burt and company, 1844. 2 v. MoSpD. 44-4395

Moultrie, James. On the organic functions of animals. Charleston, South

Carolina: Burges and James, 1844. 20 p. NcD; NNNAM; PPCP; ScU. 44-4396

Mount Holyoke College. Seventh annual catalogue of the Mount Holyoke Female Seminary, in South Hadley, Massachusetts, 1843-1844. Amherst: J.S. and C. Adams, printers, 1844. 16 p. MiD-B. 44-4397

Mount Holyoke College. Eighth annual catalogue of the Mount Holyoke Female Seminary, in South Hadley, Massachusetts, Amherst: J.S. and C. Adams, printers, 1844. 16 p. IaU; MA; MAJ; NbCrD. 44-4398

Mount Sinai, New York. Congregational Church. Confession of faith and covenat... New York: 1844. 10 p. MBC. 44-4399

Mowatt, Anna Cora. Autobiography of an actress; or, eight years on the state, Boston: Ticknor, Reed and Fields, 1844. 448 p. CVal. 44-4400

Mudge, Enoch. Farewell discourse. Delivered before New Bedford Port Society, July 14, 1844. Lynn: Kimball and Butterfield, 1844. 12 p. IEG; MBNMHi. 44-4401

Mudge, Enoch. This tract is the substance of the farewell discourse of Rev. Enoch Mudge, delivered before the New Bedford Port Society, July 14, 1844, and published by their executive board, for distribution among seamen. Lynn, Massachusetts: Kimball and Butterfield, printers, [1844?] 12 p. MNBedf. 44-4402

Munk, Edward, 1803-1871. The metres of the Greeks and Romans. A manual for schools and private study, translated from the German of Edward Munk, By Charles Beck and C.C. Felton. Boston: James Munroe and company, 1844. 349 p. CSansS; IaPeC; NjP; PAtM; RPB. 44-4403

Munson, Samuel B. A new map of the western rivers. [Cinconnati: E.S. and J. Applegate] 1844. 1 p. PHi. 44-4404

Murdock, James. Modern philosophy... Second edition. Hartford: John C. Wells, 1844. [7]-201 p. ArCH; IaCec; MiD; NNUT; RPaw. 44-4405

Murray, Charles Augustus. The prairie bird. ....New York: Harper and brothers, 1844. 207 p. ICHi; OClWHi; PPL; RPB. TXShA. 44-4406

Murray, Hugh. Historical and descriptive account of British India. New York: Harper and brothers, 1844. 3 v. InCW; MdBS; MeAu; OCX; WaPS. 44-4407

Murray, John, 1741-1815. The life of the Rev. John Murray, written by himself. Eighth edition, stereotyped and improved, with notes and appendix, by Rev. L.S. Everett. Boston: A. Tompkins, 1844. 324 p. CBPac; CtY-D; GEU-T; MMeT-Hi; NCaS. 44-4408

Murray, John. Life of late minister of the reconciliation, and senior pastor the Universalists, congregated in Boston. A records, contains anecdotes of the writer's infancy, and are extended to some years after the commencement of his public labors in America, etc. Notes, etc by L.S. Everett. Boston: 1844. MB. 44-4409

Murray, Lindley, 1745-1826. Abridgement of Murray's English grammar. Boston: R.S. Davis, etc., etc., 1844. CtHWatk; ICU; MH. 44-4410

Murray, Lindley, 1745-1826. English exercises, adopted to Murray's English grammar. New York: W.E. Dean, 1844. 8-108 p. KyDC. 44-4411

Murray, Lindley, 1745-1826. The English grammar, adapted to the different classes of learners. With an appendix containing rules and observations for assisting the more advanced students to write with perspicuity and accuracy. New York: Bolles and Williams, 1844. 232 p. IaScT; MdBD; TxHR. 44-4412

Murray, Lindley, 1745-1826. The English grammar, adapted to the different classes of learners. With an appendix containing rules and observations for assisting the more advanced students to write with perspicuity and accuracy. New York: H. and S. Raynor, 1844. 264 p. KyLxT. 44-4413

Murray, Lindley, 1745-1826. The English reader: or pieces in prose and poetry, selected from the best writers; designed to... improve their language and sentiments and to include... Newark, New Jersey: Benjamin Olds, 1844. 252 p. OClWHi; PWCHi. 44-4414

Murray, Lindley, 1745-1826. The English reader: or pieces in prose and poetry, selected from the best writers, with a few preliminary observations on the principles of good reading. New York: Robinson, Pratt and company, 1844. NPV; NWatt; NWattJHi. 44-4415

Murray, Lindley, 1745-1826. English reader, or pieces in prose and verse, from the best writers. Designed to assist young

persons to read with propriety and effect. New London: Bolles and Williams, etc., 1844. MH. 44-4416

Murray, Lindley, 1745-1826. English reader; ....with a few preliminary observations on the principles of good reading. ....New London: Bolles and Williams; New York: Collins, brother and company, 1844. 252 p. MH; NNC; NNT-C. 44-4417

Murray, Lindley, 1745-1826. Introduction to the English reader, or, a selection of pieces in prose and poetry calculated to improve the younger classes of learners in reading.... New York: John S. Taylor and company, 1844. 189 p. ScCoB. 44-4418

Murray, Lindley, 1745-1826. Key to the exercises adapted to Murray's English gramar. Calculated to enable private learners to become their own instructers, in grammar and composition. By the author of the exercises. Stereotyped from the last English edition. New York; Philadelphia: Grigg and Elliot, 1844. 168 p. NNC. 44-4419

Murray, Lindley, 1745-1826. Murray's English exercises.... with which the corrseponding notes, rules, and observations in Murray's grammar are incorporated.... revised, prepared and particularly adapted to the use of schools.... Boston: Robert S. Davis; Philadelphia: Thomas, Cowperthwait and company, 1844. MH; TxU-T. 44-4420

Murray, Lindley, 1745-1826. Sequel to the English reader, or elegant selections in prose and poetry. Designed to improve the highest class of learners in reading to establish a taste for just and accurate composition; and to promote the interests of piety and virtue. New York: J.S. Taylor and company, 1844. MH. 44-4421

Musical counting room almanac for 1845. Boston: H.W. Day [1844] Broadside. MWA. 44-4422

Mutter, Thomas D. Cases of deformity of various kinds, successfully treated by plastic operations. Philadelphia: Merrihew and Thompson, 1844. 38 p. MH-M; NBMS; PHi. 44-4423

Mutter, Thomas D. Introductory for 1844-5, on the present position of some of the most important of the modern operations of surgery. By Thomas D. Mutter, M.D. Philadelphia: The class, 1844. 34 p. JeffMedC; MoSMed; NBMS. 44-4424

Mutual Insurance Company of the City and County of Albany. Act of incorporation and by-laws. May, 1836. Albany: 1844. 12 p. MHi. 44-4425

Mutual Life Insurance Company of New York. Treatise on the life insurance: being an explanation of the principles and the useful application of the mutual system to the different situations of life. New York: Dean, printer, 1844. 36 p. MB; MH-BA; MHi; Mi; RPL. 44-4426

My mother's funeral... Massachusetts Sabbath School Society, 1844. 32 p. DLC; MeBaT. 44-4427

My native village, or the recollection of twenty-five years. Philadelphia: American Sunday School Union, 1844. 139 p. AmSSchU; ICBB; PAtM. 44-4428

Myers, Peter D. The zion songster; a collection of hymns and spiritual songs, generally sung at camp or prayer meetings, and in revivals of religion; revised and corrected by the compiler. New York, New York: Collins, 1844. 319 p. CLCM; CtHWatk; NcU. 44-4429

The mysteries of Nashua: or revenge punished and constancy rewarded... Nashua: C.T. Gill, 1844. 40 p. CU; DLC; MH; N; Nh-Hi. 44-4430

N

A narrative of facts in the recent conversion of a Romanist. New York: American Protestant Society, 1844. 8 p. ICP. 44-4431

Narrative of the extraordinary life of John Conrad Shafford, known by the name of the Dutch Hermit, who for the last fifty years has lived a secluded and lonely life in a log hut, in a remote part of the village of Dundee, [Lower Canada] where he died on the 24th of April last, [1842] at the age of between and 80 and 90 [New York: C. L. Carpenter, 1844] 22 p. NN. 44-4432

Nash, Simeon. The principles of protection vindicated. A lecture delivered before the Gallipolis Lyceum, on the evenings of January 27, and February 3, 1844. Gallipolis: William Nash, printer, 1844. 24 p. OCHP; OClWHi; OMC. 44-4433

National Academy of Design, New York. Catalogue of the nineteenth annual exhibition. 1844. New York: Israel Sackett, 1844. 32 p. PPPM; RNR. 44-4434

National Academy of Design, New York. Report of committee to examine the constitution and by-laws of the National Academy of Design, made December 5, 1844. New York: Sackett, 1844. 13 p. NNC; PPPM. 44-4435

National bank, shall we but it

again?....Democratic address. Philadelphia: 1844. PPL. 44-4436

National clay almanack, 1845. Philadelphia, Pennsylvania: Desilver and Muir, [1844] MWA. 44-4437

The national clay almanack....1845....carefully calculated for the horizon of Pennsylvania, Ohio, Maryland and Virginia....By Seth Smith....Philadelphia: Uriah Hunt, [1844?] 34 p. WHi. 44-4438

The National clay club. One thousand dollar reward! Philadelphia: 1844. 8 p. MH-BA; PHi. 44-4439

The national clay melodist; a collection of popular and patriotic songs. Boston: Adams, 1844. OMC. 44-4440

The national clay melodist, second edition. Boston: 1844. DLC; ICN; MBAt; MH. 44-4441

The national clay minstrel. And true Whig's pocket companion, for the presidential canvass. Boston: J. Fisher, [1844] 126 p. MLow; OClWHi. 44-4442

The national clay minstrel. And the true Whig's pocket companion, for the presidential canvass of 1844. Philadelphia: G. Hood, [1844] 126 p. CSt; ICN; NIC; TxU. 44-4443

National Convention of Silk Growers

and Silk Manufacturers. New York. 1843. The silk question settled. The testimony of one hundred and fifty witnesses. Report of the proceedings of The National Convention of Silk Growers and Manufacturers, held in New York, October 13th and 14th, 1843. New York: Saxton and Miles, 1844. 80 p. MB; MdBJ; MH; RPB. 44-4444

National Convention of Silk Growers and Silk Manufacturers. New York, 1843. The silk question settled.... Report of the proceedings of the national convention....held in New York, October 13th and 14th, 1843. ....Second edition, with additions. Boston: T. R. Marvin, printer, 1844. 79 p. MH; MHi; NcAS; NNT-C. 44-4445

National Convention of Silk Growers and Silk Manufacturers. New York, 1843. The silk question settled. Report of the proceedings of the national convention of silk growers and silk manufacturers, held in New York, October 13th and 14th, 1843. Published under the direction of the American Institute. Second edition, with additions. Boston: T.R. Marvin, printer, 1844. 79 p. MB. 44-4446

National Lord's Day Convention. Address to the people of the United States. Philadelphia: Ashmead, 1844. PPPrHi. 44-4447

The National magazine. Literature, art, religion. New York: Carlton and Porter, 1844-1858. 14 v. NE. 44-4448

The National Protestant magazine. New York: 1844-1846. 3 v. KyU; MH. 44-4449

National Sabbath Convention. Address of the National Sabbath Convention to the people of the United States. Resolutions adopted by the convention. Baltimore: November, 1844. 19 p. CBPSR; PPPrHi. 44-4450

Native American Central Executive Committee of Philadelphia. Preamble and by-laws. Philadelphia: 1844. 11 p. PHi. 44-4451

Native American circular.... Philadelphia: 1844. PPL. 44-4452

Native American committee.... Philadelphia: 1844. PPL-R. 44-4453

Nativism; or the office hunter under a religious cloak. By a friend to equal rights. Philadelphia: 1844. 12 p. CtV. 44-4454

Natural history of the whale. Concord: Rufus Merrill, 1844. 24 p. MB; NBuG. 44-4455

Nau, L. A new scale, or a short, easy and sure way to learn the French reading and pronunciation. By L. Nau. First edition. Boston: 1844. 12 p. MHi. 44-4456

Nauvoo Legion. Revised laws of the Nauvoo legion, from the constitution of the United States. By authority. Nauvoo, Illinois: John Taylor, printer, 1844. 36 p. CtY; MoInRC; NjP; USlC. 44-4457

Neal, Daniel, 1678-1743. The history of the Puritans; or Protestant Non-conformists, from the reformation in 1517, to the revolution in 1688 comprising an account of their principles. New York: Harper and brothers, 1844. 2 v. DLC; NcD; OCl; PPC; WaS. 44-4458

Neal, Joseph Clay, 1807-1847. Charcoal sketches; or scenes in a metropolis. Illustrated by David C. Johnston. New edition. Philadelphia: Carey and Hart, 1844. 3-222 p. LU; MeSaco; NjP; PPL; REd. 44-4459

Neal, Joseph Clay, 1807-1847. Peter Ploddy, and other oddities. ....With ten illustrations.... from original designs by Darley. Philadelphia: Carey and Hart, 1844. 181 p. DLC; FOA; MB; PPL; RPA. 44-4460

Neander, August, 1789-1850. The history of the Christian religion and church, during the three first centuries. Translated from the German by H.J. Rose. Second edition. Philadelphia: Campbell, 1844. PPPrHi. 44-4461

Neander, August, 1789-1850. The history of the Christian religion and church, during the three first centuries. Translated from the German by H.J. Rose. Fifth edition. Philadelphia: 1844. MH-AH; OO. 44-4462

Neander, August, 1789-1850. History of the planting and training of the Christian church by the apostles. By Dr. Augustus Neander.... Translated from the third edition of the original German, by J.E. Ryland. Philadelphia: J.M. Campbell and company; New York: Saxton and Miles, 1844. 330 p. IaDm; MiU; NNUT; PWW; WHi. 44-4463

Neander, John Augustus William, 1789-1850. The history of the Christian religion and church during the three first centuries. Translated from the German by Henry J. Rose. Second edition. Philadelphia: Campbell, 1844. 1 v. PPPr-Hi. 44-4464

Neander, John Augustus William, 1789-1850. The history of the Christian religion and church during the three first centuries, by Dr. Augustus Neander. Translated from the German by Henry John Rose. Fifth edition. Philadelphia: J.M. Campbell, 1844. 471 p. CoDI; MH-AH; OO; PLT; WHi. 44-4465

Necker, Albertine Adrienne [de Saussure] Study of the life of woman, translated from the French. Philadelphia: Lea, 1844. 288 p. MNBedf; OCo; PPL-R; RPA. 44-4466

Neilson, Charles. An account of Burgoyne's campaign and the battles of Bemis Heights, September 19, and October 7, 1777; and map. Albany, New York: J. Munsell, 184. 291 p. MBL; MDeeP; NR. 44-4467

Neilson, Charles. Burgoynes campaign and the memorable battles of Bemis Heights. Albany: J. Munsell, 1844. 290 p. IGK; MB; OCad; O; PHi. 44-4468

Neilson, Charles. An original, compiled, and corrected account of Burgoyne's campaign, and the memorable battles of Bemis Heights, September 19, and October 7, 1777, from the most authentic sources of information; including many interesting incidents connected with the same. Albany: J. Munsell, 1844. 291 p. InU; MWA; NUt; Vi; WHi. 44-4469

Neineke, C. Music for the church containing sixty-two psalm and hymn tunes, in four parts; together with chants, doxologies and responses, for morning and evening prayer, and Holy Communion. Composed for the use of the choir of St. Paul's Church, Baltimore.

Baltimore: J. Cole by F.D. Benteen, 1844. 100 p. MBC; MdBD. 44-4470

Nelaton, Auguste, 1807-1873. Elemens de pathologie chirurgicale, par A. Nelaton... Paris: G. Bailliere; New York: H. Bailliere; etc., etc., 1844-1857. 4 v. CtMW. 44-4471

Neligan, John Moore, 1815-1863. Medicines. Their uses and mode of administration; including a complete conspectus of the three British pharmacopoeias, an account of all the remedies, and an appendix of formulae. New York: Harper and brothers, 1844. [25]-453 p. DSG; ICJ; MNBedf; NcU; TNV. 44-4472

The Nevilles of Garretstown. New York: 1844. MB. 44-4473

Nevin, Alfred. An address delivered before the students Literary Society of Strassburg Academy, March 14, 1844. Lancaster: John W. Forney, printer, 1844. 16 p. PLERC-Hi. 44-4474

Nevin, John Williamson, 1803-1886. Die angst-bank; uebersetzt aus dem englischen, nach der 2. verm. aufl. Chambersburg [Pennsylvania] Druck erei der Christlichen zeitschrift, 1844. 154 p. DLC; PLERCHi; PPLT. 44-4475

Nevin, John Williamson, 1803-1886. The anxious bench. Second edition revised and enlarged. Chambersburg, Pennsylvania: Publication office of the German Reformed Church, 1844. 149 p. IEG; GDecCT; MdBD; NNUT; TxDaM. 44-4476

Nevin, John Williamson, 1803-1886. A funeral sermon with reference to the death of James Edgar Moore, preached in the chapel of Marshall College, June 23, 1844. Mercersburg: Diagnothian Literary Society, 1844. 18 p. IEG; MBAt; NjR; PHi; PLFM. 44-4477

Nevin, William M. National taste. An address delivered before the Gothean Literary Society of Marshall College, at its anniversary, August 28, 1844. Chambersburg, Pennsylvania: the society, 1844. 20 p. MH; PHi; PLFM; PWCHi. 44-4478

The New ballroom guide; or, dancing made easy, comprising all the latest and most fashionable figures. From the fortieth London edition, revised and much enlarged by the American editor. New York: Burgess and Stringer, 1844. 64 p. LU. 44-4479

New Bedford, Massachusetts. Congregational Church. The confession of faith and covenant, adopted and used by the Congregational Church in New Bedford. Printed at the request, and for the use of the members of said church. New Bedford, [Massachusetts]: press of Benjamin Lindsey, 1844. 12 p. MNBedf. 44-4480

New Bedford, Massachusetts. Protecting Society. Constitution and by-laws of the New Bedford Protecting Society, as amended April, 1844. New Bedford [Massachusetts]: press of Henry Tilden, 1844. 7 p. MNBedf. 44-4481

New Brighton Collegiate School. New Brighton, New York. Annual catalogue. April 3, 1844. MH. 44-4482

New Britain, Connecticut. First Congregational Church. The history, rules, confession of faith and covenant of the First Congregational Church in New Britain [Second church in Berlin, Connecticut] with a catalogue of members, January, 1844. Hartford: Printed by D.B. Mosely, 1844. 22 p. OMC. 44-4483

The new church magazine for children. v. 1-20; July, 1843-June, 1862. Boston: O. Clapp, 1844-62. 20 v. in 18. DLC; McNC; PBa. 44-4484

The New England almanac and farmers' friend for the year 1845.... By Nathan Daboll, A.M. ....New London: Bolles and Williams [1844] 30 p. CU; ICMcHi; NjR. 44-4485

New England almanack by Nathan Daboll. Norwich: L. and E. Edwards, 1844. MWA. 44-4486

The New England almanack, ...Concord, New Hampshire: John F. Brown, 1844. 48 p. MiD-B. 44-4487

New England almanack for 1845. By Nathan Daboll. Norwich, Connecticut: Bolles and Williams, [1844] MWA. 44-4488

New England almanack for 1845. By Nathan Daboll. Norwich, Connecticut: L. and E. Edwards, [1844] MWA. 44-4489

New England almanack for 1845. By Nathan Daboll. Norwich, Connecticut: Thomas Robinson [1844] MWA. 44-4490

The New England almanacs, and farmers' friend, for the year of our Lord Christ, 1845; ....By Nathan Daboll, A.M.

....Norwich: Thomas Robinson [1844] 31 p. MHa. 44-4491

The New England farmer's almanac.... 1845.... by Truman Abell. Claremont, New Hampshire: Claremont bookstore, [1844] MWA; WHi. 44-4492

New England farmer's almanack, for 1845. Dudley Leavitt. Concord, New Hampshire: John F. Brown [1844] MWA. 44-4493

New England farmer's almanack, for 1845. Dudley Leavitt. Franklin, New Hampshire: Peabody and Daniell [1844] MWA; NjR. 44-4494

The New England farmer's almanack, on an improved plan for the year 1845 by Dudley Leavitt, teacher of mathematics and astronomy. Concord: John F. Brown [1844] 48 p. ICMcHi. 44-4495

New England Mutual Life Insurance Company. Annual report of the directors [first] 1844 and later years [Boston: 1844] MH. 44-4496

New England Mutual Life Insurance Company. Exposition of the objects of the institution of the New England Life Insurance Company. Boston: Printed by Freeman and Bolles, 1844. 36 p. MHi; MWA; PPM. 44-4497

The New England primer improved for the most easy attaining the true reading of English. To which is added the Assembly of Divines, and Mr. Cotton's catechism. Hartford: Ira Webster [1844] CtHWatk. 44-4498

New England Type Foundry Company. Boston. Supplement to the specimen book of modern printing types, ornaments, and combination borders from the New England Type and Stereotype Foundry. George A. Curtis, Boston. [Boston]: Dutton and Wentworths printing house, [1844?] 45 p. NN. 44-4499

New Englandism not the religion of the Bible. Being an examination of a review of Bishop Brownell's fourth charge to his clergy, in the New Englander for January, 1844. ....By [Juris Consultus] Hartford: Henry S. Parsons, 1844. 60 p. CtSoP; MdBD; NcU; PPL. 44-4500

The new genesee farmer and gardener's journal. Devoted to agriculture and horticulture, and to rural and domestic economy. Rochester: B.F. Smith and company, 1844. NRHi. 44-4501

The New Hampshire annual register and United States calendar for the year 1845. By G. Parker Lyon. Concord: G. Parker Lyon [1844] 143 p. MiD-B; MnHi. 44-4502

New Hampshire. Final report on the geology and mineralogy of the state of New Hampshire; with contributions towards the improvement of agriculture and metallurgy. By Charles T. Jackson, M.D. Published by order of the Legislature. Concord: Carroll and Baker, State printers, 1844. 376 p. CU; DLC; GAU; MBAt; MAm. 44-4503

New Hampshire. Journal of the Honorable Senate of the state of New Hampshire, at their session, held at the capitol in Concord, commencing June 5, 1844. Concord [New Hampshire] Carroll and Baker, State printer, 1844. 282 p. IaHi. 44-4504

New Hampshire. Laws of the state of New Hampshire, passed June session, 1844. Published by authority. Concord: Carroll and Baker, state pritners, 1844. 121 p. Ky; MdBB; Nj; NNLI; Nv. 44-4505

New Hampshire. Report of the case of Kittredge vs. Emerson, decided in the Superior court of judicature. July term, 1844. Concord: Asa McFarland, 1844. 52 p. NN; NSsSC; WKenHi. 44-4506

New Hampshire. Reports of cases argued and determined in the Superior Court of Judicature of New Hampshire. July term. Concord: Printed and published by Asa McFarland, 1844. 604 p. G; LU-L; MdUL; NdU-L; Nv. 44-4507

New Hampshire. Reports of the bank commissioners and the quarterly return of the banks. June session, 1844. Concord: Carroll and Baker, printers, 1844. 30 p. MB; MH; Nh-Hi. 44-4508

New Hampshire Asylum for the Insane. Report of the Board of visitors, of the trustees and of the superintendent. June, 1844. Concord, 1844. 2 v. CtHC; MHi; MH-M. 44-4509

New Jersey. Acts of the sixty-eighth General Assembly of the state of New Jersey. At the session begun at Trenton, on the twenty-fourth day of October, 1843. Being the second sitting. Freehold: Bernard Connelly, 1844. 300 p. IaU-L; In-SC; MdBB; NjR. 44-4510

New Jersey. A Constitution agreed upon by the delegates of the people of New Jersey, in convention begun at Trenton on the 14th day of May, and continued to the 29th day of June, 1844.

Trenton, 1844. 56 p. MdBJ; MH-L; NjR; NjT. 44-4511

New Jersey. Governor. Haines, Daniel, [1843-1844] Proclamation of the governor, an act calling a convention. n.p.: 1844. 8 p. NjR. 44-4512

New Jersey. Journal of the proceedings of the Convention to form a constitution for the government of the state of New Jersey; begun at Trenton on the fourteenth day of May, 1844 and continued to the twenty-ninth day of June, 1844. Trenton: Printed by F.S. Mills, 1844. 297 p. Ct; MB; NjP; Ia; T. 44-4513

New Jersey. Loco Foco Party. A review of some of the proceedings of the Loco Foco Legislature of 1843. Trenton: State Gazette, 1844. 16 p. Nj. 44-4514

New Jersey. Minutes of the votes and proceedings of the sixty-eighth general assembly of the state of New Jersey, at a session begun at Trenton, on the twenty-fourth day of October, 1843. Being the first sitting. Somerville: Printed by Thomas S. Allison, 1844. 724 p. MH-L; Mi; NcU; Nj; WaPS. 44-4515

New Jersey. Opinion of Governor Vroom, upon the act establishing the society, for useful manufactures, and for the encouragement of the same. Trenton: Printed at the Emporium office, 1844. 8 p. MiD-B. 44-4516

New Jersey. Report of the inspectors of the New Jersey prison to the legislature of New Jersey. Trenton: Printed by Franklin S. Mills, 1844. 49 p. MdBJ; Nj. 44-4517

New Jersey. Report of the joint commit-

tee. Accounts of the late treasurer. March 1, 1844. Trenton: Franklin S. Mills, printer, 1844. 8 p. NjR. 44-4518

New Jersey. Report of the joint committee to whom was referred that part of the Governor's message on the subject of the Delaware breakwater at Cape May. February, 1844. Trenton: Franklin S. Mills, 1844. 11 p. MiD-B; PHi. 44-4519

New Jersey. Report of the judiciary committee on the subject of the colonial records of New Jersey. Trenton: Printed by Franklin S. Mills, 1844. 11 p. NjR. 44-4520

New Jersey. Rules of the Supreme Court of the state of New Jersey, published under the authority and direction of the court with an appendix. Trenton: Sherman and Harron, printer, 1844. 66 p. MH-L; NjR; NjT; RPB. 44-4521

New Jersey State Horticultural Society. Constitution adopted March 14, 1844. Burlington: The society, 1844. 12 p. DLC; PHC. 44-4522

New Jerusalem Church. The new churchman [no. II] extra: containing an historical sketch of the New Jerusalem in the United States, by a layman of that church. Philadelphia: 1844. 40 p. MH-AH. 44-4523

New London Academy. Chester County, Maryland. Catalogue of the officers and students of New London academy, Chester County, Pennsylvania. Baltimore, Maryland: John Murphy, printer, 1844. 2 v. IaHA; PHi. 44-4524

New Orleans and Carrollton Railroad Company. Plans of real estate of the New

Orleans and Carrollton Railroad Company, to be sold at public auction on the 29th day of April, 1844. [New Orleans] J. Manouvrier and P. Snell, [1844] [15] p. LU. 44-4525

New Orleans annual and commercial directory, 1844; containing the names and residences of all the inhabitants of the city and suburbs of New Orleans. J.J. Cowperthwaite and company, 1844. 359 p. NbOM. 44-4526

New Orleans, Louisiana. Prospectus of the New Orleans Medical Journal. It is proposed by the undersigned, to publish in the city of New Orleans, a journal devoted to the cultivation of medicine and the associate sciences, provided sufficient assurance be obtained that such an object is desired, and will be promoted by the members of the profession. New Orleans: 1844. TxU. 44-4527

New Orleans, Louisiana. Whig meeting, 1844. An address to the citizens of Louisiana, on the subject of the recent election in New Orleans. New Orleans: Printed at the Bee office, 1844. 16 p. DLC; MH. 44-4528

The New Orleans Medical Journal, devoted to the cultivation of medicine, and the associate sciences. Edited by Erasmus D. Fenner, M.D. and A. Hester, M.D. New Orleans: Printed by A. Dor, 1844-. MoSMed. 44-4529

The new pictorial and illustrated family magazine, established for the diffusion of useful knowledge.... 1844-1849. New York: R. Sears, 1844-49. 5 v. MB; MiU. 44-4530

The New universal letter-writer; or,

complete art of polite correspondence.... Philadelphia: Hogan and Thompson, 1844. 216 p. MoU. 44-4531

New world pictorial annual for 1844 containing choice tales, poetry, anecdotes, etc., illustrated by numerous splendid engravings. New York: 1844. 32 p. CtHWatk. 44-4532

New York [City] Annual report of the city inspector of the city of New York, for the year 1844. New York, 1844. NjR. 44-4533

New York [City] business directory. New York, 1844. PPL-R. 44-4534

New York [City] Catalogue of the library of the Mechanics' Institute, of the city of New York; regulations of the reading room and library; and circular to the public. New York: A. Baptist, Jr., printer, 1844. 64 p. DLC; MH. 44-4535

New York [City] Catalogue of the Mercantile Library in New York. New York: Printed by E.O. Jenkins, 1844. 300 p. CSf; DLC; LNH; MdHi; ScU. 44-4536

New York [City] Church of the Messiah. Chants and anthems used in the Church of the Messiah, New York. New York: Francis, 1844. 60 p. CBPac. 44-4537

New York [City] Common Council. Report, January 3, 1844 of the special committee of the board of aldermen to whom was referred the resolution presented by Alderman Tillou, May 15, 1843, in relation to the re-organization of the police department [New York: 1844] MH. 44-4538

New York [City] Croton Aqueduct Board. Annual report of the Croton Aqueduct Board, June 1844. New York [1844] M. 44-4539

New York [City] Fire Department. Annual report of the chief engineer. New York: John F. Trow and company, 1844. 4 p. M. 44-4540

New York [City] Manual of the corporation of the city of New York, for years 1843 and 1844. New York: William C. Bryan, printer, 1844. 312 p. NNLI. 44-4541

New York [City] Mercantile Library Association. Catalogue of the Mercantile Library in New York... New York: Printed by E.O. Jenkins, 1844. 300 p. DLC; MnU; NN. 44-4542

New York [City] Mercer Street Presbyterian Church. Manual for the communicants of the Mercer Street Presbyterian Church. New York, 1844. ICN. 44-4543

New York [City] Mount Washington Presbyterian Church. The story of Mt. Washington, 1844-. PPPrHi. 44-4544

New York [City] New York Gallery of the Fine Arts. Catalogue of the exhibition of the New York Gallery of the Fine Arts, founded 1844. Now open in the large saloon of the National Academy of Design. New York, 1844. 24 p. WHi. 44-4545

New York [City] An ordinance relative to charcoal carts, fish carts, fruit carts, and other carts and vehicles. Passed 1844. [New York? 1844?] 171 p. DLC. 44-4546

New York [City] Prison Association. First report of the Prison Association of New York. New York [1844] NoLoc. 44-4547

New York [City] Report of the committee on the annual apportionment, on the communications of the county superintendent, relative to the use of the Bible in public schools of the city of New York. New York: Office of the "Morning News," 1844. 8 p. NNUT. 44-4548

New York [State] Agricultural Society. Arrangements for diffusing agricultural knowledge through the instrumentality of common schools and public libraries together with the premium list and regulations of the annual fair and cattle show, 1844, prepared by Henry O'Rielly. Albany: Van Benthuysen, 1844. 24 p. MH; NRHi. 44-4549

New York [State] Annual report of the superintendent of common schools of the state of New York together with the reports of county superintendents made to the Legislature, January 13, 1844. Albany: Printed by Carroll and Cook, 1844. 699 p. NCH; NSyU; RJA. 44-4550

New York [State] Argicultural Society. Transactions of the New York State Agricultural Society. Albany: Printed by Carroll and Cook, printers to the assembly, 1844. 671 p. NbHi. 44-4551

New York [State] Canal Department. Canal regulations, rates of toll, and names of the principal places on the New York State Canals; as established by the Canal Board and in force on said canals, May, 1844. Albany: Printed by French and Cassidy, 1844. 66 p. MH. 44-4552

New York [State] Commissioners of the Canal Fund. Annual report of the Commissioners of the Canal Fund, 1843. Albany, 1844. MH. 44-4553

New York [State] Court of Chancery. Rules and orders of the Court of Chancery of the state of New York, as revised and established in 1844, with precedents of writs, orders, and bills of costs, approved by the chancellor and notes of decisions, showing the practical construction of the rules. Albany: William and A. Gould and company, 1844. 204 p. LNT-L. 44-4554

New York [State] Court of Errors. In the court for the trial of impeachments and the correction of errors. Charles Cartlidge and John Horspool, plaintiffs in error vs. Joseph J. West and James D. Oliver, defendents in error. New York: Printed by William Osborn, 1844. 38 p. IaHi. 44-4555

New York [State] Geological and Natural History Survey. Zoology of New York, or the New York fauna, by James DeKay, part 6 crustacea. Albany: Carroll and Cook, printers to the assembly, 1844. WM. 44-4556

New York [State] Hospital, Utica. Annual report, 1843- Albany, 1844-. 1st-. DLC; PPTU. 44-4557

New York [State] In the court for the trial of impeachment and the correction of errors. Moritz Wolff and Charles Hinrichs, plaintiffs in error, vs. Caspar L. Koppel, defendent in error. Case made by defendent in error. John A. Stemmler, attorney for the plaintiff. Burr, Benedict and Beebe, attorney for defendent. New York: 1844. 54 p. IaHi; ICL. 44-4558

New York [State] Journal of the assembly of the state of New York at their sixty-seventh session begun and held at the capitol in the city of Albany, on the second day of January, 1844. Albany: Carroll and Cook, printers to the assembly, 1844. 1378 p. NNot. 44-4559

New York [State] Laws of the state of New York passed at the sixty-seventh session of the Legislature, begun and held in the city of Albany, the second day of January, 1844. Albany: Printed by C. Van Benthuysen and company, for William and A. Gould company, 1844. 607 p. Az; In-SC; MH-L; Nj; NNLI. 44-4560

New York [State] Lunatic Asylum. Annual report of the managers of the State Lunatic Asylum. Made to the legislature January 18, 1844. Albany: Carroll and Cook, printers, 1844. 66 p. CtHC; TNP. 44-4561

New York [State] Report and speeches on the state prison bill in the House of Assembly, March, 1844. Albany: Printed by J. Munsell, 1844. 41 p. MHi. 44-4562

New York [State] Reports of cases argued and determined in the Supreme Court and in the Court for the Correction of Errors of the state of New York. By Nicholas Hill, Junior. Albany: William And A. Gould, 1844. 714 p. ICJ; LNT-L; MdUL. 44-4563

New York [State] Reports of the committee on canals in relation to the observances of the Sabbath on the canals, April 10, 1844. 15 p. PPPrHi. 44-4564

New York [State] Revised statutes of the state of New York and additional laws to 1845, reduced to questions and answers, for the use of schools and families by William B. Wedgwood. New York, 1844. 181 p. Ct. 44-4565

New York [State] Rules and orders of the court of chancery of the state of New York as revised and established by Chancellor Walworth, in 1844, with the precedents of writs, orders, and bills of cost, approved by the Chancellor. And notes of decisions, showing the practical construction of the rules. Albany: William and A. Gould and company; New York: Gould, Banks and company, 1844. 204 p. OClW. 44-4566

New York [State] University of the state of New York, College of Physicians and Surgeons. Annual catalogue. New York: Adee and Estabrook, printers, 1844. 12 p. NNNAM. 44-4567

New York [State] Univesity. Catalogue of and history of its graduates for fifty years. Albany, 1844. NBuG. 44-4568

New York and Erie Railroad Company. Address [at a meeting of the board of directors, October 31, 1844] [New York: 1844] 16 p. CSt. 44-4569

New York and Erie Railroad Company. Report of the board of directors, elected October 5, 1843. February 8, 1844. New York: G.F. Nesbitt, printer, 1844. 40 p. CSmH; CSt; DBRE; NN; NRU. 44-4570

New York and Erie Railroad Company. Reports of the president and superintendent.... to the stockholders. 1843-. New York: 1844-. PP; PPFrankI; PPL; PPPr-Hi; PU. 44-4571

New York and Erie Railroad Company. A review of Mr. Baker's report and the reply thereto, drawn up by Major Thompson S. Brown, chief engineer, and comprised in the late annual report of the board of directors to the secretary of state. [Published in anticipation of a quarterly which is in contemplation, and of which this may be taken as no. 1, January, 1844] New York: 1844. 30 p. CSt. 44-4572

New York and New Haven Railroad. Charter [New Haven]: n.p., 1844. 8 p. NRU. 44-4573

New York Association for Improving the Condition of the Poor. Address to the public; constitution and by-laws; and visitor's manual, of the association for the improvement of the condition of the poor. New York: January, 1844. New York: J.S. Taylor and company, 1844. 34 p. DLC; MB; MdHi; MH; MHi. 44-4574

New York Association of Friends for the Relief of Those Held in Slavery. Testimony of the association concerning Charles Marriott, deceased. New York: Piercy and Reed, 1844. 15 p. ICN; MH. 44-4575

New York Chamber of Commerce. Charter, by-laws, and organization of the Chamber of Commerce of the state of New York: Instituted April 5, 1768; incorporated March 13, 1770; re-incorporated April 13, 1784. New York: Printed by J.M Elliott, 1844. 35 p. MidD-B. 44-4576

New York dissector, a journal of medicine, surgery, magnetism, mesmerism, and the collateral sciences, with the mysteries and fallacies of the faculty. Edited by H.E. Sherwood. New York:

the editor, 1844-1847. 4 v. ICJ; ICRL; MnU; PPCP; PPWI. 44-4577

New York farmer and mechanic; devoted to agriculture, mechanics, manufactures and the arts.... S. Fleet, editor. Record office, 1844-46. 4 v. KMK; NIC-A. 44-4578

New York Female Assistance Society. Thirty-first annual report incorporated May 6, 1840. New York: Printed by William Osborn, 1844. 22 p. MiD-B. 44-4579

New York Female Association. Second annual report of the New York Female Association to aid the Swiss mission in Canada. New York: 1844. 32 p. MH-AH. 44-4580

New York Gallery of Fine Arts. Catalogue. New York: 1844. 24 p. NN. 44-4581

New York Historical Society. Commemoration of the conquest of New Netherland on its two hundreth anniversary by the New York Historical Society. New York: C.A. Alvord, printer, 1844. 87 p. LNH. 44-4582

New York Historical Society. Constitution and by-laws of the New York Historical Society.... Revised March, 1844. New York: press of the historical society, 1844. 33 p. DLC; ICN; MBC; MH; OO. 44-4583

New York Historical Society. Proceedings of the New York Historical Society.... 1843[-1849] New York: press of the historical society, 1844-49. 7 v. IGK; MdBJ; MiU-C; OFH; ViU. 44-4584

New York mirror. Volume 1 - Number 1 - October 12, 1844. 1844- No. Loc. 44-4585

New York Protestant Episcopal Tract Society. Annual report. New York: the society, 1844. 1 v. CtHT. 44-4586

New York Sabbath Tract Society. Sabbath tracts: the Sabbath and Lord's day: a history of their observance in the Christian church. New York: Sabbath Tract Society, 1844. 48 p. CtMW; NAlf. 44-4587

New York Society for the Promotion of Collegiate and Theological Education at the West. Permanent documents, New York: 1844-1859. 3 v. MH-AH. 44-4588

New York State Register, 1844. Being a supplement to the register for 1843. Edited by O.L. Holley. Albany: Published by J. Disturnell, 1844. 30 p. NUtHi. 44-4589

New York State Sabbath Convention. Proceedings of the New York State Sabbath Convention, Held at Saratoga Springs, August 28 and 29, 1844. Albany: 1844. 36 p. MiD-B. 44-4590

New York Yearly Meeting. Minute of advice from the New York Yearly Meeting of Ministers and Elders, 1844. New York: Egbert, Hovey and King, printers, 1844. Broadside. NNFL. 44-4591

Newark Female Seminary. Newark, Delaware. Circular of the Newark Female Seminary in Newark, Delaware. Philadelphia: 1844. 8 p. DLC. 44-4592

Newburyport, Massachusetts. Expenses of the town of Newburyport, for the financial year ending March, 1844. Newburyport: Watchtower office, printer, 1844. 111 p. MiD-B; MNe. 44-4593

Newcomb, Harvey, 1803-1863. The attributes of God; being a series of Sabbath evening conversations, designed to illustrate the character of God. Boston: Massachusetts Sabbath School Society, 1844. 144 p. CSto. 44-4594

Newcomb, Harvey, 1803-1863. The Dawn of divine light upon popish darkness; or an account of the rise of the reformation in German. Boston: Massachusetts Sabbath School School Society, 1844. 252 p. MBC; OO. 44-4595

Newcomb, Harvey, 1803-1863. The false prophet; or an account of the rise and progress of the Mohammedan religion; comprising the history of the church from the close of the fifth to the beginning of the seventh century. Second edition. Boston: Massachusetts Sabbath School Society, 1844. 216 p. IP; MBC; MiU. 44-4596

Newcomb, Harvey, 1803-1863. The Lollards, containing an acount of Wickliffe, Jerome, of Prague, Huss and other eminent persons, with sketches of church history during the 13th, 14th and 15th centuries. Third edition. Boston: Massachusetts Sabbath School Society, 1844. 198 p. ICRL; MA; MBC: NNC. 44-4597

Newcomb, Harvey, 1803-1863. Newcomb's scripture questions. Two parts. Boston: Massachusetts Sabbath School Society, 1844. MWHi. 44-4598

Newcomb, Harvey, 1803-1863. Questions on the shorter catechism. Part 1.

Boston: Crocker and Brewster, 1844. 18 p. DLC. 44-4599

Newcomb, Harvey, 1803-1863. Questions on the shorter catechism. Part 2. For the higher classes. Boston: Crocker and Brewster, 1844. 35 p. NNUT. 44-4600

Newcomb, Harvey, 1803-1863. The rule of life; being the second volume of a series of conversations of the Shorter catechism. Written for the Mass. Sunday School Society, and revised by the Committee of publication. Boston: Massachusetts Sabbath School Society, 1844. 82 p. DLC. 44-4601

Newcomb, Harvey, 1803-1863. Scripture questions. Boston [1844-1845] 3 v. DLC. 44-4602

Newell, D. The parlow annual; edited and published by Rev. D. Newell. New York: D. Newell, 1844. v. 1-. NRU. 44-4603

Newman, Henry. An almanack containing an account of the celestial motions, aspects etc., for the year of the Christian empire 1691. Boston: Harris, 1844. CSt; ICJ; MNS; MPiB; NNC. 44-4604

Newman, John Henry, 1801-1890. An essay of the development of Christian doctrine. New York: D. Appleton and company [1844?] [9]-206 p. CSfCW. 44-4605

Newman, John Henry, 1801-1890. Sermons, bearing on subjects of the day. By John Henry Newman. New York: Appleton, 1844. GMM; NBuDD; PLT; RPA; TMeSC. 44-4606

O

Oak hall; or, the glory of Boston. A poem in four parts; with a prologue and epilogue. By a young gentleman of Boston. Boston: Mead and Beal, 1844. 46 p. PHC. 44-4653

Oberlin College. Catalogue of the officers and students of the Oberlin Collegiate Institute, 1844-1845. Oberlin: Evangelist office, printer, 1844. 32 p. MnHi; NBuG. 44-4654

O'Brien, John G. Philadelphia wholesale business directory and United States, South America, West India, London, etc. Circular for 1844. Philadelphia: 1844. 228 p. PHi. 44-4655

O'Brien, Matthew, 1814-1855. A treatise on plane co-ordinate geometry; or, the application of the method of co-ordinates to the solution of problems in plane geometry. Part I. By the Rev. M. O'Brien.... Cambridge: Deighton, 1844. 180 p. MB; MBBC; MiU; PPAN; WU. 44-4656

Observations on excluding females from participating in the Gospel ministry. Baltimore: William Woody, 1844. 12 p. NjR; PSC-Hi. 44-4657

Obstinate, inverterate, and habitual constipation, not only totally overcome but also completely destroyed. Fifth English edition translated from the twenty-second French edition. New York: 1844. 129 p. MH-M. 44-4658

O'Callaghan, Jeremiah. The hedge round about, the vineyard, dressed up. By the Rev. Jeremiah O'Callaghan, Roman Catholic priest. Burlington: printed for the author, 1844. 360 p. ArLSJ; CSfCW; LNL; MBC; MiNazC. 44-4659

O'Connell, Daniel, 1775-1847. Irish state trials; or, the queen vs. Daniel O'Connell, and others. New York: William H. Colyer, 1844. 229 p. MH-L; NN; OClWHi; PP; RPA. 44-4660

Odd Fellows, Independent Order of. Journal of proceedings of the grand lodge, and jurisdiction thereunto belonging; from its formation, February 1821 to the close of the session, 1843. New York: 1844. 601 p. MH. 44-4661

Odd Fellows, Independent Order of. Journal of proceedings of the Right Worthy Grand Lodge of the United States of America, and jurisdiction thereunto belonging; from its formation, February 1821 to 1843. New York: McGowan and Treadwell, 1844. CtHWatk; MiD-B; IaDa; MWo. 44-4662

Odd Fellows, Independent Order of. Illinois. Constitution, by-laws, and rules of order... Chicago: Ellis and Fergus, 1844. 36 p. ICHi. 44-4663

Odd Fellows, Independent Order of. Maine. Ceremonies or dedication of the hall of Maine Lodge, Number 1, July 24, 1844; with a dedicatory address, by Bro.

Charles Holden. Portland: Case and Holden, printers, 1844. 24 p. MB; MeBa. 44-4664

Odd Fellows, Independent Order of. Massachusetts. Acushnet Lodge. Constitution, by-laws and rules of the lodge, No. 41. Boston: Br. T. Prince, 1844. 36 p. MNBedf. 44-4665

Odd Fellows, Independent Order of. Massachusetts. Constitution and by-laws of Prospect Lodge, No. 33, Waltham, Massachusetts. Instituted February 1, 1844. Boston: Printed by Bro. Alfred Mudge, 1844. 35 p. MWA. 44-4666

Odd Fellows, Independent Order of. Massachusetts. Constitution, by-laws and rules of Maverick Lodge, No. 36. Instituted February 7, 1844. Boston: Printed by Bros. Reed and Rand, 1844. 34 p. WHi. 44-4667

Odd Fellows, Independent Order of. Massachusetts. Constitution, by-laws and rules of Montezuma Lodge, No. 33. Instituted January 22, 1844, at Boston. Boston: Printed by Bro. T. Prince, 1844. 38 p. RPE. 44-4668

Odd Fellows, Independent Order of. Massachusetts. Constitution, by-laws and rules of order of the right worthy grand lodge of Independent Order of Odd Fellows, of Massachusetts. Boston: 1844. 24 p. MH. 44-4669

Odd Fellows, Independent Order of. Massachusetts. Constitution, by-laws and rules of Quinsigamond Lodge. Instituted at Worcester, May 1, 1844. Worcester: Printed by Bro. Nathan Sawyer, 1844. 31 p. MWHi. 44-4670

Odd Fellows, Independent Order of. New Hampshire. Constitution and by-laws of White Mountain Lodge No. 5. Concord: 1844. 36 p. Nh-Hi. 44-4671

Odd Fellows, Independent Order of. New Hampshire. Constitution and by-laws. Dover, New Hampshire: 1844. NhDo. 44-4672

Odd Fellows, Independent Order of. New York. Constitution, by-laws and rules of Buffalo Lodge, No. 37. Chartered, May 6, 1840. By-laws and rules as amended and adopted January 2, 1844. Buffalo: Printed by Lee and Thorp, 1844. 28 p. NBu. 44-4673

Odd Fellows, Independent Order of. New York. Halcyon Lodge. No. LVI, of the Independent Order of Odd Fellows. Constitution, by-laws and rules of, as amended, November, 1844. Troy, New York; N. Tuttle, 1844. 38 p. NoLoc. 44-4674

Odd Fellows, Independent Order of. New York. Journal of proceedings... New York: McGowan and Treadwell, 1844. 601 p. MiU. 44-4675

Odd Fellows, Independent Order of. New York. Ontario Lodge No. 116. Constitution, by-laws and rules of order, of Ontario Lodge N. 116. Held in the village of Canandaigua. Rochester: Printed by E. Shepard, 1844. 23 p. NCanHi. 44-4676

Odd Fellows, Independent Order of. Ohio. Constitution and by-laws... Hillsborough, Ohio: James Brown, printer, 1844. 32 p. OClWHi. 44-4677

Odd Fellows, Independent order of. Ohio. Constitution of the Miami Encampment of Patriarchs, No. 4. of Ohio: approved by the Grand Encampment of Ohio, March 2, 1844. Piaua: 1844. OHi. 44-4678

Odd Fellows, Independent Order of. Rhode Island. Brief history, constitution, etc. Providence: 1844. 36 p. RHi. 44-4679

Odd Fellows, Independent Order of. Rhode Island. Constitution, by-laws and rules of Ocean Lodge, No. 5, of the Independent order of Odd Fellows. Newport, Rhode Island: Bro. James Atkinson, printer, 1844. 27 p. RHi; RNR. 44-4680

Odd Fellows, Independent Order of. Rhode Island. Constitution, by-laws and rules of order. Providence: 1844-. RHi. 44-4681

Odd Fellows, Independent Order of. United States. Journal of proceedings of the Grand Lodge of the United States of America for the annual sessions. Baltimore: 1844. PHi; PPL; WKenHi. 44-4682

Odd Fellows, Independent Order of. United States. Journal of proceedings of the right worthy grand lodge... New York: McGowan and Treadwell, 1844. 601 p. WKenHi. 44-4683

Odenheimer, William Henry. The origin and compilation of the prayer book: with an appendix, containing historical facts and documents connected with our liturgy. Second edition, enlarged. Philadelphia: 1844. 189 p. MdHi; MH; NNG. 44-4684

Oertel, Maximilian. Deutsche Grammatik zum Gebrauche in Schulen und zum selbstunterrichte. Von Maximilian Oertel.... Cincinnati, Ohio: Druck und verlag bei H. Lehmann, 1844. 110 p. MiNazC; MnSS; MoSU; MoWgT. 44-4685

Ogden, David Bayard, 1775-1849. Reply to an address "to the laity of the Protestant Episcopal Church in the Diocese of New York." New York: 1844. 7 p. MiD-B; NNC; NNG. 44-4686

Ogden, Elias Dayton. Tariff; or rates of duties payable on goods, wares, and merchandise imported into the United States of America, on goods, wares, and merchandise imported into the United States of America, on and after August, 1842. Revised and corrected by E.D. Ogden. New York; Rich and Loutrel, 1844. 52 p. LNH; MH-BA; NjP. 44-4687

Ogdensburg and Lake Champlain Railroad Company complainant vs. Boston and Lowell Railroad. Corporation. Boston: Harvard Busines Branch, 1844. MB. 44-4688

Ogilby, John David, 1810-1851. The Catholic Church in England and America... New York; D. Appleton and company, 1844. 208, 16 p. LU; MWiW; PBa; RP; WNaE. 44-4689

Ohio almanac, calculated by William Lusk. Columbus: Charles Scott, 1844. MB; PHi. 44-4690

Ohio cultivator; a semi-monthly journal. 1844- . Columbus, 1844-. PPM. 44-4691

Ohio. Act for the preservation and repair of the national road, and for the collection of tolls thereon. Columbus: 1844. OClWHi. 44-4692

Ohio. An act to authorize the Governor to appoint Commissioners to take acknowledgement of Deeds, etc. Columbus, 1844. Broadside. NN. 44-4693

Ohio. Acts of a general nature, passed by the 42nd general assembly of the State of Ohio, begun and held in the city of Columbus, December 4, 1843 and in the 42nd year of said state. Columbus: Samuel Medary, State printer, 1844. 103 p. L; Nj; NNLI; W. 44-4694

Ohio. Acts of a local nature, passed by the 42nd General Assembly of the State of Ohio, begun and held in the City of Columbus; December 4, 1843 and in the 42nd year of said state. Columbus: Samuel Medary, State printer, 1844. 293 p. NNLI; W. 44-4695

Ohio. Annual report of the auditor of state to the Forty-Third General Assembly. December 3, 1844. Columbus: Samuel Medary, State printer, 1844. 85 p. Ms. 44-4696

Ohio. Eighth annual report of the trustees and superintendent of the Ohio Institution for the Education of the Blind, for the year 1844. Columbus: Samuel Medary, State printer, 1844. 30 p. O. 44-4697

Ohio. Laws of the protection of the canals of the state of Ohio. The regulation of the navigation thereof, and for the collection of tolls; also the orders, rules, regulations, and rates of toll, with tables of distances on the several public works, as established by the Board of public works, March 20, 1844. Columbus: Samuel Medary, printer, 1844. 59 p. OU. 44-4698

Ohio. Report of the majority of the standing committee on banks and currency... repeal general banking law... Bank of Wooster. Columbus: 1844. OHi. 44-4699

Ohio. Report of the minority of the standing committee on new counties, relative to the erection on the new county of Wyandot. Columbus: 1844. OHi. 44-4700

Ohio. Young Men's Democratic State Central Committee. Address to the electors of Ohio, or the coalition of 1825, or Clay's bargain with Adams. Columbus: Ohio Statesman, 1844. OHi. 44-4701

Ohio Turnpike Convention, 1844. Proceedings... for establishing uniform rates of toll, on state roads. Medary, Col.: 1844. O. 44-4702

Olcott, James S. Animal electricity: or the electric science; an application of the primary laws of nature. Boston: N.S. Magoon, 1844. 131 p. IaDaP; IaHi; MHi; WHi. 44-4703

Old Colony Club. Boston. Bill of fare, United States Hotel, for the Old Colony Club. December 21st, 1844 [Boston] Clapp's Press [1844] MHi. 44-4704

Old Colony Railroad Company. Annual report of the directors.... to the stockholders.... 1st-10th. 1844-1853. Boston; 1844-1853. OCl. 44-4705

Old Colony Railroad Company. Brief statement of facts in relation to the proposed railroad from Boston to Plymouth. Plymouth: Printed by James Thurher, 1844. 16 p. ICN; WU. 44-4706

The old farmer's almanac, calculated on a new and improved plan for the year of our Lord, 1844... By Robert B. Thomas... Boston: Jenks and Palmer, 1844. 48 p. MoU. 44-4707

Old Fort Duquesne, a tale of the early toils, struggles and adventures of the first settlers at the forks of the Ohio, 1754. Pittsburgh: Cooks Literary Depot, 1844. 79 p. MH; NN; OFH; PHi; RHi. 44-4708

The old grey goose. A most popular banjo song sung by Aken, the celebrated banjoist. Arranged for the piano forte. Philadelphia: Fiot, 1844. 2 p. MB. 44-4709

Old Michael and young Maurice or the country at all seasons. Philadelphia: George and Wayne, 1844. 180 p. NUt; PAtM. 44-4710

Old Mortality, pseud. The song of the sexton. [Albany: 1844?] MB. 44-4711

Olin, Stephen, 1797-1851. Travels in Egypt, Arabia, Petraea, and the Holy Land. With twelve illustrations on steel. Fourth edition. New York: Harper and brothers, 1844. 2 v. GEU-T; MnSSt; NFred; OCl; RPB. 44-4712

Olive branch; or, an earnest appeal in behalf of religion, the supremacy of the law and social order; with documents relating to the late disturbances in Philadelphia. Philadelphia: Printed by M. Fithian, 1844. 47 p. ICloy; OClaw; P; Phi. 44-4713

Oliver, Daniel. First lines of physiology; designed for the use of students of medicine. ....Third edition, with corrections and additions.... Boston: William D.

Ticknor and company, 1844. 517 p. KyLxT; MdBJ; NNN; OrU; RPM. 44-4714

Oliver, Daniel. Lines of physiology. Third edition revised and enlarged. Boston: Munroe and company, 1844. 517 p. LNT-M. 44-4715

Oliver, Samuel Clark. Onslow, or the protege of an enthusiastist; an historical traditionary tale of the South. Philadelphia: Ziebs, 1844. 222 p. A-Ar; AU; ICN; TxU; ViU. 44-4716

Ollendorff, Heinrich Gottfried, d. 1865. Ollendorff's new method of learning to read, write and speak: the Spanish language with an appendix.... together with practical rules for the Spanish pronunciation.... by Velazquez and T. Simonee.... New York: D. Appleton, 1844. 558 p. MdBS; NBuG. 44-4717

Olmstead, John Wesley. An ominous future. A discourse, delivered on the day of the annual fast, in the First Baptist Church, Chelsea, April 4, 1844. Boston: Printed by Tuttle and Dennett, 1844. 18 p. MB: MWA; MWelC; RPB; WHi. 44-4718

Olmsted, Denison, 1791-1859. A compendium of astronomy; containing the elements of the science, familiarly explained and illustrated, with the latest discoveries. Adapted to the use of schools and academies, and of the general reader. Sixth edition. New York: Published by Collins, brother and company, 1844. 275 p. DLC; ICU; MB; NNC; RPB. 44-4719

Olmsted, Denison, 1791-1859. A compendium of natural philosophy: adapted to the use of the general reader, and of schools and academies. A supplement containing instructions to young experimenters, with a copious list of experiments. Stereotype edition. New Haven: S. Babcock, 1844. 420 p. IaDuU; KPea; MWH; OO; RPB. 44-4720

Olmsted, Denison, 1791-1859. An introduction to astronomy; designed as a text book for the students of Yale College. Fourth edition. New York: Collins brothers and company, 1844. 288 p. CtHT; MA; NcU; OO; TNP. 44-4721

Olmsted, Denison, 1791-1859. An introduction to natural philosophy; designed as a text book.... By Denison Olmsted, LL.D., ...Second revised edition. By E.S. Snell, LL.D., ...New York: Collins and brother, 1844. 437 p. KJu; MWHi. 44-4722

Olmsted, Denison, 1791-1859. An introduction to natural philosophy; designed as a text book for the use of students in college, by Denison Olmsted, LL.D. ....and E.S. Snell, LL.D. ....Third revised edition. By Rodney G. Kimball, A.M. ....New York: Collins and brother, 1844. 495 p. KyLoS; LNB; NcStC; ODaU; PWbO. 44-4723

Olmsted, Denison, 1791-1859. An introductory to natural philosophy; designed as a text book in physics for the use of students in college. Fourth revised edition. New York: Charles Collins, and Baker and Taylor company, 1844. 465 p. MW; NcGA. 44-4724

Olmsted, Denison, 1791-1859. Rudiments of natural philosophy and astronomy; designed for the younger classes in academies, and for common

schools. ....Stereotype edition. New Haven: S. Babcock; New York: Collins, brother and company, 1844. 288 p. CU; GDecCT; MH; PHi; RPB. 44-4725

Olney, Jesse, 1797-1872. A practical system of modern geography; or a view of the present state of the world. Accompanied by a new and improved atlas. Forty-first edition. New York: Pratt, Woodfrod and company, 1844. MH; PLFM. 44-4726

Olney, Jesse, 1797-1872. A practical system of modern geography; or a view of the present state of the world. Accompanied by a new and improved atlas. Fortieth edition. New York: Robinson, Pratt and company, 1844. MH. 44-4727

Olney, Jesse, 1797-1872. A practical system of modern geography; or a view of the present state of the world. Revised and illustrated by a new and enlarged atlas. Forty-second edition. New York: Pratt, Woodford and company, 1844. 294 p. DLC; IEG; MAm; MtU; NbHi. 44-4728

Olney, Jesse, 1798-1872. The easy reader; or, introduction to the national preceptor; consisting of familiar and progressive lessons, designed to aid in thinking, spelling, defining, and correct reading. New Haven: Durrie and Peck; Philadelphia: Smith and Peck, 1844. 144 p. MShM; TxComT. 44-4729

Olney, Jesse, 1798-1872. A history of the United States, on a new plan; adapted to the capacity of youth. To which is added, the Declaration of Independence, and the Constitution of the United States, ... New Haven: Durrie and Peck, 1844. 288 p. 44-4730

Olney, Jesse, 1798-1872. Improved system of arithmetic edited by W.P. Gallup. Hartford, 1844. CtHWatk. 44-4731

Olney, Jesse, 1798-1872. Modern geography. Fourty-fourth edition. New York: 1844. MBAt. 44-4732

Olney, Jesse, 1798-1872. The national preceptor; or, selections in prose and poetry.... Sixth edition. Hartford: H. and E. Goodwin, 1844. 336 p. MiGr; NHem. 44-4733

Olney, Jesse, 1798-1872. Olney's school atlas... New York: Pratt, Woodford and company, 1844. CtHT; IU; MID-B; NcWsH. 44-4734

Olney, Jesse, 1798-1872. School atlas. New York: drawn and engraved by Sherman and Smith, 1844. RPB. 44-4735

Olney, Jesse, 1798-1872. School atlas. New York: Pratt, Woodford, [1844] 70 p. MWC. 44-4736

O'Mahoney, Edmond William. Whites confutation of Church-of-Englandism, and correct exposition of the Catholic faith, on all points of controversy between the two churches. Translated from the two churches. Translated from the original [Latin] ....Philadelphia: Henry M'Grath, 1844. 342 p. CStclU; NGH; NStC; OCX; PSerW. 44-4737

The omnibus of modern romance. New York: J. Mowatt, 1844. MH; TxU; VtU. 44-4738

Onderdonk, Benjamin Tredwell, 1791-1861. The church.... the faith.... tradition. A sermon, by Benjamin T. Onderdonk, D.D., bishop of the Diocese of New York, and professor of the nature, ministry and polity of the church, in the general theological seminary of the Protestant Episcopal Church in the United States. New York: Onderdonk and Forrest, 1844. 23 p. CtHC; IEG; MB; NcU; NGH. 44-4739

Onderdonk, Benjamin Tredwell, 1791-1861. A pastoral letter, to the clergy and people of his spiritual charge; by Benjamin T. Onderdonk, Bishop of the Diocese of New York. New York: Onderdonk and Forrest, 1844. 12, 7, 16 p. MH; MiD-B; MWA; NNC; NNG. 44-4740

Onderdonk, Benjamin Tredwell, 1791-1861. Proceedings of the court for the trial of Bishop Onderdonk, bishop of the Protestant Episcopal Church of the United States for the trial of Rt. Rev. Benjamin Tredwell Onderdonk, D.D., Bishop of New York. [1844] 330 p. MBD; NBuG. 44-4741

Onderdonk, Benjamin Tredwell, 1791-1861. Reply to a communication signed by three hundred and twenty-eight laymen of the diocese of New York. By Benjamin Tredwell Onderdonk, bp. of New York. New York: H. M. Onderdonk and company, 1844. 8 p. IEG; MB; MH; NNG; PHi. 44-4742

Onderdonk, Benjamin Tredwell, 1791-1861. To the clergy and people of my spiritual charge. New York: 1844. 3 p. NN. 44-4743

Onderdonk, Benjamin Tredwell, 1791-1861. To the right reverend the bishops of the Protestant Episcopal Church in the United States of America, their brother the undersigned, the bishop of New

York, feels himself compelled to communicate this his solemn remonstrance, protest, and demand. New York: 1844. WHi. 44-4744

Onderdonk, Henry Ustick, 1789-1850. Worship; the use of a liturgy; a charge to the clergy of the Protestant Episcopal Church in Pennsylvania, delivered in St. Andrew's Church, Philadelphia, May 17th, 1843. Second edition. By Henry Ustick Onderdonk, bp. of Pennsylvania. Philadelphia: Stavely and M'Calla, 1844. 24 p. MdBD; MH; PHi. 44-4745

Onderdonk, Henry Ustick, 1789-1858. Episcopacy tested by scripture. By the Right Reverend Henry U. Onderdonk.... New York: Protestant Episcopal Tract Society, 1844. 277 p. CBCDS; NNG. 44-4746

Onderdonk, Henry Ustick, 1789-1858. Episcopacy. Tested by scripture, by Rev. Henry U. Onderdonk, D.D. New York: Protestant Episcopal Tract Society, [1844?] 124 p. CBCDS. 44-4747

One thousand dollars reward! The leaders of the Polk party in the interior of this state, are asserting with unparalleled audacity that Polk is in favor of a protective tariff. New York: Printed for the Central Clay Committee, 1844. 11 p. MH. 44-4748

Onondaga, New York. Salt Springs. Annual report of Superintendent. February. Albany: 1844. OCHP. 44-4749

The opal: a pure gift for the Holy days; edited [by N.P. Willis, Mrs. J.S. Hale, John Keese] with nine illustrations by J.G. Chapman. New York: John C.

Riker, 1844-. IU; MPiB; NjR; PU; WU. 44-4750

Oras, John. Evenings of a working man: Being the occupation of his Scanty Leisure. With a preface relative to the author. New York: J. Winchester [1844] MB. 44-4751

Order of exercises at the dedication of Washington Street Chapel in Beverly, January 12, 1844. Salem: Salem Observer office [1844?] MBevHi. 44-4752

The Order of United Brothers of Temperance of the United States. Constitution of the Order... with the bylaws of Association No. 1 and of the Junior Order No. 1 of the State of New York. New York: Sherman's Yankee Press, 1844. 24 p. MB. 44-4753

Ordo in oratione quadraginta Horarum in Dicecesi Baltimorensi Servandus. Jussu Reverendissimi D. Archiepiscopi editus second edition. Baltimore: John Murphy, 1844. 16 p. OCX. 44-4754

Oregon. American protection to American pioneers; or, shall Oregon be surrendered to Great Britain? Washington: Published by order of a committee of the Democratic Members of Congress, 1844? 7 p. RPB. 44-4755

Oregon. Petition of a number of citizens of the territory of Oregon, praying the extension of the jurisdiction of the United States over that territory, February 7, 1844. Presented to the Senate and House of Representatives of the United States of America. Washington, 1844. 6 p. OrU. 44-4756

An original history of the religious

denominations at present existing in the United States, containing authentic accounts of their rise, progress, statistics, and doctrines. Philadelphia: J.Y. Humphreys, 1844. 734 p. NjR. 44-4757

Ormsby, Robert McKinley, 1814-1881. The American definition spelling book, on an improved plan; in which the spelling and pronunciation are generally upon the principles of Noah Webster.... designed for the use of schools in the United States.... By R.M.K. Ormsby. Improved edition. Bradford, Vermont: A. Low, 1844. 180 p. MH; NBLiHi; NhD; VtHi; VtNofNC. 44-4758

Orne, Caroline Frances, b. 1818. Sweet Auburn and Mount Auburn with other poems by Caroline F. Orne. Cambridge: John Owen, 1844. 196 p. CtSoP; GEU; ICU; NhPet; PPL-R. 44-4759

Orpheus glee book. A collection of glees, selected from the best composers. New York: Hall, 1844. 5 v. MB; MH. 44-4760

Osgood, Frances Sargent Locke, 1811-1850. Puss in boots, and the marquis of Carabas. Illustrated by Otto Speckter. New York: Benjamin and Young, 1844. 43 p. IaU; MWH; PU; RPB; ViU. 44-4761

Ossoli, Sarah Margaret (Fuller), 1810-1850. Summer on the lakes, in 1843. Boston: C.C. Little and J. Brown, 1844. 256 p. IHi; MB; MeU; OkU; RPA. 44-4762

Ostervald, J.F. Essay on the composition and delivery, of a sermon, by the late J.F. Ostervald, ...Translated from the French and illustrated with notes, by Joseph Sutcliffe, A.M. Third American

from the last London edition. Baltimore: Issac P. Cook, 1844. 233 p. GAGTh; TChU; TKimJ; WStf3F. 44-4763

Oswald, John. An etymological dictionary of the English language on a plan entirely new. By John Oswald. Revised and improved and especially adapted to the purpose of teaching English composition in schools and academies. By J. M. Keogy. Philadelphia: Edward C. Biddle, 1844. OSW; PP; ViL. 44-4764

Otis, William Foster. Report of the [Boston] Trinity Hall Sunday School. Boston: Printed by request of the rectors and teachers, 1844. 11 p. MB; MBD; NNG. 44-4765

Otway, Thomas, 1652-1685. Venice preserved. In five acts.... New York: William Taylor and company, 1844. [7]-58 p. LNH. 44-4766

Our Saviour; or a brief exposition of the birth, teaching, etc. By a teacher. Revised by the Committee of publication. Philadelphia: American Baptist publication society, 1844. 144 p. ICBB; MH; MH-AH; PPAmP. 44-4767

Ourselves our own sovereigns. American Republican candidates. New York: 1844. PPL. 44-4768

Ouseley, Gideon, 1762-1839. Old Christianity against papal novelties. Including a review of Dr. Milner's "end of controversy," by Gideon Ouseley.... First American from the fifth Dublin edition. Philadelphia: Sorin and Ball, 1844. 406 p. ArCH; KyLoS; Nh; OC. 44-4769

Ovid. Selectae Fabulas ex Libris Metamorphoseon Ovidii Nasonis, notis

Illustratae, accedunt quaedam ex Libris Tristium Elegiae, Baltimore: Ex-Typographia Metropolitana, 1844. CoHi; MdHi; MdW. 44-4770

Ovid. Works, translated by Dryden, Pope, Congreve, Addison and others. New York: Harper, 1844. 2 v. IaCorn. 44-4771

Ovidius Naso, Publius, 43 B.C.-18 A.D. Excerpta et scriptis Publii Ovidii Nasonis. Accedunt notulge anglicae et questiones. In usum scholae Bostoniensis. Cura B.A. Gould. Bostoniae: Benjamin B. Mussey, 1844. 287 p. CtHT; GDecCT; KyLxT; LNB; OCU. 44-4772

Ovidius Naso, Publius, 43 B.C.-18 A.D. Ovid, translated by Dryden, Pope, Congreve, Addison and others. New York: Harper, 1844. CtMW; LNP; MChi; TNAg; WNaE. 44-4773

Ovidius Naso, Publius, 43 B.C.-18 A.D. Selections from the metamorphoses and Heroides. With notes, grammatical references and exercises in scanning by E.A. Andrews. Boston: Crocker and Brewster, 1844. 264 p. CoCsC; KTW; MH; MNF. 44-4774

Owen, David Dale, 1807-1860. Report of geological exploration of Iowa, Wisconsin and Illinois, made under instructions from the secretary of the treasury of the United States in the year 1839. Ordered to be printed by the Senate of the United States. 1844. [Washington, D.C.: 1844?] 191 p. GU; IaCrM; MnHi; OCHp; OrU. 44-4775

Owen, David Dale, 1807-1880. Review of the New York geological reports [New Haven: 1844] 15 p. MB; MH-Z; MoS; OO. 44-4776

Owen, Griffith. Counsels to domestics. By Rev. G. Owen, Baltimore: D. Owen and son, 1844. 77 p. PAtM; PPPrHi. 44-4777

Owen, Griffith. How to be contented and useful. Baltimore: Owens, 1844. 77 p. PPPrHi. 44-4778

Owen, John, 1616-1683. The forgiveness of sin: Illustrated in a practical exposition of Psalm 130. New York: American Tract Society [1844?] 429 p. ICU. 44-4779

Owen, John, 1616-1683. Grace and duty of being spiritually minded... Carefully reprinted from the author's edition. New York: Robert Carter; Pittsburgh, Thomas Carter, 1844. 385 p. CSansS; IaDuU; MTop; NNUT; OrPD. 44-4780

Owen, John, 1616-1683. Treatise on the Holy Spirit and his operations: an Exposition of the 130th Psalm. Xenia: 1844. ScCoB. 44-4781

Owen, Robert, 1771-1858. Manifesto of Robert Owen, addressed to all governments and people who desire to become civilized, and to improve permanently the condition of all classes in all countries...Washington: Printed at the Globe office, 1844. 8 p. In; MBAt; MH; OClWHi; WHi. 44-4782

Owen, Robert Dale, 1801-1877. Native Americanism. Extract from an address delivered at Madison, Indiana, July 26, 1844. Louisville, Kentucky: Democrat office, 1844. 7 p. In. 44-4783

Owen, Robert Dale, 1801-1877. The theory of tariff protection; speech delivered in the House of Representatives, April 22, 1844, touching the claims and merits of a protective tariff system. [Washington: 1844] 8 p. MiD-B; PHi; WHi. 44-4784

Oxenford, John, 1817-1877. Tales from the German, comprising specimens from the most celebrated authors. ....New York: Harper and brothers, 1844. 110 p. MH; NjR; ViU; VtB. 44-4785

P

Packard, Levi. A sermon, preached at Spencer, Massachusetts, Sabbath, February 4, 1844. By Levi Packard, pastor of the Congregational Church in Spencer. Brookfield, Massachusetts: Merriam and Cooke, printers, 1844. 25 p. MB; MBC; MiD-B; MWA. 44-4786

Paddock, S.B. A sermon preached in Christ Church, Norwich, September 8, 1844, on the occasion of resigning the rectorship of said church. By Rev. S.B. Paddock. Norwich, Connecticut: George W. Concklin, 1844. 15 p. MiD-B; MnHi; NjR; NNG; RPB. 44-4787

Page, David Perkins, 1810-1848. Advancement in the means and methods of public instruction; a lecture delivered before the American Institute of Instruction, at its 14th anniversary at Pittsfield, Massachusetts. Boston: Ticknor, 1844. 38 p. Ia; LNH; MBC; NjR; RP. 44-4788

Page, John E. 1799-1867. The gospel light. Washington, D.C. Printed by John E. Page, editor and publisher, 1844. 16 p. USIC. 44-4789

Page, John E. 1799-1867. To the inhabitants and sojourners of Washington. Washington: 1844. 13, 4 p. USIC. 44-4790

Page, William. Pictorial illustrations of apostolical succession. By William Page, of Monroe, Michigan, bishop Presbyterian. New York: Ezra Collier, 1844.

32 p. IEG; MiD-B; NNUT; PPM; RP. 44-4791

Paget, Francis Edward. Sermon; duties of daily life, by Francis E. Paget, M.A. ....Philadelphia: Thomas Wardle, 1844. 327 p. ABBS; CoD; IU; OO; PHi. 44-4792

Paget, Francis Edward. Tales of the village. By Francis E. Paget, M.A. ....First series.... First American edition. New York: D. Appleton and company [1844] 3 v. MWiW; NcD; NcU; NNS. 44-4793

Paine, Martyn, 1794-1877. The defence of an introductory lecture on the improvement of medical education in the United States against an attack by the medico-chirurgical review. Boston: D. Clapp, printer, 1844. 4, 5 p. CSfA; KyLxT; MeB; MHi; NNN. 44-4794

Paine, Martyn, 1794-1877. A lecture on the physiology of digestion, introductory to a course of lectures on the institutes of medicine and materia medica. New York: printed for the medical class of the University, by J.H. Jennings, 1844-1845. 24 p. CtY; DNLM; MdBM; NjR; WMAM. 44-4795

Paine, Martyn, 1794-1877. A lecture on the physiology of digestion, introductory to a course of lectures on the instututes of medicine and materia medica. Second edition. New York: Jennings, 1844-1845.

24 p. DLC; DNLM; NNNAM; OClW; OrU-M. 44-4796

Paine, Martyn, 1794-1877. A lecture on the physiology of digestion, introductory to a course of lectures on the institutes of medicine and materia medica. Third edition. New York: J.H. Jennings, 1844-1845. 24 p. DLC; MH. 44-4797

Paine, Martyn, 1794-1877. A lecture on the physiology of digestion, introductory to a course of lectures on the institutes of medicine and materia medica. Fourth edition. New York: J.H. Jennings, 1844-1845. 24 p. DLC; ICU; KyU; MB; WMAM. 44-4798

Paine, Thomas, 1737-1809. Common sense: which was ordered by congress to be read at the head of all armies, before the Declaration of Independence, and by Washington, at the head of every captain's company... Reprinted by H. Mann for S. Bryant Esq., 1844. 39 p. MB; MH; MMal. 44-4799

Paine, Thomas, 1737-1809. A letter to George Washington, on the subject of a treaty concluded between Great Britain and the United States... Granville, N.J.: G.H. Evans, 1844. 95 p. NN. 44-4800

Paine, Thomas, 1737-1809. Miscellaneous letters and essays on various subjects. Granville, N.J.: G.H. Evans, 1844. 86 p. NN. 44-4801

Paine, Thomas, 1737-1809. The political writings of Thomas Paine.... To which is prefixed a brief sketch of the author's life. A new edition with additions....Granville. Middletown, New Jersey: G. H. Evans, 1844. 2 v. CBPac; IU: PMA; TxU; ViU. 44-4802

Paine, Thomas, 1737-1809. The theological miscellaneous and poetical works of Thomas Paine, also, a letter to George Washington, and letters to the citizens of the United States, after an absence of fifteen years. Granville, Middletown, New Jersey: George H. Evans, 1844. 384, 3-86, 3-24, 3-95 p. NIC; WBeloC. 44-4803

Paley, William, 1743-1805. A view of the evidences of Christianity. In three parts. By William Paley, D.D., archdeacon of Carlisle. A new edition. New York: Harper and brothers, 1844. 377 p. MiBatW; MnSS; NOg; RPE; TNS. 44-4804

Palmer, Aaron. A key to the endless, self-computing scale, showing its application to the different rules of arithmetic, &c. Boston: Smith and Palmer, 1844. 50 p. LU; MH: NNC. 44-4805

Palmer, Albert Gallatin. A discourse delivered at the one hundredth anniversary of the organization of the First Baptist Church in North Stonington, September 20th, 1843.... Boston: Gould, Kendall and Lincoln, 1844. 72 p. Ct; MB; MH-AH; RHi; RWe. 44-4806

Palmer, Albert Gallatin. The early Baptists of Connecticut; a discourse.... at the one hundredth anniversary of the.... first Baptist Church in North Stonington, September 20, 1843. Boston: Gould, Kendall and Lincoln, 1844. 72 p. CtSoP; MBC; Nh-Hi. 44-4807

Palmer, Albert Gallatin. The relations and responsibilities of the Christian ministry. A sermon delivered at the twenty-seventh anniversary of the Stonington Union Association. June 19, 1844.

Providence: 1844. 15 p. NHC-S; PCA; RHi. 44-4808

Palmer, Richard. The Bible atlas, or sacred geography delineated, in a complete series of scriptural maps, drawn from the best authorities, ancient and modern. Revised and compared with the most recent authorities, by Geor. Bush. New York: Charles Wells, 1844. 32 p. PWCHi; PWW. 44-4809

Palmer, William, 1803-1885. The Character of the Rev. W. Palmer, of Worcester College, as a controversialist; particularly on the reference to his charge against the Rt. Rev. Dr. Wiseman, considered in a letter to a friend at Oxford, by a late member of the University. From the London edition. Baltimore: Metropolitan Press, 1844. 3-96 p. MdBD. 44-4810

Palmer, William, 1803-1885. A compendious ecclesiastical history, from the earliest period to the present time. With a preface and notes, by an American editor. Fifth edition. With a series of questions, adapting the work for parochial instruction. New York: Stanford and Swords, 1844. 250 p. CtHC; IEG; NCH; NNUT; PPP. 44-4811

Pamphlets on sea walls, sustaining walls, resistance of piles, foundations in compressible soils. Washington: 1844-1868. 4 p. in 1 v. ICJ. 44-4812

Pancoast, Joseph, 1805-1882. Treatise on operative surgery; comprising a description of the various processes of the art, including all the new operations... Philadelphia: Carey, 1844. 380 p. CSt-L; IU; OCIM; PU; TU-M. 44-4813

Paradise restored, a poem. Cincinnati: R.P. Donogh, printer, 1844. 40 p. MH; OCHP; OClWHi. 44-4814

Parburt, George R. To the men of candor and reflection [Phelps, New York: 1844] 8 p. CSmH. 44-4815

Paris, John Ayrton, 1785-1856. Pharmacologia: being an extended inquiry into the operations of medicinal bodies, upon which are founded the theory and art of prescribing, by J.A. Paris.... From the ninth London edition. Rewritten in order to incorporate the latest discoveries in physiology, chemistry, and materia medica. With notes by Charles A. Lee.... New York: Harper and brothers, 1844. 353 p. CU; KyLx; LNB; NNN; PPCP. 44-4816

Parish hymns; a collection of hymns for public, social and private worship, selected and original. Philadelphia: Perkins, 1844. 466 p. CtMW; DLC; MBC; MWHi; OO. 44-4817

Parish psalmody; a collection of psalms and hymns for public worship.... to which are appended the confession of faith and shorter catechism of the Presbyterian Church in the United States.... Philadelphia: Perkins and Purves, 1844. 708 p. ICN; KyDC; NbOP; OMC; PPLT. 44-4818

Park, Edwards Amasa, 1808-1900. A discourse delivered in Boston before the pastoral association of Congregational ministers in Massachusetts, May 28, 1844. By Edwards A. Park. Andover: Allen, Morrill and Wardwell, 1844. 44 p. MBAt; NNG; OO; RHi. 44-4819

Park, Edwards Amasa, 1808-1900. A

discourse delivered in Boston before the pastoral association of Congregational ministers in Massachusetts, May 28, 1844. By Edwards A. Park, Second edition. Andover: Allen, Morrill and Wardwell, 1844. 60 p. CtHC; MBAt; MNtcA; Nh; PPPrHi. 44-4820

Park, Edwards Amasa, 1808-1900. Sermon on the duties of the New England clergy. ....Discourse delivered in Boston before the Pastoral Association of Congregational Ministers in Massachusetts, May 28, 1844. Andover: 1844. CtHWatk; MDeeP. 44-4821

Park, John Cochran, d. 1889. Address at a meeting of the descendants of Richard Haven, of Lynn, at Framingham, Massachusetts, August 29, 1844. Being the second centennial anniversary of his landing in New England. ....Boston: Samuel N. Dickinson, printer, 1844. 27 p. AzMe; Ct; MDeeP; MWA; PHi. 44-4822

Park, Roswell, 1807-1869. Pantology; or, a systematic survey of human knowledge; proposing a classification of all its branches, and illustrating their history, relations, uses and objects; with a synopsis of their leading facts and principles; and a select catalogue of books on all subjects, suitable for a cabinet library.... Third edition. Philadelphia: Hogan and Thompson, 1844. 587 p. IGK; MH; MnSM; NBu; TNJU. 44-4823

Parke, Uriah. Farmer's and mechanic's practical arithmetic. Hartford, 1844. CtHWatk. 44-4824

Parker, Daniel. Familiar letters to a brother; in two series; on the final restoration of all mankind to holiness and happiness; through a righteous judgement and an equitable retribution. Cincinnati: printed by C.W. Thorp, 1844. [9]-144 p. ICU; MiU; MMeTHi; OClWHi. 44-4825

Parker, Edward L. A sermon, delivered at the funeral of the Rev. Calvin Cutler, pastor of the Presbyterian Church in Windham, New Hampshire. February 24, 1844. By Edward L. Parker.... Andover: Allen, Morrill and Wardwell, printers, 1844. 23 p. CtHC; MBC; MH-AH; Nh; PPL. 44-4826

Parker, James W. Narrative of the perilous adventures, miraculous escapes and sufferings of Rev. James W. Parker, during a frontier residence in Texas, of fifteen years; ....to which is appended a narrative of the capture, and subsequent sufferings of Mrs. Rachel Plummer [his daughter]....Louisville, Kentucky, n.p., 1844. 95 p. ICN; WHi. 44-4827

Parker, Joel. Invitations to true happiness and motives for becoming a Christian. New York: Harper and brothers, 1844. 157 p. CtHC; IaDmD; LN; NjN; PPPrHi. 44-4828

Parker, Leonard Fletcher, 1825-1911. An essay on the mode and design of Christian baptism; in which the scriptures are carefully examined, and made the only book of appeal for positive proof.... New Philadelphia: Lutheran Standard office, printer, 1844. 304 p. IaDnU; NbOP; OClWHi; OU; PU. 44-4829

Parker, R. The tree of life. Containing moral and religious subjects, calculated to benefit and interest. [Wholly original] Written by Miss R. Parker. Lowell: 1844. 24 p. MH; NjR. 44-4830

Parker, Richard Green, 1798-1869. Aids to English composition, prepared for students of all grades; embracing specimens and models of school and college exercises, and most of the higher departments of English composition, both in prose and verse:....[first edition] Boston: R. S. Davis; New York: Robinson, Pratt and company, 1844. 418 p. ICU; LNDil; MB; MBAt; NRom. 44-4831

Parker, Richard Green, 1798-1869. Progressive exercises in English composition. Forty-first stereotype edition. Boston: R. S. Davis, 1844. MH; NRU. 44-4832

Parker, Samuel, 1779-1866. Journal of an exploring tour beyond the Rocky Mountains, under the direction of the A.B.C.F.M., containing a description of the geography, geology, climate, productions of the country, and the numbers, manners and customs of the natives; with a map of Oregon territory.... Fourth edition. Ithaca, New York: Andrus, Woodruff and Gauntlett, 1844. 416 p. KU; MWA; PU: TxHuT; WaU. 44-4833

Parker, Theodore, 1810-1860. A discourse on the transient and permanent in Christianity; preached at the ordination of Mr. Charles C. Shackford, in the Hawes Place Church in Boston. May 19, 1841. Boston: printed for the author, 1844. 48 p. MWHi. 44-4834

Parlour songster, containing a superior collection of the most popular sentimental songs, many of which are now first printed. New York: 1844. 240 p. CtHWatk; RPB. 44-4835

Parmly, Eleazer. Temperance address

as delivered to the society at Runsom, New Jersey. New York: 1844. 12 p. WHi. 44-4836

Parnell, Edward Andrew. Applied chemistry; in manufactures, arts, and domestic economy. Edited by Edward Andrew Parnell... New York: D. Appleton and company; Philadelphia: George S. Appleton, 1844. 175 p. CtHWatk; MCHi; MLow; NjR; PPL. 44-4837

Parrot, Friedrich von, 1791-1841. Journey to Ararat. New York: 1844. MB. 44-4838

Parry, Aaron Fyfe, b. 1815. Ohio citizen. Summary of the constitution and statutes of the state of Ohio. Columbus: J.H. Riley, 1844. 150 p. DLC; IaOt; MiD-B; OHi. 44-4839

Parry, William Edward, 1790-1855. Three voyages for the discovery of a northwest passage from the Atlantic to the Pacific, and a narrative of an attempt to reach the North Pole, by Sir W.E. Parry, Capt. R.N. F.R.S. In two volumes. New York: Harper and brothers, 1844. 328 p. MoSpD; PHi; PPGi; RWe. 44-4840

A parting gift to a Christian friend. Hartford: Brown and Parsons, 1844. 192 p. CtHWatk; IU; MNF; MWA. 44-4841

Paschall, Ann S. The friend's family. Intended for the amusement and instruction of children. Philadelphia: T.E. Chapman, 1844. 92 p. NBF; PHC; PPL; PSC-Hi. 44-4842

Passmore, Beulah. Reflections in prose and poetry by Beulah Passmore and G.

Rachel. Philadelphia: 1844. PSC-Hi; PPFr. 44-4843

Passmore, Beulah. Some reflections in prose and poetry. By Beulah and Rachel Passmore.... Philadelphia: J. Richards, printer, 1844. 72 p. CoCs; NjR. 44-4844

Pastor's appeal to his flock, on confirmation, showing its authority, nature, the qualifications for it, and motives to it. Hartford: 1844. 24 p. Ct; CtHT; LNB; PPL. 44-4845

A pastoral for the times. The church's chain of authority from God to minister in the word and sacraments. Burlington, New Jersey: J.L. Powell, 1844. 28 p. KyU; MdBD; NcD; NjPT; PHi. 44-4846

A pastoral letter to the clergy and members of the Protestant Episcopal Church in the United States of America. Philadelphia: Stavely and M'Calla, printers, 1844. 16 p. InID; MdBD; MiD-B; NGH. 44-4847

Paterson, Henry S. Valedictory address, delivered before the graduates of the medical department of Pennsylvania College.... By Henry S. Patterson. Philadelphia: Barrett and Jones, printers, 1844. 14 p. GDecCT; MB; NjR; OClWHi; PWW. 44-4848

Paterson, Thomas J. Speech on the civil and diplomatic appropriation bill in the House, June 14, 1844. Washington: printed by J.T. Towers, 1844. 23 p. M; NBu; NUtHi. 44-4849

Patmore, Coventry Keassey Dighton. The angel in the house. The betrothal. Boston: Ticknor and Fields, 1844. 201 p. NhPet. 44-4850

Patmore, Peter George. Chatsworth; or the romance of a week. New York: Harper, 1844. 122 p. MBAt; MdCatS; PBm; PPL. 44-4851

Patrick, Simon, 1626-1707. A critical commentary and paraphrase on the Old and New Testament and the Apocrypha. A new edition. Philadelphia: Carey and Hart, 1844. 4 v. InCW; KyLoP; ScDuE; TxU; WHi. 44-4852

Paulding, James Kirke, 1778-1860. A life of Washington. ....New York: Harper and brothers, 1844. 2 v. DLC; IAlS; LU: MWar; OCo. 44-4853

Pavilion Family School. Hartford, Connecticut. Catalogue of the instructors, pupils, and patrons, for three years preceding May 31st, 1814, with a circular annexed. Hartford: Elihu Geer, 1844. 7 p. Ct. 44-4854

Paxton, J.D. No future return of the Jews called for by the prophecy. Two sermons preached at Mulberry, August, 1844. Louisville: C.C. Hull and brothers, 1844. CtHC; MH-AH; PPPrHi. 44-4855

Paxton, James, 1786-1860. An introduction to the study of human anatomy. Fourth American edition in the additions, by Winslow Lewis. Boston: W.D. Ticknor, 1844. 24, 447 p. DNLM; NN; PPWI; UU; WU-M. 44-4856

Payne, William Winter. Speech... on the bill making appropriation for certain rivers and harbors... April 5, 1844 [Washington: 1844] 16 p. NoLoc. 44-4857

Payton, Joseph Hopkins, 1808-1845. Speech of Mr. Joseph H. Payton, of Tennessee, on the general appropriation bill. Delivered in the House or Representatives, June 5, 1844. [Washington, 1844] 19 p. DLC; IU; NN; NNC; OClWHi. 44-4858

Peabody, Andrew Preston, 1811-1893. Lectures on Christian doctrine. Boston: J. Munroe and company, 1844. 227 p. DLC; MPiB; NBu; Nh; TMeT. 44-4859

Peabody, Andrew Preston, 1811-1893. Lectures on Christian doctrine. Second edition. Boston: J. Munroe and company, 1844. 221 p. FDeS; ICN; NNUT; OO; RP. 44-4860

Peabody, Andrew Preston, 1811-1893. The wealth, industry, and resources of Portsmouth. A lecture delivered before the Portsmouth Lyceum, November 12, 1844. [Portsmouth]: 1844. 11 p. MH; MH-AH; Nh-Hi. 44-4861

Peabody, Oliver William Bourn. Life of James Oglethorpe, the founder of Georgia. Boston: C.C. Little and J. Brown, 1844. [201]-405 p. InCW; OClWHi; RPA. 44-4862

The peace almanac for 1845. New York, New York: Collins, brother and company [1844] MB; MWA. 44-4863

Pearson, John. An exposition of the creed. With an appendix, containing the principal Greek and Latin creeds. New York: D. Appleton and company, 1844. [8] 616 p. KyLoP; MiDD; PPP; TMeD; TSewU. 44-4864

Pease, L.T. A geographical and historical view of Texas, with a detailed account of the Texas revolution and war.

Hartford: H. Huntington, 1844. NN; PHi. 44-4865

Peck, George, 1797-1876. Appeal from tradition to scripture and common sense; or an answer to the question... by George Peck. New York: Carlton and Porter, 1844. 472 p. ICU; InCW; MsJMC; OBerB. 44-4866

Peck, George, 1797-1876. Appeal from tradition to scripture and common sense, or, an answer to the question, what constitutes the divine rule of faith and practice. New York: G. Lane and P.P. Sandford, for the Methodist Episcopal Church, 1844. 472 p. CBPSR; IEG; KyWA; MH; MWiW. 44-4867

Peck, John Mason. A new guide for emigrants to the west, containing sketches of Michigan, Ohio, Indiana, Illinois, Missouri, Arkansas, with the territory of Wisconsin and the adjacent parts.... New edition. Boston: 1844. 394 p. 44-4868

The peep of day; or a series of the earliest religious instruction, the infant mind is capable of receiving. Boston: American Board of Commissioners for Foreign Missions, by T. R. Marvin, 1844. 144 p. MBGCT; MCM; MH-AH. 44-4869

Peet, Harvey Prindle, 1794-1873. Vocabulary and elementary lessons for the deaf and dumb. New York: 1844. CtHWatk. 44-4870

Peirce, Bradford Kinney. The Sunday school teacher, and Bible class guide, for Sabbath school teachers, and parents, and church members. By Rev. Bradford Kinney Peirce, editor. Boston: Reid and

Rand, 1844-45. 284 p. MiOC; NjMD. 44-4871

Pellico, Silvio, 1788-1854. Memoirs of Silvio Pellico; or My Prisons. Translated by M.J. Smead and H.P. Lefebre. New York: J. and H.G. Langley, 1844. 8-96 p. KyDC; MH; OO; PPPrHi; WaPS. 44-4872

Penchant, Phillip. The mystery of Fitchburg. Fitchburg: C. Shepley, 1844. 28 p. MFiHi. 44-4873

Penn, William, 1644-1718. Primitive Christianity revived; in the faith and practice of the people called Quakers, written in testimony to the present dispensation of God through them to the world.... Salem: G.F. Read, 1844. 6-61 p. MH; PHC; TxDaM. 44-4874

Pennsylvania and New Jersey almanac for 1845. By Joseph Foulke. Philadelphia, Pennsylvania: Thomas L. Bonsal, [1844] MWA. 44-4875

Pennsylvania Historical Society. List of meetings. Philadelphia, 1844. PPL. 44-4876

The people of China; or, a summary of Chinese history. ....Philadelphia: American Sunday School Union [1844?] 234 p. ArPb; CSansS; ICBB; NNC; TxHC. 44-4877

Peoples Fire Insurance Company, Dickinson Township, Pennsylvania. By-laws of the Cumberland Valley Mutual Protection Company of Dickinson Township, Cumberland County. Chartered the 9th of March, 1843. For Cumberland and Adams Counties. Carlisle [Pennsylvania] printed by G. Sanderson, 1844. 12 p. DLC. 44-4878

Percival, Thomas, 1740-1804. Parental instruction, or, guide to wisdom and virtue for young persons of either sex, from writings of eminent physician. New York: Alex. V. Blake, 1844. 252 p. MBC; NICLA. 44-4879

Perkins and Purves' almanac for 1845. Philadelphia, Pennsylvania: Perkins and Pures [1844] MWA. 44-4880

Perkins, George Roberts, 1812-1876. Elements of algebra; designed for the use of common schools; also serving as an introduction to the "Treatise on algebra." New York: D. Appleton and company; Utica: H. Fuller and company, 1844. 244 p. DAU; IP; NUt. 44-4881

Perkins, George Roberts, 1812-1876. Higher arithmetic, designed for the use of high schools, academies, and colleges.... Second edition, revised and improved. Utica, [New York]: Bennett, Backus and Hawley; New York: Saxton and Miles, 1844. 278 p. DAU; DLC; NBuG; NUt. 44-4882

Perkins, Jonas. A sermon preached on the day of the annual Thanksgiving in the meeting house of the Union Religious Society of Weymouth and Braintree, November 30, 1843. By Jonas Perkins.... Boston: press of T.R. Marvin, 1844. 16 p. MiD-B; MWey; MWeyHi; RPB. 44-4883

Perkins, Jonas. Thanksgiving sermon. Boston: 1844. 16 p. MBC. 44-4884

Perkins, Joseph. Introductory lecture to the spring session of lectures in Castleton Medical College. Albany: Printed by C.

Van Benthuysen and company, 1844. 16 p. NjR; VtMidSM. 44-4885

Perkins, Samuel. The world as it is: containing a view of the present condition of its principal nations.... With anecdotes of distinguished characters, and numerous engravings. Seventh edition. [New Haven?] Thomas Belknap, 1844. 484 p. COT; IU; NRom. 44-4886

Perrin, Jean Baptiste, fl. 1786. A selection of one hundred of Perrin's fables, accompanied with a key.... also a figured pronunciation of the French, according to the best French works extant on the subject... by A. Bolmar... A new edition. Philadelphia: Lea and Blanchard, 1844. MH; MoU; OO; TxU-T. 44-4887

Perrin, Jean Baptiste, fl. 1786. A selection of one hundred of Perrin's fables, accompanied with a key... By A. Bolmar... A new edition. Philadelphia: Lea and Blanchard, 1844. 181 p. MBBC; MWHi; NNC. 44-4888

Perrin, Lavalette. The nation in perplexity: last sermon. New Haven: 1844. 23 p. MBC; MH-AH. 44-4889

Perry, B.F. Address before the Literary Society of Erskine College, Abbeville District, South Carolina on the fifth anniversary, September 13, 1844. Greenville, S.C.: printed by O.H. Wells, 1844. 15 p. TBriK. 44-4890

Perry, Gideon B. The Bible, the young man's guide... Philadelphia: Griffith and Simon, 1844. 60 p. MnHi. 44-4891

Persius Flaccus Aulus. Juvenal Satires, translated by Charles Badham. New edition, and satires of Persius. New York:

Harper, 1844. 227, 58 p. IaCorn; PP. 44-4892

Peter Parley's tales. Author of North and South America; the manners, customs, and antiquities of the Indians of North and South America. Boston: Bradbury, 1844. MMel. 44-4893

Pettigrew, Thomas Joseph, 1791-1865. On superstitions connected with the history and practice of medicine and surgery. Philadelphia: E. Barrington and G. D. Haswell, 1844. 213 p. IaK; NhD; Ohi; ViU; Wa-M. 44-4894

Peyton, Joseph Hopkins, 1803-1845. Remarks of Messrs. Peyton and Dickinson, in the House of Representatives... January, 1844, on the bill to refund the fine imposed upon General Jackson. Washington: 1844. DLC. 44-4895

Phaedrus. Fables with the appendix of gudius [sic] translated by Christopher Smart. New York: Harper, 1844. 74 p. C; MoSC; ScC. 44-4896

Phelps and Ensign's traveller's guide through the United States: containing stage, steamboat, canal and railroad routes, with the distances from place to place.... New York: Phelps and Ensign, 1844. 53 p. DLC; MB; MnHi; NBu. 44-4897

Phelps, Almira Hart Lincoln, 1793-1884. Botany for beginners.... Lectures on botany.... Eleventh edition. New York: Huntington and Savage, 1844. 216 p. CtY; MH; IsaMp. 44-4898

Phelps, Almira Hart Lincoln, 1793-1884. Botany for beginners; an introduction to Mrs. Lincoln's lectures on botany, for the use of common schools and the younger pupils of higher schools and academies, by Mrs. Phelps.... Twelfth edition. New York: Huntington and Savage, 1844. 216 p. CtHWatk; MH; WHi. 44-4899

Phelps, Almira Hart Lincoln, 1793-1884. Caroline Westerly; or the young traveller from Ohio. Containing the letters of a young lady of seventeen, written to her sister. New York: Harper and brothers, 1844. 233 p. KyLoS; MB; OSW. 44-4900

Phelps, Almira Hart Lincoln, 1793-1884. Chemistry. Lectures on chemistry.... Second edition. New York: 1844. 383 p. IaDaM. 44-4901

Phelps, Almira Hart Lincoln, 1793-1884. Familiar lectures on botany, practical, elementary, and physiological; with an appendix containing descriptions of the plants of the United States and exotics. Nineteenth edition revised and enlarged. New York: Huntington and Savage, 1844. MH; OSW. 44-4902

Phelps, Almira Hart Lincoln, 1793-1884. Familiar lectures on botany, practical, elementary, and physiological; with an appendix containing descriptions of the plants of the United States and exotics. Twentieth edition revised and enlarged. New York: Huntington and company, 1844. 246, 186 p. IaDaP; NIC-A; NRMA. 44-4903

Phelps, Almira Hart Lincoln, 1793-1884. Familiar lectures on botany, practical, elementary, and physiological; with an appendix containing descriptions of the plants of the United States and exotics. Twenty-first edition revised and

enlarged. New York: Huntington and Savage, 1844. 186 p. CLSU; MsCld; OO; TNP. 44-4904

Phelps, Almira Hart Lincoln, 1793-1884. Familiar lectures on botany, practical, elementary, and physiological; with an appendix containing descriptions of the plants of the United States and exotics. Twenty-second edition revised and enlarged; illustrated by many additional engravings. New York: Huntington and Savage, 1844. 246, 186 p. CtHWatk; Tx-SaUr. 44-4905

Phelps, Almira Hart Lincoln, 1793-1884. Lectures on chemistry, for the use of schools, framilies, and private students. Second edition. New York: Huntington and Savage, 1844. 383 p. GEU; IaDaM; KyLxT; PPi. 44-4906

Phelps, Amos Augustus, 1804-1847. Memoir of Ann Elizabeth Pierce. Boston: Massachusetts Sabbath School Society, 1844. MBC. 44-4907

Phelps, Amos Augustus, 1805-1847. The sabbath. Third edition. New York and Boston: Dodd, 1844. 60 p. IaB; NNUT; OO. 44-4908

Phelps, Richard Harvey. Newgate of Connecticut, a history of the prison, its insurrections, massacres, &c., imprisonment of the Tories in the Revolution, the ancient and recent working of its mines, &c., to which is appended a description of the state prison at Wethersfield. Hartford: Geer, 1844. 33 p. PPL; PU. 44-4909

Phelps, Richard Harvey. Newgate of Connecticut: a history of the prison, its insurrections, massacres, etc. ....Second edition. Hartford: press of E. Geer, 1844. 24 p. MiD-B. 44-4910

Phelps, Richard Harvey. Newgate of Connecticut: a history of the prison, its insurrections, massacres, &c., imprisonment of the Tories in the Revolution, the ancient and recent working of its mines, &c., to which is appended a description of the state prison at Wethersfield. Third edition. Hartford: 1844. 33 p. Ct; CtSoP; MHi; NBLiHi; OClWHi. 44-4911

Phelps, Samuel Shether, 1793-1855. Substance of the speech of Mr. Phelps of Vermont [o]n the subject of the tariff. Delivered in the Senate of the United States, February 16 and 19, 1844. Washington: Gales and Seaton, 184. 35 p. MB; NjR; PHi; TxU; WHi. 44-4912

Phelps, Samuel Shether, 1793-1855. To the people of Vermont. Mr. Phelp's rejoinder to Mr. Slade's "reply" [Washington: 1844] 40 p. NoLoc. 44-4913

Philadelphia, Pennsylvania. Address of the Catholic lay citizens of the city and county of Philadelphia to their fellow citizens, in reply to the presentment of the grand jury of the court of quarter sessions of May term, 1844. In regard to the causes of the late riots in Philadelphia. Baltimore: Metropolitan Tract Society, 1844. 2-12 p. MdBS; MdW. 44-4914

Philadelphia, Pennsylvania. Assessment of property in the city and county of Philadelphia. Philadelphia: 1844. PPL. 44-4915

Philadelphia, Pennsylvania. Blockley Almshouse. Auditors reports of the ac-

counts of the Blockley Almshouse for 1844. Philadelphia: 1844. PPL. 44-4916

Philadelphia, Pennsylvania. Catalogue of books added to the library of the Library Company of Philadelphia, since the large catalogue of 1835. To January, 1844. Third edition. Philadelphia: C. Sherman, 1844. [9]-182 p. PU; RPB. 44-4917

Philadelphia, Pennsylvania. Digest of acts of assembly and ordinances of the Kensington District of the Northern Liberties. Philadelphia: Perry, 1844. 286 p. PPFrankI. 44-4918

Philadelphia, Pennsylvania. Rules for the government of the Board of Guardians; its officers, bus. etc. Also the poor laws. Philadelphia: 1844. 76 p. PHi; PPCP. 44-4919

Philadelphia Library Company. Books added since 1835. Third edition. Philadelphia: 1844. MBAt. 44-4920

Philadelphia Library Company. Catalogue of books added to the library since the large catalogue of 1835. Philadelphia: 1844. PPCC. 44-4921

Philadelphia pocket almanac. Philadelphia, Pennsylvania: T.E. Chapman, 1844. MWA. 44-4922

Philip, Robert, 1791-1858. The Hannahs; or maternal influence on sons. Third edition. New York: D. Appleton and company, 1844. 306 p. CtHWatk; ICP; MWiW. 44-4923

Philip, Robert, 1791-1858. The love of the spirit; traced in his work, a companion to the experimental guide. Sixth edition. New York: Appleton, 1844. 301 p. KyBC; NCH. 44-4924

Philip, Robert, 1791-1858. The Marthas; or the varieties of female piety. Eleventh edition. New York: D. Appleton, 1844. CtHC. 44-4925

Philip, Robert, 1791-1888. The Marys; or the beauty of female holiness. Fifteenth edition. New York: D. Appleton and company; Philadelphia: George S. Appleton, 1844. 251 p. TBriK. 44-4926

Philips, L. C. The new birth; showing its necessity.... also a view of the growth of grace in the soul, a discourse upon heaven and hell, and one upon friends knowing each other in heaven.... Second edition. Cincinnati: Shepard and company, 1844.. 595 p. IP. 44-4927

Phillips, A.E. A treatise on the preservation of the teeth. Salem: Gazette office, 1844. 24 p. NjR. 44-4928

Phillips, George B. A glimpse into the world to come in a walking dream, 1844. New York: Robert Carter, 1844. 105 p. GDecCT; MLow; PWaybu. 44-4929

Phillips, Stephen C. Sunday school service book. Part first, lessons, etc. Boston: 1844. 3 parts in 1. MB; MH. 44-4930

Phillips, Wendell, 1811-1884. The constitution, a pro-slavery compact, or selections from the Madison papers etc. New York: American Anti-slavery Society, 1844. 123 p. MH; NB; WHi. 44-4931

Phillips, William, 1773-1828. An elementary treatise on mineralogy: comprising an introduction to the science. Fifth edition.... containing the latest discoveries in American and foreign mineralogy; with numerous additions by Francis Alger. Boston: Ticknor, 1844. 812 p. CU; GU; ICJ; MiU; ViU. 44-4932

Phillips Exeter Academy. Exeter, New Hampshire. Statement of facts relative to the removal of six pupils from Phillips Exeter Academy, by one of the removed.... Exeter, New Hampshire: 1844. 16 p. MHi. 44-4933

Phinney's calendar, or western almanac, ...1844. Cooperstown: H. and E. Phinney, 1844. 36 p. DLC; MiD; MWA; NUtHi; WHi. 44-4934

Phipps, Joseph, 1708-1787. The original and present state of man briefly considered, wherein is shown the nature of his fall.... New York: New York Meeting for Sufferings, 1844. 144 p. MiU; MoSpD; OU; WHi; WM. 44-4935

Phrenological almanac and physiological guide for 1845. By O.S. and L.N. Fowler. New York, New York: O.S. Fowler, [1844] MWA. 44-4936

The physiology of the London medical student and curiosities of medical experience. By "Punch." Philadelphia: Carey and Hart, 1844. 96 p. KyHoP; MB; MH-M; PPCP; TNV. 44-4937

Pickering, Ellen, d. 1843. The grandfather. By the late Miss Ellen Pickering. New York: Harper and brothers, 1844. 119 p. MBAt; NjR; RPA. 44-4938

Pickering, Ellen, d. 1843. The grumbler. By the late Miss Ellen Pickering. New York: Harper and brothers, 1844. 134 p. CtY; MB; NN; OrU; ViU. 44-4939

Picot, Charles. First lessons in French: consisting of rules and directions for the attainment of a just pronunciation; select piece, sentences, colloquial phrases, and words in general use. ....Philadelphia: Thomas, Cowperthwait and company, 1844. 132 p. KHi; MiU; Nh; ScU. 44-4940

Picot, Charles. The French student's assistant.... with a key to pronunciation, by Charles Picot. A new and improved edition. Philadelphia, Pennsylvania: Thomas, Cowperthwait and company, 1844. 48 p. MB; MBAt; MiU; NcWsS. 44-4941

The picture alphabet. Newark, New Jersey: Benjamin Olds, 1844. 15 p. MoKCM; NjP. 44-4942

Picture gallery of the new and old worlds, June 29, 1844. Volume I. New York: 1844. ICHi. 44-4943

Picture reader.... By a friend to youth. New Haven: S. Babcock, [1844] MH. 44-4944

Pierson, Cornelia Tuthill, 1820-1870. Wreaths and branches for the church. By Mrs. C. Pierson.... Second edition. Boston: Dow, 1844. 232 p. ICBB; MH; NjP. 44-4945

Pierson, Johnson, 1814-1906. The Judaid; a poem; detailing the rise and decline of the Jews, from the exodus from Egypt, to the destruction of their temple by the Romans. In eleven books. St Louis: Printed by Daniel Davies, 1844. 248 p. CtY; DLC; MH; MoSM; RP. 44-4946

Pike, John Gregory. The Christian ministry contemplated in the devotional spirit it requires, in its labors, its importance, and its results. By J.G. Pike, author of "persuasives to early piety," etc. Dover: the trustees of the F. Baptist Connection, 1844. 96 p. MeLewB; NhHi; PCA. 44-4947

Pike, John Gregory. True happiness; or the excellence and power of early religion. New York: 1844. 179 p. OO. 44-4948

Pike, Robert, Jr. Mnemonics applied to the acquisition of knowledge; or the art of memory. Boston: Published monthly by R. and W.C. Pike. 1844. 11 p. NjR; RNR. 44-4949

Pike, Robert, Jr. Mnemonics applied to the acquisition of knowledge; or the art of memory. Second edition. Boston: Printed by S.N. Dickinson, 1844. [5]-35, 39-100 p. ICBB; MWAl NjR; NNT-C; OClWHi. 44-4950

The pilgrim's legacy. A church without a bishop, a state without a king. With music. New York: 1844. 3 p. MH-AH; MNF. 44-4951

Pillow, Gideon Johnson. Speech at the mass meeting on the democracy near Columbia, Tennessee, July 13, 1844, on the annexation of Texas. Columbia, Tennessee: printed by the Tennessee Democrat Office, 1844. 16 p. RPB. 44-4952

Pimentel Andres. Juicio sobre la causa seguida contra. New Orleans, 1844. 120 p. MB. 44-4953

Pinamonti, Giovanni Pietro. The cross in the true light or the utility of sufferings.

Baltimore: Metropolitan Press, 1844. 111 p. MdBS; MoSU. 44-4954

Pinckey, Henry Laurens. An address delivered before the Cape Fear Lodge, No. 2 of the independent order of Odd fellows, Wilmington, N. C. New York: Booth, 1844. 21 p. ScC. 44-4955

Pindar. Olympic odes, Pythian odes, Nimean odes and Isthmian odes. Rev. C. A. Wheelwright, translator. New York: Harper and Brothers, 1844. 259 p. MAm. 44-4956

Pindarus. Pindar, translated by the Rev. C.A. Wheelwright, and Anacreon, translated by Thomas Bourne. New York: Harper and brothers, 1844. 66 p. CLSU; MoSM; OClW; PP; ViR. 44-4957

Pingree, E.M. Debate on universalism. Waraw, Kentucky: 1844. PCC. 44-4958

Pinkney, Edward Coate. The miscellaneous poems of Edward C. Pinkney. New York: Morris, Willis and company [1844] 16 p. ICU; MWH; RPB. 44-4959

Pinney, Norman. The complete French master; or a new method of learing to read, write and speak the French language. Mobile: Printed by Dade and Thompson, 1844. 232 p. LNH. 44-4960

The pirate boy; or, adventures of Henry Warrington. A story of the sea. By the author of the cabin boy; Ambrose and Eleanor; valley of the Mohawk.... New York: Nafis and Cornish, 1844. 112 p. CSmH; CU; KEmT; MWA. 44-4961

The pirate's almanac. Philadelphia: Turner and Fisher, 1844. MBNEH. 44-4962

The pirates own book, or, authentic narratives of the lives, exploits, and executions of the most celebrated sea robbers. With historical sketches of the Joassamee, Spanish, Ladrone, West India, Malay, and Algerine pirates. Portland: Sanborn and Carter; Philadelphia: Thomas, Cowperthwait and company, 1844. 432 p. MB; MH; ViRVal. 44-4963

Piratical and tragical almanac for 1845. Philadelphia, Pennsylvania: John B. Perry, [1844] MWA. 44-4964

Pitman, Isaac, 1813-1897. A manual of phonography; or, writing by sound; a natural method of writing all languages by one alphabet, composed of signs that represent the sound of the human voice. A complete system of phonetic writing. 1st American ed. New York: J. Donley, 1844. 16 p. CtY; DLC; MoSW; NN. 44-4965

Pitman, Isaac, 1813-1897. A manual of phonography; or, writing by sound; a natural method of writing all languages by one alphabet, composed of signs that represent the sound of the human voice; adapted also to the English language so as to form a complete system of phonetic writing, applicable to every purpose. Third edition. New York: John Donlevy, 1844. 32 p. MH; NN. 44-4966

Pitman, Isaac, 1813-1897. Phonographic class book. Bath: 1844. MB. 44-4967

Pitman, Isaac, 1813-1897. Phonographic reading book written in the third style. Bath: 1844. MB. 44-4968

Pitman, Isaac, 1813-1897. Table ... third

style of phonography. Bath: Pitman, 1844. MB. 44-4969

Pitman, J.S. Trial of T.W. Dorr for treason. Boston: 1844. MB. 44-4970

Pitts, Fountain E. A sermon delivered at the opening of the Tennessee annual conference at Gallatin, Tennessee, October 18, 1843, by Rev. F.E. Pitts. Published by order of the conference. Nashville, Tennessee: B.R. M'Kennie, 1844. 38 p. T. 44-4971

Pitts, Fountain E. Tracts on Campbellism. Nashville: printed by Cameron and Fall, office of Tennessee Agriculturist, 1844. 120 p. T. 44-4972

Pittsfield, Massachusetts. Young Ladies Institute. Third annual catalogue of the instructors and pupils in the Young Ladies' Institute, Pittsfield, Massachusetts, August, 1844. Pittsfield, Massachusetts: Charles Montague, printer, 1844. 16 p. GDecCT. 44-4973

Plain sermons, by contributors to the tracts for the times. In two volumes. Second edition. New York: James A. Sparks, 1844. 2 v. ICLoy; IGK; MdBD; MiU; NBuDD. 44-4974

Planche, James Robinson, 1796-1880. Grist to the mill; a comic drama, in two acts... New York: London: Samuel French [1844] 34 p. OCl. 44-4975

Playfair, John, 1748-1819. Elements of geometry; containing the first six books of Euclid, with a supplement on the quadrature of the circle and the geometry of solids; to which are added the elements of plane and spherical trigonometry.... From the last London

edition, enlarged. New York: W.E. Dean, 1844. 317 p. KAStB; MH; MShM; MWH; NmStM. 44-4976

Plee, Francois. Types de chaque famille et des principaux genres des plates croissant spontaement en France; exposition detaille et complege de leurs caracteres et de l'embryologie, par F. Plee. New York: Bailliere brothers, 1844-1864. 2 v. CU-A; DNA: MdBP; MH. 44-4977

The plow boy's almanac for 1845, illustrated with sixty engravings; by A. Randall, editor of the "plow boy," Cincinnati, Ohio. Cincinnati: H. Huxley, [1844] 114 p. WHi. 44-4978

Plutarchus. Delay of the deity in the punishment of the wicked, with notes by H.B. Hackett. Andover: Allen, Morrill and Wardwell, 1844. 171 p. CtHC; IaDmU; IGK; MB. 44-4979

Plutarchus. Lives, Translated from the original Greek; with notes, historical and critical; and a life of Plutarch. By John Langhorne and William Langhorne. From the last London edition. New York: 1844. 4 v. InTi; IQ; MChi; MH. 44-4980

Plutarchus. Plutarch's lives of the most select and illustrious characters of antiquity. Translated from the original Greek; with notes, historical and critical, by John Langhorne, M.D., and William Langhorne, A.M., and others. By William Mayor, LL.D. ....Complete in one volume. Ithaca: Andrus, Woodruff and Gauntlett, 1844. 432 p. ArT; IaDu; KyWA; NIC; OO. 44-4981

Pocket almanack for 1845. Boston,

Massachusetts: T. Groom and company, [1844] MWA. 44-4982

The pocket anatomist: being a summary description of the muscles, with a tabular view of the arteries and nerves. Concordant with "Dublin dissector," and "Harrison on the arteries." Fourth edition. Philadelphia: 1844. 63 p. DNLM; MBM; MH; PP; PPL. 44-4983

The pocket lawyer and family conveyancer. To which is added an abridged law dictionary, and the fee bill. Embellished with upwards of twenty pages of script, serving as a model for good writing. Compiled by a gentleman of the bar. Philadelphia: Charles Bell, 1844. 142 p. KyBC; PPiAL. 44-4984

Poe, Edgar Allen, 1809-1849. The landscape-garden by Edgar A. Poe. New York: 1844. ViU. 44-4985

The poetical works of Churchill, Parnell and Tickell; with a life of each. Boston: printed by Houghton, 1844. 352 p. AU; Ia; IU; PAlt. 44-4986

The poetical works of Coleridge, Shelley, and Keats; complete in one volume. Philadelphia: Thomas, Cowperthwait and company, 1844. 617 p. MEab; NcD; OClW; ViU; WNaE. 44-4987

The poetical works of Milton, Young, Gray, Beattie, and Collins. Philadelphia, Pennsylvania: Grigg and Elliot, 1844. 498 p. IaB; ODaU. 44-4988

The poetry of love, from the most celebrated authors, with several original pieces. Selected by the editor of "poetry of the affections"... Philadelphia: T.

Wardle, 1844. 224 p. MdBJ; NBuG; NIC. 44-4989

Poleulieder. Nus dem Nachloppe des Gropen. Nuguft bon Ploten Hollermunde. Nebft einem unhouge. Breefwechsel, New York: Druct von Gechthal and Berubart, 1844. 34 p. LNH; MH; WM. 44-4990

The political and public character of J. K. Polk. [Washington: 1844] 20 p. MH. 44-4991

The political and public character of James K. Polk of Tennessee. Second edition. [Boston: Eastburn's press, 1844?] 20 p. KyU; M; RPB; ViU. 44-4992

The political and public character of James K. Polk of Tennessee. Fourth edition. [Boston: 1844] 20 p. MWA; NN; WHi. 44-4993

The political contrast. [A compilation of authentic documents] Philadelphia: 1844. 16 p. MBAt; MnU; PPL; TxU. 44-4994

The political text book for reference, containing a complete statement of the votes thrown for William Henry Harrison and Martin Van Buren at the presidential election in 1840; together with a great variety of other useful information. Compiled from the official returns. Boston: Bradbury, Soden and company, 1844. 32 p. InHi; MB; MBevHi; MH; MHi. 44-4995

Politician's register exhibiting the complete election returns of all the states by counties, &c. 1844. Sixth edition. New York: [1844?] 32 p. PHi. 44-4996

The politician's returns, being a supplement to the Whig almanac for 1844, showing the complete election returns of all the states by counties, list of members of Congress.... third edition. New York: Greeley and McElrath, [1844] 32 p. PScr-Hi. 44-4997

Polk, James Knox, 1795-1849. Biographical sketch of James K. Polk, the democratic candidate for the presidency. Nashville: Jno. P. Heiss, printer, 1844? 16 p. WHi. 44-4998

Polk, Josiah F. A defence of the protestant Bible, as published by the Bible societies, against the charge raised against it by the Rev. Dr. Ryder, president of the College of Jesuits at Georgetowen, D.C... New York: Leavitt, Trow and company; Washington, D.C.: William M. Morrison, 1844. GEU; MBAt; NNG; PPPrHi; RPB. 44-4999

The Polk and Dallas songster, a collection of Democratic melodies for glee clubs. Ithaca: Andrus, Woodruff and Gauntlett, [1844] 8 p. CtY; MH; PPL. 44-5000

Pollok, James. Speech in defence of the tariff of 1842, in the House, May 1, 1844 [Washington: printed at Gideon's Office, 1844] 16 p. In; M. 44-5001

Pollok, Robert, 1798-1827. The course of time, by Robert Pollok, with a memoir of the author and an ample index, compiled for this edition. New York: D. Appleton and company, 1844. 3-233 p. MH; MHolliHi; NBuT; WST. 44-5002

Pollok, Robert, 1798-1827. The course of time, a poem... with a memoir of the author, by W.L. Prall. A copious index,

and an analysis prefixed to each book. Philadelphia: Anners, 1844. 256 p. MH; MiDMCh; NnStM; OO. 44-5003

Pollok, Robert, 1798-1827. The course of time, a poem with a memoir of the author. Portland: Sanborn and Carter, 1844. 288 p. CtHT-W; IEG; IU; MeHi; OCl. 44-5004

Pollok, Robert, 1798-1827. The course of time, a poem...With an enlarged index, a memoir of the author, and an analysis prefixed to each book. Revised edition. Concord, New Hampshire: Morrill, Silsby and company, 1844. 207 p. CtHWatk; MH; MnU. 44-5005

Pollok, Robert, 1798-1827. The course of time. Bound with poetical works of G. Crabbe; and poetical works of Reginald Heber. Philadelphia, Pennsylvania: printed by Grigg, 1844. USl. 44-5006

Pollok, Robert, 1798-1827. The poetical works. Philadelphia: Grigg, 1844. MChi. 44-5007

Polo, Marco, 1779-1846. Travels of Marco Polo, greatly amended and enlarged from valuable early manuscripts recently published by the French society of geography, and in Italy by Count Baldelli Boni, with copious notes, illustrating the routes and observations of the author and comparing with those of more recent travellers. New York: Harper and brothers, 1844. 326 p. CSb; MCR. 44-5008

Pomey, Francois Antoine, 1618-1673. Pantheon of the heathen gods and illustrious heroes. Revised for classical course of ed. and adpt. for use of students of every age of either sex; illus. Baltimore: Joseph Neal, 1844. 305 p. IaDuU; IEG; LN. 44-5009

Pond, Enoch, 1791-1881. First principles of the oracles of God. Boston: Sabbath School, 1844. MBC. 44-5010

Pond, Enoch, 1791-1881. Wickliffe and his times. Philadelphia: American Sunday School Union, 1844. 197 p. ScCoT. 44-5011

Pond, Enoch, 1791-1882. Mather family. Boston: Massachusetts Sabbath School Society, 1844. 180 p. CtSoP; MeBa; MnHi; TNV; ViRU. 44-5012

Pond, Enoch, 1791-1882. Mather family. Second edition. Boston: Sabbath School Society [1844] 180 p. MB; MBC; MH. 44-5013

Pond, Enoch, 1791-1882. The young pastors guide: or, lectures on pastoral duties. By Enoch Pond, D.D., professor in the theological seminary, Bangor. Bangor: E. F. Duren, 1844. 377 p. COD; ICP; MeBaT; NbCrD; TJaU. 44-5014

Pond, Samuel William, 1808-1891. Dakota wiwangapi wowapi. Catechism in Sioux. New Haven: Printed by Hitchcock and Stafford, 1844. 12 p. CtY; MBAt. 44-5015

Poor, N. Peabody. Haldeman's picture of Louisville, directory, and business advertiser, for 1844-1845. Compiled by N. Peabody Poor. Louisville, 1844. 248 p. ICP; ICU; MdHi; WHi. 44-5016

Poor Wills almanac, ...1845, ...Philadelphia: Joseph M'Dowell, [1844] [36] p. MWA; WHi. 44-5017

Porcher, Frederick A. Report on manures read before the Black Oak Agricultural Society. Charleston: Miller and Browne, 1844. 15 p. MBHo; ScCC. 44-5018

Porter, Charles Summerfield. Sermon.... [Our country's danger and security] Utica: R.W. Roberts, printer, 1844. 20 p. NCH; NjR; RPB. 44-5019

Porter, Ebenezer, 1771-1834. Lectures on homiletics and preaching, and on public prayer; together with sermons and letters. Second edition. New York: Ezra Collier, 1844. 418 p. GMM; IaB; KyLoP; MnSM; NNUT. 44-5020

Porter, Ebenezer, 1771-1834. The rhetorical reader; consisting of instructions for regulating the voice, with rhetorical notation, illustrating inflection, emphasis and modulation; and a course of rhetorical exercises. Designed for the use of academies and high-schools. ....Two hundred thirtieth edition, with an appendix. Cincinnati: W. H. Moore and company, 1844. 304 p. ICU. 44-5021

Porter, Henry Bliss, 1799?-1866. Theology in verse. New Haven: J.H. Benham, 1844. 22 p. Ct; CtHC; CtY; RPB. 44-5022

Porter, James. Lectures on come-outism. Boston, 1844. 80 p. MBC. 44-5023

Porter, James. Three lectures delivered in the First Methodist Episcopal Church, in Lynn, Massachustts, December 1843, on come-outism, ...By Rev. James Porter.... Boston: Reid and Rand, 1844. 80 p. MiD-B; MTop; NH; NjR. 44-5024

Porter, Jane, 1776-1850. The Scottish

chiefs. A romance. Hartford: S. Andrus and Son, 1844. 5 v. in 3. NoLoc. 44-5025

Porter, Jane, 1776-1850. Thadeus of Warsaw. A new and revised edition. New York: The American News Company, 1844. 536 p. MoSCBC; NdCan. 44-5026

Porter, Jane, 1776-1850. Thadeus of Warsaw. A new and revised edition, with addition of new notes. Philadelphia: Porter and Coates, 1844. 536 p. CoGP; FTa; IaLeo; ScCF. 44-5027

Porter, Jane, 1776-1850. Thadeus of Warsaw. A new and revised edition. Arlington edition. New York: Hurst and company, 1844. 461 p. IaMayr; KAn; KyWA; OO; RPaw. 44-5028

Porter, John Scott. Unitarianism the faith of the apostles. First series. No. 207. By Rev. J. Scott Porter. Boston: James Munroe and company, 1844. 46 p. IaHi; MeB; MH-AH; OClWHi; RP. 44-5029

Porter, Noah. Theodore Parker and liberal Christianity. New Haven: 1844. 33 p. MB; MBC; MCM; MH-AH. 44-5030

Porter, William Denison, 1810-1883. An oration, delivered before the Independent order of Odd Fellows of the state of South Carolina, upon their third anniversary, January 1, 1844. Charleston: Burges and James, 1844. 24 p. ScC; ScCC; ScU. 44-5031

The Portland directory....1844. By Harlowe Harris. Portland: Thurston, Ilsley and company, printers, 1844. 101 p. MBNEH; MeHi. 44-5032

Portraits of Methodist preachers; and other engravings. ....New York: G. Lane

and P. P. Sanford, for the Methodist Episcopal Church, [1844] [300] p. IEG; KMcpC. 44-5033

Portsmouth, Ohio. Common council. Additional ordinances of the town of Portsmouth, passed since 1832. Portsmouth: Tribune, 1844. 29 p. OHi. 44-5034

The position of the church: in a letter to the author of "The position of the evangelical party in the Episcopal Church." [Purparting to come] from one no longer in a false position.... Philadelphia: George and Wayne, 1844. 72 p. CSansS; MAnP; NCH; NjR; PPL-R. 44-5035

Post, Truman M. Address to the alumni association of McKendree College. Lebanon, Illinois: 1844. 20 p. MnHi. 44-5036

Potter, Alonzo, 1800-1865. Political economy; its objects, uses, and principles considered with reference to the condition of the American people. With a summary, for the use of students. ....D.D. New York: Harper and brothers, 1844. 318 p. OCY; OSW; PHC; RPE; ScGrw. 44-5037

Potter, Alonzo, 1800-1865. The school and the schoolmaster: manual for the use of teachers, employers, trustees, inspectors, etc., by Alonzo Potter and George B. Emerson. New York: Harper, 1844. 552 p. PU; WHi; WU. 44-5038

Potter, Alonzo, 1800-1865. The school: its objects, relations and uses. New York: 1844. MBC. 44-5039

Potter, Elisha Reynolds. 1811-1882. Speech of Mr. Potter, of Rhode Island, on the memorial of the Democratic members of the legislature of Rhode Island, delivered in the House, March 7, 9, and 12, 1844. Washington: 1844. 13 p. MH; MiD-B; PHi, RPA; WHi. 44-5040

Potter, Horatio, 1802-1887. Discourse on religious tendencies of the age and etc. preached in St. Peter's Church. Albany, November 23, 1844. Albany, 1844. 32 p. MB; PHi. 44-5041

Potter, Horatio, 1802-1887. Rightly dividing the word of truth. A sermon on the religious tendencies of the age, and the consequent duty of the Christian minister.... Albany: Erastus H. Pease, 1844. 32 p. CtHT; MBC; NGH; NjR; WHi. 44-5042

Potter, James Brown Mason. Oration delivered at Kingston, Rhode Isand, July 4, 1843. Boston: T.H. Webb and company, 1844. 24 p. MBAt; MiD-B; NCH; RPB. 44-5043

Potter, R.K. The Boston temperance songster; a collection of songs and hymns for temperance societies, original and selected. Boston: William White, 1844. 64 p. MB; MBC; MDovC. 44-5044

Poughkeepsie farmers almanac, for the year of our Lord 1844, being leap year; and [till July 4] the sixth-eighth year of American independence. George Nagle, 1844. 28 p. DLC. 44-5045

Power, Thomas, 1786-1868. Masonic melodies; adapted to the ceremonies and festivals of the fraternity. Boston: Published by Oliver Ditson, 1844. 105 p. DLC; MeB; MWA; NNUT; PPM. 44-5046

Power, Thomas, 1786-1868. The mountain maid's invitation. Written by Thomas Power. Arranged by Werner. Boston: Oliver Ditson, 1844? 5 p. MH; ViU. 44-5047

Powers, John. A sermon preached on the day of the annual thanksgiving, November 30, 1843. Springfield: Wood and Rupp, printers, 1844. 19 p. CtHWatk; MSHi. 44-5048

Praed, Winthrop Mackworth, 1802-1839. Lillian. New York: Morris, Willis and company, 1844. 10 p. MWH. 44-5049

Praed, Winthrop Mackworth, 1802-1839. The poetical works of Winthrop Mackworth Praed. Now first collected by Rufus W. Griswold. New York: H.G. Langley, 1844. 287 p. IaK; MWA; NbU; PPL; RPA. 44-5050

Pratt, Anne. Dawnings of genius, or, the early lives of some eminent persons of the last century. By Anne Pratt. New York: D. Appleton and company; Philadelphia: George S. Appleton, 1844. 180 p. InCW; MNBedf. 44-5051

Pratt, Enoch, 1781-1860. A comprehensive ecclesiastical and civil history of Eastham, Wellfleet and Orleans; 1644-1844. Yarmouth: 1844. 180 p. DLC; MWA; OClWHi; PHi; WaS. 44-5052

Pratt, Enoch, 1781-1860. A comprehensive history, ecclesiastical and civil, of Eastham, Wellfleet and Orleans, County of Barnstable, Massachusetts from 1644 to 1844. Yarmouth [Massachusetts] Published by W.S. Fisher and company, 1844. 180 p. ICU; MBBC; MNan; Nh-Hi; PHi. 44-5053

Pratt, Parley Parker, 1807-1857. A dialogue between Josh Smith and the devil [n.p.: 1844?] 16 p. CtY; MH. 44-5054

Pratt, Parley Parker, 1807-1857. An exile of Missouri. Appeal to the inhabitants of the state of New York; letter to Queen Victoria; the fountain of knowledge; immortality of the body; intelligence and affection. Nauvoo, Illinois: John Taylor, printer, 1844. 40 p. CSmH; NjR. 44-5055

Pratt, Parley Parker, 1807-1857. A voice of warning, and instruction to all people or an introduction to the faith and doctrine of the Church of Jesus Christ, of Latter Day Saints. Third American edition. Nauvoo, Illinois: Printed by J. Taylor, 1844. 284 p. DLC; ICN; MWA; NN; PPRF. 44-5056

Pratt, Parley Parker, 1809-1857. An appeal to the inhabitants of the state of New York, letter to Queen Victoria. Nauvoo, Illinois: John Taylor, printer, 1844? 20 p. CSmH; NNN. 44-5057

Pratt, Stillman. The two Samuels; or, the great contrast. Boston: Massachusetts Sabbath School Society, 1844. MBC. 44-5058

Pray, Lewis G. The Boston Sunday school hymn book: with devotional exercises. Boston: Benjamin H. Greene, 1844. 180 p. MB; MBAU. 44-5059

Premium treatise: Romanism incompatible with republican institutions, by Civis. New York: American Protestant Society, 1844. 107 p. GDecCT. 44-5060

Prentiss' collection of easy cotillions.

Arranged for flute, clairinet or violin. With figures. By a professor. Boston: Prentiss, 1844. 15 p. MB. 44-5061

The Presbyterian almanac adapted for use in every part of the United States.... for the year 1845.... Philadelphia: Presbyterian Board of Publication, [1844] 48 p. MWA; NGos; NjR. 44-5062

Presbyterian and Congregation Convention, 1844. Minutes of the Presbyterian and Congregational convention, held at Cleveland, Ohio. June 20, 1844. Cleveland: T.H. Smead, 1844. 23 p. OO. 44-5063

Presbyterian Church in the United States of America. Board of education. Annual report of the Board of education of the Presbyterian Church in the United States of America presented May, 1844. Philadelphia: Published by the Board, 1844. 28 p. GDecCT; TxDaM. 44-5064

Presbyterian Church in the United States of America. Board of Foreign Missions. The seventh annual report of the Board of Foreign Missions of the Presbyterian Church, in the United States of America. May, 1844. New York: Published for the Board, 1844. 42 p. TNMB; TxDaM. 44-5065

Presbyterian Church in the United States of America. Board of Missions. Annual report of the Board of missions of the general assembly of the Presbyterian Church in the United States of America. Presented May, 1844. Philadelphia: Published by the Board, William S. Martien, printer, 1844. 48 p. GDecCT; MnHi; OkHi; TxDaM. 44-5066

Presbyterian Church in the United

States of America. Board of Publication. Remarkable places mentioned in the Holy scriptures. n.p.: Presbyterian Board of Publication, 1844. KyLo. 44-5067

Presbyterian Church in the United States of America. Board of Publication. A series of tracts on the doctrines, order, and polity of the Presbyterian Church in the United States of America. Philadelphia: Presbyterian Board of Publication, 1844. DLC; TxU. 44-5068

Presbyterian Church in the United States of America. Board of Publication. Sixth annual report of the board of publication of the Presbyterian Church in the United States of America. Presented to the general Assembly, May, 1844. Philadelphia: Paul T. Jones, publishing agent. William S. Martien, printer, 1844. 16 p. GDecCT; MnHi; WHi. 44-5069

Presbyterian Church in the United States of America. Buffalo Presbytery. Trial of the Rev. Asa T. Hopkins, pastor of the First Presbyterian Church, Buffalo, before a special meeting of the Buffalo Presbytery; commencing October 22, and ending October 31, 1844 [Buffalo: 1844] 39 p. DLC. 44-5070

Presbyterian Church in the United States of America. Columbus, Georgia Presbytery. Minutes of the annual sessions of the Flint River Presbytery, held at Columbus, Georgia. April, 1844. Columbus: Printed at the Enquirer office, 1844. 14 p. NcMHi. 44-5071

Presbyterian Church in the United States of America. Fayetteville, North Carolina Presbytery. Minutes. Fayetteville, 1844. PPPrHi. 44-5072

Presbyterian Church in the United States of America. General Assembly. Parish psalmody. A collection of psalms and hymns for public worship; containing Dr. Watts' verification of the Psalm of David, entire, a large portion of Dr. Watts' hymns and psalms and hymns by other authors. Philadelphia: 1844. 708 p. IU. 44-5073

Presbyterian Church in the United States of America. Indiana. To Christians in slaveholding states by the Synod of Indiana. n.p., n.p., 1844? In. 44-5074

Presbyterian Church in the United States of America. Kind words for his young friends. By Uncle William. Philadelphia: Presbyterian Board of Publiscation, 1844. 137 p. GDecCT. 44-5075

Presbyterian Church in the United States of America. Presbyteries of Hudson. The support due to the Christian ministry. A pastoral letter from the Presbytery of Hudson, to the churches under its care. Goshen, New York: Printed by Mead and Webb, 1844. 24 p. NNUT; PPPrHi. 44-5076

Presbyterian Church in the United States of America. South Carolina. Bethel Presbytery. Both sides heard or, The independent Presbyterian and a member of Bethel Presbytery. Columbia: Issued from Morgan's letter press, 1844. 85 p. NcMHi. 44-5077

Presbyterian Church in the United States of America. South Carolina. General convention. Pastoral letter of the general convention of the Independent Presbyterian Church with extract from the minutes. Columbia, South

Carolina: issued from Morgan's Letter Press, 1844. 15 p. NcMHi. 44-5078

Presbyterian Church in the United States of America. Synod of Kentucky. An address to the Presbyterians of Kentucky for the instruction and emancipation of their slaves, by a committee of the Synod of Kentucky. Louisville: 1844. 16 p. NcMHi; NjR. 44-5079

Presbyterian Church in the United States of America. Synod of Mississippi. A catechism for the religious instruction of persons of colour. Charleston: Printed for the author, 1844. 76 p. NN-Sc. 44-5080

Presbyterian Church in the United States of America. Synod of New York and New Jersey. Minutes of the Synod of New York and New Jersey, October, 1844. New York: Printed by J.F. Trow and company, 1844. 20 p. MBC. 44-5081

Presbyterian Church in the United States of America. Synod of New York. Minutes of the particular synod of New York. October 1843 and May 1844. New York: J. Post, printer, 1844. 40 p. NcMHi. 44-5082

Prescott, William Hickling, 1796-1859. The conquest of Mexico, by N.H. Prescott. New York: Harper, 1844. 3 v. LN. 44-5083

Prescott, William Hickling, 1796-1859. History of the conquest of Mexico, with a preliminary view of the ancient Mexican civilization, and the life of the conqueror, Hernando Cortes. New York: Harper and brothers, 1844. 3 v. CU-B; MH; NSyU; OOxM; ViU. 44-5084

Prescott, William Hickling, 1796-1859. History of the reign of Ferdinand and Isabella the Catholic. Tenth edition. Boston: Charles C. Little and James Brown, [1844] 3 v. MNBedf; MsCliM; PHC. 44-5085

Presidential chart. Here's to you, Harry Clay! Next president of these United States. Whig principles are a tariff to protect every branch of Amerian industry, etc. [Boston?]: 1844. MH. 44-5086

Preston, Lyman, b. 1795. Preston's treatise on book-keeping by single entry, adapted to the use of retailers, farmers, mechanics, and common schools. Being taken from Preston's larger work on book-keeping, wich contains both double and single entry. New York: Collins, brother, and company, 1844. 224 p. MB; MH; NNC; TxU. 44-5087

Preston, Lyman, b. 1795. Stories for the whole family, young and old, male and female. New York: Huntington and Savage, 1844. 230 p. OO; UU. 44-5088

Preston, Paul. Paul Preston's voyages, travels and remarkable adventures; as related by himself. With engravings. Boston: Munroe and Francis, 1844. 336 p. NWebyC. 44-5089

Price, David. English speller. New York, 1844. NoLoc. 44-5090

Price, William. Clement Falconer; or the memoirs of a young whig... Baltimore: Printed by J. Young, 1844. 2 v. in 1. NN. 44-5091

Priest, Josiah, 1788-1851. A copy of the grants to the Van Rensselaer and

Livingston families together with a history of the settlement of Albany. Gathered from authentic sources and published for the information of the renters. Albany: Printed by J. Munsell, 1844. 32 p. CtY; MiU-C; MWA; NHi; NN. 44-5092

Prince, firm, Nurserymen, Flushing. Prince's descriptive catalogue of fruit and ornamental trees, shrubbery, etc. ....Thirty-fourth edition. New York: W. Osborn, 1844. 108 p. DLC; MiU-C; PPM. 44-5093

Princeton Theological Seminary. Society of Inquiry on Missions. Constitution and by-laws. Princeton: 1844. 16 p. MBC; OO. 44-5094

Princeton University. Examination papers in the mathematical course of the College of New Jersey. Princeton: J.T. Robinson, 1844. 78 p. DLC; NhD. 44-5095

Principles of the American government containing the Declaration of Independence; Bill of Rights; Articles of Confederation; Constitution of the United States; constitution of Pennsylvania.... Philadelphia: J. Van Court, 1844. 90 p. DLC; NN; P; PHi. 44-5096

Prindle's almanac for 1845. By Charles Prindle. New Haven, Connecticut: A.H. Maltby and company, [1844] MWA. 44-5097

Prior, Margaret Barrett Allen, 1773-1842. Walks of usefulness, or, reminiscences of Mrs. Margaret Prior. By Mrs. Sarah R. Ingram. New York: American Foreign Mission Society, 1844. 324 p. CtY; IaMp; IEG; RHi; Vi. 44-5098

Prior, Margaret Barrett Allen, 1773-1842. Walks of usefulness, or, reminiscences of Mrs. Margaret Prior. Second edition. New York: American Foreign Mission Society, 1844. 324 p. M. 44-5099

Prior, Margaret Barrett Allen, 1773-1842. Walks of usefulness, or, reminiscences of Mrs. Margaret Prior. Third cheap edition. New York: the American Foreign Mission Soceity, 1844. 324 p. MBNMHi; ViU; WM. 44-5100

Prior, Margaret Barrett Allen, 1773-1842. Walks of usefulness, or, reminiscences of Mrs. Margaret Prior. Fourth edition. New York: American Foreign Missionary Society, 1844. 324 p. MNutn; ScCoB. 44-5101

Prior, Margaret Barrett Allen, 1773-1842. Walks of usefulness, or, reminiscences of Mrs. Margaret Prior. Fifth edition. New York: American Foreign Mission Society, 1844. 324 p. Ia; IaHA; MShM. 44-5102

Prior, Margaret Barrett Allen, 1773-1842. Walks of usefulness, or, reminiscenses of Mrs. Margaret Prior. Sixth edition. New York: American Foreign Missionary Society, 1844. 324 p. MBC; NcSalL; NSyHi. 44-5103

Prison Association of New York. First report of the Prison Association of New York. December, 1844. New York: Jared W. Bell, 1844? 63 p. MB; PPM. 44-5104

Proceedings of a meeting in favor of municipal reform, held at Tammany Hall, on Friday evening, March 22, 1844. New York: W. B. and T. Smith, 1844. 24 p. WHi. 44-5105

Procter, Bryan Waller, 1787-1874. English songs, and other poems by Barry Cornwall [pseud.] Boston: William D. Ticknor and company, 1844. 228 p. CtMW; LNH; MH; PPM; OrP. 44-5106

The prodigal son....Baltimore: Metropolitan Press, 1844. 114 p. MdBLC. 44-5107

The prophet: William Smith, editor. New York: S. Brannon and company, 1844 -[1845] Vol. I. MoInRC. 44-5108

Proposed treaty with Texas, a gross usurpation of power. The annexation of Louisiana, a precedent against the constitutionality of the treaty with Texas. Inconsistency of the strict constructionists, who favor that treaty.... Philadelphia: 1844. 8 p. MH; MHi; MiD-B; RPB; Tx. 44-5109

Proscription is itself to be proscribed. Washington: 1844. 8 p. PHi; PPL. 44-5110

Protestant Episcopal Church in the United States of America. Board of Missions. Domestic Committee. Journal of a town in the "Indian Territory," performed by order of the domestic committee of the board of missions of the Protestant Episcopal Church, in the spring of 1844, by their secretary and general agent. New York: 1844. 74 p. CtY; DLC. 44-5111

Protestant Episcopal Church in the United States of America. Board of Missions. Journal of a tour in the "Indian territory" performed by order of the domestic committee of the board of missions of the Protestant Episcopal Church, in the spring of 1844, by their secretary and general agent. New York: Daniel Dana, Junior, 1844. 74 p. CtHT; IaHi; MdBD; NjR; PPL. 44-5112

Protestant Episcopal Church in the United States of America. Board of Missions. Proceedings of the Board of Missions of the Protestant Episcopal Church in the United States of America. New York: Published for the Board of Missions by Daniel Dana, Jr., 1844. 81 p. MBD. 44-5113

Protestant Episcopal Church in the United States of America. Board of Missions. Proceedings of the Board of Missions. Third triennial meeting, Philadelphia, October 3, 1844. [New York, 1844?] 304 p. MnHi. 44-5114

Protestant Episcopal Church in the United States of America. The book of Common Prayer, and administration of the Sacraments. Together with the Psalter. Hartford: Robins and Smith, 1844. 2 v. in 1. MB. 44-5115

Protestant Episcopal Church in the United States of America. The book of Common Prayer, and administration of the sacraments, and other rites and ceremonies of the church according to the use of the Protestant Episcopal Church in the United States of America; together with the Psalter or Psalms of David. Hartford: S. Andrus and Son, 1844. 309 p. DLC; MH; MH-AH. 44-5116

Protestant Episcopal Church in the United States of America. The book of Common Prayer, and administration of the sacraments, and other rites and ceremonies of the Church, according to the use of the Protestant Episcopal

Church in the United States of America. Together with the Psalter, or Psalms of David. New York: Blake, 1844. 466 p. MB; MiU-C. 44-5117

Protestant Episcopal Church in the United States of America. The book of Common Prayer, and administration of the sacraments; and other rites and ceremonies of the Church. Together with the Psalter, or Psalms of David. New York: New York Bible and Common Prayer Book Society [1844] 580 p. MB; OFH. 44-5118

Protestant Episcopal Church in the United States of America. The book of Common Prayer, and administration of the sacraments, and other rites and ceremonies of the church ...together with the Psalter, or Psalms of David. Philadelphia: Carey and Hart, 1844. 680 p. NN. 44-5119

Protestant Episcopal Church in the United States of America. The book of Common Prayer, and administration of the sacraments, and other rites and ceremonies of the church according to the use of the Protestant Episcopal Church in the United States of America, together with the psalter or psalms of David. Philadelphia: J.B. Perry, 1844. MH. 44-5120

Protestant Episcopal Church in the United States of America. Book of Common Prayer. The common prayer, and administration of the sacraments, and other rites. According to the use of the Protestant Episcopal Church in the United States of America. Hartford: S. Andrews and Son, 1844. 208 p. NoLoc. 44-5121

Protestant Episcopal Church in the United States of America. Book of Homilies. Philadelphia: Published by George and Wayne, 1844. 678 p. OrPD. 44-5122

Protestant Episcopal Church in the United States of America. Canons for the government of the Protestant Episcopal Church in the United States of America. Philadelphia: Edward C. Biddle, 1844. 51 p. MdBP; MnHi; NjR. 44-5123

Protestant Episcopal Church in the United States of America. Debates and proceedings of the general triennial convention, held in Philadelphia from October 4 to 24, 1844. Philadelphia: Stavely and McCalla, 1844. 100 p. CtHT; MB; MdBD; NBuDD; WHi. 44-5124

Protestant Episcopal Church in the United States of America. The denominations and the church. Philadelphia: 1844. PPL-R. 44-5125

Protestant Episcopal Church in the United States of America. Diocese of Alabama. Journal of the proceedings of the thirteenth convention of the Protestant Episcopal Church in the United States of America in the diocese of Alabama. Mobile: Printed by Dade and Thompson, 1844. 34 p. MBD; MiD-B; NBuDD; NN. 44-5126

Protestant Episcopal Church in the United States of America. Diocese of Connecticut. Journal of the proceedings of the sixtieth annual convention. New Haven, June 11th and 12, 1844. New Haven: Stanley and Chapin, printers, 1844. 75 p. MBD; MiD-B; NBuDD. 44-5127

Protestant Episcopal Church in the United States of America. Diocese of Delaware. Journal of the proceedings of the fifty-fourth annual convention of the Protestant Episcopal Church of the Diocese of Delaware, 1844. Wilmington: Wilson and Heald, printed by Harker and Johnson, 1844. 55 p. MBD; MiD; NBuDD. 44-5128

Protestant Episcopal Church in the United States of America. Diocese of Georgia. Journal of the proceedings of the twenty-second annual convention in St. Paul's Church, Augusta commending on the 2d May, 1844. Athens: Clayton and Flint, 1844. 47 p. MBC; NBuDD; NN. 44-5129

Protestant Episcopal Church in the United States of America. Diocese of Indiana. Journal of a special convention of the Protestant Episcopal Church in the United States of America in the Diocese of Indiana, held in Christ Church, Indianapolis, September 5th and 6th, 1844. Lafayette: Henry W. DePuy, 1844. CtHT; InID; InU; MBD; NN. 44-5130

Protestant Episcopal Church in the United States of America. Diocese of Indiana. Journal of the proceedings of the seventh annual convention of the Protestant Episcopal Church in the United States of America in the Dicocese of Indiana; held in Saint Paul's Church, Richmond, Friday, Saturday and Monday, June 7, 8, 10, 1844. Indianapolis: Printed by S.V.B. Noel, 1844. 41 p. ICU; InID; MBD; MiD-MCh; NBuDD. 44-5131

Protestant Episcopal Church in the United States of America. Diocese of Kentucky. Journal of proceedings, of the sixteenth annual convention of the

Protestant Episcopal Church in the United States of America, in the Diocese of Kentucky. To which is appended the constitution and canons of the Diocese. Louisville: Morton and Griswold, 1844. 33 p. MBD; NBuDD; NN. 44-5132

Protestant Episcopal Church in the United States of America. Diocese of Louisiana. Journal of the sixth annual convention in Trinity Church, Natchitoces, on the 18th and 22nd April; and in Christ Church, New Orleans on the 14th and 15th June, 1841. New Orleans: T. Rea, printer, 1844. 24 p. MBD; NBuDD; NN. 44-5133

Protestant Episcopal Church in the United States of America. Diocese of Maryland. Journal of the fifty-sixth annual convention of the Protestant Episcopal Church in the United States of America in Maryland. Baltimore: H. Colburn, 1844. 155 p. MdBD; MiD-MCh; NBuDD. 44-5134

Protestant Episcopal Church in the United States of America. Diocese of Massachusetts. Journal of the fifty-fourth annual convention held in Trinity Church, Boston, June 12, 13, 14, 1844 with appendix. Boston: James B. Dow, office of the Witness and Advocate, 1844. 111 p. MiD-MCh; WHi. 44-5135

Protestant Episcopal Church in the United States of America. Diocese of Mississippi. Journal of the proceedings of the 19th, 20th annual conventions of the Protestant Episcopal Church in the United States of America in the Diocese of Mississippi. Jackson: Printed at the Southern office, 1844-1846. NN. 44-5136

Protestant Episcopal Church in the

United States of America. Diocese of New Hampshire. Journal of the first twenty eight conventions of the Diocese of New Hampshire, 1802-1828, hitherto unpublished together with a reprint of the journals of later conventions (1829-1844) to the consecration of the first Bishop. Tilton: George Burnham Munsey, 1844. 290 p. NBuDD. 44-5137

Protestant Episcopal Church in the United States of America. Diocese of New Hampshire. Journal of the proceedings of the forty-fourth convention Manchester, June 26, 1844. Manchester: Printed by S.F. Wetmore, 1844. 16 p. MiD-B. 44-5138

Protestant Episcopal Church in the United States of America. Diocese of New Jersey. Journal of proceedings of the sixty-first annual convention held in grace in Grace Church, Newark, 1844. Burlington: At the the Missionary Press, 1844. 42 p. MBD. 44-5139

Protestant Episcopal Church in the United States of America. Diocese of New York. Journal of the proceedings of the sixtieth convention of the Protestant Episcopal Church in the United States of America in the Diocese of New York held in St. John's chapel in the city of New York to which is prefixed a list of the Clergy of the diocese. New York: Henry M. Onderdonk, 1844. 234 p. MiD-MCh; NBuDD. 44-5140

Protestant Episcopal Church in the United States of America. Diocese of North Carolina. Journal of the twenty-eighth annual convention of the Protestant Episcopal Church in the United States of America in the state of North Carolina held in St. Peter's Church,

Washington. On Wednesday May 22, Thursday May 23, Friday May 24, Saturday, May 25, and Monday May 27, 1844. Fayetteville: Printed by Edward J. Hale, 1844. 56 p. MiD-B; NBuDD. 44-5141

Protestant Episcopal Church in the United States of America. Diocese of Ohio. Journal of the proceedings of the twenty-seventh annual convention of the Protestant Episcopal Church, Gambier: 1844. OGaK. 44-5142

Protestant Episcopal Church in the United States of America. Diocese of Pennsylvania. Journal of the proceedings of the sixtieth convention. Philadelphia, May 21, 22, 23, 24, 1844. Philadelphia: King and Baird, printers, 1844. 115 p. MiD-B. 44-5143

Protestant Episcopal Church in the United States of America. Diocese of Pennsylvania. Journal of the proceedings of the special convention of the Protestant Episcopal Church in the United States of America in the state of Pennsylvania on Thursday, September 5, 1844. Philadelphia: Published by order of the convention, King and Baird, printers, 1844. 58 p. MB; MdBD; NBuDD; NjR. 44-5144

Protestant Episcopal Church in the United States of America. Diocese of Rhode Island. Circular to members. [Providence, 1844] 8 p. RPB. 44-5145

Protestant Episcopal Church in the United States of America. Diocese of Rhode Island. Journal of proceedings of the fifty-fourth annual convention of the Protestant Episcopal Church in the United States of America in Rhode Island held in Zion Church, Newport,

Tuesday, June 11 and Wednesday, June, 12, 1844. Providence: Samuel C. Blodget, 1844. 59 p. MBD; MiD-MCH; NBuDD; NGH; RNHi. 44-5146

Protestant Episcopal Church in the United States of America. Diocese of South Carolina. Journal of the proceedings of the fifty-fifth annual convention of the Protestant Episcopal Church in the United States of America in South Carolina, 1844. Charleston: Printed by Miller and Browne, 1844. 77 p. MBD; MiD-MCh; NBuDD; NN. 44-5147

Protestant Episcopal Church in the United States of America. Diocese of Tennessee. Journal of the proceedings of the sixteenth annual convention in Christ Church, Nashville, 1844. Clarksville: Printed by Charles Faxon, at the office of the Primitive Standard, 1844. 31 p. MBD; MBuDD; NN. 44-5148

Protestant Episcopal Church in the United States of America. Diocese of Vermont. Journal of the proceedings of the fifty-fourth annual convention. Burlington: Chauncey Goodrich, 1844. 48 p. ICN; ICU; MBD; MiD-B; NBuDD. 44-5149

Protestant Episcopal Church in the United States of America. Diocese of Virginia. Journal of the convention of the Protestant Episcopal Church in the United States of America in the Diocese of Virginia. Richmond: Printed at the office of the "The Southern Literary Messenger," 1844. 67 p. MBD; MiD-B; NBuDD. 44-5150

Protestant Episcopal Church in the United States of America. Diocese of Western New York. Journal of the proceedings of the seventh annual convention of the Protestant Episcopal Church in the United States of America in the Diocese of Western New York. Utica: Printed for the convention, H.H. Curtiss, printer, 1844. 97 p. MBD; MiD-B; MWA; NN; NUt. 44-5151

Protestant Episcopal Church in the United States of America. General Theology Seminary. The act of incorporation, constitution, and statues of the General Theological Seminary of the Protestant Episcopal Church in the United States of America. Published by order of the trustees, June, 1844. New York: Henry M. Onderdonk, 1844. 32 p. NBuDD. 44-5152

Protestant Episcopal Church in the United States of America. House of Bishops. Proceedings of the right reverend the bishops of the Protestant Episcopal Church in the United States of America, as visitors of the general theological seminary. Published by order of the House of Bishops. New York: James A. Sparks, 1844. 31 p. NNUT; PHi; TSewU. 44-5153

Protestant Episcopal Church in the United States of America. House of Bishops. Tract showing the sentiments of the bishops or the American church on some of the points recently discussed among Episcopalians in England and America. Taken from the pastoral letters of the House of Bishops from the year 1808 to the year 1844. Philadelphia: Stavely and McCalls, 1844. 24 p. NNG. 44-5154

Protestant Episcopal Church in the United States of America. Hymnal. Hymns of the Protestant Episcopal

Church in the United States of America. Hartford: Robins and Smith, 1844. 124 p. NNG. 44-5155

Protestant Episcopal Church in the United States of America. Hymnal. Hymns of the Protestant Episcopal Church in the United States of America. New York: H. and S. Raynor, 1844. [463]-570 p. NNG. 44-5156

Protestant Episcopal Church in the United States of America. Hymnal. Hymns suited to the feasts and fasts of the Church, and other occasions of public worship. Philadelphia: Carey and Hart, 1844. 286 p. NN. 44-5157

Protestant Episcopal Church in the United States of America. Journal of a tour in the Indian Territory, performed by order of the domestic committee of the Board of Missions... in the spring of 1844, by their secretary and general agent. New York: Published for the Domestic Committee of the Board of Missions by Daniel Dana, Jr., 1844. 74 p. DLC; MH; MoU; OOxM; PPL. 44-5158

Protestant Episcopal Church in the United States of America. Journal of the proceedings of the Bishops, clergy and laity, of the Protestant Episcopal Church in the United States of America. New York: James A. Sparks, 1844. 320 p. MBD. 44-5159

Protestant Episcopal Church in the United States of America. The novelties which disturb our peace. Philadelphia: 1844. PPL-R. 44-5160

Protestant Episcopal Church in the United States of America. Pastoral let-ter, 1844. New York: 1844. CtHT. 44-5161

Protestant Episcopal Church in the United States of America. The position of the church. Philadelphia: 1844. PPL-R. 44-5162

Protestant Episcopal Church in the United States of America. Proceedings of the court convened under the third canon of 1844, in the city of New York, on Tuesday, December 10, 1844, for the trial of the Right Rev. Benjamin T. Onderdonk, Bishop of New York. New York: D. Appleton and company, 1844. 333 p. NcD. 44-5163

Protestant Episcopal Church in the United States of America. Proceedings of the Right Reverend, the Bishops of the Protestant Episcopal Church as visitors of the General Theological Seminary. Published by order of the House of Bishops. New York: James A. Sparks, 1844. 32 p. CtHT; MiDMCh; MSJJPED; NBuDD. 44-5164

Protestant Episcopal Church in the United States of America. South Carolina Diocese. Circulars of the Society for the Relief of the Widows and Orphans of the Clergy of the Protestant Episcopal Church in South Carolina. Charleston: 1844. PPL. 44-5165

Protestant Episcopal Church in the United States of America. Theological Seminary of Virginia. A catalogue of the officers and students and alumni of the Theological Seminary of the Protestant Episcopal Church, in the Diocese of Virginia, 1843-1844. Fairfax County, Virginia, 1844. [Richmond: 1844] 18 p. CSansS. 44-5166

Protestant Episcopal Society for the Advancement of Christianity in South Carolina. The thirty- fourth annual report of the trustees preceded by the minutes of the anniversary meeting to which are annexed the treasurer's account, the names of the officers, a list of the life and annual members, etc and the act of incorporation and the constitution. Charleston: Printed by Miller and Browne, 1844. 530 p. ScU. 44-5167

Protestant Episcopal Sunday School Union. A descriptive catalogue of books of instruction, Sunday School requisites, and library books. New York: General Protestant Episcopal Sunday School Union, 1844. 488 p. MdBD; NjR. 44-5168

Protestant Episcopal Tract Society. The meaning of the word baptism. New York: Published by the Protestant Episcopal Tract Society, 1844. 8 p. InID; NjPT; TSewU. 44-5169

Protestant Episcopal Tract Society. The nature and benefits of Holy baptism. New York: Protestant Episcopal Tract Society, 1844. 29 p. InID; KyLoS; MBC; MiD-B. 44-5170

The Protestant trial in controverted points of faith. Philadelphia: M. Fithian, 1844. 208 p. NPStA. 44-5171

The Protestants' objections to points of Catholic doctrine; or, the Protestants' trial in controverted points of faith. By the written word. Philadelphia: Henry McGrath and sons, 1844. 208 p. ILM; MdBJ; MiDU; MoSU. 44-5172

The Providence almanac and business directory for the year 1845. By Benjamin

F. Moore. Providence: B.F. Moore, [1844] 141 p. CtHWatk; MH. 44-5173

The Providence almanac; embracing a business directory of Providence, Newport, Warren, Bristol, Pawtucket and Woonsocket, Rhode Island; also of Fall River, Massachusetts. Providence, Rhode Island: Benjamin F. Moore, 1844. MH. 44-5174

Providence, Rhode Island. By-laws of the school committee, and regulations of the public schools, in the city of Providence. Providence: Knowles and Vose, printers, 1844. 22 p. CtHT; IU; MB; RHi; RNHi. 44-5175

Providence, Rhode Island. First Baptist Church. A list of members, with the general rules and regulations of the first Baptist Church, in Providence, Rhode Island. Providence: Knowles and Vose, printers, 1844. 20 p. NjR; PCA; RHi; RNHi; ViRU. 44-5176

Providence, Rhode Island. Fourth Congregational Church. Manual of the church. Providence: B.T. Albro, 1844. 30 p. MH; RPB. 44-5177

Providence, Rhode Island. Grace Church. Annual report of the committee for the distribution of the Sunday offerings. Providence: 1844. 4 p. RPB. 44-5178

Providence, Rhode Island. Grace Church. Catalogue of books, 1844 [Providence: 1844] 12 p. RPB. 44-5179

Providence, Rhode Island. A list of persons assessed in the city tax of $81,086.04; being the amount produced by an assessment of 36 cents on each $100 of ratable property. Ordered by the city council, June, 1844; with the amount of valuation and tax of each. Providence: H.H. Brown, 1844. 74 p. RHi. 44-5180

Providence, Rhode Island. Methodist Episcopal Church. Catalogue of the sunday school library, of the Power Street Methodist Episcopal Church. Providence: B.F. Moore, printer, 1844. 16 p. RHi. 44-5181

Providence, Rhode Island. Providence directory, containing names of the inhabitants, their occupations, places of business and of residence; with lists of the streets, lanes, wharves, etc. Also, banks, insurance officers and other public institutions, municipal officers of the city, etc., etc. The whole carefully collected and arranged. Providence: H.H. Brown, 1844. 246 p. IaHA; MH; RHi. 44-5182

Providence and Worcester Railroad Company. Charters of the Providence and Worcester Railroad Company. [Providence? 1844] 16 p. RHi; RP. 44-5183

The proviso faction in New York: Its course and objects briefly and calmly stated... Albany: Argus Extra, 1844. 7 p. MiU. 44-5184

The psalmist: a new collection of hymns for the use of the Baptist churches. By Baron Stow and S. F. Smith. Boston: Gould, Kendall and Lincoln, 1844. 720 p. IaPeC; KOtU; MH-AH; Nh; OO. 44-5185

The psalmist: a new collection of hymns for the use of the Baptist churches. By Baron Stow and S. F. Smith. Philadel-phia: American Baptist Publication and Sunday School Society, Boston, 1844. 704 p. KyLoS. 44-5186

Psi Upsilon Fraternity. Catalogue. New York: J. S. and C. Adams, printers, 1844. 37 p. MdHi; MnHi; MWHi. 44-5187

Publius, pseud. Letter to the members of the Pennsylvania legislature, on the subject of the state debt. Philadelphia: King and Baird, printers, 1844. 24 p. MB; MH; MHi; PPAmP; PPL. 44-5188

Puget, Loisa, 1810-1884. Dear Mother adieu! A la grace de dieu. Romance. Translated from the French by B.S. Barclay. The music by Madelle Loisa Puget. Philadelphia: A. Fiot; New York: W. Dubois, 1844. 3 p. MB; ViU. 44-5189

Pugh, Jordan A. An address delivered on the anniversary of the first settlement of Ohio, April 8, 1844... Cincinnati: E. Morgan and company, 1844. 17 p. MdBJ. 44-5190

Pugin, Augustus Welby Northmore, 1812-1852. Glossary of ecclesiastical ornament and costume, compiled and illustrated from ancient authorities and examples... translated by Rev. Bernard Smith. New York: Covent Garden, 1844. MoK. 44-5191

Pumroy, John N. A defence of our naturalization laws, with a friendly warning to members of the Native American Party... Norristown [Pennsylvania] A. Slemmer, printer, 1844. 22 p. GAM-R; OClWHi; P; PPi. 44-5192

Punch. Bowl of "Punch"; or selections from the London Charivari. With illustrations by Leech and others.

Philadelphia: 1844. MBAt; MdBP; MH; PHi; PU. 44-5193

Punch. London medical student. Philadelphia: 1844. MB. 44-5194

Punch. Natural history of courtship. By Punch. Philadelphia: Carey and Hart, 1844. MH; NPV. 44-5195

Punchard, George, 1806-1880. A view of Congregationalism, its principles and doctrines, the testimony of ecclesiastical history in its favor, its practice and its advantages, by George Punchard. With an introductory essay by R.S. Storrs, D.D. Andover: Allen, Morrill and Wardwell, 1844. 331 p. CSansS; GDecCT; KyLoS; MAnHi; PCC. 44-5196

Punchard, George, 1806-1880. A view of Congregationalism, its principles and doctrines, the testimony of ecclesiastical history in its favor, its practice and its advantages. By George Punchard. With an introductory essay, by R.S. Storrs, D.D. Second edition. Andover: Allen, Morrill and Wardwell, 1844. 331 p. CSansS; ICT; MLaw; OO; TChU. 44-5197

Pusey, Edward Bouverie, 1800-1882. The day of judgement; a sermon preached on the twentieth Sunday after Trinity, in St. Peter's Church, Brighton.... From the second Oxford edition. Philadelphia: C. Sherman, 1844. 40 p. CtB; NNG; PHi; TMeC. 44-5198

Putnam, George, 1807-1878. An oration delivered at Cambridge, before the Phi Beta Kappa Society in Harvard University, August 29, 1844. Boston: C.C. Little and J. Brown, 1844. 36 p. ICU; MiD-B; NCH; PPAmP; RPA. 44-5199

Putnam, I.A. An oration, delivered in Pembroke, N.H., October 30, 1844, on the occasion of erecting a monument to the memory of Isaac Kinsman. Concord: Morrill, Silsby and company, 1844. 19 p. MH; MiD-B; Nh; Nh-Hi. 44-5200

Putnam, John M. A sermon, preached at Dunbarton, New Hampshire, January 7, 1844, occasioned by the death of Rev. Walter Harris, D.D. ....By John M. Putnam.... Concord: press of Asa McFarland, 1844. 24 p. MBC; MBNEH; MW. 44-5201

Pycroft, James, 1813-1895. A course of English reading. New York, 1844. 313 p. ICarbT. 44-5202

Q-R

Quackenbos, C.P.A.M. An elementary arithmetic... upon the basis of the works of George R. Perkins. New York: 1844. 144 p. VtMidSM. 44-5203

Quain, J. A series of anatomical plates, with references and physiological comments, illustrating the structure of the different parts of the human body. By J. Quain and W. J. E. Wilson. Philadelphia: 1844. MBM; ViU. 44-5204

Quarterman, James. A narrative of facts upon which is based a protest against the consecration of.... Dr. Hawks.... by James Quarterman.... Philadelphia: I. M. Moss, 1844. 8 p. CtHT; MB; NGH; NSmb; PPL. 44-5205

Quarterman, James. A reply to the speech of the Rev. F. L. Hawks, D.D. ....October 11th, 1844, before the general convention of the Protestant Episcopal Church.... Flushing, Long Island: printed for the author, 1844. CtHT; NcU; NN; NSmb; PPL. 44-5206

Quarterman, Robert. Motives and encouragements. An address before the Association for the Religious Instruction of the Negroes, in Liberty County, Georgia; delivered at the annual meeting, January 23, 1844. By the Rev. Robert Quarterman.... Savannah: Thomas Price, printer, 1844. 44 p. KyLy; TNF. 44-5207

Quaw, James E. Bible baptism, or the immerser instructed. From various sources. Third edition. Detroit: Benjamin Wood, 1844. 391 p. ICNBT; ViRut. 44-5208

Queens County, New York, Agricultural Society. Annual report of the transactions of the Queen's County Agricultural Society, containing the address of D.S. Dickinson, etc. for 1843. Hempstead, L.I.: 1844. PPL-R. 44-5209

Queens County, New York, Horticultural Society. Constitution and by-laws of the Queens County Horticultural Society. Flushing, New York: 1844. 12 p. MBHo. 44-5210

Questions for examination in Whately's elements of rhetoric. Boston: J. Munroe and company, 1844. MH. 44-5211

Quinby, George Washington. A lecture showing why females should be interested in odd fellowship, delivered in Odd Fellow's Hall, Saco, May 26, 1844, on the opening of the hall for the admission of ladies. Portland: Thurston, Ilsley and company, printer, 1844. 16 p. MH. 44-5212

Quincy, Josiah. A catalogue of the officers and students of Harvard University, for the academical year. 1844-45. Cambridge: Metcalf and company, 1844. 62 p. A-Ar. 44-5213

Raines, Aylett. A sermon against the doctrine of the serpent. By Aylete

Raines, of Paris, Kentucky. With appropriate introductory remarks, by Jesse Kennedy, September, 1844. Frankfort, Kentucky: Hodges, Todd and Pruett, 1844. 16 p. PCA. 44-5214

Ralston, Samuel. Defence of an inquiry into the propriety of using an Evangelical Psalmody in the worship of God; against the objection of Rev. John T. Pressly. Pittsburg: Printed by George Parkin, 1844. 165 p. CtHC; KyLoP; OCoC; PPiW; PPPrHi. 44-5215

Ramani, Felice, 1788-1865. Songs, duetts.... opera.... [Philadelphia: King and Baird, 1844] 24 p. DLC. 44-5216

Ramsey, Alex. Speech of Mr. Alex Ramsey, of Pennsylvania, on the tariff bill. Delivered in the House, April 29, 1844. Washington: 1844. 16 p. In; NNC. 44-5217

Ramsey, William. The millennium and the New Jerusalem contrasted. New York: Joseph Levon, 1844. 26 p. In; PPL; PPPrHi. 44-5218

Randall and Company, McCausland's Old Brewery, Baltimore, Maryland. The portable tubular steam generator. Manufactured by Randall and company, McCausland Old Brewery, Baltimore, Maryland. Baltimore: 1844. 12 p. PHi. 44-5219

Randall, Samuel Sidwell, 1809-1881. A digest of the common school system of the state of New York: together with the forms, instructions, and decisions of the superintendent.... Albany: C. Van Benthuysen and company, printer, 1844. 335 p. CtMW; MiU; NjP; OO; PU. 44-5220

Randall, Samuel Sidwell, 1809-1881. Mental and moral culture and popular education, including a special report on common school libraries. New York: C.S. Francis and company, 1844. 236 p. C; ICMe; MB; MBBC; PCA. 44-5221

Ranke, Leopold Von, 1795-1886. The history of the Popes, their church and state in the sixteenth and seventeenth century. By Leopold Ranke. Translated from the last edition of the German, by Walter Keating Kelly. Philadelphia: Lea and Blanchard, 1844. 644 p. ICU; NCH; OWoC; PAtM; WBeloC. 44-5222

Ranke, Leopold Von, 1795-1886. History of the reformation in Germany translated from the last edition of the German, by Sarah Austin. Philadelphia: Lea and Blanchard, 184. 455 p. IJI; MB; NhD; RPB; TxD-W. 44-5223

Rapp's comic almanac, 1844. Philadelphia: W. D. Rapp, 1844. PHi. 44-5224

Rathbun, George Oscar. Speech in the House, June 4, 1844, on the civil and diplomatic apppropriation bill [Washington: 1844] 8 p. MH; OClWHi. 44-5225

Rathbun, George Oscar. Speech on the resolution authorizing the committee on the Rhode Island controversy to send for persons and papers; delivered in the House, March 9, 1844. Washington: printed at the Globe office, 1844. 8 p. MH; OC; RHi; RPB. 44-5226

Rathbun, George Oscar. Speech on the right of members to their seats in the House, delivered in the House, February 12, 1844. 8 p. MH; NNC. 44-5227

Rauch, Friedrich August, 1806-1841. Psychology; or, a view of the human soul: including anthropology, being the substance of a course of lectures, delivered to the junior class, Marshall College, Pennsylvania, by Frederich A. Rauch. Second edition. New York: M. W. Dodd, 1844. 388 p. MB. 44-5228

Rauch, Friedrich August, 1806-1841. Phychology; or a view of the human soul including anthropology, being the substance of a course of lectures, delivered to the junior class, Marshall College, Pennsylvania. Third edition, revised and improved. New York: M.W. Dodd, 1844. 401 p. MB; NcD; NNUT; OClW; PPL. 44-5229

Ray, Isaac, 1807-1881. A treatise on the medical jurisprudence of insanity. Second edition. Boston: W.D. Ticknor and company, 1844. 490 p. DLC; ICRL; KyU; MH-L; WaWW. 44-5230

Ray, Joseph, 1807-1855. Eclectic series newly improved Ray's arithmetic. Part third. Thoroughly revised, enlarged, and improved. Cincinnati: Winthrop B. Smith and Company, 1844. 267 p. DLC; KySoPL; MoU; OFH; OrU. 44-5231

Ray, Joseph, 1807-1855. Ray's arithmetic, part first.... Rules and tables, revised and enlarged. Cincinnati: Winthrop B. Smith, 1844. No. Loc. 44-5232

Ray, Joseph, 1807-1855. Ray's arithmetic, part third. Practical arithmetic by introduction and analysis. Revised edition. Cincinnati: W. B. Smith, 1844. OCHP; OClWHi; OHi; WaPS. 44-5233

Raymond de l'eglise. Remarques du droit francois, confirmees por loix... Lynn, Massachusetts: Rigaud, 1844. 924 p. KyLo. 44-5234

Read, Daniel, 1805-1878. An address delivered before the Mechanics Institute of Bloomington, at the celebration of their anniversary, February 22, 1844. Bloomington, Indiana: Democrat, printer, 1844. 15 p. In; WHi. 44-5235

Read, H.A. A sermon on the criminality of the traffic in intoxicating drinks. Worcester: 1844. 23 p. MBC. 44-5236

Reading, Massachusetts. Historical address and poem, delivered at the bi-centennial celebration of the incorporation of the old town of Reading, May 29, 1844, with an appendix. Boston: Printed by S.N. Dickinson, 1844. 131 p. MGref. 44-5237

Reading, Massachusetts. Historical notices of Reading and South Reading; address at the bicentennial celebration of the town. Boston: S.N. Dickinson, 1844. MBC. 44-5238

The reading of the Bible. Boston, 1844. MA; MB. 44-5239

Redesdale, John Freeman Mitford, 1748-1830. A treatise on the pleadings in suits in the court of chancery by English bills.... Fourth edition, with additional references and notes by G. Jeremy.... New York: J.S. Voorhies, 1844. 401 p. GAWW; InU; NcD; PU-L; WaU. 44-5240

Ree, Peter De La. The American republican songster. Composed and arranged by P. De La Ree. New York:

1844. 24 p. DLC; MH; MoSM; RPB. 44-5241

Reed, Andrew. Personal effort for the salvation of men. From the London Edition. Revised by the Committee of Publication. Boston: Sabbath School Society, 1844. 80 p. NbOP; ViRut. 44-5242

Reed, John, 1738-1776. An explanation of the map of the city and liberties of Philadelphia. Philadelphia: 1844. PPL-R. 44-5243

Reed, William Bradford, 1806-1876. The model adminstration. An oration delivered before the Whig citizens of Philadelphia, on the twenty-second of February, 1844. Philadelphia: J. Crissy, printer, 1844. 22 p. IU; MH; PPL; RPB; WHi. 44-5244

Rees, William, 1802-1883. Cofiant y diweddar barch. Wm. Williams, o'r Wern;... Argraffiad Americanaidd. Remsen [New York] Argraffwyd gan J.R. and R. Everett, 1844. 165 p. CSmH. 44-5245

Reese, William James. Address delivered at the installation of officers of the Zanesville Royal Arch Chapter, January 31, 1844. Philadelphia: C. Sherman, 1844. 52 p. IaCrM. 44-5246

Reeve, Joseph, 1733-1820. The history of the Holy Bible, comprising the most remarkable events in the Old and New Testaments; interspersed with moral and instructive reflections, chiefly taken from the Holy Fathers. Waterford [Connecticut] National Commission Book and Print Shop [1844?] 458 p. IaDuC. 44-5247

Reference book of the state of Maine, for the year of our Lord 1845. Boston: White, Lewis and Potter, printers, 1844. 139 p. MBNEH. 44-5248

The reformation defended against the errors of the times. Nos 1-9. Edited by J.N. Campbell. Albany: Henry, 1844. PPPrHi. 44-5249

Reformed Church in America. Acts and proceedings of the Synod of the German Reformed Church in the United States of America, at Allentown, Lehigh County, Pennsylvania, 1844. Chambersburg: Printed at the Publication office of the German Reformed Church, 1844. 84 p. MoWgT; NcMHi. PLERC-Hi. 44-5250

Reformed Church in America. Hochdeutsch reformierte kirche leiches predigt. Chambersburg: 1844. PPeSchw. 44-5251

Reformed Church in America. Verhandlungen der Synode der Hochdeutschen Reformirten Kirche in den Vereinigten Staaten von Nord Amerika, versammelt in Allentaun, Lecha Caunty, Pa., Im Oktober ...1844. Chambersburg: Dreckerei der Hochdeutsch - Reformirten Kirche, 1844. 96 p. MoWgT; PERCHi. 44-5252

Reformed Dutch Church. Theological Seminary. Catalogue of the officers, alumni and students of the theological seminary of the Reformed Dutch Church.... New Brunswick, New Jersey: n.p., 1844. 15 p. NjR. 44-5253

A refutation, by his friends, of the calumnies against David Henshaw, in relation to the failure of the Commonwealth Bank, and the transfer of South

Boston lands to the United States. Boston: Beals and Greene, 1844. 60 p. ICN; MBC; MH; NIC; PPM. 44-5254

A refutation of the charges against John Frazee, architect, of the New York Custom House, with the decision of the Secretary of the Treasury thereon. New York: J.W. Bell, 1844. 21 p. DNA; MH; MHi. 44-5255

Reid, Adam. A historical address before the congregational church in Salisbury, Connecticut, at their first centennial celebration, November 20, 1844. Hartford: Elihu Geer, 1844. 63 p. MB; MWA. 44-5256

Reid, Alexander, 1802-1860. A dictionary of the English language, containing the pronunciation, etymology, and explanation of all words authorized by eminent writers: to which are added, a vocabulary of the roots of English words, and an accented list of Greek, Latin, and scripture proper names. New York: D. Appleton and Co., 1844. 572 p. GU-M; KWiU. 44-5257

Reid, James. King slavery's council; or, the midnight conclave: a poem by James Reid, of Hebron, New York. Troy: Daily Whig office, printer, 1844. 58 p. ICN; MPiB; N. 44-5258

Reigart, John. United States album; embellished with the arms of each state and other appropriate engravings containing the autographs of the President and cabinet, twenty-eighth Congress, Supreme Court, ministers and other officers of government. Philadelphia: Dubal, 1844. 57 p. ICHi; MoSHi; MWA; PP; THi. 44-5259

The rejoinder of the "Catholic Layman" to the "Reply" of the Rev. R.C. Grundy, to a pamphlet entitled "A brief refutation of three discourses against the Catholic Church," by the Rev. R.C. Grundy, etc. Louisville: B.J. Webb and Brothers, 1844. 26 p. CSmH; DCU; ICLay. 44-5260

Religion is your concern. Printed for the Main Western Ministerial Association. Number 2. Boston: Office of the Christian World, 1844. 14 p. ICMe. 44-5261

Religion of paradise.... Philadelphia, 1844. PPL-R. 44-5262

The religious log-book, giving some account of the last days of Mr. Theophilus Patten, who died at sea. Edited by J. Farr. Boston: office of the Christian World, 1844. 60 p. MHi; MWA. 44-5263

Religious Tract Society, London. Columbus and his times. Albany: Erastus H. Pease, 1844. NHunt. 44-5264

Religious tracts.... on infant baptism. Philadelphia: Stavely and McCalla, 1844. 16 p. NjR. 44-5265

Remarkable conversions.... from the London edition. Boston: Massachusetts Sabbath Society, 1844. 54 p. MeBat. 44-5266

Remarkable places mentioned in the Holy Scriptures. Prepared for the Presbyterian Board of Publication. Philadelphia: Presbyterian Board of Publication, 1844. 124 p. GMilvC; ICMeHi; ScClPP; ViRut. 44-5267

Remarkable visions, comprising highly important revelations concerning the life after death. From the German. Boston: Jordan and company, 1844. 92 p. LN; MHi; MNBedf; OClWHi; VtMidbC. 44-5268

Remarks upon politics and politicians, addressed to the electors of the First Congregational District [of Georgia] N.p. [1844] 19 p. MH. 44-5269

Remember the Sabbath day to keep it Holy, such is the solemn order of Him, in whose hands our breath is. Andover: Printed for the New England Tract Society by Flagg and Gould, 1844. 4 p. MWA. 44-5270

Rennie, James, 1787-1867. Natural history of birds. Their architecture, habits and faculties. New York: Harper and brothers, 1844. 308 p. MeAu; MH-Z; MSaP; RPE; ScGtw. 44-5271

Rennie, James, 1787-1867. Natural history of quadrupeds illustrated with numerous engravings. New York: Harper and brothers, 1844. 324 p. LN; MeAu; MH-Z; OSW; RKi. 44-5272

Reno, George. Buds and flowers of leisure hours... by Harry Hawser, sailor, etc. [pseud.] Philadelphia: printed and published for the author, 1844. 132 p. ICP; MBAt; MH; PHi; TxU. 44-5273

Renwick, James, 1790-1863. Applications of the science of mechanics to practical purposes. New York: Harper and brothers, 1844. 327 p. MiGr; NNC; PPi; ScCh; ScGrw. 44-5274

Renwick, James, 1790-1863. Familiar illustrations on natural philosophy... New York: Harper and brothers, 1844. 379 p. MLow; RKi; RPE. 44-5275

Renwick, James, 1790-1863. First principles of chemistry; being a familiar introduction to the study of that science, for the use of schools, academies, and the lower classes of college, by James Renwick, LL.D., professor of natural and experimental philosophy and chemistry in Columbia College. New York: Harper and brothers, 1844. 444 p. RKi. 44-5276

Renwick, James, 1790-1863. First principles of natural philosophy. Being a familiar introduction to the study of that science. By James Renwick.... New York: Harper, 1844. 530 p. IaMpI; WHi. 44-5277

Renwick, James, 1790-1863. Lives of Robert Fulton, Joseph Warren, Henry Hudson, and Father Marquette. New York: Harper and brothers, 1844. 386 p. RKi; RPE. 44-5278

A reply to the letter of the Honorable Langdon Cheves. His former opinions contrasted with this present views. ...By a southerner. [Charleston?: 1844] 24 p. IU; MB; MH. 44-5279

Report of the committee appointed to examine into the conditions of the records and archives of the General Land Office. Washington: Printed by Thomas Johnson, 1844. 14 p. NcU. 44-5280

Report of the committee of correspondence with southern ecclesiastical bodies on slavery; to the general assembly of Massachusetts... Salem: John P. Jewett and company, 1844. 23 p. MAnP; MeHi; NcMHi; RP. 44-5281

The repository of English romance: comprising all the best serial novels of the day, by James, Dickens, Lever,

Ainsworth, Lover and other distinquished writers. New York: J. Winchester, New World Press, 1844-. v. 1-. M. 44-5282

Republican Party. Address to their fellow citizens, the position of the party in relation to the public school question and the false issue attempted to be created by Bishop Hughes. New York, 1844. 7 p. NNC. 44-5283

Republican sentinel. Devoted to the support of the rights of the union, of the states and of the people, as defined by strict construction of the written constitution. Richmond, Virginia: 1844-. v. 1-. ICU; Vi. 44-5284

Revelation: Thoughts on a spiritual understanding of the book, with some remarks upon the Parousia or second coming of the Lord Jesus Christ. New York: 1844. MBC. 44-5285

Revere House, Boston. Bills of fare, Boston: 1844-1861. 2 v. MB. 44-5286

Review of Dr. R.J. Brechinridge's letters on the rights of ruling elders, from the Princeton Review, April, 1844. Princeton, New York: Robinson, 1844. 32 p. NcU. 44-5287

A review of the elementary spelling book compiled by Aaron Ely, and published under the name of Noah Webster. Extracted principally from Cobb's critical review. New York: 1844. 32 p. MH; NjR. 44-5288

A review of the reflections of Mr. A. on the subject of psalmody, which appeared in the "Presbyterian of the West," from February 15th to May 2, 1844. Pittsburgh:

Printed by William Allinder, 1844. 48 p. NbOP; PPPrHi. 44-5289

Reynolds, Catharine. Memoir of Miss Catharine Reynolds, of Poughkeepsie, New York; with selections from her diary and letters. Edited by Rev. George Coles. New York: Methodist Book Room, 1844. 212 p. IaFayU; MBNMHi; MH; NIC; NPV. 44-5290

Rhees, J.L. A scriptural view of the restoration of the Jews, the second advent of the Lord Jesus and some of the leading circumstances of that glorious event. Philadelphia: 1844. 40 p. OO; PDrop. 44-5291

Rhett, Robert Barnwell, 1800-1876. Address of Robert Barnwell Rhett to his constituents in South Carolina. Washington: 1844. PPL. 44-5292

Rhett, Robert Barnwell, 1800-1876. Speech on the western harbor and river bills in the House, April, 1844. [Washington: 1844] 8 p. MH; WHi. 44-5293

Rhoads, J. The primary arithmetic. By J. Rhoads, M.D. Philadelphia: Bast and Miller [1844] 72 p. PAtM; PU. 44-5294

Rhoads, Samuel. Considerations on the use of the productions of slavery, especially addressed to the religious Society of Friends, within the limits of Philadelphia Yearly Meeting. Philadelphia: Merrihew and Thompson, printers, 1844. 36 [2] p. IEG; MB; MiD; PHC; Tx. 44-5295

Rhoda: or the excellence of charity... Philadelphia: Sorin and Ball, 1844. 144 p. OClWHi. 44-5296

Rhode Island. Acts relating to the public schools of Rhode Island. Providence: 1844. RP; RPA. 44-5297

Rhode Island. Address to the people of the United States, October 21, 1844, by citizens of Rhode Island [Providence: 1844] 15 p. MHi; PPL. 44-5298

Rhode Island. Annual reports by the inspectors, warden and physician of the Rhode Island state prison. Providence: Knowles and Vose, printers, 1844. MiD-B; NjR; RHi; RP; W. 44-5299

Rhode Island. Charters and legislative documents illustrative of Rhode Island history. Providence: Knowles and Vose, 1844. 68 p. DLC; Mid-B; OMC; OO; PHi. 44-5300

Rhode Island. Election law. State of Rhode Island and Providence Plantations in General Assembly. An act to regulate the election of civil officers. Providence: Knowles and Vose, printers, 1844. 16 p. R; RP. 44-5301

Rhode Island. License law, passed January session, 1844. Providence, 1844. 8 p. RPB. 44-5302

Rhode Island. Protest of the Legislature against the interference of Congress in the affairs of the state. Providence, 1844. DLC; PPL; RPL. 44-5303

Rhode Island. Public laws of the state of Rhode Island and Providence Plantations, as revised by a committee, and finally enacted by the General Assembly at the session in January, 1844. Providence: Printed and published by Knwles and Vose, 1844. 594 p. IU; MH; NNLI; RPL. 44-5304

Rhode Island. Rhode Island in 1842. Minority report of the commiteee of Congress appointed to inquire into the interference of the President in the affairs of Rhode Island in 1842. Washington: Printed by Blair and Rives, 1844. R. 44-5305

Rhode Island. State of Rhode Island and Providence Plantations. An act enabling town councils to grant licenses for retailing strong liquors and for other purposes. Providence: 1844. 8 p. R. 44-5306

Rhode Island. State of Rhode Island and Providence Plantations. An act to regulate the militia. n.p., 1844? 32 p. MdBJ; R; RPB. 44-5307

The Rhode Island almanac....1844. Providence: H. H . Brown, [1844] RPE. 44-5308

Rhode Island almanack for 1845. By Isaac Bickerstaff, philom. Providence, Rhode Island: H. H. Brown, [1844] MWA; RNHi. 44-5309

Rhode Island State Temperance Society. Report of the Rhode Island State Temperance Society, for 1843. Providence: B.T. Albro, printer, 1844. 24 p. MdBJ; MH; MHi; RP; RPB. 44-5310

Rhodes, J. W. Melini; or, the victim of guilt. Boston, 1844. MB. 44-5311

Rice, Roswell. Orations on intemperance war, the atonement, Christ's second advent, the devil's preaching and death. Albany: Bentheusen, 1844. 109 p. NjR; PU. 44-5312

Rich, Ezekiel. New project for reforming the English alphabet and orthography. The memorial of the Rev. Ezekiel Rich, of Troy, New Hampshire, setting forth the plan....and praying the assistance of Congress to extend a knowldge of it over the nation. [Washington]: Blair and Rives, printers, [1844] 21 p. CU; DLC; MH; OClWHi; TxU. 44-5313

Richards, William Carey, 1818-1892. The divinity of Christ; discourse in the Baptist meeting house, New England Village, Massachusetts, January, 1844. Worcester: Church and Fiske. 36 p. CtHWatk; MB; MBC; RPB. 44-5314

Richardson, Nathaniel Smith, 1810-1883. Reasons why I am a churchman: or, The Episcopalian armed against popular objections. Providence: 1844. 36 p. MBC; MBD; RHi. 44-5315

Richardson, Nathaniel Smith, 1810-1883. Reasons why I am a churchman: or, The Episcopalian armed against popular objections. Second edition, rev. and enlarged. Hartford: Parsons, 1844. 48 p. CtHT; NjR; PPLT. 44-5316

Richardson, Nathaniel Smith, 1810-1883. Reasons why I am a churchman; or, The Episcopalian armed against popular objections. Third edition, rev. and enlarged. Hartford, 1844. 48 p. CtSoP; IEG; InU; NNG; PHi, WHi. 44-5317

Richardson, Phineas. Earnest efforts for gospel truth. A sermon delivered in the Baptist meeting house, Hollis, New Hampshire, April 7, 1844. By Phineas Richardson, pastor of the Baptist church. Nashville: Albin Beard, printer, 1844. 16 p. NHC-S. 44-5318

Richardson, Phineas. A sermon delivered in the Baptist Meeting House,

Hollis, New Hampshire, April 7, 1844. By Phinehas Richardson.... Nashville: Albin Beard, printer, 1844. 16 p. Nh. 44-5319

Richardson's Virginia and North Carolina almanac for 1845. Calculations by David Richardson. Richmond, Virginia: Drinker and Morris, [1844] CSmH; MWA; Vi; ViRVal. 44-5320

Richmond, James. Petition to abollish capital punishment [To the legislature of the state of New York] Hudson, New York: 1844. 82 p. NN. 44-5321

Richmond, Legh, 1772-1827. Annals of the poor. A new edition, enlarged, with an introductory sketch of the author. New York: J. and H.G. Langley, 1844. 239 p. CBPSR; OWoC; RBr. 44-5322

Richmond College. The second annual catalogue of the officers and students of Richmond College, 1843-1844. Richmond: H.K. Ellyson, 1844. 12 p. ViRU. 44-5323

Richter, Paul Friedrich, 1763-1825. The death of an angel. Translated from the German with a memoir of the author [New York: 1844] 16 p. IU; MB; NN. 44-5324

Ricord, Philippe, 1800-1889. Practical treatise on venereal diseases; or, critical and experimental researches on innoculation, applied to the study of these affections, with a therapeutical summary and special formurlary, ...Translated from the French by A. Sidney Drave.... Second edition. New York, [New York]: Redfield, 1844. 339 p. MdBJ; MnRM; NBMS; OCGHM; TNV. 44-5325

Ridgley, Greenburg William. Examination of Mr. Barnes' reply to the Episcopal recorder by one of the editors. Philadelphia: Stavely McCalla, 1844. 144 p. DLC; MB; MH; PPL; PPM. 44-5326

Riell, Henry E. An appeal to the voluntary citizens of the United States, from all nations, on the exercise of their elective franchise, at the approaching presidential election. New York: 1844. 16 p. DLC; NN. 44-5327

Ripley, Henry Jones, 1798-1875. The four gospels with notes. Boston: 1844. 2 v. in 1. MH. 44-5328

Ripley, Henry Jones, 1798-1875. Question book of scripture history: for Sabbath schools and family instruction... Written for the New England Sabbath School Union, and revised by the committee of publication. Philadelphia [1844] 72 p. ICRL; WHi. 44-5329

The rise, progress, and present position of the Jesuits. New York: American Protestant Society 1844. 94 p. WHi. 44-5330

Ritchie, Anna Cora Ogden Mowatt, 1819-1870. Life of Goethe. From his autobiographical papers and the contributions of his contemporaries. By Henry C. Browning [Pseud.] New York: J. Mowatt and company, 1844. 2 v. in 1. ICMe; LNT; MeB; NNC; PU. 44-5331

Ritchie, David. Address delivered before the Philomathean Literary Institute of the Western University of Pennsylvania, June 27, 1844. Pittsburgh: Printed by W. Allinder, 1844. 16 p. InU; MH. 44-5332

Ritter, Jacob, 1757-1851. Memoirs of J.

Ritter, a faithful minister in the Society of Friends. Philadelphia: T.E. Chapman, 1844. 111 p. DeWi; MdToH; MWA; NBLiHi; PSC. 44-5333

Riverview Academy. Poughkeepsie, New York. Catalogue of the trustees, teachers and pupils of the Poughkeepsie Collegiate School for 1843 and 1844. Poughkeepsie: Platt and Schram, 1844. 19 p. NP; NPV; VtMidbC. 44-5334

Rives, William Cabell, 1793-1868. Letter of Hon. William C. Rives [United States Senator from Virginia] giving reasons for preferring Mr. Clay to Mr. Van Buren for next president. [New York: office of the Tribune] 1844. 8 p. MBC; MH; OO; PPL; Vi. 44-5335

Rives, William Cabell, 1793-1868. Speech on Mr. McDuffie's proposition to repeal the tariff Act of 1842; delivered in the Senate, May 27, 1844. Washington: J. and G.S. Gideon, 1844. MdHi; MH; MWA; NcD; TxDaM. 44-5336

Rives, William Cabell, 1793-1868 Speech.... on the Texas treaty delivered in the Senate of the United States June 6, 1844. Washington: 1844? 8 p. DLC. 44-5337

Robb, Alexander. Specimen of printing types and ornaments, by Alexander Robb, letter founder. Philadelphia: 1844. NNC-Atf. 44-5338

Robberts, John Gooch. The doctrine of two natures in Christ. Printed for the American Unitarian Association. Boston: J. Munroe and company, 1844. 23 p. CtHC; DLC; ICMe; MHi; MMeT-Hi. 44-5339

Robbins, Chandler, 1810-1882. An address before the Jefferson Literary Society of Augusta College, delivered at its anniversary... August 23, 1844. Cincinnati: R.P. Thompson, printer, 1844. 3, 22 p. MBAt; MnHi. 44-5340

Robbins, Chandler, 1810-1882. Address delivered at the laying of the cornerstone of the Second Church.... Boston: I.R. Butts, 1844. 10 p. ICMe; MBAU; NNC; RPB; WHi. 44-5341

Robbins, Chandler, 1810-1882. The missionary enterprise. Boston: James Munroe and company, 1844. 16 p. DLC; ICMe; MBC; MeB; MH. 44-5342

Robbins, Chandler, 1810-1882. Two sermons before the Second Church and Society, March 10, 1844, on the occasion of taking down their ancient place of worship. Boston: I.R. Butts, 1844. CtHC; DLC; MeHi; MnHi; RPB. 44-5343

Robbins, Chandler, 1810-1882. Two sermons delivered before the Boston Second Church and Society: Two sermons on taking down their ancient place of worship. Boston: Printed by Isaac Butts, 1844. 76 p. MBC; MiD-B; MWA; RPB. 44-5344

Robbins, Eliza, 1786-1853. Elements of mythology, or classical fables of the Greeks and Romans... Fourth edition. Philadelphia: Hogan, 1844. 279 p. MdBLC; NcWsS; OO; TxD-T. 44-5345

Robbins, Eliza, 1786-1853. Tales from American history. By the author of American popular lessons. New York: 1844. 250 p. MFiHi; NcU; RPE. 44-5346

Robbins, Royal. The happiness of a long

and useful life. A sermon delivered at the funeral of Mrs. Ruth Hart, ...of Kensington, [Oberlin] Connecticut, who died.... 1844.... Hartford: D.B. Mosely, 1844. 16 p. CtSoP; MB; MiD-B; OClWHi. 44-5347

Robbins, Royal. Outlines of ancient and modern history on a new plan embracing biographical notices. General views of geography of ancient and modern nations. Hartford: Belknap and Hammersley, 1844. 228, 420 p. CLSU; CtHWatk; MH; MnM; OMC. 44-5348

Robbins, Royal. Sermon delivered at the funeral of Ruth Hart, January 15, 1844. Hartford: 1844. 16 p. CtHT; MH-AH; MW. 44-5349

Robertson, William, 1721-1793. An historical disquisition concerning the knowledge which the ancients had of India, and the progress of trade with the country, prior to the discovery of the passage to it by the Cape of Good Hope, with an appendix. New York: Harper, 1844. 146 p. CtHWatk; InRchE; MH; NjP; WM. 44-5350

Robertson, William, 1721-1793. The history of Scotland during the reigns of Queen Mary and of King James VI till his accession to the crown of England. With a review of the Scottish history previous to that period, and an appendix, containing original letters. New York: Harper and brothers, 1844. LN; MH; NjMD; OCY; ViU. 44-5351

Robertson, William, 1721-1793. The history of the discovery and conquest of America. Abridged, with a memoir of the author from that by Dugald Stewart. New

York: Harper, 1844. 551 p. MiThr; WM. 44-5352

Robertson, William, 1721-1793. The history of the reign of the emperor Charles V.... abridged edition. New York: Harper and brothers, 1844. 615 p. NcD; OCY; OSaht; OSW; RPE. 44-5353

Robinson, Horatio Nelson, 1806-1867. Universal key to the science of algebra. Cincinnati: E. Morgan and company, 1844. 167 p. InI; MiU; NjP; NjR; OO. 44-5354

Robinson, Jane. Richelieu in love; or, the youth of Charles I., an historical comedy in five acts, as accepted at the Theatre Royal, Haymarket, and prohibited by authority of the Lord Chamberlin; with a preface explanatory. New York, New York: Benjamin and Young, 1844. 53 p. MH; NcU. 44-5355

Robinson, William C. Letter giving his reasons from preferring Mr. Clay. Washington: 1844. PPL-R. 44-5356

Rochester Collegiate Institute. Rochester Collegiate Institute daily and weekly report. Rochester: Printed by Canfield and Warren, 1844. 8 p. NRHi. 44-5357

Rochester, Massachusetts. Centre church. Articles of faith and covenant of the Centre Church, ...Rochester: 1844. 8 p. Ct. 44-5358

Rochester, Massachusetts. Centre Church. Manual. Rochester: 1844. 8 p. MBC. 44-5359

Rochester, New York. Revised charter of the city... passed April 11, 1844.

Rochester: Power Press of Erastus Shepard, 1844. 253 p. IU; MH-L; NN; NRU. 44-5360

Rockhill, Thomas C. Address delivered before the reading room and calocagathian Societies of Saint Mary's College, Baltimore at the annual commencement, July 16, 1844. Baltimore: Metropolitan Press, 1844. 19 p. DLC; MdBLC; MdW. 44-5361

Rockie Hills Institute for Boys. Prospectus of the Rockie Hills Institute for Boys at Ellicott's Mills, Howard District, Anne Arundel County, Maryland. Baltimore: R.J. Matchett, 1844. 16 p. MdBD. 44-5362

Rockingham Agricultural Association. Constitution and by-laws. n.p.: [1844] Nh-Hi. 44-5363

The rococo; containing the Culprit Fay, by Joseph Rodman Drake; Lillian, by William Mackworth Praed; and the Eve of St. Agnes, by John Keats... with original notes by N.P. Willis. New York: Morris, Willis, 1844. 16 p. MdBJ; NN; TxU. 44-5364

Rogers, Abner, 1813-1844. Report of the trial of Abner Rogers, Jr. indicted for the murder of Charles Lincoln, Jr. late warden of the Massachusetts State Prison; before the Supreme Judicial Court of Massachusetts; holden at Boston, January 30, 1844. Boston: Charles C. Little and James Brown, 1844. 286 p. Ct; NjR; PHi; RPL; WvU. 44-5365

Rogers, Ammi. Memoirs of the Rev. Ammi Rogers, A.M., a clergyman of the Episcopal Church.... persecuted in the state of Connecticut on account of religion and politics.... Tenth edition. Watertown, New York: Knowlton and Rice, 1844. 264 p. Ct; MiD-B; MnHi; MtH; OSW. 44-5366

Rogers, Charles. Speech on the right of petition, in the House of Representatives, February 23, 1844. Washington: J. And G.S. Gideon, 1844. 16 p. M; MBat; MH; MWA; OClWHi. 44-5367

Rogers, George. Universalist hymn book. By George Rogers. Fourth edition. Cincinnati: R.P. Brooks, 1844. 448 p. IGK; MMeT-Hi; PPL-R. 44-5368

Rogers, Henry Darwin, 1808-1866. Address delivered at the meeting of the Association of American Geologists and Naturalists, held in Washington, May, 1844. With an abstract of the proceedings. New York: Wiley, 1844. 58, 43 p. ICJ; MWiW; NjR; PPL; WBeloC. 44-5369

Rogers, John Gray. Report of one of the commissioners appointed to reduce the common law of crimes and punishments to a systematic code. [Boston: 1844] 48 p. DLC; MH-L; MnU; NNC; OCLaw. 44-5370

Rogers, Samuel. The poetical works of Rogers, Cambell, J. Montgomery, Lamb, and Kirke White. Complete in one volume. Philadelphia: Grigg and Elliot, 1844. TKC. 44-5371

Rogers, Samuel Baldwyn. An elementary treatise on iron-making, wherein the feasibility of producing good iron from any kinds of ore and with every species of fuel, by Samuel Rogers.... by J.H. Alexander. Baltimore: F. Lucas, Junior, 1844. 189 p. LNT; MdBJ; MH; OCoY; PHi. 44-5372

Rogers, William B. Account of some new instruments and processes for the analysis of the carbonates. By Profs. William B. Rogers and Robert E. Rogers, of the University of Virginia. [New Haven? 1844?] 14 p. MB; Vi. 44-5373

Rollin, Charles, 1661-1741. The ancient history of the Egyptians, Carthaginians, Assyrians, Babylonians, Medes, and Persians, Grecians and Macedonians; including a history of the arts and sciences of the ancients. Life of the author by James Bell. Cincinnati: George Conclin, 1844. 2 v. IaDmD; IaMpI; MB; VtCas. 44-5374

Rollin, Charles, 1661-1741. The ancient history. Translated from the French to which is prefixed a life of the author. By the Rev. R. Lynam, [A.M.] New York: Pratt, Woodford and company, 1844. 8 v. CoCsC; InID; MdU; MFIL; OU. 44-5375

Rollin, Charles, 1661-1741. The ancient history of the Egyptians, Carthaginians, Assyrians, Babylonians, Medes and Persians, Macedonians and Grecians. New York: Nafis and Cornish, 1844. 4 v. KyLoS; MiU; MTaHi; NGoS; Nj. 44-5376

Rollin, Charles, 1661-1741. Ancient history: containing the history of the Egyptians, Assyrians.... from Rollin, and other authentic sources, both ancient and modern. Second edition. New York: Robert Carter, 1844. 4 v. NcCJ; NjPT; OClW; ScDuE; TxBronB. 44-5377

Roman Catholic Society of St. Joseph.

Report. Philadelphia, 1844. PPL. 44-5378

Rome's policy towards the Bible; or papal efforts to suppress the scriptures in the last five centuries. Exposed by an American citizen. Philadelphia: Campbell, 1844. 100 p. OWoC; PPL; ViRut. 44-5379

Rome's policy towards the Bible; or papal efforts to suppress the scriptures in the last five centuries. Exposed by an American citizen. Second edition. Philadelphia: James M. Campbell; New York: Saxton and Miles, 1844. 100 p. OO; PLERC-Hi; ViRut. 44-5380

Rome's policy towards the Bible; or papal efforts to suppress the scriptures in the last five centuries. Exposed by an American citizen. Third edition. Philadelphia: James M. Campbell, 1844. 100 p. OO; OWoC. 44-5381

Root, James. The horrors of delirium tremens, by J. Root. New York: Josiah Adams, 1844. 483 p. CSt-L; FOA; MBAt; NNC; PU. 44-5382

The rose; or, affection's gift for 1844. Edited by Emily Marshall. Illustrated with ten highly finished steel engravings. New York: D. Appleton and company; Philadelphia: George S. Appleton, 1844. 256 p. ICU; MBBC; MH; NjR; ViU. 44-5383

Ross, James, 1744-1827. A Latin grammar, comprising all the rules and observations necessary to accurate knowledge of the Latin classics.... With latin idioms, and a new prosody, and other important additions and emendations. By N. C. Brooks.... Philadelphia: Thomas, Cowperthwait and company, 1844. 21 p. Ia; MdBD; OCan; PPA; PPM. 44-5384

Rossini, Gioachino Antonio, 1792-1868. The stabat mater with Latin and English words. Boston: 1844. PPL. 44-5385

Roussel, Napoleon. Sacred Scenes: from the French of Napoleon Roussel. Translated for the Massachusetts Sabbath School Society, and revised by the committee of publication. Boston: Massachusetts Sabbath School Society, 1844. [7]-288 p. DLC; MA; OO. 44-5386

Rowland, Henry Augustus. The distinctive features of Presbyterianism, as exhibited in the confession of faith. A sermon, delivered in the Presbyterian Church, Honesdale, Pennsylvania, July 2, 1843.... Philadelphia: printed at the office of the Christian Observer, 1844. 18 p. ICT; MBC; NNUT. 44-5387

Roxbury, Massachusetts. Report of the committee on the inhabitants of the town of Roxbury on the petition of Ebenezer Seaver and others for a division of the town. Roxbury: 1844. MB-FA. 44-5388

Roxbury Warren Veteran Association. Constitution and records of the Roxbury Warren Veteran Association, May 15, 1844. Boston: Printed by H.L. Devereaux, 1844. 12 p. MiD-B. 44-5389

Royce, Andrew. Consideration for the people of Barre [Vermont] respecting the hostility of the Methodists. Montpelier: E.P. Walton and sons, 1844. 16 p. VtHi. 44-5390

Royston, S. Watson. An address delivered at Cumming, Georgia,

February, 1844, on the rise and progress of society, and the formation of government. New Haven: printed for the author, 1844. 16 p. Ct; CtHC; MH. 44-5391

The rubic [sic] of love: containing love thoughts by many contributors... New York: Morris and Willis, 1844. 32 p. MB. 44-5392

The rudiments of the Latin tongue, or a plain and easy introduction to Latin grammar. Philadelphia: Thomas, Cowperthwait and company, 1844. 154 p. NoLoc. 44-5393

Ruffin, Edmund, 1794-1865. An essay on calcareous manures. By Edmund Ruffin... Fourth edition. Philadelphia: L. Wallace, 1844. [13]-316 p. MAA; PJo; Vi. 44-5394

Rules of deportment and instructions for the youth. Part two, a juvenile monitor, consisting of rules of conduct for youth and children. New Lebanon, New York: 1844. 132 p. MShi. 44-5395

The Rum seller's looking glass; or, a peep behind the bar. Boston: 1844. 16 p. WHi. 44-5396

Rundell, Maria Eliza Ketelby, 1745-1828. New system of domestic cookery: founded upon principles of economy, and adapted to the use of private families; augmented and improved by the addition of more than 900 new receipts, suited to the present state of the art of cookery. Philadelphia: Carey and Hart, 1844. 274 p. CBe; MH; NjR; NNNAM; OCl. 44-5397

Rundell, Maria Eliza Ketelby 1745-

1828. A new system of domestic cookery, formed upon principles of economy, and adapted for the use of private families. By Mrs. Rundell. From the sixty-seventh London edition augmented and improved.... Philadelphia: Carey and Hart, 1844. 274 p. CU; MH; NjR; NNT-C; OCl. 44-5398

Rupp, Israel Daniel, 1803-1878. The farmer's complete farrier. Comprising a historical description of ... the horse... Selected, compiled and translated from the best German and English works... With numerous additions. Lancaster, Pennsylvania: I.L. Eshleman, 1844. 416 p. DLC; PLFM. 44-5399

Rupp, Israel Daniel, 1803-1878. He Pasa Ekklesia. An original history of the religious denominations at present existing in the United States. Containing authentic accounts of their rise, progress, statistics, and doctrines.... Projected, compiled and arranged by I. Daniel Rupp. Philadelphia: J.Y. Humphreys, 1844. 734 p. CBPac; IaHA; LNH; NCaS; OCX. 44-5400

Rupp, Israel Daniel, 1803-1878. History of Berks and Lebanon Counties.... account of Indians.... Lancaster, Pennsylvania: G. Hills, 1844. 512 p. DLC; ICN; KHi; MiD-B; PAnL. 44-5401

Rupp, Israel Daniel, 1803-1878. History of Lancaster County. To which is prefixed a brief sketch of the early history of Pennsylvania. Compiled from authentic sources. By Daniel Rupp.... Lancaster, Pennsylvania: G. Hills, 1844. 531 p. CtMW; DLC; ICN; MH; NNNBG. 44-5402

Rupp, Israel Daniel, 1803-1878. History

of Lancaster County. To which is prefixed a brief sketch of the early history of Pennsylvania. Lancaster, [Pennsylvania]: Gilbert Hills, 1844. 528 p. ICN; NjP; ODaB; PWW; TKL-Mc. 44-5403

Rupp, Israel Daniel, 1803-1878. History of the counties of Berks and Lebanon, Pennsylvania, containing a brief account of the Indians who inhabited this region of the country... Lancaster: G. Hills, 1844. 518 p. GU; InU; MWA; PCC; WaS. 44-5404

Rural life in New England. A domestic romance. By the author of "Lights and shadows of factory life." New York: J. Winchester, [1844] 114 p. DLC. 44-5405

Ruschenberger, William Samuel Waithman, 1807-1895. Anatomy and physiology, showing the structure of the human body and the functions of its various parts, in ten easy lessons. Philadelphia; New York: Turner and Fisher, 1844. 120 p. DLC. 44-5406

Ruschenberger, William Samuel Waithman, 1807-1895. Elements of botany. Philadelphia: Turner and Fisher, 1844. 161 p. IaDaM; MoS; MSaP; NjP; TxCsA. 44-5407

Ruschenberger, William Samuel Waithman, 1807-1895. Elements of botany. Second edition. Philadelphia: Grigg and Elliot, 1844. 159 p. MSaP. 44-5408

Ruschenberger, William Samuel Waithman, 1807-1895. Elements of conchology: prepared for the use of schools and colleges... From the text of Milne Edwards, and Achille Comte... Philadelphia: Grigg and Elliot, 1844. 114 p.

MSaP; NjP; OCo; PU-Z; TxU-T. 44-5409

Ruschenberger, William Samuel Waithman, 1807-1895. Elements of entomology. Philadelphia, 1844. 121 p. IaDaM. 44-5410

Ruschenberger, William Samuel Waithman, 1807-1895. Elements of herpetology and of ichthyology prepared for the use of schools and colleges by W.S.W. Ruschenberger. From the text of Milne Edwards and Achille Comte. Philadelphia: Grigg and Elliot, 1844. 145 p. MH; MiU; NIC; OMC. 44-5411

Ruschenberger, William Samuel Waithmam, 1807-1895. Elements of history, prepared for the use of schools and colleges. From the test of Milne Edwards and Archalle Compte. Philadelphia: Turner and Fisher, 1844. 161 p. NcD. 44-5412

Ruschenberger, William Samuel Waithman, 1807-1895. First books of natural history. Elements of herpetology, and of ichthyology: prepared for the use of schools and colleges. From the text of Milne Edwards and Achille Comte, Philadelphia: Grigg and Elliott, 1844. 159 p. MH; MSaP; NNN; OUrC; PPM. 44-5413

Ruschenberger, William Samuel Waithman, 1807-1895. Lessons in physiology, the structure of the human body and the functions of its various parts, in ten easy lessons, adapted to the comprehension of all readers. Philadelphia: Turner and Fisher, 1844. 143 p. PPC; PPCP. 44-5414

Ruschenberger, William Samuel

Waithman, 1807-1895. Mammalogy: natural history of mammiferous animals. Second book of natural history, prepared for the use of schools an colleges.... Philadelphia and New York: Turner and Fisher, 1844. [11]-151 p. IEG; MH; MoS. 44-5415

Ruschenberger, William Samuel Waithman, 1807-1895. Ornithology: the natural history of birds. Third book of natural history. Prepared for the use of schools and colleges. Philadelphia: Grigg and Elliot, 1844. 125 p. ABBS; IaDaM; MH; OUrC; TxU-T. 44-5416

Ruschenberger, William Samuel Waithman, 1807-1895. Physiology and animal mechanism. First book of natural history prepared for the use of schools and colleges. Philadelphia: 1844. 120 p. MB; MBM; OUrC. 44-5417

Rusling, Joseph. Original hymns, for the use of Sunday schools and young Christians. Second edition, revised. New York: Published by G. Land and C.B. Tippett, for the Sunday school union, 1844. 152 p. NNMHi; NNUT. 44-5418

Russell, Henry, 1812-1900. The spider and the fly: a comic song....arranged and adapted to a favorite melody by Henry Russell. Baltimore: W.C. Peters, 1844. 6 p. MB; WHi. 44-5419

Russell, Henry, 1812-1900. The spider and the fly: a comic song. [A. or bar. accomp. for pianoforte].... Music arranged and adapted to a favorite melody. Cincinnati: Peters and company, 1844. 6 p. MB. 44-5420

Russell, John. Ancient history of Greece and Rome. With introductory sketches of the history of the Jews, Egyptians, Carthaginians, and other nations.... By John Russell, A.M. Philadelphia: Hogan and Thompson, 1844. 266 p. ICBB; MHad. 44-5421

Russell, John. History of England, with separate historical sketches of Scotland, Wales, and Ireland; from the invasion of Julius Caesar until the accession of Queen Victoria. With questions for examination. Philadelphia: Hogan and Thompson, 1844. 244 p. LNB; NcDaD; PP; TxU-T. 44-5422

Russell, John. History of France, from the earliest times to the present day.... By John Russell, A.M. Philadelphia: Hogan and Thompson, 1844. 234 p. NdU; PReaAT. 44-5423

Russell, John. A history of the United States of America, from the period of discovery to the present time: arranged for the use of schools, with questions for the examination of students.... Philadelphia: Hogan and Thompson, 1844. 250 p. CtHWatk; NcD; PReaAT; TxU-T. 44-5424

Russell, Michael, 1781-1848. History and present condition of the Barbary States. New York: Harper and brothers, 1844. 340 p. MChi; MeAu; MsU; MWar. 44-5425

Russell, Michael, 1781-1848. Life of Oliver Cromwell. New York: Harper and brothers, 1844. 2 v. IGK; MRp; MWA; MWar; TNJU. 44-5426

Russell, Michael, 1781-1848. Palestine or the Holy Land, from the earliest period to the present time. New York:

Harper and brothers, 1844. 330 p. MeAu; MnHi; MWar; NcHil; OCo. 44-5427

Russell, William, 1741-1793. The history of modern Europe: by William Russell, LL.D., and a continuation of the history to the present time. By William Jones, esq. With annotations by an American. New York: Harper and brothers, 1844. 3 v. CSf; KyLoS; LNB; NcCJ; ViPet. 44-5428

Russell, William, 1798-1873. Primer; or, first steps in spelling and reading. Boston: Tappan and Dennet, 1844. 72 p. CtY; MB. 44-5429

Russell, William, 1798-1873. Russell's American elocutionist. Comprising lessons in enunciation, exercises in elocution, and rudiments of gesture. Boston: Jenks and Palmer, 1844. 380 p. CtHC; DLC; MH; MHi; OCU. 44-5430

Russell, William, 1798-1873. Spelling book, or, second course of lessons in spelling and reading.... Boston: Tappan, Whittemore and Mason, [1844] 160 p. ICU; MH; MPeHi; NNC. 44-5431

Rutgers Female College. New York. Anniversary commencement. July, 1844. New York, 1844. 11 p. DLC. 44-5432

Rutgers Female College. New York. Annual circular. New York: Osborn, 1844. 20 p. PPPrHi. 44-5433

Ryan, James. A treatise on gauging, and also the most important problems in mechanics; added to an introduction to mensuration. Philadelphia: 1844. 288 p. PHi. 44-5434

Ryan, John. Reflections on the late riots by candid writers in poetry and prose. Philadelphia: 1844. 43 p. DLC; PHi; RNR. 44-5435

S

The Sabbath and Lord's day: A history of their observance in the Christian Church. New York: Sabbath Tract Society, 1844. 48 p. NAlf. 44-5436

The Sabbath day book for boys and girls. By the editors of the popular library. Second edition. Boston: Benjamin H. Greene, 1844. 230 p. CtHC; MB; MNutn; NNC. 44-5437

Sabbath Day Convention, Columbus, Ohio, 1844. Sabbath day convention, at Columbus, Ohio, January, 1844. Columbus: Scott and Teesdale, printers, 1844. 14 p. OCHP; OClWHi; PPPrHi. 44-5438

Sabbath School Missionary Society. Anniversary of the Sabbath School Missionary Society, at the Methodist Episcopal Church, East Chelsea, Christmas Evening. East Chelsea, Massachusetts: J. Dunham's Press [1844] Broadside. RPB. 44-5439

Sabbath School Teacher. The New England Sabbath school minstrel, a collection of music and hymns, adapted to Sabbath schools, families and social meetings. By a Sabbath school teacher. Boston: New England Sunday school union, 1844. 63 p. CtHWatk; MBAt; MH; MH-AH. 44-5440

Sabinus. The evil and the remedy. Little Rock: Printed by B.J. Borden, 1844. 200 p. ArU. 44-5441

Sacred harp; a collection of hymns and divine songs for sabbath schools and social meetings. Portsmouth: 1844. 110 p. Nh-Hi; RPB. 44-5442

The sacred rosary: a select volume of serious poetry. Compiled by N. P. Willis. New York: Morris and Willis, 1844. 32 p. MWH; LNH. 44-5443

Sadler, L.L. An easy and familiar catechism on the gospel of St. Matthew.... Part II. Portland, [Maine]: 1844. 63 p. DLC. 44-5444

Sailor's almanac for 1845. New York, New York: [1844] 24 p. MeHi; MWA. 44-5445

St. Andrew's Society of the City of Charleston. Rules of the St. Andrew's Society, of the city of Charleston, South Carolina: founded in the year one thousand seven hundred and twenty-nine. Incorporated in 1798. Charleston: printed at the office of Burgess and James, 1844. 38 p. ScHi. 44-5446

St. John, James Augustus. The lives of celebrated travelers. New York: Harper and Brothers, 1844. 3 v. IGK; MB; NcHil; OSW; WM. 44-5447

The Saint Nicholas gift. For little boys and girls. Boston: T. H. Carter and company, 1844. 104 p. ICU; NUt. 44-5448

St. Paul's College. College Point, New York. Journal of St. Paul's College. College Point, New York. Flushing: Charles R. Lincoln, printer, 1844. CSmH; NjR. 44-5449

Salem, Massachusetts. Address of the mayor, upon the organization of the city government, March 25, 1844. With the reports of several departments for the preceding municipal year. Salem: 1844. [4]-32 p. MiD-B; MSa. 44-5450

Sales, Francis, 1771-1854. Cartilla O silabario, y metodo practico de ensenar a leer. Fifteenth edition. Boston: 1844. 52 p. MH. 44-5451

Sales, Francis, 1771-1854. Colmena espanola; o, Piezas escogidas, de varios autores espanoles, morales, instructivas, y divertidae.... Por F. Sales.... Fifth edition. Boston: J. Munroe y cia, 1844. 216 p. ViU. 44-5452

Sales, Francis, 1771-1854. Spanish hive, or, select pieces from various Spanish authors, moral, instructive, and amusing; with the various signification in English of the particles, words and idiomatic phrases at the bottom of each piece, and also in the general index: the whole accentuated with the greatest care, for the use of beginners. By F. Sales. Fifth edition. Boston: 1844. PPM. 44-5453

Salisbury, Edward Elbridge. Memoir on the history of Buddhism. Read, May 28, 1844. Boston: S.N. Dickinson, 1844. 57 p. CtHC; NIC; NN. 44-5454

Salkeld, Joseph. Classical antiquities, or a compendium of Roman and Grecian antiquities; with a sketch of ancient mythology. New York: A.V. Blake, 1844.

275, 36 p. CoDR; MH; NBuDD; OClW; WM. 44-5455

Salkeld, Joseph. Compendium of Greek and Roman antiquities. With a sketch of ancient mythology. New York: Blake, 1844. DLC; ViU; VtWood. 44-5456

Sallustius, Crispus C. Sallusts' Jugurthine war and conspiracy of Catiline, English commentary, and geographical and historical indexes. By C. Anthon....Ninth edition, corrected and enlarged. New York: Harper and brothers, 1844. 332 p. IAlS; LN; MoFayC; NvU; PMA. 44-5457

Sampson, Marmaduke Blake. Slavery in the United States. A letter to the Honorable Daniel Webster, by M. B. Sampson. New York: Wiley and Putnam, 1844. 87 p. AU; CtSoP; DLC; NNG; TxU. 44-5458

San Diego and Gila Southern Pacific Railroad Company. Report from the delegation.... San Diego: D.U. Gelwicks, state printer, 1844. 15 p. MH-BA. 44-5459

Sanborn, Dyer H. Analytical grammar of the English language, embracing the inductive and productive methods of teaching, ...and an appendix. In five parts. Sixth edition improved. Concord, New Hampshire: G. Parker Lyon, 1844. 288 p. MBevHi; Nh; NNC. 44-5460

Sanborn, P.E. The sick man's friend, being a plain, practical medical work, on vegetable or botanical principles.... by P.E. Sanborn. Second edition. Boston: William Johnson; New York: Dr. Strong,

1844. 270 p. MB; NbU-M; NNNAM. 44-5461

Sandby, George, 1799-1880. Mesmerism and its opponents: with a narrative of cases. By George Sandby, Junior, M.A. New York: Benjamin and Young, 1844. 135 p. DLC; NbO; NCH; NjP; NNC. 44-5462

Sanders, Charles Walton, 1805-1889. Sander's spelling book; containing a minute and comprehensive system of introductory orthography. Cincinnati: William H. Moore and company, 1844. 168 p. OC. 44-5463

Sanders, Charles Walton, 1805-1889. Sander's spelling book; containing a minute and comprehensive system of introductory orthography. Twelfth edition. Cleveland: 1844. NNC; OClWHi. 44-5464

Sanders, Charles Walton, 1805-1889. The school reader. Second book, by Charles W. Sanders. New York: Mark H. Newman; Rochester: Sage and brother, 1844. 180 p. NRU. 44-5465

Sanders, Charles Walton, 1805-1889. The school reader. Third book. By Charles W. Sanders, ...Twentieth edition. New York: Mark H. Newman; Cincinnati: William H. Moore and company, 1844. 250 p. NNC. 44-5466

Sanders, Charles Walton, 1805-1889. The school reader. Fourth book. Containing instructions in the elementary principles of reading, and selected lessons from the most elegant writers. For the use of academies and the higher classes in common and select schools. Cincinnati: Moore, 1844. OHi. 44-5467

Sanders, Elizabeth Elkins, 1762-1851. Tract on missions. Salem, 1844-1845. CSmH; MH; MNBedf; NjR; WHi. 44-5468

Sanderson, James Monroe. Mirror for dyspeptics, from the diary of a landlord. Philadelphia: G.B. Zieber and company, 1844. 32 p. CtY; LNH; NN; PPM; RWe. 44-5469

Sandford, Elizabeth Poole, d. 1853. Woman in her social and domestic character... Boston: Otis, Broader and company, 1844. MH. 44-5470

Sandham, Mrs. The twin sisters. A tale for youth. From the twentieth London edition. New York: D. Appleton and company; Philadelphia: George S. Appleton, 1844. 176 p. FFlo; FTa; ScCMu. 44-5471

Sanford, E.H. An epitome of phrenology. Being a clear and concise view of the science; systematically and synthetically arranged and analytically applied. Rochester, New York: Printed by Hammond and Cunnington, 1844. 36 p. DLC. 44-5472

Sanford, E.H. An epitome of phrenology... For sale at Dewey's news room, Rochester, New York... Rochester, New York: printed by Hammond and Cunnington, 1844. 36 p. DLC. 44-5473

Sanford, James. Miss Lucy Neal. An Ethiopian song. Written by James Sanford, the celebrated negro singer. Philadelphia: A. Fiot, 1844. 3 p. KU. 44-5474

Sanford, Peter P. 1781-1857. Memoirs of Mr. Wesley's missionaries to

America.... New York: G. Lane and P.P. Sanford, for the Methodist Episcopal Church, 1844. 390 p. CtY-D; IEG; InGrD; NNUT. 44-5475

Sappington, John. The theory and treatment of fevers, by Dr. John Sappington, Saline County, Missouri. Revised and corrected by Ferdinando Stith, M.D., Franklin, Tennessee. Arrow Rock: the author, 1844. 216 p. AzF; MsU; NBu; OAsht; TKL-Mc. 44-5476

Sargent, Epes, 1813-1880. The life and public services of Henry Clay. New edition, revised and enlarged and brought down to the year 1844. New York: Greeley and McElrath, 1844. 80 p. A-Ar; MH; NcD; OFH; TxU. 44-5477

Sargent, Epes, 1818-1880. The light of the light-house and other poems. New York, 1844. 16 p. RPB. 44-5478

Sargent, John, 1781-1812. Life of John Sargent. Fourth edition, from the tenth London edition. New York: 1844. 467 p. OO. 44-5479

Sargent, John, 1781-1812. A memoir of the Rev. Henry Martyn. Fourth edition from the tenth London edition, corrected and enlarged with an introductory essay and an appendix, by the American editor. New York: Robert Carter, 1844. 467 p. IEG; GMM; MdBD; PP; TxBrdD. 44-5480

Sargent, John Osbourne, 1811-1891. A lecture on the late improvements in steam navigation and the arts of naval warfare... New York: Wiley and Putnam, 1844. [7]-64 p. ICU; LNH; MB; NIC; PPM. 44-5481

Sargent, John Turner, d. 1877. The rich and poor. A sermon. Boston: Leonard C. Bowles, 1844. 14 p. MB; MBAt; MBAU; MiD-B. 44-5482

Sargent, Lucius Manlius, 1786-1867. The rumseller's money: moral suasion without law. New York: 1844. 8 p. CtY; MB; MBC; MH; WHi. 44-5483

Sargent, Lucius Manlius, 1786-1867. The temperance tales. Boston: 1844. MB; MH. 44-5484

Sargent, Nathan, 1794-1875. Brief outline of the life of Henry Clay. By Oliver Old School [pseud.] [Washington: 1844] 16 p. GEU; MH; NIC. 44-5485

Sargent, Nathan, 1794-1875. Life of Henry Clay. [Oliver Oldschool] ...Philadelphia: R.G. Berford, 1844. [17]-32 p. ICU; MeHi; MH; NUtHi; RP. 44-5486

Sargent, Nathan, 1794-1875. Life of Henry Clay. [Oliver Oldschool] ...Philadelphia; R.G. Berford, 1844. 16 p. IP; LNH; MnU; NNC; RP. 44-5487

Sargent, Nathan, 1794-1875. A sketch of the life and public services of Henry Clay. By "Oliver Oldschool," [Baltimore: Printed at the office of the American Whig by S. Sands, 1844?] 16 p. DLC; MdBJ; PPL. 44-5488

Sargent and company. New York. An account of some of the traditions and experiments, respecting Captain Kidd's piratical vessel. New York: Herald Book and Job Printing office, 1844. 12 p. DLC; MH; N; RPJCB. 44-5489

Saunders, John Simcoe. The law of

pleading and evidence in civil actions, arranged alphabetically... Fourth American edition. Philadelphia: R.H. Small, 1844. 2 v. CSt; NcD; RPL; TU; WaU. 44-5490

Saunders, Romulus Mitchell, 1791-1867. Speech against receiving, referring; or reporting on abolition petitions, delivered in the House of Representatives, January 19 and 23, 1844. Washington: 1844. 13 p. MH; MiD-B; NcD; NcU; NNC. 44-5491

Savage, Eleazer. Manual of church discipline. Rochester: Sage and brother, 1844. [13]-119 p. MiGr; NHC-S; NRC-R; NRHi. 44-5492

The Saviour: a question book on the character, offices and work of Christ, for Sabbath schools. Boston, Massachusetts: Sunday School Society, 1844. 70 p. MBC. 44-5493

Sawyer, Leicester Ambrose, 1807-1898. Critical exposton of baptism; embracing the mosaic baptisms; Jewish traditionary baptisms, John's baptism and Christian baptism; clearly establishing the scriptural authority of and of infant baptism. Cincinnati, Ohio: Henry Derby and company; New York: D. Appleton and company, 1844. 188 p. KyLoP; LNB; MH; OWervO; PPPrHi. 44-5494

Sawyer, Lemuel, 1777-1852. Auto-biography of Lemuel Sawyer, formerly member of Congress from North Carolina. New York: Published for the author, 1844. 48 p. A-Ar; DLC; MPiB; NcU; OClWHi; PPL. 44-5495

Sawyer, Lemuel, 1777-1852. A biography of John Randolph, of Roanoke,

with a selection from his speeches. New York: W. Robinson, 1844. [5]-132 p. Ct; MeHi; MWA; RPA; ScU. 44-5496

Saxton's River Seminary. Rockingham, Vermont. Catalogue... 1844. Bellows Falls, 1844. 2 v. DLC. 44-5497

Schenck, Robert Cumming, 1809-1890. Speech of Mr. Schenck, of Ohio, on the bill to refund General Jackson's fine, in the House of Representatives, January 8, 1844 [n.p.: 1844] 15 p. DLC; MB; MBAt; NBU; OClWHi. 44-5498

Schieferdecker, Chr. Charles. Vincenz Priessnitz: or, the wonderful power of water in healing the diseases of the human body. Second edition. Philadelphia: Chr. Charles Schieferdecker, 1844. 140 p. DSG; NClsM; PPHa. 44-5499

Schiller, Johann Friedrich von, 1759-1805. The poems and ballads of Schiller. ....New York: Harper and brothers, 1844. 424 p. GMar; LU; NcU; OClW; PPA. 44-5500

Schlegel, Frederich von, 1772-1829. Lectures on the history of literature, ancient and modern. From the German of Frederich Schlegel. A new edition, with a series of questions for examination in schools. By John Frost. New York: Henry G. Langley, 1844. 12, 392 p. CtHT; KBB; RJa; ScCoT; WBeloC. 44-5501

Schlegel, Frederich von, 1772-1829. Lectures on the history of literature, ancient and modern. From the German of Frederich Schlegel. A new edition, with a series of questions for examination in schools. By John Frost. New York: Henry G. Langley, 1844. 427 p. IaPeC; KyU; MoSpD; NhD; PRosC. 44-5502

Schlegel, Frederich von, 1772-1829.
Lectures on the history of literature.
Philadelphia: 1844. ODaU. 44-5503

Schmauk, John G. Erstes buch fur
deutsche schulen. Philadelphia: G.
Mentz und sohn, 1844. 156 p. ICU; PPL-
R. 44-5504

Schmid, Christoph von, 1768-1854. The
basket of flowers; or piety and truth triumphant, a tale for the young. Translated
from the French, and altered and arranged by G.T. Bedell. Eleventh edition.
Boston: O. Scott, 1844. 125, 11 p. MiU.
44-5505

Schmid, Christoph von, 1768-1854. The
basket of flowers; or piety and truth triumphant. A tale for the young. Translated from the French... Eleventh
edition. Boston: O. Scott, 1844. 125, 11 p.
MiU. 44-5506

Schmid, Christoph von, 1768-1854.
Eustachius, an episode of the first ages of
Christianity... Baltimore: Lucas, 1844.
196 p. MdBLC. 44-5507

Schmid, Christoph von, 1768-1854. The
lost child, from the German of Schmid.
Translated from the French edition, by
Rev. A. Stevens. Boston: Waite Pierce
and company, 1844. 151 p. NHem; NNC.
44-5508

Schmidt, Henry Immanuel, 1806-1889.
Education. Part 1. History of education,
ancient and modern. Part II. A plan of
culture and instruction based on Christian principles, and designed to aid in the
right education of youth, physically, in-
tellectually, and morally, ...New York:
Harper and brothers, 1844. 340 p. InRch;
MBAt; MiU; MLow; MMh. 44-5509

Schmucker, Samuel Simon, 1799-1873.
Psychology, or, elements of a new system
of mental philosophy, on the basis of con-
sciousness and common sense. Designed
for colleges and academies. By S. S.
Schmucker.... Second edition, much enlarged. New York: Harper and brothers,
1844. 329 p. CoCsC; DLC; ICJ; KWiU;
NbOM. 44-5510

Schmucker, Samuel Simon, 1799-1873.
Psychology; or, elements of a new system
of mental philosophy, on the basis of con-
sciousness and common sense.... Third
edition enlarged. New York: Harper,
1844. 329 p. PPLT. 44-5511

Schneck, Benjamin Shroder, 1806-
1874. Die deutsche kanzel; eine sam-
mlung auserlesener predigten der
neuesten zeit. Chambersburg, Pennsylvania: Druckerei der Hochdeutsch
Reformirten Kirche, 1844. 560 p. IEG;
PPLT; PPG; PPeSchw; PSt. 44-5512

The School controversy. Remarks on
the seventh annual report of Horace
Mann. Reply to the "remarks" of "thirty-
one Boston schoolmasters," &c. by
Horace Mann. [From the Boston post,
December 11, 1844. Boston: 1844] MH.
44-5513

Schoolcraft, Henry Rowe, 1793-1864.
Oneonta; or characteristics of the red
race of America. From original notes and
manuscripts. New York: Burgess,
Stringer and company, 1844-1845. 8 v. in
1. CU-B; ICN; MH; OClWHi; TxU. 44-
5514

Schott, James. The younger. A statement by.... [In regard to the proceedings
for a divorce instituted by Mrs. Schott.

Baltimore?: 1844] 49 p. MdHi; NN; PHi. 44-5515

Schuylkill Navigation Company. An address to the stockholders of the Schuylkill Navigation Company, in reply to a pamphlet circulated by the Reading Railroad Company. Philadelphia: printed for the author, 1844. 20 p. NN; NNE; PPFrankI; PHi. 44-5516

Schuylkill Navigation Company. Junius.... Philadelphia: 1844. PPL. 44-5517

Schuylkill Navigation Company. Report of the president and managers of the Schuylkill navigation company to the stockholders, January 1, 1844. Philadelphia: Joseph and William Kite, 1844. 24 p. C-S; WU. 44-5518

Scituate, Massachusetts. First Trinitarian Congregational Church of Christ. Church manual; or, the history, standing rules, discipline, articles of faith, and covenant.... with a list of members. Boston: 1844. 36 p. MHi; MWA; NBLiHi. 44-5519

Scituate, Massachusetts. First Trinitarian Congregational Church. With a list of the members. Boston: M.S. Damrell, 1844. 36 p. MB; MH; MNos; WHi. 44-5520

Scott, Orange. Church government: a work for the times, containing also a declaration of rights.... Boston: O. Scott, 1844. 128 p. MBNMHi; Nh; WWauHi. 44-5521

Scott, Orange. The Methodist Episcopal church and slavery; containing also the views of the Wesleyan Methodist Church, with regard to slavery; and a treatise on the duty of seceding from all pro-slavery churches.... By Rev. Orange Scott. Boston: Orange Scott, 1844. 128 p. MB; NBuG; NjMD. 44-5522

Scott, Walter, 1771-1832. Marmion: tale of Flodden Field. A poem, in six cantos. New York: D. Appleton and company, 1844. GMar; MH; NcD; RPB; ViU. 44-5523

Scott, Walter, 1771-1832. The poetical works of.... by J.W. Lake. 1 vol. Philadelphia: J. Crissy, 1844. 443 p. MShW; NN. 44-5524

Scott, Walter, 1771-1832. The poetical works.... with a life of the author. New York: D. Appleton and company; Philadelphia: G. S. Appleton, 1844. 624 p. PPA. 44-5525

Scott, Walter, 1771-1832. Waverly novels, with the author's last corrections and additions. Complete in five volumes. Philadelphia: Carey and Hart, 1844-1849. 5 v. NN; OCl. 44-5526

Scott, Walter, 1771-1832. Waverly novels, with the author's last corrections and additions. New edition. Complete in five volumes. Philadelphia: Carey and Hart, 1844. 5 v. NN. 44-5527

Scotts Charitable Society, Boston. Constitution, adopted May 9, 1843; with list of members from 1657-1844. Boston: The society, 1844-1896. DNLM; MB; MH; PPPrHi. 44-5528

Scribe, Augustin Eugene. Judith, or, the opera box [New York: Morris and Willis, 1844] 10 p. MB. 44-5529

Scribner, Isaac W. Review of the Rev. U. C. Burnap's sermon on Bible servitude. ....Published by request of the friends of the slave in Lowell. [Lowell?]: J. G. Pillsbury, printer, 1844. 22 p. IaHi; MdBJ; OClWHi; RPB; WHi. 44-5530

Scribner, J.M. A practical system of mensuration of superficies and solids: designed especially for advanced scholars in schools and academies by Rev. J.M. Scribner, A.M. ....Auburn: H. and J.C. Ivison, 1844. 123 p. DLC; ICBB. 44-5531

Scribner, J.M. A practical system of mensuration of superficies and solids. New York: A. V. Blake, 1844. 123 p. DAW; DLC. 44-5532

Scribner, J.M. The ready reckoner; being a correct measurement of scantling, plank, square timber, saw logs, wood, etc. Rochester: Fisher and Co., 1844. 64 p. NRU. 44-5533

Seabrook, Whitemarsh Benjamin, 1795-1855. A memoir on the origin, cultivation and uses of cotton, from the earliest ages to the present time, with a special reference to the sea-island cotton plant.... located in Georgia and South Carolina.... Charleston: Miller and Browne, 1844. 62 p. CU; LU; NjP; PPAN; ScC. 44-5534

Seabrook, Whitemarsh Benjamin, 1795-1855. Origin, cultivation and uses of cotton. Charleston: 1844. MB. 44-5535

Seabury, Samuel, 1801-1872. Discourse, death of Reverend Arthur Carey. New York: 1844. CtHT; MB; PHi; PPL. 44-5536

Seabury, Samuel, 1801-1872. The joy of the saints: a discourse on.... the death of.... Arthur Carey.... by.... Samuel Seabury.... New York: J.A. Sparks, 1844. 28 p. MH; MiD-B; MWA; NjR; NNG. 44-5537

Seabury, Samuel, 1801-1872. The joy of the saints. Second edition. New York: J.A. Sparks, 1844. InU; MB; MBAt; MH; NBuDD; NN. 44-5538

Seabury, Samuel, 1801-1872. The joy of the saints: a discourse.... Third edition. New York: James A. Sparks, 1844. 28 p. NBuG. 44-5539

Seabury, Samuel, 1801-1872. The relation of the clergy and laity: a discourse preached in St. Paul's Chapel and St. Clement's Church, New York. By the Rev. Samuel Seabury, D.D., rector of the Church of the Annunciation. New York: Henry M. Onderdonk, 1844. 24 p. InU; MH; MiD-B; MWA; NNG. 44-5540

Sealsfield, Charles, 1793-1864. The cabin book; or sketches of life in Texas, by Sealsfield [Charles Sealsfield, pseud.] translated from the German by Professor C.F. Mercsh. New York: Winchester, 1844. 155 p. CtHT; LNH; MH; PPL; TxU. 44-5541

Sealsfield, Charles, 1793-1864. Life in the new world; or, sketches of American society, by Sealsfield [pseud] Translated from the German by Gustavus C. Hebbe and James Mackay. New York: J. Winchester [1844] 349 p. CSmH; LU; NjR; PPL-R; PU. 44-5542

Sealsfield, Charles, 1793-1864. North and south; ....New York: J. Winchester

[1844] 118 p. CtHT; DLC; LNH; MH; Tx. 44-5543

Sears, Barnas, 1802-1880. The ciceronian; or the Prussian method of teaching the elements of the Latin language... Boston: Gould, Kendall and Lincoln, 1844. 184 p. IaGG; MAmP; NjP; OO; PCA. 44-5544

Sears, Edmund Hamilton. A discourse occasioned by the death of Rev. Isaac Allen, of Bolton, preached at Lancaster, March 24th, 1844. By Edmund H. Sears. Worcester: Jonathan L. Estey, 1844. 16 p. ICMe; MB; MH-AH; MWA; RPB. 44-5545

Sears, James H. A standard spelling book; or, the scholar's guide to an accurate pronunciation of the English language.... revised edition. Newark, New Jersey: Benjamin Olds, 1844. 144 p. NjN. 44-5546

Sears, M. The American politician; containing the Declaration of Independence, the constitution, the inaugural and first annual addresses and messages of all the presidents and other important state papers. Sixth edition. Boston: Bela Marsh, 1844. 564 p. MB; MH; MiD-B; OCl. 44-5547

Sears, Robert, 1810-1892. Bible biography; or the lives and characters of the principal personages recorded in the sacred writings... Edited by Robert Sears.... Twelfth edition. New York: Sears and Walker, 1844. 491 p. CtMW; KBB; MB; MoSpD; OWoC. 44-5548

Sears, Robert, 1810-1892. The guide to knowledge; or repertory of facts; forming a complete library or of entertaining in-

formation, in the several departments of science, literature, and art. New York: Sears and Walker, 1844. 484 p. MiU; MNan; MoS; ScDuE; ViU. 44-5549

Sears, Robert, 1810-1892. A new and popular pictorial description of the United States: containing an account of the topography, settlement, history, revolutionary and other interesting events, statistics, progress in argriculture... New York: R. Sears, 1844. 608 p. OClWHi. 44-5550

Sears, Robert, 1810-1892. A new and complete history of the Holy Bible, as contained in the Old and New Testaments, from the creation of the world to the full establishment of Christianity. Second edition. New York: Sears and Walker, 1844. 2 v. in 1. MB; MH; NN; RPB; ViU. 44-5551

Sears, Robert, 1810-1892. A new and complete history of the Holy Bible, as contained in the Old and New Testaments, from the creation of the world to the full establishment of Christianity. Third edition. New York: Sears and Walker, 1844. 2 v. in 1. McA-S. 44-5552

Sears, Robert, 1810-1892. A new and complete history of the Holy Bible, as contained in the Old and New Testaments, from the creation of the world to the full establishment of Christianity. Fourth edition. New York: Sears and Walker, 1844. 2 v. in 1. CtY; FSar; MA; NWiN; PPLT. 44-5553

Sears, Robert, 1810-1892. The wonders of the world, in nature, art and mind, comprising library of useful and entertaining knowledge... Sixth edition, New York: R. Sears and E. Walker, 1844. 528

p. IEG; MLow; MH; NbOP; WSteT. 44-5554

Seaver, Ebenezer. The register or Odd Fellow's guide to all encampments, grand and degree lodges in the New England states. Boston, 1844. MH. 44-5555

Seaver, James Everett, 1789-1827. Deh-he-wa-mis: or, a narrative of the life of Mary Jemison: ....by Ebenezer Mix. Third edition. Batavia, New York: W. Seaver and son, 1844. 192 p. DLC; ICN; NN; WHi; WNaE. 44-5556

Seaver, James Everett, 1789-1827. Life of Mary Jemison. Third edition. Batavia: 1844. ICN. 44-5557

Sedgwick, Catharine Maria, 1789-1867. A love taken for children. Designed for Sunday school libraries. New York: Harper and Brothers, 1844. 142 p. MH; MHi. 44-5558

Sedgwick, Catharine Maria, 1789-1867. Means and ends, or, self-training. By the author of Redwood, Hope Leslie, Home.... Second edition. New York: Harper and brothers, 1844. 278 p. RJa. 44-5559

Sedgwick, Catharine Maria, 1789-1867. Tales and sketches. Second series. By the author of "Hope Leslie, Home," &c, &c. New York: Harper and brothers, 1844. 396 p. DLC; ICU; MH; PPL-R; RPA. 44-5560

Sedgwick, Susan Anne Livingston [Ridley] 1789-1867. Alida; or, town and country.... [anon.] New York: Henry G. Langley, 1844. 176 p. CtHT; IU; PPL; RPB; ViU. 44-5561

Sedgwick, Theodore, 1811-1859. Thoughts on the proposed annexation of Texas to the United States. First published in the New York Evening Post, under the signature of veto. New York: D. Fanshaw, printer, 1844. 55 p. CU-B; MeB; RPB; TxGR. 44-5562

Sedgwick, Theodore, 1811-1859. Thoughts on the proposed annexation of Texas to the United States. First published in the New York Evening Post, under the signature of veto, [Theodore Sedgwick] together with the address of Albert Gallatin, LL.D., delivered at the tabernacle meeting, held on the 24th of April, 1844. Second edition. New York: S. W. Benedict and company, 1844. 56 p. CU-B; MH-AH; OCl; PPL; WHi. 44-5563

The seed.... New York: 1844. DLC. 44-5564

Seidenstucker, Johann Heinrich Phillip. An elementary practical book for learning to speak the French language, expressly adapted to the capacity of children. Translated from the German by Mrs. Barbara O'Sullivan Addicks. New York: Collins, brother and company, 1844. MH; NN; PHi. 44-5565

Select anecdotes and extracts, on moral and religious subjects, by various authors. Philadelphia: Tract Association of Friends, [1844?] WHi. 44-5566

Select theological library; containing valuable publications principally treating the doctrine of universal salvation. Philadelphia: Gihon, Fairchild, and company, 1844. MH; MH-AH; NCaS; OrPD; VtReg. 44-5567

The self instructor's assistant in stenography, or, the act of shorthand writing.... Albany, New York: Munsell and Tanner, printers, 1844. MHi; NAl. 44-5568

Self-examination: or plain questions for professors of religion. Boston: 1844. DLC. 44-5569

Semaine Litteraire du Courrier des etats unis. Recreif Shoise de Romans, Feuilletons, ouvrages Historiques et Dramatiques en prose et en vers, des autenes Modernes Les plus Renommes. Troisieme Serie. New York: F. Caillardet, editeur, Bureau du Courrierdes Etas Unis, 1844. CSf; LNB; LNT; MB. 44-5570

Semple, James. Remarks of Mr. Semple of Illinois, on the resolution introduced by him relative to the occupancy of the Oregon Territory. Delivered in the Senate of United States, January 25, 1844. Washington: Blair and Rives, 1844. 19 p. CSmH; CU-B; Or; PPL. 44-5571

Sentiment and poetry of flowers. Boston: 1844. 61 p. MWA. 44-5572

Severance, Luther, 1797-1855. Speech of Mr. Severance of Maine, on the right of petition. Delivered in the House of Representatives, February 16, 1844. Washington: Printed by J. and G.S. Gideon, 1844. 16 p. DLC; ICU; MH; NBU; PU. 44-5573

Seward, William Henry, 1801-1872. The elements of empire in America; address before the literary society of Amherst College. New York: 1844. 39 p. CBPSR; ICN; MBC; MWA; PU. 44-5574

Seward, William Henry, 1801-1872.

Governor Seward and Gerrit Smith. Letter from Governor Seward to the Whig Young Men of Rochester. Auburn, April 10, 1844. [Utica: Jackson and Chaplin, 1844] 8 p. N. 44-5575

Sewell, Elizabeth Missing, 1815-1906. Amy Herbert. By a lady. Edited by the Rev. W. Sewell, B.D. ....New York: Harper and brothers, 1844. 133 p. KSalW; MeBa; NjR; RPB; ViU. 44-5576

Sewell, Elizabeth Missing, 1815-1906. The rectors visits; or stories on the Lords prayer. New York: Republished by the General Protestant Episcopal Sunday School Union, 1844. 108 p. ICU. 44-5577

Sewell, Richard Clarke, 1803-1864. A treatise on the law of sheriff, with practical forms and precedents. Philadelphia: John S. Littell, 1844. 472 p. W. 44-5578

Sewell, William, 1654-1720. The history of the rise, increase and progress of the Christian people called Quakers, intermixed with several remarkable occurrences.... Written originally low Dutch, and translated by himself into English. To which is prefixed a brief memoir of the author, compiled from various sources.... New York: Baker and Crane, 1844. 2 v. in 1. InU; MoSM; OO; RJa; ScC. 44-5579

Sewell, William, 1804-1874. Christian morals. By the Rev. William Sewell, M.A., fellow and tutor of Exeter College, and professor of moral philosophy in the University of Oxford. From the latest London edition. Flemington, New Jersey: J.R. Dunham, 1844. 152 p. CtMW; MsJMC; TMeD. 44-5580

Sewell, William, 1804-1874. Christian morals; from the third London edition.

Baltimore: Robinson, 1844. 423 p. MBC; ODaB; PPLT; ViU; WHi. 44-5581

Seymour, David Lowrey, 1802-1867. Remarks delivered in the House of Representatives.... January 9, 1844 [upon the resolution offered by Mr. Wise that so much of the president's message as relates to the policy of attending to the lakes and rivers of the west, be referred to the committee on commerce] [Washington: 1844] 7 p. MiD-B; MnHi; WHi. 44-5582

Seymour, David Lowrey, 1802-1867. Revenue: minority report, April 6, 1844. [Washington] 1844. ICN. 44-5583

Sforzosi, Luigi. A compendious history of Italy, translated from the original Italian, by Nathaniel Greene. New York: Harper and brothers, 1844. 319 p. InCW; MeAu; NOg; OWoC. 44-5584

Shakespeare, William, 1564-1616. The dramatic works of William Shakespeare, with a life of the poet, ...Boston: Charles C. Little and James Brown, 1844. 7 v. KyLo; NcU; O; PU. 44-5585

Shakespeare, William, 1564-1616. The dramatic works of William Shakespeare, ...Complete in one volume. Hartford, Connecticut: S. Andrus and sons, 1844. 844 p. IU. 44-5586

Shakespeare, William, 1564-1616. Loves of Venus, with all the suppressed passages. Boston: Wm. O. Page and company, 1844. 32 p. MWA. 44-5587

Sharon, Massachusetts. First Congregational Church. Articles of faith and covenant of the First Congregational Church, Sharon, Massachusetts. May,

1844. Boston: Samuel N. Dickinson, printer, 1844. 8 p. MBC; MWA. 44-5588

Sharp, Daniel, 1783-1853. Christian Mourning. A discourse delivered at the funeral of Rev. Lucius Bolles. Boston: Gould, Kendall and Lincoln, 1844. 44 p. CtSoP; ICMe; NHC-S; PCA; RPB. 44-5589

Sharp, Daniel, 1783-1853. A discourse delivered at the funeral of Rev. Lucius Bolles, D.D. By Daniel Sharp. Boston: Gould, Kendall and Lincoln, 1844. 44 p. ICNBT; MB; MPeHi; NNC; PCC. 44-5590

Sharp, Daniel, 1783-1853. Recognition of friends in Heaven; discourse. Fourth edition. Boston: J. Putnam, 1844. MBAt. 44-5591

Shea, J.A. Who feeleth not a rapture? A Whig banner song. The poetry by J.A. Shea, esq. The music by Alexander Kyle. New York: J.F. Nunns, 1844. 5 p. CSt. 44-5592

Shecut, John Linnaeus Edward Whitridge, 1770-1836. The scout; or, the fast of Saint Nicholas. A tale of the seventeenth century. By the author of the eagle of the Mohawks. New York: C. L. Stickney, 1844. 312 p. DLC; RPB; ScU; WHi. 44-5593

Shedd, William Greenough Thayer, 1820-1894. The influence of temperance upon intellectual discipline: a discourse before the Temperance Society of the University of Vermont, April 30. Burlington: 1844. 31 p. IaB; KWiU; MH; RPA; VtHi. 44-5594

Shehane, C.F.R. A sermon on the

parable of the rich man and Lazarus. Wetumpka: Charles Mancey, printer, 1844. 15 p. MMeT. 44-5595

Sheil, Richard Lalor, 1791-1851. ....The apostate, a tragedy in five acts, by Richard Sheil, esq. ....Philadelphia and New York: Turner and Fisher, [1844?] 63 p. DLC; MH. 44-5596

Shenstone, William, 1714-1763. Poetical works with life, critical dissertations, and explanatory notes by Rev. George Gilfillan. New York: D. Appleton and company, 1844. 284 p. ScC. 44-5597

Shepard, Charles Upham, 1804-1806. A treatise on mineralogy. Second edition. New Haven: A.H. Maltby, 1844. 168 p. MH; NNE; NRU; OClW; TWcW. 44-5598

Shepard, Isaac Fitzgerald. Hymn. Boston: Crocker and Brewster, 1844. 24 p. RPB. 44-5599

Shepard, Isaac Fitzgerald. Poetry of feeling, and spiritual melodies. Boston: Lewis and Sampson, 1844. 128 p. MB; MH; MWat; RPB. 44-5600

Shepard, James Biddle. An address delivered before the two literary societies, of the University of North Carolina in Gerard Hall by James Shepard, June 5, 1844. Published by order of the society. Raleigh, North Carolina: printed by T. Loring, at the office of the Independent, 1844. 18 p. MH; NcAS; NN; PHi; WHi. 44-5601

Shepherd, William, 1768-1847. A history of the American revolution. First published in London under the superintendence of the Society for the Diffusion

of Useful Knowledge. Revised and enlarged by Rev. J.L. Blake.... New York: A.V. Blake, 1844. 252 p. DLC; MiGr; NBU; OrU; ViU. 44-5602

Sheppard, John Hannibal, 1789-1873. Address delivered at Portland before the Grand Lodge and Chapter of Maine and visiting lodges. By John H. Sheppard, P.H. and K.T. Tuttle and Dennett, printers, 1844. 80 p. Me; MH; NNFM; PHi; WHi. 44-5603

Sherman, Henry, 1808-1879. An analytical digest of the law of marine insurance, containing a digest of all the cases adjudged in this state, ...by Henry Sherman. New York: Gould, Banks and company, 1844. 315 p. IU; PU-L. 44-5604

Sherman, Henry, 1808-1879. Governmental history of the United States of America, from the earliest settlements to the adoption of the present constitution.... New York: M.H. Newman, 1844. 282 p. DLC; ODW. 44-5605

Sherman, John, 1772-1828. A description of Trenton Falls, Oneida County, New York. New York: W.H. Colyer, 1844. 23 p. CtMW; MBC; OClWHi; PPl; RWe. 44-5606

Sherwin, Thomas, 1799-1869. An elementary treatise on algebra, for the use of students in high schools and colleges. By Thomas Sherwin, A.M. Second edition. Boston: Benjamin B. Mussey, 1844. 300 p. CtWatk; MB; MH; NNC. 44-5607

Sherwood, Henry Hall. Motive power of organic life and the symptoms and treatment of chronic diseases. Second edition enlarged. By Henry Hall Sherwood, M.D. New York: Wiley and Putnam, 1844. 268 p. CLCM; MNS; NIC; OUrC; PV. 44-5608

Sherwood, Mary Martha Butt, 1775-1851. History of little Henry and his bearer. New York: 1844. IEG. 44-5609

Sherwood, Mary Martha Butt, 1775-1851. The lady of the manor: being a series of conversations on the subject of confirmation, intended for the use of the middle and higher ranks of young females.... New York: Harper and brothers, 1844. 4 v. RPB; ViU. 44-5610

Sherwood, Mary Martha Butt, 1775-1851. The lily of the valley. New York: J.S. Taylor and company, 1844. MDeeP; NN. 44-5611

Shew, Joel, 1816-1855. Facts in hydropathy; or, water cure; ....By Joel Shew, M.D. ....New York: Burgess, Stringer and company, 1844. 108 p. MBC; NNN. 44-5612

Shew, Joel, 1816-1855. Hand-book of hydropathy; or, a popular account of the treatment and prevention of diseases by means of water. New York: Wiley and Putnam, 1844. 144 p. ICU; LNOP; MWA; PPCP; WU-M. 44-5613

Shew, Joel, 1816-1855. Hydropathy or the water cure: By Joel Shew, M.D. New York: Wiley and Putnam, 1844. 304 p. IGK; MBM; NbU; PPCP; RPM. 44-5614

Shew, M.L. Water-cure for ladies; a popular work on the health, diet and regimen of females and children, and the prevention and cure of diseases; with a full account of the processes of water cure.... revised by Joel Shew.... New

York, New York: Wiley, 1844. 156 p. MoSpD; NcD; OO; PU; VtU. 44-5615

Shimeall, Richard Cunningham, 1803-1874. Prophecy, now in course of fulfillment, as connected with the 2,300 days of Daniel VIII: 14: a sermon, in two parts in Daniel XI: 14, last clause, showing the predicted rise, career and subversion of Millerism.... delivered in the large chapel of the New York University.... February 18th and 25th, 1844. New York: 1844. 51 p. MH-AH; WHi. 44-5616

Shinning it; a tale of a tape-cutter, or, the mechanic turned merchant. By one who knows. New York: M. Y. Beach, 1844. 32 p. MH. 44-5617

Shoberl, Frederic, 1775-1853. Persecutions of popery: historical narratives of the most remarkable persecutions occasioned by the intolerance of the church of Rome, by Frederic Shorberl. New York: Harper and brothers, 1844. 183 p. CSansS; MB; PPPrHi; TxDaM; ViU. 44-5618

Short miscellanies for young people. Philadelphia: Paul T. Jones, 1844. 117 p. GDecCT. 44-5619

Short, Thomas Vowler. What is Christianity? New York: Stanford and Swords, 1844. 165 p. CtHT; IU; MPiB; NNMer; OrPD. 44-5620

Shunk, Francis R. Broadside relative to his participation in a Catholic procession. Philadelphia: 1844. PPL. 44-5621

Siddons, Leonora. The female warrior; an interesting narrative of the sufferings and adventures of Miss L. Siddons....

New York: Barclay, 1844. 23 p. ICU; PHi; PPAmP. 44-5622

Siegvolk, Paul. The everlasting gospel, commanded to be preached by Jesus Christ, judge of the living and the dead unto all creatures, concerning the eternal redemption found out by him whereby devil, sin, hell and death shall at last be abolished, and the whole creation restored.... Written originally in German. Philadelphia: Gihon Fairchild and company, 1844. 43 p. MH; MMeT-Hi; MWA; PPL; PReaHi. 44-5623

Sigourney, Lydia Howard Huntley, 1791-1865. The book for girls, consisting of original articles in prose and poetry. New York: Turner and Hayden, 1844. 243 p. RPB. 44-5624

Sigourney, Lydia Howard Huntley, 1791-1865. The child's book. Consisting of original articles, in prose and poetry. New York: Turner, 1844. CtHT; IaU; MB; PPM. 44-5625

Sigourney, Lydia Howard Huntley, 1791-1865. The pictorial reader, consisting of original articles for the instruction of young children. ....New York: Turner and Hayden, 1844. 141 p. CtHT; MH; NBuG. 44-5626

Sigourney, Lydia Howard Huntley, 1791-1865. Pleasant memories of pleasant lands. ....Second edition. Boston: J. Monroe, 1844. 373 p. GU; KPea; NcAS; VtU; WaS. 44-5627

Sigourney, Lydia Howard Huntley, 1791-1865. Pocahantas, and other poems. ....New York: Harper, 1844. 283 p. CtSoP; ILM; MLow; OM; WU. 44-5628

Sigourney, Lydia Howard Huntley, 1791-1865. Poems, by Lydia H. Sigourney. Philadelphia: J. Locken, 1844. 256 p. MeLewB; Mi; MLow. 44-5629

Sigourney, Lydia Howard Huntley, 1791-1865. Scenes in my native land [Hartford, Connecticut: 1844] 288 p. Mbev. 44-5630

Sigourney, Lydia Howard Huntley, 1791-1865. Select poems. Fourth edition. Philadelphia, Pennsylvania: Edward C. Biddle, 1844. 320 p. CtHWatk; NcDaD; NjHo; NTEW; ViSWC. 44-5631

Sigourney, Lydia Howard Huntley, 1791-1865. Sketches by Mrs. Sigourney. Amherst: J.S. and C. Adams, 1844. 216 p. NN; WPta. 44-5632

The Silver lake. Words by Percival. Adapted to a celebrated Tyrolean melogy. Boston: George P. Read, 1844. 3 p. IaU; MNF. 44-5633

Simcoe, John Graves, 1752-1806. A history of the operations of a partisan corps, called the Queens Rangers commanded by Lt. Col. J.G. Simcoe during the war of the revolution. New York: Bartlett and Welford, 1844. 13-328 p. CaBVa; DLC; MiU; OCl; Vi. 44-5634

Simcoe, John Graves, 1752-1806. Military journal; history of the operation of the Queen's rangers during the American revolution, by Lieut. Col. J. Graves Simcoe. Now first published, with a memoir of the author. New York: Bartlett and Welford, 1844. 328 p. MnM; OMC; RNR; ScC; WHi. 44-5635

Simm's Monthly Magazine. The Southern and Western monthly

magazine and review edited by W. Gilmore Simms. Charleston: 1844-1845. 2 v. LU; MiU; PSt. 44-5636

Simmons, Mr. Speech of Mr. Simmons of Rhode Island.... to reduce the duties on imports. Delivered in the United States Senate, March 27, 1844. Washington: 1844. 32 p. In; OO; PPL. 44-5637

Simmons, Charles, 1798-1856. A scripture manual, alphabetically and systematically arranged, designed to facilitate the finding of proof texts. By Charles Simmons.... Second edition, enlarged and revised. Boston: Crocker and Brewster; Providence: I. Wilcox, 1844. 539 p. IU; MB; MiU; OO; WHi. 44-5638

Simms, Frederic Walter, 1803-1865. A treatise on the principal mathematical instruments employed in surveying, levelling, and astronomy: explaining their construction, adjustments and use. With an appendix and tables. By Frederic W. Simms.... Second American edition.... Revised and with additions, by J. H. Alexander. Baltimore: F. Lucas, junior [1844] 134 p. MdBD; MiD; OClWHi; PPL; TNP. 44-5639

Simms, William Gilmore, 1806-1870. Castle dismal; or, the bachelor's Christmas. A domestic legend.... [anon.] New York: Burgess, Stringer and company, 1844. 192 p. CSmH; DLC; MB; NN; TxU. 44-5640

Simms, William Gilmore, 1806-1870. The life of Francis Marion. New York: H.G. Langley, 1844. 347 p. IaAS; KEmT; MoS; PSt. 44-5641

Simms, William Gilmore, 1806-1870.

The life of Francis Marion... Eighth edition. New York: George Cooledge and brother [1844] 347 p. KyHI; OCHP; WaU. 44-5642

Simms, William Gilmore, 1806-1870. The life of Francis Marion... Tenth edition. New York: George Cooledge and brother, 1844. 347 p. InU; LU; MNS; PLFM; Vi. 44-5643

Simms, William Gilmore, 1806-1870. The prima donna: a passage from city life.... Philadelphia: Louis A. Godey, 184. 24 p. CtY; MWA. 44-5644

Simms, William Gilmore, 1806-1870. The Yemassee: a romance of Carolina.... [anon.] New York: 1844. 2 v. in 1. MdBJ. 44-5645

Simons, Samuel, 1792-1847. Remarks on the resolution to appoint a standing committee on printing and engraving maps and charts, delivered in the House of Representatives of the United States, March 16, 1844. Washington: 1844. 8 p. WHi. 44-5646

Simpson, Stephen, 1789-1854. The life of Thomas Jefferson. With a portrait, and a parallel... Philadelphia: J.G. Russell, 1844. 1890389 p. MH; ViU. 44-5647

Singer's own book: a well selected collection of the most popular sentimental, patriotic, naval and comic songs. Philadelphia: 1844. CtHWatk. 44-5648

Six months ago; or, the eventful Friday and its consequences: an epic poem. By R.... Philadelphia: 1844. 16 p. PHi; PPL-R. 44-5649

Sketches of sermons preached in

various parts of the United Kingdom and on the European continent. Furnished by their respective authors. Vol. III, First American edition. Philadelphia: Sorin and Ball, 1844. 396 p. ArPb; C-S; IaFay-U; InID; PRea. 44-5650

Sketches of the lives of Jesus Christ and the twelve apostles. Watertown, New York: Knowlton and Rice [1844] 12 p. NN. 44-5651

Skinner, H.B. Family doctor, or guide to health. Thirteenth edition. Boston: the author, 1844. MoKU. 44-5652

Skinner, H.B. Family doctor, or guide to health. Sixteenth edition. Boston: the author, 1844. 56 p. IEN-M. 44-5653

Skinner, H.B. Family doctor, or guide to health. Twentieth edition. Boston: Skinner and Blanchard, 1844. CtHT; OrU-M. 44-5654

Skinner, H.B. Family doctor, or guide to health. Thirty-second edition. Boston: J.K. Wellman, 1844. 56 p. NNC. 44-5655

Skinner, John Stuart, 1788-1851. Address delivered before the Agricultural Society of Newcastle County, Delaware, at the annual meeting, held September 11, 1844. Newcastle county, Delaware: 1844. 28 p. MH; PPL. 44-5656

Skinner, Otis Ainsworth, 1807-1861. Family worship; containing reflections and prayers for domestic devotion. Fourth edition. Boston: A. Tompkins and B.B. Mussey, 1844. 216 p. FSar; IaU. 44-5657

Skinner, Otis Ainsworth, 1807-1861. Lessons derived from the death of the young; address, August 4, 1844, funeral of Miss Evelina T. Stevenson. Boston: A. Tompkins, 1844. 16 p. MMeT-Hi; RPB. 44-5658

The slave power. From an address to the voters of the Second Congressional District of Ohio. 1844. 4 p. ICu; OClWHi. 44-5659

The slave's cry. Vol. 1, no. 1. December 23, 1844. New London, Connecticut: 1844-. V. 1-. MB. 44-5660

Slavery; a treatise showing that slavery is neither a moral, political, nor social evil. Penfield, Georgia: Benjamin Brantly, 1844. 40 p. MH; MNtCA; NjMD; NNG; OClWHi. 44-5661

Sleeper, John Sherburne, 1794-1878. Tales of the ocean, and essays for the forecastle, containing matters and incidents humorous, pathetic, romantic and sentimental. By Hawser Martingale. New York: R.P. Bixby, 1844. 431 p. IU. 44-5662

Slidell. Speech of Mr. Slidell, of Louisiana, on the tariff. In the House of Representatives, April 27, 1844. 15 p. In; MH; NBu. 44-5663

Sloan, R.R. The character of the present age, and the responsibilities of the literary men. An address delivered before the students of Ashland Academy, Commencement Day, October, 1844. Mt. Vernon, Ohio: E.J. Ellis, printer, 1844. 16 p. OClWHi. 44-5664

Slocum, John, b. 1787. An authentic narrative of the life of Joshua Slocum: containing a succinct account of his revolutionary services, together with other interesting reminiscences! and thrilling incidents in his eventful life. Carefully compiled by his eldest son, John Slocum. Hartford: Printed for the author, 1844. 105 p. MdBJ; MiD-B; OHi; WHi. 44-5665

Smallwood, G.B. The Christian church in the first century.... Rossville, Ohio: J. M. Christy, 1844. 189 p. OClWHi; OOxM. 44-5666

Smedley, Edward. Sketches from Venetian history. New York: Harper, 1844. 2 v. in 1. InCW; LN; MWar; NcU; RPE. 44-5667

Smellie, William, 1740-1795. The philosophy of natural history. By William Smellie, ...with an introduction and various additions and alterations, ...By John Ware, M.D. Stereotype edition. Boston: William J. Reynolds, 1844. 344 p. MH; MPiB; RRu; TNP; TxU-T. 44-5668

Smiley, Thomas Tucker, d. 1879. A complete key to Smiley's new federal calculator, or, scholar's assistant; ....Designed to facilitate the labour of teachers, and assist those who have not the advantage of a tutor's aid.... Philadelphia: Grigg and Elliott, 1844. 177 p. DAU; NNC. 44-5669

Smiley, Thomas Tucker, d. 1879. The new federal calculator, or scholar's assistant: ....for the use of schools and counting houses. By Thomas J. Smiley, ...Philadelphia: Griggs and Elliott, 1844. NoLoc. 44-5670

Smith, Albert, 1805-1870. Speech of Mr. Albert Smith of New York, on the subject of the tariff. Delivered in the House of Representatives, April 30, 1844. Washington: J. and G.S. Gideon, printers, 1844. 15 p. ICU; NBU; NNC; TxU; WHi. 44-5671

Smith, Alexander B. The mode and subjects of baptism, being the substance of two discourses preached at Cedar Creek Church, Anson County, North Carolina, September 17, 1843, in reply to two discourses on the same subject, delivered... by the Rev. R. Furman. Charleston, South Carolina: Southern Christian Advoccate, 1844. 112 p. CtHT; NcD; NcU. 44-5672

Smith, Andrew M. Brief history of Evangelical missions, with the date of commencement and progress and present state. Hartford: Robins and Smith, 1844. 193 p. CSansS; MB; OWoC; RPB; ViRut. 44-5673

Smith, B.B. A sermon, preached on occasion of the funeral of the Rev. William Jackson, on Lord's day afternoon, February 25, 1844. In St. Paul's Church, Louisville, Kentucky. By Rt. Rev. B.B. Smith, D.D. Louisville: Morton and Griswold, 1844. 18 p. InID; MdBD; MiD-B; NGH; NN. 44-5674

Smith, Benjamin Mosby, 1811-1893. The exclusive claims of prelacy, stated and refuted: a discourse delivered in.... Staunton: Harper, 1844. GDecCT; MB; MH-AH; PPPrHi. 44-5675

Smith, Caleb Blood, 1808-1864. Effects of a protective tariff on agriculture: speech on the subject of the tariff, delivered in the House of Representatives of the United States April 20, 1844. Washington: J. and G.S. Gideon, 1844. 16 p. DLC; NNC; WHi. 44-5676

Smith, Caleb Blood, 1808-1864. Speech in the House of Representatives, February 9, 1844 on the constitutionality of the second section of apportionment act. Washington: 1844. 12 p. DLC; OCHP; OCl; OClWHi; WHi. 44-5677

Smith, Caleb Blood, 1808-1864. Speech of Mr. Caleb B. Smith, of Indiana, on the subject of the tariff. Delivered in the House... April 29, 1844. Washington: Printed by J. and G.S. Gideon, 1844. 16 p. In; MBevHi. 44-5678

Smith, Caleb Blood, 1808-1864. Speech on the constitutionality of the second section of the apportionment act... delivered in the House... February 9, 1844. Washington: 1844.12 p. DLC; OClWHi. 44-5679

Smith, Caleb Blood, 1808-1864. Speech on the memorial of the democratic members of the legislature of Rhode Island. Delivered in the House, March 14, 1844. Washington: Office of the Whig standard, 1844. 16 p. CSmH; DLC; ICN; MMC; PHi. 44-5680

Smith, Charles Billings, d. 1890. The church, the world's reformer. A sermon delivered at the First Baptist Church, of Buffalo, New York. By C.B. Smith. Buffalo [New York] A.M. Clapp, 1844. 30 p. CSmH; N; NHC-S; NNUT. 44-5681

Smith, Elisha. The botanic physician, being a compendium of the practice of medicine, upon botanic principles... Revised, corrected and improved by Isaac S. Smith... New York: printed for the editor, by D. Adee, 1844. 508 p. CSt-L; MdUM. 44-5682

Smith, F.L. Memoir of Sarah Maria Stearns. Boston: 1844. DLC; MBC. 44-5683

Smith, George G. Topographical map of Massachusetts compiled from astronomical, trigonometrical and various local surveys; made by order of the legislature. Simeon Borden, superintendent. [New York]: H.F. Walling, 1844. RPB. 44-5684

Smith, Gerrit, 1797-1874. Gerrit Smith's constitutional argument. Utica: Jackson and Chaplin, 1844. 16 p. DHU; NIC; NN; PHi; WHi. 44-5685

Smith, Gerrit, 1797-1874. To the friends of the slave in the town of Smithfield: Pardon me for again warning you against the most guilty and corrupting body of men in the land. I mean the clergy... Peterboro: 1844. NSyU. 44-5686

Smith, Gerrit, 1797-1874. To the proslavery voters of the County of Madison. Peterboro, April 20, 1844 [Peterboro? New York: 1844] 3 p. WHi. 44-5687

Smith, Gibson. Trial for slander. Rev. Gibson Smith vs. John R. Clark... New Portland, September, 1843. Bangor: Printed for the publisher, 1844. 24 p. MeHi. 44-5688

Smith, Henry Foster. An essay on human magnetism: or the infant magnetism enrobed in its panoply. Second edition. Philadelphia: printed by William S. Young, 1844. 96 p. InU; MnHi; OC. 44-5689

Smith, Henry Hollingsworth, 1815-1890. Anatomical atlas, illustrative of the structure of the human body. By Henry H. Smith.... Philadelphia: Lea and

Blanchard, 1844. 200 p. CLU; ICJ; MiOC; RPB; ScAb. 44-5690

Smith, Horatio, 1779-1849. Arthur Arundel, a tale of the English revolution. By the author of "Brambletye house," etc. New York: Harper and brother, 1844. 159 p. KSalW; LNH; MB; RPB; ViU. 44-5691

Smith, Horatio, 1779-1849. Festivals, games, and amusements, ancient and modern, with additions, by Samuel Woodworth, esq., of New York. New York: Harper and brothers, 1844. 355 p. LN; MeAu; MWar; OCX; RWe. 44-5692

Smith, Hugh. Heart delineated in its state of nature and as renewed by grace. New York: Harper and brothers, 1844. 330 p. GDecCT; InLW; LN; MB; NjP. 44-5693

Smith, J.R. Key to the panorama of Boston, from an original drawing in 1839. Boston: 1844. CtHC. 44-5694

Smith, James Strudwick. To the voters of Wake, Person and Orange. Hillsborough: Aughor, 1844. [1] p. NcU. 44-5695

Smith, John Calvin. Guide through Ohio, Michigan, Indiana, Illinois, Missouri, Wisconsin and Iowa, showing the township lines of the United States surveys. New York: Colton, 1844. In. 44-5696

Smith, John Calvin. Map of Long Island, with the environs of New York and the southern part of Connecticut. New York: J.H. Colton and company, 1844. NIC. 44-5697

Smith, John Cross, 1803-1878. The religion and patriotism of '76. A discourse delivered in the city of Washington on the Fourth of July, 1844.... Second edition. Washington: J. and G.S. Gideon, 1844. 24 p. CBPac; MeLewB; MWA; NAuT; PPPrHi. 44-5698

Smith, John Hyatt. National oration, by J. Hyatt Smith, esq., and temperance oration, by Isaac Edwards, esq., delivered at Guilderland Centre, July 4, 1844.... Albany, [New York]: E. H. Pease, 1844. 40 p. MH; MWA; NBLiHi; NjR; WHi. 44-5699

Smith, John Reubens. The juvenile drawing book. Third edition. Philadelphia: J.W. Moore, 1844. MH; PPL. 44-5700

Smith, John William, 1809-1845. A selection of leading cases on various branches of the law: with notes, by John William Smith. With additional notes, and references to American decisions, by J.I. Clark Hare and H.B. Wallace. Philadelphia: T. and J.W. Johnson, 1844. 2 v. DLC; IU; NcD; OO. 44-5701

Smith, John William, 1809-1845. A selection of leading cases on various branches of the law: with notes. By John William Smith. With additional notes, and references to American decisions, by J.I. Clark Hare and H.B. Wallace. Second law library, from the last London edition. Philadelphia: J.S. Littell, 1844. 2 v. CU; MdBJ; MH-L; NIC-L; PP. 44-5702

Smith, John. Romanism in Mexico; being a reply to an article by the Rev. Mr. Verot, against Mayer's Mexico, in the United States Catholic magazine, for

March, 1844. By John Smith, junior. Baltimore: D. Brunner, 1844. 31 p. ICU; MdBD; MdHi; PPL; VtU. 44-5703

Smith, Joseph, 1805-1844. Correspondence between Joseph Smith, the prophet and Col. John Wentworth.... New York: John E. Page and L.R. Foster, elders of the church of Latter Day Saints, 1844. 16 p. CSmH; IHi; NN; USIC. 44-5704

Smith, Joseph, 1805-1844. The doctrine and covenants of the Church of Jesus Christ of Latter Day Saints; carefully selected from the revelations of God... Second edition. Nauvoo, Illinois: Printed by John Taylor, 1844. 448 p. CtY; MH; NN; OClWHi; WHi. 44-5705

Smith, Joseph, 1805-1844. General Smith's views of the powers and policy of the government of the United States. Nauvoo, Illinois: Taylor, 1844. 12 p. CtY; IEdS; MoS; NjP; OC. 44-5706

Smith, Joseph, 1805-1844. General Smith's views of the powers and policy of the government of the United States. New York: E.J. Bevin, printer, 1844. 41 p. CSmH; IHi. 44-5707

Smith, Joseph, 1805-1844. General Smith's views of the powers and policy of the government of the United States. Philadelphia: Printed by Brown, Bicking and Gilbert, 1844. 12 p. CtY. 44-5708

Smith, Joseph, 1805-1844. General Smith's views of the powers and policy of the government of the United States. Pontiac, Michigan: 1844. 12 p. USIC. 44-5709

Smith, Joseph, 1805-1844. The voice of truth, containing General Joseph Smith's correspondence with General James Arlington Bennett; appeal to the Green Mountain boys, etc., also, correspondence with the Hon. Henry Clay. Nauvoo, Illinois: J. Taylor, printer, 1844. 64 p. IHi; MH; NN. 44-5710

Smith, Leonidas L. The Christian race, a sermon By Rev. L. Smith of Norflok, Virginia. Savannah: Printed by Thomas Purse, 1844. 56 p. PPL; Vi. 44-5711

Smith, M. Hale. Sermon delivered before First Church and Society in Nashua, New Hampshire, November 14, 1844. Thanksgiving day. Boston: S.N. Dickinson, 1844. 27 p. MBNMHi; MeBat; MLow; Nh. 44-5712

Smith, M.G. Synopsis of phrenology. Concord: 1844. 11 p. Nh-Hi. 44-5713

Smith, Marcus A. The Boston speaker; being a collection of pieces in prose, poetry, and dialogue. Sixth edition, enlarged and improved. Boston: Joseph Dowe, 1844. 234 p. NNC. 44-5714

Smith, Marion. The life of Marion Smith, written by her niece. Boston: 1844. 12 p. RPB. 44-5715

Smith, Martha, 1787-1841. Letters of Martha Smith, with a short memoir of her life... New York: Piercy and Reed, 1844. 230 p. MH; NjR; OClWHi; PHC; PSC-Hi. 44-5716

Smith, Matthew Hale, 1810-1879. The blessings yet left us. A sermon delivered before the First Church and Society in Nashua, New Hampshire, November 14, 1844. Being the day of annual thanksgiving. By M. Hale Smith, pastor. Boston:

S.N. Dickinson, printer, 1844. 27 p. CBPSR; MB; MiD-B; Nh-Hi; RPB. 44-5717

Smith, Matthew Hale, 1810-1879. Universalism examined, renounced, exposed; Twelfth edition. Boston: Tappan and Dennet, 1844. 396 p. CoD; IaMP; MnSS; NbCrD; PU. 44-5718

Smith, Robert. Both sides of Universalism. Covington, Kentucky: Grihfield, 1844. PPPrHi. 44-5719

Smith, Roswell Chamberlain, 1797-1875. Arithmetic on the productive system, accompanied by a key and cubical blocks. Stereotype edition. Hartford: John Paine, 1844. MH; NjR. 44-5720

Smith, Roswell Chamberlain, 1797-1875. Atlas to accompany Roswell C. Smith's geography for schools, 1844 or 1845. [Hartford: 1844?] 22 l. MH; WHi. 44-5721

Smith, Roswell Chamberlain, 1797-1875. English grammar on the productive system. A method of instruction recently adopted in Germany and Switzerland, designed for schools and academies. Cincinnati: W.T. Truman, 1844. 192 p. IaHA; InICC; MH; MHad; NNC. 44-5722

Smith, Roswell Chamberlain, 1797-1875. English grammar on the productive system, a method of instruction recently adopted in Germany and Switzerland; designed for schools and academies. Philadelphia: Butler and Williams, 1844. 192 p. MH; OO. 44-5723

Smith, Roswell Chamberlain, 1797-1875. Smith's atlas.... designed to accompany the geography.... 1843. Hartford: J. Paine, 1844. MH. 44-5724

Smith, Roswell Chamberlain, 1797-1875. Smith's geography. Geography on the productive system.... Revised and improved. Accompanied by a large and valuable atlas. ....Hartford: John Paine, 1844. 312 p. AzU; GMM; MH; IU; OClW. 44-5725

Smith, Roswell Chamberlain, 1797-1875. Smith's new arithmetic. Arithmetic on the productive system; accompanied by a key and cubical blocks. By Roswell C. Smith, author of practical and mental arithmetic, the productive grammar, the productive geography, &c. Stereotyped edition. Rochester: William Alling, 1844. 311 p. N; NNC. 44-5726

Smith, Roswell Chamberlain, 1797-1875. Smith's new grammar. English grammar, on the productive system: a method of instruction recently adopted in Germany and Switzerland. Designed for schools and academies.... New stereotype edition. Philadelphia: Butler and Williams, 1844. 192 p. MDeeP; OO; WU. 44-5727

Smith, Samuel Francis, 1808-1895. Lyric gems: a collection of original and select sacred poetry. Boston: Gould, Kendall and Lincoln, 1844. 128 p. CtHWatk; MnU; NcD; OO; RPB. 44-5728

Smith, Sarah Pogson. The Arabians; or the power of Christianity. Philadelphia: Hooker, 1844. 69 p. OO; RPB. 44-5729

Smith, Sydney, 1771-1845. Letters on American debts. New York: J.

Winchester, New World Press, 1844. 13 p. Ct; DLC; KHi; MiD-B; NNC. 44-5730

Smith, Sydney, 1771-1845. The works of the Rev. Sydney Smith. New York: Edward G. Taylor, 1844. 333 p. CoU; InThR; LNB; MH; TJaU. 44-5731

Smith, Sydney, 1771-1845. The works of the Rev. Sydney Smith. Philadelphia: Carey and Hart, 1844. 3 v. ArAO; LNB; MH; MnS; PPA. 44-5732

Smith, Thomas W. A narrative of the life, travels and sufferings of Thomas W. Smith: comprising an account of his early life, adoption by the gipsy's, his travels during eighteen voyages to various parts of the world, during which he was five times shipwrecked.... written by himself. Boston: William C. Hill, 1844. 240 p. MB; MH; MoKU; Nh; Nh-Hi. 44-5733

Smith, Thomas, 1775 or 6-1830. The origin and history of missions; a record of the voyages, travels, labors, and successes of the various missionaries.... compiled from authentic documents.... by John O. Choules and Rev. Thomas Smith. Seventh edition. New York: Robert Carter, 1844. 2 v. CtMW; KyLoP; MiU; MnSM; PPPrHi. 44-5734

Smith, Wesley, 1815-1902. The Methodist Episcopal Church against the charges of having obtained her form of government by fraud.... Cadiz, Ohio: Printed at the Standard office, 1844. 55 p. NjR. 44-5735

Smith, William D. d. 1848. Bible, confession of faith and common sense being a series of dialogues between a Presbyterian minister and a young convert... doctrines of the confession of faith of the Presbyterian Church; to which are added five dialogues on the ground and causes of the division of the Presbyterian Church in 1837 and 1838. Springfield: 1844. 251 p. CSansS; InCW; KyLxT; NbOP; OO. 44-5736

Smith, William Henry, 1806-1872. The drunkard; or the fallen saved. By the author of the moral drama of the same name which has been performed nearly one hundred times at the Boston Museum. Boston: E.P. Williams [1844] 38 p. MH. 44-5737

Smith, William Henry, 1806-1872. The drunkard; or the fallen saved; a moral domestic drama, in five acts...New York: Samuel French [1844] 64 p. MS; OCl; TNP. 44-5738

Smith, William R. The duty of supporting the ministry. A sermon preached... before the Northumberland Presbytery at McEwensville... Sunbury, Pennsylvania: Office of the "Sunbury American," 1844. CSmH; MB; PPPrHi. 44-5739

Smither, James. A noisy member, and a silent monitor; discourse, Baptist Church, Plainfield, December, 1843. Hartford: Burr and Smith, printers, 1844. 12 p. Ct; MBAt; MiD-B; PCA. 44-5740

Smithville Seminary. North Scituate, Rhode Island. Catalogue of the officers and students of Smithville Seminary, for the year ending August 22, 1844. Pawtucket: B. W. Pearce, printer, 1844. 16 p. RHi; RPB. 44-5741

Smollett, Tobias George, 1721-1771. The expedition of Humphry Clinker. Newark, New Jersey: B. Olds, 1844. 2 v. CtY; ICU. 44-5742

Smollett, Tobias George, 1721-1771. The history of England, from the revolution in 1688 to the death of George the Second. Designed as a continuation of Hume. Philadelphia: T. Davis, 1844. [15]-967 p. AAP; MH; MSda; OCo; TSewU. 44-5743

Smyth, Thomas, 1808-1873. An address delivered before a meeting of the Friends of Sunday Schools in... Charleston, South Carolina. Philadelphia: American Sunday School Union [1844] MH; MnHi; NNUT; PPL; PPPrHi. 44-5744

Smyth, Thomas, 1808-1873. Claims of the Free Church of Scotland to the sympathy and assistance of American Christians. Second edition. New York: Leavitt, Trow and company, 1844. 146 p. ScDuE. 44-5745

Smyth, Thomas, 1808-1873. Ecclesiastical catechism of the Presbyterian Church; for the use of families, Bible classes, and private members. Fourth edition. New York: 1844. 113 p. GOgU; MiU; NN; ViRut; WHi. 44-5746

Smyth, Thomas, 1808-1873. Exodus of the Church of Scotland; and the claims of the Free Church of Scotland to the sympathy and assistance of American Christians; Second edition. New York: Leavitt, Trow and company, 1844. 146 p. ICU; NCH; NjP; NN; PPPrHi. 44-5747

Smyth, Thomas, 1808-1873. The life and character of Calvin, the reformer, reviewed and defended. Philadelphia: Presbyterian Board of Publication, 1844. 120 p. CSt; GDecCT; MnSM; PPPrHi; ScDuE. 44-5748

Smyth, Thomas, 1810-1873. The history, character, and results of the Westminster Assembly of Divines.... By Thomas Smyth, D.D. New York: Leavitt, Trow and company, 1844. 124 p. CSans-S; IEG; MiD; PPPrHi; RPA. 44-5749

Smythies, Harriet Maria Gordon, 1838-1883. The jilt. A novel. New York: Harper and brothers, 1844. 131 p. DLC; LNH. 44-5750

Snodgrass, William D. Discourses on the apostolical succession, by W.D. Snodgrass.... Troy, New York: Stedman and Redfield, 1844. 283 p. IaDuU; MBC; NjR; OU; RPB. 44-5751

The social pioneer, and herald of progress. [Published under the superintendence of the New England Social Reform Society] Boston: J.P. Mendum, [1844] 96 p. ICU; IU. 44-5752

Social reform: or, an appeal in behalf of association, based upon the principles of a pure Christianity.... Northampton: John Metcalf, printer, 1844. 72 p. NNCo-Ci. 44-5753

Society for the Promotion of Collegiate and Theological Education. Annual report. New York: 1844. 1st.-. CtHT; IGK; NjR; PPL; TxU. 44-5754

Society for the Promotion of Collegiate and Theological Education. First report. New York: J.F. Trow and company, 1844. 16 p. ICP; InU; MAnP; NNUT; TxHuT. 44-5755

Society for the Promotion of Collegiate and Theological Education. Permanent documents.... New York: J.F. Trow,

1844. v. 1-. Ct; CtY; CU; ICJ; MB. 44-5756

Society of Jesus in North America. Secret instructions of the Jesuits; with an appendix.... Philadelphia: F.C. Wilson, 1844. 72 p. NjR. 44-5757

Solar almanac. New York: Sun office, 1844. MWA. 44-5758

Sommers, Charles George. Memoir of the Rev. John Stanford, together with an appendix, comprising brief memoirs of the Rev. John Williams, Rev. Thos. Baldwin and Rev. Richard Furman. New York: Stanford, 1844. 417 p. ICU; KyLo; PCC. 44-5759

Songs, duets, choruses and finales in the new fairy tale of Fortunia and his seven gifted servants.... New York: J.C. House, printer, 1844. 8 p. NjR. 44-5760

Songs for the Sabbath. By various authors. Boston: Oliver L. Perkins, 1844. 128 p. CtMW; MBNMHi; NcWsM; OrU; WU. 44-5761

Songs for the Sabbath. [New York: Morris and Willis, 1844?] 16 p. MWA; MWH; NN; OrU; RPB. 44-5762

Sons of Temperance of North America. Constitution and by-laws of the Harmony Division, No. 5 of the Sons of Temperance, of New Haven, Connecticut. Adopted May 16, 1844. New Haven: Printed by B.L. Hamlin, 1844. 33 p. PHi. 44-5763

Sons of Temperance of North America. Journal of the proceedings of the National Division of the Sons of Temperance, Second annual session. Philadelphia: S.

Douglas Wyeth, 1844-. v. 1-. IaHA; IU; MoSpD; NcD; OMC. 44-5764

Sons of Temperance of North America. Proceedings... from the commencement of the order until the formation of the Grand Division of the state of New York. Philadelphia: S. Douglas Wyeth [1844?] 115 p. OClWHi. 44-5765

Sons of temperance. New York. [Journal of grand division of New York, 1842-1844] Philadelphia: stereotyped by S. Douglas Wyeth, [1844?] 115 p. MnHi. 44-5766

Sophocles, Evangelinus Apostolides, 1807-1883. A catalogue of Greek verbs. For the use of colleges. Hartford: H. Huntington, 1844. 319 p. CtMW; CU; ICU; NBu; TxU-T. 44-5767

Sophocles, Evangelinus Apostolides, 1807-1883. Dramas; translated by Thomas Franklin. New York: Harper, 1844. NPtc. 44-5768

Sophocles, Evangelinus Apostolides, 1807-1883. A greek grammar, for the use of learners. By E.A. Sophocles. Ninth edition. Hartford: H. Huntington, 1844. 284, 12 p. ICU; MH; NNC; OO; ScCC. 44-5769

Sophocles, Evangelinus Apostolides, 1807-1883. A greek grammar, for the use of learners. By E.A. Sophocles. Tenth edition. Hartford: H. Huntington, 1844. 284 p. MH; NbCrD; NNC. 44-5770

Sophocles, Evangelinus Apostolides, 1807-1883. Sophocles. Translated by Thomas Franklin, D.D., Greek professor in the University of Cambridge. New

York: Harper and brothers, 1844. 343 p. LNH; MChi; MH; RWe; ViU. 44-5771

Soulie, Frederic, 1800-1847. The mysteries of the heaths; or the chateau de Chevalaine. From the French of Frederic Soulie. Translated by George Fleming. New York: H.G. Langley, 1844. 168 p. CtY; MdBP; OU. 44-5772

South Carolina. Acts of the General Assembly of the State of South Carolina, passed in December, 1843. Printed by order of the Legislature and designed to form a part of the eleventh volume, commencing with the acts of 1839. Columbia: Pemberton, State printer, 1844. 59 p. IaU-L; L; MH; Nj; Nv. 44-5773

South Carolina. Cases at law, argued and determined in the court of appeals of South Carolina. From November, 1843 to May 1844, both inclusive. By R.H. Speers, State reporter. Columbia: A.S. Johnston, 1844. 2 v. L; Me-LR; MoU; Nv; W. 44-5774

South Carolina. Equity cases, argued and determined in the Court of appeals of South Carolina from November, 1842 to May, 1844 by R.H. Speers. Columbia: A.S. Johnston, 1844. 676 p. Ct; In-SC; Me-LR; Mn; W. 44-5775

South Carolina. Governor's message, no. 1. November 26, 1844. 14 p. ScU. 44-5776

South Carolina. Governor. 1842-44. J.H. Hammond. Letter of His Excellency Governor Hammond to the free church of Glasgow on the subject of slavery. Columbia: A.H. Pemberton, 1844. 7 p. MH. 44-5777

South Carolina. Journal of the House of Representatives of the state of South Carolina, being the annual session of 1844. Columbia: A.H. Pemberton, 1844. 192 p. In-SC; Nj; T. 44-5778

South Carolina. Journal of the Senate of the state of South Carolina. Being the annual session of 1844. Columbia: A.H. Pemberton, State printer, 1844. 178 p. In-SC; MH; Nj; Sc; T. 44-5779

South Carolina. Report of the proceedings in the cases of the Bank of South Carolina, and the bank of Charleston, upon scire facias to vacate their charters for suspending specie payments in the years, 1842 and 1843. Printed by order of the legislature of South Carolina. Charleston: W. Riley, 1844. 550 p. NN; NNG; ScU. 44-5780

South Carolina. Report of the regents of the lunatic asylum. 23 p. A-Ar; WHi. 44-5781

South Carolina. Report on the geological and agricultural survey of the state of South Carolina, 1844. By M. Tuomey, geological surveyor of the state. Columbia: Printed by A.S. Johnston, 1844. 8 p. MdBJ; NNC; OCU; TxU; WM. 44-5782

South Carolina. Reports and resolutions of the General Assembly of South Carolina, passed at its regular session of 1844. Columbia: A.H. Pemberton, State Printer, 1844. 204 p. IaU-L; MH; Nj; Sc. 44-5783

South Carolina. University. Treasurer's report to the board of trustees. Columbia, 1844-. ScU. 44-5784

South Carolina College. Catalogue of

the trustees, faculty and students of the South Carolina College. January, 1844. 12 p. GDecCT. 44-5785

South Cove Corporation. Boston. Catalogue of 128 lots of land....to be sold at auction.... Boston: Crocker and Brewster, 1844. 8 p. MH-BA. 44-5786

South Hadley, Massachusetts. First Congregational Church. Articles of faith and covenant, with a list of members, Northampton: J.H. Butler, 1844. 11 p. MBC; NN. 44-5787

South, Robert, 1633-1716. Sermons preached on several occasions. By Robert South.... A new edition, in 4 volumes, including the posthumous discourses....Philadelphia: Sorin and Ball, 1844. 4 v. CBB; ICU; MH-AH; OCX; TJaL. 44-5788

Southern almanac, ...by Robert Grier. Americus, Georgia: T.P. Ashmore, [1844] 44-5789

Southern Christian Sentinel. No. 1/5-1841-. Charleston, South Carolina: Hussey, 1844. PPPrHi. 44-5790

Southern rights, free trade and anti-abolition tract no. I. Contents letters of the Hon. Langdon Cheves. Speech of the Hon. Daniel Webster at Fanieul [sic] Hall, 1820. Bancroft's speech in New York. Jackson's letter on Texas. Address of the Democratic Association at Washington. John Quincy Adams disunion letter. Charleston: Walker and Burke, printers, 1844. 40 p. DLC; NNC; OCHP; ScHi; TxU. 44-5791

Southey, Caroline Anne Bowles, 1786-1854. Autumn flowers and other poems.

Boston: Saxton, Peirce and company, etc., etc., 1844. CSmH; DLC; MH. 44-5792

Southey, Robert. The book of the church. From the fifth London edition. Flemington, New Jersey: J.R. Dunham, 1844. 266 p. IaDa; MB; NGH; PLOR; PPP. 44-5793

Southgate, Horatio, 1812-1894. A letter to the members of the Protestant Episcopal Church in the United States, from...Horatio Southgate, their missionary at Constantinople. New York: Stanford and Swords, 1844. 39 p. MH-AH; NNG. 44-5794

Southgate, Horatio, 1812-1894. Narrative of a visit to the Syrian [Jacobite] Church of Mesopotamia; with statements and reflections upon the present state of Christianity in Turkey, and the character and prospects of the eastern churches, by the Rev. ....New York: D. Appleton and company; Philadelphia: G. S. Appleton, 1844. 275 p. ArBaA; ICT; MnHi; PHC; RPA. 44-5795

Southgate, Horatio, 1812-1894. Vindication of the Rev. Horatio Southgate: a letter to the members of the Protestant Episcopal Church in the United States, from the Rev. Horatio Southgate, ...New York: Stanford and Swords, 1844. 39 p. CtHC; IEG; MBC; PPPrHi; RPB. 44-5796

Southgate, Horatio, 1812-1894. Visit to the Syrian Church of Mesopotamia. New York: 1844. 275 p. LNP MB; MBL. 44-5797

Southwark Fire Engine Company.

Philadelphia. Charter and by-laws. Philadelphia: 1844. 21 p. PHi. 44-5798

Southwestern law journal and reporter. Edited by Milton A. Haynes.... Nashville: Cameron and Fall, 1844. 284 p. ICU; MiU-L; TMeC; ViU; WaU-L. 44-5799

Spalding, Martin John, 1810-1872. D'Augibne's "history of the great reformation in Germany and Switzerland," reviewed; or, the reformation in Germany examined in its instruments, causes, and manner, and in its influence on religion, government, literature, and general civilization. By M.J. Spalding, D.D. Baltimore: John Murphy; Pittsburgh: George Quigley, 1844. 379 p. MoSU; NhD; PPiD; RPB; WNaE. 44-5800

Spalding, Martin John, 1810-1872. Sketches of the early Catholic missions of Kentucky, from their commencement in 1787 to the jubilee of 1826-7. Louisville: B. J. Webb [1844] 398 p. InHi; KyHi; MnS; NN; WHi. 44-5801

Sparks, Jared, 1789-1866. Letters on the ministry, ritual and doctrines of the Protestant Episcopal Church addressed to the Rev. Wm. E. Wyatt, in reply to a sermon. Second edition. Boston: James Munroe and company, 1844. 240 p. MdBP; NNC; ScNC; WNaE. 44-5802

Sparks, Jared, 1789-1866. The library of American biography. Boston: Charles C. Little and James Brown, 1844. 10 v. IUr; ViW. 44-5803

Sparks, Jared, 1789-1866. Life and treason of Benedict Arnold. New York: Harper, 1844. 335 p. KyLx; MChi; MPri; NNC; RNHi. 44-5804

Sparks, Jared, 1789-1866. The life of George Washington. Boston: Tappan and Dennet, 1844. 562 p. CSmH; ICN; MeB; ODW; PPFr. 44-5805

Sparks, Jared, 1789-1866. Lives of John Stark, Charles Brockden Brown, Richard Montgomery and Ethan Allen. By Jared Sparks. New York: Harper and brothers, 1844. 356 p. NSon. 44-5806

Sparks, Jared, 1789-1866. Ministry, ritual and doctrines of the Protestant Episcopal Church. 2d edition. Boston, 1844. MB. 44-5807

Sparrow, William, 1801-1874. Annual sermon, before the bishops, clergy, and laity, constituting the board of missions of the Protestant Episcopal Church in the United States of America, preached in the Church of the Ascension, New York, June 19, 1844. New York: Daniel Dana, Jr., 1844. 20 p. MdBD. 44-5808

Spear, Charles, 1801-1863. Capital punishment of death. Fourth edition. Boston: the author, 1844. 237 p. CtY; MB; MBS; PU. 44-5809

Spear, Charles, 1801-1863. Essays on the punishment of death. Second edition. Boston: the author, 1844. 237 p. MBAt; MH-L; NjR; PP; RNR. 44-5810

Spear, Charles, 1801-1863. Essays on the punishment of death. Third edition. Boston and London: 1844. MB; MH; MHi; OCLaw. 44-5811

Spear, Charles, 1801-1863. Essays on the punishment of death. Fourth edition. Boston: the author, 1844. 237 p. IU; MeAug; MMeT-Hi; MnU; PU. 44-5812

Spear, Charles, 1801-1863. Essays on the punishment of death. Fifth edition. Boston: the author, 1844. 237 p. MB; MH; MnU; MPiB; NRAL. 44-5813

Spear, Charles, 1801-1863. Essays on the punishment of death. Sixth edition. Boston: the author, 1844. 238 p. StTeach-C. 44-5814

Spear, Charles, 1801-1863. Essays on the punishment of death. Seventh edition. Boston: the author, 1844. 237 p. MMeT-Hi; NhConC; NNIA. 44-5815

Spear, Charles, 1801-1863. Essays on the punishment of death. Eighth edition. Boston: the author, 1844. CSt; MdBE; MH-AH; MiU; WHi. 44-5816

Spear, Charles, 1801-1863. Essays on the punishment of death, Ninth edition. Boston: the author, 1844. 237 p. IaUL; MBC; MoU; OrP. 44-5817

Spear, Charles, 1801-1863. Essays on the punishment of death. Twelfth edition. Boston: the author, 1844. 237 p. NN. 44-5818

Spear, Charles, 1801-1863. Names and titles of the Lord Jesus Christ. Sixteenth edition. Boston: C. Spear, 1844. DLC; IaMP; MBC; MH. 44-5819

Spear, William Wallace. The holy Catholic Church, the communion of saints. A sermon.... Philadelphia: J.M. Campbell; New York: Saxton and Miles, 1844. 26 p. MB; MWA; NNG; PHi; RPB. 44-5820

The spectator. With sketches of the lives of the author, an index, and explanatory notes.... Philadelphia: J. Cris-sey, 1844. 12 v. in 6. CMC; KyLoP; NLock; OAk; ScP. 44-5821

Speeches of the Rev. Drs. Tyng, Parker, and Everts, at the Boston meeting... May 29, 1844. Philadelphia: American Sunday School Union [1844] 40 p. NjPT; PHi. 44-5822

Speed, Joseph John. A letter from J.J. Speed, esq. of Baltimore to the representatives of Maryland, in the congress of the United States on the subject of the canal. Baltimore: printed by Buel and Tuttle, 1844. 18 p. CSmH; DLC; MdHi; MiU; NNE. 44-5823

Spencer, Jesse Ames, 1816-1898. The Christian instructed in the ways of the gospel and the church; a series of discourses delivered in St. James's Church, Goshen, New York, during the years 1840-42. New York: D. Appleton and company, 1844. 325 p. CBCDS; InID; NNS; OrPD; WHi. 44-5824

Spencer, Thomas, 1793-1857. Documents and analysis of facts, showing the pecuniary and moral obligations between the board of professors of the medical Institution, and the board of trustees of Geneva College, 1843 to 1844, furnished in answer to an official call upon the medical faculty by the standing committee of trustees on the medical institution. Albany: 1844. 96 p. MB; NNC; WHi. 44-5825

Spindler, Karl, 1796-1855. The Jesuit; a historical romance, illustrating the principles and practices of the celebrated society of the Jesuits during the early portion of the 18th century. New York: J. Winchester [1844] 110 p. ICU; MH; MoSHi; NjP; RPB. 44-5826

Spindler, Karl, 1796-1855. The Jew. New York: Harper and brothers, 1844. 173 p. CL; KyU; PPDrop; RPA; RPB. 44-5827

The spirit and his bride. The wearer of many crowns. The faithful and true. The word of God. New York: Tribune printer, J.A. Fraetas, 1844. 16 p. NjR. 44-5828

Spirit of the nation. American edition. Boston: Donahoe, 1844. 72 p. MB; PV. 44-5829

The spirit of the nation: and other select political songs. By the writers of the Dublin newspaper press. New York: Boston: Montreal: D. and J. Sadlier and company, 1844. 2 v. in 1. LNX. 44-5830

The spirit of the nation: and other select political songs. Part I. By the writers of the Dublin Newspaper Press. First American from the last correct Dublin edition, with additions. New York: Casserly and sons, 1844. 74 p. CtHWatk; MdBLC. 44-5831

The spiritual mirror or looking-glass; exhibiting the human heart as being either the temple of God, or habitation of devils [exemplified by a series of ten engravings] Anciently published in the French language from which it is now translated by Peter Bauder. Sixth American edition. Newburyport: C. Whipple, 1844. 80 p. OKentU; MB; MH. 44-5832

The spoliation of American commerce, first by the French and then by our own government. [From the Democratic Review for February. New York: 1844?] 7 p. DLC; NN; OClWHi. 44-5833

Spooner, John Aiden. The death of Christians precious to the Lord. A sermon, preached in Trinity church, Granville, New York, Saturday, 10th August, 1844, at the funeral of the Rev. Palmer Dyer. Troy, New York: Press of N. Tuttle, 1844. 44 p. MB; N. 44-5834

Spooner, John Alden. A sermon, preached in Trinity Church, Granville, New York, Saturday, 10th August, 1844, at the funeral of Rev. Palmer Dyer, A.M., formerly director of that parish. By the Rev. John Alden Spooner, A.M. Troy, New York: press of N. Tuttle, 1844. 44 p. CtHT; MdBD. 44-5835

Spooner, Lysander, 1808-1887. The unconstitutionality of the laws of Congress prohibiting private mails.... New York: Tribune Printing Establishment, 1844. 24 p. IU; MdBJ; MH; PPL; OClW. 44-5836

Sprague, William Buell, 1795-1876. An address at the Young ladies' institute, Pittsfield, Mass. Pittsfield: E.P. Little; Albany: C. Van Benthuysen and Company, printers, 1844. 32 p. CtY; MWiW; NjR; RPB. 44-5837

Sprague, William Buell, 1795-1876. Address delivered at the close of the annual examination of the young ladies institute, Pittsfield, Massachusetts, September 28, 1844. Pittsfield: Little, 1844. 32 p. KHi; MPiB; MWA; OO; RPB. 44-5838

Sprague, William Buell, 1795-1876. A discourse pronounced July 30, 1844, before the Philomathesian Society in Middlebury College, by William B. Sprague.... Albany: E.H. Pease, 1844. 67 p. CSt; MiD-B; NUtHi; PHi; RPB. 44-5839

Sprague, William Buell, 1795-1876. Occasional discourses. Albany? 1844-1865. 18 v in 1. MnU. 44-5840

Sprague, William Buell, 1795-1876. On true magnanimity addressed particularly to young men, and delivered in the Second Presbyterian Church in Albany, February 25, 1844. By William B. Sprague.... Albany: E.H. Pease, 1844. 56 p. AB; CSt; MHi; NjR; OO. 44-5841

Sprague, William Buell, 1795-1876. A sermon on the danger of political strife addressed to the Second Presbyterian Congregation, Albany. October 13, 1844. Albany: Munsell and Tanner, printers, 1844. 23 p. MB; MHi; MWA; NjR; WHi. 44-5842

Spring Garden Mutual Insurance Company. Charter, with original act of incorporation. Philadelphia: Hogan and Thompson, 1844. 12 p. NNC; PHi. 44-5843

Spring, Gardiner, 1785-1873. The church in the wilderness, and other fragments, from the study of a pastor. New York: John S. Taylor and company, 1844. 160 p. ICLRL; InUpT; MDeeP; OSW. 44-5844

Spring, Gardiner, 1785-1873. A discourse delivered before the general assembly of the Presbyterian church at Louisville, Kentucky, May 1844, by Gardiner Spring. New York: M.W. Dodd, 1844. 51 p. MAnP. 44-5845

Spring, Gardiner, 1785-1873. A dissertation on the rules of faith; delivered at Cincinnati, Ohio, at the annual meeting of the American Bible Society, and published at their request.... New York:

Leavitt, Trow and company, 1844. 104 p. CtHC; ICU; MiU; NoU; PCA. 44-5846

Spring, Gardiner, 1785-1873. The obligations of the world to the Bible: a series of lectures to young men by Gardiner Spring. New York: John S. Taylor and company, 1844. 404 p. CSansS; KyLoP; MoSpD; PP. 44-5847

Spring, Gardiner, 1785-1873. Obligations of the world to the Bible. New edition. Philadelphia: Presbyterian board of publication [1844] CtHC. 44-5848

Spring, Gardiner, 1785-1873. The Saviour's presence with his ministers. A discourse delivered before the general assembly of the Presbyterian Church in the United States, at the opening of their sessions at Louisville, Kentucky, in May, 1844.....New York: M. W. Dodd, 1844. 51 p. In; MWA; OMC; PPPrHi; RP. 44-5849

Springs, John. To the voters of York district. Springfield, York District, South Carolina, June, 1844. n.p.: 1844. [4] p. ScU. 44-5850

Squarey, Charles. Popular treatise on agricultural chemistry. Philadelphia: 1844. PPL. 44-5851

Squib almanack. By H. P. Grolton. Boston: George Roberts, 1844. MWA. 44-5852

Stael-Holstein, Anne Louise Germaine Necker, 1766-1817. Corinne, ou L'Italie. Nouvelle edition. Boston: Otis Brouders, et compagnie, 1844. 431 p. CU; KyDC; MdBP; NCats; RPB. 44-5853

Stael-Holstein, Anne Louise Germaine

Necker, 1766-1817. The influence of literature upon society. Translated from the French of Madame De Stael-Holstein to which is prefixed, a memoir of the life and writings of the author..... Hartford: S. Andrus and son, 1844. 112 p. NBuCC; TxW. 44-5854

Stanley, Arthur Penrhyn, 1815-1881. The life and correspondence of Thomas Arnold, late head master of Rugby School and Regius Professor of Modern History in the University of Oxford. Fifth American edition. Boston: Ticknor and Fields, 1844. 400 p. NJaM; NTEW. 44-5855

Stanley, Arthur Penrhyn, 1815-1881. Life and correspondence of Thomas Arnold, sometime head master of Rugby school. New York: New Amsterdam Book company, 1844. 548 p. OKentU. 44-5856

Stanley, Arthur Penrhyn, 1815-1881. The life and correspondence of Thomas Arnold. New York: Scribner [1844] 2 v. in 1. InU; MdBE; OSal; PAlt. 44-5857

Stansbury, George A. Tables of interest by months and days.... computed at seven per cent and adapted to other rates. Decimally arranged under the head of time. Together with factors for calculating discount, and convenient time tables. By George A. Stansbury.... New York: Harper and brothers, 1844. 184 p. CtSoP; LNP. 44-5858

Stanton, Robert Livingston. Prelacy examined: being strictures upon three discources [sic.].... New Orleans: A. Brusle, 1844. 235 p. ICP; MBC; NcMHi; NjR; TxU. 44-5859

Starr, Peter. An address, delivered at Westfield, August 14, 1844, at a meeting of the present and former pupils of Westfield Academy. Northampton: John Metcalf, printer, 1844. 16 p. MBC; MH. 44-5860

State Sabbath Convention. Proceedings of the state Sabbath convention held at Harrisburg on the 30th and 31st days of May, A.D. 1844. Philadelphia: Isaac Ashmead, printer, 1844. 43 p. OSW; PCA; PLT. 44-5861

Statement of the sugar and rice crops made in Louisiana.... New Orleans: [1844]-96. 20 v. NjP. 44-5862

Stations of the Holy Cross; with other devotions suited to the holy season of Lent. From the most approved sources. Jersey City: James Walsh, 1844. 128 p. MoSU. 44-5863

Staunton, William. A dictionary of the church, containing an exposition of terms, phrases and subjects connected with the external order, sacraments, worship, and usages of the Protestant Episcopal Church.... Third edition. New York: Onderdonk, 1844. 473 p. IC; NBuG; NNS; OClW; OrPD. 44-5864

Stearns, John Glazier, 1795-1874. An antidote for the doctrine of universal salvation. Second edition revised. Geneva: 1844. 96 p. NHC-S; NNUT. 44-5865

Stearns, Jonathan French. Obstacles and encouragements; two discourses at the anniversary of the author's ordination, Newburyport, September 22, 1844. Newburyport: Tilton, 1844. CtSoP; IEG; MiD-B; MWA; RPB. 44-5866

Stearns, Jonathan French. Two discourses delivered in the First Presbyterian Church in Newburyport.... Newburyport: John G. Tilton, 1844. 36 p. MeBat; MNe; NjR; PPPrHi. 44-5867

Stearns, William Augustus, 1805-1876. Infant church membership; or the relation of baptized children to the church. Boston: Crocker and Brewster, 1844. 165 p. CtHC; KWiU; MB; NhD; PPPrHi. 44-5868

Stebbins, Rufus Phineas, 1810-1885. Two sermons preached before the First Congregational Church and Society in Leominster, September 15, 1844. Boston: Printed by Freeman and Bolles, 1844. CtY; DLC; NIC; WHi. 44-5869

Steele, John Hardy. Message to the legislature, November 20, 1844. Concord: 1844. 6 p. MBC; Nh-Hi. 44-5870

Steele, Oliver Gray, 1805-1879. Steele's Niagara Falls port-folio, containing eight new views of Niagara Falls taken from the most striking points.... Lithographed by Hall and Mooney. Buffalo: Steele's press, 1844. 2 p. DLC. 44-5871

Steele's Albany almanack for 1845. Albany, New York: Steele and Durrie [1844] MWA. 44-5872

Steenrod, Lewis. Speech on the bill to refund General Jackson's fine, delivered in the House of Representatives, January 8, 1844. Washington, 1844. 8 p. WHi. 44-5873

Stelle, Allen. The foundation of success, an address, delivered before the Cleosophic Society of Yates Academy, August 15, 1844, by the Reverend Allen

Steele.... Rochester: D. Hoyt, printer, 1844. 24 p. MoS; NCH; NNC; NRHi; TxDaM. 44-5874

Stephen Girard Charity Fund. Rules for the government of the stewards of the Stephen Girard Charity Fund: with an extract from the will. A.L. 5844. Philadelphia: printed for the use of the stewards, 1844. [24] p. PPFM. 44-5875

Stephens, Alexander Hamilton. Speech of Mr. Stephens, of Georgia, against the tariff bill. Reported by the Committee of Ways and Means. Delivered in the House of Representatives. May 7, 1844. Washington: John T. Towers, 1844. 32 p. MH; MWA; NNC; OClWHi; PHi. 44-5876

Stephens, Alexander Hamilton. Speeches of Mr. Stephens of Georgia, on the right of members to their seats in the House of Representatives, February 9, 1844. Washington: Globe office, 1844. 12 p. MHi; NBu; NcD; NjR. 44-5877

Stephens, Alexander Hamilton. To the people of Georgia, in reply to Mr. Stiles. Washington: 1844. DLC; MBAt. 44-5878

Stephens, Ann Sophia Winterbotham. Alice Copley: a tale of Queen Mary's time. Boston: Yankee office, 1844. 48 p. MWA; NN. 44-5879

Stephens, Ann Sophia Winterbotham. High life in New York. By Jonathan Slick.... of Weathersfield, Connecticut.... Part I; Third edition. New York: Burgess, Stringer and company, 1844. 48 p. NjR. 44-5880

Stephens, Archibald John, 1808-1880?. The law of nisi prius, evidence in civil actions and arbitration and awards; with notes by George Sharswood. Philadelphia: Carey and Hart; Boston: Little and Brown; New York: Gould, Banks and company, 1844. 3 v. AzU-L; MAnP; MH-L; PU-L; TSewU. 44-5881

Stephens, John Lloyd, 1805-1852. Incidents of travel in Central America, Chiapas, and Yucatan. Illustrated by numerous engravings. Twelfth edition. New York: Harper and brothers, 1844. 9-424 p. KyLxT; MC; ScDuE; TJoV. 44-5882

Stephens, John Lloyd, 1805-1852. Incidents of travel in Egypt, Arabia, Petraea and the Holy Land. By an American. Tenth edition, with additions. New York: Harper and brothers, 1844. 2 v. MDW; PU; TNJU; TNP. 44-5883

Stephens, John Lloyd, 1805-1852. Incidents of travel in Greece, Turkey, Russia, and Poland. With a map and engravings... Seventh edition. New York: Harper and brothers, 1844. 2v. CU; KHi; MiU; PSC; TxAu. 44-5884

Stephens, Thomas. A new system of broad and small sword exercise, comprising the broad sword exercise for cavalry and the small sword cut and thrust practice for infantry; to which are added instructions in horsemanship.... Philadelphia: Henry Korn, 1844. 119 p. C; Nh-Hi; WHi. 44-5885

Sternberg, A.W. An address delivered for the Schoharie County Bible Society, at its twenth-eighth anniversary, held in St. Paul's Church, Schoharie C.H. January 9, 1844. Schoharie, New York: 1844. 13 p. N. 44-5886

Sterndale, Mary. The sisters.... Boston: Munroe and Francis, 1844. 96 p. MFiHi. 44-5887

Sterne, Lawrence. The works of Lawrence Sterne, ...Philadelphia: Grigg and Elliot, 1844. 416 p. CLSU; MdBJ; MeBaT. 44-5888

Stetson, Caleb. The principles of reform. A sermon preached at the ordination of John Pierpont, junior, as pastor of the Second Congregational Church in Lynn, October 11, 1843, by Caleb Stetson. Second edition. Boston: B. H. Greene, 1844. 36 p. CBPac; ICMe; MiD-B; MMe; MWA. 44-5889

Stetson, Lemuel. Speech of Mr. Stetson, of New York, touching the opinions of Mr. Van Buren on the right of suffrage, in reply to Mr. Caleb B. Smith: delivered in the House of Representatives, March 20, 1844. Washington: Printed at the Globe office, 1844. 8 p. FC; MH; TxU. 44-5890

Stevens, Abel, 1815-1897. Sketches and incidents; or, a budget from saddlebags of a superannuated itinerant. New York: Lane and Sanford, 1844. DLC; MiD-B; OMC; OO. 44-5891

Stewart, Alvan. The creed of the Liberty Party Abolitionists; or their position defined, in the summer of 1844, as understood by Alvan Stewart. Utica: Jackson and Chaplin, 1844. 8 p. CtY. 44-5892

Stewart, Andrew. Rede.... zur vertheidigung des tarifs und der vertheilung des ertranges der offentlichen landereien unter die staaten, gehalten im Hause der reprasentanten der ver. st. am

13. marz, 1844. Washington: J. and G.S. Gideon, 1844. InU. 44-5893

Stewart, Andrew. Speech in defence of the tariff and distribution, in the House of Representatives of the United States. March 13, 1844 by Andrew Stewart. Washington: J. and G. S. Gideon, printers, 1844. 16 p. GEU; In, M; NjR; PPi. 44-5894

Stewart, Andrew. Speech in favor of Western improvements in the House of Representatives, of the United States, Jan. 16, 1844, by Andrew Stewart. Washington: J.T. Towers, 1844. 16 p. M; MHi; MiD-B; NBU; TB. 44-5895

Stewart, Charles. Biographical sketch of Charles Stewart. Philadelphia, 1844. PPWa. 44-5896

Stewart, James, 1799-1864. A practical treatise on the diseases of children by James Stewart.... Second edition, carefully revised and enlarged. New York: J. and H. G. Langley, 184. 544 p. ICU-R; MdBJ-W; NNN; PPCP; PU. 44-5897

Stewart, Lispenard, 1809-1867. In the matter of proving the last will and testament of the late Robert Stewart. New York, 1844. 65 p. CtY; MH; NjR; NN. 44-5898

Stewart, William. An address delivered in the university chapel before the Athenian Society, Feb. 12, 1844. Bloomington, Indiana: Brandon and Richards, 1844. 16 p. InU. 44-5899

Stier, F. Arguments designed to show that Jesus Christ is the true God. New York: Printed by Piercy and Reed, 1844. 29 p. MdBMP. 44-5900

Stiles, William Henry. Speech of Mr. Stiles of Georgia on the right of petition, in the House of Representatives, January 28 and 30, 1844. Washington, 1844. MH; MHi; NBU. 44-5901

Stimpson's Boston directory containing the names of the inhabitants, their occupations, places of business, and dwelling houses, and the city register, with lists of the streets... Boston: Charles Stimpson, 1844. 580 p. WHi. 44-5902

Stirling, Edward, 1807-1894. Aline; or, the rose of Killarney. A drama, in three acts, by E. Stirling, esq., author of "the Pickwick club" ...."Ondine," etc., etc. ....As performed in the London and American theatres. New York: Samuel French, 1844. 35 p. NNC; OCl. 44-5903

Stockton, Robert Field. Speech delivered at the great democratic meeting at New Brunswick, New Jersey. New York: Printed by Jared W. Bell, 1844. 12 p. LU; MH; MH-BA; NjP; NjR. 44-5904

Stockton, Thomas Hewlings. Floating flowers, from a hidden brook.... Philadelphia: W.S. Young, 1844. 168 p. DLC; MB; RPB. 44-5905

Stokes, George, 1789-1847. The lives of the British reformers... Philadelphia: Presbyteian Board of Publication, 1844. 404 p. CSansS; CtHC; IP; NbOP; PLT. 44-5906

Stokes, George, 1789-1847. The manners and customs of the Jews, and other nations mentioned in the Bible. Second American stereotype edition. Hartford: Henry Berton, 1844. 172 p. ICBB; MB; WU. 44-5907

Stokes, William Axton, 1814?-1877. "Justice to Jackson." An oration, by William A. Stokes, delivered on the first of April, 1844, by the request of the Democratic citizens of Philadelphia. Philadelphia: Mifflin and Parry, printers, 1844. 16 p. CtY; MdW; MiD-B; PPL; WHi. 44-5908

Stokes, William Axton, 1814?-1877. An oration on the character and services of Washington .... 1844 at the Philadelphia Museum. Philadelphia: printed at the office of the National Catholic Register, 1844. 12 p. MBAt; NjR; PHi. 44-5909

Stokes, William, 1804-1878. A treatise on the diagnosis and treatment of diseases of the chest. Diseases of the lung and windpipe. Second edition.... with notes by the American editor. Philadelphia: E. Barrington and G. D. Haswell, 1844. 528 p. ICU-R; LNX; MdBJ-W; NBMS; ViU. 44-5910

Stone, Alice I. Young raven's cry: or, incidents of providence. Boston: 1844. 111 p. Nh-Hi. 44-5911

Stone, Edwin Martin. Hymns and tunes for vestry and conference meetings. By Edwin M. Stone. Boston: William Crosby, 1844. 95 p. MB. MWey; RHi. 44-5912

Stone, John Seely, 1795-1882. Institution of the Sabbath. New York: Blake, 1844. CtHC. 44-5913

Stone, John Seely, 1795-1882. Lectures on the institutions of the sabbath, by the Rev. John S. Stone. New York: Alexander V. Blake, 1844. 186 p. CtB; NjP; OO; PPPrHi; ScCoT. 44-5914

Stone, John Seely, 1795-1882. Memoir of Alexander Viets Griswold. Philadelphia, 1844. CtHWatk; MB; RPB. 44-5915

Stone, John Seely, 1795-1882. Memoir of the life of the Rt. Rev. Alexander Viets Griswold, bishop of the Protestant Episcopal Church in the Eastern Diocese; with an appendix to which are added a sermon, charge and pastoral letter of the late bishop. Philadelphia: Stavely, 1844. 620 p. ICN; MPiB; NcD; OCl; RNR. 44-5916

Stone, John Seely, 1795-1882. Mysteries opened; or scriptural views of preaching and the sacraments as distinguished from certain theories concerning baptismal regeneration and the real presence. New York: Harper, 1844. 396 p. GDecCT; LNB; OrPD; PPA; ScCoT. 44-5917

Stone, Timothy Dwight Porter, 1811-1887. Child's reader... Fifth edition. New York: 1844. CtHWatk. 44-5918

Stone, Timothy Dwight Porter, 1811-1887. Stories to teach me to think. Fifth edition, improved. Boston: Tappan and Dennet, 1844. 180 p. CoU. 44-5919

Stone, William Leete, 1792-1844. Life of Joseph Brant-Thayendanegea; including the border wars of the American revolution, and sketches of the Indian campaigns of Generals Harmar, St. Clair, and Wayne. Cooperstown [New York] 1844. 2 v. CSfA; ICHi; NGlf; NN; PHi. 44-5920

Stone, William Leete, 1792-1844. The poetry and history of Wyoming.... containing the history of Wyoming, from its discovery to the beginning of the present century.... Second edition enlarged. New York: M. H. Newman, 1844. 398 p. MiD-B; OCY; PHi; RPB; WHi. 44-5921

Storer, Bellamy, 1798-1875. An address, delivered before the Literary Society of Granville College, Ohio; at the annual commencement, July 17, 1844. By Bellamy Storer... Cincinnati: printed at the Daily Atlas office, 1844. 26 p. MdBJ; MH; NCH-S; OFH; ViRU. 44-5922

Stories and travels. New York: Leavitt and Allen, 1844. 228 p. IaDL; MB. 44-5923

Stories illustrative of the Lord's Prayer. By a clergyman. Baltimore: Protestant Episcopal Female Tract Society, 1844. 36 p. MdBD. 44-5924

Storrs, Richard Salter, 1787-1873. American slavery, and the means of its removal. A sermon preached in the First Congregational Church, Braintree, April 4, 1844. By Richard Storrs, Pastor of the church. Boston: press of T.R. Marvin, 1844. 31 p. MBC; PU; RPB; TxU; WHi. 44-5925

Storrs, Richard Salter, 1787-1873. A sermon, preached in the First Congregational Church, Braintree, ...By Richard S. Storrs, D.D., pastor of the church. Boston: press of T.R. Marvin, 1844. 31 p. MWey. 44-5926

Story, Joseph, 1779-1845. Commentaries on equity pleadings, and the incidents thereof, according to the practice of the courts of equity, of England and America. Third edition, revised, corrected and enlarged. Boston: C.C. Little and James Brown, [etc., etc.] 1844. 923 p.

Ct; OCLaw; PU-L; TxU-L; WvW-L. 44-5927

Story, Joseph, 1779-1845. Commentaries on the law of agency as a branch of commercial and maritime jurisprudence, with occasional illustrations from the civil and foreign law. Second edition. Boston: Charles C. Little and James Brown, 1844. 667 p. MdBP; NcD; OU; PU-L; WaU. 44-5928

Story, William Wetmore, 1819-1895. Nature and art: a poem, delivered before the Phi Beta Kappa Society of Harvard University.... Boston: Charles C. Little and James Brown, 1844. 48 p. ICN; MWH; RNR; TxU; WHi. 44-5929

Story, William Wetmore, 1819-1895. A treatise on the law of contracts not under seal. ....Boston: C. C. Little and J. Brown, 1844. 472 p. CU-Law; IaU-L; LU-L; Me-LR; TU. 44-5930

The stove almanack. Boston: L. V. Badger, 1844. MWA. 44-5931

Stow, Baron, 1801-1869. Daily manna for Christian pilgrims. Boston: Gould, Kendall and Lincoln, 1844. 128 p. IEG; MBC; OO; PCA; TxElpL. 44-5932

Stowe, Calvin Ellis, 1802-1886. The religious element in education; an address delivered before the American Institute of Instruction, at Portland, Maine, August 30, 1844. Boston: W. D. Ticknor and company, 1844. 34 p. ICP; MBC; NNUT; OClWHi; WHi. 44-5933

Stowe, Harriet Elizabeth Beecher, 1811-1896. The Mayflower; or, sketches of scenes and characters among the descendants of the Pilgrims. By Mrs. Harriet

Beecher Stowe. New York: Harper and brothers, 1844. 324 p. CSt; KyU; LNH; MW; TxU. 44-5934

Stowe, W.R. Sound doctrine; or, scriptural faith in one God, one mediator, and the Holy Spirit. Norfolk: press of William E. Cunningham and company, 1844. 29 p. ICMe; OO. 44-5935

Strange, Robert, 1796-1854. Life and character of Hon. Wm. Gaston. A eulogy delivered by appointment of the officers and members of the Fayetteville Bar, on Monday, November 11, 1844. Fayetteville [N.C.] Printed by E.J. Hale, 1844. 29 p. DLC; NcU; RPB. 44-5936

Stray sunbeams, being selections from the "planetarium," a weekly paper, conducted by the young ladies of the Albany Female Academy. Published for the benefit of the orphan asylum. Albany: Erastus H. Pease, 1844. 24 p. MB. 44-5937

Street, Alfred Billings, 1811-1881. Drawings and tintings. New York: Burgess, Stringer and company; Boston: Redding and company, 1844. 48 p. CtY; DLC; MHi; NjR; WHi. 44-5938

Street talk about an ordinance of councils, passed the 11th July, 1844, organizing a military force for the government of Philadelphia. Philadelphia: 1844. 22 p. DLC; MiD-B; PHi; PPL; PPAmP. 44-5939

Streeter, Russell. Familiar conversations: in which the salvation of all mankind is clearly exhibited and illustrated... Third edition. Philadelphia: Gihon, Fairchild and company, 1844. 83 p. MB; MH; MMeT-Hi. 44-5940

Strickland, G.G. A sermon delivered in the Universalist Meeting House, ...on Thanksgiving Day, ...Newburyport: Watchtower office, printer, 1844. 16 p. MBAt; MiD-B; RPB. 44-5941

Strickland, William Peter. Address delivered at Masonic convocation, held at Lithopolis, August 10, 1844, by Rev. William P. Strickland; published at request of the convention. Columbus: Bro. Charles Scott, printer, 1844. 12 p. IaCrM; NNFM; OCHP. 44-5942

Stuart, Alexander Hugh Holmes, 1807-1891. Anniversary address before the American Institute of the city of New York, at the Broadway Tabernacle, October 18, 1844, during the seventeenth annual fair by the Honorable Alexander H.H. Stuart. New York: James Van Norden and company, printers, 1844. 27 p. DLC; MiD-B; NNC; NSyHi. 44-5943

Stuart, Moses, 1780-1852. Mr. Webster's Andover address and his political course while secretary of state. Essex County, Massachusetts: Published for distribution, 1844. 20 p. DLC; MB; OClWHi; PU; RPB. 44-5944

Sturgis, J. Sketch of his character and services. Boston, 1844. MB. 44-5945

Sturtevant, Julian Monson. A discourse, delivered at the funeral of Honorable Joseph Duncan, ex-governor of the state of Illinois, January 16, 1844. By Professor J.M. Sturtevant, of Illinois College. Jacksonville: A.V. Putnam, printer, 1844. 16 p. IaDaM; ICHi. 44-5946

Suddards, William, 1805-1883. The British pulpit; consisting of discourses by the most eminent living divines in England, Scotland, and Ireland: accompanied with pulpit sketches: to which is added, scriptural illustrations: and selections of the office, duties and responsibilities of the Christian ministry. 6th ed. New York: Carter, 1844. CSaT; DLC; OU; PPLT; WaWW. 44-5947

Suddards, William, 1805-1883. The British pulpit; consisting of discourses by the most eminent living divines in England, Scotland, and Ireland.... Sixth edition.... New York: Robert Carter, 1844. 7 v. CSansS; IaPeC; ICP; NbOP; NBuDD. 44-5948

Sue, Eugene, 1804-1857. Arthur. A novel. Translated from the French of Eugene Sue by P.F. Christin, esq. New York: Harper and brothers, 1844. 166 p. CSto; DLC; NN; PU; ViU. 44-5949

Sue, Eugene, 1804-1857. Colonel De Surville: a tale of the empire. [1810] Translated from the French. New York: William H. Colyer, 1844. 46 p. DLC. 44-5950

Sue, Eugene, 1804-1857. The female bluebeard; or, Le morne-au-diable. By Eugene Sue.... New York: J. Winchester, [1844] 115 p. ViU. 44-5951

Sue, Eugene, 1804-1857. Le juif errant. New York: Gaillardet, 1844-1845. 10 parts in 1 v. C-S; MH; MNt; PPD. 44-5952

Sue, Eugene, 1804-1857. Marquis de Leto riere; or, the art of pleasing, a romance of real life.... translated from the French by Thomas Pooley.... New York: Burgess, 1844. 57 p. CL; CtY; NN. 44-5953

Sue, Eugene, 1804-1857. Matilda; or, the memoirs of a young woman. A novel. By Eugene Sue. Translated from the French by Henry William Herbert. New York: J. Winchester, 1844. 418 p. LNH; NIC. 44-5954

Sue, Eugene, 1804-1857. Les mysteres de Paris. New York: Press of du New World, J. Winchester, 1844. 2 v. in 1. CU; DLC; MWA; OCX; PPL. 44-5955

Sue, Eugene, 1804-1857. The mysteries of Paris; a romance of the rich and poor. Translated from the French by Henry C. Denning. New York: Winchester New Yorld Press, 1844. 346 p. MeAu; NcD; PPM; RPB; ViU. 44-5956

Sue, Eugene, 1804-1857. The salamander. A naval romance, by Eugene Sue.... Translated from the French by Henry William Herbert.... New York: J. Winchester, [1844] 115 p. CL; ICU; MH; ViU. 44-5957

Sue, Eugene, 1804-1857. The wandering Jew. New York: Harper and Brothers, 1844. 598 p. MtHi; NNC. 44-5958

Sue, Eugene, 1804-1857. The wandering Jew. New York: J. Winchester, New World Press, 1844. MH; NN; PU. 44-5959

Sue, Eugene, 1804-1857. The wandering Jew [Philadelphia: T.B. Peterson and Brothers] 1844? 558 p. MsSM. 44-5960

Suffield, Connecticut. First Baptist Church. Summary of the faith and practice with the articles of the covenant. A.M. Tasket, pastor. Hartford: 1844. 8 p. NHC-S. 44-5961

Sullivan, Marion Dix. The blue Juniata. Arranged for the pianoforte by E.L. White. Boston: Ditson, 1844. 2 p. MB. 44-5962

Sullivan, Marion Dix. Oh! Boatman row me o'er the stream. A duet. Arranged by Edward L. White. [With accompaniment for pianoforte] Boston: Ditson, 1844. 3 p. MB. 44-5963

Sullivant, Joseph. To the Liberty Party in Ohio [Columbus, Ohio: 1844] 7 p. MWA. 44-5964

Summerbell, N. The review; or, the young Christian's reply to the Presbyterian doctor. Also, three different trinities and a two nature scheme presented to view.... Philadelphia: Gihon, 1844. MB; MBrZ; PPPrHi. 44-5965

Summerfield, John, 1798-1825. Sermons and sketches of sermons by the Rev. John Summerfield, late a preacher in connexion with the Methodist Episcopal Church with an introduction by the Rev. Thomas E. Bond. New York: Harper and brothers, 1844. 437 p. KyLxT; MH-AH. 44-5966

Summers, George William, 1804-1868. Speech of Mr. Summers of Virginia, on the contested election of the members of the House of Representatives, elected by the general ticket system in the states of New Hampshire, Georgia, Missouri and Mississippi. Delivered in the House of Representatives, February 10, 1844. Washington: Gales and Seaton, 1844. 22 p. IC; MH; MoHi; NBU; OClWHi; TxU. 44-5967

Sunday morning reflections. New York: Calhoun, printer, 1844. 78 p. ICMe. 44-5968

Susquehanna and Tide Water Canal Company. Annual report of the president and managers of the Susquehanna and Tide Water canals, submitted at the meeting of stockholders, May 13, 1844. Baltimore: John Murphy, printer, 1844. 20 p. DLC; MdHi; OClWHi; PPAmP; PPL. 44-5969

Sutton, Christopher, 1565?-1629. Disce vivere. Learn to live. Second American edition. New York: Appleton, 1844. 338 p. ICMe; MWelC; OC; PPM. 44-5970

Suydam, James. Cheap Jimmy's opinion of Henry Clay. His opinion about one of the big whig guns they are shooting at Poke. New York: Suydam, 1844. 20 p. CtY; PU. 44-5971

Svinine, Paul. Some details concerning General Moreau, and his last moments. Followed by a short biographical memoir. Charged to accompany the General on the continent. Second American from the London edition.... Translated from the French. Boston: Printed by Rowe and Hooper, 1844. 156 p. MPiB. 44-5972

Swan, Thomas, 1795-1857. Missionary success; or encouraging features in the present aspect of the times as it respects missions. Philadelphia: 1844. 8 p. NHC-S; NRAB. 44-5973

Swan, William Draper, 1809-1864. District school reader, or, exercises in reading and speaking. Boston: C. Little and J. Brown, 1844. 468 p. USlC. 44-5974

Swan, William Draper, 1809-1864. The

primary school reader. Boston: C[harles] C. Little and J[ames] Brown, 1844. 3 v. MH; SWa. 44-5975

Swan, William Draper, 1809-1864. The grammar school reader, consisting of selections in prose and poetry, with exercises in articulation... Philadelphia: Thomas Cowperthwait and company; Cincinnati: Desilver and Burr, [etc., etc.] 1844. 248 p. MB; MH. 44-5976

Swan, William Draper, 1809-1864. Questions adapted to Emerson's North American arithmetic, part third. Boston: Jenks and Palmer, 1844. MH. 44-5977

Swedenborg, Emanuel, 1688-1772. Angelic wisdom concerning the divine providence by Emanuel Swedenborg. Boston: Otis Clapp, 1844. 387 p. MCNC. 44-5978

Swedenborg, Emanuel, 1688-1772. Angelic wisdom concerning the divine providence. Originally published in Latin at Amsterdam in 1764. Third American edition. A new translation. Boston: Otis Clapp, 1844. 387 p. CtMW; GMM; OWoC; PPiW; RP. 44-5979

Swedenborg, Emanuel, 1688-1772. Concerning heaven and its wonders, and concerning hell.... Translated from the Latin of Emanuel Swedenborg. Boston: T.H. Carter and company and Otis Clapp. New York: John Allen, 1844. 361 p. MeWa; MLow; NbOM; PPiW; WvW. 44-5980

Sweet, Waterman. Views of anatomy and practice of natural bonesetting, by a mechanical process different from all book knowledge. Schnectady: I. Riggs, 1844. 124 p. IEN-M; MBM; NBMS; NNN; PPHa. 44-5981

Swett, Josiah, 1814-1890. An English grammar, comprehending the principles and rules of the language. Improved edition. Claremont, New Hampshire: Claremont Manufacturing Company, 1844. 192 p. DLC; MH; Nh-Hi; NNC. 44-5982

Swett, Josiah, 1814-1890. Swett's grammar. An English grammar, comprehending the principles and rules of the language, illustrated by appropriate exercises: on the basis of Murray. By J. Swett, junior, A.M. ....Improved edition. Claremont, New Hampshire: Claremont Manufacturing Company, 1844. 192 p. NCas; NhD; NNC. 44-5983

Swift, Jonathan, 1667-1745. The poetical works of Jonathan Swift.... With a life, by Rev. John Mitford. Boston: Little, Brown and company, 1844. 3 v. MHins. 44-5984

The Swiss boy, or, the double discovery, by the author of the factory boy, etc. Philadelphia: American Baptist Publication Society, 1844. 36 p. ViRU. 44-5985

Sword's pocket almanack for 1845. New York, New York: Stanford and Swords [1844] MWA. 44-5986

Syracuse, New York. First Baptist Church. A brief history, together with the declaration of faith, church covenant and list of members, of the first Baptist Church of Syracuse. Syracuse: printed at the Sentinel office, 1844. 4 p. NSy. 44-5987

T

Tables of logarithms; to which is added traverse tables adapted to the course of mathematics used in the American colleges. New Haven: 1844. 90 p. CtY; PHC. 44-5988

Tacitus, Cornelius. C. Cornelii Taciti Historiarum, libri quinque. Accedit dem oribus Germanorum libellus: Julii Agricolae vita: de oratoribus dialogus. ....Editio quarta. Jac L. Kingsley.... New York: Blake, 1844. 329 p. OkHi; NNC; OBerB; PU; TxU. 44-5989

Tacitus, Cornelius. C. Cornelii Taciti Historiarum, liber quinque. Accedit De moribus Germanorum libellus. Julii Agricolae vita. De oratoribus dialogus. Cum excerptis variorum notis. Editio quinta. Edited by James L. Kingsley. Philadelphia: Uriah Hunt and son, [1844] 329 p. CLSU. 44-5990

Tacitus, Cornelius. C. Cornell Taciti historiarum libri quinque. ....Edited by James L. Kingsley. Philadelphia: Uriah Hunt's sons, 1844. 329 p. OCU. 44-5991

Tacitus, Cornelius. Historiaruni libri quinque; acc. De moribus Germanorum, Agricolae vita De oratoribus cum var. nat. New York: A.V. Blake, 1844. 329 p. DLC; NR; OCU; PPL; PU. 44-5992

Tacitus, Cornelius. The works of Cornelius Tacitus; with an essay on his life and genius, notes, supplements, &c. By Arthur Murphy, ...A new edition with the author's last corrections. Philadelphia: Thomas Wardle, 1844. 742 p. LNH; MeBa; OClW; PU; TBriK. 44-5993

Talbott, John L. The western practical arithmetic.... particularly adapted to the currency of the United States; to which is added a short system of book-keeping.... Revised and improved. Cincinnati: E. Morgan and company, 1844. InG; InU; MiU. 44-5994

A tale of kidnapping. Lowell: 1844. 12 p. MB. 44-5995

Talfourd, Thomas Noon. Ion; a tragedy in five acts. New York: J. Mowatt and company, 1844. MB; MH; PU; VtU. 44-5996

Tallmadge, James, 1778-1853. Remarks on the commercial policy of England affecting the interests of American agriculture.... Second edition. New York: Van Norden, 1844. 16 p. MHi; NCH; RPB. 44-5997

Tallmadge, James, 1778-1853. Remarks on the Honourable J. Tallmadge at the agricultural convention on the commercial policy of England, affecting the interests of American Agriculture, etc. New York: 1844. 19 p. DLC; MdBP. 44-5998

Tallmadge, James, 1778-1853. Remarks on the Honourable J. Tallmadge at the agricultural convention on the commercial policy of England, affecting the interests of American Agriculture, etc. New York: J. Van Norden and company, 1844. 16 p. ICU; KyU; MWA; NNC; RPB. 44-5999

Tallmadge, James, 1778-1853. Remarks on the Honourable J. Tallmadge at the agricultural convention on the commercial policy of England, affecting the interests of American Agriculture, etc. Second edition. New York: 1844. NoLoc. 44-6000

Talmage, Samuel Kennedy, 1798-1865. A lecture delivered before the Georgia Historical Society, February 29th and March 4th, 1844. On the subject of education.... Savannah: press of Locke and Davis, 1844. 24 p. MH; NjR; RPB; ScCC; WHi. 44-6001

Talmud. The Talmud. Selections from the contents of that ancient book.... also, brief sketches of the men who made and commented upon it. Translated from the original, by H. Polano.... Philadelphia: E. B. Stuart, [1844] ABBS; MMe. 44-6002

Tandy, David C. Political paradise an unrealised ideal. An address delivered before the C.P. and L. Society of Centre College, on the 22nd of February, 1844. Lexington: Inquirer office, printers, 1844. 14 p. CSmH; ICU; KyLx. 44-6003

Tanner, Henry Schenck, 1786-1858. The American traveller, or, tourists' and emigrants' guide through the United States.... Ninth edition.... New York: T.R. Tanner, 1844. 144 p. DLC; IHI; MH; MnHi; ViU. 44-6004

Tanner, Henry Schenck, 1786-1858. The central traveller, or, tourist's guide thorugh the states of Pennsylvania, New Jersey, Delaware, Maryland, Virginia, the District of Columbia and parts of New York, and the other adjoining states.... Second edition. New York: Tanner, 1844. 524 p. IaPeC; MH; NcD; NNA; NUtHi. 44-6005

Tanner, Henry Schenck, 1786-1858. Handbook from New York and Canada. New York: 1844. MB. 44-6006

Tanner, Henry Schenck, 1786-1858. A new picture of Philadelphia, or the stranger's guide to the city and adjoining districts: ....Third edition. New York: T.R. Tanner, 1844. 156 p. Ct; DLC; OClWHi; PHi. 44-6007

Tanner, Henry Schenck, 1786-1858. A new picture of Philadelphia, or the stranger's guide to the city and adjoining districts: ....Fourth edition. New York: T.R. Tanner, 1844. 156 p. MBAt; MWA; NHi; NN. 44-6008

Tanner, Henry Schenck, 1786-1858. A new universal atlas, containing maps of the various empires, kingdoms, states and republics of the world, with a special map of each of the United States, plans of cities, &c. Comprehended in seventy sheets and forming a series of one hundred and seventeen maps, plans and sections. ....Philadelphia: Carey and Hart, 1844. ICU; MBAt; MdBP; PHi; PPB. 44-6009

Tanner, Henry Schenck, 1786-1858. Stranger's guide to the city of New York and its environs containing a general description of the city and adjacent country, with brief accounts of the public buildings... New York: T.R. Tanner, [1844] 36 p. MBAt; NNS; WHi. 44-6010

Tanner, Henry Schenck, 1786-1858. The travelers' handbook for the state of New York and the province of Canada.... Second edition. New York: J.R. Tanner, 1844. 166 p. DLC; MHi; NIC; NjR; WHi. 44-6011

Tappan, Henry Philip, 1805-1881. Brief memorials of an only daughter. New York: Wiley and Putman, 1844. 285 p. CtY; DLC; MiOC; NN. 44-6012

Tappan, Henry Philip, 1805-1881. Elements of logic, together with an introductory view of philosophy in general, and a preliminary view of the reason. New York and London: Wiley and Putnam, 1844. 461 p. IaGG; PU; RPB; ViU; WNaE. 44-6013

Tappan, Henry Philip, 1805-1881. Logic: By Henry P. Tappan. New York: 1844. UU. 44-6014

Tappan, William Bingham, 1794-1849. Daughter of the isles. Boston: William D. Ticknor and company, 1844. 256 p. IaDum; MB; MBAt; MH. 44-6015

The tariff.... [Washington? 1844?] 16 p. ICU. 44-6016

The tariff. Martin Van Buren, the people's friend and candidate... Henry Clay, the candidate of politicians and speculators... Whiggery exposed [Columbus, Ohio: 1844?] 8 p. DLC. 44-6017

The tariff: a tract for the times by a citizen of Virginia. Prepared by order of Honorable Willis Green, chairman of the executive committee of the Whig members of Congress [Washington?

1844?] 20 p. In; NIC; OClWHi; TxDaM; TxU. 44-6018

The tattler, with notes, and a general index. Philadephia: M'Carty and Davis, 1844. 444 p. IaB; IJMac; IaB; ILM; ScDuE; ScMar. 44-6019

Tayler, Charles Benjamin, 1797-1875. The records of a good man's life... New York: Stanford and Swords, 1844. 298 p. MnHi; MsSM. 44-6020

Taylor, Bayard, 1825-1878. Ximena; or, the battle of the Sierra Morena, and other poems, by James Bayard Taylor.... Philadelphia: H. Hooker, 1844. 84 p. DLC; MB; NjP; PPM; RPB. 44-6021

Taylor, C.B. Allgemeine geschichte der vereingten staath von Amerika. New York: Ezra Strong, 1844. InValU. 44-6022

Taylor, C.B. A universal history of the United States of America. Early discoveries. Hartford, [Connecticut] Ezra Stone, 1844. 612 p. IU; In; NUtHi; TxD-T. 44-6023

Taylor, Charles, 1756-1821. Apostolic baptism. Facts and evidences on the subjects and mode of Christian baptism... New York: Saxton and Miles; Boston: Saxton Peirce, and company, 1844. 236 p. CSansS; ICP; MiU; OO; PPP. 44-6024

Taylor, Charles Coffin. The communion of saints: a discourse, delivered at St. Andrews Church, Ann Arbor, Michigan, at the funeral of Mrs. Mary Ann Kellogg, October 15, 1844. By the Rev. Charles C. Taylor, rector of said church. Published by request of the family of the deceased. Troy, New York:

Kneeland and company's press, 1844. 20 p. MiD-B; NT; RPB. 44-6025

Taylor, Charles D. The records of a good man's life by the Rev. Charles E. Taylor, M.A. ....New York: Stanford and Swords, 1844. 298 p. MdBD; NCH; Nh; PAtM; ScDuE. 44-6026

Taylor, Emily, 1795-1872. The boy and the birds. Boston: 1844. 128 p. MB. 44-6027

Taylor, Isaac, 1759-1829. The mine. From the London edition. Revised by the editors. New York: G. Lane and C.B. Tippett, 1844. OCl; RPB. 44-6028

Taylor, J.N. Law of landlord and tenant. New York: Voorhies, 1844. 477 p. MWCL. 44-6029

Taylor, James W. The useful and the beautiful - their relations and their harmony. An address delivered before the Alpha Delta Phi Society of Hamilton College at its twelfth anniversary, Clinton, New York. By James W. Taylor, esq., of Cincinnati. Utica: R.W. Roberts, printer, 1844. 24 p. CtSoP; N; NCH; NUt. 44-6030

Taylor, Jane, 1783-1824. The contributions of Q.Q. to a periodical work: with some pieces not before published. By the late Jane Taylor. New York: Saxton and Miles; Boston: Saxton, Peirce and company, 1844. IP; KWiU; NFred. 44-6031

Taylor, Jeremy, 1613-1667. Bishop Taylor on Episcopacy. Published by D. Appleton and company, 1844. 361 p. ArPb. 44-6032

Taylor, Jeremy, 1613-1667. Offices of Episcopacy asserted and maintained. New York: Appleton and Company, 1844. 361 p. OrPD. 44-6033

Taylor, Jeremy, 1613-1667. Sacred order and offices of Episcopacy asserted and maintained; to which is added a discourse of the office ministerial, by Rev. Jeremy Taylor. New York: Appleton, 1844. 361 p. GDecCT; IU; NBuDD; TxDaM; WNaE. 44-6034

Taylor, John Neilson, 1805-1878. American law of landlord and tenant. New York: 1844. 477 p. MH-L; PU-L. 44-6035

Taylor, John Neilson, 1805-1878. A treatise on the American law of landlord and tenant; having reference to the statutory provisions and decisions of the several United States, with a selection of procedents. ....New York: J.S. Voorhies, 1844. 477 p. AzU-L; CU-Law; DLC; NcD; ViU. 44-6036

Taylor, Oliver Alden, 1801-1851. Memoir of Andrew Lee. Boston: Sabbath School Society, 1844. 215 p. MB; MiOC. 44-6037

Taylor, Oliver Alden, 1801-1851. Piety in humble life: a memoir of Mr. Andrew Lee.... By Rev. Oliver A. Taylor. Boston, Massachusetts: Sabbath School Society, 1844. 216 p. CoCsC; DLC; MBC; MoSpD; ScNC. 44-6038

Taylor, Samuel. A discussion of baptism by immersion. Frankfort: G.W. Snyder, printer, 1844. 96 p. CSmH. 44-6039

Taylor, William Cooke, 1800-1849. History of Ireland, from the Anglo-Norman invasion till union of the country with

Great Britain.... with additions, by William Sampson. New York: Harper and brothers, 1844. 2 v. MMh; OSW; ScDuE. 44-6040

Taylor, William Cooke, 1800-1849. A manual of modern history; containing the rise and progress of the principal European nations, their poetical history, and changes in their social condition; with a history of the colonies founded by Europeans. Eighth edition, revised, with a chapter on the history of the United States. New York: D. Appleton and company, 1844. 797, 54 p. OkOkU. 44-6041

The teacher's companion, and young gentleman's friend; or, a complete system of theoretical and practical arithmetic. Adapted to the currency of the United States.... Compiled from the best authorities by William T. Barr,.... Philadelphia: King and Baird, printers, 1844. 347 p. ICBB; NNC. 44-6042

Teale, William Henry. The life of Lucius Cary, Viscount Falkland. Flemington, New Jersey: J.R. Dunham, 1844. 48 p. CBCDS; ICU; MiDD; NBuDD; PP. 44-6043

Teeth almanac for 1845. Boston, Massachusetts: Saxton, Peirce and company [1844] MWA. 44-6044

Teller, Thomas. The pleasant journey; and scenes in town and country. New Haven: Babcock, 1844. 64 p. TxDaM. 44-6045

Temperance, pseud. Hints to the honest tax payers of Boston. [Boston: 1844?] 8 p. MH. 44-6046

Temperance almanac by G.R. Perkins. Albany: J. Munsell, 1844. MWA. 44-6047

Temperance almanac for 1845. Albany, New York: J. Munsell, printer, [1844] MWA. 44-6048

Temperance almanac for 1845. Troy, New York: [1844] MWA. 44-6049

The Temperance almanac, of the Massachusetts Temperance Union, for the year of our Lord 1845: ....Calculations by Benjamin Greenleaf, esq. ....Boston: Massachusetts Temperance Union [1844] 36 p. MHa; MWA; WHi. 44-6050

The Temperance almanac, of the Massachusetts Temperance Union.... 1845.... calculated by Benjamin Greenleaf.... Boston: Massachusetts Temperance Union, 1844. 32 p. MHa. 44-6051

The Temperance almanac, vol. I., no. 7, of the Massachusetts Temperance Union; ....1845: ....Calculations by Benjamin Greenleaf, esq., author of Greenleaf's arithmetic, etc. ....Boston: Massachusetts Temperance Union [1844] 34 p. MMal. 44-6052

Temperance almanac. By G. R. Perkins. Albany, Varied edition. New York: 1844. MWA. 44-6053

Temperance almanac. New York: Greeley and McElrath, 1844. MWA. 44-6054

Temperance almanack. Boston: Temperance Union, 1844. MWA. 44-6055

Temperance song for the Fourth. [Buf-

falo Creek reservation, New York: 1844]
CSmH. 44-6056

Templeman, George. Catalogue of part
of the laws, documents, registers of
debates and journal of Congress and of
the law books and rare and scarce books,
political registers and newspapers.
Washington: William Greer, printer,
1844. 8 p. DLC; RPB. 44-6057

Tennant, J.E. The elephant. New York:
Harper, 1844. PHatU. 44-6058

Tennessee. Acts passed at the first session of the twenty-fifth General Assembly of the state of Tennessee; 1843-1844.
Published by authority. n.p.: L. Gifford
and E.G. Eastman, printers, 1844. 356 p.
In-SC; Ky; L; MdBB; Mo. 44-6059

Tennessee. Journal of the House of
Representatives of the state of Tennessee, at the twenty-fifth General Assembly, held at Nashville on Monday, the
20th day of October, 1843. Knoxville:
E.G. Eastman and L. Gifford, printers to
the state, 1844. 812 p. NN; T; TNV; TU.
44-6060

Tennessee. Report of the board of commissioners, appointed to investigate the
branch of the Bank of Tennessee, at
Trenton. December, 1843. Nashville:
W.F. Bang and company, and B.R.
M'Kennie, printers, 1844. 11 p. T. 44-
6061

Tennessee. Report of the commissioners appointed by the General Assembly to investigate the Bank of
Tennessee and branches. Printed by
order of the Senate. Nashville: W.F.
Bang and company, and B.R. McKennie,
printers, 1844. 13 p. T. 44-6062

Tennessee. Report of the commissioners appointed to examine the branch
bank at Clarksville. December, 1843.
Nashville: W.F. Bang and company, and
B.R. M'Kennie, printers, 1844. 6 p. T. 44-
6063

Tennessee. Report of the commissioners appointed to examine the branch
bank at Shelbyville. December, 1843.
Nashville: W.F. Bang and company, and
B.R. M'Kennie, printers, 1844. 8 p. T. 44-
6064

Tennessee. Report of the commissioners appointed to examine the branch
bank of Tennessee at Sparta. Printed by
order of the Senate. Nashville: W.F.
Bang and company, and B.R. McKennie,
printers, 1844. 14 p. T. 44-6065

Tennessee. Report of the commis-
sioners appointed to examine the branch
of the Bank of Tennessee at Columbia.
Printed by order of the Senate. Nashville:
W.F. Bang and company, and B.R. Mc-
Kennie, printers, 1844. 8 p. T. 44-6066

Tennessee. Seventh geological report
to the twenty-fifth General assembly of
the state of Tennessee, made November,
1843. By G. Troost, geologist to the state.
Nashville: W.F. Bang and company, and
B.R. McKennie, printers, 1844. 45 p.
MoS; NNA; OO; T. 44-6067

Tenney, Timothy J., 1807-1854. The
destruction of soul and body in hell. A
discourse on Matt 10:28 preached in
Norway, 1842 by T.J. Tenney. Portland,
Maine: Ira Berry and Company, 1844. 12
p. CSmH. 44-6068

The terrific almanac for 1844. New
York: 1844. 10 p. MWA. 44-6069

Teste, Alphonse. Practical manual of animal magnetism.... the methods employed in producing the magnetic phenomena.... its application to the treatment and cure of diseases, translated by D. Spillman. First American edition. Philadelphia: Brown, 1844. 321 p. CtHC; DSG; LN; MMal; PPA. 44-6070

Texas. The annexation of Texas to the United States fully and fairly discussed; together with all the important documents connected with the question. Published under the direction of the Central committee. Nashville: Printed by John P. Heiss, Union office, 1844. 14 p. T. 44-6071

Texas. Annual report of the treasury department, to the Ninth Congress of the Republic of Texas. Washington, Texas: Printed at the Vindicator office, 1844. 29 p. TxWFM. 44-6072

Texas. Journals of the House of Representatives of the eighth Congress of Texas. Published by authority. Houston: Cruger and Moore, Public printers, 1844. 470 p. DLC; TxWFM. 44-6073

Texas. Journals of the Senate, eighth Congress of the Republic of Texas. Published by authority. Houston: Cruger and Moore, Public printers, 1844. 245 p. TxWFM. 44-6074

Texas. Laws passed by the Eighth Congress of the Republic of Texas. Houston: Cruger and Moore, Public Printers, 1844. 120 p. CSmH; CU-B; MdBB; Nj; NNLI. 44-6075

Texas. Report of the committee appointed to examine into the condition of the records and archives of the general

land office. Washington, Texas: Printed by Thomas Johnson, 1844. 14 p. TxWFM. 44-6076

Texas. Thoughts on the proposed annexation of Texas to the United States. New York: D. Fanshaw, printer, 1844. 55 p. NNUT. 44-6077

The Texas question, reviewed by an adopted citizen, having twenty-one years of residence in the United States. New York: 1844. 28 p. CU-B; MiD-B; NNC; PHi; WHi. 44-6078

Thacher, James, 1754-1844. American medical biography: or, memoirs of eminent physicians embracing principally those who have died since the publication of Dr. Thacher's work on the same subject. Greenfield: 1844. 664 p. ArU-M; NBu; RPM. 44-6079

That same old coon. No. 1-25, April 12, 1844-November 16, 1844. Dayton, Ohio: R.N. and W.F. Comly, 1844. CtY; DLC; ODa. 44-6080

Thatcher, Benjamin Bussey, 1809-1840. Indian traits: being sketches of the manners, customs, and character of the North American natives.... New York: Harper and brothers, 1844. 2 v. Mi; MiD-B; NjN; NN. 44-6081

Thayer, Caroline Matilda, d. 1844. Religion recommended to youth. Sandford, New York: Published by Lane, 1844. 157 p. WBaraHi. 44-6082

Thayer, Foster. The commencement of the religious life. New York: Henry M. Onderdonk, 1844. CtHT; MdBD; MH; NNC. 44-6083

Thayer, J. The widow's son. Boston: Isaac Tompkins, 1844. MWA; NNC. 44-6084

Thayer, Sylvanus. Special report on the sea wall, built in the year 1843, for the preservation of Ram Head at the northwest end of Lovell's Island, in the harbor of Boston... Washington: W.Q. Force, 1844. [4-213]-232 p. CSt; CU; MdBJ; MH; NNC. 44-6085

A theme for the meditation of the members of Zion. By a layman. Charleston: B. Jenkins, 1844. 59 p. KyLoS. 44-6086

Thenat, Jean Pierre, 1803-1857. Practical perspective, for the use of students translated from the French. New American edition. New York: Saxton and Miles, 1844. MBU-A; NNC. 44-6087

Theological sketch book, or, skeletons of sermons carefully arranged in systematic order so as to constitute a complete body of divinity. Baltimore: 1844. GDecCT; ICU; MdBLF; MH; ScCoT. 44-6088

Thiers, Louis Adolphe, i.e. Marie Joseph Louis Adolphe, 1797-1877. The history of the French revolution. By M.A. Thiers. Translated, with notes and illustrations, from the most authentic sources, by Frederick Shoberl. Third American edition. Philadelphia: Carey and Hart, 1844. 4 v. CtHC; DLC; KTW; MnM; OEaC. 44-6089

Think: act: pray: ....New York: J.S. Redfield; Boston: Saxon, Pierce and company, 1844. CBPSR; NRock; PPL. 44-6090

Tholuck, Friedrich August Gottreau,

1799-1877. Exposition of St. Paul's epistle to the Romans: with extracts from the exegetical works of the fathers and reformers. Translated from the original German by Robert Menzies. First American from the second revised Edinburgh edition. Philadelphia: Sorin and Ball, 1844. 432 p. CtHC; KyLoP; MeBat; NBu; PMA. 44-6091

Thomas a Kempis, 1380-1471. Of the imitation of Christ; four books. First complete American edition. New York: D. Appleton and company, 1844. 324 p. Ct; MdBD; NNS; OrSaw; TChU. 44-6092

Thomas, Frederick William, 1806-1866. The beechen tree; a tale told in rhyme. New York: Harper and brothers, 1844. 95 p. CtMW; ICU; LNH; NjP; RPB. 44-6093

Thomas, J.B. Incarnation and miscellaneous poems; also Infidelity, a tale of the Revolution. Covington, Kentucky: R.C. Langdon, 1844. 5-96 p. CSmH; ICN; KEmT; NcD; RPB. 44-6094

Thomas, M. Catalogue of law and miscellaneous books from the library of Peter S. Du Ponceau. Philadelphia: 1844. MBAt. 44-6095

Thomas, R. The glory of America. By R. Thomas. Philadelphia: Leary and Getz, 1844. 574 p. MoSW; MoWg. 44-6096

Thomas, R. A pictorial history of the United States of America, from the earliest discoveries by the northmen,..... to the present time.... Hartford: E. Strong, 1844. 755 p. DLC; MiD-B; OClWHi; OHi; PWCHi. 44-6097

Thomas, Thomas Ebenezer. A review of the Rev. Dr. Junkin's synodical speech, in defence of American slavery; delivered September 19th and 20th, and published December 1843: with an outline of the Bible argument against slavery.... Cincinnati: printed at the daily atlas office, 1844. 136 p. MB; MH-AH; NNUT; OWoC; WHi. 44-6098

Thompson, Abraham G. Remarks.... relative to the auction business, duties, etc., and the New York and Albany Railroad to advance the prosperity of the city of New York. New York: Francis Hart, printer, 1844. 12 p. MB; MH-BA. 44-6099

Thompson, Jacob, 1810-1885. Speech of Hon. Jacob Thompson, of Mississippi, on the right of members to their seats in the House of Representatives, delivered February 9, 1844. Washington: 1844. 8 p. NNC. 44-6100

Thompson, Joseph Parrish, 1819-1879. Life of Joseph Thompson. New Haven: 1844. 148 p. OO. 44-6101

Thompson, Joseph Parrish, 1819-1879. A memoir of the late Timothy Dwight; with the sermon delivered on the occasion of his death. By Joseph P. Thompson. New Haven: J.H. Benham, printer, 1844. 148 p. CU; NNUT; OO; PHi; RPB. 44-6102

Thompson, Pishey, 1784-1862. To the honorable, the Judges of the Circuit Court of the District of Columbia sitting as a Court of Chancery. [Washington: 1844] DLC. 44-6103

Thompson, R.G. Auction of businesses. New York, 1844. DLC. 44-6104

Thompson, Waddy. Letter... on the annexation of Texas. Washington: 1844. 14 p. ICN; Nh; PPL. 44-6105

Thompson, William Tappan, 1812-1882. Major Jones's [pseud.] courtship: detailed, with other scenes, incidents, and adventures in a series of letters, by himself. Second edition. Philadelphia: Carey and Hart, 1844. 200 p. CtY; DLC; MdBE; MH; MWH. 44-6106

Thompson, William Tappan, 1812-1882. Scenes in Georgia. By Major Jones. Philadelphia: T.B. Peterson and brothers, 1844. 195 p. GMtvBP; MdBLC. 44-6107

Thomson's almanac. Boston: 1844. MWA. 44-6108

Thompson's bank note reporter. New York: J. Thompson, 1844-. 3 v. NjR. 44-6109

Thomson, James, 1700-1748. The seasons. A new edition. Boston: Lewis and Sampson, 1844. 154 p. MPeaHi; NN. 44-6110

Thomson, James Bates. Elements of geometry: on the basis of Dr. Brewster's legendre. To which is added a book on proportion; with notes and illustrations. New Haven: Durrie and Peck, etc., etc., 1844. 12, 237 p. MB; MH; MoS; Nh; PU. 44-6111

Thomson, James Bates. Elements of geometry: on the basis of Dr. Brewster's legendre. To which is added a book on proportion; with notes and illustrations. Second edition. New Haven: Durrie and Peck, 1844. [3]-237 p. NjR; RPB. 44-6112

Thomson, James Bates. Elements of geometry: on the basis of Dr. Brewster's legendre. [sic] To which is added a book on proportion; with notes and illustrations. Third edition. New Haven: Durrie and Peck, 1844. CtHWatk. 44-6113

Thomson, James Bates. Higher arithmetic. One hundred and twentieth edition. New York: Ivinson, 1844. 422 p. MiU. 44-6114

Thomson, John Renshaw, 1800-1862. The slanderer rebuked; or, the private character and public services of John R. Thomson, the originator of the constitution of New Jersey. Camden: 1844. 8 p. PHi. 44-6115

Thomson, Samuel Harrison, 1813-1882. Review of Mr. MacMaster's speech before the synod of Indiana, October 4, 1844. Madison: Jones and Lodge, 1844. 16 p. In; InU. 44-6116

Thorburn, James M. Catalogue of kitchen garden, flower, tree and grass seeds.... New York: Vinten, printer, 1844. 60 p. MiD-B. 44-6117

Thoughts about water. Boston, 1844. 16 p. DLC; MBB; MBC. 44-6118

Thoughts about water. Boston: 1844. 3-17 p. DSG. 44-6119

Thoughts of peace for the christian sufferer. A selection of short passages from scripture and sacred poetry. From the fourth London edition. Philadelphia: Herman Hooker, 1844. 238 p. LNB. 44-6120

Thrifty almanac, for 1845. By an old farmer. Cincinnati, Ohio: A. Randall, [1844] MWA. 44-6121

The thrilling and romantic story of Sarah Smith and the Hessian: An original tale of the American Revolution. To which is added: female heroism exemplified. An interesting story, founded on fact... Philadelphia: 1844. 24 p. DLC. 44-6122

Thucydides. History of the Peloponnesian war. Translated from the Greek of Thucydides. By William Smith. A new edition corrected and revised. New York: Harper and brothers, 1844. 2 v. AzU; DLC; NcU; RWe; ScCliTO. 44-6123

Thucydides. History of the Peloponnesian war. Translated from the Greek of Thucydides. By William Smith. A new edition corrected and revised. Philadelphia: Wardle, 1844. 2 v. FOA; ICP; LNT; OCad; RPB. 44-6124

Tibbatts, John W. Speech of Mr. Tibbatts, on the question of the reannexation of Texas; together with.... remarks on the tariff; delivered in the House of Representatives, May 7, 1844. 16 p. MH; MHi; NjMD; TxU. 44-6125

Ticknor, Caleb B. The philosophy of living; or, the way to enjoy life and its comforts.... New York: Harper and brothers, 1844. 336 p. AMaJ; GHi; InCW; KyBC; MB. 44-6126

Ticknor, Caleb B. Quacks and quackery; by a physician of New York. New York: Mark H. Newman, 1844. 273 p. CtY; DLC; ICJ; NNN. 44-6127

Ticknor, firm, publishers. Boston.

Catalogue of medical books comprising all the late publications on anatomy, medicine, surgery, midwifery.... for sale by William Ticknor and company. Boston: 1844. 35 p. MH; MHi. 44-6128

Tillinghast, N. Elements of plane geometry, for the use of schools. Boston: Lewis and Sampson; New York: Robinson, Pratt and company, 1844. 96 p. MB; MH; Nh; NN; TxU-T. 44-6129

Timbs, John, 1801-1875. Knowledge for the people; or, the plain why and because. Familiarizing subjects of useful curiosity and amusing research. ....Domestic series. Hartford: S. Andrus and sons, 1844. 294 p. MLow; NN; NPot; OCX; TN. 44-6130

Tinker, Reuben, 1799-1854. The book of God. An address delivered before the Lake County Bible Society, and the Painesville Female Bible Society; August 31, 1844.... Hudson: Ohio Observer, 1844. 16 p. CBPac. 44-6131

Tinsley, Isaac S. The nature and effects of faith, a discourse delivered in the hall of representatives on the fourth Lord's day in January, 1844. ....Washington: 1844. 11 p. ICN; MBC; MiD-B; N; PPL. 44-6132

To the citizens of Greene County [annexation of Texas] n. p. 1844? MH. 44-6133

To the Democratic citizens of Pennsylvania [Signed: a voice from a friend] Phialdelphia: 1844. 8 p. MB; NN; PHi. 44-6134

To the Democratic party of the United States on the presidential election. To which is appended, a biographical sketch of Commodore Charles Stewart. Philadelphia: Printed for the committee, 1844. 27 p. MdHi; MH; PPWa. 44-6135

To the electors of the sixteenth district of New York. Philadelphia: 1844. MB. 44-6136

To the freemen of New Hanover County. Fellow Citizens: We respectively announce ourselves as candidates for seats in the Commons of the next General Assembly... Alexander McRae, Griffith J. McRee. Wilmington, North Carolina: 1844. 1 p. NcU. 44-6137

To the friends of home industry, protection. [n.p.] 1844. PPL. 44-6138

Tochman, Gaspard. Lecture delivered before the members of the state legislatures of New York, Massachusetts, New Hampshire, [etc.] and before the members of New Jersey state convention, on the subject of the social, political and literary condition of Poland, and her future prosects.... by Major G. Tochman.... Baltimore: John D. Toy, printer, 1844. 48 p. CU; MB; MnHi; PPL; RPB. 44-6139

Tochman, Gaspard. Poland, Russia, and the policy of the latter towards the United States. Baltimore: John D. Toy, printer, 1844. 48 p. In; MiD-B. 44-6140

Tochman, Major G. "Strike, but hear" Poland, Russia and the policy of the latter towards the United States. A lecture. Baltimore: 1844. 48 p. MBC. 44-6141

Todd, John, 1800-1873. The angel of the iceberg, and other stories, illustrating great moral truths. Designed chiefly for the young. Northampton: Bridgman and Childs, etc., 1844. 374 p. MPiB. 44-6142

Todd, John, 1800-1873. The foundations of success. An oration pronounced before the Philomathaean and Phrenakosmian Societies of Pennsylvania College, Gettysburg, September 19, 1843. By Rev. John Todd.... Second edition. Gettysburg: H.C. Neinstedt, printer, 1844. 28 p. MnHi; N; NCH; PHi. 44-6143

Todd, John, 1800-1873. Hints addressed to the young men of the United States. [n.p.] 1844. PPWa. 44-6144

Todd, John, 1800-1873. Little Lewis; by John Todd. Pittsfield, Massachusetts: E.P. Little, 1844. 44 p. MBUPH. 44-6145

Todd, John, 1800-1873. Moral influence connected with great cities. Northampton: 1844. MB. 44-6146

Todd, John, 1800-1873. A mountain cottage. Pittsfield, Massachusetts: E.P. Little, 1844. 35 p. MB; MH. 44-6147

Todd, John, 1800-1873. The pastor's daughter.... Pittsfield: P.E. Little, 1844. 48 p. DLC; RPB. 44-6148

Todd, John, 1800-1873. The pulpit tested. A sermon delivered at the centennial anniversary of the Congregational Church in Great Barrington, [Massachusetts] December 23, 1843. [Also] an appendix: containing a history of the Congregational Church....by J.W. Turner. Pittsfield, [Massachusetts] Little, 1844. CSmH; MBC; OO; PPPrHi; WHi. 44-6149

Todd, John, 1800-1873. A sermon delivered at the Centennial anniversary of the Congregational Church in Great Barrington, December 23, 1843. Pittsfield: 1844. 123 p. MB; MH-AH. 44-6150

Todd, John, 1800-1873. The student's manual: designed, by specific directions, to aid in forming and strengthening the intellectual and moral character and habits of the students. Twelfth edition. Northampton: J.H. Butler, 1844 392 p. NN. 44-6151

Todd, John, 1800-1873. Sunday school teacher; designed to aid in elevating and perfecting the Sabbath school system. Eighth edition. Manchester: S. Johnson and son, 1844. MH. 44-6152

Todd, John, 1800-1873. The young man: hints addressed to the young men of the United States. Northampton: J.H. Butler; Buffalo: J.H. Butler and company, 1844. 355 p. GMilvC; MDeeP; MTop; NNUT; OCY. 44-6153

Token of friendship. Boston: Cottrell, 1844. NMtv. 44-6154

Tomley, Archer H. Helen Maria waltz, dedicated to Phineas S. Fiske, by Archer H. Townley. Prentiss, 1844. 3 p. KU. 44-6155

Tonna, Charlotte Elizabeth Browne, 1790-1846. Alice Benden; or the bowed shilling, and other tales. New York: John S. Taylor, 1844. 177 p. NN; NNC; PPPrHi. 44-6156

Tonna, Charlotte Elizabeth Browne, 1790-1846. The daisy and other floral illustrations. By Charlotte Elizabeth. New

York: M.W. Dodd, 1844. 107 p. NmStM. 44-6157

Tonna, Charlotte Elizabeth Browne, 1790-1846. The female martyrs of the English reformation. By Charlotte Elizabeth. Selected from "English martyrology;" for the use of the Sabbath schools. New York: John S. Taylor and company, 1844. 180 p. GEU; MH; NcRSh; NNUT; ScCoB. 44-6158

Tonna, Charlotte Elizabeth Browne, 1790-1846. The flower garden, or, chapters on flowers....By Charlotte Elizabeth [pseud.] New York: John S. Taylor and company, 1844. 330 p. KyLx; MH; TChU. 44-6159

Tonna, Charlotte Elizabeth Browne, 1790-1846. The flower garden, or, chapters on flowers; a sequel to floral biography. By Charlotte Elizabeth [pseud.] New York: M.W. Dodd, 1844. 329 p. IaDuU-Sem; KyLx; NIC; PPM; ViU. 44-6160

Tonna, Charlotte Elizabeth Browne, 1790-1846. Helen Fleetwood. New York: John S. Taylor and company, 1844. 332 p. NjMD. 44-6161

Tonna, Charlotte Elizabeth Browne, 1790-1846. Helen Fleetwood. New York: M.W. Dodd, 1844. 184 p. MB; MdHi; MiU. 44-6162

Tonna, Charlotte Elizabeth Browne, 1790-1846. Helen Fleetwood. Second American edition. New York: John S. Taylor, 1844. 332 p. VtMidSM. 44-6163

Tonna, Charlotte Elizabeth Browne, 1790-1846. Israel's ordinances. A few thoughts on their perpetuity in a letter to the Right Rev. the Bishop of Jerusalem. New York: Labagh, 1844. 24 p. MB; PPPrHi. 44-6164

Tonna, Charlotte Elizabeth Browne, 1790-1846. Judah's lion. New York: M.W. Dodd, 1844. 406 p. DeU; DSI; MB; MH; OCH. 44-6165

Tonna, Charlotte Elizabeth Browne, 1790-1846. The lace runners. New York: J.S. Taylor and company, 1844. 112 p. MBC. 44-6166

Tonna, Charlotte Elizabeth Browne, 1790-1846. Letters from Ireland. New York: M.W. Dodd, 1844. [367]-494 p. CtY. 44-6167

Tonna, Charlotte Elizabeth Browne, 1790-1846. Personal recollections by Charlotte Elizabeth [pseud.] From the London edition. New York: J.S. Taylor and company, 1844. MH; NjMD; RKi; ViRut. 44-6168

Tonna, Charlotte Elizabeth Browne, 1790-1846. Personal recollections by Charlotte Elizabeth. New York: M.W. Dodd, 1844. 126 p. CSansS; MPiB; ViRut; WHi. 44-6169

Tonna, Charlotte Elizabeth Browne, 1790-1846. Personal recollections. New York: J.S. Taylor, 1844. 357 p. MH; OO; TxU. 44-6170

Tonna, Charlotte Elizabeth Browne, 1790-1846. Phelan. Combination, a tale founded on facts. New York: 1844. 209 p. MeBat; MiGi; NbU; NNC. 44-6171

Tonna, Charlotte Elizabeth Browne, 1790-1846. Phelan. Combinations, though hand join in hand the wicked shall not be unpunished. New York; Dodd, 1844. OM. 44-6172

Tonna, Charlotte Elizabeth Browne, 1790-1846. Principalities and powers in heavenly places. By Charlotte Elizabeth [pseud.] With an introduction by the Rev. Edward Bickersteth. New York: J.S. Taylor and company, 1844. 298 p. CU; ICBB; KyLx. 44-6173

Tonna, Charlotte Elizabeth Browne, 1790-1846. Ridley, Latimer, Cramer, and other English martyrs. Selected from "English martyrology," for the use of Sabbath schools. New York: J.S. Taylor and company, 1844. 300 p. GEU; ICN; MWA; NN; PPL. 44-6174

Tonna, Charlotte Elizabeth Browne, 1790-1846. The rockite, an Irish story. Fourth edition. New York: J.S. Taylor and company, 1844. NN; PPL. 44-6175

Tonna, Charlotte Elizabeth Browne, 1790-1846. The siege of Derry; or, sufferings of the Protestants: a tale of the revolution. By Charlotte Elizabeth [pseud.] Second American edition. New York: J.S. Taylor and company, 1844. 322 p. CSt; MBBC; NjMD; PPL-R; RKi. 44-6176

Tonna, Charlotte Elizabeth Browne, 1790-1846. Tales and illustrations, chiefly intended for young persons. New York: J.S. Taylor, 1844. MH. 44-6177

Tonna, Charlotte Elizabeth Browne, 1790-1846. The works of Charlotte Elizabeth [pseud.] With an introduction by Mrs. H.B. Stowe.... New York: M.W. Dodd, 1844-45. 3 v. DLC; InCW; OClW; PP; WMMD. 44-6178

Tonna, Charlotte Elizabeth Browne, 1790-1846. The wrongs of woman.... Third edition. New York: M.W. Dodd, 1844. 4 parts. NPee; OSW. 44-6179

Tonna, Charlotte Elizabeth Browne, 1790-1846. The yew tree, and other stories. New York: M.W. Dodd, 1844. 100 p. MDux; NcD. 44-6180

Toole, Henry Irwin. Address delivered before the two literary societies of Wake Forest College on the 20th of June, 1844, at the solicitation of the Philomathesian Society. Raleigh: Holden, 1844. 35 p. NcU; NcWfC. 44-6181

Topsfield. Schools committee. Report of the school committee of the town of Topsfield, 1843-44. Salem: printed at the Gazette office, 1844. MA. 44-6182

Torrey, Henry Warren, 1814-1893. An English-Latin lexicon, prepared to accompany Leverett's Latin-English lexicon. Boston: J.H. Wilkins and R.B. Carter, 1844. 318 p. MBevHi; MH; NbCrD; NIC. 44-6183

Torrey, Jesse. The moral instructor and guide to virtue being a compendium of moral philosophy... for the use of schools and families. Philadelphia: Grigg and Elliot, 1844. 300 p. IaMp; ILM; KyU; PPM; TxD-T. 44-6184

Torrey, R.C. An address delivered before Alabama Lodge, No. 3, on the anniversary of St. John the Baptist. June 24, A.L. 5844. Mobile: Dade and Thompson, printers, 1844. 16 p. MWA. 44-6185

Toumey, Michael. Report on the geological and agricultural survey of the state of South Carolina, 1844, by Michael

Toumey. Columbia, South Carolina: Johnson, 1844. 63 p. MH-Z; NcD; NcWfc; PPAN; ScU. 44-6186

Town, Ithiel. Catalogue of.... books.... ancient and modern.... New York: Tribune Printing office, 1844. 37 p. DLC. 44-6187

Town, Salem, 1779-1864. An analysis of the derivative words in the English language. New York: R.C. Root, 1844. 164 p. DLC; NjP. 44-6188

Town, Salem, 1779-1864. An analysis of the derivative words in the English language; by Salem Town, A.M. Twenty-first edition, carefully revised, enlarged, and adapted to schools of all grades. New York: R.C. Root and company, 1844. 164 p. MdBF; MH; MnU; NNC; RKi. 44-6189

Town, Salem, 1779-1864. An analysis of the derivative words in the English language; by Salem Town, A.M. Thirtieth edition. New York: R.C. Root, 1844. 164 p. KHi; MH; NRU; WWauHi. 44-6190

Town, Salem, 1779-1864. An analysis of the derivative words in the English language; or a key to their precise analytic definitions, by prefixes and suffixes. Thirtieth edition. Rochester, New York: Fisher and company, 1844. 164 p. MH; NjP; NRU; PWCHi. 44-6191

Town, Salem, 1779-1864. Spelling and defining book; containing rules for designating the accented syllable in most words in the language, being an introduction to Town's analysis. One hundredth edition. New York: Root, 1844. 167 p. CtHWatk; OO. 44-6192

Town, Salem, 1779-1864. Town's first reader, consisting of easy and attractive lessons; to be used in connection with any speller. Cooperstown: H. and E. Phinney, 1844. 128 p. DLC. 44-6193

Town, Salem, 1779-1864. Town's spelling and defining book, being an introduction to Town's analysis and also to Town's readers, in four parts. Auburn, New York: Made and sold by H. and J.C. Ivison, 1844. 160 p. NAuHi. 44-6194

Town, Salem, 1779-1864. Town's spelling and defining book. One hundreth edition, critically revised and corrected. New York: R. C. Root, 1844. MH. 44-6195

Towndrow, T. Guide to caligraphy.... Part 1, [4, 7] Salem: J.P. Jewett and company; Cincinnati: J.P. Jewett, 1844. MH. 44-6196

Townes, G. Chemistry; a prize essay. New York: 1844. NPV. 44-6197

Townes, Samuel A. The history of Marion, sketches of life, &c. in Perry County, Alabama, by S.A. Townes. Marion, Alabama: Dennis Dykous, 1844. [64] p. A-Ar; NcD; TxU; WHi. 44-6198

Townsend, W. Thompson, 1806?-1870. Whitefriars; or, the days of Claude du Val; a drama in three acts, from the celebrated romantic novel of the same title. New York: Samuel French and son, [1844?] 48 p. OCl. 44-6199

Townshend, Chauncey Hare, 1798-1868. Facts in mesmerism, ...by the Rev. Chauncey Hare Townshend, A.M. ....New York: Harper and brothers, 1844.

388 p. MAm; NB; NcC; NNS; OMC. 44-6200

The tract distributor. Honeoye, New York, 1844. V. 1-. No. 1-. OO. 44-6201

Tract showing the sentiments of the Bishops of the American Church on some of the points recently discussed among Episcopalians in England and America taken from the pastoral letters of the House of Bishops, from the year 1868 [sic] to the year 1844. Philadelphia: Stavely and McCalla, 1844. 24 p. MdBD. 44-6202

Tracts on the doctrines of the church. Baltimore: Joseph Robinson, 1844. v. 1. WNaE. 44-6203

Tracy, Joseph, 1793?-1874. Colonization and missions. A historical examination of the state of society in Western Africa, as formed by Saganism, and Muhammadanesm. Slavery, the slave trade and piracy, and of the remedial influence of colonization and missions. Boston: T.R. Marvin, 1844. 40 p. KyDC; MH-AH; PPPrHi; RPB; VtU. 44-6204

Tracy, Joseph, 1793?-1874. Historical account of state of society in western Africa, &c. Boston: 1844. 40 p. OCHP. 44-6205

Tracy, Joseph, 1793?-1874. A historical examination of ... Western Africa... and of the remedial influence of colonization and missions. Boston: 1844. DLC. 44-6206

Tracy, Joseph, 1793?-1874. A historical examination of the state of society in western Africa, as formed by paganism and muhammedanism, slavery, the slave

trade and piracy, and the remedial influence of colonization and missions. Boston: Board of directors, 1844. 40 p. DLC; MeBat; NbCrD. 44-6207

Tragic almanac for 1845. New York: T.W. Strong, 1844. MWA. 44-6208

Transmontanus, pseud. What is baptism? An essay, being chiefly a review of the first part of a work entitled an "exposition of the law of baptism," by the Rev. Edwin Hall, by Transmontanus. Boston: Gould, Kendall and Lincoln, 1844. 164 p. ICNBT; KyLoS; MNtCA; ViRU. 44-6209

Transportation. Brief statement of facts relative to the proposed railroad from Futchburg [sic] to Brattleborough, under charters lately obtained in the states of Massachusetts and Vermont. Boston: Dutton and Wentworth, 1844. VtMidbC. 44-6210

Transylvania University, Lexington, Kentucky. Annual announcement of Transylvania University for 1843-1844. Lexington, Kentucky: Observer and Reporter, printer, 1844. 16 p. KyLxT; KyU; PPPrHi; PWW. 44-6211

Trapier, Paul. Pastoral counsel affectionately tendered to the congregation of St. Michael's Church. Charleston: Miller and Browne, 1844. 4 p. WHi. 44-6212

Trautwine, John Cresson, 1810-1883. Report on the survey for a railroad from Blossburg to Ralston, by John C. Trautwine. Philadelphia: Young, 1844. 8 p. DBRE; ICJ; PHi; PPF. 44-6213

Travels in Denmark, Sweden and Nor-

way. New York: Lane, 1844. 163 p. NcD.
44-6214

Treadwell, Francis C. Treason defined;
by Francis C. Treadwell to which are
added the Declaration of Independence
and the Constitution of the United
States. New York: published at the
People's Rights office, 1844. 32 p. MWA;
RP. 44-6215

A treatise on the virtues and efficacy of
the saliva, or fasting spittle; being con-
veyed into the intestines, by eating a crust
of bread.... By a physician.... Salem:
Henry Whipple, 1844. 23 p. NjR. 44-6216

Trial of the pope of Rome, the anti-
Christ, or man of sin, described in the
Bible, for high treason against the son of
God, tried at the sessions house of truth.
Second American edition with an appen-
dix. Boston: Tappan, 1844. 176 p. CtHT;
MH; MPeHi; PU; WAsN. 44-6217

Tribune almanac and political register.
Politician's register; being a supplement
to the Whig almanac for 1844. Showing
the complete election returns of all the
states by counties; list of members of
Congress. Fifth edition. New York:
Greeley and McElrath, [1844] PP; PPL.
44-6218

The tribune almanac and political
register.... New York: 1844. CS; CSf;
MH-BA. 44-6219

Trimmer, Mary. A natural history of the
most remarkable quadrupeds, birds,
fishes, serpents, reptiles and insects by
Mrs. Mary Trimmer. Boston: S.G.
Simpkins, 1844. 233 p. IEG; PAtM. 44-
6220

Trinity College. Hartford, Connecticut.
Athenaeum Society. Catalogue of the
library and members of the Athenaeum
Society of Washington College.
Hartford: Case, Tiffany, 1844. CtSoP;
MA; MH; RPB. 44-6221

Trowbridge, Asa R. The temperance
melodeon, a melodeon, a collection of
original music, written expressly for this
work, and designed for the use of
temperance meetings, picnic parties, social circles, and choirs. Boston: [1844] 56
p. MB; MHi. 44-6222

Troy almanac for 1845. Troy, New
York: Stedman and Redfield [1844]
MWA; NT. 44-6223

Troy Conference Academy. West
Poultney, Vermont. Catalogue of the
corporation, faculty and students....year,
1844. Troy, New York: press of N. Tuttle,
1844. 20 p. NN. 44-6224

Troy Conference. Baptist Church. The
mode of baptism, by a member of the
Troy Conference. New York: printed for
the author, 1844. 34 p. NjR. 44-6225

The Troy fuel-saving magazine.
Published semi-annually. Troy: P. Low
and company, 1844. 22 p. NT. 44-6226

Troy register, business directory and advertiser. Troy, New York: H. Merriam,
1844. v. 1. No. 1. CSmH; NT. 44-6227

The true Catholic. Baltimore: 1844.
CSmH; DLC; IEG; NBuG; PPL. 44-6228

A true declaration of the estate of the
colony in Virginia, with a confutation of
such scandalous reports as have tended
to the disgrace of so worthy an enterprise.

Published by advice and direction of the councel of Virginia. London: W. Barret; [Washington: 1844] 27 p. CtHT; ICU; MdBP; MiU-C; OClWHi. 44-6229

The true midnight cry. ....Edited by S. N. Snow, ...Haverhill, Massachusetts: 1844. v. 1. no. 1. 4 p. MHa; MiU-C. 44-6230

True statement of the first fire on Sunday evening, July 7, 1844. Philadelphia: 1844. 8 p. MH; PHi; PPL. 44-6231

The true Wesleyan. Boston, 1844-1845. 2 v. DLC; MBAt; MiU-C; MWA; OrU. 44-6232

Truman, George. Narrative of a visit to the West Indies, in 1840 and 1841. By George Truman, John Jackson, and Thomas B. Longstreth. Philadelphia: Merrihew and Thompson, printers, 1844. 130 p. DeWi; ICN; MBBC; OClWHi; PHi. 44-6233

Trumball, Henry. History of the Indian wars: to which is prefixed a short account of the discovery of America by Columbus, and of the landing of our forefathers at Plymouth, with their most remarkable engagements with the Indians in New England, from their first landing, in 1620, until the death of King Philip in 1679.... New edition. Boston: George Clark, 1844. 320 p. CtSoP; DLC; IHi; NN; WaPS. 44-6234

Trumble, Alfred. Red Mary; or the mariner of the Pacific, by the author of "The mysteries of New York." Boston: 1844. 32 p. RPB. 44-6235

Truth unveiled; or a calm and impartial exposition of the origin and immediate cause of the terrible riots in Philadelphia on May 6-8, 1844, by a Protestant and native of Philadelphia. Philadelphia: M. Fitchian, 1844. 24 p. IaU; MdW; NcD;OCX; PPM. 44-6236

Truth unveiled; or a calm and impartial exposition of the origin and immediate cause of the terrible riots in Philadelphia on May 6th, 7th, and 8th, 1844; by a Protestant and native Philadelphian. Philadelphia: 1844. 24 p. CSmH; DeU; MH-AH; NN; PU. 44-6237

Tuberville, Henry. An abridgement of the Christian doctrine, with proofs of scripture on points controverted. By the way of question and answer. Composed in 1649 by Rev. Henry Tuberville, D.D. ....New York: Edward Dunigan, 1844. 151 p. IaDuTM; MBBC; OCX. 44-6238

Tucker, Ephraim W. A history of Oregon containing a condensed account of the most important voyages and discoveries of the Spanish, American and English navigators on the north west coast of America; Buffalo: A.W. Wilgus, 1844. 84 p. CU; DLC; NN; WaU. 44-6239

Tucker, Henry St. George, 1780-1848. A few lectures on natural law, by Henry St. George Tucker.... Charlottesville, [Virginia] J. Alexander, 1844. 128 p. MHi; MiU; NcD; ViU. ViW. 44-6240

Tucker, Henry St. George, 1780-1848. Lectures on Government, by Henry Tucker, Professor of law in the University of Virginia. Charlottesville:... 1844. 224 p. DLC; MHi; ViU. 44-6241

Tucker, J.N.T. The liberty harp: containing liberty hymns, songs, etc. Syracuse: J.N.T. Tucker, 1844. 60 p. DLC; NSy. 44-6242

Tucker, Luther. The farmer's museum. A monthly devoted to agriculture, etc. Albany: 1844. NN. 44-6243

Tuckerman, Samuel Parkman, 1819-1890. The Episcopal Harp.... a collection of original music adapted to the morning and evening service of the Protestant Episcopal Church in the United States. CtY; ICN; MB; NBuG; NN. 44-6244

Tudehope, Archibald. Church manual for the use of the Ninth Presbyterian Church, Philadelphia. Philadelphia: Wm. F. Geddes, 1844. 23 p. MiU-C; WHi. 44-6245

Tupper, Martin Farquhar, 1810-1889. Heart, a social novel.... New York: William H. Colyer, 1844. 140 p. CtY; MWA; PU. 44-6246

Tupper, Martin Farquhar, 1810-1889. The crock of gold, a rural novel. New York: Winchester, 1844. 64 p. NN. 44-6247

Turner, Sharon, 1768-1847. The sacred history of the world, attempted to be philosophically considered, in a series of letters to a son. By Sharon Turner, F.S.A., R.A.S.L..... New York: Harper and brothers, 1844. 3 v. CMtv; LN; MsU; OCX; OSW. 44-6248

Turner's comic almanack for 1845. Boston, Massachusetts: James Fisher, [1844] MWA. 44-6249

Turner's improved almanac and family recipe book.... New York: Turner, [1844?]-. PPTU. 44-6250

Turner's improved housekeeper's al-

manac for 1845. New York, New York: Turner and Fisher, MWA. 44-6251

Turner's Lowell directory and annual register, for the year of our Lord 1844. Lowell: J.G. Pillsbury, printer, [1844]-45. 2 v. MBNEH. 44-6252

Turney, Edmund. The triumph of the Gospel; or, an exposition of Rev. XX:1-9: a discourse delivered November 19, 1843, at Granville, Ohio: By Rev. Edmund Turney. Columbus: Scott and Teesdale, printers, 1844. 29 p. CSmH; MiD-B; MNtcA; OClWHi; PPPrHi. 44-6253

Tuson, Edward William, 1802-1865. The dissector's guide; or, student's companion.... By Edward William Tuson.... Third American edition with additions by Winslow Lewis, junior.... Boston: W.D. Ticknor and company, 1844. 220 p. DSG; MiDW-M; MoU; NNN; PPCP. 44-6254

Tustin, Septimus. The doubting communicant encouraged. Washington, D.C.: Anderson, 1844. 110 p. PPPrHi. 44-6255

Tuthill, Louisa Caroline Huggins, 1798-1879. The belle, the blue and the bigot; or three fields for woman's influence. Providence: S.C. Boldget, 1844. 322 p. CU; ICU; MiU-C; NjP; ViU. 44-6256

Tuthill, Louisa Caroline Huggins, 1798-1879. I will be a gentleman. A book for boys. Boston: Crosby, 1844. MB-FA. 44-6257

Tuthill, Louisa Caroline Huggins, 1798-1879. I will be a gentleman. Boston:

Andrews, Prentiss and Studley, printers, 1844. 148 p. RLa. 44-6258

Tuthill, Louisa Caroline Huggins, 1798-1879. Onward! Right onward! Twentieth edition. Boston: Crosby, Nichols and company, 1844. 169 p. NN. 44-6259

Tuthill, Louisa Caroline Huggins, 1798-1879. The young lady's reader; arranged for examples in rhetoric. Second edition. New Haven: 1844. 456 p. IU. 44-6260

Tuthill, Louisa Caroline Huggins, 1798-1879. The young lady's reader: arranged for examples in rhetoric for the higher classes in Seminaries. Second Edition. New Haven: S. Babcock, 1844. 5-436 p. IaHA; IU; MWHi; NbU; ViL. 44-6261

Tuttle, Timothy, 1781-1864. A sermon: preached at the dedication of the New Congregational Church in Ledyard, December 6, 1843.... Norwich, Connecticut: Cooley's Printing Establishment, 1844. 12 p. Ct; CtNwchO; Mhi. 44-6262

Twiss, Horace, 1787-1849. The public and private life of Lord Chancellor Elden, with selections from his correspondence. By Horace Twiss.... London: J. Murray; Philadelphia: Carey and Hart, 1844. 2 v. ArL; KyDC; MBL; OCY; PCC. 44-6263

The two May-days. Second edition. Boston, Massachusetts: Sabbath School Society, [1844] MNS. 44-6264

Tydings, Richard, 1783-1865. A refutation of the doctrine of uninterrupted apostolic succession, with a correction of errors concerning Rev. John Wesley and Dr. Coke. In answer to the Rev. G.T. Chapman, D.D., and others. By Richard

Tydings.... To which is appended a sketch of the author's life....Louisville [Jeffersonville, Iowa: A.S. Tilden, printer] 1844. 364 p. GEU-T; KyBgW; LNB; NcD; TxDaM. 44-6265

Tyler, Bennet, 1783-1858. Memoir of the life and character of Rev. Asahel Nettleton.... By Bennet Tyler.... Hartford: Robins and Smith, 1844. 372 p. ArCH; CtMW; MWA; NjR; ViRu. 44-6266

Tyler, Bennet, 1783-1858. Memoir of the life and character of Rev. Asahel Nettleton, ...Fourth edition. Boston: Doctrinal Tract and Book Society, 1844. 367 p. MiD. 44-6267

Tyler, Edward Royall, 1800-1848. Congregational catechism, containing a general survey of the organization, government and discipline of Christian churches. New Haven: A.H. Maltby, 1844. 137 p. ICU; MiD; MCH; MWA; OWoC. 44-6268

Tyler, George Palmer, 1809-1896. A sermon, adapted to the times, delivered at the ordination and installation of Rev. W.E. Knox.... February 14, 1844. ....Watertown, New York: Knowlton and Rice, 1844. 16 p. CSmH; MBC; MH-AH; N. 44-6269

Tyler, John, 1790-1862. Address of John Tyler, jr. before the Democratic Association of Portsmouth, Virginia. Washington: 1844. PPL. 44-6270

Tyler, John, 1790-1862. Address of John Tyler, Junior, esq., delivered before the Democratic Association of Portsmouth, Virginia, during the canvass of 1844. Washington, [D.C.]: J.E. Dow and company, printer, [1844?] 21 p. Vi. 44-6271

Tyler, John, 1790-1862. Life of John Tyler, president of the United States up to the close of the second session of the twenty-seventh congress.... 1844. [New York]: Harper and brothers, 1844. 256 p. IP; MdBE; MeB; MiGr. 44-6272

Tyler, Joseph D. The duty and advantages of educating the deaf, dumb and blind. A sermon preached in Staunton, Virginia, 1842. Raleigh: reprinted by Western R. Gales, 1844. 16 p. NcU. 44-6273

Tyler, Samuel. A discourse of the Baconian philosophy. Frederick City, Maine: E. Hughes, 1844. 178 p. ArBaA; CSmH; GU; MWA; NjMD; NRU. 44-6274

Tyng, Stephen Higginson, 1800-1885. The beloved physician. A discourse addressed to medical students, delivered in the Church of the Epiphany, Philadelphia, February 4, 1844. Philadelphia: King and Baird, 1844. 15 p. MBC; MdBM; PPM; PPPrHi. 44-6275

Tyng, Stephen Higginson, 1800-1885. Bible companion, designed for the assistance of Bible classes, families... Fourth American from the last London edition. Revised. Baltimore: 1844. MdBJ. 44-6276

Tyng, Stephen Higginson, 1800-1885. Lectures on the law and the gospel. Third edition, revised and enlarged. Philadelphia: Stavely and M'Calla, 1844. CtHC; GDecCT; ICU; NBuDD; OU. 44-6277

Tyng, Stephen Higginson, 1800-1885. A

plea for union. A sermon preached before the special convention of the Protestant Episcopal Church, in the state of Pennsylvania, in St. Andrew's Church, Philadelphia, September 6th, 1844. By Stephen H. Tyng.... [Philadelphia] Stavely and M'Calls, printers, 1844. 23 p. DLC; MdBP; MH; OO; PPM. 44-6278

Tyng, Stephen Higginson, 1800-1885. Sermons. Epiphany Church. Philadelphia: 1844. PHi. 44-6279

Tyng, Stephen Higginson, 1800-1885. Sermons. St. Andrew's Church. Philadelphia: 1844. PHi. 44-6280

Tyng, Stephen Higginson, 1800-1885. Speeches at the Boston meeting, on behalf of the American Sunday school Union, May 29, 1844. Philadelphia: American Sunday school Union, 1844. 39 p. ICRL; NcD. 44-6281

Tyrer, John. Taxidermy made easy, being plain and practical directions for preserving, selling and embellishing in the most approved style all kinds of quadrupeds, birds, fishes, reptiles, insects, etc. ....Chatham: 1844. PPAN. 44-6282

Tyson, Job R. Discourse before the Young Men's Colonization Society of Pennsylvania, October 24, 1834... Philadelphia: 1844. 63 p. PHi; PPL; PPM. 44-6283

Tytler, Patrick Fraser. Historical view of the progress of discovery on the more northern coasts of America, from the earliest period to the present time. New York: Harper and brothers, 1844. 360 p. InCW; LU; MeAu; PHi. 44-6284

U

Uncle Barnaby: or, recollections of his character and opinions. Second edition. New York: M.W. Dodd, 1844. 316 p. ICBB; MdHi; NGlc; NIC; WHi. 44-6285

Uncle Ben's New Jersey almanac for 1844. Princeton, New Jersey: R.E. Horner, [1844] 32 p. InU; MWA; NHi; NjR; NjHi. 44-6286

Uncle Ezekiel's youths cabinet volume I. Concord, New Hampshire: J.F. Witherell, 1844. 188 p. MCanHi. 44-6287

Uncle Sam's large almanac, for 1845.... Philadelphia: William W. Walker, [1844] 34 p. PPTU; ViU; WHi. 44-6288

Union Academy. Durham, [New Hampshire] Catalogue of the officers and students. Exeter: 1844. 12 p. Nh-Hi. 44-6289

Union Club of American Republican Men. Address of.... New York: 1844. DLC. 44-6290

Union College, Schenectady, New York. Annual catalogue of donations to the library, apparatus and museum of the Union College. 1843-1844. Schenectady: Riggs, 1844. NN; PPPrHi; WHi. 44-6291

Union College. Schenectady, New York. Nomina senatus academici.... Schenectadiae: typis Stephani S. Riggs, 1844. 35 p. NN. 44-6292

Union League of Philadelphia. Art Association of the Union League of Philadelphia. Annual Reports. Philadelphia: 1844-. PHi. 44-6293

Union Missionary. New York: 1844-. V. 1-. MBC; OO. 44-6294

Union Mutual Insurance Company. A further supplement to an act entitled an act to incorporate. Philadelphia: Walker, printer, 1844. 8 p. PhInsLib. 44-6295

Union Singing Association. Selections for the Providence children and youth's Union Singing Association. Providence: 1844. 126 p. RHi. 44-6296

United Brethren. Regeln und ordnungen der Bruder. Gemeinen in Gnadenhutten, Saron und Dover, Tuscarawas County, Ohio. Pittsburgh: Printed in the printery of the Lutheran Church, 1844. 20 p. PNazMHi. 44-6297

United Brothers of Temperance. Constitutions of the order of United Brothers of Temperance of the United States, ...New York: Sherman's Yankee Press, 1844. 24 p. DLC; MB; MH. 44-6298

United Hebrew Beneficient Fuel Society, Philadelphia. Constitution and by-laws.... adopted Sivan 8, 5604, May 26, 1844. [Society organized in Feburary, 1841] Philadelphia: [1844] 20 p. OCH; PPDrop. 44-6299

The United States almanac; or complete ephemeris, for the year 1844; containing the length and increase of days and the sun's rising and setting... By Freeman Hunt... Philadelphia: E.H. Butler, 1844. 316 p. CoCsC; IaHi; M. 44-6300

The United States almanac; or complete ephemeris, for the year 1844; containing the length and increase of days and the sun's rising and setting... By John Downes... Philadelphia: 1844. 315 p. MHi; WHi. 44-6301

The United States almanac; or complete ephemeris, for the year 1844; containing the length and increase of days and the sun's rising and setting... By John Downes... Philadelphia: E.H. Butler, 1844. 323 p. MWHi; PMA. 44-6302

The United States almanac; or, complete ephemeris. Philadelphia: E.H. Butler, 1844-45. 2 v. NBLiHi; NCH; OClW; PHC; PWW. 44-6303

United States constitution almanac for 1845. New York, New York: [1844] MWA. 44-6304

United States exploring expedition, 1838-1842. United States exploring expedition.... Under the command of Charles Wilkes, United States navy.... Philadelphia: C. Sherman, printer, 1844-74. 23 v. in 21. CLU; MH-Z; Mi; NbU; PU. 44-6305

United States farmers' almanac for 1845. New York, New York: David Felt and company, [1844] MWA. 44-6306

The United States farmers' almanac, for the year of our Lord and Savior 1845. [....]

Fitted to five different meridians; and calculated for the whole United States, British provinces, and Texas. [....] Milwaukee, Wisconsin territory: P. C. Hale, [1844] [36] p. WHi. 44-6307

United States Hotel. Boston, Massachusetts. Bill of fare for the Old Colony Club. December 21, 1844. [Boston] Clapp's Press [1844] MHi. 44-6308

United States liberty almanack for 1845. By W.B. Jarvis. Columbus, Ohio: Thrall and Glover, [1844] MWA. 44-6309

United States practical receipt book: or, complete book of reference.... By a practical chemist. Philadelphia: Lindsay and Blakiston, 1844. 359 p. MBP; MdBM; MH; PPL-R; RPA. 44-6310

United States statistical and chronological almanac for 1845. Rochester, New York: M. Miller and company, [1844] MWA; NRU. 44-6311

Universal salvation. Select theological library.... Philadelphia: 1844. PPL. 44-6312

Universalist quarterly and general review. Boston: A. Tompkins, 1844-91. 48 v. DLC; IC; MB; NcD; PP. 44-6313

Universalist year book. The Universalist companion, with an almanac and register, containing the statistics of the denomination for 1845. Calculations for the almanac, by George R. Perkins, A.M. Utica: Grosh and Walker, [1844] 64 p. MeB; MH; MMeT-Hi; MWA; OClWHi. 44-6314

Upfold, George. The duty of charity: A

sermon, delivered in Trinity Church, on Quinquagesima Sunday, February 18, 1844. By George Upfold, pastor or the Parish. Pittsburgh: printed by A. Jaynes, 1844. 30 p. MdBD; MHi; NNG. 44-6315

Upham, Thomas Cogswell, 1799-1872. Elements of mental philosophy abridged and designed as a text book for academies and high schools. New York: Harper and brothers, 1844. 480 p. IaPeC; MH; MoSpD; RPB; TU. 44-6316

Upham, Thomas Cogswell, 1799-1872. Principles of the interior or hidden life, designed particularly for the consideration of those who are seeking assurance of faith and perfect love. Second edition. Boston: Waite, Pierce, 1844. 520 p. CBPac; MWA; NBuU; OZAN; RP. 44-6317

Upham, Thomas Cogswell, 1799-1872. Ratio discipline, on the constitution of the Congregational churches, examined and deduced from the Congregational writers, and other ecclesiastical authorities, and from usage. Second edition. Portland, Maine: Hyde, 1844. 324 p. IEG; MnHi; OO; PPPrHi; RPB. 44-6318

Upper Merion, Pennsylvania. Swedish Lutheran Congregation of Christ Church. Charter of incorporation and by-laws. Norristown: 1844. 14 p. PHi. 44-6319

Ure, Andrew, 1778-1857. A dictionary of arts, manufactures, and mines; containing a clear exposition of their principles and practice. By Andrew Ure, M.D. ....From the third London edition corrected. New York: D. Appleton and company [1844] 2 v. KyLx; MB: RPB; VtU. 44-6320

Ure, Andrew, 1778-1857. Recent improvements in arts, manufactures, and mines; being a supplement to his dictionary. New York: D. Appleton and company, 1844. Cu-M; IC; NT; P; PU. 44-6321

Utica, New York. First Presbyterian Church. State and condition of the First Presbyterian Church and Society, in Utica: with a brief review of certain late proceedings and published statements of the minority relating to it. Utica: R. W. Roberts, printer, 1844. 32 p. MWA; N; NjR; NUt-Hi; PPPrHi. 44-6322

Utica, New York. Regulations of the common schools and of the school district library. May, 1844. Utica: 1844. 8 p. CtY. 44-6323

Utica, New York. Report of the common schools and of the school district library. Utica: 1844. 8 p. CtY. 44-6324

Utica, New York. School District Library. Supplement. Books added.... up to May 1, 1844. [Utica: 1844] 3 p. N; NN. 44-6325

Utica, New York. Utica Female Academy. Annual circular and catalogue of the officers and members of the Utica Female Academy, during the year ending August 4, 1844. Utica: Bennett, Backus and Hawley, 1844. 16 p. NUt. 44-6326

The Utica city directory. Compiled by William Richards. Utica, New York: H.H. Curtiss, printer, 1844. 150 p. MWA; NUt. 44-6327

V

The vacation; or, the four cousins. New Haven: S. Babcock, 1844. 16 p. CtY. 44-6328

Valpy, R. The elements of Greek grammar, with additions by C. Anthon. Twelfth edition. New York: W.E. Dean, 1844. 301 p. NccQ; PALT; PPL-R. 44-6329

Van Alstyne, Frances Jane Crosby, 1820-1915. The blind girl and other poems... New York: Wiley, 1844. 159 p. CtB; ICMe; MB; PPPIB; TxU. 44-6330

Van Buren, Martin, 1782-1862. Life of Martin Van Buren. Philadelphia: Mifflin and Parry, 1844. 16 p. MiD-B; Vi. 44-6331

Van Buren, Martin, 1782-1862. The Van Buren platform, or facts for the present supporters of Martin Van Buren. n.p., n.p. 1844? 8 p. WHi. 44-6332

Van Camp, A. Inquiries answered on a few brief remarks concerning the proper management of the teeth. Nashville, Tennessee: B.R.M. Kennie, 1844. MdUM; T. 44-6333

Van Heuvel, Jacob Adrien, 1787-1874. El Dorado; being a narrative of the circumstances which gave rise to reports, in the sixteenth century, of the existence of a rich and splendid city in South America... New York: J. Winchester, 1844. 165 p. KyLx; MH; MoSM; NBuG; PPL. 44-6334

Van Kleeck, Robert Boyd. An address, on the occasion of laying the cornerstone of the Free Mission Church of the Holy Cross, in the city of Troy. Troy, New York: Young and Hartt, 1844. 18 p. CtHT; MBC; NCH; NjR; PPL. 44-6335

Vanarsdall, Peter, b. 1787? Memoirs of Peter Vanarsdall, 1844-1857. 221 p. ICU. 44-6336

Vandenhoff, George. A plain system of elocution; or, logical and musical reading and declamation, with exercises in prose and verse, distinctly marked for the guidance of the ear and voice of the pupil. ....New York: C. Shepard, 1844. 164 p. IaDuU; NNQ; NNS; ScNC. 44-6337

Vanderburgh, Federal. An appeal for homoeopathy; or, remarks on the decision of the late Judge Cowen, ...by F. Vanderburgh, M.D. New York: William Radde, 1844. 29 p. MH; NNN; NNNAM; OC; PPHa. 44-6338

Vanvalkenburg, Sylvester. The mysteries of Haverhill. Haverhill: John Scott and company, 1844. MHa; MHaHi; MWA. 44-6339

Vattel, Emmerich de, 1714-1841. The law of nations; or principles of the law of nature, applied to the conduct and affairs of nations and sovereigns. From the

French of Monsieur de Vattel.... Sixth American edition, from a new edition by Joseph Chitty... Philadelphia: T. and J.W. Johnson, 1844. 500 p. ABBS; CtMW; MoU; PPB; ScSp. 44-6340

Vega Carpio, Lope Felix de, 1562-1635. Seleccion de obras maestras dramaticas de Lope de Vega y Calderon de la Barca; can indice y observaciones esenciales; al uso de los colegios y de las universidades de los Estados Unidos. Preparado, revisado, y corregido conforme a la mas reciente ortografia de la Academia espanola, por F. Sales.... Boston: J. Munore and company, 1844. 292 p. ArU; CLU; InU; MH; ViU. 44-6341

Vegetable substances used for the food of man. New York: Harper and brothers, 1844. 271 p. InRch; LN; MeAu; O; RJa. 44-6342

Venn, Henry. The complete duty of man: or the system of doctrinal and practical Christianity. Designed for the use of families. A new edition, carefully revised and corrected by Rev. H. Venn, of St. John's Holloway. New York: American Tract Society [1844] 430 p. ArCH; InEvW; MdBD. 44-6343

Verbesserter calender...Gedruckt: bey J.C.F. Egelmann, Berechnet von Carl Friederich Egelman, Reading, Pennsylvania: 1844. 31 p. PReaHi. 44-6344

Verbesserter Calender, 1845. Bei Carl Friderich Egelmann. Reading, Pennsylvania: I.C.F. Egelmann, [1844] MWA. 44-6345

La Verdad. Periodico del Nuevo-Mejico [weekly] [Santa Fe?: 1844] CSmH. 44-6346

Veremigten Staaten Calender fur 1845. Philadelphia, Pennsylvania: Edmund T. Schelly, [1844] MWA. 44-6347

Vergilius Maro, Publius. The Aeneid of Virgil, with English notes, critical and explanatory, a metrical clavis, by Charles Anthon, LL.D. New York: Harper and brothers, 1844. 942 p. LNP; NcC; WMHi; WvSht. 44-6348

Vergilius Maro, Publius. Virgil. The ecologues translated by Wrangham, the Georgics by Satheby, and the Aeneid by Dryden. New York: Harper and brothers, 1844. 2 v. KAStB; MBBC; MPiB; NN. 44-6349

Vergilius Maro, Publius. Maronis opera; or the works of virgil.... to which is added, a table of reference. By the Rev. J.G. Cooper. Ninth stereotype edition. New York: Robinson, Pratt and company, 1844. 615 p. IaMvC; OCan; ODaB; TChU; VtWood. 44-6350

Veritas, [pseud.] A brief statement of the argument for the abolition of the death punishment. In twelve essays. Published originally in the Nazarene, over the signature of Veritas.... Philadelphia: Gihon, Fairchild and company, 1844. 26 p. MB; MH; MMeT-Hi; OCLaw; WHi. 44-6351

Vermilye, Thomas Edward, 1803-1893. A funeral discourse, occasioned by the death of Mrs. Cornelia Van Rensselaer.... delivered in the North Dutch Church, Albany, on Sabbath, the first September, 1844. New York: Henry Ludwig, printer, 1844. 32 p. CtHC; MnHi; NjR; PPPrHi; WHi. 44-6352

The Vermont almanac, pocket

memorandum, and statistical register for the year.... Woodstock: Haskell and Palmer, 1844-[1849] NjR. 44-6353

Vermont and Massachusetts Railroad Company. Brief statement of facts relative to the proposed railroad from Fitchburg to Brattleborough, under charters lately obtained for the same in the states of Massachusetts and Vermont. Boston: Dutton and Wentworth, printers, 1844. 24 p. CSt; MB; MeHi; MFiHi; NjR. 44-6354

Vermont and Massachusetts Railroad Company. Report. First. Lowell: 1844-. CtY; DLC; ICU; MWiW; PPAmP. 44-6355

Vermont Medical College. Annual announcement....Woodstock: 1844-5. Nh. 44-6356

Vermont Medical College. Catalogue of the trustees, examiners, faculty and students of.... for the year 1844; and since its foundation in 1830. Woodstock, May, 1844. Woodstock: 1844. 16 p. Nh. 44-6357

Vermont year book for....1845.... Astronomical calculations by Zadock Thompson, A.M. Montpelier: E.P. Walton and sons, [1844] 126 p. Ct; MH; MHi; Mi; Nh-Hi. 44-6358

Vermont. Acts and resolves passed by the legislature of the state of Vermont, at their October session, 1844. ....Burlington: Chauncey Goodrich, 1844. 54 p. MdBB; MiD-B; Mi-L; NNLI; TxU-L. 44-6359

Vermont. Governor. [Slade, William] Legislature of Vermont.... October session, 1844. Governor's message. n.p.: [1844] 18 p. ICJ; VtMidbC. 44-6360

Vermont. Journal of the Senate of the state of Vermont, October session, 1843. Published by authority. Montpelier: E.P. Walton and sons, 1844. 191 p. CSmH; M; MB; MH; Mi. 44-6361

Vermont. University. Report of the commissioners to examine. 1844. 7 p. MBC. 44-6362

Very little tales for the very little children; First American from the sixth London edition. Philadelphia: George S. Appleton; New York: D. Appleton and company, 1844. 192 p. MH; NNC; PPL. 44-6363

Vethake, Henry, 1792-1866. The principles of political economy. ....Second edition. Philadelphia: J.W. Moore, 1844. 415 p. CtMW; MdBJ; MsU; NBu; OC. 44-6364

Vic., Seyatto de, pseud. Runzy, the last of the tribunes. Hartford: Printed by D.B. Moseley, 1844. 16 p. Ct. 44-6365

The Vicksburg almanac, for the year 1844; being bissextile or leap year. Calculated for the meridian of Vicksburg, latitude 32 20' north, longitude 91 west of Greenwich. Containing a complete and accurate court calendar for the states of Mississippi and Louisiana. Vicksburg: O.O. Woodman, 1844. MH; MsJs. 44-6366

Vidocq, Francois Eugene, 1775-1857. Memoirs of Vidocq; third edition.... Philadelphia: Carey and Hart, 1844. 311 p. NBronC; NjR; PWW. 44-6367

Vincennes University, Vincennes, Indiana. Petition of the trustees of the University of Vincennes. Indianapolis: 1844. 8 p. OO; WHi. 44-6368

Vindes y Gardoque, Francisco. Memorial respecting the right of Mr. John Wade Damon.... of Havana, to the ownership of the contract made with the municipality of said city.... for the supply of ice to the exclusion of Mr. Frederick Tudor, merchant of Boston.... Boston: Samuel N. Dickinson, 1844. 29 p. M; MB; MWA. 44-6369

Vinton, Francis. The church of her Lord's almoner to the world; a sermon preached before the convention of the Protestant Episcopal Church in the diocese of Rhode Island. Providence: Samuel G. Blodget, 1844. 32 p. IEG; MiD; NBLiHi; NNG; RNR. 44-6370

Vinton, Francis. A pastoral letter, by the reverend Francis Vinton. New York: A.V. Blake, 1844. 17 p. MdBD; NNG. 44-6371

Vinton, Francis. A remembrance of former days; being the farewell discourse to Trinity Church, Newport, Rhode Island. ....Providence: S.C. Blodget, 1844. 33 p. CtHT; MdBD; MiD; NBLiHi; Nh-Hi. 44-6372

Vinton, Samuel Finley. Speech of Mr. Vinton, of Ohio, on the contested election of the members of the House of Representatives, elected by the general ticket system in the states of New Hampshire, Georgia, Missouri and Mississippi. Delivered in the House of Representatives, February 12, 1844. Washington: J. and G.S. Gideon, 1844. 16 p. OCHP; OClWHi. 44-6373

Virginia's cure; or an advisive narrative concerning Virginia: discovering the true ground of that churches unhappiness, and the only true remedy. As it was presented to the Right Reverend Father in God Gilbert lord bishop of London, September 2, 1661.... London, printed by W. Godbid for H. Brome, 1662. [Reprinted. Washington: W.Q. Force, 1844] 19 p. CSt; ICU; MH; MnHi; TxU. 44-6374

Vogelbach, Ehrw. J. Abschieds-Rede des Ehrw. J. Vogelbach. Philadelphia: Schreifer und Schwacke, 1844. 15 p. NoLoc. 44-6375

Voices of the true-hearted....No. 1-. Philadelphia: Merrihew and Thompson, 1844-. 1 v. MB; NBuG; NIC; PHi; PWcHi. 44-6376

Voltaire, Francis Marie Arouet de, 1694-1778. La Henriade: poeme, par Voltaire. Edition stereotype, revue, corrigee, et annotee, par C.L. Parmentier. Boston: James Munroe and company, 1844. 171 p. ArCh; MeB; NGH; OFH; PBa. 44-6377

Voltaire, Francis Marie Arouet de, 1694-1778. Histoire de Charles XII, roi de Suede. Mouvelle edition. revue et corrigee par J. et P. Mouls. New York: W.E. Dean, 1844. MH. 44-6378

Voyages round the world, from the death of Captain Cook to the present time; including remarks on the social condition of the inhabitants in the recently discovered countries: their progress in the acts; and more especially their advancement in religious knowledge. New York: Harper and brothers, 1844. 401 p. WWaN. 44-6379

W

Wabash College. Crawfordsville, Indiana. A catalogue of the officers and students of Wabash College, July 17, 1844. Indianapolis: Chamberlain and Spann, printers, 1844. 19 p. In; MH; MiD-B. 44-6380

Waddell, Francis L. Texas. Tale of San Antonio. Death of Milan. Goliad and other poems. New York: Printed by William Applegate, 1844. 26 p. CSmH; CtY; NhPoA; RPB. 44-6381

Wadsworth Gallery, Hartford. Catalogue of paintings, now exhibiting in Wadsworth Gallery, Hartford. Hartford: Press of Elihu Geer, 1844. 28 p. CtSoP; DLC; MB; MiD-B. 44-6382

Wagner, Rudolph, 1805-1864. Elements of comparative anatomy, designed especially for the use of students. Edited by Alfred Tulk. [Part 1. The anatomy of mammalia. [complete]] New York: 1844. 64 p. DLC; MB; MH-M. 44-6383

Wainwright, Jonathan Mayhew, 1792-1854. Can there be a church without a bishop? Controversy between Rev. Drs. Wainwright and Potts. New York: Greeley and McElrath, etc., etc., 1844. 45 p. CtHC; IU; MH; NCaS; PPM. 44-6384

Wainwright, Jonathan Mayhew, 1792-1854. Controversy between Jonathan M. Wainwright and George Potts; "Can there be a church without a bishop?" New York: 1844. 45 p. CSfCW; N; PHi. 44-6385

Wainwright, Jonathan Mayhew, 1792-1854. No church without a bishop; or, the controversy between the Rev. Drs. Potts and Wainwright. With a preface by the latter, and an introduction and notes by an anti-sectarian. New York: Harper and brothers, 1844. 176 p. MH; NjR; PPPrHi; RPB. 44-6386

Wakely, Thomas, 1795-1862. The mother's medical adviser, on the diseases and management of children. With original recipes. First American from the tenth London edition. New York: Wilson and company, 1844. 64 p. DLC; MH-M. 44-6387

A walk about Vicksburgh, an [sic] other poems. By a gentleman of nature, ...Boston: J.V. Pierce, 1844. 304 p. IU; MB; MnU; MsJS; NIC. 44-6388

Walker's Buffalo city directory, containing a list of civil and military officers, religous, benevolent and philanthropic societies, local and miscellaneous statistics. With the names, residence and occupation, of the business population, heads of families, etc. By Horatio N. Walker. Buffalo: Lee and Thorp's press, 1844. 236 p. DLC; MH; NN; OClWHi; WHi. 44-6389

Walker, Alexander. Intermarriage; or the mode in which beauty, health, and intellect result from certain unions, and deformity, disease, and insanity from others. New York: H.G. Langely, 1844. 384 p. MB; NN; OCLaw; PPeSchw; ViU. 44-6390

Walker, Charles V. Electrotype manipulation: part 1. Being the theory and plain instructions in the art of working in metals.... Illustrated by wood cuts. From the thirteenth London edition. Philadelphia: Carey and Hart, 1844. 72 p. KyU; LNH; MB; MLow; PPL-R. 44-6391

Walker, George, J.S. Oration, pronounced on the Fourth of July, 1844 at Taylor's Stream Mills, Dallas County, Alabama. Cahawba: printed at the Dallas Gazette office, 1844. 15 p. GEU. 44-6392

Walker, John, 1732-1807. Walker's critical pronouncing dictionary, and expositor of the English language abridged by the Rev. Thomas Smith, London.... Cincinnati: E. Morgan and company, 1844. 416 p. In; LNH. 44-6393

Walker, John, 1732-1807. Walker's critical pronouncing dictionary, and expositor of the English language. Abridged by Thomas Smith, to which is added a chronological table, containing the principal events of the late war between the United States and Great Britain. Cooperstown, New York: H. and E. Phinney, 1844. MH; NRCR. 44-6394

Walker, John, 1732-1807. Walker's critical pronouncing dictionary, and expositor of the English language...To which are prefixed principles of English pronunciation...Likewise, rules to be observed by the natives of Scotland, Ireland and London...New London: Bolles and Williams, 1844. 71, 609, 103 p. NBuG; PAtM; ViU. 44-6395

Walker, Robert James, 1801-1869. Abstract of Mr. Walker's speech on the Texas treaty. Delivered in the United States Senate, May 20, 1844. Washington City: J. Heart, printer, 1844. 8 p. LU; MH; OClWHi. 44-6396

Walker, Robert James, 1801-1869. Letter of Mr. Walker of Mississippi, relative to the reannexation of Texas: in reply to the call of the people of Carroll County, Kentucky, to communicate his views on that subject. Washington: printed at the Globe office, 1844. 32 p. A-Ar; DLC; MB; PHi; TxH. 44-6397

Walker, Robert James, 1801-1869. Speech delivered in the Senate, May 20 and 21, in secret session on the treaty for the reannexation of Texas. Washington: 1844. 20 p. TxU; TN; WHi. 44-6398

Walker, Timothy, 1806-1856. Introduction to American law. Second edition. Cincinnati: U.P. James, 1844. 747 p. MiDU-L; OC; OHi. 44-6399

Walker, Warham. Church discipline: an exposition of the scripture doctrine of church order and government. Boston: Gould, Kendall and Lincoln; Utica: Bennett, Backers and Hawley, 1844. 156 p. GMM; ICU; MH-AH; ScCoB; ViRU. 44-6400

Walker, William, 1809-1875. The Southern harmony and musical companion: containing a choice collection of tunes, hymns, Psalms, odes and anthems; selected from the most eminent authors in the United States. Philadelphia: William Walker, 1844. 228 p. NcD; MsU. 44-6401

Walker, William F. God's covenant: a sermon, preached on the thirteenth Sunday after Trinity, in Trinity Church, Chicago, Illinois: by the rector. Chicago: Ellis and Fergus, printers, 1844. 32 p. CSmH; DLC; NBuDD. 44-6402

Walkly, Nelson. Two years experience in the employment of magneto-electricity, as a remedial agent in disease. By Dr. Nelson Walkly, Tuscaloosa, Alabama. Tuskaloosa: M.D.J. Slade, printer, 1844. 59 p. DLC. 44-6403

Wallace, B.J. Spiritual ambition: a sermon preached before the synod of Pennsylvania, in the Clinton Street Church, Philadelphia, ...October 29, 1844. By B.J. Wallace.... Philadelphia: printed at the office of the Christian Observer, 1844. 24 p. CSfCW; KyDC; MBC; NjR; PHi. 44-6404

Wallace, John William, 1815-1884. The reporters, chronologically arranged with occasional remarks upon their respective merits.... From the American Law Magazine. Philadelphia: Bailey, 1844. 77 p. PHi; PP; PPB; PPL. 44-6405

Wallis, Severn Teackle, 1816-1894. Lectures on the philosophy of history, and some of the popular errors which are founded on it. Delivered before the Calvert Institute, January 24, 1844. Baltimore: Printed by John Murphy [1844] 32 p. CSmH; DLC; NjP; PP; ScU. 44-6406

Walpole, Horace, 1717-1797. Letters of Horace Walpole, Earl of Oxford, to Sir Horace Mann, His Britannic Majesty's

resident at the court of Florence, from 1760 to 1785. Now first published from the original mss. Concluding series... Philadelphia: Lea and Blanchard, 1844. 2 v. AMob; FTa; PWW; ScC; Vi. 44-6407

Walpole, Massachusetts. Report of the school committee. [1844, 59] Dedham: 1844-59. MB. 44-6408

Walpole, Massachusetts. The town of Walpole in account with Warren Clap, treasurer, from March 24th, 1843, to March 26th, 1844. Dedham: Herman Mann, printer, 1844. 8 p. MB. 44-6409

Walshe, Walter Hayle, 1812-1892. The anatomy, physiology, pathology, and treatment of cancer. By Walter Hayle Walshe. With additions by J. Mason Warren. Boston: W.D. Ticknor and company, 1844. 351 p. CSt-L; ICJ; MdBJ; PPCp; TNN. 44-6410

Waltham, Massachusetts. The annual report of the character and condition of the schools in Waltham. Waltham: Josiah Hastings, printer, 1844. 13 p. MWal. 44-6411

Waltham, Massachusetts. Report of the committee, appointed at a meeting, to investigate the statements made in a report of Messrs. Whitney and Smith. Waltham: J. Hastings, printer, 1844. 12 p. MWal. 44-6412

Walton, Izaak, 1593-1683. The complete angler; or contemplative man's recreation, by Izaak Walton and Charles Cotton, edited by John Major. New York: Burt, 1844. 354 p. MSIntY; NcD; OkCla. 44-6413

Walton, Izaak, 1593-1683. The complete angler; or contemplative man's recreation, by Izaak Walton and Charles Cotton, edited by John Major. From the fourth London edition. New York: Crowell, 1844. 418 p. CMiC; ICMundC; IU. 44-6414

Walton, Izaak, 1593-1683. The complete angler; or contemplative man's recreation, by Izaak Walton and Charles Cotton. Philadelphia: Lippincott and company, 1844. 445 p. CtY; NjP; PU. 44-6415

Walton, Izaak, 1593-1683. The complete angler; or the contemplative man's recreation of Izaak Walton and Charles Cotton. Philadelphia: J.B. Lippincott and company [1844] 445 p. CtY; NjP; PU. 44-6416

Wanostrocht, Nicolas, 1745-1812. Recueil choisi de traits historiques et de contes moraux. Avec la signification des mots en anglais au bas de chaque page.... Nouv. ed., rev., cor. avec soin, et enrichie de plusieurs notes grammaticales.... Par Paul Mouls.... New York: W.E. Dean, 1844. 308 p. AzPr; DLC; MH; ScU. 44-6417

Ward, Samuel Dexter, 1788-1871. Remarks upon the oration delivered at Cambridge by George Putnam, before the Phi Beta Kappa Society, in Harvard University, August 29, 1844, by a member of the Suffolk Bar. Boston: Ticknor, 1844. 35 p. MA; MB; MH; MiD-B; MNBedf. 44-6418

Ward, Thomas, 1652-1708. Errata of the Protestant Bible; or the truth of the English translations examined; ... A new edition, carefully revised and corrected; to which are added, the celebrated preface of the Rev. Doctor Lingard.... and a vindication, by the Rt. Rev. Dr. Milner.... New York: D. and J. Sadlier, 1844. 118 p. DLC; ICU; MB; MPiB; TxU. 44-6419

Ward, William. The French importer's ready calculator; for the use of importers and dealers in French goods.... By William Ward. New York: J.S. Redfield, 1844. 36 p. DLC; LNSou. 44-6420

Ware, Henry, 1794-1843. The life of the Darwin. Boston: 1844. MH. 44-6421

Ware, Henry, 1794-1843. Memoirs of the Rev. Noah Worcester, D.D. By the Rev. Henry Ware, Junior, D.D. With a preface, notes, and a concluding chapter, by Samuel Worcester. Boston: J. Munroe and company, 1844. 155 p. CBPac; IEG; MdBP; Nh-Hi; PSC; RPB. 44-6422

Warfield, Catherine Ann [Ware] The wife of Leon, and other poems. By two sisters of the West. New York: D. Appleton and company; Philadelphia: G.S. Appleton, 1844. 256 p. DLC; ICU; NcAS; PU; RPA. 44-6423

Warne, Joseph Andrews, 1795-1861. A concise introduction to the study of the Holy Scriptures, containing an outline of the evidence of the genuineness, authenticity and inspiration of the sacred writings.... Franklin, New Hampshire: Peabody and Daniell, 1844. 1171 p. NoLoc. 44-6424

Warnung eine wehrhaft thatsache. Philadelphia: Conrad Zentler, 1844. PPeSchw. 44-6425

Warren Ladies' Seminary. A catalogue of the trustees, instructors, and pupils of the Warren Ladies' Seminary, for the academical year ending November, 1843. With an outline of the course of study. Boston: George Coolidge, printer, 1844. 12 p. RHi. 44-6426

Warren, James. Annual descriptive catalogue of fruits and ornamental trees... cultivated at Warrens Gardens... Nonantum Vale, Brighton. Boston: 1844. 60 p. MH; MHi. 44-6427

Warren, Jonah Goulding. A discourse on the history of the Westfield Baptist Association and church composing [it] Springfield: 1844. 36 p. MiD-B; MNtCA; NHC-S; OClWHi; RPB. 44-6428

Warren, Josiah, 1798-1874. Letter.... on equitable commerce. New Harmony: Warren, amateur printer, 1844. 16 p. InHi. 44-6429

Warren, Josiah, 1798-1874. A new system of notation. J. Warren. New Harmony, Indiana: 1844. 96 p. InHi; InNhW; NN. 44-6430

Warrock's Virginia and North Carolina almanack for 1845. Calculated by David Richardson. Richmond, Virginia: John Warrock, [1844] MWA. 44-6431

Warsaw signal. Warsaw, Illinois: Sharp and Galloway, 1844-46. USlC. 44-6432

Warsaw signal and agricultural, literary and commercial register. Published every Wednesday morning on Main Street, by Sharp and Head, at one dollar and seventy five cents per annum in advance. New series. No. 1. Warsaw, Illinois: 1844. KWiU. 44-6433

Washburn, William. Report of the case of Washburn, et al, vs. Gould, heard before Mr. Justice Story, in the circuit of the United States, for the district of Massachusetts. At Boston, May term, 1844. By William W. Storey. ....Boston: Freeman and Bolles, 1844. 55 p. MB; MBAt; MH-L. 44-6434

Washington, George, 1732-1799. Facsimiles of letters for his Excellency George Washington, president of the United States of America, to Sir John Sinclair... on agricultural and other interesting topics. Washington: F. Knight, 1844. 72 p. ICN: MB; OCHP; RPJCB; ViU. 44-6435

Washington, George, 1732-1799. Farewell address to the people of the United States.... Boston: Joseph G. Torrey, printer, 1844. 24 p. CSmH; MB; MBAt; NWHi; NN. 44-6436

Washington, George, 1732-1799. His farewell address to the people of the United States of America. Harrisburg: I.G. M'Kinley, state printer, 1844. 13 p. DLC; MB; MWHi. 44-6437

Washington, George, 1732-1799. Monuments of Washington's patriotism; containing a facsimile of his public accounts, kept during the revolutionary war, and some of the most interesting documents connected with his military command and civil adminstration. Fourth Edition. Washington: Franklin Knight, 1844. 108 p. IaHi; MdHi; NjN; OFH; ViRVal. 44-6438

Washington, George, 1732-1799. Revolutionary orders of General Washington issued during the years 1778-1782, selected from the MSS. of John Whiting, and edited by Henry Whiting. New York and London: Wiley and Putnam, 1844. 255 p. C-S; KyLx; LNH; MH; PPL-R. 44-6439

Washington, D.C. Washington Democratic Association. Another Whig slander refuted. [Washington: 1844] 4 p. N. 44-6440

Washington almanack for 1845. By Seth Smith. Philadelphia, Pennsylvania: Uriah Hunt, [1844] MWA; NCH. 44-6441

Washington College. Catalogue of the library and members of the Athenaeum Society, of Washington College. Hartford: Press of Case, Tiffany and Burnham, 1844. 14, 25-52 p. InID. 44-6442

Washington College. Chestertown, Maryland. Regulations of Washington College, [Chestertown, Maryland].... To which is prefixed an historical sketch of the college and address to the public. Baltimore: John D. Tay, printer, 1844. 24 p. MiD-B; PPL; RPB; TU. 44-6443

Washington College. Washington College, Tennessee. Catalogue of the officers, alumni and students of Washington College, East Tennessee. For MDCCCXLIV. Jonesborough, Tennessee: printed at the Whig office, 1844. 16 p. OCHp; PPW; TU. 44-6444

Washington Insurance Company. [Cincinnati] Charter and by-laws. 1844. IU; OCHP. 44-6445

Washington Temperance Society. Baltimore. An address of the Washington Temperance Society of Baltimore to their brethren throughout the United States. Setting forth the principles upon which the temperance reformation was based... Baltimore: Printed by Richard J. Matchett, 1844. 12 p. MdHi. 44-6446

Washington Total Abstinence Society, Dorchester, Massachusetts. Appeal to inhabitants. Boston, 1844. 20 p. DLC; MB. 44-6447

Washingtonian almanac for 1844. New York: E. Kearn, 1844. MB; MWA. 44-6448

Washingtonian almanac for 1845. New York, New York: E. Kearny, [1844] MWA. 44-6449

Waterford, Connecticut. Second Baptist Church at Waterford. Covenant of the Second Baptist Church. Waterford: 1844. 12 p. Ct. 44-6450

Waterloo Academy. Waterloo, New York. Annual catalogue of the officers and students.... for the year ending June, 1844. Waterloo: Pew and Marsh, printers, 1844. 8 p. MB. 44-6451

Waterman, Henry. The dead in Christ; a discourse pronounced at the interment of Mrs. L. Jenks Farnum, Waterford, Massachusetts, March 24, 1844. Providence: 1844. 32 p. CtSoP; RHi. 44-6452

Waterston, Robert Cassie, 1812-1892. The Thursday lecture. Discourse delivered on occasion of resuming the Thursday lecture, Dec. 14, 1843. Boston: William Crosby, 1844. 19 p. CBPac; ICMe; MH-AH; OClwhi; WHi. 44-6453

Waterston, Robert Cassie, 1812-1893. Address delivered at the installation of

Rev. George M. Rice, as pastor of the First Church in Chelsea, September 18, 1844. Boston: Leonard C. Bowles, 1844. 8 p. ICU; MH; MLy; MoSM; OClWHi. 44-6454

Waterston, Robert Cassie, 1812-1893. An address on pauperism, its extent, causes and best means of prevention; delivered at the church in Bowdoin Square, February 4, 1844. Published by the Society for the prevention of Pauperism. Boston: C.C. Little and J. Brown, 1844. 52 p. CtHC; ICMe MB; MDeeP; MH. 44-6455

Waterston, Robert Cassie, 1812-1893. The keys of the kingdom of heaven; a sermon at Windsor, Vermont, December 18, 1843 at the ordination of Frederick Hinckley. Boston: 1844. 23 p. MBAt; RPB. 44-6456

Waterston, Robert Cassie, 1812-1893. The Keys to the kingdom of heaven; a sermon preached at the ordination of Rev. Martin W. Willis, as pastor of the church of Christ in Walpole, New Hampshire. Boston: 1844. 24 p. CtHC; MB; MeU; Nh-Hi; WHi. 44-6457

Waterston, Robert Cassie, 1812-1893. A sermon on the true church of Christ. By R.C. Waterston. Boston: Benjamin H. Greene, 1844. 24 p. MeU; Nh. 44-6458

Waterston, Robert Cassie, 1812-1893. Thoughts on moral and spiritual culture.... Second edition revised. Boston: William Crosby and company, 1844. 320 p. MH; NCaS; OUrC; PMA. 44-6459

Watertown, New York. Black River Literary and Religious Institute....

Catalogue.... Watertown: J. Green, 1844. 24 p. N. 44-6460

Waterville College. Catalogue of the officers and students of Waterville College, Maine. For the academical year 1844-5. Hallowell: Glazier, Masters and Smith, 1844. 15 p. MeHi. 44-6461

Watmough, Edmund Carmick, 1796-1848. Scribblings and sketches, diplomatic, piscatory, and oceanic; by a fisher in small streams. Second edition with additions. Philadelphia: 1844. 189 p. DeWi; KyLo; MH; PHi; PPL. 44-6462

Watson, John Fanning, 1779-1860. Annals of Philadelphia and Pennsylvania in the olden time; being a collection of memoirs, anecdotes and incidents of the city and its inhabitants. Second edition. Philadelphia: published for the author, 1844. 2 v. DeU; NUt; PHi; Vi; WaS. 44-6463

Watson, Richard, 1781-1833. A biblical and theological dictionary. New York: G. Lane and company, 1844 [-1854] 2v. MBU-A; MoFayC; ScGrwL. 44-6464

Watson, Richard, 1781-1833. An exposition of the gospels of St. Matthew and St. Mark, and of some other detached parts of holy scripture. New York: Lane and Sandford, 1844. 538 p. CLSU; KWS; OCO; TNT; TxWB. 44-6465

Watson, Robert. Tables of interest, determining, by means of the differences of logistic squares, the interest on every whole sum to 10,000, for any length of time not exceeding 400 days, at the rates of 6 and 7 percent. New York: Wiley, 1844. 42 p. PU. 44-6466

Watson, Thomas. The Bible and the closet; or how we may read the scriptures with the most spiritual profit... edited by J.O. Choules. By Rev. Thomas Watson and Rev. Samuel Lee. Boston: Gould, Kendall and Lincoln, 1844. 128 p. 128 p. CSansS; CtHC; ICBB; MBC; NPlaK. 44-6467

Watson, Thomas, 1792-1882. Lectures on the principles and practice of physic; delivered at King's College, London... Philadelphia: Lea and Blanchard, 1844. 13 [9]-920 p. AMob; CSt-L; IU-M; NcU; TNV. 44-6468

Watson, William. Sermon, November 3, 1843, at the funeral of Mrs. Adaline E. Welton. Hartford: 1844. 21 p. CtHT. 44-6469

Watson, William Robinson, 1799-1864. The Whig party; its objects, its principles, its candidates, its duties, and its prospects; an address to the people of Rhode Island. ....Providence: Knowles and Vose, 1844. 44 p. IaU; MH; NjR; OClWHi; RPB. 44-6470

Wattles, John O. A few thoughts on marriage. Salem, Ohio: H. Painter, printer, 1844. 28 p. OClWHi. 44-6471

Watts, Anna Mary Howitt, 1824-1884. An art student in Munich by Anna Mary Howitt... Boston: Ticknor, 1844. 470 p. CO. 44-6472

Watts, Isaac, 1674-1748. Horae lyricae... to which are added the divine songs and moral songs from children, with a life of the author by Robert Southey. Boston: Little and Brown and company, 1844. 368 p. MHoly; OTifH. 44-6473

Watts, Isaac, 1674-1748. Hymns and spiritual songs... Philadelphia: Thomas, 1844. 240 p. PPLT. 44-6474

Watts, Isaac, 1674-1748. Infant hymns: designed for young children. New Haven: S. Babcock, 1844. 16 p. MWal. 44-6475

Watts, Isaac, 1674-1748. Logic. Sixth American edition. Boston: West, Richardson and Lord, 1844. 288 p. PScrM. 44-6476

Watts, Isaac, 1674-1748. Psalms, hymns and spiritual songs of Isaac Watts. To which are added select hymns, from other authors. New edition... Boston: Crocker and Brewster, 1844. 776 p. CU; DLC; MH-AH; NNUT. 44-6477

Watts, Isaac, 1674-1748. Songs, divine and moral, to which is prefixed a memoir of the author. Philadelphia: Smith and Peck, 1844. 191 p. MB; MBD; MH; WHi. 44-6478

Watts, Joshua. The museum of remarkable and interesting events, containing historical and other accounts.... Improved and enlarged. Cleveland, Ohio: Sanford and Hayward, 1844. 2v. in 1. KyHop; MB; NN; OCl; OCY. 44-6479

Wayland, Francis, 1796-1865. The elements of moral science. Abridged and adapted to the use of schools and academies. Boston: Gould, Kendall and Lincoln, 1844. 239 p. CLSU; GAGTh; KyBgW; RPB; TBriK. 44-6480

Wayland, Francis, 1796-1865. The elements of moral science. Twenty-second thousand. Revised and stereotyped. Boston: Gould, Kendall and Lincoln, 1844.

398 p. LNB; MWH; NCas; PU; TxDaTS. 44-6481

Wayland, Francis, 1796-1865. The elements of moral science. Twenty-fifth thousand. Boston: Gould, Kendall and Lincoln, 1844. 398 p. CoDI; MH; MLow; NNG; NNUT; ScCliTO. 44-6482

Webb, George James, 1803-1887. The odson: a collection of secular melodies, arranged and harmonized for four voices. Designed for adult singing schools, and social music parties by G.J. Webb and Lowell Mason. Fifth edition. Boston: J.H. Wilkins and R.B. Carter, 1844. 304 p. NcD. 44-6483

Weber, Moritz Ignaz, 1795-1875. Explanation of the anatomical atlas of the human body in natural size of Dr. M.J. Weber... New York: George Endicott, 1844. 54 p. DNLM; NNN. 44-6484

Webster, Augustus. A statement of the facts alluded to in "an address to the ministers and members of the Methodist Protestant Church, in the Maryland District." [Baltimore?: 1844] 21 p. MdBP; MdHi. 44-6485

Webster, Chauncey. Reasons of protest against a decision of the Associate Synod of North America in the case of Joseph J. Cooper, by C. Webster and F. W. McNaughton. Philadelphia: 1844. 24 p. MH-AH; PHi; PPPrHi. 44-6486

Webster, Daniel, 1782-1852. Andover address and his political course while Secretary of State, by Prof. Stuart of Andover. Essex County: 1844. 28 p. OCHP; PHi. 44-6487

Webster, Daniel, 1782-1852. A defence

of the Christian religion, and of the religious institution of the young, February 10, 1844, in the case of Stephen Girard's will. New York: M.H. Newman, 1844. 76 p. CSansS; KyDC; MH; Nh-Hi; PHi. 44-6488

Webster, Daniel, 1782-1852. A defence of the Christian religion, and of the religious institution of the young, February 10, 1844. Second edition. New York: Mark H. Newman, 1844. 72 p. MAnP; MiD-B; PHi. 44-6489

Webster, Daniel, 1782-1852. A defence of the Christian religion, and of the religious instruction of the young. Delivered in the Supreme Court of the United States, February 10, 1844, in the case of Stephen Girard's will. Second edition. New York: Newman, 1844. 72 p. MiU-C; NcMHi; NjP; PHi; PPPrHi. 44-6490

Webster, Daniel, 1782-1852. Mr. Webster's speech in defense of the Christian ministry... delivered in the Supreme Court of the United States, February 10, 1844, in the case of Stephen Girard's will. Washington: Printed by Gales and Seaton, 1844. 60 p. CoCs; ICU; MiD-B; MnU; WHi. 44-6491

Webster, Daniel, 1782-1852. Speech of Daniel Webster of Massachusetts, delivered at the great Whig mass convention, held at Philadelphia, on the first day of October, 1844. Philadelphia: 1844. 22 p. CSmH; MH; Nh; NN; PPL. 44-6492

Webster, Daniel, 1782-1852. Speeches and forensic arguments. Boston: Tappan, 1844. 2 v. PMA. 44-6493

Webster, Daniel, 1782-1852. Speeches

and forensic arguments. Eighth edition. Boston: Tappan and Dennet, 1844. 482 p. LN. 44-6494

Webster, James. Address to the graduates of Geneva Medical College. Delivered in the Presbyterian Church, Geneva, January 23, 1844. Geneva, New York: Scotten and Van Brunt, printers, 1844. 18 p. IEN-M; NBuU-M; OClM. 44-6495

Webster, L.S. Chirography, announcement. Boston: 1844. MB. 44-6496

Webster, Noah, 1758-1843. An American dictionary of the English language exhibiting the origin, orthography, pronunciation and definition of words. By Noah Webster. New York: Harper and brothers, 1844. 1079 p. CU; MB; OClWHi; ViAl; WHi. 44-6497

Webster, Noah, 1758-1843. The elementary spelling book being an improvement on the American spelling book. Portland [Maine] Sanborn and Carter, 1844? 168 p. MH. 44-6498

Webster, William Greenleaf, 1805-1869. A sequel to Webster's elementary spelling book; or a speller and definer. Third edition, revised and greatly improved. Louisville, Kentucky: Morton and Griswold, 1844. 172 p. IcU; In. 44-6499

Webster, William Greenleaf, 1805-1869. A sequel to Webster's elementary spelling book; or a speller and definer. Third hundred thousand. New York: G. F. Cooledge and brother, [1844] MH. 44-6500

Webster, William Greenleaf, 1805-

1869. A speller and definer... Third edition. Louisville: 1844. PPL. 44-6501

Webster, William Greenleaf, 1805-1869. A spelling book and dictionary. Revised and improved to Webster's elementary spelling book; or a speller and definer.... New York: George F. Cooledge and brother, 1844? 168 p. Ia-Keos. 44-6502

Webster's calendar. Howland's Albany almanack for 1845. Sandy Hill, New York: G. and E. Howland, [1844] MWA; PP. 44-6503

Webster's calendar, or, the Albany almanack. By G.R. Perkins. Albany: E.W. and C. Skinner, 1844. MWA. 44-6504

Webster's calendar, or, the Albany almanack. By G.R. Perkins. Varied edition. Albany: E.W. and C. Skinner, 1844. MWA. 44-6505

Webster's calendar, or the Albany almanack for 1845. Albany, New York: E.W. and C. Skinner, [1844] MWA; WHi. 44-6506

Webster's calendar, or the Albany almanack for 1845. Albany, New York: James Henry, [1844] MWA. 44-6507

Webster's calendar, or the Albany almanack for 1845. Albany, New York: W.C. Little, [1844] MWA. 44-6508

Wedgwood, William B. The constitution and revised statutes of the United States, and additional laws to 1844, reduced to questions and answers, for the use of schools and families. Philadelphia: Thomas, Cowperthwait and company,

1844. 196 p. InRch; MoSU; PPM; OCX; WU. 44-6509

Wedgwood, William B. The revised statutes of the commonwealth of Massachusetts, and additional laws to 1844, reduced to questions and answers for the use of schools and families. Boston: Tappan and Dennet, 1844. 116 p. CtHT; MB; MBev-F; MCanHi; MWinchrHi. 44-6510

Wedgwood, William B. Statutes of the state of Connecticut and additional laws to eighteen hundred forty-four reduced to question and answers, for the use of schools and families; ....Hartford: Gordon Robins, 1844. 104 p. Ct; MB; MH; OCLaw; OO. 44-6511

The week-day book for boys and girls. By the editors of the popular library. Portland: S.H. Colesworthy, 1844. 232 p. IEG; MeHi; MHi. 44-6512

Weems, Mason Locke, 1759-1825. The life of Benjamin Marion. Philadelphia: Lindsay and Blakiston, 1844. 208 p. InCW. 44-6513

Weems, Mason Locke, 1759-1825. The life of George Washington; with curious anecdotes, equally honourable to himself, and exemplary to his young countrymen.... Embellished with six engravings. By M.L. Weems, formerly rector of Mount Vernon parish.... Philadelphia: Allen, 1844. 244 p. Ct; KHi; MLaw; OO; PHi. 44-6514

Weinzoepflein, Roman. Report of the trial and conviction of Roman Weinzoepflein, a Roman Catholic priest, for rape, committed upon the person of Anna Maria Schmoll, while at confes-sional, in the Catholic Church at Evansville, Ind. [Evansville? 1844 80 p. DLC; InHi; InU; MH-L. 44-6515

Weinzoepflein, Roman. Trial of Roman Weinzoepflen...on a charge of rape, preferred by Mrs. Anna Maria Schmoll; held at Princeton, Indiana. Reported by A. E. Drapier. Louisville: Haldeman, 1844. 147 p. KyHi; MoU; OCLaw; PP. 44-6516

Weiss, John, 1818-1879. An address on temperance before the Watertown Washingtonian Society, November 10, 1844. Boston: Printed by White, Lewis and Potter, 1844. 16 p. MB; MH; NN. 44-6517

Welch, Archibald, 1794-1865. The annual address to the candidates for degrees and licences, in the medical institution of Yale College... New Haven: Printed by B.L. Hamlen, 1844. 22 p. Ct; NNN; OClM; WMAM. 44-6518

Welch, Oliver. Welch's improved American arithmetic, adapted to the currency of the United States. To which is added a concise treatise on the mensuration of planes and solids. Compiled by Oliver Welch. Improved and illustrated with questions adapted to the rules, for the use of schools and academies. Boston: R.H. Sherburne, 1844. 222 p. DLC; MoK. 44-6519

The well-spring. Published weekly. Edited by Rev. Asa Bullard. Boston: Massachusetts Sabbath School Society, 1844[-45] 2 v. DLC; MB; NNC; MPeaHi; PP. 44-6520

The well-bred boy, or, new school of

good manners. Boston: T.H. Carter and company, 1844. 94 p. MH. 44-6521

Weller, John B. Remarks in reply to Mr. Stewart of Pennsylvania, House of Representatives, January 17 and 18, 1844 [relative to the improvement of the navigation of the western waters. Washington: 1844] 7 p. OClWHi; WHi. 44-6522

Weller, John B. Speech.... on the bill to refund General Jackson's fine: delivered in the House of Representatives, etc. Washington: 1844. NoLoc. 44-6523

Wells, Albert. The Babcock family. [Albany: Munsell and Rowland, printers, 1844] 4 p. M. 44-6524

Wells, Charles. Sabbath school premium; familiar conversations explanatory of the New Testament. New York: Wells, 1844. VtVe. 44-6525

Wells, Daniel. Argument of Daniel Wells, esq. on the trial of William Wyman, at Lowell, November, 1843, on an indictment against himself and others for embezzlement of the funds of the Phoenix Bank, Charlestown, Massachusetts, before the Hon. Charles Allen.... Greenfield, Massachusetts: Printed by A. Phelps, 1844. 75 p. MB; MH-L; NHD; OCLaw. 44-6526

Wells, George Wadsworth, 1804-1843. Practical discourses by G.W. Wells. With a memoir. Boston: Crosby, 1844. 290 p. CBPac; MdBS; MH; MH-AH; NhPoA. 44-6527

Wells, H.T. Wells' book keeping and mechanic's lawyer; explaining the method of keeping accounts. Containing forms.... and supplement with questions, for the use of schools. Hartford: J.C. Wells, 1844. 60 p. CtMW. 44-6528

Wells, Horace. Specimen of printing types and ornaments from the Cincinnati Type Foundry. By Horace Wells, agent. Cincinnati, [Ohio]: 1844. 243 p. IaHi. 44-6529

Wentworth, John, 1815-1888. Remarks of Mr. Wentworth on the tariff. In the House of Representatives, Decmeber 17, 1844. [Washington, 1844] 1 p. TxHU. 44-6530

Wentworth, John, 1815-1888. Speech of Mr. Wentworth, of Illinois, on the Oregon Territory; delivered in the House of Representatives, January 24, 1844. Washington: Printed at the Globe office, 1844. 8 p. CU; OrP; WHi. 44-6531

Wesley, John, 1703-1791. Letters by the Rev. John Wesley, and the Rev. T. Coke. Second edition. Baltimore: D. Brunner, 1844. 22 p. MdBD; NNG; PHi. 44-6532

Wesley, John, 1703-1791. A plain account of Christian perfection. New York: G. Lane, etc., 1844. 60 p. MH. 44-6533

Wesley, John, 1703-1791. Sermons on several occasions. By the Rev. John Wesley, A.M., sometime fellow of Lincoln College, Oxford. New York: G. Lane and C.B. Tippett, 1844. 2 v. LNB; MdBE; NcD; NjMD. 44-6534

Wesley, John, 1703-1791. Treatise on baptism, by the Rev. John Wesley. Baltimore: D. Brunner, 1844. 15 p. MdBD; NNG. 44-6535

Wesleyan Academy. Wilbraham, Massachusetts. Nineteenth annual catalogue of the officers and students of the Wesleyan Academy, Wilbraham, Massachusetts, 1843-1844. Springfield: Smith and Taylor, printers, 1844. 16 p. MiD-B. 44-6536

Wesleyan College, Macom, Georgia. Catalogue of the trustees, officers, and students of the Georgia Female College [at Macon] New York [1844] DLC; MiU; PU. 44-6537

West Brookfield Anti-Slavery Society. An exposition of difficulties in West Brookfield, connected with anti-slavery operations, together with a reply to some statements.... West Brookfield, Massachusetts: the anti-slavery society, 1844. 59 p. MA; MB; MHi; WHi. 44-6538

Westboro', Massachusetts. Agricultural Society. Transactions of the Agricultural Society of Westboro' and Vicinity, for the year 1843. Boston: press of T.R. Marvin, 1844. 35 p. MWA. 44-6539

Western almanac. By William Luok. Columbus: E. Glover, 1844. MWA. 44-6540

Western almanac and Franklin calendar for 1845. Rochester, New York: M. Miller and company, [1844] MWA. 44-6541

Western almanac for 1845. By P. Johnson. Cincinnati, Ohio: A. Randall, [1844] MWA. 44-6542

The western and oneida almanac, for the year of our Lord 1845:.... By George R. Perkins, A.M., professor of mathematics. Utica, New York: R.W. Roberts, [1844] 36 p. MWA; NUtHi. 44-6543

The western farmer and gardener and horticultural magazine. Edited by Edward James Hooper, ...and Charles W. Elliott, ...Cincinnati: E.J. Hooper, 1844. 288 p. NNNBG; OCHP. 44-6544

Western farmer's almanac. By Horace Martin. Auburn, New York: H. Oliphant, 1844. ICN; MWA; NCH. 44-6545

Western farmer's almanac for 1845. By Horace Martin. Syracuse, New York: J.R. Gilmore, [1844] MWA. 44-6546

Western farmer's almanac; for 1845.... Calculations by Horace Martin. Syracuse: J.R. Gilmore, [1844?] [30] p. MWA. 44-6547

Western farmer's comprehensive almanac, for the year of our Lord 1844. ....Louisville, Kentucky: Morton and Griswold, 1844. 48 p. OC. 44-6548

The western literary journal and monthly review, Cincinnati: 1844-. V. 1-. IGK; OCHP; TxU. 44-6549

The western mirror and literary magazine. ....Cincinnati: O.G.W. Phillips, Junior, 1844-. v. 1-. KyLx; OC; OClWHi. 44-6550

Western Mutual Improvement Association. The constitution and by-laws of the Western Mutual Improvement Association. Organized in New York, April 3, 1844. New York: New World Press, 1844. 12 p. MiD-B. 44-6551

The western patriot and Canton almanack, for the year of our Lord 1845.... by Charles T. Egelmann; under this title the thirteenth, but in all the twenty-eighth edition. Canton, Stark County,

Ohio: Peter Kaufmann and company, 1844. 28 p. WHi. 44-6552

Western reserve almanac, for 1845. Astronomical calculations by Ansel Young. No. 2. Cleveland, Ohio: Sanford and Hayward, [1844] MWA. 44-6553

Western Reserve University, Cleveland, Ohio. Catalogue.... 1843-1853. Cleveland: 1844-1853. MB. 44-6554

Western Reserve University, Cleveland Ohio. Catalogue of the officers and students....1844-5. Hudson, Ohio: printed at the office of the Ohio Observer, 1844. 28 p. MiD-B; NBuG; NN; OC; WBeloC. 44-6555

Western side-saddle scenes, and young lady's equestrian manual. Edited by a citizen. Rochester: 1844. NoLoc. 44-6556

Western Theological Seminary. Allegheny, Pennsylvania. Catalogue of the officers and students of the Western Theological Seminary at Allegheny City, Pennsylvania, 1843-1844. Allegheny: Kennedy and brothers, 1844. 8 p. CSans-S; MBC; PPL; PPPrHi; PPWe. 44-6557

Westman, Habakkuk O., pseud. The spoon, with upwards of one hundred illustrations, [primitive, Egyptian, Roman, mediaeval, and modern] ....New York: Harper and brothers, 8144. 72 p. LU; NjT; PU; PWW; WHi. 44-6558

Westminster Assembly of Divines. The shorter catechism of the Westminster Assembly. Auburn: 1844. 30 p. MWA. 44-6559

Westtown Boarding School. Information for parents and others, inclining to send children to Friends' Boarding School at Westtown. Philadelphia: J. Kite and company, 1844. 8p. PHC. 44-6560

Wethered, John. Speech of Mr. Wethered, of Maryland, on the tariff. Delivered in the House of Representatives, April 24, 1844. Washington: Printed by J. and G.S. Gideon, 1844. 13 p. ICU; MdHi; MiD-B; PHi; WHi. 44-6561

What wait I for? Printed for the Main Western Ministerial Association. No. 5. Boston: office of the Christian world, 1844. 18 p. ICMe. 44-6562

Whately, Richard, 1787-1863. Elements of logic, comprising the substance of the article in the encyclopaedia metropolitana, with additions, etc. Boston: James Munroe and company, 1844. 359 p. KWiU; MB; MoU; ODaU; PReaA. 44-6563

Whately, Richard, 1787-1863. Elements of logic, comprising the substance of the article in the encyclopaedia metropolitana, with additions, etc. New York: Harper and brothers, 1844. 29-396 p. NN. 44-6564

Whately, Richard, 1787-1863. Elements of rhetoric; comprising the substance of the article in the encyclopaedia metropolitana...Boston: Munroe, 1844. 347 p. NRU; PU; ViRu. 44-6565

Whately, Richard, 1787-1863. Historic doubts relative to Napoleon Buonaparte.... Philadelphia: American

Sunday School Union, 1844. 60 p. KyDC; NjR; OMC. 44-6566

Wheat, John Thomas. Thorough churchmanship the highest style of Christian character; a sermon, preached at the funeral of Mrs. Belinda Dickinson Polk, ...By The Rev. J.T. Wheat. Clarksville, Tennessee: Charles Faxon, printer, 1844. 11 p. T. 44-6567

Wheaton, Homer. The church as it is: a sermon, preached at St. Paul's chapel, in the city of New York, on occasion of the joint anniversary celebration of the New York Bible and Common Prayer Book Society, and the Protestant Episcopal Tract Society, on the evening of Wednesday the 25th of September, 1844. By the Rev. Homer Wheaton. New York: James A. Sparks, 1844. 24 p. MB; NBuG; RPB. 44-6568

Wheaton College, Norton, Massachusetts. Catalogue of the officers and members of Wheaton Female Seminary, at Norton, Mass. for the winter and summer terms of the year ending July, 1844. Boston: Press of Crocker and Brewster, 1844. [4]-12 p. DLC; ICJ; MiD-B; NjP; PU. 44-6569

Wheeler, Alfred. Immortality or the pilgrim's dream and other poems.... New York: Saxton and Miles, 1844. 88 p. DLC; ICU; MB; MH; NBuG. 44-6570

Wheeler, Noyes. The phrenological characters and talents of Henry Clay, Daniel Webster, John Quincy Adams, William Henry Harrison, and Andrew Jackson. Boston: Dow and Jackson, 1844. 36 p. CtY-M; DLC; IaHi; ICN; MBAt. 44-6571

Wheeling, West Virginia. Northwestern Bank and Merchants and Mechanics Bank. [Document number 44] Northwestern and Merchants and Mechanics Bank. [....] January 29, 1845. [Richmond: Samuel Shepherd, printer, 1844] 3 p. WHi. 44-6572

Wheildon, William Wilder, 1805-1892. The new custom house; strictures on an article in the North American Review for April, 1844, entitled Architecture in the United States. Boston: Ticknor and company, 1844. 23 p. MB; MCon; MH; MHi; NIC. 44-6573

Whelpley, Samuel. A compend of history, from the earliest times. Twelfth edition. New York: Collins, Brother and company, 1844. 502, 69 p. MeLew. 44-6574

Whelpley, Samuel. A compend of history, from the earliest times; comprehending a general view of the present state of the world. Twelfth edition with corrections and important additions and improvements by Rev. Joseph Emerson. New York: Collins, brother and Co., 1844. 218 p. MoSpD. 44-6575

Whelpley, Samuel. A compend of history, from the earliest times; comprehending a general view of the present state of the world.... by Samuel Whelpley, A.M. Twelfth edition with corrections and important additions and improvements by Rev. Joseph Emerson.... New York: Collins, brother and company, 1844. 2 v. in 1. NHem; OOxM; OSW. 44-6576

Whig almanac. Seventh edition. New York: Greeley and McElrath, 1844. MWA. 44-6577

Whig almanac and politicians register for 1845. New York: Greeley and McElrath, [1844] IaDaM; IaHi; NAl; NRHi. 44-6578

Whig almanac and politician's register, being a supplement to the Whig almanac for 1844. Showing the complete election returns of all the states by counties, list of members of Congress, etc. Fifth edition. New York: [1844] NoLoc. 44-6579

The Whig almanac and United States register for 1844. New York: Greeley and McElrath, 1844. 72 p. KHi; MiD-B; PScrHi. 44-6580

The Whig almanac and United States register for 1845. New York: Greeley and McElrath, [1844] 53 p. MsJS. 44-6581

The Whig almanac and United States register for 1845. New York: Greeley and McElrath, [1844] 64 p. CoU; CtHWatk; MWHi; NvHi; WMOSC. 44-6582

Whig almanac for 1845. New York, New York: Greeley and McElrath, [1844] MBevHi; MWA. 44-6583

Whig banner melodist. Published for the Whigs of the Union. Philadelphia: 1844. 64 p. DLC; MB; TxU. 44-6584

The Whig banner songster, a choice collection of popular Whig melodies.... Life of Henry Clay.... Baltimore: 1844. PPL. 44-6585

Whig Congressional Committee, 1843-1845. Prospect before us, or locofoco impositions exposed. To the people of the United States. Washington: Printed at Gideons office [1844] 32 p. DLC; GEU; MBAt; MoS; OClWHi. 44-6586

Whig Congressional Committee, 1843-1845. Tariff doctrine. Washington: Gideon's office, printer, [1844?] 16 p. MoKU; MH-BA; PPL; TxU. 44-6587

Whig Party. Arkansas. Address of the Whig state convention to the people of Arkansas. Little Rock: Printed by B.J. Borden, 1844. 29 p. TxU. 44-6588

Whig Party. National convention. Baltimore. 1844. ....Proceedings of the great Whig national conventions, held in Baltimore on the 1st and 2d of May, 1844, for the nomination of president and vice president of the United States, to be recommended to the support of the people at the presidential election in 1844. [16] p. MdHi; MHi; MiD; MiU. 44-6589

Whig Party. New York. Canal policy of the state of New York [New York: 1844?] 8 p. MH-BA. 44-6590

Whig Party. Virginia. Convention. Whig state convention. Richmond: P.D. Barnard, 1844. 16 p. NcD; Vi. 44-6591

Whig Party. Virginia. The farmer's mechanic's and laboring man's ticket. For president, Henry Clay, For vice president, Theodore Frelinghuysen [Richmond: 1844?] Broadside. ViU. 44-6592

Whig songs for 1844. New York: Published at the New York Tribune, by Greeley and McElrath, 1844. 16 p. MB; MHi. 44-6593

Whig songs of the national club. Philadelphia: 1844. PPL-R. 44-6594

Whig songs: selected, sung and

published by the choir of the National Clay Club. Philadelphia: National Clay Club, 1844. 48 p. IU. 44-6595

Whig text book, or, democracy unmasked. To the people of the United States. [Washington: 1844] 31 p. MH; NIC; PPL; PU; Vi. 44-6596

Whig [and Tribune] almanac. 47. Volumes as follows: 1843 to 1854, 1856 to 1890. New York: 1844-1890. 44-6597

White, Alexander. White's confutation of the Church of Englandism and correct exposition of the Catholic Church, on all points of controversy between the two churches. Translated from the original [Latin] by Edmond Wm. O'Mahoney. Philadelphia: Henry M'Grath, 1844. 342 p. GMM; IaDuC; LNP; NBuCC; WNaE. 44-6598

White, B.F. The sacred harp, a collection of psalm, hymn tunes, odes and anthems, selected from the most eminent authors: together with nearly one hundred pieces never before published. Suited to most metres, and well adapted to churches of every denomination, singing school, and private societies.... Philadelphia: T.K. Collins,junior, 1844. 354 p. GU; OkGoP; PU; TKL-Mc. 44-6599

White, Charles, 1795-1861. Goodness, an essential element of true greatness: a baccalaureate address, delivered July 17, 1844. Indianapolis: Printed By Chamberlain and Spann, 1844. 30 p. CSmH; IENM; In; MH-AH; PPM. 44-6600

White, Daniel Appleton, 1776-1861. An address delivered before the society of the Alumni of Harvard University, on their anniversary, August 27, 1844. Cambridge: J. Owen, 1844. 42 p. CBPac; IEG; MBC; NjR; PPAmP. 44-6601

White, E.L. Oh! Poor Miss Lucy Neale! And Dandy Jim. Arranged as a quick step by Edward L. White. Boston: Oliver Ditston, 1844. 2 p. MB. 44-6602

White, Henry, 1812-1880. Elements of universal history of a new and systematic plan from the earliest times to the treaty of Vienna. Philadelphia: Lea and Blanchard, 1844. 525 p. DLC; KyLoS; NcGA; PU; RNR. 44-6603

White, Henry Kirke, 1785-1861. Memoir and poetical remains of Henry Kirke White; also melancholy hours. With an introduction by Rev. John Todd.... Philadelphia: Perkins and Purves, 1844. 11-480 p. CSansS; InNd; MdBG; MHa; ScDuE. 44-6604

White, Henry Kirke, 1785-1806. The works of Henry Kirke White. Containing his life, poems and melancholy hours. New York: Hurst [1844?] 414 p. CU; InU. 44-6605

White, Hugh. The believer: a series of discourses, by the Rev. Hugh White.... First American from the seventh Dublin edition. New York: Robert Carter; Pittsburg: Thomas Carter, 1844. 252 p. GHi; LNB. MBC; NbOP. 44-6606

White, Hugh. Meditations and addresses on the subject of prayer. Fourth American from the tenth Dublin edition. New York: Robert Carter, 1844. 237 p. NcHil; NjP. 44-6607

White, James C. Brief history of the Tabernacle church.... Cincinnati:

Jeremiah Faulkner, printer, 1844. 16 p. PLT. 44-6608

White, Jeremiah. The restoration of all things: or, a vindication of the goodness and grace of God to be manifested at last in the recovery of His whole creation out of their fall. First American edition. Philadelphia: Gihon, Fairchild and company, 1844. 88 p. CtHC; MBC; MeBat; MMeT-Hi; PHi. 44-6609

White, Samuel. Address on insanity, delivered before the New York State Medical Society, February 5, 1844. Albany: J. Munsell, 1844. 20 p. MH; MHi; N. 44-6610

White Plains, New York. Bloomingdale Hospital. Extracts from the twenty-fourth annual report of the Bloomingdale Asylum for the Insane. [New York? 1844] 16 p. OO. 44-6611

Whitehead, John, 1740?-1804. Life of the Rev. John Wesley... with the life of the Rev. Charles Wesley. Boston: J. Mc-Leish, 1844. 2 v. CBPSR; MBC; NNS; PPA; WvU. 44-6612

Whiting, N.N. Origin, nature, and influence of neology. Boston [1844] 51 p. MH. 44-6613

Whitman, Jason. A letter to a friend, on the duty of commencing at once a religious life. Boston: office of the Christian World, 1844. MWA. 44-6614

Whitman, Jason. Unbelief exposed. Boston: Office of the Christian World, 1844. 28 p. MWA. 44-6615

Whitney, Louisa [Goddard] The burning of the convent. A narrative of the destruction, by a mob, of the Ursuline School on Mount Benedict, Charlestown, as remembered by one of the pupils. Cambridge, Massachusetts: 1844. MH. 44-6616

Whitney, Thomas Richard, 1804-1858. Evening hours; a collection of poems. New York: Leavitt, 1844. 118 p. CtMW; MB; MWiW; NRU. 44-6617

Whitsitt, James. The old thing on the atonement, or twelve objections to the new thing on it. Nashville: W.F. Bang and company, printers, Republican Banner office, 1844 24 p. LNB. 44-6618

Whittemore, Thomas. The plain guide to Universalism designed to bad inquires to the belief of that doctrine and believers to the practice of it. Boston: published by the author, 1844. 408 p. MMeT-Hi; MSwan; NCaS; OHi. 44-6619

Whittingham, William Rollinson. A pastoral letter to the people of the diocese of Maryland.... Baltimore: Daniel Brunner, 1844. 12 p. MdBD. 44-6620

Whittingham, William Rollinson. The apostle in his master's house; a sermon preached in St. Paul's Church, Baltimore... Baltimore: H. Colburn, 1844. 32 p. MdBD; MiD-MCh; NjR; NNG; TSwV. 44-6621

The whole truth. To the freemen of New England. Woodstock, Virginia: John Tatewood, 1844. 24 p. NcD. 44-6622

Wickens, Stephen B. The life of John Bunyan... By S.B. Stephen. New York City, New York: Printed by Carlton and

Porter, 1844. 344 p. CBe; IU; NNer; UPB; ViNew. 44-6623

Wickford [Rhode Island] Baptist Church. Brief history comprising the principal facts connected with the late difficulties which resulted in its dissolution April 4, 1844. Providence: 1844. 36 p. MHi; RHi; RP; RPB; RWe. 44-6624

Wieland, C.M. Oberon. Poems. New York: 1844. MB. 44-6625

Wiggins, Francis S. The American farmer's instructor, or practical agriculturist; comprehending the cultivation of plants, the husbandry of the domestic animals, and the economy of the farm; together with a variety of information which will be found important to the farmer. By Francis S. Wiggins.... Philadelphia: 1844. 504 p. Ct; OClW. 44-6626

Wiggins, Richard. New York expositor; or, fifth book, being a collection of the most useful words in the English language. By Richard Wiggins. To which is added a vocabulary of scientific terms. By J. Griscom.... New York: S.S. and W. Wood, 1844. 285 p. PMA. 44-6627

Wight, Lyman. An address by way of an abridged account and journal of my life from February, 1844, up to April, 1848, with an appeal to the Latter Day Saints. By Lyman Wight. Black River Falls, Wisconsin: [n.p.: 1844] 16 p. MoInRC. 44-6628

Wilcox, Phineas Bacon, 1796-1863. Digest of the first twelve volumes of the Ohio reports... all cases ever reported at law and in equity. Columbus, 1844. 607 p. OCl; OO; OU. 44-6629

Wilkes, Charles, 1798-1877. Narrative of the United States exploring expedition. During the years 1838, 1839, 1840, 1841, 1842. By Charles Wilkes, United States Navy, commander of the expedition.... Philadelphia: C. Sherman, printer, 1844. 5 v. CU; FU; In; NNF; OFB. 44-6630

Wilkes, George. The mysteries of the tombs, a journal of thirty days imprisonment in the New York city prison; for libel... New York: 1844. 64 p. ICJ; MWA; PHi. 44-6631

Wilkes, J. Wimpleton. The mysteries of Springfield; a tale of the times. Springfield, Massachusetts: William R. Brockett, 1844. 40 p. MSHi; MWA. 44-6632

Wilkins, William. Mr. Wilkin's address to the people of the twenty-first congressional district of Pennsylvania. Washington: Blair and Rives, printers, 1844. 8 p. MiD-B; MH; TxU. 44-6633

Wilks, Thomas Egerton, 1812-1854. A mistaken story; a farce, in one act... New York: Samuel French, [1844?] 22 p. OCl. 44-6634

Willard, Emma Hart, 1787-1870. Abridged history of the United States or republic of America.... Fourth edition. Philadelphia: A.S. Barnes and company, 1844. 336 p. GHi; MH; OHi; PMA; ScU. 44-6635

Willard, Emma Hart, 1787-1870. Address to the pupils of the Washington Female Seminary. By Emma Willard. Pittsburgh: printed by George Parkin, 1844. 23 p. CtHWatk; MBAt, MWA; PPL. 44-6636

Willard, Emma Hart, 1787-1870. Ancient geography, as connected with chronology, and preparatory to ancient history; accompanied with an atlas. By Emma Willard. Also problems on the globes, and rules for constructing maps. To accompany modern geography by W.C. Woodbridge. Revised edition. Hartford: Belknap and Hamersley, 1844. 96 p. KWiU; MB; MH; NT; ScC. 44-6637

Willard, Emma Hart, 1787-1870. History of the United States, or Republic of America. Philadelphia: A.S. Barnes and company, 1844. 443 p. ABBS; CtSoP; IaHi; MW; OKentC. 44-6638

Willard, Emma Hart, 1787-1870. A system of universal history in perspective. Philadelphia: Barnes, 1844. 496 p. FOC; MB; OClWHi; PU; ScU. 44-6639

Willard, John H. The primary arithmetic.... Second edition. Providence: 1844. RPB. 44-6640

Willett, William Marinus. Woman's true sphere. Newbury, Vermont: Hayes and company, 1844. 14 p. MBNMHi; MH; Nh. 44-6641

Willetts, Jacob, 1785-1860. Mental and practical arithmetic; designed chiefly for the use of district and common schools in the United States. Poughkeepsie: William Wilson, 1844. 216 p. NP. 44-6642

Willetts, Jacob, 1785-1860. Scholar's arithmetic.... Fifty-fifth edition, revised and enlarged... Poughkeepsie: 1844. CtHWatk. 44-6643

Williams, C. D. A review of professor C.B. Coventry's introductory lecture, delivered before the class of medical students of Geneva College, session of 1843-4. By Dr. C.D. Williams. Geneva: Ira Merrell, printer, 1844. 24 p. DSG; NSyU; PPHa. 44-6644

Williams, Charles James Blasius, 1805-1889. Principles of medicine.... with.... additional notes, explanatory and critical by the editor of the select medical library and bulletin of medical science. Philadelphia: E. Barrington and G. D. Haswell, 1844. 395 p. ICJ; KyLxT; MeB; MH; WBeloC. 44-6645

Williams, Charles James Blasius, 1805-1889. Principles of medicine: comprising general pathology and therapeutics.... With additions and notes by Meredith Clymer.... Philadelphia: Lea and Blanchard, 1844. 383 p. CSt-L; LNOP; PPA; ViU. 44-6646

Williams, Henry. To the citizens of Boston [On the Water Question] Boston: 1844. 9 p. MBC. 44-6647

Williams, P. Table of rates of toll on the Erie Canal. By P. Williams, accountant. Buffalo: Thomas, printer, 1844 [99] p. DLC. 44-6648

Williams, R.O. A historical sketch of universalism, in Norwich, Connecticut. A sermon delivered before the Universalist society in that place, on the fifth of May, 1844. By R.O. Williams, pastor.... Norwich, Connecticut: George W. Concklin, 1844. 32 p. CtSoP; MBC; MHi; Nh-Hi; NNUT. 44-6649

Williams, Thomas. Address on the subject of the tariff, and the relations of the two great parties and their candidates thereto, delivered by request, before the Clay Clubs of Allegheny and Pittsburgh.

Pittsburgh: Published by order of the Clubs, 1844. 30 p. MoWgT. 44-6650

Williams, Thomas, 1806-1872. A song, to be read, said, or sung; inscribed to the Hon. Henry Clay, the candidate for the office of President of the United States of America. By an old bard of Narragansett. Providence: printed for the author, 1844. 8 p. IU; RHi; RP. 44-6651

Williams, William R., 1804-1885. The conservative principle in our literature. An address before the literary societies of the Hamilton Literary and Theological Institution [Madison County, New York] Tuesday, June 13, 1843. New York: Gray, 1844. 51 p. IGK; MH; MNtcA; NCH; PCA. 44-6652

Williams, William R., 1804-1885. The conservative principle in our literature. An address before the literary societies of the Hamilton Literary and Theological Institution [Madison County, New York] Tuesday, June 13, 1843. Second edition. New York: Lewis Colby, 1844. 135 p. CtMMHi; MiD; NNUT; RPA; RPB. 44-6653

Williams College. Williamstown, Massachusetts. Catalogue of the officers and students of Williams College, 1844-5. Troy, New York: press of J.C. Kneeland and company, 1844. 20 p. NN; NNC. 44-6654

The Williams miscellany. 1844. v. 1, 2 [no. 1] CU; MB; NjR; NN; NNUW. 44-6655

Williamsburgh, New York. Charter of the village of Williamsburgh and the several acts relating thereto, with the by-laws and ordinances of said village, as revised and amended in May, 1844, and also forms of proceedings. Williamsburgh: 1844. 84 p. MH-L; NN; NNMuCN. 44-6656

Williamsburgh, New York. The charter of the village of Williamsburgh, and the several acts relating thereto; with the by-laws and ordinances of said village, as revised and amended in May, 1844, and also, forms of proceedings. Williamsburgh: L. Darbee, 1844. 93 p. MH. 44-6657

Williamson, Isaac David, 1807-1876. An argument for the truth of Christianity in a series of discourses by I.D. Williamson. New York: C.L. Stickney, 1844. 252 p. MVh; NCaS; OClWHi. 44-6658

Willis, Nathaniel Parker, 1806-1867. The harp with a Sabbath tone: containing Montgomery's world before the flood.... New York: Morris and Willis, 1844. 32 p. LNH; NN. 44-6659

Willis, Nathaniel Parker, 1806-1867. Lecture on fashion: delivered before the New York Lyceum, by N.P. Willis. [New York: Morris and Willis, 1844] 16 p. ICU; MB; MBAt; MH; MiU. 44-6660

Willis, Nathaniel Parker, 1806-1867. Letters from under a bridge. [New York: 1844] 32 p. IU; LNH; MB; MoK; WU. 44-6661

Willis, Nathaniel Parker, 1806-1867. Pencillings by the way: written during some years of residence and travel in France, Italy, Greece, Asia Minor, Turkey, and England, by N.P. Willis.... First complete edition. New York: Morris and Willis, 1844. 216 p. LNH; MH; NNS; PU; RPA. 44-6662

Willis, Nathaniel Parker, 1806-1867. The poems, sacred, passionate, and humorous. New York: Clark and Austin, 1844. 331 p. InEv; MH; NNC; PPL-R; ScC. 44-6663

Willis, Nathaniel Parker, 1806-1867. The poems, sacred, passionate, and humorous. Third edition. New York: Clark and Austin, 1844. 331 p. IaSc; IU; MH; MSa; NAlbi. 44-6664

Willis, Nathaniel Parker, 1806-1867. Tortesa, the userer [and Bianca Visconti; or, the heart overtasked] by N.P. Willis. [New York: Morris Willis and company, 1844] 31 p. IaU; MWH; TxU. 44-6665

Willis, Nathaniel Parker, 1806-1867. Two ways of "dying for a husband." New York: Morris and Willis, [1844] 31 p. ICU. 44-6666

Willison, John. The afflicted man's companion: or, a directory or persons and families afflicted with sickness, or any other distress: ....By the Rev. John Willison, ... A new edition, revised and improved. Philadelphia: W.A. Leary, 1844. 252 p. MdHi; MWiW; NbOP; TxD-T; ViRut. 44-6667

Williston, Seth, 1770-1851. Slavery not a scriptural ground of division in efforts for the salvation of the heathen.... New York: M.W. Dodd, 1844. 24 p. CtSoP; MB; MiD-B; NNUT; OO. 44-6668

Williston Seminary. Easthampton, Massachusetts. Catalogue of the trustees, teachers and students.... for the fall term ending November 19, 1844. Easthampton, Massachusetts. Northampton: John Metcalf, printer, 1844. 16 p. MA; MBC; MiD-B; OO. 44-6669

Willmot, Robert Eldridge Aris, 1809-1863. The poets of the nineteenth century. Selected and edited by the Rev. Robert Aris Willmott, incumbent of Bearwood. With English and American additions, arranged by Evert A. Duyckinck, editor of the cyclopedia of American literature. Illustrated with one hundred and forty engravings, drawn by eminent artists. New York: Harper brothers, 1844. 674 p. NoLoc. 44-6670

Wilmington, North Carolina. Proceedings of the safety committee: for the town of Wilmington, North Carolina [1774-76].... Raleigh: 1844. 76 p. DLC; MB; MdHi; MHi; NcD. 44-6671

Wilson, Caroline Fry, 1787-1846. Christ our example. New York: Richer, 1844. 285 p. ICU; LNP; OO; PAtM; TBriK. 44-6672

Wilson, Daniel. An address to young persons about to be confirmed. By Daniel Wilson.... Edited by Benjamin Dorr.... Second edition. Philadelphia: R.S.H. George, 1844. 105 p. NcD; NNG. 44-6673

Wilson, Erasmus, 1809-1884. A system of human anatomy, general and special. Second American edition edited by Paul B. Goddard.... Philadelphia: Leo and Blanchard, 1844. 607 p. CSt-L; ICU-R; PPCP; NNN; WBeloC. 44-6674

Wilson, Erasmus, 1809-1884. A system of human anatomy, general and special. Second American edition. Edited by Paul B. Goddard. Two hundred illustrations, by Gilbert. From the second London edition. Philadelphia: Lea and Blanchard, 1844. 554 p. IaDaM. 44-6675

Wilson, Erasmus, 1809-1884. The dissector; or, practical and surgical anatomy. By Erasmus Wilson.... With one hundred and six illustrations. Modified and rearranged by Paul B. Goddard.... Philadelphia: Lea and Blanchard, 1844. 444 p. CU; GU-M; MdBJ; NNN; OMC. 44-6676

Wilson, James G.V. Report of the case on application for an injunction, Circuit Court United States, District of Maryland at Baltimore, on the 21st-23rd and 26th of November, 1844. Baltimore: 1844. 38 p. MH-L. 44-6677

Wilson, John. The history of Switzerland, from B.C. 110, to A.D. 1830. New York: Harper and brothers, 1844. 21-288 p. GMW; NNF; RPE; ViLxW. 44-6678

Wilson, John. A treatise of grammatical punctuation designed for letter writers, authors, printers and correctors of the press and for the use of academies and schools. Manchester: 1844. MB; MBAt; MHi. 44-6679

Wilson, Thomas, 1663-1755. Sacra privata: the private meditations, devotions, and prayers, of the Right Rev. T. Wilson.... [The only complete American edition] New York: D. Appleton and company; Philadelphia: G.S. Appleton, 1844. 310 p. NbOM; NBuDD. 44-6680

Winchester, Elhanan, 1751-1797. Ten letters addressed to Mr. Paine, in answer to his pamphlet entitled The age of reason: containing some clear and satisfying evidences of the truth of divine revelation... Third edition. Philadelphia:

Gihon, Fairchild and company, 1844. [3]-37 p. DLC; MMeT; MWA; PHi; PPL. 44-6681

Winchester, George W. Theoretical and practical penmanship. Book 3. Hartford: J.H. Mather and company [1844] MH. 44-6682

Winchester, George W. Theoretical and practical penmanship.... No. 1-4. Hartford: 1844. CtHWatk. 44-6683

Windsor, Lloyd. An inquiry into the ministerial commission. Claremont, New Hampshire: S. Ide, 1844. 214 p. Nh; OO; PPM; PPPrHi. 44-6684

Windsor, Lloyd. Inquiry into the ministerial commission. Claremont, New Hampshire: 1844. 210 p. RPB; WFonBG. 44-6685

Windsor, Lloyd, b. 1812. An inquiry into the ministerial mission. By the Rev. Lloyd Windsor.... New York: William Hinton, 1844. 210 p. GAGTh; ICBB; MnSH; NBuDD; WNaE. 44-6686

Windsor, Lloyd, b. 1812. A letter addressed to Rev. William C. Wisner being a review of "A review, etc." By Rev. Lloyd Windsor. Lockport: printed by T.P. Scorell, 1844. 44 p. MH-AH; N. 44-6687

Winebrenner, John, 1797-1860. Popular treatise on regeneration founded on John, chapter III, verse 7, comprising the substance of a series of practical sermons preached before the church of God, in the city of Lancaster, in the year 1842. Philadelphia: Lindsay, 1844. 264 p. CtMW; OO; PHi. 44-6688

Winslow, Hubbard, 1799 or 1800-1864.

The Christian doctrines. By Rev. Hubbard Winslow... Boston: Crocker and Brewster, 1844. [13]-360 p. CSansS; IaDmU; NCH; OrP; RPB. 44-6689

Winsted, Massachusetts. Congregational Church and Society. Minutes of the proceedings of the Congregational Church of Winsted in relation to the settlement, etc. Hartford, 1844. 8 p. MBC. 44-6690

Winthrop, John. Selections from an ancient catalogue of objects of natural history.... New Haven: B.L. Hamlen, printer, 1844. 11 p. MdBP; MH; MWA; PPL-R. 44-6691

Winthrop, Robert Charles, 1809-1894. American seamen in foreign ports, etc., May 16, 1844 [Report from the Committee on Commerce. Washington: 1844] 8 p. MH. 44-6692

Winthrop, Robert Charles, 1809-1894. Speech of Mr. Winthrop, of Massachusetts, on the Oregon question. Delivered in the House of Representatives of the United States, March 18, 1844 [Washington: 1844] 16 p. ICN; MWA; OrP; PHi, WaU. 44-6693

Winthrop, Robert Charles, 1809-1894. Speech of Mr. Winthrop, of Massachusetts, on the right of petition; delivered in the House of Representatives of the United States, January 23d and 24th, 1844. Washington: Gales and Seaton, 1844. 19 p. CU; IaGG; KHi; MWA; PU. 44-6694

Winthrop Juvenile Association. Catalogue of books belonging to the Winthrop Juvenile Association. B.H. Aurora Press, 1844. 17 p. MB. 44-6695

Wirt, William, 1772-1834. The letters of the British spy. Tenth edition, revised and corrected. To which is prefixed a biographical sketch of the author. New York: Harper and brothers, 1844. 7-260 p. AB; LN; NdHi; MGeno; OO. 44-6696

Wirt, William, 1772-1834. Sketches of the life and character of Patrick Henry. By William Wirt of Richmond, Virginia. Ninth edition, corrected by the author. Philadelphia: Thomas, Cowperthwait and company, 1844. 468 p. AZ; GMWa; NT; TNV; WJan. 44-6697

Wisconsin. Journal of the council, second annual session of the fourth legislative assembly of Wisconsin. Commenced on Monday, December 4, 1843, and terminated Wednesday, January 31, 1844. Madison: George Ryer, 1844. 383 p. In; MH; W; WBeloC; WM. 44-6698

Wisdom in miniature: or, gems of wisdom: being a collection of sentences from distinguished authors on religion, morals, and literature. New York: Alexander V. Blake, 1844. 106 p. MLow; NNUT; PPFHi. 44-6699

Wisner, William, 1782-1871. The line of demarcation, between the secular kingdoms of this world, and the spiritual kingdom of the Lord Jesus Christ. A sermon preached in the First Presbyterian Church, at Ithaca, April 14, 1844. Ithaca, New York: A. and S. Spencer, printers, 1844. 22 p. CSmH; IaB; ICP; MBC; NCH. 44-6700

Wisner, William Carpenter, 1808-1880. The biblical argument on slavery. Begin principally a review of T.D. Weld's "Bible against slavery." New York: Leavitt,

Trow and company, 1844. 40 p. NjR; OClWHi. 44-6701

Wisner, William Carpenter, 1808-1880. A letter in reply to one received from Rev. Lloyd Windsor, on the subject of prelacy and parity... Lockport, New York: Crandall and Brigham, 1844. 50 p. CtHT; MiD; NbOP; NLock. 44-6702

Wisner, William Carpenter, 1808-1880. Prelacy and parity, discussed in several lectures; comprising a review of Rev. Lloyd Windsor's argument on the ministerial commission. New York: Leavitt, 1844. 180 p. CtMW; GDecCT; NbOP; OMC; PPPrHi. 44-6703

Wistar, Henry. Wistar's balsam of wild cherry, nature's own remedy, etc. [An advertisement] New York?: 1844? NoLoc. 44-6704

Witherow, Samuel. The union clay glee book, a choice collection of original and select national airs and patriotic songs. Gettysburg, Pennsylvania: 1844. 90 p. DLC; ICJ. 44-6705

Woburn, Massachusetts. First Congregational Church. The rules and regulations, and confession of faith and covenant of the First Congregational Church in Woburn... July, 1844. Somerville: Edmund Tufts, 1844. 24 p. MB; MiD-B; MWA; MWo. 44-6706

Woman's worth, or, hints to raise the female character. First American from the last English edition, with a notice by Emily Marshall. New York: n.p., 1844. 180 p. MH; NICLA; PPL-R; WHi. 44-6707

Wood, Benjamin. A sermon occasioned

by the death of Mrs. Maria Legg, wife of Captain William Legg, who died February 9, 1843. Aged XLII. By Rev. Benjamin Wood, pastor of the church in Upton. Worcester: Massachusetts Spy office, printer, 1844. 12 p. MB; MiD-B; MWHi; OO; RPB. 44-6708

Wood, C.A.F. The Irish broom-maker; or, a cure for dumbness; a farce, in one act, as acted by Barney Williams. New York and London: Samuel French, [1844?.] OCl. 44-6709

Wood, George Bacon, 1797-1879. Syllabus of the course of lectures on materia medica and pharmacy delivered in the University of Pennsylvania. Philadelphia: Lydia R. Bailey, 1844. 70 p. GEU-M; LNT-M; NhD; PPCP; RPM. 44-6710

Wood, Horatio. Evil speaking. A sermon preached in the Congregational Church in Tytngsborough, [sic] February 4, 1844, by Horatio Wood, pastor of that church. Boston: James Munroe and company, 1844. 12 p. ICMe; MB; MH-AH; MiD-B; WHi. 44-6711

Wood, Robert Serrell. An attempt to explain the nature of electricity, and its intention in the economy of the universe. Philadelphia: printed by C.F. Town, 1844. 90 p. ICJ; IU; MH; MdAN. 44-6712

Woodbridge, John. An address delivered before the society of inquiry on missions in Amherst College. Amherst: J.S. and C. Adams, 1844. 32 p. CSfCW; MA; MAJ; NjR. 44-6713

Woodbridge, John. The duties of American scholars. An address delivered before the Society of Inquiry on Missions, in Amherst College, on the evening preceding commmencement in that institution, August 7, 1844. Amherst: J.S. and C. Adams, printers, 1844. 32 p. MBC; NNG; NNUT; RPB; TxU. 44-6714

Woodbridge, William, 1780-1861. The dead bird. Boston: 1844. MBC. 44-6715

Woodbridge, William, 1780-1861. Speech delivered in the Senate of the United States, February 14, 1844, on the bill to remit the fine imposed upon General Jackson, and upon the incidental question of the right assumed by the legislature of a state to instruct a member of the Senate of the United States. Washington: 1844. 8 p. DLC; WHi. 44-6716

Woodbridge, William Channing, 1794-1845. Modern school geography, on a plan of comparison and classification... With an atlas... Hartford: Belknap, 1844. 352 p. CsSoP; MH; MoSpD; OO; TNV. 44-6717

Woodbridge, William Channing, 1794-1845. System of modern geography, on the principles of comparison and classification. Illustrated with maps and engravings; and accompanied by an atlas. Improved edition. Hartford: Belknap and Hamersley, 1844. 474 p. GHi; MiD; MLaw; OCo; OO. 44-6718

Woodbridge, William Channing, 1794-1845. Woodbridge and Willard's universal geography... Accompanied by modern and ancient atlases... [New edition, revised and enlarged] Hartford: Belknap and Hamersley [1844] [11]-38, [49]-474, [9]-96 p. DLC; NBuU; OO. 44-6719

Woodbury, Levi, 1789-1851. Speech in executive session, on the treaty for the reannexation of Texas to the United States, delivered in the Senate of the United States, June 4, 1844 [Washington: 1844] 20 p. OOxM; WHi. 44-6720

Woodbury, Levi, 1789-1851. Speech in executive session, on the treaty for the reannexation of Texas to the United States, delivered in the Senate of the United States, June 4, 1844 [Washington: 1844] 30 p. DLC; NNU-W; TxU; ViW; WHi. 44-6721

Woodbury, Levi, 1789-1851. Speech of Mr. Woodbury, of New Hampshire, on the tariff: delivered in the Senate of the United States, February 7 and 8, 1844. Washington: printed at the Globe office, 1844. 30 p. In; MBAt; P; Vi. 44-6722

Woodhouselee, Alexander Fraser Tytler, 1747-1813. Elements of general history, ancient and modern. To which is added a succinct history of the United States by an American gentleman. Concord, New Hampshire: J.F. Brown, 1844. 527 p. ABH; DLC. 44-6723

Woodhouselee, Alexander Fraser Tytler, 1747-1813. Universal history of the creation of the world to the beginning of the eighteenth century. Boston: Benjamin B. Mussy, 1844. 2 v. MAbD; MH; MiOC; TNP. 44-6724

Woods, Leonard, 1774-1854. Lectures on church government. Objections to episcopal scheme. New York: Turner and Hayden, 1844. 198 p. CSt; ICP; MBC; OO; RPB. 44-6725

Woodsworth, C. Discourse on public education. Boston: 1844. MB. 44-6726

Woodward, E.F. Roads and etc. in the town of Brookline [Brookline: 1844] M; MB; MH. 44-6727

Woodward, Joseph Addison, 1806-1885. Speech of Mr. Woodward, of South Carolina, on the power of congress to regulate elections in the states. Delivered in the House of Representatives, February 7, 1844. Washington: Printed by Blair and Rives, 1844. 15 p. MiD-R; ScU. 44-6728

Worcester, Joseph Emerson, 1784-1865. A comprehensive pronouncing and explanatory dictionary of the English language: with pronouncing vocabularies of classical, scripture and modern geographical names.... Carefully revised and enlarged. Boston: Jenks and Palmer, 1844. 424 p. MH; NNC. 44-6729

Worcester, Joseph Emerson, 1784-1865. Elementary dictionary for common schools...Cincinnati: Jewett and Mason, 1844. MnU; OClWHi. 44-6730

Worcester, Joseph Emerson, 1784-1865. Elementary dictionary... Boston: 1844. CtHWatk. 44-6731

Worcester, Joseph Emerson, 1784-1865. Elements of ancient, classical and scripture geography. With an atlas. Boston: Lewis and Sampson, 1844. 74 p. MBAMC; MH; Nh-Hi; RPB. 44-6732

Worcester, Joseph Emerson, 1784-1865. Elements of geography, modern and ancient, with a modern and ancient atlas. Revised and improved edition. Boston: Lewis and Sampson, 1844. 6, 257, 74 p. ICU; KyBC; MH; NjR; PV. 44-6733

Worcester, Joseph Emerson, 1784-1865. Elements of history, ancient and modern. Boston: William J. Reynolds, 1844. 386 p. GWay, MBAt; NIC; NRHi; RKi. 44-6734

Worcester, Joseph Emerson, 1784-1865. Worcester's ancient classical and scripture atlas. Improved edition. Boston: Lewis and Sampson, [1844] 10 maps. MH. 44-6735

Worcester, Joseph Emerson, 1784-1865. Worcester's modern atlas. New edition, revised and improved. Boston: Lewis and Sampson [1844] MH. 44-6736

Worcester, Samuel Austin, 1798-1859. Cherokee Hymns. Compiled from several authors and revised. Seventh edition. Park Hill: Mission Press, 1844. DLC; MBAt. 44-6737

Worcester, Samuel Thomas, 1804-1882. The American primary spelling book. Fourth edition. Boston: James Munroe and company, 1844. MH. 44-6738

Worcester, Samuel Thomas, 1804-1882. Sequel to the spelling book. Boston: J. Munroe and company, 1844. MWbor. 44-6739

Worcester, Samuel, 1793-1844. A fourth book of lessons for reading; ....Boston: Charles J. Hendee, and Jenks and Palmer, 1844. 408 p. MB; MeHi; MH; NjP; RPB. 44-6740

Worcester, Samuel, 1793-1844. Introduction to the third book for reading.... Boston: 1844. CtHWatk. 44-6741

Worcester, Samuel, 1793-1844. Third book for reading and spelling. One hundred and seventh edition. Boston: C.J. Hendee, 1844. MBAt; MH. 44-6742

Worcester Agricultural Society. Premiums, rules and regulations. Worcester: Church and Fiske, printers, 1844. 16 p. MWHi. 44-6743

Worcester Branch Railroad. First annual report of the Worcester Branch Railroad Company for the honorable Senate and House of Representatives of the Commonwealth of Massachusetts. [Worcester] 1844. 2 p. MH-BA. 44-6744

Worcester County, Massachusetts. Articles of faith adopted by several Baptist churches in Worcester County with the covenant. Worcester: 1844. 20 p. MH. 44-6745

Worcester County Mechanics' Association. Constitution of the Worcester County Mechanics' Association, as amended and adopted April, 1844. Worcester: press of James M. Stone, 1844. 20 p. MWA. 44-6746

Worcester Natural History Society. Worcester, Massachusetts. Catalogue of books in library. Worcester: Henry J. Howland, printer, 1844. 24 p. MWHi. 44-6747

Words from the law and the testimony, in answer to several important inquiries. Boston: office of the Christian World, 1844. 16 p. ICMe. 44-6748

Wordsworth, William, 1770-1850. The complete poetical works of William Wordsworth; together with a description of the country of the lakes in the north of England, now first published with his works... edited by Henry Reed...

Philadelphia: J. Kay, Jr. and his brother; Pittsburgh: C.H. Kay, 1844. 25-551 p. MB; OU; PHi; RPB; ViU. 44-6749

Wordsworth, William, 1770-1850. Poems from the poetical works of William Wordsworth....[selected by Henry Reed] Philadelphia: J. Locken, 1844. 281 p. CtHT; NIC; OO; TBriK. 44-6750

Workings of the tariff. Baltimore: 1844?. PPL-R. 44-6751

The world before you; or, the log cabin. Second edition. Philadelphia: George S. Appleton; New York: D. Appleton and company, 1844. 207 p. KyHi. 44-6752

The world we live in. A semi-monthly journal of useful and entertaining literature, ...Boston: John B. Hall and company, 1844. v. 1-. 192. p. MBBC. 44-6753

Worth, Edmund. A sermon delivered in the Baptist meeting house in Boscawen. Concord: Charles Young, printer, 1844. 16 p. NjR. 44-6754

Worth, Edmund. Tests of discipleship. A sermon delivered in the Baptist meeting house in Boscawen, July 7, 1844. By Edmund Worth. Published by request. Concord: Charles Young, printer, 1844. 16 p. MNtCA; NHC-S; Nh-Hi; RPB. 44-6755

Worth, Gordon A., d. 1856. Sketches of the character of the New York press. By O.P.Q. New York: 1844. 47 p. LU; MBC; MH; NBuG; NCH. 44-6756

Wrentham, Massachusetts. School committee. Annual report. 1844/45-1919. MH. 44-6757

Wright, A.S. The American receipt book, or the complete book of reference.... By A.S. Wright. Philadelphia: Lindsay and Blakiston, 1844. 359 p. DSI; NN. 44-6758

Wright, Alfred, 1788-1853. Chahta uba isht taloa holisso, or Choctaw hymn book. Third edition, revised. Boston: Marvin, 1844. 175 p. CtHWatk; MsJS; NN. 44-6759

Wright, Edward. A sermon, delivered at the funeral of Rev. Stephen W. Stebbins, senior pastor of the Congregational Church in West Haven: August 16, 1843. By the junior pastor. Published by request. New Haven: William Storer, printer, 1844. 16 p. Ct; MBC; MBNEH; MiD-B; OCl. 44-6760

Wright, Joseph Albert, 1810-1867. Remarks of Joseph A. Wright, of Indiana, on the right of petition. Delivered in the House of Representatives, January 27, 1844. [Washington: 1844] 7 p. In; M; MBAt; MH; OClWHi. 44-6761

Wright, Joseph Albert, 1810-1867. Speech on the tariff, delivered in the House of Representatives, April 22 and 23, 1844. Washington: 1844. 13 p. In; WHi. 44-6762

Wright, Joseph Hall. Breakfast table science; or the philosophy of common things, written expressly for the amusement and instruction of young people. New York: Alexander V. Blake, 1844. 193 p. IaDuU; InCW; MB; MoSpD; MPiB. 44-6763

Wright, Joseph W. Language and belles lettres: ....New York: R.W. Barnard and company; Philadelphia: Hogan and Thompson, 1844. 48 p. DLC; MH, NjR. 44-6764

Wright, Marmaduke Burr, 1803-1879. A lecture delivered to the students of the Medical College of Ohio, at the opening of the session, 1843-1844. Cincinnati: R.P. Donogh, 1844. 16 p. NBMS; OCGHM; OClWHi. 44-6765

Wright, Silas, 1795-1847. Speech of Mr. Wright of New York, on the tariff. Delivered in the Senate of the United States, April 19 and 23, 1844. n.p.: 1844?. 23 p. N; OClWHi; WHi. 44-6766

Wright, Silas, 1795-1847. The tariff. Mr. Wright's speech at Watertown. n.p [1844?] 7 p. N. 44-6767

Wright, Stephen Smith. Narrative and recollections of Van Dieman's land, during three years captivity of Stephen S. Wright. New York: J. Winchester [1844] [5]-80 p. MHi; NbO; NCH; NIC; WHi. 44-6768

Wright, Stephen Smith. Narrative of the battle of Prescott in Canada and recollections of Van Dieman's land....New York: 1844. PPL. 44-6769

Wright, Thomas, 1810-1877. St. Patrick's purgatory; an essay on the legends of purgatory, hell and paradise, current during the middle ages. New York: J. Winchester, New World Press, 1844. 67 p. CSansS; DLC; NIC; PPL; PU. 44-6770

Wright, William H. Brief practical treatise on mortars; with an account of the processes employed at the public works in Boston harbor. Boston: Ticknor, 1844. 148 p. IaU. 44-6771

Wrongs and rights of Ireland, depicted by distinguished Americans in their speeches and letters on occasion of the "simultaneous meetings throughout the world in defense of Irish rights and human freedom" ....and other proceedings connected with the project of the Albany repealers for simultaneous meetings throughout the world. Albany, New York: Jones, 1844. 29 p. CSmH; MBBC; NRHi. 44-6772

Wyckoff, Isaac Newton, 1792-1869. Christian example; a sermon occasioned by the death of Christian Miller, for sixty years a member of the church in the Dutch Reformed Connection; delivered in the Second R.P. Dutch Church, Albany, on Sunday, December 15, 1844. Albany: Pease, 1844. 31 p. IEN-M; MB; MiD-B; N; NjR. 44-6773

Wyman, Thomas W. Tables of allowances of equipment, outfits, stores, etc., for each class of vessels in the navy of the United States, by Captain Thomas W. Wyman, ...Washington: Alexander and Barnard, printers, 1844. 85 p. MH; NNE; PPFrankI. 44-6774

X-Y-Z

Xavier University. Cincinnati, Ohio. Calendar. St. Xavier College. Catalogue. St. Xavier College. Catalogue. Xavier University. 1844-45. MH. 44-6775

Xenophon. The Anabasis. Translated by Edward Spelman, Esq. New York: Harper and Brothers, 1844. 17-292 p. CoU;GOgU; ViRU. 44-6776

Xenophon. The Anabasis of Xenophon: chiefly according to the text of L. Dindorf; with notes, for the use of schools and colleges. Fourth edition. New York: Leavitt, Trow and company, 1844. 368 p. InRch; MB; MH; MH-AH; PU. 44-6777

Xenophon. The cyropaedia. Translated by Edward Spellman, esq. [v. 1] and Honorable Maurice Ashley Cooper [v. 2] Harper's stereotyped edition. ....New York: Harper and brothers, 1844. 2 v. GHi. 44-6778

Xenophon. The Cyropaedia. Translated by Hon. Maurice Ashley Cooper. New York: Harper and brothers, 1844. 2 v. MsJPED; NGeno; OM. 44-6779

Xenophon. A narrative of the expedition of Cyrus the younger, and of the retreat of the ten thousand. By Xenophon of Athens....Edited by Alpheus Crosby....Boston: James Munroe and company, 1844. 282 p. CtY; MBC; MBU-E. 44-6780

Xenophon. Xenophon. Translated by Honorable Maurice Ashly Cooper. New York: Harper and brothers, 1844. 2 v. MBBC. 44-6781

Xenophon. Xenophon's expedition of Cyrus, with English notes. By Charles D. Cleveland, translator. Boston: B. J. Mussey, 1844. 306 p. IEG; MoSC; NNC; OMC; ViNew. 44-6782

Yale, Elisha. Divine method of raising charitable contributions. Boston: T.R. Marvin, 1844. Mwiw. 44-6783

Yale University. Catalogue of the officers and students in Yale College, 1844-5. New Haven: B.L. Hamlen, printer, 1844. 39 p. Ct; KHi; MeB; MNBedf; MoSM. 44-6784

Yale University. Catalogus Senatus Academici, Et Eorum Qui Munera Et Officia Academica Gesserunt, Quique Aliquovis Gradu Exornati Fuerunt, in Collegio Yalensi, Novi-Portus, in Republica Connecticutensi. Novi-Portus: B.L. Hamlen, typographo, 1844. 133 p. MiGr; MNBedf. 44-6785

Yale University. Department of Theology. A triennial catalogue of the theological department in Yale College; published by the students, August, 1844. New Haven: J. H. Benham, 1844. 32 p. MH-AH; NNUT. 44-6786

Yates, John. The Washingtonian harp: a collection of hymns, songs and odes, for temperance meetings and festivals. Rochester: E. Shepard, 1844. 160 p. NRHi; TxU. 44-6787

Yeadon, Richard, 1802-1870. Speech of Richard Yeadon, on the constitutionality of the tariff or protective system, and in vindication of Henry Clay against the charge of a breach of the compromise of 1833. Charleston: Burges and James, 1844. 11 p. ScCC; Vi. 44-6788

Yeadon, Richard, 1802-1870. Speech of Richard Yeadon... at the court house, in Madison, Georgia... on the evening of July 31, 1844. Charleston: Published by request of the Clay Club of Charleston, South Carolina, 1844. 28 p. GHi; MB; NcD; ScU. 44-6789

Yorke, A. Absorption: A rational and consistent system of mesmerism; exposing many of the fundamental errors prevalent upon this subject... Philadelphia: Grubb and Reazor, 1844. [7]-46 p. MH; WHi. 44-6790

Youatt, William, 1776-1847. The horse, by William Youatt. A new edition... Together with a general history of the horse; a dissertation on the American trotting horse, how trained and jockeyed, an account of his remarkable performances; and an essay on the ass and the mule. Philadelphia: Lea and Blanchard, 1844. 17-448 p. CU; NNN; ViU. 44-6791

Youatt, William, 1776-1847. The stock raiser's manual: a guide to the raising and improvment of cattle, being a treatise on their breeds, management and diseases by William Youatt, with numerous il-

lustrations. Philadelphia: Grigg and Elliot, 1844. 600 p. NGlc; NJam. 44-6792

Young, Alcinous. Marriage dinner: in answer to Dr. Fairchild's great supper. Pittsburgh: Parkin, 1844. PPins. 44-6793

Young, Alexander, 1800-1854. Chronicles of the pilgrim fathers of the colony of Plymouth, from 1602 to 1625. Now first collected from original records and contemporaneous printed documents, and illustrated with notes. Second edition. Boston: C.C. Little and J. Brown, 1844. 502 p. CtMW; IU; MeBa; MWiW; PPAmP. 44-6794

Young, Alexander, 1800-1854. The stay and the staff taken away. A discourse occasioned by the death of the Hon. William Prescott, LL.D., delivered in the church on Church Green, December 15, 1844. Boston: Charles C. Little and James Brown, 1844. 34 p. CBPac; ICN; MeB; RPB; WHi. 44-6795

Young, Isaac. Illustrated advertisement of saddles, harness [sic], and trunks made by Isaac Young. Cincinnati: 1844. Broadside. OHi. 44-6796

Young, J. Thomas. Strong consolation: or three letters to a friend in spiritual dejection, with an introduction. Charleston: Burges and James, 1844. 62 p. GDecCt. 44-6797

Young, James Alexander. The age of brass: or the fun dynasty: containing the political morals of certain political characters... Baltimore: G.W. Wilson, 1844. 48 p. ICU; MdHi; MHi; PHi. 44-6798

Young, James Hamilton, b. 1793. The

tourist's pocket map of Ohio. Philadelphia: 1844. 1 p. PHi. 44-6799

Young, James Hamilton, b. 1793. The tourist's pocket map of Pennsylvania, exhibiting roads, etc. Philadelphia: 1844. p. PH. 44-6800

Young, John C. Foreign missionary chronicle. A sermon by John G. Young. Louisville: 1844. KyDC. 44-6801

Young, John C. Sermon before the Board of Missions. Louisville: 1844. PPL. 44-6802

Young, Loyal. Features of the last time: an address, delivered before the alumni of the Western Theological Seminary... Pittsburgh: printed at the Spirit of the Age office, 1844. 8 p. NjR; PPL; PPPrHi. 44-6803

Young, Samuel. The orphan and other tales. Pittsburgh: A.A. Anderson, 1844. 107 p. DLC. 44-6804

Young, Thomas John. The time and measure of almsgiving. A sermon preached in St. John's Church, John's Island on the fourth Sunday after Epiphany being the 28th January, 1844. Charleston: printed by Miller and Browne, 1844. 20 p. MBC; MdBD; NNG; ScU. 44-6805

Young Bible reader. Cincinnati: William T. Turner, [1844] 24 p. CtY. 44-6806

Young hickory almanac for 1845. Rochester, New York: M. Miller, [1844] MWA. 44-6807

Young hickory banner. August 10th-31, 1844. New York: [A. Dinsmore] [1844] v.

1, No. 1. A-Ar; CtY; MB; OClWHi; PPL. 44-6808

Young Kate; or, the rescue. A tale of the great Kanawha. ....New York: Hayer and brothers, 1844. 2 v. in 1. DLC; ICU; OClWHi; ViU; Wv. 44-6809

The young mechanic: by the author of the young merchant... New York: Saxton and Miles, 1844. 233 p. MoSU; Nifi; NjR. 44-6810

Youth's new drawing book.... New York: P.J. Cozans, [1844] MH. 44-6811

Youth's ornithology. Concord, New Hampshire: Rufus Merrill, 1844. 24 p. MiHi; Nh-Hi; NIC. 44-6812

The youth's parlor annual. Edited and published by Rev. D. Newell. New York: [1844]-1845. 431 p. CSt; FSa; MH; NGrn; NKings. 44-6813

Youth's penny gazette. Philadelphia: 1844-. PP. 44-6814

Youth's temperance lecture. Boston: 1844. 32 p. MBC. 44-6815

Youth's zoology.... with.... engravings. Concord, New Hampshire: Rufus Merrill, 1844. 24 p. ICU; Nh-Hi; NjR. 44-6816

Zabriskie, James C. Address of the Democratic state convention, to the people of New Jersey, as reported by James C. Zabriskie, esq., chairman of the committee. Trenton: Emporium office, printer, 1844. 11 p. NjP; P; PHi. 44-6817

Zacharie, I. Surgical and practical observations on the diseases of the human foot. New York: 1844. IEN; IU-M. 44-6818

Zetsche. Return quick step. Composed by Zetsche, arranged for the pianoforte by Simon Knaebel. Boston: Keith's Music Publisning House, 1844. 3 p. MBNEC; MHi. 44-6819

Zeuner, Charles, 1797-1857. The American harp: being a collection of new and original church music, under the control of the Musical Professional Society in Boston.... Boston: Samuel G. Simpkins, 1844. 392 p. MH; MLe; NhD; OCl. 44-6820

Zimmermann, Johann Georg, ritter von. Solitude.... with the life of the author....By Johann Georg Zimmermann.... New York: Kearny, 1844. 296 p. NjP; TBriK; UU. 44-6821

Zion's harp; for prayer, conference, class meetings and families; comprising the most approved spiritual hymns, ...Dover, New Hampshire: trustees of the Free Will Baptist Connection, 1844. 144 p. ICU; MeLewB; NBuC; NcU; Nh-Hi. 44-6822

Zollikefer, Johannes. Himmilischer Welhraushschatz; order, Vollstandiges gebet-buch auf allerlei zeiten, angliegen und personen anwendbar.... vielfaltig vermehrt und zum druck befordert von A.L. Herman, nobst einem starken antang communicos-gebete order andachtsuebungen.... Vierto auflage. Philadelphia: Lippincott, 1844. 688 p. KyDC; MBC; OCl. 44-6823

Zschokke, Heinrich, 1771-1848. Hours of meditation and devotional reflection, upon the religious, moral, and social duties of life. By Heinrich Zschokke. Translated from the German. By James D. Haas. New York: J.S. Redfield, 1844. 243 p. CtB; IEG; InCW; NCaS; OAsht. 44-6824

Zschokke, Johann Heinrich Daniel. Incidents of social life amid the European Alps. Translated from the German of J. Heinrich Zschokke. By Louis Strack. New York: D. Appleton and company, 1844. 373 p. MNF; OWoC; PHatU; PPL-R. 44-6825

Zumpt, Carl Gottlob, 1792-1849. Syntax of the Latin language, chiefly from the German of C.G. Zumpt. By Charles Bech.... Second edition. Boston: J. Munroe and company, 1844. 200 p. ICU; MH; RPB; TxU-T; VtU. 44-6826

Zumpt, Carl Gottlob, 1792-1849. Latin syntax, chiefly from the German of C.G. Zumpt. Second edition. Boston: 1844. MC. 44-6827

ABOUT THE AUTHORS

SCOTT BRUNTJEN (B.A., University of Iowa; M.A., University of Iowa; M.A. Shippensburg University of Pennsylvania; D.A. Simmons College) is the Executive Vice President of Acquisitions Management Corporation of Colorado. Prior to this he served for twenty years in various library capacities from reference librarian to creator and then Director of the Iowa Locator, the first CD-ROM based statewide library computer database. Dr. Bruntjen began work on The *Checklist of American Imprints* project in 1972 and has been active in its development for the past twenty-one years. In the late 1970's he co-directed an HEA Title IIc project to bring initial control to the then unorganized WPA files which form the basis of the *Checklist*. He has more than forty publications to his credit ranging from the basic text on preparing library data for computer input (*Data Conversion*) to a bio-bibliography of Douglas C. McMurtrie (*Douglas C. McMurtrie, Bibliographer and Historian of Printing*).

CAROL R. RINDERKNECHT is a graduate of Shippensburg University of Pennsylvania. She is currently the President of Acquisitions Management Corporation of Colorado which owns and operates several smaller resort properties along the Front Range of The Rocky Mountains. She has worked on the American Imprints project since 1972 and in that capacity has published sixteen volumes in the *Checklist* series. She co-directed an HEA Title IIc project in the late 1970's at Rutgers University which brought order to the basic WPA files used in the production of the *Checklist*.